Bears vs. Cardinals

Bears vs. Cardinals
The NFL's Oldest Rivalry

Joe Ziemba

McFarland & Company, Inc., Publishers
Jefferson, North Carolina

ISBN (print) 978-1-4766-8851-0
ISBN (ebook) 978-1-4766-4733-3

LIBRARY OF CONGRESS AND BRITISH LIBRARY
CATALOGUING DATA ARE AVAILABLE

Library of Congress Control Number 2022035366

© 2022 Joe Ziemba. All rights reserved

No part of this book may be reproduced or transmitted in any form or by any means, electronic or mechanical, including photocopying or recording, or by any information storage and retrieval system, without permission in writing from the publisher.

On the cover: (top, left to right) John "Paddy" Driscoll, George Halas, and Charley Trippi (University of Georgia); (bottom) Bears halfback Red Grange (right) carries the ball against the Cardinals on Thanksgiving Day, November 26, 1925, at Cubs Park in Chicago

Printed in the United States of America

*McFarland & Company, Inc., Publishers
Box 611, Jefferson, North Carolina 28640
www.mcfarlandpub.com*

To Steve Thomas—A great friend and mentor.
To Rosemary Coffeen—Always with love, Big Mick!
To Carol—Of course, and still in awe!

Table of Contents

Acknowledgments — ix
Preface — 1
Introduction — 4

ONE—The Cardinals' Slippery History — 9
TWO—Famous Chicago Cardinals — 22
THREE—Order of the Broken Jaw — 29
FOUR—Yankees, Bobcats, and Owls! — 40
FIVE—Pro Football: The Beginning — 53
SIX—NFL's Oldest Rivalry — 68
SEVEN—Lawyers, Gum, and Money — 84
EIGHT—That Al Capone Crowd! — 104
NINE—The Grange Effect — 113
TEN—The NFL's First Scandal — 136
ELEVEN—Betrayals and Empty Bank Accounts! — 155
TWELVE—Programs and Sir Duke — 179
THIRTEEN—Bidwill Saves the Bears! — 201
FOURTEEN—Bronko, Spies, and Foolish Magnates — 225
FIFTEEN—Mergers, Titles, and Missing Halfbacks — 245
SIXTEEN—Windy City Warriors — 271
SEVENTEEN—The Last Hurrah — 284

Chapter Notes — 307
Bibliography — 327
Index — 331

Acknowledgments

As with any project of this scope, there are many individuals and organizations to thank. Since this book covered over 100 seasons of professional football (60 with the Chicago Cardinals and 40 with the Decatur Staleys/Chicago Bears), I was fortunate to rely on many authors and other experts who willingly shared their particular expertise in discussing key matters pertinent to individuals and organizations during the early days of professional football.

In particular, Jon Kendle of the Professional Football Hall of Fame was gracious and accommodating during my many visits to study and absorb the magnificent Dutch Sternaman collection housed in the Ralph Wilson, Jr. Pro Football Research and Preservation Center. Mr. Kendle is the director of archives and football information at the Hall of Fame and an invaluable resource on any topic related to pro football history. The Sternaman collection captures a fascinating period in pro football, and Dutch Sternaman's insightful retention of material from his tenure as the co-owner of the Chicago Bears is perhaps the most significant assemblage housed in the Pro Football Hall of Fame. It is an honor to share some of the wealth of "new" information (as well as photos) from the Sternaman collection and it is with gratitude that Jon Kendle is acknowledged for his exceptional assistance.

My valued friend and mentor Steve Thomas once again served as the initial editor of this book. His extraordinary capabilities ensured that this document remained on course, while his astute background as an attorney allowed me to be a recipient of his sage advice on legal matters discovered in the Bears-Cardinals rivalry over the years. In addition, Steve corralled another legal associate, Doug Graham, for help on locating old court documents.

In my humble opinion, the finest collection of ancient newspapers and documents related to the Chicago area resides at the Chicago History Museum. Under the direction of Ellen Keith and Lesley Martin, the many volumes of obscure articles and invaluable editions were located and sprang to life. All of which allowed this book to include forgotten information that might have otherwise been overlooked. Thank you, Ellen, Lesley, and the capable staff at the Chicago History Museum Research Center!

As mentioned, several excellent authors provided wonderful comments on specific events pertaining to the early days of football or items related to the Bears-Cardinals rivalry. These include Dr. Dominic Pacyga, author of *Slaughterhouse: Chicago's Union Stock Yard and the World It Made*; Robert Pruter, author of *The Rise of American High School Sports and the Search for Control*; Chris Serb, author of *War Football: World War I and the Birth of the NFL*; Chris Willis, head of the research library at NFL Films, and author of *Joe Carr: The Man Who Built the National Football League* and *Red Grange: The Life and Legacy of the NFL's First Superstar*; Jeff Miller, author of *Buffalo's Forgotten Champions: The Story of Buffalo's First Professional Football Team and The Lost 1921 Title*; and Richard J. Shmelter, author of *Chicago Assassin: The Life and Legend of "Machine Gun" Jack McGurn and the Chicago Beer Wars of the Roaring Twenties*.

Other good friends and pro football history aficionados who freely gave of their time and knowledge were John Steffenhagen, noted historian of the Rochester Jeffersons; Mark Sorensen, author of numerous articles on the Decatur Staleys and a respected historian; Bob Harley, the grandson of Bill Harley, an early partner in the Staleys/Bears organization; Justin Lenhart, museum curator at the Oklahoma Sports Hall of Fame in Oklahoma City, which also houses the Jim Thorpe Museum; and Upton Bell, the son of former NFL Commissioner Bert Bell and himself a general manager in the National Football League. My time with Upton was entertaining, educational, and honest. I will always be grateful for his time and advice!

I am grateful for family members of former Bears and Cardinals players who graciously shared stories and information about their relatives. They include Patrick Glynn, nephew of Jack Glynn, the secretary of the Racine Cardinals; Toni Nagel Mason, daughter of Cardinals player Ray Nagel; Carol Judge, granddaughter of Cardinals founder Chris O'Brien; Mary Zoia Zentner, daughter of 1920s Cardinals lineman Clyde Zoia; George King, grandson of Chicago Bears great Bill Karr; Wendy Snyder, relative of Jimmy Snyder; and Cathy Markee Smith, granddaughter of William Thompson. While some of the names of the players mentioned may not be recognized by football fans today, all were important contributors to the story of the NFL's oldest rivalry!

In addition, I was provided with great information from Justin Conn, sports editor of the *Decatur Herald & Review*; Michael Walsh, communications coordinator at De La Salle Institute in Chicago; and Joe Skibinski, Archivist at the Indianapolis Motor Speedway. Thanks to my colleagues at the Sports History Network, Arnie Chapman and Darin Hayes, for their support and encouragement. A special thanks to readers of the manuscript who honestly shared suggestions for improving the document: Mike Coffeen, Margaret Achenbach, and Rosemary Coffeen.

Many libraries and research facilities were utilized for research purposes, including the following: University of Illinois Sports Information Department; University of Illinois, Office of Admissions and Records; Chicago Public Schools, Student Record Services; Anderson Public Library, Lawrenceburg, Kentucky; Frankfort Public Library, Frankfort, Illinois; Annie Halenbake Ross Library, Lock Haven, Pennsylvania; Hackley Public Library, Muskegon, Michigan; Hammond Public Library, Hammond, Indiana; Harold Washington Library, Chicago, Illinois; Hastings Public Library, Hastings, Michigan; Rockford Public Library, Rockford, Illinois; St. Louis Public Library, St. Louis, Missouri; Staley Museum, Decatur, Illinois; University of Notre Dame, South Bend, Indiana; and the University of Illinois Library, Champaign, Illinois.

A special thanks to football coach and scout Jon Cooper, who is probably the most knowledgeable and enthusiastic fan of the old Chicago Cardinals. Thank you, Coach!

I am very grateful to the professional staff at McFarland, including Susan Kilby, Lisa Camp, and Mark Durr, for allowing me to be a part of their impressive literary family! The professionalism, care, and attention to detail exhibited by the McFarland staff were evident from the beginning.

And finally, there is no greater attribute than to have the support of your family. Thanks to my children, Joseph A. Ziemba and Angela Kim Ziemba, for their ongoing support through many wacky football endeavors, and to my wife, Carol Lynn, who tirelessly and relentlessly reviews every single word multiple times for accuracy, credibility, and common sense. Thank you is never enough.

Preface

It was just a box.

Old and dusty, tattered and ripped, but holding a treasure.

As I moved through life, and from home to home, there was always this single box that made each trip. It was a box full of stuff, my father's stuff, and I never really looked through it. I knew what was in there but not "what" was in there.

As a kid, I poked around at the contents, which included scrapbooks and other weary and odd items from his football career in the 1930s and '40s. Born in the Polish neighborhood of Hegewisch on the South Side of Chicago, my father played football at Mt. Carmel High School and then traveled west to attend St. Benedict's College in Atchison, Kansas. For some, it was known as the "Notre Dame of the West" because not only was the school a winner on the football field, but its roster also contained several players from Chicago—similar to Notre Dame, but on a smaller scale.

Along the way, St. Benedict's encountered teams such as Creighton, New Mexico State, and Wichita State and my father eventually earned first team (small college) All-American honors from *Collier's* magazine. Good stuff, but he never really talked about it … nor did he ever share what was in the box. But as an adult, after the seventh or eighth move, I thought it might be time to fully investigate the box and determine if the contents, now decades old, were worth keeping. That's when the treasures revealed themselves!

From under a crumbling scrapbook filled with faded newspaper clippings, a letter appeared, and then another and another. One was from George Halas of the Chicago Bears, urging my father to join his team. There was one from the Detroit Lions, another originating from a minor league club in the east, and even one from a team called the Chicago Cardinals. None promised riches, but all offered the opportunity to play pro football as well as the team's assistance in locating off-season employment. There was an NFL draft in place back then (1940) and my father was selected by the Chicago Cardinals as the overall 131st choice. The letter from Cardinals coach Jimmy Conzelman contained instructions for the upcoming 1940 training camp as well as my dad's signed rookie contract with the Cardinals. It was for the fabulous amount (not!) of $110 per game, but the players would need to provide their own cleats and shoulder pads! That was the NFL in 1940.

Instead, my father reinjured his knee in training camp and ended his time with the Cardinals, figuring (correctly) that he could earn more money coaching high school football than he could playing pro football. Where his football-playing career ended when he "retired" from the Cardinals, my search for hidden football history began. I wanted to learn more about his experience as an "almost" NFL player and then it only seemed natural to explore the escapades of the Cardinals, the forgotten NFL team that long ago vacated its home on the South Side of Chicago.

Beginning with the contents of the tattered cardboard box that housed his football relics, the quest to find out more about the Cardinals eventually led to the publication of my book called *When Football Was Football: The Chicago Cardinals and the Birth of the NFL*. It has been a pleasant journey, and the research regarding the history of the Cardinals has never wavered. The organization can be traced to its fragile beginnings in 1899 when the team consisted of neighborhood teenagers who called themselves the Morgan Athletic Association. Yet one thing eerily stood out in this research: the published history of the Cardinals was woefully inaccurate from everything concerning the date of the team starting to the origin of the nickname to the identities of the early owners. As for the other half of this gridiron partnership, it was a natural transition to address some questionable history of the Chicago Bears as well.

In 1920, George Halas became affiliated with the Decatur (Illinois) Staleys, a team that shortly thereafter became the Chicago Bears. Since both clubs were based in Chicago, their rivalry endured for 40 years until the Cardinals left Chicago in early 1960. As such, this project includes 100 years of football history: 60 years for the Cardinals and 40 years for the Bears, with emphasis on the interactions of the teams rather than extended studies of individual players. As with my previous study of the Cardinals, there was also much to learn about the history of the Bears. Once again, a great deal has been written about the team's history, but precious few words have been contributed regarding the early academic history of George Halas, specifically his high school, college, and military experiences that helped establish his love of football. Much of what we do know about this period emanates from his invaluable autobiography, which, however, was written a half century after some of the events occurred and is thus prone to some errors as well.

The intent of this book, then, was to correct the extant early history of both organizations through careful evaluation of newspapers, along with interviews, other resources, and input from family members. Most important, I was honored to have the opportunity to fully analyze the recently available personal records of Edward "Dutch" Sternaman, the co-owner of the Chicago Bears with George Halas until 1932. The Sternaman collection in the Professional Football Hall of Fame reveals an enormous amount of information on the finances, travel, salaries, and personalities of the early NFL. Perhaps most intriguing, the collection unveils the financial agreements between the Bears and Red Grange—the formidable superstar who took the NFL by storm in 1925 and changed the course of professional football.

This book follows the two teams, and the maturing of the National Football League, in chronological order as all move forward during the early part of the 20th century searching for both recognition and survival. Through brawls, aggressive playmaking, hard-nosed competition, and, sometimes, cooperative endeavors, the

Bears and the Cardinals remain the two lone survivors from the founding members of the National Football League in 1920. Their perseverance and loyalty through the murky early days of the NFL pushed the league to survive and blossom. For those who never knew, or may have forgotten, the critical contributions and intense rivalry of the Bears and the Cardinals, these are their stories.

Introduction

> *"The Chicago Cardinals were celebrating a great victory, for yesterday they defeated their hated brothers of the Windy City, the Chicago Bears."*
> —*Dayton Herald*, December 1, 1922

In the beginning, there were two.
Two men, two competitors, two pioneers.
Just two.
One a legend, one largely forgotten...
The Chicago Bears and the Chicago Cardinals spent 40 seasons battling each other for football supremacy in the Windy City. From the first contest in 1920 through the final battle in 1959 (when both were still in Chicago), the teams knocked heads about twice a season on an annual basis. More often than not, the players were pleased to engage in nonathletic whims on the field, such as punching, gouging, biting, and other preferred means of gridiron endearment. Meanwhile, the fans on both sides would amuse themselves with generous support of their favorites but might also set fire to the bleachers or join the action on the field when circumstances seemed to invite such unusual participation.

And then, suddenly, in March 1960, the Cardinals surprised the city with their plans to immediately relocate to St. Louis, albeit with a healthy nudge from the owner of the Bears. While the teams have continued to play each other sporadically since that time, the luster, the lipstick, and the glow of the intense rivalry quickly withered away. It simply wasn't the same with each team no longer stationed within shouting distance of its primary nemesis.

Therefore, the goal in these pages is not to bemoan what no longer exists but to retrieve and celebrate what was ... and it all starts with the two founding fathers of professional football in Chicago: George Halas and Chris O'Brien. You might respond, "We know all about Halas, but who the heck is Chris O'Brien?" In order to understand the evolution of pro football's oldest rivalry, we must first understand the critical roles of those two individuals and their pioneer teams.

We may accurately consider the Bears-Cardinals rivalry as the oldest in the National Football League (NFL), since it started in 1920 and still continues whenever these old counterparts meet according to the league schedule makers. It is, for example, older than the Bears–Green Bay rivalry, thought by some to be the league's oldest. As we shall examine later, that rivalry is merely the third oldest in NFL history.

Introduction

With their longevity, the Bears and Cardinals share a voluminous history, and one that parallels the NFL itself.

The Cardinals' origins date to 1899 when a haphazard group of neighborhood kids on the South Side of Chicago created the informal Morgan Athletic Association. By 1917, the organization was incorporated as the Racine Cardinal Pleasure Club (we can't make that up!), or the "Racine Cardinals" for short, under the management of the aforementioned local businessman Chris O'Brien.

Meanwhile, in central Illinois, a prominent Midwest manufacturer sponsored a strong-armed football roster, known simply as the Decatur Staleys, that represented the Staley Manufacturing Company in Decatur, Illinois. In 1920, Mr. Augustus Eugene (A.E.) Staley, the owner of Staley Manufacturing, invited a young University of Illinois graduate from the North Side of Chicago named George Halas to organize, recruit, coach, and play on the Staley football team.

With both of these key figures in place for their respective football teams, O'Brien and Halas were present on September 17, 1920, in Canton, Ohio, when the historic meeting was held to establish the American Professional Football Association (APFA), the forerunner of the National Football League. Both individuals are now recognized as two of the founders of the NFL, although their legacies have wandered somewhat in different directions over the last century. In truth, one (Halas) became a legend in professional football circles, while the other (O'Brien) has been largely forgotten.

Because of those early efforts by O'Brien and Halas, we now enjoy the juggernaut that is the NFL, a circuit of 32 teams that engages our undivided attention each year from late July through early February.

That's just the "playing" season, including all of the elements such as preseason games, the regular schedule, and the wildly popular playoffs—all of which culminate in America's greatest non-holiday event … the Super Bowl.

Then, it's all over way too quickly and we usually wait about 24 hours (or less) to begin talking about the next season with new hopes, dreams, and aspirations for our favorite team. The savvy marketing arm of the NFL, however, does not rest as we are quickly drawn into the discussion, anticipation, and imagination of the annual player draft, a three-day behemoth that rivals the Super Bowl in terms of interest and speculation. And, of course, we cannot avoid the presence of off-season training sessions, college player combines and pro days, free agent movements, coaching changes, trades, and roster adjustments that keep the NFL in our focus for several months even when no games are being played.

It's hard to believe with all of this grand spectacle and attention that once upon a time, America cared little about professional football. As such, this book will focus heavily on the growth and evolution of the game before 1940 and will be top-heavy on those years before its popularity exploded with the advent of televised competition.

Back in the early part of the 20th century, baseball was still the national pastime and college football clearly ruled the gridiron portion of the national sports scene. Professional football was largely unknown, but even then looked upon with a general abundance of both skepticism and suspicion (if not disdain). After all, why would an intelligent college graduate bother to grovel in the mud and slime of the irresponsible and classless pro football mire? The effort to launch the APFA in 1920 was largely ignored by the media, even by the hometown newspapers of the original 11 teams attending the organizational meeting: Canton (Ohio) Bulldogs, Cleveland (Ohio) Indians, Dayton (Ohio) Triangles, Akron (Ohio) Professionals, Massillon (Ohio) Tigers, Rochester (New York) Jeffersons, Rock Island (Illinois) Independents, Muncie (Indiana) Flyers, Hammond (Indiana) Pros, Decatur (Illinois) Staleys, and the Racine (Wisconsin) Cardinals.

Wait! Is that last item a typo? The Racine (Wisconsin) Cardinals?

Not really a typo, but an honest mistake by the new league secretary, Art Ranney (owner of the Akron Pros), who mistook the "Racine" portion of the team's name to coincide with the more familiar "Racine, Wisconsin," rather than a franchise that was, in reality, named after a street in Chicago. The minutes from that historical first meeting were never corrected.

Another misnomer from the list of potential 11 original teams was the imminent disappearance of Massillon as a charter member. Massillon fell out of the pack even before the first league meeting concluded back on September 17, 1920. However, before the dust had settled on the construction of a new professional circuit, four more clubs would be added to the mix, bringing that initial first-year total to 14 with the inclusion of the Buffalo (New York) All-Americans, the Chicago (Illinois) Tigers, the Columbus (Ohio) Panhandles, and the Detroit (Michigan) Heralds.

When the wire services shared the news of the bold decisions created at the September 17 meeting, few noticed, although the brief release was captured by numerous publications throughout the country. Pro football, after all, was not an occupation to which a college man should be attracted, with rampant rumors of debauchery or, even worse, gambling, frightening the misinformed observer.

Even the biggest media market in the league (Chicago) barely stifled an extended yawn. Pro football continued to be shunned by the major newspapers while the upper crust of the college coaching fraternity, e.g., Amos Alonzo Stagg of the University of Chicago, would never succumb to praising the eventual promise and opportunities of postgraduate football. Many pro players melted into the rosters of the early NFL clubs under assumed names, afraid to be identified by either family members or former coaches, or both, for their embarrassing participation. Almost immediately, professional management (among them, the Cardinals) anxiously snared these players and welcomed them into their lineups, no matter what name they chose to play under.

While the new league went to great lengths to distinguish itself from the vastly popular collegiate version of the game, it would still struggle initially with self-inflicted problems concerning equitable scheduling, inconsistent rosters, and guaranteed paychecks for players. One of the primary objectives of the APFA was to forbid the recruiting of current college players to its ranks, which was a main concern of the sporting public. It was feared that the "pros" would harvest the best collegiate football talent, seduce the players with tarnished riches, and ruin the honest reputation of collegiate competition. With such dreadful perceptions, the APFA appeared to be buried in a losing effort from the start, especially with the perceived lack of the old college "spirit" that was hardly feasible when players were being paid for their efforts. Perhaps there would never be a chance for the professional game to initiate a foothold in the American sporting world where baseball, boxing, horse racing, tennis, and college football all enjoyed an established, and successful, stake in the favor of the sporting public.

In time, however, the game of professional football began to slowly emerge from its murky reputation and gradually secure some acceptance from both the media and fans. The escalating rivalry between the Bears and the Cardinals certainly helped to bridge that divide as followers of both teams in Chicago began to harness their support behind the championship aspirations of their chosen club. With the Chicago White Sox and the Chicago Cubs dividing the city's baseball allegiances, it soon became apparent that the Bears and Cardinals would do likewise on the gridiron. Unlike Major League Baseball competition where the Chicago teams would compete only on an exhibition basis (or in a World Series) due to being in separate leagues, the Bears and the Cardinals would meet in meaningful battles within the league's annual schedule. This was especially true in 1925, when the Bears inked the gifted halfback Red Grange to a contract following his final collegiate game with the University of Illinois. His first opponent? The Chicago Cardinals!

Following that initial professional encounter, which sold out Wrigley Field in Chicago (a most unusual occurrence), the Bears and Grange embarked on a lengthy tour (actually two of them) in 1925–1926 that attracted the largest crowds seen to date in the early history of pro football, thus providing a much-needed lifeline for the struggling NFL.

What originated as a North Side (Bears) vs. South Side (Cardinals) territorial conflict in Chicago soon evolved into something much more personal between the two clubs. Whether the battles were on the field for gridiron superiority, or off the field in terms of roster raiding, spying, lawsuits, or plain orneriness, the Bears and Cardinals matchups offered continuous entertainment throughout the years. Through it all, NFL championships were captured by both organizations, successful gridiron campaigns were likewise ruined, and nervy backroom politics were not only anticipated but expected. The early cooperative ventures between Halas and O'Brien grew chilly as each of the owners was driven to succeed. Even after one of the mainstays (O'Brien) was no longer in the picture, the competitive feud between the rivals continued unabated. While the Cardinals have been owned by only three families throughout the team's long history, ironically George Halas was instrumental in arranging for two of these sales. Of course, the Halas family has always owned the Bears, despite a few bumps in the process early on in the journey. So, while the two oldest NFL clubs at one time shared a city, a stadium, and a radio contract, their differences were colossal, if not extraordinary. In short, the Bears and the Cardinals have enjoyed a tempestuous relationship, one based on competition, but stirred, when needed, with animosity, greed, and distrust.

Now let's pull back the curtain of time and journey back to the dawn of pro football and the game's oldest rivalry…

ONE

The Cardinals' Slippery History

> *"They might just as well ask me why I do not nail cranberry jelly to the wall. It would not be my fault or the fault of the nail; it would be the fault of the jelly."*—Theodore Roosevelt, April 9, 1912

Long before the Chicago Bears became a reality, the Cardinals were a dominant football force on the South Side of Chicago. Indeed, the history of the latter club drifts back over 20 years before the advent of the Decatur Staleys/Chicago Bears enterprise. While the history of the Bears is well-documented and verified, the history of the Cardinals is less clear; in fact, it is, unfortunately, a blur.

By the time these two teams first met in 1920 to initiate what is now the oldest rivalry in the history of the National Football League (NFL), each had established its own distinct history. As the only two remaining "original" members of the NFL (also first known as the American Professional Football Association), the Bears and Cardinals experienced a parallel growth spurt in those very early years, although the Bears eventually enjoyed a stronger financial foundation as both organizations shared Chicago as their home base through the 1959 season. But this left a full 40 years of regularly scheduled competition for the teams to growl, snarl, and grapple with each other. With respect to the eldest of these two Chicago football institutions, the curious early history of the Cardinals will be examined first in these pages before we ease into the more familiar creation of the Bears.

Calling Themselves the Morgan Athletic Club

Somewhere, somehow, an interesting quote evolved similar to the Theodore Roosevelt statement at the top of this chapter that noted: "Writing intellectual history is like trying to nail jelly to a wall." Think about that one…

Actually, this simple statement was attributed in 1945 to famed Civil War historian and author William B. Hesseltine.[1] After considering this casual passage, perhaps one might think that the respected Mr. Hesseltine was referring to the quizzical history of the Chicago (now Arizona) Cardinals. Like jelly, the Cardinals' history is a bit slippery and has changed shape and form on a regular basis throughout the team's lengthy existence.

Little of the Cardinals' early published history is accurate. Countless scribes have shared existing information over the past few decades and confidently repeated the magical episodes of Cardinals football history that, in truth, never took place.

And why not? If that slippery history is clearly claimed by the current team itself, as well as by the Pro Football Hall of Fame, why question it?

Yet, the Cardinals' actual history is quite evasive. This is not unusual for the only NFL club that can trace its roots back to the 19th century. Now, as the NFL eases past its 100th anniversary, it is an opportune time to wipe the Cards' historical slate (or jelly) clean and adjust that proud history of the NFL's oldest team. In this reconstruction, several pseudo-historical facts will need to be addressed and altered. To begin, let's review the "beginning" history of the team as it appears on the current website of the Pro Football Hall of Fame: "A charter member of the National Football League, the Cardinals trace their history back to 1898 when Chris O'Brien formed the Morgan Athletic Club. A few years later, he bought used jerseys from the University of Chicago. He described the faded maroon coloring as 'Cardinal red' and the team, then playing at 61st and Racine Street, became the Racine Street Cardinals."[2]

The *2019 Arizona Cardinals Media Guide* shares a nearly identical description: "The Cardinals were founded in 1898 … playing under the name Morgan Athletic Club. The team later was acquired by Chris O'Brien, a painting and decorating contractor, and soon its playing site changed to Normal Field, prompting the new name Normals. In 1901, the team gained long standing identification when O'Brien bought used jerseys from the nearby University of Chicago. The jerseys were faded maroon in color, prompting O'Brien to declare, 'That's not maroon, it's Cardinal red!' The club's permanent nickname had been born."[3]

And, of course, Wikipedia chimes in with another interpretation: "The franchise's inception dates back to 1898, when a neighborhood group gathered to play in the Chicago South Side, calling themselves the Morgan Athletic Club. Chicago painting and building contractor Chris O'Brien acquired the team, which he relocated to Normal Field on Racine Avenue. The team was known as the Racine Normals until 1901, when O'Brien bought used jerseys from the University of Chicago. He described the faded maroon clothing as 'Cardinal red' and the team became the Racine Street Cardinals."[4]

If all of the above information is incorrect, then where and when did the initial trail of inaccuracies begin?

One of the earliest examples of Cardinals history appeared in the *Official Guide of the National Football League* in 1935. Since this was the first year that the NFL published the *Official Guide*, it is one of the more accurate references to the very early days of the professional circuit. The history of the Cardinals merited just a brief mention, but nonetheless, was fairly on-target: "The Cardinals were the first major professional football team in Chicago. Organized originally by Chris O'Brien as an amateur club in the Racine Avenue neighborhood in 1899, they were known as the Cardinals and played under that name until 1903. They were reorganized in 1917 as the Racine Cardinals."[5]

However, overall, there was very little else written about the Cardinals' history from 1899 until 1947, when an article appeared in the team's game-day programs pertaining to the club's deep history. This was nearly two decades after original owner Chris O'Brien sold the team in 1929 to Dr. David Jones, the former physician for the city of Chicago. In those 1947 game programs, Cardinals public relations chief Eddie McGuire updated the team's history as follows:

> The game has come a long way since the days when Chris O'Brien organized the Morgan A.C. [Athletic Club] back in 1899.... In 1901 the lads purchased some red jerseys and took the name Racine Cardinals because they played in the neighborhood of 61st and Racine. Chris and his teammates played amateur ball until running out of competition in 1906, when they disbanded. Chris loved the game and the excitement it provided so in 1913—he was in the painting business at the time, he again organized the team. In 1917, the "raggedy kids" became big-time when they, for the first time, had a coach and classy uniforms. However, it didn't last long due to the war and a "flu" epidemic. Following Armistice Day in 1918, the team was reorganized and in 1919 presented a strong club.[6]

So, starting with Mr. McGuire's interpretation above in 1947, the published history of the Cardinals began to resemble the jelly on the wall mentioned previously. It has been, simply—all over the place—with very little of it being correct. Over the next few chapters in this book, a more accurate portrayal of the team's history will be established. But first, if such inaccuracies are to be traced to Eddie McGuire, it is only fair that we step back and take a look at the career of McGuire, and his own importance within the Cardinals organization.

Few People Knew More Good Times Than Eddie McGuire

Eddie McGuire, who handled publicity for the Cardinals for nearly 20 years, was a creative genius, with a gift for both the written and spoken word. He joined the Cards in 1941 while continuing to work for owner Charles Bidwill in a variety of capacities, such as handling public relations for Bidwill's Chicago Bluebirds women's softball team. McGuire also served in a similar capacity for both the All-American Girls Professional Baseball League and the National Girls Baseball League. He was a popular man in Chicago, constantly working his media contacts, showing up at crowded events, and being a "regular" on the local pallbearer circuit where noteworthy Chicagoans would serve as honorary pallbearers during the services of respected citizens. For example, for the funeral in 1938 for John O. Seys, the vice president of the Chicago Cubs, McGuire was one of 75 honorary pallbearers, part of a massive list that included Chicago Mayor Edward Kelly, baseball Commissioner Keneshaw M. Landis, Cubs owner William Wrigley, and Chicago Bears owner George Halas.[7] McGuire, it seemed, was everywhere!

If a sport needed publicity back then in the Chicago area, McGuire was the guy to handle it. Over his career, he was the publicity guru behind the Cardinals, the Bluebirds, those two baseball leagues, the Chicago Majors of the American Basketball League (and the league itself), the Harlem Globetrotters, the Midwest Invitational Pocket Billiards Tournament, various racing interests, and many others. *Chicago Tribune* columnist David Condon once said of McGuire: "Few people in this man's town [Chicago], and in this great racket, knew more good times than Eddie McGuire. His presence at any affair always ensured a great time for the others on hand."[8]

McGuire started out as a sportswriter for the long-gone *Chicago American*, and his byline later appeared in numerous other newspapers over articles he penned in praise of his beloved Cardinals. Quick with his wit, and holding an ever-present cup of coffee and cigarette, McGuire loved to share stories, exchange tall tales, and rub elbows with the working press around the country. Because of his solid reputation and perpetual presence, McGuire was trusted by both his employers and the media—connecting the interests of both sides by providing insight to the reporters and keeping the name of his employer in front of the reader. It was a wonderful time to work in the press as various news outlets looked for the "scoop" while publicity representatives, like McGuire, were never hesitant to provide the inside stories.

With the respect that McGuire rightfully developed and pursued, there were often examples of minor skirmishes with the truth—tiny excursions into slight exaggeration that were not intended to be harmful nor misleading. For example, in 1961, Leo Sugar, a former Cardinal then with the Philadelphia Eagles, was asked about his significant weight gain during his first training camp with the Eagles. The *Chicago Tribune* reported: "Sugar's weight was a sweet surprise to the Eagles. When the former Purdue star stepped on the scales the day he reported to camp, it was discovered he weighed 232 pounds, 22 more than his refined poundage as a Cardinal. 'I haven't weighed 210 since I first joined the Cards,' Leo explained. 'They never changed my weight on the program because Eddie McGuire, the Cardinal publicity director, liked to brag that I was the smallest defensive end in the league. I was 240 most of last year!'"[9]

Certainly, this was a minor stretch of the truth, but for a good newsman such as McGuire, it made for an interesting story in perpetuating a small misinterpretation concerning a player's weight. According to Mr. Sugar, no one ever questioned the basis of the story, including his new employer! All of which extends into the creation of the history of the Cardinals, where a slight detour to the truth here, or a quiet embellishment there, never stood in the way of a good story. During McGuire's lengthy tenure with the Cardinals, his words wiggled and danced throughout the years, often landing in the slightly ajar door of a newly created story line. Slight historical alterations were never noticed, nor did they matter. The Cardinals' imagined history had been captured, caged, and delivered under the byline of Eddie McGuire, where it continues to flourish today.

You Bucked a Fortification!

About the only item that is consistent with the various documentations of the Cardinals' history is the persona of Chris O'Brien. Mr. O'Brien is credited with being the founder, as well as the first owner, of the Cardinals, and some of that verbiage is true to a limited extent, especially since the existence of today's Arizona Cardinals can be traced directly to O'Brien. Born on October 23, 1881, in Ireland, Chris O'Brien was just 17 years old when he and a group of neighborhood friends organized an informal football team in the summer of 1899 (not 1898) called the Morgan Athletic Association. At the time, O'Brien, and his brother, Pat, lived at 1038

West 53rd Place in the South Side Chicago neighborhood known as Englewood. This would place the O'Brien brothers' residence just west of Morgan Street, and in an era where local athletic teams often snatched the name of the nearest major street or avenue to serve as the name of their sports squad, the O'Briens easily labeled their football club as the Morgan Athletic Association. Apparently, the brothers sought to distinguish their creation from other local teams by adding "athletic association" to the name, although the gridders quickly became more commonly known as the Morgans.

While the name "Morgan Athletic Association" certainly sounded professional, the team could clearly be classified as a "prairie" club, a loosely organized unit that took over neighborhood vacant lots and prairies in order to mark off a field for their games against local rivals. There was no owner, no business manager, nor any stockholders. It was strictly a group of young men who bonded together to play some football in the shadows of Chicago's infamous Union Stockyard. In 1899, the game of football was much different than it is over 120 years later. The players wore little protection, uniforms didn't match, helmets were optional and largely ignored, and rosters were set at the bare minimum. The ball was remarkably different, more closely resembling a swollen bowling ball in shape rather than the sleek sphere utilized today. According to the *Spalding's Official Football Guide* for the 1899 season, the field needed to be "330 feet in length and 160 feet in width, enclosed by heavy white lines marked in lime upon the ground."[10] The longer field in 1899 was just one of the significant differences from the game that many regard as the nation's prevalent sport today.

Scoring was quite different as well with both a touchdown and field goal being worth five points. Because of the rotund shape of the early football (as well as stringent rules regarding passing, which would be illegal until 1906), much of the scoring was achieved through the field goal route. Instead of the *placekick* attempt that evolved over the years, field goal artists in 1899 relied on the dependable *dropkick*, especially on dry fields. As its name implies, for a dropkick the football was dropped to the ground by the kicker, who then timed his attempt after the ball bounced back off the turf. Many booters bemoaned a wet surface on a rainy day, since the "dropped" ball would likely hit the muddy ground and stay there, thus minimizing the success rate for the dropkicker.

While teams could be "coached" by an individual during practices or before a contest, no actual coaching was allowed during the games. If such a serious infraction was noted by the game officials, the offender would be warned once to cease the coaching activity. If a second infringement of the coaching rules occurred, the officials would be required to "exclude him for the reminder of the game from the neighborhood of the field of play; i.e., send the offender behind the ropes or fence surrounding the field of play."[11] As such, those witnessing a gridiron clash in 1899 were likely to view quite a boring game as the teams stood toe-to-toe, and rushers "bucked" (i.e., smashed) the line in an effort to secure the five yards required to establish a first down. Aside from the shorter distance (five yards) needed to achieve a first down, the offense was allowed just three downs in order to reach that objective (fourth down was not added until 1912, with 10 yards needed for the first down).

In fact, teams often elected to punt the ball on first or second down in order to possibly acquire better field position by hopefully pinning the opposition a bit deeper into its own territory. In 1945, James Hopper, who played for the University of California in 1899, provided some interesting memories from participating in football at the turn of the century: "The difference came out of the absence of the forward pass. There being no forward pass, and hence no fear of a forward pass, the team on the defense lined up tight, its line a solid wall, its backs close up. When you lowered your head and bucked that, you bucked a fortification. You had help, though. The help was not so much ahead, in the form of blocking, as it is today; it came from behind. As you bucked, your whole team massed at your tail and enthusiastically shoved you through. [And] Through you went like a straw driven through a fence by a Middle Western cyclone."[12]

Another observation of early football logistics in the 1890s was provided later in his life by Judge Michael McKinley, who played for the University of Iowa during that early decade: "Flying wedges, mass formations, clipping and everything else was a part of the game. It was always a case of slaughter them or be slaughtered. All the coaches hammered into us was 'Run low, tackle hard and be sure to knock down your man.' Instead of quarters there were two halves of forty-five minutes each. A fellow not in shape couldn't stand that. All they gave us were moleskins and jerseys. The only protection for the head was a three-month growth of hair. We generally stopped cutting it in June!"[13]

In a final bit of football rules antiquity, once the ball carrier was tackled, it did not mean that the play was over in 1899. Whereas today, we can view multiple camera angles to determine when an elbow, knee, or rear end touched the ground to conclude an offensive play, back in 1899 the rusher could continue to crawl or stumble to secure additional yardage after being tackled. This, of course, was done at the ball carrier's own peril, since his intention to continue his movement, even while already prone on the ground, would encourage the defense to swiftly join the enlarging pile on top. It was then up to the official (or the pleading ball carrier, who would yell "down") to finally end the play. Such was the game of football embraced by the fledgling Morgan Athletic Association prior to its first contest in 1899.

Bridgeport Stench

While Chris and Pat O'Brien eventually became the standout players on the Morgan football squad, it was their neighbor Tom Clancy who appeared to absorb most of the organizational responsibilities for the new outfit. Clancy resided at 948 West 53rd Street (just a few houses east of the O'Brien family).[14] Clancy was a mere 18 years old during that initial season but was listed as the contact person in local newspapers and flyers when the Morgans began to schedule games in the early fall of 1899.[15]

It was up to Clancy to secure both opponents and a home field for the new organization. The latter selection was easy; Clancy arranged to utilize a spare patch of land at 52nd and Morgan to serve as the team's home base, and then began working on the Morgans' 1899 schedule. News releases were prepared for small, neighborhood newspapers that served readers who were largely employed either by the city of Chicago or by the Union Stockyard, whose boundary ended at 47th Street, just a few blocks north of the home field of the Morgans. The impact of the stockyards on the Englewood neighborhood where the O'Briens and their teammates resided was enormous. "At its peak, during World War I, the stockyards employed nearly 50,000 workers," stated Dr. Dominic Pacyga, author of *Slaughterhouse: Chicago's Union Stock Yard and the World It Made*.[16] With Englewood positioned so close to the packing facilities, employment opportunities were significant for the residents, both for labor and management responsibilities. "At that time," added Pacyga, "Englewood was considered more of an upper-class neighborhood—a place you moved to—rather than from. So many of the Englewood people held management positions at the stockyards and that had a great economic impact on Englewood."

Pacyga, who is the emeritus professor of history at Columbia College in Chicago and the author of several books on Chicago and its environs, worked at the stockyards as a livestock handler and security guard while completing his collegiate education. His memories of that experience, and from growing up in a neighborhood adjacent to the facility, include an indelible reference to the atrocious odor that was common before the stockyards closed for good in 1971. "The smell could be horrendous and could be overpowering at times," said Pacyga. "When the stockyards opened in 1865, the odor was originally known as the 'Bridgeport Stench.' The winds tended to blow the stench through Bridgeport over to Hyde Park and into downtown Chicago. Even when I was growing up in the Back of the Yards [a neighborhood bordering the stockyards], we sang a little ditty":

> *Roses are red,*
> *Violets are blue,*
> *The stockyards stink*
> *And so do you!*

The residents in the areas surrounding the stockyards were often at the whim of ugly, obnoxious odors. As the wind shifted, so did their moods. If caught by surprise by a sudden change in the direction of the wind, residents reluctantly inhaled gulps of the putrid, ghastly stench. One never became accustomed to the polluted atmosphere on the South Side of Chicago; it never seemed to disappear. It was always there. Spit it out. Gag a bit. Get rid of it. Pray for a shift in the wind…

Despite living in the shadows of the sprawling stockyards, the players on the Morgan Athletic Association football team and their neighbors could never shake the maleficent smells drifting down to their home playing field, affectionately referred to as "The Woods." But the players would work through it, just as other residents had for decades. At times, the smell was so challenging that it deserved its own headline, such as in a *Chicago Tribune* article from 1899: "Stock Yards Stench Again. Vile Odors from Bridgeport Spread Over the City, Disgusting and Sickening the People. Almost before the people of Chicago living north of the Stock-yards had recovered from the last visit of the Bridgeport stench another wave of fetid odors has engulfed them."[17]

Club Netted a Snug Sum of Money

The long-forgotten *Chicago South Side Daily Sun* was the first newspaper to announce the formation of the local contingent and its initial gridiron success. The Morgans defeated a local adversary called the Shermans by a robust score of 29–0 on Sunday, October 15, 1899, with the *Sun* providing ample game coverage the very next day: "The Morgan A.A. football team defeated the Shermans in a one-sided game by a score of 29–0. The game was very monotonous on account of the playing of the Shermans, who were unable to cope with the center rush or the end runs of the Morgans. The features of this game were the punting of Green, the ground gaining of Kendrick, Ward, P. O'Brien, and Kennedy of the Morgans and a phenomenal run of 15 yards by Corcoran of the Shermans."[18]

Chris O'Brien started at left end for the Morgans while Tom Clancy was penciled in at left tackle. Kirk Green, who was also listed as the coach of the Morgans, tallied three touchdowns and booted four extra points to account for 24 of the team's total of 29 (touchdowns were still worth just five points at the time). All in all, it was a nice start for the upstart Morgans. Except for an 11–5 defeat at the hands of the Dearborn Athletic Association, the Morgans (6–1–1) pitched shutouts in all six of their other games in 1899, winning five and tying one, and outscored their opponents 94–11 on the season. The final game finished in a scoreless tie with the host Kensington Tigers, and the game report provided by the *South Side Daily Sun* included some very interesting insight into the game of football in 1899. While the newspaper noted that over 700 fans attended the game, it also mentioned that "From a financial standpoint the game was a success, netting the club [Morgans] a snug sum of money." Since the Morgans likely did not share in any gate receipts, the above comment strongly suggests that the players, and their followers, participated in some ambitious wagers on the side. Furthermore, the efforts of some of the individual players were highlighted: "The Morgans' backs, Daly, [Chris] O'Brien, Noonan, and Corcoran, played the game of their life, always gaining whenever they had the ball, the punting of P. O'Brien was also of high order. For the Kensingtons, Padden, Warren, Mericer and a player whom the Kensingtons had hired, and whose name they would not tell, played a good game."[19]

Even in 1899, "ringers" were a problem as players jumped from roster to roster on any given day for either a little bit of action or perhaps in the hopes of grabbing some quick cash. But it is quite interesting that the *Daily Sun* would so boldly mention that one of the opponents preferred to remain nameless! For a group of mostly teenage players, the 1899 campaign was quite successful for the Morgans. While the opponents were likely scheduled on a weekly basis, the Morgans went only one week without a game once the season started and actually played a pair of contests on November 16, grabbing some revenge in a 6–0 win over the Dearborns, and then easing past the Kensingtons 11–0 after a brief respite.

A season-ending dinner party was hosted by Coach Green at the affluent Kinsley's restaurant in downtown Chicago with left end Willie Ward serving as toastmaster. But the football dynasty of the Morgan Athletic Association would be short-lived. After just that lone inaugural season, the players on the Morgan A.A.

were absorbed by the new Morgan Athletic Club. On August 24, 1900, the formation of a new neighborhood athletic club with grand ambitions was announced in a neighborhood newspaper: "The Morgan Athletic Club, a new organization composed of young men who reside in the vicinity of Fifty-third and Halsted streets, was formed last Friday evening." Then just three weeks later, more pertinent information about the club surfaced:

> The Morgan Athletic Club, recently organized, bids fair to become the leading organization of its kind.... Its membership includes many of the prominent merchants, politicians and athletes of the south side.... The club has fitted up an elaborate and complete gymnasium at 5256 Halsted street and has facilities for boxing, wrestling, fencing, handball, etc., and its members will compete in the indoor meets this winter. The football team captained by Christy O'Brien, composed of members of last year's Morgans, are already in training under the guidance of Kirk Green, of the University of Chicago.[20]

While Chris and Pat O'Brien, along with trusted sidekick Tom Clancy, organized and assembled the Morgan football squad, the sport was just one of many offered to the membership. Boxing and track were extremely popular and the Morgan A.C. routinely entered teams of its athletes in just about any type of competition offered on the South Side. Dances and picnics were well supported with numbers in the thousands. By 1907, for example, the annual picnic sponsored by the club was so strongly attended that special trains were reserved to ferry the participants out to the southwest suburbs: "The Morgan Athletic Club is going to pull off its annual picnic athletic events tomorrow at Santa Fe Park, regardless of weather conditions. Officials announced that 12,000 tickets already have been sold.... Trains will leave the Polk Street station every half hour from 9 a.m. until 2:30 p.m."[21]

Around the turn of the century, athletic and social clubs were sprouting up all over the South Side of Chicago. The clubs provided not only an escape for older members, but a viable athletic alternative for younger participants. "Many of the athletic clubs basically evolved from street gangs that were politically connected," said author Dominic Pacyga. "When the gangs became athletic clubs, they appeared to be more responsible within the community."[22]

Team Blames Loss on Stag Party

The Morgan Athletic Club swiftly became quite popular in the Englewood area and was incorporated in the state of Illinois on February 2, 1901. The signees on the corporate documents were local businessmen George Reker, Frank Corcoran, Cornelius Murphy, and John Casey, with the club's objectives being "to promote and encourage athletic and gymnastic exercises, and for the furtherance of field and indoor sports."[23] Aside from athletic activities, the club quickly sponsored its first dance on Friday, September 14, 1900, with over 150 people in attendance, prompting exceptional praise from those in attendance: "An excellent string orchestra dispensed music during the evening. The affair started at 8 and continued until 12 o'clock, when all left for their homes after bestowing much laudation upon the efforts of the club to become a leader among organizations of its kind on the south side."[24] One of the committee members responsible for the festivities was

Christopher O'Brien, suggesting that the ambitious young man intended to become involved with more than just football for the Morgan A.C. In fact, O'Brien was already being recognized for his work on the Morgan's newly minted baseball squad: "The Morgan Athletic Club's team defeated the Englewoods yesterday afternoon in a well-contested game at Sixty-third street and Centre [Racine] avenue by a score of 7 to 5. Pitcher O'Brien, of the Morgans, kept the Englewoods guessing throughout the game, and their inability to reach his twisters was soon apparent."[25]

Of course, the above information shatters a couple of more misnomers about the history of the Cardinals. Since the Morgan Athletic Club did not surface until 1900 (and was not incorporated until 1901), the 21st-century history lessons indicating the team was part of the Morgan A.C. in 1898 or 1899 could not be accurate if the club itself did not exist until 1900. We also usually hear that Chris O'Brien was the owner of the Morgan Athletic Club. While still a teenager in 1900, O'Brien was certainly in charge of football operations but was not one of the owners of the corporation.

As he did the year before, Thomas Clancy developed the schedule for the gridiron representatives of the Morgan Athletic Club with Kirk Green once again serving as the coach. On the field, the Morgans enjoyed another superlative season, finishing 6–2–1 against a schedule stacked with competing athletic clubs. One of the intriguing aspects of the journalistic coverage of the local games was the pure honesty of the reporting. After an early season loss (5–0) to the neighboring Hyde Park Columbias, the Morgans pinned the defeat on an unusual, but familiar, foe: "The members of the defeated team lay the blame to a stag party which was given at their clubhouse Saturday evening, lasting until an early hour Sunday morning."[26]

While most of the games were arranged on the vacant lot at 52nd and Morgan Streets, the team soon began attracting hefty crowds, such as the 2,000 fans who stood and encircled the field during a 22–5 victory over the Dearborns on Sunday, October 28, 1900. Another 1,000 attendees were on hand for an away game at the Pullman Kensingtons on November 11, boosted by over 200 followers of the Morgans who grabbed a seat on a special train to enjoy the trek out to what was then the far-south suburbs around 111th Street. With a 6–1–1 record, the Morgans suddenly found themselves in the spotlight when a final "championship" game was arranged with the undefeated Delawares (8–0) on December 2 at what was then called "Comiskey's Park," the home of the newly arrived Chicago White Sox baseball club. Located at 39th (now called Pershing) and Wentworth, the ballpark had wooden stands that could accommodate nearly 15,000 fans for baseball, cricket, or football events. It was a huge upward step for the Morgans and their fans, who were more familiar with football fields situated on empty lots and lacking any permanent seating facilities.

White Sox owner Charles Comiskey constructed the grandstands for his team's first season in Chicago and the club remained in that location for the remainder of the decade. For the Morgans and the Delawares, the importance of the football game also provided some significant recognition for the sport itself, according to author Floyd Sullivan: "On December 2, 1900, the team [Morgan A.C.] played a Chicago city championship game against the Delawares at the home of the new American League Chicago White Stockings.... A precedent was set for football in Chicago. The new sport's growing popularity demanded that an important football game be played in a professional sports arena, specifically a baseball park."[27]

Although attendance figures for the landmark contest at Comiskey's Park were not published, a likely strong crowd watched as the Delawares edged the Morgans 6–0 to preserve their undefeated (9–0) campaign, while the 1900 Morgan Athletic Club finished with a successful 6–2–1 mark. Chris O'Brien remained with the team for nearly 30 years and eventually became its owner; Pat O'Brien split off eventually to become an electrician and also co-owned a series of local businesses with his brother Chris. Tom Clancy moved over into law enforcement, achieving the position of sergeant with the Chicago Police Department. He passed away at the age of 55 in 1936.[28]

Bezdek Is Unquestionably the Greatest Fullback

Yet there are three others from that early team who left a significant impact on life away from the Morgan Athletic Club: guard Nick Bruck, fullback Hugo Bezdek, and administrator and sometimes lineman Frank Ragen. Bruck was one of the best bowlers not only in the city and state but also in the country. At one time, Bruck (1877–1934) held the world's record in bowling "doubles" and later served as president of the National Bowling Proprietors' Association and the Chicago Bowling Proprietors' Association.[29] Hugo Bezdek, on the other hand, was just a very young man when he joined the Morgans in 1900. Born in the Czech Republic in 1884, Bezdek was a shade under 5'7" but a solid 170 pounds. As a teenager, he loved boxing, baseball, and the game of football but there was one major drawback. His high school (Lake High School, later Tilden Tech) offered challenging academics but did not field a football team.

This problem was quickly solved as Bezdek was added to the Morgan Athletic Club grid squad while a mere 16 years old! Bezdek proved to be a punishing and valuable workhorse in the backfield. After two seasons under the tutelage of Chris O'Brien, Bezdek matriculated to the powerful University of Chicago squad in 1902, where he was the happy responsibility of legendary coach Amos Alonzo Stagg. By his senior campaign in 1905, Bezdek achieved All-American honors in an undefeated (11–0) season later marked by the retroactive awarding of the national championship crown for Stagg and his determined band of Maroons. In the final contest of the season, Chicago edged Michigan by the strange score of 2–0, thus ending Michigan's 56 game unbeaten streak. The respected coach was more than pleased with the play of the aggressive Bezdek: "Bezdek is unquestionably the greatest full back of the year east or west. It is likely to be quite a time before we will have another man as good as Bezdek to buck the line. Not only is he a great line bucker, but he is a great player in every department of the game. He is a star in defensive work as well as in the art of interfering for his fellow backs. He certainly should be put on the All-American team this year."[30]

Of course, Stagg did see his wish come true as Bezdek secured those

All-American honors for the dominant champs of the Western (later Big Ten) Conference. It does seem ironic that at a time when there was an unrelenting succession of finger-pointing and accusations by one school or another regarding the presumed "professionalism" of other teams' players, no one ever closely examined Bezdek's background. In other words, why did Stagg or others not comprehend that Bezdek played two seasons of "prairie" football *before* he entered the vaunted halls of the University of Chicago? As will be discussed later in this book, Stagg abhorred even the thought of one of his players straying into the professional ranks (as slim as that chance was in the early 1900s). It should be noted that in 1904, the University of Illinois accused Bezdek of being a "professional," but in boxing! Bezdek was later acquitted of these charges, but he was never reprimanded for his dalliance with Chris O'Brien over that two-year period in 1900 and 1901 when, under normal circumstances, he would have been playing for his high school team.

After graduation, Bezdek immediately began a lifelong career in the coaching profession as he accepted the head football coaching position at the University of Oregon in 1906. Over the next dozen years, Bezdek crisscrossed the country with one impressive job after another: "After his college playing days were over, Bezdek went to Eugene, Oregon, and helped to develop the athletic stars at State college. Two years later he returned to help [Amos Alonzo] Stagg coach his old team, and then became coach at the University of Arkansas. Then he returned to the University of Oregon as athletic director."[31]

Not content to remain focused solely on football, Bezdek also served major colleges as both a baseball and basketball coach. He was the head football coach at Penn State from 1918 to 1929 and at Delaware Valley in 1949. Along the way, Bezdek achieved a coaching honor that has never been duplicated. He is the only person to assume the role of head coach of an NFL club (the Cleveland Rams from 1937 to 1938) as well as serve as the manager of a Major League Baseball team (Pittsburgh Pirates from 1917 to 1919). Bezdek is also the only football coach to bring three of his teams (Oregon, Penn State, and Mare Island) to the Rose Bowl. Bezdek was eventually voted into the College Football Hall of Fame after his long and successful career.

But Bezdek also remained in contact with his old gridiron friends in Chicago, often attending the reunions of the Morgan Athletic Club. And the Morgans loved Hugo in return, as club President Frank Ragen stated a few years later: "In the world of athletics, too, our boys made a fine record. One old [member] is Hugo Bezdek, now the famous coach of the football team at Penn State. I could cite many others who became well known in the athletic world. I think these things should be recalled in writing the obituary of the club."[32]

As for Frank Ragen, he quickly became president of the Morgan Athletic Club and was a master organizer for the group, planning huge events (such as the annual picnic) and related athletic competitions. He eventually broke away from the Morgans around 1908 and formed his own club called the Ragen Athletic and Benevolent Association, often known as "Ragen's Colts." But in 1901, the Morgan Athletic Club was thriving, and plans were quickly developed for the club to construct a new, larger headquarters. On the football front, Hugo Bezdek and his cohorts would be back for another season of sure success on the gridiron along with the glut of free publicity that a winning team generates.

Except for one problem: the O'Brien brothers and their pigskin teammates were on the move again. For the third time in as many seasons, the O'Briens would be playing under a different team name. And this time, the moniker would stick around for the next 120 years or so!

Two

Famous Chicago Cardinals

> *"The Cardinals football team, which formerly played under the colors of the Morgan Athletic Club, has organized for the season."*
> —*South Side Daily Sun*, September 27, 1901

On September 27, 1901, the *South Side Daily Sun* announced the creation of still another local community entity—The Cardinals Social and Athletic Club: "The Cardinals club will open the season with an informal dance at Masonic Hall. Forty-second and Halsted Streets, Friday, October 18. The Cardinals football team, which formerly played under the colors of the Morgan Athletic Club, has organized for the season with a line of about 160 pounds, and, aided by a competent coach, will endeavor to maintain its former reputation. Managers of teams averaging 140 pounds or over desiring games, are requested to send challenges to J.P. [Pat] O'Brien, captain, 1038 Fifty-third Place."[1]

While most of the members from the previous season's Morgan A.C. team remained with the Cardinals, the club sought to elevate itself above the "prairie" (or schoolyard) level of competition by joining a new organization called the Associated Football Clubs of Chicago, which welcomed over 30 teams under its umbrella. Tom Clancy and Pat O'Brien represented the Cardinals at the organizational meetings held to establish the league and develop more organized scheduling of games among its members.[2] The inception of such a union demonstrated the emerging popularity of independent football in the Chicago area. Baseball was still the local king, but the readily available baseball fields in the area could easily be converted into football gridirons during the late summer in order to accommodate the increasing number of games scheduled throughout the week, and especially on Sundays. While the Cardinals played an abbreviated schedule in 1901, the club finished with a successful 4–0–1 mark, the first undefeated campaign in the team's history that has now stretched across three centuries.

In the very early part of the 20th century, the game of football was still in transition. Without a national professional league, colleges and universities were the subject of increased fan appreciation, although greater emphasis was now being placed on the number of deaths and injuries incurred by participating players across the country. Meanwhile, schools that are now considered major colleges continued to sprinkle their schedules against much smaller institutions and high schools. For example, in 1901 Hyde Park High School in Chicago fell to the University of

Wisconsin 63–0 but defeated the University of Chicago 6–0. Englewood High School in Chicago dropped a pair of games to the University of Chicago, while also absorbing a 39–0 shellacking at the University of Illinois. In time, high schools disappeared from collegiate schedules, especially when students and alumni demanded tougher competition as the college game continued to grow and expand. Looming in the background, however, was the increasing concern over the number of injuries and fatalities suffered on the gridiron.

Meanwhile, the Cardinals breezed through the abbreviated 1901 schedule, paced by a diminutive 145-pound quarterback named Maurice O'Shea. In an era when passing was largely nonexistent, O'Shea teamed with Hugo Bezdek and the O'Brien brothers to provide the Cardinals with a quick and evasive backfield. Bezdek was especially impressive in the final game of the campaign, a 14–5 decision over the Columbias: "Bezdek, star end of the Cardinals, carried the ball to the Columbias 50-yard line. And from this point, the ball was finally sent across Columbia's goal line by L.C. Bliss and O'Shea for another touchdown. P. O'Brien kicked a difficult goal from side line at 25 yards."[3]

Off the field, the O'Brien brothers started a neighborhood business that offered "paints, oils, glass, wallpaper, etc., at lowest prices." This advertisement appeared on a regular basis in the *South Side Daily Sun* and encouraged customers to visit the O'Brien brothers at 751 West 43rd Street. Although Chris O'Brien was a struggling business owner at the age of 19, his role in the inception of the Cardinals Social and Athletic Club refutes another myth about the origination of the Cardinals team nickname. As mentioned in the previous examples of the existing Cardinals history, O'Brien (incorrectly defined as the owner of the team) supposedly purchased used jerseys from the University of Chicago and likened the faded maroon colors to "cardinal red." And that, apparently, was when and how the team name of Cardinals originated. Of course, since O'Brien did not own the team, it is highly unlikely that Coach Amos Alonzo Stagg would have sold any property to a semiprofessional team. When the NFL was born almost 20 years later, Stagg stubbornly dug in his heels, declaring his vociferous opposition to the professional game: "To patronize Sunday professional football games is to cooperate with forces which are destructive of the finest elements of interscholastic and intercollegiate football…. To cooperate with Sunday football is to work against the best interests of interscholastic and intercollegiate football and cooperate with forces destructive to the school and college game."[4]

Comparisons of extant photos from the University of Chicago football teams of 1899 and 1900 and those of the 1901 Cardinals club cannot define the uniforms as being similar. Again, it appears that the feel-good story about the origination of the Cardinals name evolved from the creative pen of Eddie McGuire in the late 1940s. No mention of O'Brien purchasing used uniforms from Stagg surfaced until then. So, the account of the team's history that still comes closest to accuracy is that of the 1935 *Official Guide of the National Football League* as noted previously: "Organized originally by Chris O'Brien as an amateur club in the Racine Avenue neighborhood in 1899, they were known as the Cardinals and played under that name until 1903."

Chris O'Brien and friends did return as the Cardinals in 1902. That season was highlighted by the first out-of-town trip taken by the team (a 15–5 loss at Michigan

City, Indiana). The local newsmakers gloated after that game about the vastness of the victory by stretching the accomplishments of the visitors: "The famous Chicago Cardinals, for the past five years champions of the gridiron game in Cook County, Ill., outside of the college teams, met the first defeat that they have suffered in that period."[5] Not bad for a team that didn't exist five years before! Other than that blemish, the Cardinals grabbed victories in their other five contests to finish 5–1. By ignoring the Michigan City defeat, the Cards claimed the championship of Cook County by sweeping past all foes in the county.

Enter the Normals!

If we consider the early history of the Cardinals a bit slippery, it became downright murky after that 1902 season. Chris O'Brien, and his teammates, virtually vanished from the local newspapers in 1903. The Cardinals Social and Athletic Club, it seems, was no longer in existence. Meanwhile, the Morgan Athletic Club continued to grow and prosper under the leadership of Frank Ragen. Its football team in 1903, also coached by Ragen, played a full schedule, prompting the *South Side Daily Sun* to decree: "The Morgan Athletic Club has never been defeated in three seasons."[6] If the O'Briens were maintaining a low profile in 1903 or were simply not mentioned in the neighborhood chronicles, a new opportunity emerged in that same year with the announcement of the Normal Athletic Association, albeit without a football team. "The Normal Athletic Association clubrooms are located at Sixty-ninth street and Lowe Avenue, and the club has a membership in the neighborhood of 200. The Normal Athletic baseball team has held an important position in amateur baseball this season."[7] The club actually remitted its $10 fee to incorporate on February 7, 1903, with offices at 755 West 69th Street in Chicago.[8] Its five-member board consisted of E.J. Kane, O.H. Reins, S.J. Fisk, C.H. Carlson, and P. Warner. Football would become part of the club's offerings in 1904 when the O'Brien brothers, and many of their familiar comrades, showed up when the Normals first took the football field on October 9 for a scoreless tie with the nearby Hamilton Athletic Club. Games were played at what was called the "Normals' Grounds" or the "Normal Athletic Association Park" at 69th and Green (one block west of Halsted Street) in Chicago.[9] Conditions were not ideal on this field as recounted years later by one William Coyne: "The fellows played in the lot at 69th and Halsted Streets, the same lot that was used by the circus. One difficulty had to be overcome, however, in every game. The field was 15 yards too short because of a large sign board standing at one end of the gridiron. When a player [on offense] reached the sign board, he was automatically downed and the ball placed 15 yards from the sign board. Play would resume with the attacking team needing that distance for a touchdown. What pileups they had! When a man was tackled, everybody piled on to make sure he wouldn't go any further!"[10]

Both the Normals and the Morgans became members of the new Chicago Football League in the fall of 1904. After a convincing 12–0 win over the Maplewoods on November 20, 1904, the Normals were 3–0–1 and earned some praise in the city press after each of the O'Brien brothers scored a touchdown: "The Normal Athletics clinched the championship of the city in the heavyweight division by defeating the strong Maplewood team by the score of 12–0. The features of the game were the playing of C. O'Brien, P. O'Brien, St. John, and Morrisey of the Normals…. The Normals will play their last game of the season next Sunday with the Morgans at American League park for $150 a side."[11]

Since the separation of the O'Brien team members from the Morgan Athletic Club following the 1902 season, the two neighboring clubs had not met on the field. That was about to change as the spotlight once again shifted to the home of the Chicago White Sox at 39th and Wentworth, where the two unbeaten squads would face off on November 27, 1904. After a tremendous buildup, the two clubs battled to a 0–0 deadlock. While this would prove to be the final contest of the campaign for the Morgans, the Normal Athletic Club reined in one more opponent: the dangerous Clover Athletic Club. Behind a touchdown from Chris O'Brien and the successful extra point by Pat O'Brien, the Normals escaped with a 6–5 victory and another undefeated season (4–0–2), earning the team the heavyweight championship of the city of Chicago. The win capped a rather satisfying personal year for Chris O'Brien. Aside from the successful season and the growth of his business, O'Brien had married the former Frieda Benecke on July 28, 1904.

Football Must Be Radically Reformed or Abolished

The growth of local football in Chicago continued unabated in 1905, despite the increased concern over the number of deaths and injuries extending over all levels of the game. The *Chicago Tribune*, as well as many other publications elsewhere in the country, tabulated regular lists of the injured and deceased resulting from football activities. The relentless call for reform culminated in a lengthy exposé on November 27, 1905, entitled "Sound Knell of Brutal Football," which included flaming opinions from key educators and scholars representing leading universities such as Harvard, Northwestern, California, and the University of Chicago. All were united in their call for massive reform of the gridiron game: "Football as it is played must be immediately and radically reformed or abolished. This is the opinion of university and college presidents all over the country, telegraphed to the Tribune in answer to a message calling attention to the 19 deaths and 138 injuries of the season now drawing to an end. From the Pacific to the Atlantic coast the game as it is played is universally condemned. The urgent necessity for a national conference of university authorities to reform the game and eliminate its brutality is strongly emphasized by a majority of university and college presidents."[12]

With the frank encouragement and personal involvement of President Theodore Roosevelt, representatives of major colleges such as Harvard and Yale met at the White House to bring some lifesaving rules changes to the sport—all in the spirit of significantly decreasing the mayhem and violence on the field. Designated as the "Football Reform Platform," the college reps agreed to universally focus on minimizing the carnage that had become so prevalent: "Brutality and foul play, however, should receive the same summary punishment given to a man who cheats at cards, who strikes a foul blow in boxing…. It would be a real misfortune to lose so manly and vigorous a game as football, and to avert such a possibility the college authorities in each college should see to it that the game in that college is clean.'"[13]

Beginning with the 1906 season, several key rules changes were implemented, including the creation of a neutral zone on the line, increasing the first-down distance to 10 yards (although offenses were still allowed just three downs to accomplish this feat!), and legalizing the forward pass. Although the rules would continue to be evaluated and massaged over the years, these initial attempts succeeded in subduing, but not eliminating, some of the deaths associated with football. The changes did, however, save the game itself from being possibly abolished. Fortunately, football did have an ally in President Roosevelt, whose own philosophy captured his feelings on the state of the game at this time. "In life, as in a football game, the principle to follow is: Hit the line hard; don't foul and don't shirk, but hit the line hard!"[14]

Back in Chicago, the O'Brien brothers reversed course once again and retreated back to the roster of the Morgan Athletic Club for the 1905 season. Pat O'Brien was swiftly appointed as the team's captain. Working under the auspices of new coach James Ragen (brother of Frank), the football squad rolled into the finale of the season undefeated when they tested the Deering Maroons for the title of the Chicago Football League. The circuit had matured to the point where the leaders from the South Side of Chicago (Morgans) would clash with the North Side frontrunners (Maroons) for the overall city title. Roster movement was still not a concern as the Morgans added University of Chicago All-American Hugo Bezdek to the squad prior to kickoff. Bezdek's presence was not disguised. In fact, he began "coaching" the team four days per week in mid–October, while still in the midst of Chicago's incredible 11–0 season. After the collegiate season concluded with that 2–0 landmark win over Michigan on November 30, Bezdek was the object of Coach Stagg's reported affection in the postgame locker room bedlam: "Bezdek, who had just completed his four years of football, was seated, minus jersey, on a bench in another part of the room. Unmindful of the grime and the visage of the stocky full back, the veteran coach threw his arms about him. 'Beautiful, Bezdek—beautiful!' said Stagg, and Bezdek grinned back his happiness at the coach."[15]

Just three days later (December 3), Bezdek was in the Morgans lineup to face the Deering Maroons.[16] Sadly, the final score of that title tilt is nowhere to be found in any of the Chicago-area papers. There were mentions a year later that the Maroons were the defending city champions, so we might surmise that the Morgans fell to Deering in that contest, likely finishing the season with a 4-1-1 record. While Red Grange would stun the sporting world 20 years later by participating in a professional game a week after his final collegiate game, no one seemed to notice that Hugo Bezdek set the precedent for such activity way back in 1905.

While Bezdek would move on to begin his coaching career in 1906, local teams such as the Morgans faced a new problem that was directly correlated to the massive new rules changes. In Chicago, city park administrators under the guise of the South Park Commission initiated several mandates intended to eradicate, or at least stifle, the brutality of football. These measures included limiting football access to park-owned fields, encouraging the scheduling of games between teams of similar overall weight averages, and requiring that park directors oversee the scheduling of games. Perhaps most important for the local clubs, admission fees were banned for games played on city park grounds. Teams were also required to secure a permit to schedule a game and all players were now forced to undergo a physical prior to playing in one of the battles on the park district property. Coupled with the new rule that required a 10-yard gain for a first down with only three downs (four downs would not be placed into the mix until 1912, the same year that a touchdown achieved its present value of six points), the games were slow and basically boring. For Edward DeGroot, athletic director for the commission, the changes were not only necessary, but also welcome: "The park commissioners have done well to recommend changes in the game as it is played in the parks, as there is a much greater need for reform among these players than among properly coached college teams."[17]

Since many, if not all, of the local football teams had utilized city park spaces in the past to host their competitions, the tighter hold on these fields may have forced some athletic clubs to capitulate and drop their football programs. While the Morgans and the Normals continued with their popular and successful baseball teams, any mention of their previous football powerhouses were few and far between. The Normals did have an advantage since the club apparently owned or leased property for its football field as mentioned in a 1908 article: "The Normal Athletic Club football team will play the South Chicago Athletic Club team on the Normals grounds, 69th and Green Streets, Sunday afternoon at 3 o'clock. It will be a good game."[18]

The Normals grabbed a 16–0 decision over South Chicago and managed to advance to the championship game of the Chicago Football League in 1908 against Anson's Colts. After a 5–5 decision on December 13 failed to decide a winner, the two clubs met a week later, but no final score was reported.[19] Again box scores and rosters became increasingly sparse in area newspapers, leaving no trace of the O'Brien brothers or their former teammates after the 1905 season. With no available tangible evidence to trace their whereabouts, it was thought that the O'Briens simply discontinued their participation on the local gridirons. Both were older now, engaged in a growing business, and Chris at least (Patrick never married) was enjoying married life. In 1910, Chris and Frieda O'Brien welcomed the birth of their only child, Edward.

And then on December 15, 1918, an article in the *Chicago Herald and Examiner* disclosed that Chris O'Brien had never stopped playing football. After years as a quick halfback or end for various teams, in 1918 he was now employed in the trenches for his own club called the Racine Cardinals: "Chris was a fleet halfback in the good old days, but after nearly twenty years of service had slowed him down, he went into the forward wall, and since then has been playing all guard and tackle. He is built more along the lines of a halfback than of a line man, yet, despite the fact that he yields weight in the ordinary run of opponents, Chris continues to shine. In a recent game he outplayed a husky tackle who a couple of years ago was regarded as a member of the Ohio State University eleven."[20]

While the article did not document which specific teams O'Brien played for throughout the years (except the Morgans), it mentioned that he would be playing that afternoon in his 168th game of "amateur and semi-pro football on the prairies and sand lot gridirons of Chicago." The article served as a bridge between 1918 and

O'Brien's early playing days when "football was little known outside of the colleges and the Morgan A.A. team with which Chris was connected attracted crowds composed mostly of people who gathered from curiosity."

While the 37-year-old O'Brien was preparing for his 168th football contest, a skinny young Navy man named George Halas was about to embark on a trip to California for a football game that would change his life—and football—forever.

But first—his backstory.

Three

Order of the Broken Jaw

"Halas is the hard luck man of Illinois football. In the last two years injuries have retired him before the season was well started."
—*Wisconsin State Journal*, October 15, 1917

While in *high school*, George Halas was all over the sports pages. But not for football.

While in *college*, Halas was once again all over the sports pages. But not for football.

While considered too small to make an impact in high school football, and then too often injured in college, Halas early on found that his first love was baseball. He was so good in the sport that he earned a spot on the New York Yankees in 1919 and later dabbled in a minor league baseball career. Halas was also an excellent basketball player who played professionally for the Whiting (Indiana) Red Crowns. So, some who view Halas as purely a football man might be surprised that he was good enough in all three major sports to play at the professional level in football, basketball, and baseball.

While a multitude of articles and books on Halas have appeared over the last few decades, there is much more to his athletic resume than is evident in his more famous football accomplishments with the Chicago Bears. Born on February 2, 1895, on the near west side of Chicago, Halas grew up learning responsibility and determination from his strict parents, Frank and Barbara, both immigrants from Bohemia. With older brothers Frank and Walter serving as mentors, George engaged in neighborhood sports, particularly baseball. In his autobiography, Halas discussed his athletic hopes and dreams at that age: "By the time I was ten, I was a roaring Cubs baseball fan. My heroes were the infield double-play trio—Tinkers to Evans to Chance…. At every opportunity, I would present myself at the entrance to Cubs' Park, then at Polk and Wood Streets, about a mile and a quarter from home…. At the park, we would hang about the pass-gate and call to our heroes as they entered…. I dreamed of the day when the big league star would be George Stanley Halas."[1]

Halas entered Crane Technical High School in the fall of 1909 weighing a scrawny 110 pounds. At that time, high school football teams were divided by weight limitations, rather than by class years. Therefore, a slight senior weighing less than 150 pounds might be placed on the "lightweight" football squad whereas a heavier sophomore over 150 pounds would likely find a role on the "heavyweight" team. The annual yearbooks for Crane Tech reveal that during his time there Halas never advanced above the lightweight level. In fact, he claimed in his autobiography that he graduated as a senior in 1913 weighing just 120 pounds.

Seeking to satisfy his athletic ambitions, Halas did discover some solace in baseball, particularly with Crane's famous indoor baseball team, which grabbed three city championships during his tenure at the school. Yet, the indoor version of baseball was vastly different from that of the outdoor game. Observers today might describe indoor baseball as being similar to softball. The game of softball originated in Chicago and is typically played today with a 16" ball that is rock hard at the beginning of each contest. Defensive players do not wear gloves and proudly display bent fingers as badges of honor from their playing days. It is a game that differs from "fast pitch" softball (with a 12" ball) in that the 16" pitch must be tossed (with an arc) slowly toward the batter, although the pitcher, at times, may use certain fakes or gestures to confuse the hitter. Near the end of the game, the ball will likely be softened up a bit, making it less difficult to field for the defense, but tougher for the offense to hit long balls. The magical part of 16" softball is the ability of crafty hitters to not "kill" the ball for distance, but to place their hits strategically around the diamond, collecting singles and doubles in bunches rather than relying solely on the long ball.

In 1910 indoor baseball was played with a very soft 17" ball and a thin bat (just two and three-quarters feet in length) that more closely resembled a broomstick without the brushes. Since there were few facilities that could accommodate any type of regular baseball inside, the high school version of indoor baseball was played in existing gymnasiums, armories, or available "open" indoor meeting spaces. This resulted in limited dimensions for the playing "fields" themselves with the bases spaced only 27 feet apart. No gloves were worn and pitches were hurled underhanded from 22 feet away. Any batted ball hitting a wall or ceiling fixture was considered a fair ball, as long as it crashed into something within the foul lines. Fast balls and curves were the weapons of choice for pitchers as the batters also faced the annoyance of having two "shortstops" setting up on either side of the pitcher just 10 feet from the batter.[2] It was a crowded atmosphere that rewarded speed and agility by the players.

Author Robert Pruter (*The Rise of American High School Sports and the Search for Control*), a prominent high school sports historian, explained the popularity of the indoor baseball game over basketball during the time George Halas, and his older brothers, were in high school:

> When it [indoor baseball] started in 1887 it was the *only* indoor athletic game. Within a few years in the early 1890s there were some 100 teams playing, and a bunch of leagues. The game preceded basketball, so it had a head start in attracting fans and players. The first years of basketball in Chicago, the game was primarily seen as a YMCA game. In 1896, when the Cook County High School League decided to add an indoor sport to their schedule, there was a vote among the schools and indoor baseball was favored over basketball by a vote of 7 to 2. Up to 1900, the high schools saw basketball as primarily a female game. The Cook County League only added basketball for boys in 1900.[3]

When George Halas entered Crane Tech in 1909, he was paired, albeit briefly, with his brother Walter on the Crane indoor baseball team. Walter was the star pitcher and three years older than George, so the younger Halas, who also fancied

George Halas (bottom row, second from left) was just a freshman at Chicago's Crane Tech High School when this photograph was taken in 1910. His brother Walter Halas (top row, third from left) was an excellent pitcher on the school's indoor baseball team. Both of the Halas brothers later played baseball at the University of Illinois (SDN-008471, *Chicago Daily News* collection, Chicago History Museum).

himself a pitcher, settled in at right shortstop. This was the position that was unique to indoor baseball in that his defensive placement was within a few feet to the side of the pitcher. Crane opened its season with an easy 22–3 win over Evanston Academy on February 5, 1910, in which Walter Halas clubbed four home runs, and then North Division High School fell in another romp: "The speedy team from Crane demonstrated its superiority in the Cook County High School baseball league yesterday by shutting out North Division 14–0. By its victory, Crane looms up as the strongest contender for premier honors in the league. [Walter] Halas, the Crane pitcher, was invincible and allowed the North Division team but two hits."[4]

As the dangerous leadoff hitter, freshman George Halas contributed two hits and a couple of stolen bases. Walter ended up striking out 14 in the big win. But just a month later, Walter Halas, and his teammates, received a jolt when an anonymous source accused Walter of being a "professional." Apparently, Walter was guilty of playing with an independent team called the Pilsens while still representing Crane Tech. In addition, "He was declared a pro for receiving five dollars playing on the Darby Social team," noted Pruter. The decision by the high school Board of Control on March 16, 1910, was swift and decisive. Walter Halas denied all charges but his appeal was rejected a week later and the league reinforced its own mandate that a student could not play for a team outside of the school during the academic year. If Walter was indeed guilty of playing for the Pilsens, it was never mentioned that his brothers Frank and young George were both in the lineup with Walter for a game with the Pilsens on March 6, 1910.[5]

While Walter Halas was declared ineligible for the remainder of the school year, the judgment against him was altered to imply that his punishment was due to his participation in still another amateur game where he was fully aware that the umpire had accepted money for his services.[6] In other words, a high school kid was punished because an umpire received a reputed payment in exchange for his responsibilities. Despite the loss of Halas, the Crane team was not accused of any wrongdoing, nor did it affect Walter's exceptional collegiate pitching career later at the University of Illinois. Brother George would join Walter at Illinois in a few years, even if his journey would prove to be a bit circuitous.

But first, George Halas would help Crane capture the 1910 indoor baseball title without the presence of Walter, the first of numerous accomplishments George would achieve over the remainder of his prep career. In 1911, Crane secured its fourth straight Cook County Indoor League crown by defeating Medill High School 4–2. Leadoff man Halas "carried away the hitting honors annexing a single and ripping a three sacker."[7] The only failure in indoor baseball that Halas experienced in high school was when Crane fell to Lane Tech 3–2 in the 1912 Cook County finals. By this time, Halas was doing the pitching, and he incurred the loss in the Lane contest despite striking out eight and allowing only five hits.[8]

Halas Was an Enigma

In his senior season (1912–1913), Halas was even more dominant on the "mound" during the indoor baseball season. By the middle of March, Halas had tossed six one-hitters and then struck out 17 in a win over Wendell Phillips High School that qualified Crane for a trip to the Cook County finals. Halas and Crane Tech then secured a bit of revenge against the defending 1912 champion Lane Tech squad, by

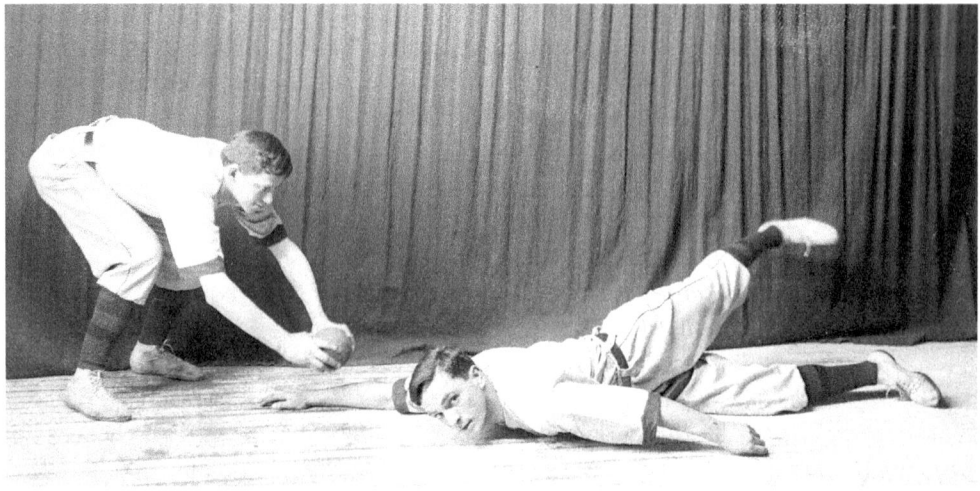

This may be the earliest photograph of George Halas in athletic action. Although posed, Halas (left) is ready to tag B. Croutch during an indoor baseball practice at Crane Tech High School in Chicago in 1911. Halas played little football during his prep years but was a baseball standout (SDN-009260, *Chicago Daily News* collection, Chicago History Museum).

defeating Lane 11–4 in the title tilt. After a slow start, wrote the *Herald-Examiner*, "Halas was an enigma. All together Lane got only five hits, not two of those came together. He also breezed [struck out] 15 batsmen and was a factor offensively with two singles."[9] Overall, Crane Tech secured three indoor baseball championships with Halas in the lineup, but that was just part of his busy athletic career. He played second base on Crane's "outdoor" baseball team and was an integral part of the track team as well, representing Crane in what was then called the "Three Standing Broad Jumps" (triple jump) and the broad jump during the indoor track season. Once again, he served his school well: "Halas in the triple jump and Frye in the half mile were the Crane winners. The broad jumpers had a battle royal in the triple jump. Halas of Crane finally carried off the prize by registering the distance of 28 feet, five inches."[10] Off the field, Halas also served as the athletics (sports) editor for the monthly student journal.

But what about football? The man who would one day be perhaps the most recognizable name in professional football caused hardly a ripple on the gridiron during his high school years. Halas was relegated to the lightweight team for those players under 150 pounds but found service as an undistinguished lineman. In a preview of the 1912 season, Halas received a rare press mention for his presence on the Crane Tech football team: "Not satisfied with having won the lightweight football championship last year, Crane Tech will attempt to take both the lightweight and the heavyweight titles this season. Sixty-two men have reported for practice, among them being, however, but two regulars of last year's pennant winners. Promising candidates are Halas, center; Howe, guard, Plant, guard; and Cella, tackle."[11]

That weight worked out just fine for Halas during his senior year football season of 1912 when the school dropped its heavyweight program for the season when not enough players (out of an all-male enrollment of over 1,000) showed any interest in playing. The Crane Tech *Science and Craft* journal sadly reported: "Crane withdrew from the heavyweight football division because not enough heavy men came out to try for the team."[12] Halas started at right tackle for the lightweight team throughout its nine-game schedule, which included Oak Park, Lane Tech, and Evanston high schools. Crane finished 4–4–1 when it dropped a season-ending 48–9 tilt to Dubuque, Iowa. Earlier in the year, tackle Halas somehow managed to score a touchdown in a 52–0 romp over Austin High School.

In just a few years, Halas would be known throughout the football universe, but in 1912, he was struggling just to win a spot on a high school lightweight football squad. His stardom in "indoor" baseball did not translate well into collegiate baseball opportunities, and he never played basketball at Crane Tech. Nonetheless, Halas was the epitome of determination as he shared with his family his intent to follow brother Walter to the University of Illinois and play both baseball and football at that institution. His father, Frank J. Halas, had passed away in December 1910, but his mother and older brothers convinced George to delay college and work for a year, especially if he was serious in his efforts to play collegiate sports. The family decision was not an easy one for Halas to accept, but a late-night discussion with his brother Walter convinced George that the decision was pragmatic:

Walter came in and sat on the bed. "How much do you weigh, Kid?" he asked.

"Over 120."

"Well, Kid, if you weigh over 120, you don't weigh over 122," he said. "You really should work and get some meat on that skinny frame. You could do all right at baseball. Your speed will see you through. But the speed will make you terrific at football if you can put on some weight."

I knew Walter was speaking sense. Anyway, I didn't have any options. The family had decided.[13]

During his year away from academics, Halas procured employment at the Western Electric Company and continued to play baseball wherever and whenever possible. He played on the Commodore Barry Council indoor team with his older brother Frank that grabbed its second straight Knights of Columbus league title in 1914. George was also a mainstay on the Sigma Circles indoor club that same winter.[14] When George Halas finally matriculated at Illinois in September 1914, his weight still hovered around 140 pounds. With freshmen ineligible for varsity competition at that time, Halas accepted a reserve role on the yearling football squad as a halfback while pursuing engineering coursework. As the year progressed, he also joined the freshman baseball team. During the summer of 1915, Halas returned home to Chicago and once again worked for the Western Electric Company. "I played outfield on the payroll department's baseball team. I was hitting well and had picked up a lot of speed."[15]

George Halas Was Presumed Dead

One of the major events on the company's calendar was its fifth annual picnic on July 24, 1915, in Michigan City, Indiana, just a brief boat excursion away from Chicago via the waters of Lake Michigan. As part of the festivities, the Western Electric baseball teams would enjoy some competition as well. Transportation would be provided for employees on five steam vessels, including the SS *Eastland* departing from the Chicago River in downtown Chicago. George Halas was looking forward to the event and purchased an advanced ticket for his fare on the *Eastland*, which was scheduled to depart at 7:30 a.m. Much to his chagrin, Halas was running late that morning and feared that he would literally "miss the boat" and the full day of festivities in Michigan City. However, upon his arrival near the Clark Street Bridge, Halas discovered the horrible site of the overturned *Eastland* as it lay on its side in the Chicago River. At 7:28 a.m. that morning, the overcrowded ship capsized and 844 lives were lost.[16] Five years before he was to become a founder of the National Football League, George Stanley Halas was presumed dead…

In the immediate aftermath of the tragedy, Chicago newspapers attempted both to reconstruct the cause of the accident and to identify those lost or missing. Working from Western Electric employee ledgers and comparing the confirmed dead with those who were still missing, the *Chicago Tribune* published a comprehensive list of those who had not yet been accounted for since the ship overturned. The tardy Halas initially failed to report that he was indeed a survivor. Hence, the names of the dead and missing were published on July 27, 1915, in alphabetical order including the following: "Halas, G.S., Dept. 4110."[17]

Perhaps it was luck that helped protect Halas from the tragedy of the Eastland. However, nothing but bad luck seemed to plague him during his first two seasons on the Illinois varsity football team. His dream was to emulate the stardom of his childhood baseball heroes, and Halas finally found himself in the national spotlight in 1915 but, unfortunately, not for the right reason. While struggling to impress Illinois coach Robert Zuppke with his hustle and determination, it appeared that during his sophomore season, the still scrawny Halas would be relegated to a nice, cozy spot on the Illinois bench. Somehow, Halas worked his way into the on-field action as the reserve left end and impressed the local media in the opening 36–0 rout of the Haskell Indians ("Halas, at the other end, did noticeable work") and in a 75–7 pasting of Rolla School of Mines in the second contest.[18]

Less than a month later, Halas finally achieved the spotlight that he so often craved as a youth when the wire services picked up an intriguing article on a pair of rare injuries on the Illini football squad: "A new society, 'The Order of the Broken Jaw,' has been organized at Illinois University. Potsy Clark, famous quarterback, was the first member. George Halas, end, was next. George has it on Potsy, though, because his jaw is broken in two places; Potsy's in only one. Clark was hurt in a game against Rolla School of Mines. He knew something was wrong, but didn't know what, and played through the contest. His jaw was the first broken at Illinois in 25 years."[19]

The injury to Halas basically ended his sophomore season and he later claimed that the injury occurred while he was making a tackle during a practice session. A photo of Clark and Halas accompanied the article and brought both players some national attention. Clark, of course, went on to a very successful career as a coach at both the collegiate and professional levels, winning an NFL title with the Detroit Lions in 1935. As for Halas, his playing time in 1915 was limited to brief appearances in those two early blowout victories, although he did accompany the team (as a reserve) to the final game at the University of Chicago on November 20 but did not play in the 10–0 Illinois win. Due to his limited time on the field in 1915, Halas did not earn a letter, nor did he attend the team banquet for the 5–0–2 Illini on November 29 when Bart Macomber was named the team captain for the 1916 season.[20]

During the spring of 1916, Halas shook off any ill effects from the broken jaw and quickly established himself as the star right fielder for the Illinois baseball team. Reunited on the playing field for one last season with his older brother Walter, George helped Illinois to snare the Big Ten championship and finish with an overall 17–5 record (8–1 in league play) and earned his coveted "I" letter. Walter was a dependable starting pitcher for the club and it was not unusual for the brothers to combine their talents to the dismay of the opposition. After Illinois struggled through a season-opening southern road trip with a 4–4 mark, the impact of the Halas brothers in the first home win, 13–4 over Wabash, was significant: "[Walter] Halas held the collegians without much trouble and Klein succeeded him in the fifth. George Halas led the stickers with three hits, one a home run."[21] Walter Halas concluded his Illinois career in a season-ending 6–0 exhibition win over the touring Waseda University squad from Japan. While Walter's collegiate eligibility had ended, George Halas looked forward to a couple of more years of competition in both football and baseball.

Zuppke's Sagacity in Sizing Up Halas

Following a long summer of baseball back home and more work at Western Electric, Halas returned to Champaign in September 1916 eager to secure a spot as a regular on the Illinois football team under Coach Zuppke. Listed as a 175-pound junior end in early press reports, Halas was quickly moved to fullback for the squad's first scrimmage on September 21. He apparently left a nice impression with his coach: "Zuppke's sagacity in sizing up Halas as a full back seemed to be demonstrated by the performance of the baseball man last night."[22] With the broken jaw behind him, Halas wasted little time in pursuing his all-out effort to secure that prized spot in the starting lineup, propelling himself into consideration at fullback: "The able showing which George Halas, sub end and backfield man of last year, has made in the three days of work at fullback, is a pleasant surprise to Zuppke."[23] The once-scrawny flanker was now described as "husky" by the press with those 175 pounds packed onto his six-foot frame. After scoring a touchdown for the varsity in its annual tune-up with the freshman team, Halas was announced as the Illini's starting fullback for its opener against Kansas on October 7. His future partner with the Chicago Bears, Dutch Sternaman, was penciled in at the starting right halfback slot as Illinois blasted Kansas 30–0 to kick off the 1916 campaign. Halas sprinted around left end for one 20-yard gain, and provided ample blocking and pass protection when needed, earning him praise from the local press: "George Halas, groomed as a fullback, is one of the fastest men on the field. He gained fame as a base-runner on Huff's championship nine last season."[24]

Next up was eastern power Colgate University on October 14. To take advantage of the speed of Halas, Zuppke moved his prized pupil to right halfback. Colgate entered the contest with an undefeated 2–0 record after finishing with an impressive 5–1 mark in 1915, including decisive wins over both Army and Yale. Meanwhile, Illinois had not suffered a loss in over two years, with a 5–0–2 ledger in 1915 following an undefeated 7–0 slate in 1914 when Illinois was recognized by many as the national champion. The Colgate game, and Halas, would be in the spotlight that the Crane Tech grad had envisioned for himself many years ago. Yet just 48 hours before the Colgate kickoff, word drifted around campus that Halas was injured, prompting the *Daily Illini* to report the day before the game that "the greatest blow came last night when it was announced that George Halas would not be able to be at right half because of a bum ankle. Halas was looking like one of the best bets in the Illini offense, and this combined with his defensive ability is going to make his loss felt—badly felt."[25] Without Halas, Illinois fell quite convincingly to Colgate 15–3, the first loss for the Illini since a 19–9 defeat against Minnesota on November 22, 1913.

During the first two weeks of the season, the bothersome injuries suffered by Halas were described by various newspaper accounts as a charley horse, a bum ankle, and a bad leg. Whatever the ailment, Halas returned to action as the left halfback in a 7–6 loss to Ohio State on October 21. There was little offense in this defensive struggle that was decided by the successful extra point kick late in the game by Chic Harley of the winners. During the battle, Halas apparently reinjured his leg and was replaced when he "began to limp."[26] Halas was on the practice field the following week, in preparation for the Purdue contest, but apparently in discomfort, according to the *Daily Illini*: "George Halas was in uniform last night, but is barely able to move faster than a walk, so there will be no chance of his getting in [the Purdue game]."[27] It may have been around this time, as Halas recounted in his autobiography, that he and Coach Zuppke locked horns over the apparent injury:

> One afternoon, I limped from the field. I thought I had merely pulled a muscle or had been awarded a bruise. So did the trainer. Coach Zuppke called the team together to explain the practice the next day. As he ended, he pointed at me and said: "Halas, stop loafing! Get in there and hit!" I blew up. That is the only way to put it. My temper is always near the surface. That afternoon it went up like an explosion. I pulled off my helmet and threw it at Coach Zuppke. I was so angry. I couldn't even throw straight. I missed him.... The trainer sent me to the hospital. An x-ray showed the leg bone was broken.[28]

With Halas unable to perform, the Illini split the last four games to finish 3-3-1 in 1916. However, he remained with the team and began to visualize football strategies from a coach's perspective, carefully observing how Zuppke prepared and guided the team. Despite being a starter when he suffered the injuries, Halas failed to secure his letter in football for the second straight year when his name was not called at the annual team banquet. What he did receive at that dinner was a subtle message from his coach that would remain with him forever: "Coach Zuppke spoke. His message was short: 'Just when I teach you fellows how to play football, you graduate and I lose you.' His words were to govern the rest of my life."[29] At the time, Halas was much more adept—and promising—in baseball rather than football. Yet, Zuppke's words, especially when considering that a national football league did not exist, seemed to influence the future thinking of Halas. With his 1915 and 1916 football season virtually wiped out due to injuries, Halas would likely have just one more opportunity at Illinois to prove himself on the gridiron, and that would most likely be the last time one would expect to see George Halas as a player on a football field.

By December 1916, with his leg healed, an inexperienced Halas showed up for the Illinois basketball team under Coach Ralph Jones and earned a spot on the second team. He started at left guard against nearby Millikin College in what might be described as a junior varsity tilt in a 28-16 Illini win. In early January, Coach Jones elevated Halas to the first team, although not yet a starter; that would occur later as Halas would direct the club from his guard position and eventually help lead the team to the Big Ten championship with a 10-2 record (13-3 overall). At the end of the season, Halas would tally only 10 points in total, but his leadership and defensive tenacity were so impressive that he was selected as the team captain for the 1917-1918 Illinois basketball squad.[30] The *Daily Illini* provided a glowing summary of the growing list of his accomplishments:

> The main business of the evening was the election of George Halas as captain of next year's team. Halas was the logical candidate for the position. He played regularly through the entire season as standing guard. Coming out for the team a green candidate, Halas was developed into one of the best guards in the conference. Although a junior, this was his first year on the

basketball team. Halas won his first "I" last spring in baseball. He also went out for football this fall but a broken ankle put an end to his activities. By developing into a star basketball man, Halas looms up as one of Illinois' most versatile athletes.[31]

No matter what era, it was a remarkable accomplishment for Halas to crack the starting lineups of all three major sports at the University of Illinois. Only a very talented athlete could absorb the nuances of the game of basketball without any real taste of organized hoops beforehand … and then easily slide into the baseball season without missing a beat. By the time his junior year in baseball rolled around in 1917, Halas was already hearing whispers regarding a professional career. Indeed, he was "reserved" by Davenport (Iowa) of the Three I League in September 1916 for a possible contact for the following season.[32] Unfortunately, that club disbanded before the 1917 summer campaign, but it was clear at this point in Halas's career that baseball was likely his only option for post-collegiate participation.

Meanwhile, the 1917 Illinois baseball team saw its hopes for a fourth straight Big Ten title vanish under a 13–7 record, which was still good for second place. Halas enjoyed another banner year at the plate, delivering several multihit games such as three hits against Ohio State and then a monster game in a win over the University of Chicago: "Led by George Halas with two home runs and a single, the Illinois batters cleaned up on the Maroon pitchers, winning by a score of 8 to 4."[33]

Finally, with his status as one of the most versatile athletes in Illinois history firmly established, Halas embarked on his final gridiron schedule, hoping, for once, that he could complete the season injury-free. Or would he?

Halas May Not Play Football

Apparently, Halas was experiencing some second thoughts regarding his commitment to football. And who could blame him? With a promising baseball future in front of him, and two dreadful football injuries behind him, Halas was likely debating if the next football injury might be even more catastrophic. On September 17, 1917, the *Chicago Examiner* simply stated: "Halas may not play football."[34] Another week evaporated and Halas still had not returned to campus. Then, on September 24, Halas slipped through the clouds of doubt and stepped onto the Illini practice field. For a guy who still had not secured a football letter, the presence of Halas was greeted with unrestrained joy per the *Daily Illini*: "Smiles appeared on the faces of Coach Zuppke and his assistants yesterday—smiles that were decidedly noticeable. The cause for the symbols of good spirits was the appearance of George Halas, at present Illinois' most versatile athlete, upon the field in a [football] suit. The decision of Halas to again try for the team comes after several days of indecision. Halas was a member of the squad for the last two years, but due to injuries, has been unable to be a consistent contender for a position on the team."[35]

Halas started the season at right halfback as the Illini defeated Kansas (22–0), Oklahoma (44–0), and Wisconsin (7–0). Coach Zuppke tinkered with the lineup following the Wisconsin win in an effort to improve all aspects of the Illinois game, as reported by the *Daily Illini*: "Left end is another place that came in for the little coach's attention. Yesterday, George Halas was shifted from the backfield to the far corner…. The change seemed to be an improvement."[36] In the very next game, a 27–0 stomping over Purdue, Halas proved that Zuppke had made the correct moves, scoring on a short touchdown reception: "George Halas won his spurs as an end against Purdue, beyond all doubt."[37] Down the stretch, the Illini faltered, winning just one more contest in the final four to finish 5–2–1. The last game was an exhibition against the Camp Funston (Kansas) service eleven led by former Illinois quarterback Potsy Clark. Although the Illini breezed to an easy 28–0 victory in front of 30,000 fans in Kansas, the game would provide a lasting memory for Halas. In the final period of his final game for Illinois, Halas grabbed a 10-yard touchdown pass for the last touchdown of his Illini career. During his three years on the varsity, Halas managed to participate in just 12 games, starting five in the backfield and five at right end. He was finally awarded his "I" letter in football at the team's annual banquet on December 1, 1917. And then it was on to his final season on the Illinois hardcourt for the defending Big Ten champions as noted on December 12: "Basketball now is attracting attention at the University of Illinois. While only one man from last year's team which tied for the championship is back this year Coach Ralph Jones is optimistic and believes that from the material he has, he can turn out a winner. George Halas, who played on the varsity football team all season, is the only veteran to don the basket togs. The defensive and the offensive will be centered on him. His game at guard will probably decide whether or not this year's team will play in top notch form."[38]

The Illini cagers burst out of the gate quickly, snapping up two easy wins over Millikin before breaking for the holidays. During his sojourn back in Chicago, Halas struggled with a decision that would not only impact his athletic career at Illinois but also contribute a distant nudge toward the formation of the National Football League.

After three more basketball games in early January 1918, Halas was suddenly done with college sports. He would never again play for the University of Illinois…

Four

Yankees, Bobcats, and Owls!

"You may say for me that George Halas will start in right field for the Yankees ... but if I am any judge of a ball player, Halas is a star."
—Miller Huggins, New York Yankees Manager, April 4, 1919

On January 3, 1918, George Halas left his collegiate athletic career behind and proudly enlisted in the United States Navy. While the country had reluctantly been drawn into World War I the previous April, he likely assumed that his personal participation in the hostilities would not begin until he completed his university degree. While a military draft had been instituted to bolster the ranks of the various branches of the service, Halas boldly elected to select his own path forward as he noted in his autobiography:

> For several months the United States had been at war with Germany. Gradually the events in Europe began to crowd sport from my mind. I talked to Mother about enlisting but she asked would I please first get my degree. But in January of 1918 I decided the time had come for me to serve the country which had been so good to the Halas family. I would soon be 23. I must add that the draft was getting close to students such as myself. I went to Great Lakes Training Station, volunteered for the navy and asked to be sent to sea on a submarine chaser. The university promised to forgive the six remaining hours and in June to mail the degree to me wherever I was. The offer mollified Mother but coach Jones was upset at losing his basketball captain.[1]

Halas's decision was not completely surprising, owing to the acceleration of the war effort. It took an enormous amount of courage for Halas to not only voluntarily leave the protective umbrella of the university campus for possible war action but to also sacrifice his final year with both the basketball and baseball teams. Halas did manage to play in five basketball games with Illinois that season, with the Illini winning each of those contests. His final appearance in an Illinois uniform occurred on January 14, 1918, when the University of Minnesota visited Urbana-Champaign. As expected, the local media was not only kind but also a bit introspective when commenting on Halas's final collegiate performance: "Captain George Halas of the basketball team will play his last game for Illinois when the team meets Minnesota tomorrow night. Halas has enlisted in the public works force of the navy and will leave for the Great Lakes Naval Station as soon after the game as possible. He passed all his examinations for graduation in the College of Engineering during the past week. Halas is probably one of the greatest all around athletes the university has ever produced."[2]

Landing a training assignment at Great Lakes turned out to be an ideal situation for Halas. Not only could he pursue his military studies in the officer training school, but he was also encouraged to participate in the many sports activities offered by the base. After completing officer training, Halas would receive his commission as an ensign. However, instead of being shipped out for active naval duty, preferably on a submarine, Halas was placed in the sports program at Great Lakes. In other words, most of his military service would be spent representing Great Lakes on the football, basketball, and baseball squads. The Great Lakes Training Center was a massive base, with 775 buildings sprawling over 1,000 acres in Lake Bluff, Illinois, just north of Chicago. Completed in 1911, the training center would welcome in excess of 125,000 trainees through its stringent boot camp during World War I.[3] With those sheer numbers, the Blue Jackets' sports teams (nicknamed the "Jackies") could dip into a very deep pool of athletic talent from the collegiate and professional ranks to stockpile the various squads.

The Most Sensational Game Ever Played in Sheboygan

George Halas's arrival on base was heralded immediately. A Great Lakes press release drifted out later that same week on January 18, 1918, lauding the station's upcoming basketball season: "An almost entirely new Jackie basketball team will face Purdue Saturday night at Lafayette, Indiana, according to the plans of coach Herman Olcott. The mentor figures he will be able to keep the Boilermakers stepping with his revamped aggregation. Within two weeks, Great Lakes will have one of the most formidable fives in the country. At that time Bill Johnson, former I.A.C. whale, and George Halas, this season's Illinois captain, will be available. Manager Eddie Fall today announced that a trip will be taken through Michigan the third week in February."[4]

The Great Lakes team booked any and all challengers, from major colleges to other service teams to town teams. For example, the *Sheboygan Press* in Wisconsin excitedly touted a contest on March 8 against the local Hilleman-Resch club after listing the starters for Great Lakes (including Halas): "That is the way the Great Lakes team will line up against the locals in what is expected to be the most sensational game ever played in Sheboygan. The visitors will invade the city fresh from a general clean-up of university teams in the middle west. The quintet has defeated Camp Custer 32 to 24 at Battle Creek; Fort Zachary Taylor, 37 to 22; and has won from the University of Chicago, Northwestern University and the University of Michigan."[5]

As soon as the basketball season concluded, Halas quickly moved over to the Great Lakes baseball team, where he joined a solid group of players buoyed by several individuals with major league experience, including Dutch Leonard (Boston Red Sox), Bill Johnson (Philadelphia Athletics), Lefty Anderson (Philadelphia Athletics), Red Faber (Chicago White Sox), Verne Clemons (St. Louis Browns), and Joe Leonard (Washington Senators). In addition, John "Paddy" Driscoll, a former Chicago Cub and Northwestern University standout, would hold down second base for the squad. The big bat of George Halas would grab one of the outfield spots as Great

Lakes embarked on an ambitious Midwest and East Coast schedule. His ability to not only play but also start and "star" with this group of exceptional baseball talents proved once again that Halas possessed incredible athletic ability. During his stint with the Jackies, Halas was a consistent force both at the plate and in the field. In a game in Chicago against Garden City of the Chicago League on June 8, Halas knocked out three hits, including two home runs, in an 8–6 victory: "The sailors played a great game of ball, combined sixteen hits, and showed class. George Halas, former University of Illinois star, knocked two home runs. Pattie [sic] Driscoll, ex-Cub, and Joe Leonard of Washington also were in the navy lineup, each getting three blows."[6]

Another typical outing for Halas took place on July 25 when Great Lakes slammed the Naval Auxiliary Reserve Officers Training School and pitcher Jeff Pfeffer 7–0, as reported by the *Decatur Daily Review*: "George Halas was the slugging star for Great Lakes, pounding out four hits in five attempts."[7] Just a week before, Pfeffer had been on the mound for the Brooklyn Dodgers (while on furlough) and weaved a two-hit shutout over the Chicago Cubs. So, the workday for Halas proved to be twice as productive against Pfeffer as the entire Cubs team!

How was Great Lakes able to attract such a cadre of talented athletes? Much of that responsibility resided with the commandant of the base, Captain William A. Moffett. He was the architect of a massive buildup of the station in 1917 with the government's intent to establish Great Lakes as "the largest naval training station in the world."[8] But Moffett was also a keen marketing savant. He realized that successful, and very visible, athletic teams would greatly increase the reputation of the base. As such, Moffett directed his staff to actively recruit recognized athletes, as *Collyer's Eye* reported during the 1918 baseball season: "Any major league player anxious to join the United States Navy will have no trouble in that direction if he will address Captain William A. Moffett, commandant at this point. He says he wants the best men he can get and he will sign up every healthy professional baseball player who cares to come here."[9]

Clearly, it would be beneficial to include "professional athlete" on your resumé if seeking acceptance at Great Lakes during World War I. Chris Serb, author of the insightful *War Football: World War I and the Birth of the NFL*, explained in an interview for this book how Great Lakes became an attractive option for gifted athletes looking to fulfill their military service at the time:

> Why did so much talent flock to Great Lakes? The simplest answer is, to avoid getting drafted into the army! The draft was expanding greatly during 1918, and many young men figured: better to volunteer for the navy than get drafted into the army. George Halas admitted in his autobiography that the draft was in the back of his mind when he joined the navy at Great Lakes in January 1918. Paddy Driscoll had already been drafted by the army but enlisted at Great Lakes in February 1918 before his call-up was completed. For many young men, service on a transport convoy, while risky, seemed more appealing than infantry duty in the trenches. And if you volunteered for the navy, you had a better-than-average chance of going to Great Lakes, where about one out of every four sailors trained during the World War I years.
>
> But these guys didn't end up at Great Lakes by accident. Great Lakes actively and aggressively recruited athletes. The base's commandant, Captain William Moffett, used sports

as part of a PR strategy to be not only the best but also the best-known training base in the country. Great Lakes competed at a high level in just about everything: football, baseball, boxing, swimming, track and field, even ski jumping. And the life of an athlete was pretty cushy, compared to the life of the average sailor: time off from naval training for practices and games, a fast track into officer's candidate school, a dedicated athletic barracks, a training table, professional massages, and all sorts of extras that regular sailors didn't get.[10]

Better Football Men Than George Halas ... Cannot Be Found

While the basketball and baseball clubs at Great Lakes enjoyed successful seasons and contributed greatly to the visibility of Great Lakes, perhaps the most glittering of the athletic gems at the base was the football squad. With both the war and a raging influenza epidemic tearing at the country, the 1918 football season would be patched together and look dramatically different from any other before it. With collegiate schedules whittled away by local health regulations, and with other teams struggling to field a competitive eleven with so many players in the military, traditional rivalries and normal interconference game excursions were swept away by the unusual circumstances. Colleges and universities scrambled to schedule games that often collapsed at the last minute. As a result, major teams such as Indiana (four games), Michigan (five), Princeton (three), Washington (two), and Baylor (four) participated in just a handful of contests. During that brief moment in time, military teams, usually overflowing with an abundance of talent, were encouraged to schedule key collegiate clubs.

For Great Lakes, the grid season opened with informal practices the week of August 13, 1918, under the watchful eye of Coach Herman Olcott (also the basketball mentor). Expectations were high, even with members of the baseball and track teams still competing in their respective battles, according to the *Lansing State Journal*: "Great Lakes is preparing for a championship team; a machine to cope with the creations of [Fielding] Yost, [Robert] Zuppke, and [John] Wilce and equal to the eastern turnouts. The sailors have the material—the coach, the navy spirit and one of the greatest athletic fields in this country. The pick of the college players are in the navy. Better football men than George Halas, Hugh Blacklock of the Michigan Aggies, Paddy Driscoll of Northwestern ... cannot be found."[11]

With the advent of the 1918 Great Lakes football season, a subtle yet significant perception of football was emerging on the American landscape. The service teams consisted of talented and experienced players brought together not only to defend their country but also to publicly represent their specific military base. Before the season concluded, enormous crowds would gather to witness these clubs in action while thousands of others could follow the expanded media coverage of the service teams as they crisscrossed the country in search of competition. Games were often scheduled on short notice and wherever possible. Unlike the Great Lakes baseball team, the football eleven was not composed of both collegiate and professional stars primarily because pro football had not yet claimed a professional foothold on a national basis. Yet the 1918 season left us with two compelling results. Not only could post-collegiate teams (such as the military all-star squads) provide an exciting brand of football, but the general public was willing to support these clubs, as demonstrated by the large crowds that followed the Great Lakes juggernaut in 1918 that finished 7–0–2 and won what is now known as the Rose Bowl. Author Chris Serb provided further insight into the phenomenon that was the Great Lakes football team:

> Every army camp or navy base in the country, even the small ones, had some sort of big-time football talent in 1918. Great Lakes simply had more talent than anyplace else. More than 500 players showed up for initial tryouts in August. Great Lakes had at least one player, Gil Runkel, who would be a starter in the early NFL but didn't even make the main station team and had to play regimental football for his barracks team. Another player, quarterback Jimmy Conzelman, was good enough to make the Pro Football Hall of Fame but not good enough to keep the starting job at Great Lakes. Conzelman started two games, then was pushed to the bench by another future Hall-of-Famer, Paddy Driscoll. A whopping 17 players from Great Lakes in 1918 (16, if you don't count Runkel) would play in the early NFL.[12]

George Halas's key role on the successful grid squad was a personal reward after his injury-plagued Illinois career. The opportunity to start on this talent-laden squad was ultimately surpassed by his being named the MVP of the Rose Bowl. It was a huge move up the football ladder for Halas during his brief time with Great Lakes! By being injury-free and recognized for his talent on the field, Halas could enjoy his time with the Great Lakes squad. Over 20 years later, Edward Prell of the *Chicago Tribune* would write: "As a member of the Great Lakes Naval eleven he found he [Halas] was having more fun than ever at the sport."[13]

While the magical season enjoyed by the Jackies was not without its challenges, it was apparent early in the season that the assembled team was a potential powerhouse. With universities also losing personnel to the war effort, the overall balance of power on the "collegiate" level was already shifting. Prior to the first game of the season between Iowa and Great Lakes, former football great Walter Eckersall of the *Chicago Tribune* speculated on the impact of the veteran service teams competing with rather inexperienced collegians: "Not only will the results have an important bearing on the two teams' prospects but it will determine the chances a young, inexperienced team has against one composed of veterans, some of whom have played football for four and even six years. It will show whether the younger players have become imbued with enough fighting spirit and determination to offset their lack of experience."[14]

Merging the almost mythic talent available on the Great Lakes roster was left to coaches Herman Olcott and Lt. C.J. McReavy, although in his autobiography Halas claimed that he, Paddy Driscoll, and Charlie Bachman did the actual coaching during the practice week. Unfortunately, there is a lack of documentation to verify that statement, although it would not be unusual for a veteran player or players to assist in the day-to-day practice regimen. If anything, Halas was receiving some valuable coaching insight on the post-collegiate level that would serve him well in the near future.

In truth, with so much available talent, the Great Lakes squad of 1918 was a player-driven ensemble as men combined rigid military training with the added responsibility of football preparation. In a little over two months of the "regular" season, Great Lakes squeezed in eight games. Beginning on September 28 with an opening 10–0 win over Iowa (and future Pro Football Hall-of-Famer Duke Slater) including an easy 27–0 romp over Purdue on November 30, Great Lakes enjoyed not only an undefeated (6–0–2) season but also a warm embrace from a nation of football fans. Halas earned applause for his work against Illinois in a 7–0 victory: "George Halas, former all-around athlete of the University of Illinois, was one of the stars in the open field playing of the visitors."[15]

A pair of ties followed the Illinois contest as Great Lakes and Northwestern played a scoreless deadlock and then Notre Dame earned a 7–7 draw in a game that included a most unusual number of football legends. With future Pro Football Hall of Fame members George Halas and Paddy Driscoll in the Great Lakes lineup (and another Hall of Famer in the person of Jimmy Conzelman on the roster), the Irish were clearly viewed as the underdogs in this battle. But the Notre Dame squad included some football luminaries as well in Pro Football Hall of Famer fullback Curly Lambeau, College Hall of Famer guard Hunk Anderson, and the well-known George Gipp at halfback. Driscoll scored all of the Great Lakes points while Gipp contributed the sole Notre Dame extra point. After the game Notre Dame coach Knute Rockne stated: "I am satisfied with the game. We went into the game the underdogs and gave them a good fight. The game shows we have as good a team as any in the west."[16]

As the season unfolded, the most visible player on the Great Lakes eleven was Northwestern graduate Paddy Driscoll. The smallish (5'8") quarterback astounded the football world in a game on November 16 when the visitors dismantled undefeated Rutgers 54–14 in front of 10,000 spectators. Bouncing back from a 14–0 deficit in the first half, Great Lakes relied on the gifted legs of Driscoll to tally the final 54 points of the game. Driscoll was truly spectacular, scoring six touchdowns and adding five extra points to impress both Rutgers and the attendant media. Reporter Charles Taylor of the *New York Tribune* was effusive in his praise of Driscoll after the unworldly performance: "Ebbets Field was the scene yesterday afternoon of the biggest surprise of the season. And a new name has been added to the list of football heroes along with the Poes, the Brickleys, the Eckersalls, and the like. The new name is Paddy Driscoll. It was Paddy who upset all the dope ... and practically single-handed brought victory to the Great Lakes Training Station in its game with the Rutgers College team."[17]

Just a week after the Rutgers romp, Great Lakes faced perhaps its sternest foe in the United States Naval Academy. Navy entered the contest with a spotless 4–0 mark, mostly against service bases, but was fresh off a 127–0 pounding of Ursinus College the week before. That unreal total was the result of 19 touchdowns that led to an embarrassing 107–0 score at the end of three periods. "Long end runs and heavy line bucks for great gains, together with an aerial attack that the visitors were utterly powerless to cope with, featured the work of the middies, and every lad in the Navy backfield played a game of the stellar order," reported the *Baltimore Sun*.[18] That lofty point total remains the highest for a Navy team in one game in the history of the program.

On the morning of the big game, an interesting report slipped out of California that Great Lakes was being considered as one of the participants in a postseason game in Pasadena: "Southern California football fans may see the famous Great Lakes eleven in action at Pasadena New Year's Day. While it has not been definitely decided whether or not the Great Lakes team can make the western trip, negotiations are now underway and the football committee of the Rose Tournament is hopeful of having the middle westerners meet one of the strongest teams on the coast."[19]

Sensational Incident Seldom Witnessed on a Gridiron

The New Year's Day extravaganza is known today as the Rose Bowl, but back in 1918, the game was dubbed as the "Tournament East-West Football Game." Basically, postseason games were scarce. In fact, the future Rose Bowl was the only bowl game staged after the conclusion of the 1918 season. The concept for the 1919 clash would be to pit the top two service squads in the country against each other for the national service championship. While it appeared that Great Lakes would be anointed from the eastern part of the country, it would take a few weeks for the West Coast adversary to be named. Meanwhile, there were still three games remaining on the Great Lakes schedule, including the huge matchup with Navy.

Navy proved to be more than ready for their counterparts from the Midwest, grabbing a 6–0 lead in the third quarter, and then battling the invaders on even terms throughout most of the second half. The usually reliable Paddy Driscoll missed three dropkick field goal attempts before Navy surged deep into Great Lakes territory with less than three minutes left in the game. It was then that a brilliant defensive play, replete with a scene straight out of a *Three Stooges* movie, carried Great Lakes to a surprising comeback victory. Defensive back Harry Eileson, covering the right side of the Jackies' defense, picked up an errant Navy fumble at his own 10-yard line, weaved through several would-be tacklers and found some breathing room heading down the sideline with three more Midshipmen in hot pursuit. The swift Eileson sped past the Navy bench around the 30-yard line with no chance of being upended, when he was suddenly pulled down from behind. Unfortunately for Navy, the tackler was not a member of the vaunted defense, but rather a refugee from the bench! The chaos that ensued was captured verbally by the Rochester *Democrat and Chronicle*: "The game was a thriller from start to finish and was marked by a sensational incident—one that is seldom witnessed on a college gridiron these days. It happened after the Great Lakes runner had sprinted to within thirty yards of the Navy's goal line and the last of the pursuing tacklers had been disposed of by his interference, when Saunde, one of the Middies' first string substitutes, dashed from his seat on the bench, out into the football arena and brought the fleeing runner down from behind. General excitement prevailed for a time and some of the supporters of Great Lakes, made a rush for the intruding Middie and began pummeling him, but quiet was soon restored and the game proceeded."[20]

Eileson was quickly awarded a touchdown, and with the successful extra point, Great Lakes escaped with the 7–6 victory.

As the 1918 football season drew to a close, coinciding with the armistice signifying the end of World War I, the long, slow process of returning the country to a peacetime situation began with plans to ease military personnel back into the general population. For the most part, the Great Lakes football team temporarily remained intact, although there were persistent changes to the roster throughout the fall. By the end of November, Great Lakes had secured a spot in the upcoming New Year's Day championship battle, but an opponent was yet to be announced. Speculation about that mystery team on the West Coast continued, including potential participants such as undefeated Rockwell Field and unbeaten Mather Field. In particular, manager Herman Spitzel of Mather Field was confident in the ability of this team: "Really, we're feared in the North [California] as much as influenza. We have the best team on the coast. It is a veritable cyclone when in action.... We're after that New Year's Day game with Great Lakes."[21]

Two more games remained on the schedule as Purdue fell 27–0 on December 1 when Halas opened the scoring after snaring a pass from Driscoll. A final "home" game took place on December 16 when Great Lakes subdued their colleagues from the Seventh Regiment, the Great Lakes regimental champs, 26–0 as Halas scored the first touchdown. Although the game was billed as being for the championship of the base, the *Great Lakes Bulletin* described it otherwise: "Rolling, sliding, gliding, and almost swimming … it was more for the mud championship than anything else, it was hard for the players involved to determine which man was of his own machine, the field being quite sloppy."[22] Shortly thereafter, it was announced that the Mare Island Blue Jackets, considered the foremost service team on the Pacific coast, would oppose Great Lakes on January 1, 1919. Pushed back to the rear of the sports pages that week was another key announcement that would impact the immediate future for Halas, as Great Lakes shared some exciting baseball news. Both outfielder Halas and shortstop Johnny Jones of Great Lakes signed to play baseball for the New York Yankees. The release stated: "Halas is a left-handed hitter, but throws with the port side. He weighs 170 pounds and is said to be ready right now to step into major league society."[23]

With his post–Navy job secured, Halas joined his football teammates on December 19 for the long train trip to California. Journalist Walter Eckersall of the *Chicago Tribune*, who would also serve as the referee for the upcoming game, joined Halas and company on the westbound hegira. Eckersall filed reports from various points on the trip and complained about delays, meal times, and crowded conditions: "Last night at Kansas City, hundreds of soldiers, who had been discharged from Camp Funston, boarded the train. With so many service men aboard, the train resembled a wartime special."[24]

Little Knock-Kneed Irishman

In the battle between the unbeaten service teams, Mare Island (10–0) faced off with the Jackies (6–0–2) at Tournament Park in Pasadena for the military championship of the United States. The *Los Angeles Times* provided extensive coverage of the day's events and quickly designated the visitors from Illinois as the crowd favorite:

"From the moment that the Great Lakes team lumbered onto the turf, the tall youthfully big youngsters were favorites. Their manifest health and condition made their size, as well as the easy grace with which they handled the ball, instantly popular with the crowd.... Everybody wanted to see Driscoll, and could easily distinguish the little knock-kneed Irishman by his diminutive size."[25]

Driscoll failed to disappoint the 26,000 in attendance. During a defensive struggle in the first half that was dominated by a series of exchanged punts, Driscoll impressed the attendees with his kick returns that ultimately provided Great Lakes with some field advantage: "The ball scarcely seemed to be in his hands when the little Irishman was off swerving to the right and to the left like a swallow flying low in the morning."[26] Ends George Halas and Richard Reichle both earned praise as well: "While on his [Driscoll's] own high spirals the Marine backfield men were downed in their tracks by Reichle and Halas, the splendid Great Lakes ends."[27] Driscoll nailed a 35-yard field goal late in the first quarter to ease the visitors ahead 3–0, and then Andrew Reeves added to that advantage with a two-yard plunge in the second stanza, leaving Great Lakes with a 10–0 halftime margin. In addition to his defensive heroics, Halas garnered the final touchdown for the visitors in the third period when he snared a soft pass from Driscoll and turned it into a 32-yard score. Halas also snuffed out a possible scoring drive by intercepting a pass and returning it 80 yards to the Mare Island 10-yard marker. The stingy Great Lakes defense did the rest and the Jackies cruised to the 17–0 victory. In his postgame article, referee-turned-reporter Walter Eckersall struggled with determining the best player for the winners:

> Paddy Driscoll put on his usual stellar game. He made the first score by sending a [field] goal from the thirty-five-yard line in the first period, while his great returns of punts and open field runs electrified the spectators. He handled punts cleanly and caught them in his usual sure manner. George Halas was not far behind Driscoll. The former Illini was everywhere at the right time. One of his great feats was an eighty-yard run after he had intercepted a forward pass on his own ten-yard line. In the third quarter he caught a forward pass from Driscoll and romped over the goal line for the last score. His tackling, especially on punts, was hard and sure.[28]

The impressive performance by Halas was recognized when he was selected as the MVP for the game. In all likelihood, he had played his last football game. In fact, an article published the day before the game boldly predicted that both Halas and Driscoll were done with the game: "Paddy Driscoll will play with the Chicago Cubs next year and will no further risk injury to life and limb. George Halas, the star right end, will go south with the New York Yankees in the spring, and this New Year contest is his last."[29]

Originally, Great Lakes hoped to play at least one more game on the West Coast but finally turned down the opportunity to play Camp Lewis in Tacoma, Washington. The team arrived back in Chicago on January 8 and several players anticipated their imminent discharge from the service. Others, such as Driscoll, Halas, and Conzelman, resumed coursework in an effort to secure commissions as ensigns. Also, on January 8, Halas learned that the godfather of football, Walter Camp, had selected him as a member of the second unit of the All-Service team (Driscoll was a first-team honoree). Within a few weeks, Halas was released from the service as an ensign and was ready to embark on his next athletic adventure as a rookie outfielder for the New York Yankees.

Football Was Over for Me

During that lengthy train ride back to Chicago, Halas had plenty of time to contemplate both his future and the options before him. Most likely, he was done with football. There really were no professional opportunities that could equal those in professional baseball, so the decision to pursue a direct line to the major leagues was a pragmatic one as Halas later recalled: "We returned to Chicago. I went home on leave. The papers had been full of the Rose Bowl game. Mother was concerned I might be seriously injured. I assured her that I played end and was apart from the rough stuff. 'Well, if that is so, how did you happen to break your jaw and leg at Illinois?' Mother asked. I told her football was over for me. I said I still loved the sport but would devote my athletic efforts henceforth to baseball."[30]

Although we now know that the sojourn of Halas away from football was a brief one, the experience at Great Lakes would remain with him as his athletic pursuits continued to evolve over the next two years. Following the football campaign, Halas and Driscoll rejoined the Great Lakes basketball team, which allowed them both to stay in shape for their respective baseball spring training objectives, Halas with the New York Yankees and Driscoll with the Chicago Cubs. Both were released from the Navy on March 12, 1919, and within 10 days, Halas was on his way to Jacksonville, Florida, for the Yankees' spring training camp in an effort to make the major league roster.[31] Once drills began at South Side Park in Jacksonville, Halas quickly grabbed the attention of manager Miller Huggins. His quick bat, swift feet, and cannon-like arm from the outfield prompted Huggins to state with confidence: "You may say for me that George Halas will start in right field for the Yankees. Of course, I do not know just how he will act against American League pitching, but if I am any judge of a ball player, Halas is a star. He has every action of a great player, and so far, he has been hitting. That boy learns faster than any youngster I yet have tackled and he is there to stick."[32]

By the time the camp ended, Halas was told that he would be added to the Yankees' roster, although there were some concerns about his hitting. Halas was also bothered by what the team called a "charley horse" but what Halas termed a nagging hip injury. Due to the injury, Halas did not make his first appearance for the Yankees until May 6, 1919, two weeks after opening day. He started in right field and was the leadoff hitter in a 3–2 loss to Philadelphia, finishing 1–4 from the plate. He duplicated that performance two days later in a 2–0 conquest of the Athletics but went 0–9 in two more starts before being banished to the bench.[33] After seeing little action thereafter and batting an ugly 2–22 in 12 games overall, Halas was sent to the St. Paul Saints of the American Association minor league on July 11. Halas made his first start for St. Paul as a leftfielder on July 18 in a doubleheader at the Louisville Colonels, finishing the day with a combined 1–6 from the plate. The local media was not impressed: "George Halas made his debut with the Saints yesterday. The former collegian showed plenty of speed afield and on the bases. He performed no wonders with the bat, however."[34]

Such was to be the scourge of Halas during his short-lived professional baseball career. "I could hit a fastball, but I couldn't hit a curve," Halas later lamented.[35] Although he spent the rest of the 1919 season with the St. Paul Saints, his playing time was limited and he finished the year hitting .273 over 39 games.[36] While the baseball season was grinding to a close, Halas was already being mentioned as a candidate for a professional football team based in nearby Hammond, Indiana, called the Hammond Bobcats. Managed by 27-year-old Paul Parduhn, a local Oldsmobile car dealer and general entrepreneur, the Bobcats' roster included several well-known former college players who were anxious to take advantage of Parduhn's generous offer of $100 per game. By this time Halas had secured a position with the Chicago, Burlington and Quincy Railroad using his engineering degree in the bridge design department for a weekly salary of $55, but his love of football encouraged him to join the Bobcats. He later wrote: "I ached for the excitement of a good game, for the competition, for the challenge to the muscles, for the joy of victory."[37] Halas was back in the game...

The $20,000 Stars

The *Hammond Times* was unfailing in its support of this talented professional football venture and as early as September 19, 1919, Halas was identified as being a key member of the club: "George Halas, who has already drawn the left end position, is an All-America man, a former star at Illinois, and last year [was] with the Great Lakes eleven."[38] Parduhn was clearly ambitious, and he rented out Weeghman Park (also known as Cubs Park; now Wrigley Field) in Chicago in an effort to attract both large crowds and nationally known competition. It was an interesting concept: a team from a smaller town would base its home games out of a major city, thus playing the majority of its contests away from its true "home" location. His lofty payroll quickly earned the team a somewhat derisive nickname of the "$20,000 Stars" since that was rumored to be the size of the club's financial commitment for the season. So, whether known as the "Bobcats" or the "All Stars," the Hammond contingent embarked on what would be a nine-game schedule in 1919 against the leading professional teams in the Midwest. Halas was at one of the starting end positions throughout the season and was joined by such reputable teammates as center Shorty Des Jardien from the University of Chicago, Hugh Blacklock (Michigan State), quarterback Milt Ghee (Dartmouth), fullback/coach Dick King (Harvard), guard Jerry Jones (Notre Dame), and, later in the season, Paddy Driscoll (Northwestern), who was a teammate of Halas's on the Great Lakes Rose Bowl team. Famed football scribe Walter Eckersall was quoted as saying that Hammond was "the greatest team in the game today, bar none."[39]

For Halas, the Hammond experience offered a taste of the unpredictable daily life in the formative early days of pro football. For example, Hammond traveled to Detroit on October 5 with a full entourage of players, staff, and followers, only to discover that the management of the Heralds refused to hold the game even though both teams and 3,000 fans were already present at the stadium. The reason? Not enough folks in attendance, prompting the *Hammond Times* to chastise the host team: "The behavior of the Detroit manager in calling off the game was the worst we have seen in years. There was no hilarity amongst the Hammond players or the fans who made this trip. The real remorseful person on the trip was Paul Parduhn, the Hammond club owner, who quietly ducked to a corner to write out checks for his stars, and before the big games [in Chicago] start … it is costing Parduhn a neat little fortune."[40]

Parduhn was certainly making the effort to help his club succeed by guaranteeing that his players would receive their expected salary even with the absence (and share of the receipts) of a scheduled game. Other irksome problems faced by eager pro teams in 1919 were revolving rosters, college athletes playing under assumed names, and haphazard scheduling. All would need to be addressed if the professional sport could be taken seriously in the future. On the field, Parduhn contracted with talented players and the coaching staff prepared the well-paid gridders with a collegiate-like practice system: "To each of the stars comprising the Hammonds, football has become a business each fall. They command high salaries because of their ability to play the game. And so, it is a case of football seven days a week; nothing else to interfere. They practice as a college or university team does. Every afternoon the men are out under the coaching of King, fullback and former Harvard star."[41]

Although Hammond did not overwhelm its opposition in 1919, finishing with a 4–2–3 record, the team did participate in a pair of games that turned a few heads. One of Parduhn's intended goals for the season was to meet and defeat the best professional teams available. In particular, Parduhn had his eyes focused on the Canton Bulldogs, with star player Jim Thorpe. The two clubs finally met on November 9 at Cubs Park and battled to a 3–3 deadlock before 10,000 in attendance. The teams enjoyed the game so much that a second contest was scheduled for November 27, again at Cubs Park on Thanksgiving Day. This time, Paddy Driscoll was in the Hammond lineup after joining the club the previous week and his team was clad in new orange-and-black jerseys. Thorpe scored the game's only touchdown in the first quarter on a short run, but his 82-yard punt was the highlight of the fracas as the Bulldogs held on for the 7–0 win. More important, 12,000 were in the stands, demonstrating that there was indeed some interest in professional football, even in its present struggling state. But, when all seemed to be well for the Bobcats, team unity was shattered when paychecks "bounced" that were written to the Hammond players just before the Canton game. Some irate team members encouraged the arrest of Parduhn and he was jailed on December 15 in Oak Park, Illinois, a western suburb of Chicago, and held in lieu of payment of a $12,000 bond. Parduhn was charged with violating the Illinois "bad check law" since most of the Hammond players actually lived in Illinois. The publication of the details of the arrest did provide accurate information regarding the weekly payments to the individual players: "It was alleged that checks running from $100 to $250 with which he paid his players on November 26 were returned from the bank marked 'no funds.' Parduhn's bond was placed at $12,000, in default of which he was remanded to jail."[42]

Unfortunately for Parduhn, the story sped across the wire services, allowing other publications to add their own interpretation of the situation, such as the *Evansville Press* statement: "Such stuff as that will give professional football a black eye at the very start."[43] Although Halas enjoyed a successful season, both on offense and defense, he would not return to the Hammond club in 1920. But with a secure railroad job, and another season of professional baseball on the horizon, Halas spent the winter playing pro basketball with the Whiting (Indiana) Red Crowns. Among his teammates would be former Hammond football stars Paddy Driscoll and Shorty Des Jardien.

During the week before the start of spring training with the Yankees, Halas learned that his services would no longer be required by the parent club. Instead, he would begin the year back with St. Paul. Baseball pundits, such as J.V. Fitz Gerald of the *Washington Post*, were not reluctant to pinpoint the reason for the demotion: "Halas looked good in spring practice, but when he took a peek at big league pitching wares, once the Yankee heavers worked the kinks out of their arms, it was a different story. So, it looks, unless manager Huggins is dead wrong, that the big-league ways are not for Halas."[44] And then, George Halas received a phone call…

Five

Pro Football: The Beginning

"It will do away with irresponsible fly-by-night football organizations."
—*The Daily Times* (Davenport, Iowa), September 18, 1920

"In March of 1920, a man telephoned me at the railroad office and asked if I could meet him at the Sherman Hotel," recalled George Halas in his autobiography. "He said his name was George Chamberlain and he was general superintendent of the A.E. Staley Company at Decatur."[1]

Halas and Chamberlain did schedule a meeting at the Sherman, and Halas walked away with a dream opportunity to work and play baseball and football for the Staley Company. The decision to accept the generous offer obliterated any thoughts that may have lingered for Halas regarding the resumption of his professional baseball career in the Yankees organization. Under the terms of his agreement with owner A.E. Staley himself, Halas would be employed full-time, play for the company baseball team, and both manage and coach the Staley football team. "In between times I would learn how to make starch, putting my engineering and chemical training to use and starting a lifetime career in the fast-growing concern," added Halas.[2]

For an intelligent, athletic young man, the move into sports management with a reputable and successful company was an ideal situation. The Staley Company was a leading manufacturer of corn-related products and owner A.E. Staley was continually seeking new areas to embrace, such as soybean processing. He was also astute enough to recognize the importance of athletic endeavors, especially the positive publicity that successful teams could bring to a local business. Halas indicated that Mr. Staley sponsored competitive baseball and football squads to not only bolster employee morale but also to attract publicity for the company. The Staley baseball team emerged in 1917 and was chaperoned by former 1905 World Series star "Iron Joe" McGinnity, a member of the Baseball Hall of Fame since 1946. In 1919 the company formed football, basketball, and indoor baseball teams under the auspices of the Staley Fellowship Club. The basketball team was coached and managed by "Buster" Woodworth, the high-scoring veteran from Sparks Business College who was one of the stalwarts of the Staley baseball team and also the Staley Company tennis champ.[3]

The story of Halas and the Decatur Staleys is fairly well known, especially how he quickly elevated a local industrial club into one of the top 11s in the country. While there is scant documentation remaining from the files of A.E. Staley regarding the football team, an interesting question needs to be addressed. Was Halas the first choice of Staley management to direct the football program? According to Edward "Dutch" Sternaman, the former teammate of Halas at Illinois and his future partner in the Chicago Bears, Halas was not the original chosen one. In fact, Sternaman claims that the job was offered to him (Sternaman) a year earlier in 1919, but he declined the position. As we scratch our heads over that one, there is some evidence from Sternaman delineating the entire process. In recent years, the family of Dutch Sternaman donated his personal documents from a lifetime in the game to the Pro Football Hall of Fame as noted by Jon Kendle, archivist at the Professional Football Hall of Fame in Canton, Ohio: "The Pro Football Hall of Fame acquired the Dutch Sternaman Collection from his daughter Margaret 'Peg' Holmes. Former Pro Football Hall of Fame Executive Director Joe Horrigan and Peg formed a friendship many years ago over the mutual love and admiration for the early history of the National Football League. Peggy had done an incredible job organizing and preserving her father's collection and decided in 2010 to donate it to the Pro Football Hall of Fame to be preserved and shared with fans for generations to come."

The collection is an extraordinary treasure chest of contracts, documents, and financial reports from the dark ages of the Chicago Bears in the NFL's first decade. The Sternaman archives provide us with a peek into everything from team travel expenses to the contents of the Bears' checkbook, revealing intimate details regarding how the Bears, and the league, struggled to survive in those first few years. This book will dip liberally into the Sternaman collection in upcoming pages, sharing numerous details that have not been published before. Kendle explained the importance of the Sternaman documents: "The Dutch Sternaman Collection might be the most historically significant archival collection we preserve at the Pro Football Hall of Fame. It not only chronicles the signing of Harold 'Red' Grange, the first major college football superstar to sign a professional contract, and subsequent barnstorming tour by the Chicago Bears, but it showcases in remarkable detail how NFL franchises were managed both on the playing field and in the front office during the 1920s and 30s."[4]

As for Sternaman's rather confident assertion that he was the original selection to manage the Staley football team, a deep dig into the archives at the Pro Football Hall of Fame uncovered an unpublished mini-memoir from Sternaman dictated in 1972. In it, Sternaman provides a detailed recollection of his courtship with the Staley Company that began when Sternaman recruited a team of talented players from various Midwest colleges to play for Arcola, Illinois, against the Staley Company in a game that was scheduled for Sunday, November 30, 1919. Apparently the Staleys learned of Sternaman's recruitment efforts of top-flight collegiate players and decided not to participate in the game. However, A.E. Staley, the company owner, arranged for the Arcola players to still be paid $150 each as promised. Sternaman was a senior at the University of Illinois at the time, but his football eligibility had expired. We'll pick up Sternaman's story at that point:

> On Sunday afternoon [November 30] we all left Arcola and went our separate ways. I was headed back to school at Champaign. The next Tuesday [December 2, 1919] I received a call from a man who wanted to come down to school to see me. He came that week and said he was a representative of Mr. Staley of Decatur, who would like to have me talk to him about football. I told him I would be glad to see Mr. Staley but would not be able to do so until Christmas vacation. On the way home to Springfield [Illinois] for Christmas, I stopped off in Decatur at Mr. Staley's office…. Little did either of us realize back in December, 1919 that we, too, were laying the foundation for a dream that would one day become the National Football Conference. Mr. Staley said that he would like to get a hold of a football team and really develop football. He asked me if I would run the team for him but I told him that I didn't think that I wanted to play any more football.

After returning to Illinois, Sternaman continued his studies but reconsidered the offer from Mr. Staley:

> Later in the winter I had further talks with Mr. Staley. I had decided by now, that I would work for Staley's [sic] after Mr. Staley promised me that I could work in the boiler rooms of the starch works and learn combustion engineering. I was still in school and had the last semester to finish. I did write a few letters to ask some of the ballplayers if they were interested in the arrangement with Staley's…. Mr. Staley was anxious to get things together and get going. A former Illinois teammate of mine, George Halas, was working at Staley's and took over the job of writing the contact letters. After graduation in June, 1920 I arrived at Staley's to finish putting together the football segment of Mr. Staley's athletic organization.[5]

Sternaman's version regarding the creation of the 1920 Staley football team does not, of course, align with that of George Halas, nor any currently published testimony involving the history of the Decatur Staleys. This does not mean that it could not have transpired, and if it did, Sternaman should be duly noted for his contributions. Within a couple of years, Halas and Sternaman would be recognized as the co-owners of the new Chicago Bears, but the role of the latter in the development of the Staleys remains in the shadows. In all probability there was some conversation between A.E. Staley and Sternaman in 1919, but any records of those discussions are lost forever, except in Sternaman's unpublished memoir. Author and historian Mark W. Sorensen has written extensively about the Staleys, including the preparation of comprehensive biographies of the 1920 players for the Staley Museum in Decatur, Illinois. As the former president of the Illinois State Historical Society and the retired assistant director of the Illinois State Archives, Sorensen questions whether the Sternaman claim is accurate. "It is hard to believe that it's true," said Sorensen. "Sternaman did tell that version, according to his relatives, but A.E. Staley did not keep any records, except a letter in October of 1921 that indicated the team was not doing well financially."[6]

Alibis Galore Were Presented

We do know that the employment of Sternaman was announced on June 14, 1920, when a release stated that Dutch "accepted a position with the A.E. Staley Company and will play football with the factory team this fall."[7] Halas, while playing on the Staley baseball team that summer, also spent time recruiting for the football team. If A.E. Staley was intent on quickly building a nationally competitive squad, then Halas was focused on doing so. Utilizing his numerous contacts from college, the service, and his one season with the professional Hammond Bobcats, Halas could draw from an impressive pool of gridiron talent if he could convince those players to accept the challenge of living and working in Decatur, Illinois. It should be noted that Halas was not the "founder" of the Decatur Staleys. The football team began a year previously in 1919 and managed to finish with a 6–1 record and claim the Illinois state championship. The company published a monthly publication called the *Staley Fellowship Journal*, which provided biased, albeit informative, coverage of the season. Since the players were employees of the plant, they were allowed to practice daily, which was a distinct advantage for the club and one that Halas would continue to utilize in 1920. In particular, the *Journal* was awash with praise for its team after a 21–7 win in the most important game of the 1919 campaign against the nearby Taylorville Independents, the defending state champions: "The shock of the defeat to the famous Taylorville Independents by the newly organized Staleys virtually numbed the Christian County fans, but as soon as they could regain the use of their voices, alibis galore were presented. Some paid the Staley backfield the high compliment of being the backfield of the Hammond All Stars—others thought they were taken direct from Notre Dame. One of the boys from the reclamation plant was picked out as being a famous kicker from the University of Illinois."[8]

In truth, the majority of the Staley players were "locals" (including future Major League Baseball manager Chuck Dressen), but that was about to change under the tutelage of George Halas, who arrived in Decatur on March 28, 1920. "In August I set off on probably the first professional football recruiting journey," recalled Halas. "At Madison, Wisconsin, I signed Ralph Scott, All-American tackle; I got Guy Chamberlin, All-American end at Nebraska; Hugh Blacklock, who had made his name with the Michigan Aggies and Great Lakes; and Jimmy Conzelman, from Washington University at St. Louis and Great Lakes. I wanted Paddy Driscoll but he had joined the Chicago Cardinals."[9] There are several "contradictions" in the Halas autobiography between his written word and actual reported situations, and the Driscoll recruitment may have been one of them since the *Decatur Daily Review* reported on July 26, 1920, that Driscoll would join the Staleys: "When Superintendent G.E. Chamberlain of the A.E. Staley Co. announced the signing of Paddie [sic] Driscoll Sunday, he turned a trick that half of the great professional teams in the United States were attempting, for the Chicago boy was one of the most sought for athletes in the country…. To George Halas must go a lot of the credit for landing the great star."[10]

It was an intriguing month for Mr. Driscoll, who played baseball with the Stewart-Warners in Chicago on July 17, ventured over to Tipton, Iowa, on July 23 to handle first base for the West Branch, Iowa, town team, and then sped east to join the Chicago Pyotts for contests with the Decatur Staleys on July 24 and July 25, before signing a football contract with the Staleys during his visit. The following week, it was reported by the wire services that Driscoll had also signed a contract with baseball's New York Giants of the National League and would report to the team on August 1. Ultimately, in what must have been a keen disappointment to both Georges Halas and the New York Giants, Driscoll would play for neither team in 1920. The Staley offer of a steady job and a share of the gate receipts was soon overshadowed by another bidder.

On September 8, 1920, Paddy Driscoll agreed to an offer from Chris O'Brien and the Racine Cardinals of Chicago in which Driscoll would benefit from a staggering $300-per-game contract to play quarterback and captain the South Side club. O'Brien had swept in and stolen the services of Driscoll from Halas.[11] It was likely the first salvo fired in the contentious rivalry that would develop between the NFL's two oldest clubs.

Cleaning Up the Place Generally

Chris O'Brien never wavered in his love for football in the early years of the 20th century. By 1916, while in his late 30s, he was still an active player and a visible figure in local sporting events on the South Side of Chicago. While living at 5622 South Racine Avenue, O'Brien also understood the local economic impact of a newly constructed baseball stadium that opened down the street on May 2, 1915. Called the Normal Park Baseball Field, the facility was a privately owned enterprise that was ideal for high school, club, and semiprofessional baseball games (and not to be confused with the field at 69th and Green used by the Normals). It occurred to O'Brien that the new compact field at 6100 South Racine was large enough to be configured for use during the football season as well, prompting him to organize a new football club in 1916 called the Racine Cardinals.

It was strictly a neighborhood endeavor, with O'Brien selecting the primary name based on the street location of his home and returning to the Cardinals name that he first utilized with the Cardinals Social and Athletic Club back in 1901. O'Brien recruited, coached, and managed that first effort in 1916, meeting with woeful results. The Cardinals stumbled through the season with a record of 0–5 while failing to score a single point! Starting with a 12–0 defeat at the hands of the North Ends on October 8 and finishing with a 20–0 shutout loss to the Alpines on November 19, the Cardinals were outscored by a margin of 107–0. Undaunted, O'Brien planned for a bigger, stronger, and more competitive team in 1917. But first, he organized a group to both invest in and support his new project. On January 10, 1917, the "Racine Cardinal Pleasure Club" was incorporated in the state of Illinois.[12]

Despite the odd, and somewhat misleading, name, the Racine Cardinal Pleasure Club was intended to field football and baseball squads that could successfully compete with the numerous local athletic teams popular in the area, in leagues such as the Chicago Football League and the City Baseball League. The construction of the new Normal Park, with a long grandstand constructed along the south side of the field, would also provide a professional, and inexpensive, home field for the Racine Cardinals.[13] Normal Park could be rented for just $15 per game with ample seating and additional space for standing-room crowds. When used for baseball, home plate was tucked into the southwest corner of the facility with the left field wall fronting 61st Street and the right field wall abutting Racine Avenue. For football games, the gridiron would be placed in an east-west direction in order to fit into the cramped confines. "The seating facilities at Normal Park are adequate for most games, as the grandstand and bleachers can take care of 2,500, while standing room will accommodate 3,000 or 4,000 more," reported the *Chicago Tribune*, which also indicated that the rental at Weeghman Park on the North Side (home of the Chicago Cubs) was a more costly $200 for the day. Renters at Normal Park could also save money if they would "take a hand by marking off the field whenever necessary and cleaning up the place generally."[14] It was a perfect facility for an eager semipro football team with little or no funding!

The "owners" of the Racine Cardinal Pleasure Club were not rich and famous, but they did share their common interest in promoting local sporting activities. The directors listed in the incorporation documents were Chris O'Brien, Donald Maher, and John McCarthy. They pledged to ensure that the organization met its objectives of "sociability and pleasure," which again seems to be a distant purpose for an athletic organization. One of the signatories for the club appearing on the official papers was a 17-year-old named John J. "Jack" Glynn, who worked at the nearby Union Stock Yards. While George Halas left behind his autobiography, which documents both his personal experiences and the history of the Bears, there is very little left from the Cardinals' side of town from those pre–NFL days. Glynn, despite his youth, served as the team secretary for the Cardinals and might, today, be considered the general manager. It was Glynn's responsibility to maintain a list of available players and their contact information for O'Brien to refer to as needed. If the Cardinals would be short of players for a specific game, Glynn would be the man who would track down the replacements. Working from a small, brown notebook, Glynn included names, addresses, and even those rare phone numbers for certain players. The importance of the "Glynn Papers" (which as detailed below have surfaced only recently) is that we now have some written documentation about the early Cardinals. We can see that most of the players from 1917 to 1919 lived in, or near, the Englewood neighborhood, but that Chris O'Brien also was determined to enlist the very best football players available on the South Side of Chicago.

For research purposes, since Glynn included the correct spelling of the players' names, as well as their addresses, it becomes a bit easier to trace the individual histories through the years, as well as follow the transition of the team from mostly high school standouts to a club representing numerous major universities. And yet, the history of the notebook's (and other documents) survival over 100 years is also intriguing. Jack Glynn's nephew, Patrick Glynn, shared the story:

> The Cardinals material resided with my aunt, Jack's sister Honora "Nonie" Troller, until her death in 1987. From all those materials, the notebook somehow ended up with my sister, Sister Helen Glynn OP, Dominican sister. She discovered the roster notebook among some items in a drawer. My sister was a medical missionary in Bolivia for 25 years and then taught at Marist High School in Chicago for many years. I have no idea how she ended up with just the notebook. She was in Bolivia when my aunt died. Crazy stuff this historical research! If the Lord steps in on this research someday, other Cardinal items may someday surface in my sister Helen's "stuff." She was and still is a diehard football fan![15]

From the Glynn notebook, the players from 1917 through 1919 are clearly identified, some of whom continued with the Cardinals after the team entered what would become the NFL in 1920. Among the key players (with their college and Chicago addresses) were end Red O'Connor (De Paul, 7748 South Calumet), quarterback Marston Smith (Chicago, 5455 South Harper), end Paul Florence (Loyola/Georgetown, 10250 South Vincennes), and center Bill Whalen (no college or address). Aside from playing for the 1920 Cardinals in the new American Professional Football Association, Florence made the big leagues in baseball, playing with the New York Giants in 1926, and then enjoyed a long career in baseball management and administration.

Following the incorporation of the Cardinals club in January 1917, the members wasted little time in generating some funding for its teams by hosting a reception and dance on February 2: "The Racine Cardinals, who made a great name on the football field last fall, have organized a large club and again appear in the limelight at their reception at White City ballroom tonight. The club has a membership of 300 and is only in its infancy. Receipts will go to fit out baseball and football teams."[16]

Low Ceiling Interfered with Footwork

With the team properly "outfitted" after the fundraiser, O'Brien entered the Cardinals in the Chicago Football League in 1917, a circuit consisting of 16 "amateur" clubs loaded with former high school and college players. O'Brien was well-known on the local gridiron circuit and was recognized for his longevity by the *Hammond Times* prior to a game with the Pullman Thorns in November: "It's been sixteen years since manager O'Brien of the Racine Cardinals has led his warriors to Pullman, when he handed the Clovers, who were then the champions of Pullman, a 6–0 defeat. The Cardinals are booked to meet the speedy Thorns of the Chicago league Sunday in their league fracas. Both are high in the standings and a desperate battle is expected to be waged."[17]

The Cards finished with an improved 3–2–4 regular season record (3–3–6 overall) in 1917, but since tie games were discarded in the standings, the club managed to grab the league's final playoff berth that led to a most unusual conclusion to its football season! Due to inclement weather, the league playoffs were held indoors at the Dexter Park Pavilion, the site of which would later become the International Amphitheater adjacent to the Union Stock Yards. The opening game of the playoffs on December 23, 1917, would prove to be memorable for the Cardinals. On that day, a team from suburban Evanston, Illinois (just north of Chicago), would tie the Cards 0–0, behind the work of quarterback Paddy Driscoll. Never one to go very long without participating in some type of athletic activity, Driscoll had played for Hammond during the 1917 regular season before sliding over to Evanston for the playoffs. While Driscoll could not produce a score, he did provide some excitement as he struggled to complete the game due to an unusual circumstance (specific to indoor football), as reported by the *Hammond Times*: "Paddy Driscoll, the Hammond star, performed with the Evanston squad and for the second time this season played almost an entire half while 'out on his feet.' He struck his head against the wall early in the game, and when the half was over could not recall a play he had made. He came back for the final quarter, however, and furnished one big thrill when he attempted a sixty-yard drop kick in the last second of play. The ball missed by only a few inches. The low ceiling interfered somewhat with the footwork and both teams missed all their kicking attempts."[18]

The game provided Chris O'Brien with the opportunity to personally observe the wondrous footwork, and talented toe, of Driscoll for probably the first time. Anyway, after a weather postponement, and another tie game, the Racine Cardinals would finally be ousted 21–7 by the Tornadoes on January 20, 1918, ending the lengthy season. Ironically, this time frame would coincide with the induction of George Halas into the U.S. Navy, where he would begin still another chapter in his illustrious athletic career. While Halas would garner national acclaim for his work with the 1918 Great Lakes football team, O'Brien continued to toil in near obscurity with the Cardinals. Playing both guard and tackle in 1918, the aging O'Brien was the acknowledged leader of his team both on and off the field. In addition, he was elected president of the Chicago Football League, and his expert leadership would be tested during a season decimated by war and the flu epidemic. The Cardinals managed to squeeze in just six games during 1918, finishing with an acceptable 3-2-1 mark. Former University of Chicago standout William Marston Smith served in the dual role as the Cardinals player/coach for the season. He was known locally as simply Marston Smith, and Smith also coached the nearby Hyde Park High School football squad in 1918. Then, to avert any connection to a famous common cough suppressant, Smith legally changed his name in 1928 to William Smith Marston, explaining: "As one of the Smith brothers, I got tired of hearing people say 'not a cough in a carload.'"[19]

While Driscoll and Halas rode the Great Lakes football wave into the 1919 Rose Bowl, O'Brien and Glynn began the process of transforming the Cardinals from a strong neighborhood team into one that could compete with the best semiprofessional clubs in the Midwest. Moving away from adversaries such as the East Chicago Gophers, the 1919 Cardinals scheduled significantly stronger teams in the opening weeks of the season with the Hammond (Indiana) Bobcats and the Moline (Illinois) Fans Association. As mentioned previously, the Hammond team was a star-studded group put together by Paul Parduhn to attract big crowds in Chicago (its home base) against more highly visible Midwest teams. When the Cardinals and Hammond opened the season with a 0–0 tie on September 28 in front of just 1,500 fans, the outcome was viewed as an "upset" in favor of the Cardinals. Hammond followers lamented that their team was missing a couple of key players, but the result also indicated that the largely unknown Cardinals club might have some talent of its own. Of more importance was the fact that this game was the initial meeting between George Halas and Chris O'Brien on a football field; it would be the first of many over the next decade.

A 6–0 Racine win over the defending state champion Pullman Thorns followed the Hammond deadlock, setting up an interesting match with the Moline Fans Association (M.F.A.) on October 19. With this contest, the Cardinals received their first significant press coverage outside the Chicago area. Advance stories provided anxious local readers with ample insight into the planning of the game:

Five. Pro Football: The Beginning

Christy O'Brien, president and manager of the Racine Cardinals Athletic Club of Chicago will be in Moline to complete the details for the contest, according to a letter received this morning at M.F.A. headquarters. O'Brien also enclosed newspaper clippings from Chicago, showing that the victory of the team over the Thorns last Sunday was one of the surprises of the season and indicates that the Cardinals will be the principal contender for the heavyweight title in Chicago. In the three games the team has played this season, they have been successful, including a scoreless tie with the famous $20,000 team [Hammond]. In the Cardinal lineup are men who have made college and professional football popular in the last few years, including O'Malley, McGurk, Mensch, Murphy, Whalen, Nelson, Carey, O'Connor, Vinage, Breen, Shanks and H. McInerney. Many of these men have seen service with Notre Dame, Purdue, Chicago and other universities.[20]

While O'Brien and Glynn had successfully bulked up the Racine roster for the 1919 campaign, an article the day before the game (published on October 18) discreetly noted two more blatant issues attendant to pro football at the time: the use of college players and betting: "The Cardinals will present a strong lineup against the M.F.A. Sunday afternoon. Three of the men are college students who are playing under assumed names for obvious purposes ... the Cardinals appear to be slight favorites in the betting line, although there is plenty of Moline money to be had and the wagers will probably be made at even money when the game starts."[21]

Rosters were still very fluid in 1919, and various mysterious names would appear in the lineups throughout the season. Who were they? We'll probably never know. Many hopeful gridders played for the Cardinals whose true names are now likely lost forever. As for the wagers, it was common for the local newspapers to openly publicize the odds and the betting favorites prior to each game. Certainly, players could bet on their own teams in the Wild, Wild West environment of 1919 pro football, but the majority of the prognosticators were the loyal fans who embraced this new professional football concept.

Hair-Raising Finish!

Meanwhile, the Cardinals watched as victory slipped away at Moline on virtually the last play of the game. With a 7–0 lead and just under two minutes to play, the Cardinals' defense sagged under the unrelenting Moline ground attack and surrendered the equalizing touchdown as time elapsed. "In a hair-raising finish, Moline succeeded in tying the famous Racine Cardinal eleven at Browning Field 7–7," reported the local press. "Moline plunged and tugged and skirted the ends for a touchdown just as the whistle blew to end the game. [Coach Mark] Devlin kicked a beautiful goal to tie the score."[22]

That same week, Paul Parduhn of the Hammond Bobcats finalized a contract with the Chicago Cubs to use Cubs Park for eight Sunday football games during the fall of 1919, according to the *Daily Times*: "The idea is to test the popularity of professional football in Chicago and endeavor to establish it on some such basis as in other western cities. It's in the contract between the Chicago club and Manager Parduhn that the games must be clean and free from the rough stuff that has characterized some of the games between professional elevens in Chicago in previous years."[23]

Whether the competitors remained "free from the rough stuff" in the remaining battles at Cubs Park remains debatable. The Hammond season ended in heartache and disarray when the players' checks began bouncing late in the season. Hammond finished with a less-than-gaudy 4–2–3 record, but the two profitable games with Canton proved that intersectional play on the professional level could be successful. The Racine Cardinals, with a less recognizable roster than Hammond, finished with a similar 4–2–2 mark, but were also burdened with anguish when team secretary John "Jack" Glynn passed away suddenly on December 29, 1919, at the age of 20. While the Hammond players lost a possible paycheck, the Cardinals organization lost a key part of their young team. If Chris O'Brien was the architect of the transformation of the Cardinals into a regional power in the pre–NFL years, Glynn was certainly the foreman who did the heavy lifting. His passing was met with shock and sadness by the local football community: "Independent football circles were startled yesterday with the news that John Glynn, secretary of the Racine Cardinals football club, had died suddenly at St. Bernard's Hospital. Glynn contacted a severe cold at a recent game of his team and it took a bad turn last Tuesday which necessitated his going to the hospital. Glynn was a popular lad and his death means a vacancy in the official list of the Cardinal club that will be hard to fill."[24]

Although Glynn was just 20 at the time of his death, he had been instrumental in the construction of the Cardinals' roster. He not only developed a list of football contacts locally but began to insert some influence on a more national level. For example, his family shared his efforts to add the legendary George Gipp of Notre Dame to the team's roster once Gipp concluded his collegiate career after the 1920 season. Although George Gipp died at the age of 25 on December 14, 1920, he and

This rare photograph of the 1919 Racine Cardinals was found in the papers of Jack Glynn, secretary of the team. Glynn, fifth from the left in the top row, passed away suddenly in December 1919, but he was responsible for helping Chris O'Brien move the club from a neighborhood team into a more competitive, regional organization (courtesy Jack Glynn family).

Jack Glynn had developed a friendship, according to Glynn family legend. "My uncle traveled to Notre Dame at some point to visit with George Gipp and determine if he might be interested in playing football with the Cardinals after Notre Dame," said Patrick Glynn. "Gipp and Jack were also said to have met at a pool hall around 63rd and Halsted at some time during or after the season. My aunt and older siblings recall seeing communications with Gipp among our uncle's papers."[25]

Shortly after the passing of Jack Glynn, the Cardinals were back in action in early 1920 when the semifinals of the Chicago Football League began on January 4. While the results of this game with the Tornadoes at the indoor Dexter Park Pavilion have vanished, the contest demonstrated the efforts of O'Brien to continue his building of a more dominant team. For this contest, O'Brien added tackle Fred Gillies of Cornell; guard J.L. McGregor, a former teammate of George Halas's at Illinois; and the talented Paddy Driscoll at quarterback. This was the start of a long relationship between Driscoll and the Cardinals and the end of a long weekend for Driscoll. As a member of the Whiting (Indiana) Red Crowns professional basketball team, Driscoll scored six points on Thursday, January 1, in Janesville, Wisconsin, as the Red Crowns swept aside the Lakota Cardinals 32–17. Then on January 2, Driscoll was held scoreless as the Red Crowns dropped their first game of the season, falling 27–18 in Beloit, Wisconsin, to the Fairbanks-Morse quintet.[26] His signing with the Cardinals on January 3 was announced by the *Chicago Tribune*: "Driscoll returned to Chicago yesterday morning from a trip north with the Red Crowns basketball team and immediately signed with Chris O'Brien."[27] Years later, Driscoll, who eventually became the head coach of the Chicago Bears, remembered his initial stint with the Cardinals: "Well, you know I began with Hammond, but it seems to me that I also played a couple of games with the old Racine Cardinals—forerunners of today's Cardinals—in the old Dexter Park armory. Some boys just becoming stars at Notre Dame were with us. But that wasn't unusual. When I played for Hammond against Pine Village, a DePauw boy was to play end for Pine Village. Charley Bachman, the DePauw assistant coach, heard about it and played instead of the boy. But Bachman gave the boy his pay!"[28]

We Expect to Step Out Among the Top Notchers

With his unique athletic ability, and smallish 150-pound stature, Driscoll managed to position himself to collect a paycheck no matter what the sports season. Like George Halas, Driscoll competed in professional football, basketball, and baseball, reaching the major leagues briefly in 1917 with the Chicago Cubs. While Halas labored throughout the summer of 1920 with the Staley baseball team, Driscoll spent his sunny days with the Pyotts in Chicago before determining that his immediate football future would be with the Racine Cardinals. As the 1920 baseball season was concluding, the football teams representing the Decatur Staleys and the Racine Cardinals were preparing for the fall campaign. Both teams had been busy stockpiling former college players, although the Cardinals still filled out their roster with a few sturdy, but reliable, men who had not advanced beyond high school in terms of formal education. In Decatur, hopes for a successful season were very high, despite the failure of the team to secure the services of Driscoll as originally planned. The *Staley Fellowship Journal* was especially encouraged by the athletes assembled for the campaign: "Not satisfied with having one of the strongest industrial baseball teams in the country this season, we expect to step out among the top notchers in the gridiron game and if the men who have been lined up for the team live up to their past reputations, the name of the Staley eleven will be carried to all corners of the United States. For the past two months Mr. Chamberlain and George Halas have been busy signing the best available football players in the central West, and many an athlete who won his spurs on a university or college team will be out there on the gridiron."[29]

In the few months since George Chamberlain had initially contacted Halas to recruit him for the Staley athletic program, Halas had provided enormous contributions to the company. With the baseball team finishing 36–23–1, Halas was the captain of the squad and topped the team in hitting (.315), stolen bases (26), hits (64), runs (42), and doubles (11). In addition, he succeeded in finding both the time and the resources to attract a stellar roster for the upcoming football season. Folks around Decatur were quite excited to determine if the ability of the players could possibly match the expectations.

The announcement on September 8, 1920, that Paddy Driscoll had signed with the Cardinals did not seem to damper the enthusiasm in Decatur. While Halas was quietly scheduling games for the upcoming season, Chris O'Brien was doing the same in Chicago and both anxiously hoped to secure the biggest prize: Jim Thorpe and the Canton, Ohio, Bulldogs. On September 12, The *Decatur Herald* cautiously predicted a prominent list of opponents: "Although a schedule has not been definitely arranged, the Staleys will play ten games this fall and will meet … Jim Thorpe's Canton eleven, Dayton Triangles, Rock Island and Peoria."[30] The Cardinals sought similar prey: "Games with Akron, Canton, Massillon, and Fort Wayne are already being framed. O'Brien will open his season in town [Chicago] with three of the best of the local clubs and will then tackle the big outside clubs."[31]

Interest in the concept of legitimate professional football was expanding but remained restrained. Halas realized that further and more permanent growth would necessitate a more careful organizational structure in order to succeed: "Pro football was pretty much of a catch-as-catch-can affair. Teams appeared one week and disappeared the next. Players came and went, drawn by the pleasure of playing. If others came to watch, that was fine. If they bought tickets or tossed coins into a helmet passed by the most popular player, that was helpful. I thought the Staleys had gone beyond this mobile situation. I wrote various teams suggesting games. Replies were indifferent and vague. We needed an organization."[32]

With both clubs eyeing the big prize of scheduling a lucrative game with Thorpe and the Canton Bulldogs, Halas and O'Brien were probably both honored to receive an identical telegram from Thorpe (representing a quartet of Ohio teams) inviting them to attend a meeting on September 17 in Canton, Ohio, for the purpose of evaluating the possibility of a new professional football league. Supporters of the Rock Island Independents were overjoyed when they received the same invitation, prompting an explosion of civic pride: "The invitation was taken as a criterion that the outside football world recognizes in the Independents as an opponent worthy of the class of previous competition, and that Rock Island has earned the respect and admiration of the general football and sporting field for its clean sportsmanship and grand achievements."[33]

Naturally, Rock Island was also interested in hosting a game with the great Jim Thorpe and all three teams representing the state of Illinois were keen to learn more about the proposed new professional league.

A preliminary meeting had been held in Canton on August 20 where four teams (Dayton Triangles, Thorpe's Canton Bulldogs, Akron Pros, and Cleveland Tigers) created the American Professional Football Conference (APFC) and agreed on both a schedule and an understanding regarding the recruitment of current college players: "An agreement was reached last night which will do much to wipe out opposition which has developed against the 'pro' game in the past. No college player who is now in school is to be molested or accepted on either the Canton, Akron, Cleveland or Dayton teams. Players who have been signed and attempt to jump the club with which they are affiliated in the hopes of holding up rival backers for higher pay are to be outlawed."[34]

With this pronouncement, the APFC clearly addressed two of the biggest issues facing pro football in 1920: the use of college players (often under assumed names) and the blatant raiding of other teams' rosters. Whether these temptations would truly be banished in the new league remained to be seen. Perhaps most important, the proposed professional circuit would need to overcome the often boisterous and questionable public perception that the pro game itself was rife with exploitation of young, innocent athletes. The APFC's giant first step, in an attempt to address the acceptance of a national professional organization similar to Major League Baseball, was to share the concept with other leading clubs to determine the public interest level. The bait, of course, would be the potential opportunity for member teams to garner a nice gate with an appearance by Jim Thorpe. Others, like Rock Island, appeared to be happy merely with the recognition of their grid team on the national level. Either way, the telegram from Thorpe inviting the attendees and outlining the objectives of the September 17, 1920, meeting was the unquestioned impetus behind the formation of what would become the National Football League.

As multiple trains and buses from various parts of the country pointed toward tiny Canton, Ohio, on the eve of the anticipated meeting, hopes were lofty in Decatur, as the town oozed with confidence over the recruitment successes of Halas, noting that the A.E. Staley Company was "Expecting to have one of the greatest teams in the history of professional football."[35] Even the departure of Halas for the Canton confab was worth mentioning in the local press: "George Halas, who will have charge of the Staley football team this fall, and Morgan O'Brien, secretary, left last night for Canton, Ohio, where a meeting of coaches and managers of the leading professional football teams of the country will be held. The object of the meeting is to organize a professional football league. Jim Thorpe, the famous Carlisle Indian, and manager [Ralph] Hay of the Canton club, have invited the managers of the foremost professional teams of the country to the session and an American Conference is expected to be formed."[36]

It is interesting to note that each of three Illinois clubs balanced their financial requirements differently. The Staleys were sponsored by a rather large industrial firm, while the Cardinals pushed forward thanks to the zeal and support of local investors. Finally, the Independents relied on small contributions from individual citizens, who earnestly ignited fundraisers for items such as blankets for the players. Yet all three realized that their participation in the fledgling pro enterprise could encourage profitable gate receipts when well-known players and teams visited, courtesy of an organized professional league. As such, Chris O'Brien of the Cardinals, Walter Flanigan of the Independents, and George Halas of the Staleys all converged on Canton with visions, within reach, of economic stability and increased visibility for each of their teams.

Apparently, the invitation did not request an RSVP from attendees, so the meeting space originally allotted in Ralph Hay's Hupmobile dealership in Canton quickly proved to be inadequate when a larger-than-expected crowd of inquisitive football men showed up. Moving the location from his office to the display floor, Hay reluctantly began the session with not enough seating for the participants as Halas recalled: "The showroom was big enough for four cars—Hupmobiles and Jordans—occupied the ground floor of the three-story brick Odd Fellows building. Chairs were few. I sat on a runningboard. We all agreed on the need for a league. In two hours, we created the American Professional Football Association."[37]

The meeting itself in Canton was brief, but the results of the discussions were landmark in nature and lightly documented in a two-page set of minutes prepared by Frank Nied and signed by Art Ranney, both of the Akron Pros. That team's letterhead was utilized when the official minutes were typed for distribution to the attendees. In all, 15 individuals representing 11 teams were on hand, with those original clubs being the Cardinals and the Staleys, along with the Canton Bulldogs, Cleveland Indians, Dayton Triangles, Akron Professionals, Massillon Tigers, Rochester Jeffersons, Rock Island Independents, Muncie Flyers, and the Hammond Pros. Massillon was out of the league by the end of the initial meeting and Jim Thorpe was selected to serve as the president of the newly renamed American Professional Football Association (APFA). Following the September 17 meeting, four more clubs would join the APFA ranks: the Chicago Tigers, Columbus Panhandles, Detroit Heralds, and the Buffalo All-Americans, leaving the league with a robust number of 14 contenders for the inaugural APFA championship.

Overall, the real victor in the league's inception was likely Ralph Hay, owner of the Canton Bulldogs, who fostered a dream that something like the NFL could indeed succeed. Hay prepared the invitation list, hosted the initial meeting, and actually turned down the offer to head the league, noting that Thorpe possessed the nationally known reputation and visibility that could help the circuit achieve early acceptance. As with the APFC formed in August, the APFA would still need to actively stare down the biggest obstacles lurking on the path of success for the league: escalating salaries, the use of college players, and the bouncing of players from one roster to another. While these three items were not listed in the minutes from the September 17 meeting, they were most likely discussed at some point during the session since there was mention of such in newspaper accounts from the meeting: "A decision was reached at the meeting to refrain from luring players out of colleges for the professional game and an agreement was made that the clubs will not play men who jump from other clubs in the league."[38]

But for the time being, a national professional football league was in place. Whether it could survive was another challenge. Teams were still left on their own regarding scheduling and recruiting players, although the APFA required that rosters be submitted by January 1, 1921, to league secretary Art Ranney in an effort to minimize, and hopefully eliminate, talent raids by competing clubs. While some scheduling arrangements were discussed in Canton, big questions remained for the individual league members. Now that a pro organization existed, how would the champion be determined? How should scheduling be approached? And, how should professional football be marketed? Above all, will people attend these games? Will they come?

George Halas probably tossed these thoughts around as he headed back to Decatur on Saturday, September 18, 1920. But not for long. After all, there was still one more baseball game to be played on Sunday, September 19, against the visiting Halvolines from Lawrenceville, Illinois. Before taking his usual position in the Staley outfield, Halas had about 24 hours before he called his first football practice on Monday, September 20. Then, and finally then, Halas could concentrate solely on football…

Six

NFL's Oldest Rivalry

"We are not ready to call the Cardinals gutter champions."
—George Halas, *The Dispatch* (Moline, Illinois), December 3, 1920

After the hurried courting for the football talents of Paddy Driscoll just a week or so before, George Halas and Chris O'Brien sat in the Hupmobile showroom in Canton, Ohio, as two of the founders of what would become the National Football League. No chairs were thrown, nor were any scornful insults exchanged. At least for a moment, all was well between the two soon-to-be competitors. Perhaps the only negative takeaway from Canton was the fact that the meeting minutes mistakenly identified the Cardinals as being from Racine, Wisconsin, rather than from Chicago, Illinois. While the minutes were never corrected, O'Brien would take a significant step in adjusting that perception shortly. Overall, everyone seemed pleased with the results of the groundbreaking meeting, except that not much of the rest of the world seemed to care. Press coverage was light, especially in Chicago, which represented the largest city in the league. Publications such as the *Chicago Tribune* and *Collyer's Eye* failed to even mention the new circuit's formation.

Meanwhile, both the Cardinals and the Staleys were engaged in preparing for the 1920 season. The Cards contracted to lease Normal Park for three years while the Staleys began practice on Monday, September 20. Then, on September 21, 1920, the newborn Chicago Tigers swept in and reserved Cubs Park on the North Side of Chicago for its home games.[1] The Tigers, a late arrival into the league membership rolls, consisted of several key players who were on the 1919 roster of the Hammond Bobcats. The financial repercussions from the bounced Hammond checks at the conclusion of the previous season likely encouraged some of the prominent players to seek greener pastures: "The Hammond professional team of last season was harassed by player dissensions and broke up before the end of the season. [Shorty] Des Jardien and [Milt] Ghee, center and quarterback of last year's team, are running a team in Chicago known as the Tigers. [Hugh] Blacklock, [George] Trafton and Halas are with the Staley team."[2]

Although there was indeed a new professional league, it lacked seasoned business leadership and mandated rules. While Jim Thorpe was clearly the president, his appointment was based on his name recognition as the world's greatest athlete, not for his prowess as a business manager. Among the loosely connected members, however, a lucrative gate for a game with Thorpe and his Canton Bulldogs would be the optimum benefit of league membership. The Decatur Staleys announced two upcoming games with Canton on October 10 to be held in Canton and on November 21 back in Decatur, although the *Staley Fellowship Journal* cautioned that "the tentative dates ... will no doubt be changed in some cases."[3]

At the same time, the Rock Island Independents actively, perhaps desperately, pursued a date with Canton. The date? November 21—the same day claimed by the Staleys. The only setback was that the game would be played at Canton, thus depriving the locals of the opportunity to catch Thorpe and his comrades in person. However, careful financial negotiations were pursued by Rock Island manager Walter Flanigan, which would ensure a golden economic opportunity for the visitors: "Canton has agreed to split 50–50 on the gross receipts with Rock Island, something never done before. The field capacity in Canton is about 9,000. With this split, 9,000 tickets at $2.20 each will amount to a total gate of $19,800. Splitting this amount 50–50, the Islanders would receive $9,900 for their end, so local fans will see the benefits of the game, even though they will be denied the chance of witnessing the great battle."[4]

If it sounded too good to be true for Rock Island, sadly, it was. Neither the Staleys nor the Independents were able to pull off a meeting with the great Jim Thorpe on the gridiron in 1920. In fact, the only Illinois representative to do so was the team from Chicago's North Side—the Chicago Tigers—which lost at Canton 21–0 on November 14.

With attendance the primary source of revenue for the early pro teams, the need to attract fans was of great importance in that initial season. Securing local media coverage was paramount to success and teams pestered newspapers with redundant press releases, game reminders, and advertising, all in the hopes of achieving consistent pre- and post-game coverage on the community level. While the Tigers and Cardinals resided in the league's largest market, the efforts to receive more than a couple of lines of coverage in the various newspapers was a difficult challenge. Aside from the Tigers' home base of Cubs Park with seating for about 18,000, the stadiums used for other clubs was minimal. Even if the Staleys attracted a full house to Staley Field in Decatur, that would equal just 1,500 seats. For the Cardinals, Normal Park appeared to max out at a capacity of 4,000. Most teams grabbed the opportunity to promote the presence of "famous" college stars in their games and all hoped for a successful word-of-mouth campaign among the locals in those "quiet" days before radio and television coverage.

A Michelangelo Job with the Football

In Decatur, Halas enjoyed a distinct advantage in that his players were also employed by the Staley Company, which also was underwriting the football-related expenses. Gate receipts were also diminished at Staley Field, where tickets cost just $1.50, but all Staley Company employees received a generous 50 cents off the ticket price. In addition, the Staley players were promised a share of the final gate income at the end of the season. All in all, it appeared that Halas would need to worry only about the product on the field, rather than any bottom line in 1920. Author and

Decatur Staleys' historian Mark Sorensen verified the payment arrangements for the Staley players: "They each received $50 per week and a share of the gate receipts, but remember they were expected to work all year round at the plant. Although the players received full wages, they were also getting off work two hours early for football practice."[5]

This was a significant advantage for Halas in that he was assured that practices with a full squad would take place on a daily basis. Other pro teams managed to squeeze in practices when they could, but often were relegated to a couple of midweek sessions, especially if players did not reside in the immediate area. For the Cardinals, Chris O'Brien faced more severe challenges in rounding up players for a typical practice as recalled by former team "water boy," the late Monsignor Ignatius D. McDermott:

> Chris O'Brien was a house painter.... In the early days, the Racine Cardinals were made up of guys who didn't go to high school. They practiced at Sherman Park at 55th and Racine. I was a water boy for the team. We used to go over to practice. Those guys were working from 9 a.m. to 5 p.m. in those days, and they'd come over and practice after work. They'd practice in Sherman Park because there were two lamp posts there. Chris O'Brien was the author of what he called "Ghost Football." In order for those fellows to see the football better in the dark, he would do a Michelangelo job with the football, which he painted white. So, I'm convinced he was the father of Ghost Football![6]

While the Staleys welcomed a squadron of imported players to Decatur, the Cardinals presented an array of home-grown talent from the immediate South Side metropolitan area, even as the team evolved into more of a national power. "The Cardinals belonged to us even more than the Chicago White Sox did because the Cards were part of our neighborhood," said McDermott.[7]

With question marks galore facing the American Professional Football Association (APFA) at the start of the 1920 season, the league shuffled forward with its first games involving league teams on October 3, when Columbus fell to Dayton 14–0 and Rock Island trounced the Muncie Flyers 45–0. Meanwhile, the Staleys hosted an out-classed club from Moline, Illinois, subduing the Universal Tractors (soon to be the Moline Athletic Club) 20–0 in front of 1,500 in Decatur.

The more conventional opening day commenced on October 10 with several APFA contests, including those involving the Cardinals and the Staleys. It was not known at the time if anyone would attend these games, or if anyone really cared. But then a spark appeared prior to the opening game between the Cardinals and the Chicago Tigers: the Chicago newspapers noticed that the APFA was going ahead with its planned games. Add the fact that the Tigers' own "home" facility of Cubs Park was considered "big-time," and there was a slight move toward positive recognition of the new league. The *Chicago Daily News* broke the ice with its preview article on the Wednesday before the game: "Professional football in Chicago will be launched for the 1920 season next Sunday in a game between the Chicago Tigers and Chris O'Brien's Cardinals at Cubs Park. The meeting will be one of many over the country, the teams of the Professional Football Association starting their season at the same time. Manager Chris O'Brien of the Cardinals has twenty players, seventeen of which have played on leading school teams, and from that selection expects to pick a formidable eleven. Paddy Driscoll, formerly of Northwestern, will be the mainspring in the intricate Cardinal machinery."[8]

On game day (October 10), the *Chicago Tribune* chimed in along with a welcome wink regarding the hopefully strict rules that the pros would abide by during the campaign: "College and university stars of other years who still like the gridiron pastime have their first big day of the 1920 season today. Two dozen of them will mix in lists at Cub Park this afternoon and from advance indications their clash, Chicago Tigers vs. Racine Cardinals, will be a display of football class similar to that of Big Ten conference games. Rules of the American Professional Football Association do not permit dickering with college stars, but alumni who desire to play are in abundance."[9]

Staleys Fought Savagely

With the newfound media recognition apparently helping, an estimated 10,000 fans found their way to Cubs Park to take a peek at the professional gridders in action. Newspaper reports indicated that 26 former college stars were on the field during the 0–0 tie, headlined by Cardinals coach and quarterback Paddy Driscoll, but the most important result was the surprisingly strong attendance. Meanwhile, the Staleys continued their campaign on October 10 in Decatur by hosting the Kewanee Walworths before a packed house of 1,500 at Staley Field. Dutch Sternaman scored three times in the easy 25–7 win. The supportive *Decatur Herald* anxiously summarized the proceedings: "Staleys fought savagely in the second quarter, tearing holes in the Kewanee line and skirting the ends for big gains, and put two more touchdowns over during the period. Their scores were made mainly by means of straight football. The half ended with Staleys on the long end of a 25 to 0 score. Coach Halas sent his second-string men in for the third quarter."[10]

A week later, it was back to reality for the Cardinals. After performing in front of a nice crowd at Cubs Park, the team was relegated to entertaining the Moline Athletic Club at a Chicago high school field. With Normal Park being utilized by the semipro Standards club, Chris O'Brien hurriedly secured the nearby St. Rita High School field for the nonleague meeting with Moline. After the listless, scoreless tussle with the Chicago Tigers, the Cardinals' offense blossomed against Moline, securing an easy 33–3 win in front of about 4,000 fans. As the new league struggled to attract attendees, some teams were also experiencing difficulty in scheduling games. The allure of contracting with the Canton Bulldogs and the great Jim Thorpe was becoming more of a dream than a reality. The previous announcement from Decatur stating that the Staleys would travel to Canton on October 10, and then host the Bulldogs on November 21, never materialized, thus prompting Halas to schedule the Kewanee Walworths instead of the Bulldogs on October 10. Meanwhile, a 44–0 loss by Hammond to host Dayton on October 17 hurt both teams on a couple of levels. For Dayton, the small crowd was disconcerting: "Dayton furnished a crowd of probably 2,000 and promoters of the game stand to lose heavily," predicted the *Hammond Times*. On the other hand, Hammond was experiencing difficulty for both short- and long-term scheduling, according to the *Times*: "Before leaving for Hammond

George Halas (seated front row, center) was hired to coach and manage the Decatur Staleys football team in 1920. Halas initiated what was likely the first recruiting trip for a pro football team that summer and then led the club to a 10-1-2 record and a second-place finish in the inaugural year of what would become the National Football League (courtesy the *Decatur [IL] Herald & Review*).

[from Dayton] last night, manager Doc Young was undecided as to where his team would play next Sunday. A game had been tentatively scheduled with the Racine Cardinals early in the season, but this is still up in the air, he said. It is possible the team will play at Chicago, but this will not be decided until later in the week."[11]

Also, on October 19, 1920, Halas and the Staley Company announced that it would move its upcoming home game against the Chicago Tigers from Decatur to Cubs Park in Chicago. Although the local support for the team in Decatur was solid, Staley Field could hold only 1,500. Even though the team was sponsored by the A.E. Staley Company, there was little hope of achieving any return on the investment from gate receipts at home games with the limited capacity, especially with the employee discount. "The Staleys transferred their Chicago engagement owing to lax patronage in Decatur, it being reported that 1,500 is a top crowd for the Starchmakers on their home lot," reported the *Rock Island Argus*.[12]

It must have been a difficult decision for A.E. Staley to address. His intent to develop a powerful football squad to both promote and publicize his company had surely been successful—even this early in the season. However, it is reasonable to assume that the gridiron club was becoming both too unwieldly and too expensive. No one in business management is comfortable with a negative bottom line. The bleachers at tiny Staley Field were packed for the first two home games but the problem persisted that there were simply not enough seats. With the shift of the Tigers game to Chicago on October 24, the Staleys would play in front of the home Decatur crowd only one more time during the 1920 season. However, the early season clash with the Tigers (1–0–1) took on new meaning for the Staleys (3–0) when someone decided that the contest would be a championship battle: "The game between the Staley eleven and the Chicago Tigers, originally scheduled for Decatur Sunday, has been transferred to the Cub Park in Chicago, where the two great elevens will play for the professional title of the central west."[13]

Henceforth Would Be the Chicago Cardinals

The suggestion that this particular contest would be for the championship of anything was not unusual in 1920, with sensational headlines created on an almost daily basis to attract the eyes of the reader. Yet this declaration of the championship caliber of the game was certainly premature at this early juncture in the schedule, but to fans not knowing the uncharted wilderness of the new professional circuit, it might provide enough incentive to journey out to the ballpark to catch the game. Meanwhile, the Cardinals, who were apparently neglected from consideration when discussing title hopes three weeks into the season, scooped up some brief mentions with an announcement that scarcely drew any journalistic interest. On October 20, 1920, Chris O'Brien spread the word that the name of his team henceforth would be the Chicago Cardinals. The Racine nomenclature would be dropped forever. It was a fitting adjustment, since the change corrected the earlier APFA error in the organizational meeting minutes that the Cardinals were from Racine, Wisconsin. Also, affiliating O'Brien's team with a large city rather than a street added status to the organization. In its preview of the upcoming game on October 24 between the Cards and Rock Island, the *Daily Times* in Davenport, Iowa, did take notice of the new name: "Tomorrow's game at Douglas Park against the Racine or Chicago Cardinals, as they are now known, will either reset the Independents on the local pedestal of fame or cause a complete reorganization of the squad."[14]

Coverage by local newspapers of the trials and tribulations of the Independents in the Quad-City area (Rock Island and Moline, Illinois; Davenport and Bettendorf, Iowa) provided excellent documentation of the early days of professional football and included some intriguing honesty when discussing all aspects of the game. Prior to the battle with the Cardinals on October 24, the local media carefully outlined the various schemes of the Independents' management to attract new players—all of which were perfectly legal. While these efforts were intended to field a stronger team, the quest went beyond that. By securing players who would agree to reside in the area, the club could then multiply its number of practices each week. Team manager Walter Flanigan explained his recruiting efforts in a *Quad-City Times* interview:

> "I signed these men because they have agreed to make their homes in Rock Island during the playing season. We find that it is impossible to put out a winning team when the players practice only on Saturday afternoon." Flanigan declared that after Sunday's game scrimmages would be on the training program twice a week. "It is the only way to get a team in shape. Thus far this season we have not held a single scrimmage and that's why we were defeated last Sunday. The players who can [not] arrange to stay in Rock Island might just as well make up their minds to quit for if they don't, we'll have to tie a can to them."[15]

While the word "wager" was once a naughty unmentionable when discussing sporting events, the folks in the Rock Island media gladly shared such information leading up to the big game with the Cardinals: "Today's game is a difficult one to dope. Betting is not brisk on the contest and it is not probable that a great deal of money will be wagered between now and the time the game is called. Several Chicagoans arrived in the Island City last night with money to wage at 7 to 10 that the Cardinals would win. Rock Island fans, however, held for even money and but few bets were posted. The Windy City fans appear to be unwilling to lay their money at even."[16]

Within just a few days of perusing local newspapers, an interested follower of pro football could secure a peek at most of the challenges facing the APFA during its first month of competition: player movements, scheduling, attendance, financial problems, and betting. Could this newborn athletic organization possibly survive? With an improved lineup, Rock Island bounced back from its 7–0 defeat at the hands of the Staleys (with Jimmy Conzelman scoring the first TD in the Staleys/Bears initial win in APFA/NFL competition) to edge the Cardinals by the identical score of 7–0. The reliable *Rock Island Argus* not only provided an insightful play-by-play account of the game, but also published seemingly accurate statistics revealing that the winners outgained the Cards 263 yards to 153 while picking up eight first downs to Chicago's six in what the newspaper called the "most spirited game of championship pro derby."[17]

On that same day (October 24, 1920) George Halas and his Staleys entertained the Tigers in what would be the first "home" game for the Decatur club in Chicago. Halas brought his club north a day early so that the team could enjoy the football game between the University of Chicago and the University of Iowa. Then on Sunday, the Tigers and the Staleys took to the field at Cubs Park in front of a nice crowd of 5,000, thus verifying the reason for the move of the game out of Decatur. The Staleys emerged with a 10–0 win, sparked by a 55-yard scoring jaunt by Pard Pearce and a 22-yard dropkick field goal from Jimmy Conzelman. Fans of the familiar orange and blue colors of the Bears today might be surprised that the players on the 1920 version of the team did not wear those proud colors, according to Staleys historian Mark Sorensen: "For their first three years, the players on the Staleys wore red."[18] Another interesting facet of this trip was the addition of guard Hub Shoemake to the Staleys' roster. Shoemake, a native of Oskaloosa, Iowa, had previously been a member of the University of Illinois freshman football team before jumping to the professional ranks. Shoemake played in six games during the 1920 season with Decatur before finishing his three-year collegiate career with (wait for it!) Bethany College in West Virginia.[19]

By the end of October 1920, historical "firsts" in the world of pro football were occurring on almost a weekly basis. On October 31, the Cardinals became the latest team to reserve Cubs Park for a league game when the Detroit Heralds visited. It seemed like an optimum destination when the semipro Standards once again booked Normal Park on that date, squeezing the Cards elsewhere! With a record of 0–1–1 in APFA competition, the Cardinals had yet to score a point up to this stage in the 1920 campaign. The honor of scoring the first points in the Cardinals APFA/

NFL history fell to lineman Lenny Sachs (literally) during the 21–0 win over Detroit. Sachs established an improbable record when he blocked three Detroit punts in the third quarter, all of which led to quick Racine touchdowns. With the score deadlocked at 0–0, Sachs blocked his first kick and pounced on the ball in the Heralds' end zone, moving the Cards ahead 7–0 and scoring the team's first touchdown ever in league play. A second blocked punt by Sachs was also recovered in the end zone while a third interruption of a boot by Sachs allowed the Cardinals to quickly score another touchdown, resulting in the final 21–0 score.[20]

Getting into Chris O'Brien's Hair!

Next on the Cardinals ledger was still another example of an affiliated team legend that was initiated long after the actual event took place involving a high-stakes rivalry that really never existed. After an opening-day scoreless draw with the Chicago Tigers that drew an attractive crowd of 10,000 to Cubs Park, the two teams agreed to meet again at the same location on November 7, when the Cardinals escaped with a narrow 6–3 victory thanks to a Paddy Driscoll touchdown. Nothing special about that, even though the winners improved to 2–1–1 while the Tigers slipped to 1–3–1 for the season. What was special was the aura about this game established by a quaint story that began circulating over 30 years later. Basically, the legend persisted that Cardinals manager Chris O'Brien was feeling the pressure of sharing the city of Chicago with another professional team, in this case, the unsuspecting Chicago Tigers. In order to address this significant issue, O'Brien supposedly challenged the Tigers to that second game in the 1920 season with an unusual proposition: the loser would forfeit its franchise to the winner and leave Chicago forever! While this tall tale did not appear in early histories of the team, a version surfaced in the 1955 Cardinals media guide: "In 1920, there was a team operating under the name Chicago Tigers, owned by Gil Falcon, and getting into the late Chris O'Brien's hair. They were playing at Wrigley Field and questioning the Cardinals' supremacy. O'Brien challenged the Tigers, the stake being the losers' franchise as a pro team. The Cardinals defeated the Tigers, 6 to 3, when Paddy Driscoll ran 40 yards for the only touchdown of the game and O'Brien owned two franchises."[21]

This intriguing story remains an inaccurate myth. The article in the media guide was written by none other than Eddie McGuire, the Cardinals' longtime publicity director. Mr. McGuire was mentioned previously in this book for his diehard enthusiasm for the Cardinals, as well as his tendency to sometimes stretch the truth a bit regarding the team's lengthy history. In this case, the episode regarding the challenge issued to the Tigers by Chris O'Brien appears to have first surfaced a few years after O'Brien's death in 1950 and was then routinely reprinted in team manuals for years to come. No one questioned its accuracy and certainly there was no reason to do so. It simply was a great story that seemed to align with the mischief and mayhem of the early days of pro football. In truth, although the Cardinals won the game in question, the Tigers did not disband immediately, nor did Chris O'Brien secure the rights of the Tigers, according to any corporate records in the state of Illinois. Both teams continued with their schedules and the Tigers completed their 1920 slate with an overall 2–5–1 record. Following the season, the Tigers vanished, but it was likely due to financial challenges, and not because of an imaginative wager with the Cardinals' owner.

Softies, Punks, and Rowdies!

That same weekend, the Decatur Staleys were pulled into an equally imaginative situation when the creative sports editor of the *Rock Island Argus* newspaper helped stage a remarkable instant rivalry. After the Staleys claimed a 7–0 victory over Rock Island on October 17, Bruce Copeland of the *Argus* actively pushed for a quick rematch, citing his adverse reaction to what he sensed was a demeaning attitude of the Staleys organization following the first game between the two Illinois clubs: "Since defeating Rock Island, the Staleys have done everything in their power to belittle the Independents grand playing record. They have referred openly to the Islanders as 'softies,' 'punks,' 'rowdies,' 'small-towners,' and other epithets equally as distasteful." But Copeland was not done. In the same article, he shared some comments from the Staleys' rugged center, George Trafton, that were certain (whether real or imagined) to grab the attention of both the Rock Island players and their fans: "George Trafton, Staley center, declared that the Independents were the softest playing proposition that he had ever opposed. Leave it to Trafton for that…. He spreads it on thick."[22]

Rugged center George Trafton of the Staleys/Bears was so despised by opposing fans that he was chased out of Rock Island, Illinois, after a particularly brutal game in 1920. Trafton went on to play 12 years with the Bears before retiring in 1932. He was elected to the Pro Football Hall of Fame in 1964 (courtesy Pro Football Hall of Fame, Dutch Sternaman Collection).

Perhaps sensing that the unrelenting media broadsides might provoke some unwanted animosity toward his players off the field, Halas made the decision to move his team's local headquarters away from downtown Rock Island. In his autobiography, Halas recalled that decision: "Local feelings were against us there [Rock Island] because of the money Staley backers had made on our last game. Being cautious—off the field—I made our overnight headquarters at Hotel Davenport in Davenport, Iowa, across the Mississippi River from Rock Island."[23] But even this deception failed to dissuade local fans from approaching the fearsome Trafton in the hotel lobby the night before the game, as noted in the *Quad-City Times*: "Trafton was personally challenged in the Davenport hotel Saturday evening, and a handful of these birds from Rock Island heckled and razzed him into bets that he would be forced to take time before the end of the first quarter. Trafton bet til his money was gone and went into the game hammer and tongs."[24] Although clearly a marked man during the contest, which ended in a scoreless tie, Trafton parlayed his role as the villain to great success on the field—being personally responsible for knocking four of his opponents out of the game. The *Staley Fellowship Journal* later noted that "Trafton played a whale of a game, although he was a marked man because of some dizzy sports writer quoting him as saying he would get the Islander players."[25]

With Trafton wreaking havoc on the field, Halas was devising a quick, and safe, escape for both Trafton and his team as the boisterous crowd pressed forward near the end of the game. "The Rock Island fans were extremely upset by the ... continued aggressive tackling by our George. We foresaw trouble for our George. Fortunately, as the end neared, we had the ball. We devised a play that had George running toward the exit. As the gun fired with the score still 0–0, George went out the gate. We threw him a sweatshirt to hide his numerals. He headed for the bridge and Iowa. A car stopped and carried him safely across the river and the state line."[26] Yet the simmering feelings evolved into real danger after the game when someone tossed a bottle at the Staley players as they were departing the premises. While no one was injured as the errant throw went wide, bruised emotions were evident on both sides following the game. The *Staley Fellowship Journal* proclaimed, "Never in the history of Staley athletics have we ever seen such poor sportsmanship on the part of an organization or its supporters as that of the Rock Island Independents."[27] Not surprisingly, Bruce Copeland of the *Rock Island Argus* continued to simmer, countering the Decatur claim with his own stark headline blasting the opposition: "Staleys Win World's Dirt Title." Copeland added: "With a foul player like Trafton, the Staleys' best gutter champion roaming the field at large against teams whose ideals are cloaked in nothing but clean sport-the Staleys will soon find the best professional elevens in the country turning their backs on them."[28] Halas later documented the escape from Rock Island in his autobiography and how Trafton provided one more contribution to the Staleys' effort that day: "Our share of the gate was $3,000 in cash. At the hotel I gave it to Trafton to bring to the train. I knew if we did encounter obstreperous Rock Island fans, I would run for the money ... but Trafton would run for his life!"[29]

Not Wishing to Become Suddenly Dead

As the inaugural 1920 APFA season melted down to its final few games, both the Cardinals and the Staleys had played contests with other "regional" teams such as Rock Island, Moline, and the Chicago Tigers, yet neither team had committed to meeting each other. The Staleys (9–0–1) were breezing along undefeated behind a staunch defense that had allowed only 14 points in those first 10 battles, while the Cardinals (5–1–1) were just a step behind while also providing a strong defensive unit that had been dented for just 10 points in seven outings. Although the Staleys eased past the Tigers 6–0 on Thanksgiving Day (November 25, 1920) at Cubs Park, Halas was receptive to the suggestion that the team remain in Chicago for a couple of more days to take on the Cardinals at Normal Park on Sunday, November 28. This offer originated after the Cardinals' own game against the local Logan Square Athletic Club was canceled due to the death of Paddy Driscoll's father. So, on Thanksgiving morning, O'Brien decided to schedule a Sunday game with the Staleys, as reported in the *Chicago Tribune*: "Chris O'Brien of the Cardinals will make an effort to sign the Decatur Staleys eleven for an attraction at Normal Park Sunday, providing the strong downstate outfit is successful in this afternoon's clash with the Chicago Tigers."[30]

With the scheduling of the game finalized, Halas remained apprehensive about playing a game just three days after the previous contest. It was anticipated that this would be the final day of competition for the professional teams, although there was speculation that the undefeated Staleys would sweep past the Cardinals and then perhaps challenge the likewise unbeaten Akron Pros from distant Ohio for the overall professional title. In 1920, scheduling and rosters remained fluid and flexible throughout the season and there was really no concrete method for determining the APFA champion. Neither the Staleys nor the Cardinals likely even considered that the game on November 28, 1920, would be the first in what would become the NFL's oldest rivalry. The Staleys, for example, were more concerned with defending their self-appointed claim as the "professional champions of the west." Of course, if the Cardinals could pull off the upset, then perhaps they could likewise claim that mythical championship banner. Neither team mentioned the preseason squabble between the two clubs when nimble Paddy Driscoll initially signed with the Staleys but was swayed by the tempting monetary offer from Chris O'Brien and signed with the Cardinals for that lofty $300 per game. Instead, the real fear was that no one would show up to witness the hastily arranged game, scheduled just days before.

But then, a strange thing happened. People came to the game! Lots of people. They filled the stands at tiny Normal Park, stood tightly along the sidelines, watched from neighboring roofs, and peeked through holes in the stadium fencing. Maybe 5,000 of them, all drawn to this fascinating new project called professional football. There was the aura of seeing the big stars of the day up close and personal, from the extraordinary Paddy Driscoll of the Cardinals to the hard-nosed George Trafton of the Staleys. The game itself was an exciting match with the only two touchdowns secured as a result of fluke plays. On the opening kickoff, Bob Koehler of the Staleys grabbed a fumble by the Cardinals return man and returned it for a score with just seconds gone in the game. However, Hugh Blacklock, a teammate of Halas and Driscoll's on the 1919 Great Lakes team, missed the important extra point. The score remained 6–0 through the first half despite several threats by the hosts to knot the score. Then, early in the second half, end Len Sachs of the Cardinals picked up a loose Decatur fumble on the Staleys' 20-yard line and scampered untouched by the Staleys along the crowded sideline and into the end zone. Well, almost untouched, as it would be recalled years later by columnist Red Smith, as he described the reaction from George Halas: "George's eyes still flash when he remembers how a referee robbed the Bears in 1920, when they were the Decatur Staleys. The Staleys were leading the Racine Cardinals 6–0 late in the game when the Cardinals [runner] ducked behind a knot of spectators who had crowded onto the field and with his civilian interference ran in for a touchdown. Not wishing to become suddenly dead, the referee allowed the score."[31]

Driscoll added the extra point to provide the Cardinals with the final score in a 7–6 upset of the Staleys. That controversial noncall on the questionable crowd interference not only protected the Cardinals victory, but it also "dismayed" the volatile Halas, especially since it was the only touchdown the Staleys allowed all season. It was fitting that the very first meeting between the NFL's oldest rivals ended in controversy. Indeed, it was the first time, but it would certainly not be the last!

With the win, the Cardinals soaked up some much-needed positive publicity from the Chicago newspapers, including this applause from the *Herald and Examiner*: "Chris O'Brien's Chicago Cardinals sprang the biggest surprise of the football season yesterday when they walloped [sic] the hitherto undefeated Staleys of Decatur in a thrilling 7 to 6 contest at Normal Park. More than 5,000 fans saw the pastime, which was as full of football strategy and skill as three ordinary contests. The Cardinals not only outscored them, but also outplayed them every inch of the way, gaining almost twice as much ground and breaking up almost every play that was attempted."[32]

With Halas fuming over the conflicted ending of the contest, and both teams savoring the strong attendance at compact Normal Park, a rematch was quickly scheduled within 24 hours for the following Sunday, December 5, with the venue moved to the more expansive Cubs Park on the North Side of Chicago. "The Starchmakers are considerably worked up over the defeat, as it spoiled one of the greatest records made among pro football teams in this section. The Staleys, in fact, until that game were styling themselves champions of the middle west," reported the *Chicago Daily News*.[33] In Decatur, there were some murmurs that the scheduling of three games in eight days had resulted in the costly loss to the Cardinals, which robbed the Staleys of their unbeaten season. Revenge was clearly on the mind of the Staleys in the upcoming battle, which the *Decatur Herald* now called a "keen rivalry … developed between the two teams because of the trimming given the Staley warriors at the hands of Paddy Driscoll's eleven Sunday."[34] Aside from the revenge factor, Halas hoped that a return victory over the Cardinals might still pave the way for a postseason meeting with the undefeated Akron Pros for the championship of the APFA. After a scoreless first quarter, Bob Koehler of the Staleys scored the only touchdown of the game on a two-yard run. Then, in the third stanza, the Staleys took advantage of a Cardinals fumble as Dutch Sternaman booted a field goal for the final points in a 10–0 victory. Injuries to Paddy Driscoll and Len Sachs of the Cardinals certainly hampered the team's effort, although the Staleys dominated the battle on both sides of the ball.

From a financial viewpoint, the game was a success for Halas as well. "The largest crowd that has ever seen a professional football contest in this city, numbering about 11,000, witnessed the game," reported the *Chicago Herald and Examiner*. "The Staleys presented a wonderful all-around offense and seemed to be equally skillful in gaining on forward passes, line plunges or end runs."[35] Pleased with both the victory and the nice crowd, Halas pushed forward with an effort to entice the Akron Pros to visit Chicago for an APFA "championship" game. Again, the league did not provide any firm guidance regarding a title quest, nor did it specify any qualifications for such an event. In terms of a pragmatic solution, we can suggest that the teams with the best records should be considered for any first-place laurels. But the APFA left its members with little guidance. Since tie games did not count for anything at the time, should nonleague games be discarded as well? For Halas, it seemed logical that the Staleys (10–1–1) overall would capture the crown by defeating Akron (8–0–2), thus finishing with a better overall mark with three more victories. However, if only games played against APFA members were considered, Decatur (5–1–1) could only claim a share of the title by knocking off Akron (6–0–2). But then, what about the Buffalo All-Americans? After slugging it out with Akron on December 5 in a scoreless tie, Buffalo finished its campaign with a solid 9–1–1 record (4–1–1 in the APFA). Of course, it appeared that this could all be settled by a clear-cut victor in the upcoming Akron-Decatur battle. If only Akron would agree to play the game…

No Team the Equal of the Akron Pros

Its season concluding with the deadlock at Buffalo, the Akron Pros began planning for a West Coast tour that would bring "eastern" professional football to the Pacific. Frank Nied, manager of the Pros, was confident that his players would handily defeat any opponent: "I am satisfied that only a fluke could beat them. There is no team the equal of the Akron Pros."[36] Through a series of frantic telegrams and phone calls from Halas, the Pros finally agreed on Tuesday, December 7, to meet the Staleys on the following Sunday in Chicago. The Pros would delay their West Coast excursion to finally complete the 1920 season and settle the ownership of the first APFA title in the duel at Cubs Park. In Chicago, the media welcomed the two mighty clubs even though neither of them would be considered a true "home" team for this outing. It was all or nothing for the participants as the *Herald and Examiner* carefully outlined the credentials for each team: "Akron claims the national title at present and is admitted to have a clear hold on it with the one exception of the Staleys. The latter team clinched the western title last Sunday when they downed the Chicago Cardinals on the North Side in the play for the title, while Akron defeated Jim Thorpe's Canton Bulldogs twice this year in decisive fashion."[37]

With kickoff approaching, word leaked out of Decatur that Halas had recruited a formidable adversary to join the Staleys for one game in quest of the national title. Ignoring one of the initial precepts of the APFA, Halas added the Cardinals' Paddy Driscoll to his roster in what might be defined as a mild misinterpretation of the rules. Halas figured there were no restrictions on adding the South Side superstar to the Staleys' lineup since the Cardinals' season was over. The local *Decatur Herald* scoffed at this idea, claiming, "It is very doubtful that Coach Halas will break up his present combination in order to put other stars in the game."[38]

Although Driscoll did not start for the Staleys, his role was prominent throughout the day as both sides struggled to move the ball: "Paddy Driscoll substituted at the start of the second period. It didn't take Paddy long to convince manager George Halas of the Staleys that he hadn't made a mistake in borrowing him from the Chicago Cardinals for the afternoon."[39] Driscoll's running and passing (including a late 35-yard toss to Halas) provided most of the offense against Akron, but the Staleys were unable to score, mostly due to the fine defensive efforts of the Pros' Fritz Pollard. A graduate of nearby Lane Tech in Chicago and Brown University, Pollard was the league's first Black superstar, who was also a threat each time he rushed or returned a punt. But even with the gifted backs Pollard and Driscoll on the field, neither team was able to dent the goal line in the cold and wet conditions. The closest either club came to scoring was when the Staleys' Dutch Sternaman missed a 22-yard field goal in the third stanza, despite changing into a dry shoe for the boot. Surprisingly, Halas did not use Driscoll for that crucial kick, despite his being perhaps the most accurate dropkicker in the circuit. Since tie games did not count in the 1920 standings, nothing was accomplished in terms of defining the league champion. Akron was now 8–0–3 overall, while the Staleys completed their schedule with a 10–1–2 mark. If anything significant was generated from the "title" game, it was the strong crowd estimated at 12,000 along with a long-awaited recognition by the national media. This came in the form of the syndicated press coverage of the game by Walter Eckersall of the *Chicago Tribune*. It was not uncommon at the time for team managers such as George Halas or Chris O'Brien to quickly write up game summaries and push them out to local newspapers in hopes of securing some press clippings in the next day's editions. Most "game" articles on pro football, therefore, did not even include an author byline, which is where the Eckersall input was so important. Years later, Edward Prell of the *Tribune* recalled this journalistic breakthrough: "In December of 1920, pro football was dignified for the first time by Walter Eckersall, the *Tribune* expert, official, and college football's most potent voice in public prints. Eckie covered a match on December 12 between the Staleys and Akron for the professional football championship. While both were members of the American Professional Football Association, this affiliation seldom was mentioned in game reports. The teams, to all intents and purposes, still were in the wildcat era."[40]

Eckersall's reporting of the game appeared in a condensed version in the *Chicago Tribune* but ran as a longer article in both Decatur and Akron, along with other cities. Pro football, finally, was receiving the recognition that its founders cherished. While the growing pains would continue for several years, one imminent challenge was to determine the winner of the APFA's initial season. With the tie, Akron held a 8–0–3 overall mark, followed by the Staleys (10–1–2), Buffalo (9–1–1), the Cardinals (6–2–2), and Rock Island (6–2–2). Against APFA opponents only, Akron still held the advantage with its 6–0–3 record, edging both Decatur (5–1–2) and Buffalo (4–1–1). By tossing out the tie games, Akron clearly retained the top slot, although that honor would not be verified until the next league meeting in early 1921.

By the middle of December, the football season was finally over—or was it? In his postgame summary, Eckersall stated that Halas immediately suggested a rematch with the Pros for December 19 at Cubs Park, but that an answer would be forthcoming when the team returned to Akron. The Staleys' request ultimately would be denied, primarily because the Pros had a much bigger excursion in mind—that previously mentioned tour to the West Coast with a possible additional destination: "With the California trip arranged, owners Frank Nied and Art Ranney expect to receive word today whether the Akron Pros will be sent to China and Japan, following the games in the west."[41] While the visit to Asia did not materialize, the Pros garnered four victories on their California tour, which generally introduced the new world of pro football to the coast. Apparently, there was some fear that the acceptance of the professionals might irreversibly harm the growing popularity of the collegiate version of the game. Sensing this concern, the *Los Angeles Record* attempted to soothe any apprehension with a calming statement: "America's greatest football authorities have said that the game as played by this team [Akron] is not harmful to the general good of the sport in the least. The teams play clean, hard, fast ball and have a splendid assortment of plays."[42]

Back in Chicago, Cardinals manager Chris O'Brien was likely irate that the Staleys had blatantly "borrowed" his star player, Paddy Driscoll, for its showdown with Akron. After losing out on the large gate receipts enjoyed by the Staleys and Pros in their championship match, O'Brien scheduled one final game against the local semipro Chicago Stayms on December 19—but with a twist. While Driscoll would return to the Cardinals' backfield, the Stayms' roster would add a few players from O'Brien's new impertinent rival: the Staleys. George Halas, Hugh Blacklock, and Hub Shoemake agreed to play with the Stayms. "Halas is trying to sign other Staley stars for the game in hopes of administering a defeat to Chris O'Brien and stopping his challenges for the western title, now held by the Decatur team," explained the *Herald and Examiner*.[43] Statistically, it would have been impossible for the Cardinals to equal the record of the Staleys, since the South Siders already had two losses, but the media jousting could serve to encourage attendance at the smallish Pyott Field on the west side of Chicago.

Keeping up with the recent trend in pro football clashes at the conclusion of the 1920 season, the battle between the Cardinals and the Stayms ended up in a 14–14 tie. Little had been decided in terms of the overall standings, but the player roster jumping during the month of December, and the difficulty in determining a champion, demonstrated that the APFA still needed some fine-tuning in any effort to secure universal recognition from the sporting world.

Somewhat of a Financial Flop

Akron (8-0-3 overall/6-0-3 in APFA) clearly achieved the best record over the Staleys (10-1-2/5-1-2), but the official crowning of the Pros did not occur until the APFA meeting on April 30, 1921. At that time, Akron was voted champion of the circuit and presented with the Brunswick-Balke Collender Cup to dignify this accomplishment. More important, league officials elected Joe Carr as the APFA's new president, succeeding Jim Thorpe. It proved to be a wise and worthy decision, as Carr would prove to be the ideal person to lead the league through its difficult formative years.

Undaunted, years later, Halas still claimed in his autobiography that the Staleys captured the initial APFA title. The 7–6 loss to the Cardinals, with or without the sideline interference, still gnawed at Halas as the only blemish on an otherwise undefeated season. Because of his baseball commitment with the Staleys, Halas was unable to attend the APFA meeting where the 1920 champion was determined. His absence likely silenced what would have been the most important voice in the discussion.

Meanwhile, Halas could also reflect on the success of his team: "Back in Decatur we were an artistic success, but somewhat of a financial flop. Our 1920 loss of $14,406.36 was assumed by the Staley Company, which charged the football team the two and one-half hours each man lost from his job each day due to practice."[44] And, although the numbers have changed over the years, each member of the Staleys football team shared in the combined gate receipts for the season, believed to be between $1,800 and $2,100 each, a very nice bonus for the 13-game schedule in 1920. An unidentified document, probably authored by a Staley employee, located in the archives of the Pro Football Hall of Fame, described the season-ending Staleys football banquet and the reaction of Mr. A.E. Staley to the success of his football team: "Mr. Staley spoke of the pleasure he had received from following the work of the team, especially during the period when his mind was heavily taxed with business matters. He told of being approached by one of the officials of the Chicago Cubs baseball club who suggested the possibility of the Staley team using Cubs Park as their home grounds next season. He also expressed his strong desire to have even a better team in 1921. These words from the big boss, that he wanted even a stronger team, were music to the ears of player-coach Halas."[45]

The hint that the Staleys might move their home games to Chicago in 1921 remains intriguing. After all, the team hosted only four "home" games in 1920, with two of those being presented in Decatur. The comparative attendance figures were obvious. The 1,500 seats in Staley Field were not conducive to establishing financial success for a football team, whereas the promise of crowds of 12,000, like that for the Akron game at Cubs Park, was quite attractive. Despite the national acclaim that his football team achieved in 1920, Mr. A.E. Staley would need to carefully evaluate if the financial losses assumed by his club were equitable with the marketing value earned by that performance. With his promise to allow his players to split the yearly gate receipts while he absorbed their combined hefty salaries, Staley was virtually in a no-win situation in terms of gridiron economic sanity. Was the exposure of the Staley Company name before a few thousand fans each week a worthy reward for Mr. Staley or would he be forced to consider a managerial maneuver that would likely cripple the newly minted football giant that he had so recently constructed? Ultimately, a rather sensible conclusion by George Halas may have provided the impetus for Staley to arrive at a critical decision in his corporate planning and provide even more traction in the NFL's oldest rivalry.

Seven

Lawyers, Gum, and Money

"It is our wish and plan that when the football team goes to Chicago, it remain there until the end of the season."—A.E. Staley, October 6, 1921

As the calendar expired on 1920 and slipped into January 1921, the usually relentless frigid weather in Chicago seemed to pause. Instead of standing firm with single-digit temperatures, the thermometer was content to settle in above the freezing mark during the first week of the new year. Perfect football weather in Chicago!

Since most of the Cardinals lived in the area and were not reluctant at the prospect of receiving an extra paycheck, Chris O'Brien quickly arranged a game with the familiar Stayms team from the west side of Chicago for Sunday, January 9, 1921. Although the Chicago indoor football season was well underway at nearby Dexter Park Pavilion, O'Brien stunned some observers by scheduling this contest outdoors at friendly Normal Park. "The weather man is especially tolerant thus far toward the 'pro' football players and all that manager O'Brien asks is that he continues so for 24 hours longer. The gridiron at Normal Park is reported to be in perfect condition for a great game in the novelty encounter."[1]

In a game likely played with very little practice time, but in a balmy 29 degrees, the Cardinals outlasted the Stayms 6–0 in front of a surprisingly strong crowd of 3,000. Quarterback Paddy Driscoll paced the team in rushing, although halfback Bernie Halstrom, a graduate of nearby Hyde Park High School, scored the game's only touchdown on a short plunge in the first quarter. Ironically, on that same day, members of the Decatur Staleys were also in action in Chicago, albeit in an indoor setting. Partnering with the Pullman Thorns under the moniker of the Thorn-Staleys, the Staleys succumbed 14–7 to the Rock Island Independents in a game staged at the Dexter Park Pavilion. In later years, the site of this facility would become the International Amphitheater at 4220 South Halsted Street. Most of the key Staleys players were in the lineup, such as George Halas, Dutch Sternaman, George Trafton, and Hugh Blacklock. The *Quad-City Times* described the unique field conditions for the contest: "The game was played under strange conditions. The field, 80 yards in length, necessitated special ground rules. It was agreed that a touchdown on straight football [i.e., running plays] was possible only after a team went over the 80-yard line and then again after the ball was put in play at the 19-yard line. A touchdown via the aerial route however, eliminated this rule."[2]

Perhaps piqued by the loss, as well as the good attendance of 3,500, Halas clamored for a rematch on January 23, although this time, the Staleys would play under their own name. While Halas waited for a response from Rock Island, the Staleys were surprised by the semipro Logan Squares of Chicago, who tied their downstate brethren 0–0 at Dexter Park Pavilion on January 16. Nevertheless, Halas moved ahead with finalizing the game with Rock Island, once again at the Dexter Park location. But then, just three days before the game, Rock Island abruptly pulled out for financial reasons, as explained by manager Joe Prendergast of the Independents: "I am through with them [the Staleys], and you can tell the world they don't want to play us again. I gave manager Halas to understand that we would play for the original guarantee, and would have even compromised further. His utter indifference to our just claims does not warrant our consideration."[3] Obviously, Prendergast was incensed that Halas would attempt to change the agreed-upon original understanding that would include expenses, plus a share of the gate receipts, and instead offer only an expense payment for the Independents' trip to Chicago. As such, sportswriter Bruce Copeland of the *Rock Island Argus*, a staunch nemesis of Halas, added: "Having assumed many risks themselves, the Rock Island management could not understand why the Staleys remained so obdurate, proposing something altogether unusual in professional football."[4] It would not be the last time in his long career that George Halas would be the target of barbs for his capricious financial practices.

Apparently, Rock Island was so upset by the current status of the APFA (and its blossoming rivalry with the Staleys) that it expressed interest in joining a new professional league being organized in Omaha, Nebraska. The planned organization, called the Western Professional Football Association, sought to include teams from cities such as St. Louis, Rock Island, Des Moines, and Minneapolis, dividing the eight clubs into two conferences with the winners meeting for the postseason championship. Unwisely, the league owners assumed that the APFA, for some reason, was finished, as suggested by the *Rock Island Argus*: "If the general plan materializes, it will be the first major league professional football organization in the country. Jim Thorpe's National Association of Football Clubs, as launched last fall, failed to complete its functions to the satisfaction of all concerned, and it is believed to have expired on the rocks."[5]

Miraculously, the APFA returned for the 1921 season, including Rock Island once again as one of its members. If the APFA 1920 season contained myriad surprises amid its growing pains, 1921 would only add to the confusion. In the short span of about 18 months following the completion of the 1920 campaign, the league would witness franchise shifts and drops, welcome a new member, kick out that same member, anoint a controversial champion, and then slap down that champion for its alleged dirty deeds involving the recruitment of another club's star player. In other words, it was a normal season for the infant professional league.

Halas in Charge of All Athletics

In Chicago, astute Cardinals manager Chris O'Brien was busy securing financial supporters for his team, as well as overseeing improvements to the neighborhood

Normal Park stadium. Realizing that his club could not financially compete with other APFA members while relying solely on gate receipts from smallish Normal Park, O'Brien worked to increase seating capacity. This would not be an easy task since the field was virtually landlocked with very little space for expansion. Still, O'Brien would not be deterred, reported the *Chicago Tribune*: "Chris O'Brien, manager of the local eleven, is enlarging the seating capacity and 3,500 additional seats will be available."[6] O'Brien also addressed another "new" problem facing organizers of sporting events: parking. With more automobiles available to consumers in the early 1920s, that mode of transportation to attend football games was slowly increasing. The solution for O'Brien was to secure some empty space adjacent to the field. "Chris has leased an open plot across the street from the playing plot and it will be turned over for parking space," announced the *Tribune*.[7]

On the personnel side, both the Cardinals and the Staleys continued to fine-tune their rosters, with the Staleys (under Halas) implementing the more significant changes. When the dust had settled, the 1921 version of the Staleys retained only seven players from the previous campaign. Halas also appeared to be amassing more power within the Staley business community when he was appointed as the company's athletic director, as reported in the March 1921 edition of the *Staley Fellowship Journal*: "George Halas, our star all-around athlete, has been named Athletic Director of the company and in the future will be in charge of all branches of athletics. George came to the company a year ago and since that time has made hundreds of friends among the officials and employees besides the fans of Decatur and cities where our teams have shown."[8]

Always the innovator, Halas started and played on an indoor baseball team for the Staleys and then returned to the company baseball team for its outdoor season in 1921. As with football, Halas attempted to upgrade the Staleys' baseball schedule, including tentatively booking a game (that did not occur) with the major league St. Louis Cardinals on June 30, 1921. With the Staley baseball team booked each weekend over the summer, Halas missed his second straight APFA league meeting on June 18 in Cleveland, Ohio. Morgan O'Brien represented the Staleys at the meeting while Chris O'Brien (no relation) attended on behalf of the Chicago Cardinals. While Halas was patrolling left field in an 11–1 loss to Janesville, Wisconsin, in the finale of a three-game series in Decatur, the APFA leaders concluded their football business in Cleveland without him.

During the discussions in Cleveland, the APFA attempted to tighten up some loose ends, including a clarification of the league standings. Beginning in 1921, only games with fellow league members would count in the standings. In addition, the new president, Joe Carr, would compile "official" standings in an effort to determine the true champion at the end of the season and avoid the controversy and confusion that muddled the end of the 1920 campaign. The APFA also approved its first constitution, thereby implementing a structure with rules and regulations moving forward. In particular, teams were asked to submit their rosters from the previous season to Joe Carr by May 15, 1921. Two of the objectives of this decree were to prohibit the raiding of one team's roster by another as well as to ensure that an individual player did not represent two teams in the same week of competition. This would halt examples such as when Paddy Driscoll played for both the Cardinals and the Staleys late in the 1920 season.

Once again, would the member organizations abide by their own rules? However, with Joe Carr now heading the APFA, replacing Jim Thorpe, the league owners hired someone who could confidently manage the business aspects of the league. Chris Willis, head of the research library at NFL Films, and author of *Joe Carr: The Man Who Built the National Football League*, explained why Carr's election was so crucial to the new league:

> After the APFA was founded and played its first season in the fall of 1920, the newly formed league was in need of some good leadership. Jim Thorpe was elected the league's first president but was an athlete, not an administrator. So, in April 1921, the league elected Joe F. Carr to be the new president. He was the best choice because he was a natural-born leader and that's what the league needed desperately. Most of the owners were former players but not businessmen or administrators. Carr was both. With his experience of being a sports writer and team manager, Carr understood all aspects of the sport of football. He would establish rules, regulations, handle the media, and other league details, which made him the perfect choice to be APFA president.[9]

Prior to the start of the 1921 season, the APFA would field a loop with 21 members, including newcomers such as the Washington (D.C.) Senators, the Evansville (Indiana) Crimson Giants, the Louisville (Kentucky) Brecks, and the Green Bay (Wisconsin) Packers. It appears that Rock Island was pleased to be back in the fold after a brief flirtation with the proposed Western Professional Football Association. An optimistic, but cautious, Walter Flanigan, manager of the Independents, told the team's fans: "This association is the real thing. These clubs are going into this in earnest and I believe the fellows are going to put it over. If they do, everyone in the organization, especially among the smaller and outlying centers, will have to show the speed or be dropped. If we get by this year, we're sitting pretty, if we don't make the grade and the association continues, we'll have a hard time breaking into the big class stuff the fans expect to see."[10]

Just a week later, Halas was with the Staley baseball club as it moved into southern Wisconsin for a two-game set in Kenosha with the Simmons Company. While Kenosha swept the series and Halas managed just one hit in the pair of defeats, the left fielder had other plans to consider on this business trip. As the rest of the Staleys players headed back to Decatur, Halas took a detour and remained in Chicago for a special meeting on Monday, June 27, with the management of the Chicago Cubs baseball team. It was not the intent of Halas to secure a playing position with the Cubs. His focus was on negotiating for the use of the club's field for the upcoming football season. The outcome was positive for Halas, as announced by the *Chicago Tribune* two days later: "George Halas, athletic director of the Staley Company ... was successful in leasing the Chicago National League ball park for October, November, and December. The Staleys expect to put out another great eleven this fall and will use the Cubs' park as their home grounds."[11]

If anything, the timing for this agreement was unusual, since it directly contradicts information (that will be discussed shortly) presented in Halas's autobiography, which states that the Staleys' lease on Cubs Park was not consummated until

October 1921. It also emerged during a challenging economic time for the Staley Company, when the plant was temporarily shut down for at least two weeks due to a lack of orders, as indicated by A.E. Staley himself on June 8 in the *Decatur Herald*: "I'm still very optimistic, but we're running in the usual season and so I expect the plant will not grind steadily for the next two months or so," said A.E. Staley in regard to the temporary shutdown of the plant. "I expect that by fall we will run steadily, but until then we will have to shut down now and then."[12]

By the middle of 1921, the United States economy was beginning to emerge from a postwar downswing. The Staley Company was not an exception to these financial challenges, forcing the company to lay off workers and close its doors as needed. But things were looking up. A.E. Staley was part of a group of Decatur businessmen who met with automobile manufacturer Henry Ford on June 25. Instead of hearing a somber message, Ford was quite positive in his remarks: "The times are not bad. They are good because they make us think. We are learning a lot now. Of course, there is a lot to be done now." Ford encouraged paying workers higher wages, such as the lofty $6 per day earned by Ford's railroad track laborers. "A man has something to work for. There's hope and he earns his money. If he don't, the others crowd him out."[13] The economy, and the fortunes of the A.E. Staley Company, rebounded nicely later in the year. So much so, that the company nearly established a monthly record for corn grind production. "We're going to have a big grind [production] this month, but not as big as we thought we would have," said Staley in early October.[14]

Cross Between Music and Cannon Fire

As the 1921 baseball season began winding down, thoughts among sports fans in Decatur turned to football. There was still some simmering disappointment over the awarding of the 1920 APFA title to Akron, owing to that sole defeat the Cardinals administered to the Staleys. The *Staley Fellowship Journal* noted: "The professional championship for 1920 was awarded to the Akron Indians, which eleven went through the season without a defeat. While it would take considerable argument to convince the 12,000 fans who saw the Akron-Staley game that the Ohio team had anything on the starch workers for 1921, the fact that we lost a one point battle to the Cardinals was enough to give the Indians the title, although Halas' team demonstrated their superiority over them in the second contest."[15]

Although the correct name of the Akron team was the "Pros," it was clear that the Staleys expected an even bigger and better team in 1921. Halas made the biggest splash in the remaking of his roster by adding three former Ohio State standouts: halfback Chic Harley, quarterback Pete Stinchcomb, and guard Tarzan Taylor. Both Harley and Stinchcomb were All-Americans at Ohio State, but the former was absolutely one of the biggest names in the history of college football. A native of Chicago, Harley led the Buckeyes to an incredible 21–1–1 record from 1916 through the 1919 season, while serving in the Army Air Service during World War I in 1918. Just 5'8" and 160 pounds, Harley was an elusive runner and punishing defender, with the ability to run, pass, or punt the football. Perhaps his teammate at Ohio State, and with the Staleys, Pete Stinchcomb described him best: "Harley could do everything, he was the complete player. Chic was like a cat. You know how hard it is to catch a cat? It usually takes more than one person. It always took more than one player to catch Harley."[16] He was such a gifted player that words often were not enough to paint the full picture of Harley's abilities, as one Ohio sportswriter wrote: "If you never saw him run with a football, we can't describe it to you. It was kind of a cross between music and cannon fire, and it brought your heart up under your ears. With his famous side-step, his reliable toe, his dashing runs and his cool judgement, Harley paved the way for Ohio State's first two conference championships. His fame was so great and spread so far that people came to look upon him as a wizard."[17]

Harley would be a perfect fit in the Decatur backfield with the reliable Dutch Sternaman. Halas was so anxious to secure the services of Harley that he entered into a contractual agreement with Chic Harley and his brother Bill for the 1921 season and wrote: "The new man I sought most for the football team was Chic Harley.... He could pass, kick, run. His brother Bill offered to supply the team with Chic, Pete Stinchcomb, also an All-American, and John R. Taylor, an aggressive guard known as Tarzan, in return for a percentage of the profit. I accepted."[18]

Although the signing of Harley was announced on August 16, 1921, in the *Chicago Tribune*, the contract between the Harley brothers was actually finalized almost a month earlier.[19] In his book *NFL Century*, Joe Horrigan, the former executive director of the Professional Football Hall of Fame, addressed the agreement that was finalized on July 21, 1921, between the Harleys, Halas, and Dutch Sternaman. In this document, the four individuals would serve as partners in the management of the Staley football team. Along with those responsibilities, each would also "share equally in the profits and losses of said team." Horrigan added that this handwritten document included the precept that the four football managers would "present to Geo. E. Chamberlain periodically during the football season of 1921 a sum of money to be designated therein."[20] Chamberlain, of course, was the Staley Company general superintendent who initially contacted Halas about overseeing the football team in early 1920.

While Halas anxiously added three talented players to his Decatur roster, he also now had three individuals who would share in the gate receipts of a team that was still owned by A.E. Staley. Did this now exclude the shares of the other men on the roster? The split of the gate at the end of the 1920 season had served as a prime selling point in the recruitment process of players by Halas. Also, aside from Bill and Chic Harley, why did Halas invite Dutch Sternaman to participate on the management team? Some of these questions would be answered early in the upcoming football season.

In Chicago, Chris O'Brien tinkered with the makeup of the squad that finished 6–2–2 in 1920, but the key players from the previous season all returned, including the versatile Paddy Driscoll at quarterback. The *Chicago Daily News* reported: "Manager Chris O'Brien of the Cards will use virtually all the same lineup that sent his team to fame in the big games last season. Among the new additions to the Cardinals is Norman Barry, who starred at Notre Dame and this year is varsity coach at De LaSalle High School [in Chicago]. Barry while in college was a noted halfback and was running mate with the famous George Gipp. His defensive work attracted attention wherever he played and he is expected to cut no small figure in pro football circles this year."[21]

In an unusual scheduling quirk, the Cardinals played their entire 1921 schedule in Chicago, with their only two "away" games also being staged in the city. The opening exhibition game against the Racine, Wisconsin, Horlicks on September 25 resulted in an easy 27–0 win at the newly enlarged Normal Park and attracted 4,500 fans as well as an interesting analysis by a Racine newspaper: "Twenty-seven seems to have figured prominently in the game. The Horlicks held the Cardinals scoreless for the first twenty-seven minutes of play. The Cardinals tried out twenty-seven players in the game, and the score was 27–0 in their favor at the end."[22]

With Paddy Driscoll at the helm, the Cardinals opened APFA play on October 2, 1921, with a 20–0 rout of the Minneapolis Marines. Driscoll tallied one touchdown on a 45-yard run and tossed a 33-yard TD pass to left end Rube Marquardt. On that same day, Chic Harley made his debut with the Staleys in a convincing 35–0 win over the Waukegan Legions. Harley's passing efforts were especially notable: "The former Ohio State star shot the ball with deadly accuracy throughout the game, completing passes to [Guy] Chamberlin, Sternaman and Halas. The prettiest play of the day came in the third quarter, when Harley hurled the ball to Halas, 40 yards down the field, for a touchdown, after dodging three tacklers."[23]

A few days later, the world of George Halas changed forever...

While the sequence of events is now familiar, it bears repeating (no pun intended!). According to Halas, he was called into the office of A.E. Staley, apparently after the Waukegan game. At this time, Staley simply said to Halas: "George, I know you are more interested in football than the starch business, but we simply can't underwrite the team's expenses any longer. Why don't you move the team up to Chicago? I think pro football can go over in a big way there—and I'll

Paddy Driscoll is a member of the Pro Football Hall of Fame and former head coach of the Chicago Bears. During the football off-season, Driscoll continued to play semipro baseball. In 1921, he was a member of the Chicago Pyotts (shown here). Driscoll also spent a short time in the big leagues as a member of the Chicago Cubs (SDN-062652, *Chicago Daily News* collection, Chicago History Museum).

give you $5,000 to help you get started. All I ask is that you continue to call the team 'The Staleys' for one season."²⁴

The preceding quote appeared in a syndicated 21-part series by the *Chicago Tribune* that began on January 22, 1967. The articles, all written by Halas (then turning 72), chronicled his lifetime of experiences in pro football and the series seems to have been the basis for his memoir *Halas: An Autobiography*, which appeared a dozen years later in 1979. In the autobiography, Halas recalls that after this meeting with Mr. Staley, Halas immediately grabbed a train to Chicago and began negotiating for the use of Cubs Park with William Veeck Sr., who was representing Chicago Cubs owner William Wrigley Jr., the head of the well-known chewing gum family. However, in the *Tribune* series, Halas noted a different time frame from the October 1921 sequence delineated in his autobiography: "In addition to securing the Chicago franchise and a lease on Wrigley Field [still known as Cubs Park in 1921], I'd also acquired some problems. It was early February. The start of the '21 football season was almost eight months away. Obviously, I had to get a job to support myself until the club started making money—always assuming it made money. And there were other details—like signing players, arranging a schedule, writing publicity—to be attended to. Frankly, it looked like too much work for one man, so I asked Staley teammate Ed [Dutch] Sternaman to be my partner."²⁵

It is not clear why the time frame was inconsistent between the Halas *Tribune* series in 1967 and the publication of his autobiography in 1979. If the 1967 statements are accurate, it would explain why Sternaman was considered a partner in the Chic Harley agreement later in 1921, and it would also validate why Halas secured the lease for Cubs Park in June 1921. Author and Decatur Staleys historian Mark Sorensen offers another viable suggestion: "A.E. Staley left absolutely no correspondence about any of his business dealings so most of the world only knows what Halas has said."²⁶ If one reliable source of written information has survived regarding this situation, it is the somewhat terse letter sent by A.E. Staley to Halas on October 6, 1921. The letter served as a pact, signed by both Staley and Halas, "confirming our verbal agreement with you [Halas]." In it, the Staley Company agreed to retain no more than 19 football players on the payroll at a weekly compensation of $25 each, even though they would no longer be employed at the plant in Decatur. Staley would also purchase $3,000 worth of advertising in the team programs. The sum of the payroll payments and the advertising would equal the $5,000 that Staley previously offered to Halas in order to financially assist with the move of the team to Chicago. The final requirement would be that the "team is to operate under the name of the Staley Football Club" until the mutual agreement expired at the conclusion of the 1921 football season. Just so there was no mistake in the separation of the football team from the Staley Company, Staley included one more sentence: "It is our wish and plan that when the football team goes to Chicago on October 15th, it remain there until the end of the season."²⁷

It certainly doesn't matter at this point as to when the exact divorce between Staley and Halas occurred in 1921, but it seems more likely that it was in October, especially since Halas did play a full baseball season with the Staleys earlier in the year, an event that would be unlikely if he left the company in February 1921. He also mentioned that the separation occurred before the Rock Island game on Monday, October 10. The story does conflict again when discussing the lease of Cubs Park with William Veeck Sr., the president of the Chicago Cubs, which would have taken place in June 1921, according to published reports mentioned previously in this chapter. Halas was fearful that Veeck would require a fixed rental fee to utilize the stadium and was relieved when Veeck asked only for 15 percent of the gate receipts and the concessions. Halas would retain revenue from any program sales. If Halas surmised that his favorable rental agreement with Veeck was advantageous to the Staley company at that time, it perhaps prompted Mr. Staley's decision to discontinue his support of the football team later that year. Author Mark Sorensen offered an explanation: "Staley may have been miffed that Halas had rented Cubs Park."[28]

In later years, Joey Sternaman, another former Staleys and Bears player (and brother of Dutch Sternaman), provided some additional "insider" information on the situation: "He [Dutch Sternaman] and George Halas went there and ran the football team and worked for Staley in his plant there. They became the big shots on the Staleys. The team didn't do all that well, I guess, or something went wrong down there, and Staley washed his hands of it."[29]

By the fall of 1921, the U.S. economy was moving forward and the Staley Company was doing very well. So well in fact that it was too busy to accept a very large starch order from Germany in late October: "Printing presses in Germany would have to run overtime to print enough marks to pay for an order for starch which A.E. Staley turned down the other day. A concern in Hamburg wanted the Staley Company to ship approximately 300 carloads of starch valued at about $450,000 in good American money. Mr. Staley's plant is too busy to take on an order of that size at this time.... Business, Mr. Staley says, is very good."[30]

In a final analysis, the decision to drop football by Staley was probably not linked to the overall financial health of the company. The recession was over and the plant shutdowns were completed. In November 1921, the company enjoyed its biggest month of production in history, prompting Mr. Staley to remark: "The starch trade is very good both in the country and abroad and it looks like it will remain that way."[31] By that time, the football team was long gone to Chicago and Mr. Staley had eliminated one obvious deficit center from his budget.

From the time that the Staley/Halas agreement was finalized on October 6 until the next game with Rock Island on October 10, Halas had just four days to prepare for his new role as "owner" of the football team. However, since Cubs Park had been rented previously by Halas, and the Rock Island contest was held in Decatur, the challenge might not have been so difficult. The hard deadline would have been October 15 (as specifically mentioned in the agreement letter), when the players packed up and departed Decatur permanently for an eagerly anticipated match with the Rochester (New York) Jeffersons on Sunday, October 16, at Cubs Park in Chicago. It would be the first of 10 straight battles scheduled for the Staleys at Cubs Park as Halas deftly avoided all "away" games, and the ensuing travel expenses, during the 1921 season. In his autobiography, this was about the time that he added a partner to help with management and expenses. Dutch Sternaman had been a teammate of Halas's at Illinois, and a veteran of the 1920 Staleys season when he led the team in scoring. But

Halas noted that Sternaman was not his first choice for the position: "The problem of running a team seemed endless. I decided to take a partner. I wanted Paddy Driscoll, but he wasn't available. So, I looked around the team and settled on Dutch Sternaman. He was our most successful scorer. I offered him a 50–50 partnership. He would have taken less.... He and I agreed to take $100 each a game, same as the players—if any money were still in the bank."[32]

Running with the Speed of an Antelope

Halas's infatuation with Driscoll will be discussed shortly as Halas continued to pursue Driscoll to join his ownership team in the postseason. For the 1921 campaign, Driscoll would remain under contract to the Chicago Cardinals and enjoy another spectacular year. On October 16, the same day that the Staleys edged Rochester 16–13 in the team's first home game at Cubs Park, the Cardinals hosted the tough Rock Island Independents. After dropping an ugly 23–0 verdict to Akron the week before, the Cards looked for revenge against the Independents, now coached by tackle Frank Coughlin, a former Notre Dame star. Ironically, it was a homecoming of sorts for Coughlin since he grew up in the Normal Park neighborhood and graduated from nearby Englewood High School. Rock Island also boasted of a talented backfield star in Jimmy Conzelman and had suffered a tight 14–10 loss the previous Monday in the last Staleys game played in Decatur. History will show that Rock Island defeated the Cardinals 14–7 as the marquee names of Driscoll and Conzelman both provided thrills before a crowd of 4,000 at Normal Park. However, the game also provided a pair of historical footnotes before the day was over. Driscoll initiated the scoring in the first quarter with a remarkable 80-yard punt return that left even the *Rock Island Argus* reporter a bit breathless: "Paddy took a punt from his own 20-yard line and zig-zagging his way through a broken field placed the ball securely behind the Rock Island goal. The crowd went into spasms of delight; that is, all of it but the Rock Island fans who made the journey to see the locals in action. Running with the speed of an antelope, knees high in the air with each step, Paddy shook off tackler after tackler and to top it off slipped away from the outstretched arms of Conzelman, who made a desperate lunge in an attempt to bring the runner to earth."[33]

The Driscoll scoring romp provided the Cardinals with an early 7–0 lead, but the visitors rebounded to grab the 14–7 victory when Conzelman recovered an onside kick for a touchdown that was strenuously objected to, albeit unsuccessfully, by Cards manager Chris O'Brien: "Shortly after the touchdown the visitors registered another score by virtue of a questionable onside kick. One official and the Cardinal players claimed Conzelman was not behind the oval when it was kicked. The referee, according to manager Chris O'Brien, ruled the play legal with the result the touchdown was allowed, and this proved to be the winning play as neither team scored in the second half."[34]

The loss dropped the Cardinals to a 1–2 mark in APFA play, but the game itself was memorable for two reasons: an unknown player suddenly showing up in the Cards' lineup, and the ascension of Conzelman to coach of the Independents. A halfback listed simply as "McMahon" entered the Chicago backfield and carried the ball for 21 yards throughout the game. Actually, two players named McMahon were on the field for the Cardinals in 1921 and both were real-life brothers playing under assumed names. Their given names were Ralph and Arnie Horween, both natives of Chicago's South Side, and each enjoyed outstanding football careers at Harvard. Why the fake names? Ralph Horween's son Ralph Stow explained the situation: "It was out of respect for their mother, who was a fairly straitlaced Victorian lady and had qualms about whether it was respectable to play pro football."[35] Ralph continued with the Cardinals through the 1923 season, while Arnie completed his Cardinals career in 1924. Both were part of the Horween Leather Company, which supplies leather for footballs still used today in the current National Football League. Arnie Horween also coached the Cardinals in 1923 and 1924.

As for Conzelman, he was part of another unique episode from the early days of pro football. With the Cardinals leading 7–0 in the Rock Island game on October 16, 1921, he later shared the story that a substitute named Ed Healey (more on him in the next chapter) reported in the game for tackle/coach Frank Coughlin. "He tapped Coughlin on the back and said, 'you're out.' Then he pointed at me and said, 'You're the new coach; Mr. [team owner Walter] Flanigan wants you to take over.'"[36] Since that time, now over 100 years later, this is the only time that an APFA/NFL team changed coaches during a game. While this account may be true since the respected Conzelman shared it, the current availability of research tools tells a different version. While Coughlin was relieved of his coaching duties for Rock Island, that decision was not announced until two days later when Coughlin, along with Dave Hayes and Grover Malone, were dropped by the Independents. The reason given was that Flanigan wanted his players living full-time in Rock Island, as reported in the *Daily Times*: The shakeup is aimed to bring a purely residential team to Rock Island. Coughlin, coach of the team as well as captain, resides in South Bend, Indiana, and only spent three days a week in Rock Island, while both Hayes and Malone came down each week from Chicago. Conzelman has been named to take Coughlin's place both as captain and coach, the change to take effect at once."[37]

On a side note, access today to local newspapers from a century ago often unveil certain facts that can stick a needle into the balloon of any legendary tale. While this tidbit is less than consequential, the *Rock Island Argus* game summary reported on the number of substitutions from that game with the Cardinals: "The Cardinals kept a constant steam of fresh men running into the battle but the Independents worried along with only one substitution, that of Healey for Travis, until the last few minutes, when Duggan and Hanson replaced Vanderloo and Keefe."[38] The very specific "play-by-play" account published by the *Argus* following the game disclosed that Coach Frank Coughlin never came out of the action. Either way, Jimmy Conzelman was the new leader of the Rock Island Independents, perhaps accumulating gridiron knowledge that he would utilize 20 years later as the coach of the Cardinals!

Dutch and I Were Flat Broke

On the North Side of Chicago, the Staleys did edge Rochester 16–13 on October 16, but Halas faced another obstacle even before the game started in terms of a financial shortfall. In the brief time that the team had been in Chicago, the surplus funds were seemingly already exhausted, according to Halas: "Our [Chicago] debut against Rochester attracted about 8,000 fans, and we rallied for a touchdown in the final minutes to win 16–13. I also recall that Dutch and I were flat broke before the opener. All of our $5,000 operating capital—which Mr. Staley had provided to assist our move to Chicago—had been spent on uniforms and other expenses. In fact, I waited at the box office when the grandstand gates opened and grabbed the first $20 which came in thru the window, so I could run over to the corner drugstore to buy the tape and other medical supplies our players needed for the game."[39]

With both the Cardinals and Staleys now based in Chicago for the remainder of the year, it would seem logical that the quick pairing of the two neighbors would be both pragmatic and profitable, yet neither team seemed interested in playing the other. And so, the schedule eased into November with the Staleys leading the league and the Cardinals a step behind. On November 20, 1921, the Staleys were still undefeated with a 5–0 ledger in league competition while the Cardinals had improved to 3–2. On that day, the Staleys would bounce the visiting Cleveland Indians 22–7, while the Cardinals would welcome one of the new members of the league—the Green Bay Packers—to Normal Park. The Cardinals had not played since November 6 after a November 10 date with the Canton Bulldogs was wiped out by the weather. Chris O'Brien had envisioned a huge crowd for the Canton clash, even though the great Jim Thorpe was no longer with the team. After promising Canton a nice guarantee for the trip to Chicago, O'Brien leaped ahead with an ambitious plan. He, too, would rent Cubs Park for the day. Since the Staleys were busy using the field on Sundays, O'Brien opted for a Friday clash with Canton on November 11 when it was still known as Armistice Day. For Canton business manager Ralph Hay, any day would have been a good day to play, especially if the game was not held in Canton. A frustrated Hay announced on November 9 that his team would no longer host any "home" games during the 1921 season: "Home games have not been financially successful. We have to go on the road to pull through without a tremendous loss. When it takes more than $2,500 to put a team on the field, to say nothing of guarantees and expenses of visitors, quite a crowd is needed to make things meet. Canton failed to respond."[40]

Sadly, O'Brien's dreams of a big payday were washed away when a torrential storm resulted in the field being unplayable. In 1921, the scheduling of games was often initiated on very short notice, so O'Brien began working on an opponent for the following Sunday and grabbed the attention of the Packers. He completed negotiations on November 15 for a contest to be staged at Normal Park on November 20. As usual, players continued to bounce around the APFA rosters. While Green Bay was headed by Curly Lambeau, the squad had also added former Cardinal Norman Barry as well as Frank Coughlin, late of Rock Island. Packers fans could keep in touch with their heroes by attending the game in person (as about 400 of them did) or gathering (for a nominal fee) at Turner Hall in Green Bay for a slightly delayed telegraph announcement of each play: "Mulligan Scroogy will handle the megaphone and his amusing antics ought to be a big attraction of the afternoon game. Each play will be given off the wire by downs and although the players can't be seen in action, a little use of the imagination will probably add more excitement than if one were present at the game itself."[41]

Despite the football excitement in Green Bay, a local newspaper in Appleton, Wisconsin, scoffed at the idea of paying $9.69 for the train ride to Chicago, plus room and board, just to watch the Packers: "When 400 fans are willing to spend that much money to see a professional team play we wonder what they would do if they had a team that played real football, say like Lawrence College, in their town."[42] It was apparent that not everyone was ready to embrace this new concept of professional football in 1921! As for the game itself, the weather plagued O'Brien again as only 2,000 attendees, many of them from Wisconsin, showed up to watch the teams battle to a 3–3 deadlock. Lambeau and Driscoll provided the only points for each team with field goals in the second half. After the game, Driscoll provided a rare player interview and complimented the visitors: "You've got a sweet little machine. I would like to see your backs in action on a dry field, providing you were not playing my team!"[43]

The NFL's Oldest Rivalry

A week later on November 27, the Packers returned to the Windy City for the team's first meeting ever with the Staleys. The hosts breezed past the Packers 20–0 as both Halas and Sternaman scored touchdowns for the Staleys. While many gridiron followers today lean toward anointing the Bears and the Packers for being participants in pro football's oldest rivalry, the fact remains that the Cardinals and Packers met a week before that coupling. Of course, the Cardinals and the Bears first fought in 1920, leaving the following three games as the oldest rivalries in league history:

- November 28, 1920: Cardinals 7 Decatur Staleys 6 (Staleys became the Chicago Bears)
- November 20, 1921: Cardinals 3 Green Bay Packers 3
- November 27, 1921: Staleys/Bears 20 Packers 0

After the games on November 27, the Staleys were 8–1 (7–1 in the APFA), just behind the Buffalo All-Americans (7–0–2) in the APFA title race. The lone blemish on the Staleys' ledger was a tight 7–6 loss inflicted by Buffalo a few days earlier on November 24 when a missed Sternaman extra point attempt proved to be the difference. But what about the Cardinals (3–2–1)? Chris O'Brien was eager to schedule the Staleys in an effort to establish the local bragging rights, as reported in the *Chicago Tribune*: "Chris O'Brien, manager of the Cardinals, is pointing his team for a battle with the Staleys to determine the city championship and this encounter probably will be staged at the Cubs Park early next month if the Staleys' management accepts the challenge of the Cardinals."[44] Halas had other immediate plans. His eye was on the top prize for 1921, the APFA championship. However, with tie games still not counted in the standings and no playoff system in place, the only way for the Staleys to crawl back in contention was to defeat Buffalo in a second match. Would the All-Americans be receptive to his challenge?

Indeed they were, although under some very odd circumstances. It would have been understood if Buffalo had decided to end its season at the end of November and retired for the year undefeated. If that was the case, Buffalo would have finished 8–0–2 after edging the Dayton Triangles 7–0 on November 27 and the club would have been awarded the league title. No questions asked. Surprisingly, All-Americans owner Frank McNeil agreed to a difficult two-game set to finish the season, arranging to meet the Akron Pros on Saturday, December 3, in Buffalo and then grabbing an all-night train for the over 500-mile ride to Chicago to face the Staleys the next day. This would be a nearly impossible assignment for Buffalo, even in the current days of jet travel. On the other hand, it was certainly a huge advantage for the Staleys to play a team that not only was in action the previous day, but also one that just spent the entire night on a train. And—the APFA championship was at stake!

Jeff Miller, author of *Buffalo's Forgotten Champions: The Story of Buffalo's First Professional Football Team and The Lost 1921 Title*, believes that Frank McNeil, owner of the Buffalo team, may have been maneuvered into accepting the extra final game with the Staleys by Halas: "The Buffalo ownership was not very strong. To me, Frank McNeil was a businessman and not a sports person. I got the feeling that he wasn't as serious about the situation as Halas. Halas was certainly savvier than Frank who believed that the last two games were exhibitions."[45]

Once the teams agreed to meet, supposedly for the league title, the APFA issued a statement on December 1, 1921, indicating that Sunday, December 4, would be the final day of the season. This release originated in Chicago but was distributed around the country, including in Buffalo: "Action by the officials of the National Professional Football League [APFA] has made it certain that the winner of Sunday's game between the Buffalo All-Americans and the Staleys will be champion. The decision was to make Sunday, December 4th the closing date of the season so far as the championship is concerned. There will doubtless be battles after that, but they will have no bearing on the national pro title."[46]

Also, on December 1, Halas announced that the Staleys season would continue into December by booking home games with the Cardinals on December 11, followed by a match with the defending champion Akron Pros on December 18. But first, the all-important "playoff" with Buffalo was in sight. Over the years, there has been speculation that Buffalo considered the games with Akron and the Staleys to be merely exhibitions. In other words, neither game, no matter what the outcome, would count in the official league standings.

Although Buffalo defeated Akron 14–0 on December 3, the team fell to the Staleys 10–7 the very next day. Jeff Miller indicated that Buffalo owner Frank McNeil may have been unaware of the toll the two games might have taken on his players: "McNeil had declared the All-Americans as the league champions a week or so before, but to his credit, he scheduled two more games in what he thought were exhibitions. He was also foolish enough to think his players could play two games in two days. He didn't take into account the human element, especially since they did not use substitutions in the Chicago game."[47]

In 1956, former Buffalo quarterback/coach Tommy Hughitt recalled the circumstances of those final two games in 1921, stating that the battle with the Staleys was a "post-season game, and was arranged with that understanding by Frank McNeil, our manager. We'd certainly have been silly to risk our championship if it was to be listed as a regular season game. And the Bears [Staleys] never would agree to come to Buffalo."[48] Miller concurred, noting: "If they hadn't played those two extra games, ostensibly exhibitions, Buffalo would have won the championship."[49] Even with the loss, Buffalo (9–1) completed its season on December 4 ahead of the Staleys (8–1) in the 1921 standings without the ties included. Still, Halas was convinced that the win over Buffalo (along with no tie games by the Staleys) would secure the championship for his team, despite the equal records: "The Decaturs claimed the championship immediately following the game. Coach Halas of the Illinois eleven, based what he claimed was the superior claim of the Western team on two tie games played by the Buffalo team. He pointed out that the Buffalos and the Decaturs were each defeated in one game this year but the Staleys have no tie games to mar their record."[50]

But would the final game with the All-Americans count in the standings, especially if Buffalo presumed it would be an exhibition? Just to be sure, Halas went ahead and played two more games on the calendar, although Canton replaced Akron on the schedule for the December 11 contest. The 10–0 win pulled the Staleys even with the All-Americans since each team was now sitting on a 9–1 record. Again, would this game count for the Staleys since the APFA had already closed the door on the schedule effective December 4?

Assuming that all of the aforementioned games would "count" in the title chase, Halas could quell any questions by simply defeating the Cardinals (6–3–1/3–3–1) in the absolute final game of the year on December 18. Although it was merely the third game played between the two Chicago neighbors in two years, the rising competition factor among fans, and the players, was addressed in the buildup to the kickoff: "There is intense rivalry between the teams, and this has spread to their supporters. A big crowd of south side fans is expected to invade the north side, and more rooting is looked for than is usually noted at a pro game."[51]

In an effort to boost attendance, the ever-innovative Halas placed an ad in the *Chicago Tribune* under the "Amusements" section. Sandwiched in between ads for *Bits-o-Broadway* at the Columbia Theater and *Enter Madame* at the Playhouse, one could find a tiny mention for the big game between the Staleys and the Cardinals at Cubs Park. On game day, with temperatures dropping to single digits, neither team could generate any offense, resulting in a 0–0 tie, meaning the possession of the mythical city championship would need to wait for another year. The Cardinals also stopped cold the Staleys' bid for the outright APFA crown. A win for the Staleys would have brought that elusive 10th victory, a step ahead of Buffalo, while the tie meant virtually nothing. The freezing conditions kept the crowd away with only about 2,700 fans showing up to witness the season finale. Including tie games, the final standings for 1921 showed the Staleys with a 9–1–1 record, while Buffalo finished with a 9–1–2 mark. The Cardinals picked up ninth place with a 3–3–2 ledger. All that remained now was for the APFA honchos to determine whether the Staleys, or the All-Americans, would be proclaimed as the 1921 champs.

By the end of the season, the Halas contingent was referred to frequently as the Chicago Staleys. Halas knew he would never return to Decatur, although the Staley Company had not formally announced any discontinuation of its football program.

Behind the scenes, Halas and his lawyers moved quickly to establish a corporation that would formally serve as the foundation for his club. Certainly, he would need to devise a name for his team and quickly adopted the "Bears" in deference, and perhaps gratitude, to the helpful management of the Chicago Cubs. "My obligation to the A.E. Staley Company ceased. I considered naming the team the Chicago Cubs out of respect for Mr. William Veeck, Senior, and Mr. William Wrigley, who had been such a great help. But I noted football players are bigger than baseball players; so if baseball players are cubs, then certainly football players must be bears!"[52]

Vicious Circle Formed

Over in Decatur, rumors were spreading about the future of the sports program at the A.E. Staley Company. In response, A.E. Staley issued a statement on January 8, 1922, offering encouragement to those fearing that baseball would be discontinued: "You can rest assured that we will have a team in the field and we hope it will be the strongest that ever represented the city."[53] Yet, at the end of the month, Staley decided that his company would no longer support sporting events, stating: "As long as the teams were composed of factory players the proposition served its purpose but

The above cartoon first appeared in the *Staley Fellowship Journal*, published by the A.E. Staley Company in January 1922. Its creator noted that the football team seemed to be drawing more interest than the plant's primary manufacturing products. At that time, the decision to drop sports by the Staley Company had not yet been announced. George Halas moved the Staleys to Chicago in late 1921 as the Chicago Staleys. A year later, the team was known as the Chicago Bears (courtesy Decatur Public Library).

when the competition became keen for the high-priced players the sport failed to serve its purpose for a business institution such as ours. Our directors have decided that we will confine our efforts to manufacturing, producing and marketing our products and that we cannot afford to continue in professional sport.... There will not be a Staley football team next year, in fact there will be no sport at the Staley plant that is not self-supporting."[54]

Staley's decision prompted a scathing editorial in the local media, which sadly explained the circumstances surrounding the rapid growth of the Staley sports program while also predicting a swift demise for pro football:

> Expensive players were brought in for the public was not satisfied with second-raters. But gate receipts in games played in Decatur were not enough to meet swollen salaries. Consequently, games must be staged in Chicago. Thus, the vicious circle was formed. The very purpose for which the teams were created—to strengthen the morale of the workmen [and] to entertain the Decatur public was defeated. Professionalism outreached itself. Industrial athletics, in Mr. Staley's opinion, have had their day. *The Herald* having in mind athletic history for 25 years has maintained that professional football was doomed. It may have a revival here and there, but it will not last.[55]

During the APFA meeting on January 28, 1922, in Canton, Ohio, the Chicago Staleys were finally awarded the 1921 championship over Buffalo despite both teams finishing with 9–1 records (omitting tie games). Author Jeff Miller indicated that the decision was influenced by the insistence of Halas that the second game played between the two clubs should be weighed more heavily: "Halas went to the league meeting and said that although the teams had identical records, the Bears had won the second game with Buffalo and should therefore be considered the champion. Joe Carr and the others agreed with Halas."[56]

While Halas managed to succeed in his quest to be awarded the title, an unexpected development during the meeting may have helped nudge Mr. Staley to accelerate his "no sports" decision a couple of days later. During the meeting, Halas and Sternaman needed to apply for their own APFA franchise in Chicago since the former Decatur Staleys organization was owned by A.E. Staley. Now that the split between Halas and Staley was complete, Halas and Sternaman anticipated a swift approval of their franchise application during the Canton sessions. However, another attendee in Canton was there with a similar intention: Bill Harley. Bill and his brother Chic claimed that the agreement signed with Halas and Sternaman in 1921 was still valid, meaning that the Harleys maintained an interest in the Staleys/Bears football team. Halas recalled: "Unexpectedly, Bill Harley produced a startling demand for one-third ownership because of our agreement the past year. He came to the Association meeting and asked that the Staley franchise be given to him."[57]

When the dispute could not be rectified satisfactorily, the group called A.E. Staley in Decatur to discuss his version of the managerial events. Staley stated that he had placed the team in the hands of Halas during the fall of 1921. By the time of the league meeting in early 1922, could Staley have been completely weary of sports and convinced that he no longer needed that annoyance? With that discussion concluded, the owners and managers of the APFA initiated a vote to determine the apparent "owners" of the franchise, as recounted in an article in the *Coffin*

Corner: "Then, in a vote that wasn't even close, the moguls awarded the franchise to 'ol George and Dutch. A couple of years later, Harley took his argument that he was part owner of the long-departed Staley franchise to court, claiming a piece of the new franchise. He lost."[58]

Bill Harley was eventually awarded an NFL franchise in Toledo, Ohio, and was later in charge of Mills Stadium in Chicago. The great Chic Harley suffered from emotional and physical injuries that restricted him to assisted living facilities for most of his life before he passed away in 1974 at the age of 79.

We Are in Business to Stay!

One more momentous decision was finalized at the Canton meeting when the Green Bay Packers were dropped from the league. This action would prove to be brief, as Curly Lambeau managed to have the Packers readmitted during the next league get-together in June 1922. But for the moment, the Packers were ousted for admitting to using college players during the season—a big *no-no* in a league that boasted of its honesty and aversion to the use of undergrads. The league itself then reiterated its opposition to such practices by strengthening its punishments for any team utilizing the services of a collegiate player. President Joe Carr added: "We want to get along happily with the colleges, and we will go out of our way to do just this, but the colleges and their organizations do not need to think we are going to lay down and quit because they don't like us. We are in business to stay."[59] The Cardinals' Chris O'Brien, who normally preferred to work behind the scenes, supported Carr with a blistering epistle on this same subject in February 1922, while urging that any college players who snuck into the professional ranks while still in school be blacklisted:

> They aren't any good to themselves, the college they are supposed to represent, or the team they are playing for. I'm a promoter. I'm a professional. I couldn't stay in sport six months if I didn't make any money out of it, or if it didn't pay me at least my expenses. But, I do want to say that the "cheater" has no more place in professional ranks than he has in amateur. Promoters of professional football realize that their sport is founded upon the integrity of the college game. If the college game is allowed to die, professional football will die with it. We're only watching our own selfish interests when we try to safeguard the college game.[60]

While George Halas appeared to emerge unscathed from the Canton meeting with both the Chicago Bears franchise and the 1921 title in his pocket despite extenuating circumstances, his next move was both questionable and less than honorable. In his eagerness to continuously upgrade his roster, Halas made Cardinals superstar Paddy Driscoll a unique offer in the winter of 1922. Driscoll was believed to be the highest-paid player in the league at $300 per game, but Halas brushed aside that potential weekly obligation and moved right on to the serious stuff. In exchange for his services on the football field, Driscoll would share equally in the ownership of the new corporation called the "Chicago Bears Football Club Inc." Along with Halas and Sternaman, Driscoll would control all 75 total shares, each share worth $100. The three partners would also serve as directors of the corporation. The corporate documents were signed and filed on April 1, 1922.[61] But Halas forgot one major component in all of this planning: Driscoll was still under contract to the Cardinals. Chris O'Brien was livid!

In the preparation of this book, attorney Steve Thomas of Chicago reviewed the corporate papers filed by the three owners of the Chicago Bears in April 1922. These documents are still on file with the state of Illinois, indicating that they were indeed presented to the state with the intention of confirming John "Paddy" Driscoll as one of the owners of the Chicago Bears. In his evaluation of the corporate filings, Steve Thomas confirmed this intent and offered additional insight into the transaction:

Paddy Driscoll was the highest-paid player in the very early days of the NFL at $300 per game in 1920. Although George Halas offered Driscoll a partnership in the Bears, he remained a member of the Cardinals from 1920 to 1925 (courtesy Pro Football Hall of Fame, Dutch Sternaman Collection).

> The incorporation documents clearly show that the original equity of the Bears would be equally owned by Halas, Driscoll, and Sternaman. The document identifies each of the three as *"subscribers to the capital stock and the amount subscribed* <u>and paid in by each</u>*..."* as $2,500. Whether this was true in fact or not cannot be determined based solely on the incorporation document. Further, once a corporate charter was issued, nothing would prevent any one of the three from transferring some or all of their shares to each other or to a third party. These transfers, if they took place, would be part of internal corporate records and documents, and not subject to any public filing required by the State of Illinois.
>
> It is, however, common at present for shareholders of a closely held corporation by agreement among themselves to limit their ability to transfer their shares. Also, I have no doubt that the National Football League by league rule or regulation maintains strictly observed records on who is in an ownership position among the various league members. This may not have been true in 1922 in the formative years of the NFL. In modern times it is not so common for the original owners/investors in a new corporation to be identified by name and address in the incorporation documents. The requirement of the Illinois statute (then and now) is simply that there be three identified incorporators who must be subscribers to the capital stock. These days such incorporator/subscribers often are convenient nominees who subscribe to one share and, upon incorporation, assign their subscriptions to the real parties in interest who may never be publicly identified under the corporation law. Directors, by contrast, as well as key officers (but not shareholders), must be identified in a public corporate annual report. Directors and officers are often shareholders as well, but the law does not require that directors or officers be investors/shareholders in the enterprise.

Seven. Lawyers, Gum, and Money 103

So, I think it is clear from the document how the Bears started out as a corporation, or at least how they represented themselves to the state of Illinois. How long they maintained that ownership structure or whether they even in fact did what the document states would require confirmation from other sources such as financial statements, tax returns, internal corporate records, contemporaneous outside evidence such as public statements, correspondence, speeches, news articles, confirmation from Driscoll or Sternaman, NFL records, and the like.[62]

At the next league meeting in Cleveland on June 24–25, Halas was not present. This did not prohibit his colleagues for reprimanding him through a motion passed during the meeting. It simply stated: "Motion made and seconded that the management of the Chicago Bears be notified that Patty [sic] Driscoll is the property of the management of the Chicago Cardinals and shall not be tampered with until he receives his release from the Cardinals. Carried unanimously."[63] During the meeting, the league adopted a new constitution, established a roster limit of 18 players, decided that referees would be assigned by the league, and approved a motion by O'Brien that would bar any college players who played in the league while still holding collegiate eligibility. Finally, and perhaps most important, the APFA bosses agreed to change the name of the circuit to the National Football League!

As the summer of 1922 drifted into another football season, the Decatur Staleys were no more, the Chicago Bears would defend their league championship, and Chris O'Brien could do little to hide his distaste for his North Side competition. An article in the *Rock Island Argus* hinted at the mood of O'Brien toward Halas following a recent league meeting: "At the last confab, one of the arguments centered on the recognition of the champions. The choice was between the Staleys and Buffalo. In the heat of this Chris O'Brien, manager of the Chicago Cardinals, told all present that if any championship was presented it ought to go to Rock Island. Then Chris recounted the luck that attended the Staleys' victory in that memorable contest at Cubs Park. The supposition is that Chris disliked the Staleys more than he did Rock Island."[64]

With the blatant effort by Halas to woo Driscoll away from the Cardinals, the fledgling rivalry was turned up a notch and would soon explode into an on-field sea of violence like nothing ever seen before in the early days of pro football.

Eight

That Al Capone Crowd!

"I stood there in amazement. A couple of days earlier, I'd signed for a hundred bucks and now I'm out here liable to be killed!"
—Ed Healey, Chicago Bears

Three teams in two days?

In the early days of the National Football League (NFL), the practice of players bouncing from one roster to another was discouraged but not uncommon. But near the conclusion of the 1922 season, tackle Ed Healey of the Rock Island Independents was about to become a historical footnote.

When the financially fragile Independents were scheduled to invade Chicago for a November 19, 1922, battle at Cubs Park (now Wrigley Field) there were already whispers that the negative bottom line in the Rock Island accounting book (along with some internal bickering) was about to destroy the remainder of the team's campaign should the Bears prevail in the upcoming contest.

Still, the atmosphere in Rock Island was both supportive and proud of the local club, which boasted a solid 4–1–1 mark in league play compared with the Bears' 7–2 slate. *The Daily Times* noted that "the squad will not be lonesome for everyone in Rock Island is asking: 'When are you traveling for the Independent-Bear game?'"[1] Indeed, the Rock Island media outlets were very confident, with the *Argus* reporting: "The Independents right now appear to be at the top of their form, and with every man in first class condition the Bears should be in for the most interesting afternoon of their career."[2]

In Chicago, the *Tribune* was wary of the powerful Independents, especially the recent accomplishments of the visitors: "In their recent games the Independents have been rolling up enormous scores, having an attack that has smothered all opposition…. Their tackles, Duke Slater of Iowa and Ed Healey of Dartmouth, are considered the equal of any in the league…."[3] Of course, both Slater and Healey are now enshrined in the Pro Football Hall of Fame, but in 1922, each of these tough linemen was just beginning to establish their gridiron reputations in the fledgling professional circuit.

While a crowd of over 8,000 gathered at Cubs Park for the 2:15 kickoff, eager fans back in Rock Island assembled, as usual, outside the offices of the *Argus* newspaper for a play-by-play update of the game as relayed by wire from Chicago. "Fans are urged to come early and gain the vantage points," warned the newspaper. "A mammoth crowd is sure to be on hand when the whistle blows, and space in front of the Argus plant is necessarily limited."[4] As for the game itself, the anticipated thrills and chills were missing for fans in Chicago and Rock Island alike, as the teams battled deep into the fourth quarter without scoring. Rock Island's best scoring chance occurred after Healey blocked a Bears punt in the first quarter, but Rock Island was unable to score from the Bears' 29-yard line. Ultimately, the Bears managed to sneak away with the victory on a late field goal by Dutch Sternaman for the only points of the game, as reported by the *Daily Times*: "The Rock Island Independents went down, 3–0, yesterday, but they went down fighting as they never fought before. Facing the Chicago Bears at Cubs' Park, before one of the largest crowds ever assembled in Chicago to see a grid game in the professional league, the Islanders lost by a margin of a place kick from the 29-yard line by Dutch Sternaman in the last two minutes of play."[5]

Unfortunately for his local fans, the loss to the Bears would mark the final game that Ed Healey would ever play for the Rock Island Independents. Despite the apparent strong support of the community, in truth, the Independents were struggling financially. With only a handful of home games scheduled before the season, the Independents and their ambitious manager, Walter Flanigan, hoped for both attractive opponents, as well as good weather, in order to attract significant crowds to those Rock Island events. With four straight home games to start the 1922 campaign, the best the Independents could do in terms of attendance was the 4,749 loyal supporters who showed up for a 10–6 loss to the Bears on October 8. Otherwise, the 1,200 rain-drenched fans shivering in the stands for a 43–0 bludgeoning of the Dayton Triangles on November 12 was more typical of the usual attendance figures. Finally, the lower-than-anticipated gate guarantee received after the Bears game in Chicago (and a canceled game with the Milwaukee Badgers on November 5) apparently underscored more than the usual frustration and exasperation by the players following a tough game. In short, the team was unable to meet its payroll, prompting a round of complaints, both public and private, that forced Independents management to cease operations for the season on November 20, 1922, even as the team was still in NFL title contention with its 4–2–1 record.

Just a couple of weeks earlier, the local press had questioned the team's stamina (and desire) following a tough 0–0 tie with Green Bay: "Ugly rumors are being circulated. It is said some of the members of the team are finding late hours and 'soda pop' poor physical conditioners. If this be true, it's time for a reckoning."[6] Now, with the added concern over lost wages, the players met informally to air their gripes and demand payment for their services, according to the *Daily Times*:

> A street corner conference of most of the stars of the Rock Island Independents this noon revealed that the sentiment of the great majority of the team members is strongly in favor of disbanding for the season, because of Manager Walt Flanigan's inability to pay his players for their services in last Sunday's game with the Chicago Bears and in future games. The consensus of opinion seemed to be that immediate release of all members of the eleven should be demanded of Flanigan, so all can affiliate with other teams without danger of being branded an outlaw [by league officials].[7]

This is where Ed Healey's strange NFL journey began. With the Independents in utter financial chaos, it was agreed that the team's season would conclude prematurely and that the players, in most cases, would be free to pursue other gridiron employment opportunities for the remainder of the NFL schedule in 1922. Rock Island then turned down the opportunity to play at the Minneapolis Marines on November 26, even with a $1,500 guarantee from the hosts. The entire situation was also evolving into a civic embarrassment for the city of Rock Island. The local chamber of commerce announced that it would assign a group of local citizens to examine the "books" of the Independents not only to determine if there was any mischief evident but also to begin repairing the business structure of the team in an effort to again field a squad in 1923.[8]

Although manager Flanigan was eventually cleared of any wrongdoing (and the Independents would return in 1923), the 1922 roster was rapidly disappearing after the team dissolved for the year. Quarterback Jimmy Conzelman fled to Milwaukee, end Tillie Voss signed with Akron, and halfback Dutch Lauer joined the Packers. Healey was rumored to be negotiating for a spot with an eastern club until it was announced that both he and end Jerry Johnson were added to the roster of the Racine (Wisconsin) Horlicks on November 25.[9] Later in life, Healey recalled that his destination was actually planned for Green Bay, which included a brief train stop in Chicago:

> My own intention was to go up to Green Bay and play the rest of the season for the Packers. But Mr. [Walter] Flanigan called me in and told me to report to [Bears' owners George] Halas and [Dutch] Sternaman, that they wanted to talk to me. So, I said, "well, yeh, I might do that.... I went to Chicago and talked with Halas and Sternaman in their 'private' office, which was the lobby of the Planters Hotel. They offered to pay me seventy-five dollars a game." I said, "I wouldn't sit on your bench for seventy-five dollars a game." So, after a discussion of renumeration which lasted two hours, they agreed, and rightfully so, to pay me a hundred bucks a game.[10]

In his autobiography, George Halas provided some additional information on the transaction: "I had long coveted a Rock Island player, Ed Healey, former Dartmouth star. The Rock Island owner, Walter Flanigan, owed me $100. I offered to cancel the debt if he would give me Healey.... There was one problem. I offered Ed $75 a game. He wanted $100. I could not resist his charm. I rejoice that I succumbed."[11]

Football Players Sold for Real Money Like Baseball Players

The journey of Healey from Rock Island to Racine/Green Bay to Chicago in a couple of days was quickly documented by the media for what it was: the first "sale" of a player in the National Football League. Since the Independents had disbanded for the season, the club announced that it had "loaned" Healey to Racine for the remainder of that team's schedule in 1922. Instead, Healey interrupted his journey in Chicago to plant the seed for his acquisition by the Bears as noted by the recollections of both Healey and George Halas above. However, the sale of Healey apparently did contain some specific language indicating that Healey's return to Rock Island might be an alternative for his former team, as well as being prophetic regarding the future of player movement within the pro football universe:

Healey was sold with an option clause attached so if the Independents desire his services next year he can be purchased back at the same figure or be traded for a couple of players from the Bears' team.... The significant fact of the sale is not so much in the purchase price as of how professional football has advanced in the last year. A year ago, no manager would think of buying a player from another team. That was considered unnecessary. If a manger wanted a player from the other team he got in touch with the player and made him an offer.... In the next two years football players will probably be sold for real money like baseball players are in organized baseball.[12]

As news of the "sale" of Healey emerged, it quickly spread across the eastern football world: "The first sale of a player's contract ever received in professional football was made between the Rock Island Independents and the Chicago Bears when Ed Healey, old 1919 Dartmouth star, was sold for $100...The Independents have started to rebuild the old team for next season and the sale is one result."[13]

Within a week, Halas maintained his end of the bargain by sending a check for $100 to Flanigan, which was duly noted in the *Argus*: "One hundred dollars has been added to the fund which W.H. Flanigan says is to be raised to pay off the indebtedness of the Rock Island Independents football organization. The money was received in the form of a check from the Chicago Bears for the services of tackle Ed Healey."[14]

When comparing the remembrances of Halas with the reporting of the contemporary newspaper accounts in 1922, there exists a bit of confusion regarding the true price of the Healey transaction. If Halas forgave the apparent $100 owed to him by Walter Flanigan, and still sent a check for $100 to Rock Island, then the true cost of the Healey deal was $200, not $100, but still an exceptional price for what would become a future Hall of Fame lineman!

Meanwhile, the Bears wasted little time in preparing Healey for his next assignment, a rapidly approaching intracity battle in the blossoming rivalry with the neighboring Chicago Cardinals scheduled for Thursday, November 30, 1922. The big Thanksgiving Day tilt would be just the fourth battle between the two Windy City clubs, both in their third year of membership in the National Football League. Each team had captured one victory thus far, while a third contest had ended in a tie. Both clubs were developing solid fan support, with the Cardinals based on the South Side of Chicago while the Bears encamped on the North Side of the city. It wasn't long before both fans and the media were comparing the budding rivalry to their more well-known baseball contemporaries in the city, as noted by the *Chicago Tribune* prior to the game: "The back fields of the Bears and Cardinals have given rise to arguments as partisan as ever existed between Cubs and Sox."[15]

Off the field, the rivalry was already brewing between the management of both squads. The Cardinals were managed by Chris O'Brien, a local painter and entrepreneur who had been with the team since its earliest inception in 1899 while the Bears were controlled by George Halas and Edward "Dutch" Sternaman, a pair of University of Illinois graduates. In the very early days of the NFL, when both scheduling and rosters were often unstable, an apparent misconception between the clubs emerged a week earlier (on November 23) that endangered the playing of the anticipated Thanksgiving clash. While O'Brien claimed that the game was scheduled previously for November 30, Sternaman countered in the *Tribune* with the contention that:

"The game was canceled because we could not agree on the park. Followers of our team wanted us to play on the north side, while O'Brien was insistent about the Sox park. This happened in June, and we then drew a line through this game. At the time we notified O'Brien and Carl Storck, secretary and treasurer of the league. Storck has copies of this letter and so have we. One was also sent to O'Brien. As a result of our failure to agree on a park we have scheduled the Toledo club for Thanksgiving Day." O'Brien claims an agreement was reached to play the game at the Sox park. The Cardinals manager asserted no change was suggested until two days ago, when the Bears demanded the contest be played at the Cubs park or not at all. The original schedule was approved by the league, according to O'Brien, who expects the officers to make the Bears or any other team live up to it.[16]

Perhaps Sternaman was participating in a bit of gamesmanship since several published articles contradicted his statement regarding the schedule changes. In late August, newspapers began publishing the league schedule for 1922 and the Thanksgiving date of November 30 showed the Bears playing at the Cardinals on that day. Other sources posted that the Bears would be at Green Bay on Thanksgiving Day and Rock Island would travel to Toledo on the same date.[17] All of which was nothing unusual in the early years of the NFL where changes and surprises regarding scheduling always seemed to lurk around the corner. Yet, O'Brien's "insistence" on playing at home (Comiskey Park) was likely expected when dealing with George Halas and the Bears, especially after Halas nearly swept Cardinals superstar Paddy Driscoll away from O'Brien earlier in 1922 until NFL President Joe Carr squashed the movement decisively. That open wound had not yet healed for O'Brien.

Miraculously, the two sides finally reached an armistice on Tuesday, November 28, and the eagerly anticipated contest was scheduled for an 11 a.m. kickoff at Comiskey Park on November 30. But why did this ugly dispute ever happen? Most likely it was over the dreaded home-field advantage brought about by less-than-stringent scheduling habits fostered by the teams. Or it was possible that O'Brien might still have been peeved at the Bears' unsuccessful recruitment of Driscoll and was hesitant to bend under any pressure brought on by the strong-willed Halas.

There were no shortages of "home" games for the Cardinals in 1922, since the team played all but one of its games on the South Side, either at Normal Park or for the first time at the larger Comiskey Park, when the Cards defeated Minneapolis 3–0 on October 22, 1922. On the other hand, the Bears at this point in the season had played seven straight games at home, with just a pair of opening road games on the schedule. Thus, no one was willing to travel, even if the competing ball clubs were housed only a few (eight) miles away from each other. Once the two Chicago teams agreed to play on November 30, a second contest was tentatively planned for December 10, presumably at Cubs Park so that each organization could host one of the city battles.

As Thanksgiving Day dawned with temperatures hovering around the freezing mark, fans of both the Bears and Cardinals alike crowded elevated trains for the ride over to 35th Street. Nearly 14,000 showed up in the frosty conditions, the biggest home turnout thus far for the Cardinals during their initial three years in the NFL. On the field, the Bears (8–1) and the Cardinals (6–2) both harbored hopes of catching undefeated Canton (7–0–2) for the league championship as the 1922 campaign slipped into its final three weeks. And the simmering rivalry between the two Chicago teams was about to become even more intense…

A Fist Flew, Then a Couple More

Newly acquired tackle Ed Healey did not start for the Bears in the Cardinals game, but his recent acquisition was noted by the local press: "The two rivals are well fortified with subs, the Bears recently being the first 'pro' eleven on record to purchase a player from another team. The man in question is Healey, the great 1919 Dartmouth tackle, who was secured from Rock Island."[18] Although Healey was not on the field at the beginning of the contest, he was certainly out there at the end and likely enjoyed the bizarre activity that was about to take place on the nearly frozen Comiskey Park gridiron.

As the two clubs battled after the late-morning kickoff, neither team was able to initiate any type of offensive success. Only a 20-yard dropkick field goal by Paddy Driscoll of the Cardinals late in the second stanza solved the defensive stalemate: "Honors were even during the first period, when both machines resorted to the ancient and honorable line-bucking system to gain yardage, but in the second quarter the Cardinals uncorked their aerial offensive and proceeded to pile up distance…. The half ended with the count standing 3 to 0 in favor of the Cardinals. In the third period, the Bears, enraged by the drop kick registered by Driscoll in the second quarter when he dropped back to the twenty-yard line and booted a perfect drop kick for the three points that spelled victory, resorted to rough measures."[19]

Let's set the stage. Midway through the third quarter, the reliable Driscoll raced around his left end but was met by the staunch defense of George Halas and Joey Sternaman (brother of Dutch Sternaman). In what might be termed unnecessary roughness to the extreme, the pair of Bears stood Driscoll up and then unceremoniously body-slammed him (headfirst) into the unforgiving Comiskey Park turf. The groggy Driscoll shook off the effects of the rambunctious tackle and came up swinging, immediately decking the diminutive 5–6 Sternaman and sending him to the ground with an apparent knockout. He then turned to take on the taller Halas when all bedlam broke loose on the field as described by the *Herald* newspaper: "In less than nothing after Driscoll had leaped to his feet, mad as a hatter, players of both teams and the officials rushed up. A fist flew, then a couple more. Out of the dugouts and over the low fence in front of the boxes came fully a hundred excited fans eager to get a closer view of the scene. Three or four policemen went with them."[20]

By this time, mayhem had ensued on the field as opposing players, fans, and police were all involved in the fracas. With flimsy leather helmets, no faceguards, and less-than-ample padding, the players merged into a conflagration around the original participants tossing punches, pulling off adversaries, and screaming invectives at their opponents. Briefly, order was restored, until the officials announced that only Driscoll had been tossed from the game for his role in the fisticuffs. Enraged, Driscoll returned to the fray along with dozens of other fans, and the short interlude of peace erupted again into a mob scene for several more minutes.

George Halas carefully recalled the incident in his autobiography:

> What happened was this: Paddy Driscoll made a good run, reaching our 20. Joe Sternaman and I thought that must not be allowed to happen again. On the next play, Driscoll set off with the ball. Joey and I brought him down with all the force we could muster, which was

considerable. Paddy was down but not out. He pulled himself to his feet, wobbled toward Joey and started pummeling him with both fists. That is when the thugs came out. So did reserve players. So did fans from both stands. The police came out, too, wielding sticks and blowing whistles and shouting. In time, in quite a time, order was restored. The referee ordered Paddy to leave the field for slugging Joey, and that started the disagreement all over again.[21]

Only one other personal oral account remains from that on-field battle, that being from the newly acquired Ed Healey, who shared his still-vivid observations many years later. After being with the Bears for only a few days, Healey was instantly exposed to the burgeoning rivalry between the Bears, the Cardinals, and their respective fans. It was clearly like nothing he had previously experienced in the world of pro football. Chicago, it appeared, presented its own grand style of fan support when fights broke out between the teams:

> I played ... on Thanksgiving Day against the Chicago Cardinals and learned a lot about Chicago and the atmosphere that existed there.... And then, holy cow! Out from the Cardinal bench poured a group of men with rods [guns] on! They were going out there to protect their idol, Paddy Driscoll. As you may recall, the vogue at that time was that all the gangsters in the world were functioning in Chicago. You had Ragen's Colts from back in the yards. You had the O'Donnell crowd. You had the Al Capone crowd.... So here came that bunch of South Side rooters, flowing out from the bench with rods on. Immediately I stopped in my tracks. I stood there in amazement. All I could think of was that a couple of days before, I'd signed up for a hundred bucks, and now I'm out here liable to be killed![22]

While Healey appeared to profess his innocence in the brawl, Halas offered quite a different interpretation: "In truth, Healey did not just stand there, hands and eyes in prayer position. No indeed. He was punching away with his teammates."[23]

In the ensuing round of hostilities, both Halas and Joey Sternaman were ejected, although Halas had offered a peace pipe

Ed Healey was considered the first "free agent" in NFL history when he joined the Chicago Bears in 1922. Healey managed to participate in the infamous 1922 brawl between the Bears and the Cardinals that was broken up by police and perhaps a few local gangsters (courtesy Pro Football Hall of Fame, Dutch Sternaman Collection).

to the referees by suggesting that Driscoll be allowed to continue his participation. Apparently, that olive branch was not accepted, and the festivities continued, as reported by the *Chicago Daily News*: "A battle royal was in the process of getting under way when the police reached the scene. In the argument that followed, Driscoll's banishment, Halas and Sternaman became heated and after Halas had been knocked down both he and Sternaman were sent off the field."[24] Rumors abounded for years after the game that Halas was pushed to the ground and straddled by an inquisitive fan who just happened to hold a pistol to Halas's head!

All good things must come to an end, and the biggest brawl game in the early history of the NFL finally concluded with the Cardinals securing a very tough 6–0 victory with the final three points coming from the foot of Ralph Horween. In the aftermath of the extremely physical encounter, the management of both teams quickly assessed the possibility of another strong crowd and agreed to a rematch on December 10. The NFL's oldest rivalry was now in full gear and the infamous 1922 Thanksgiving Day brawl was just the first of what would be many physical confrontations between the two clubs. As for Halas, he ironically noted in his autobiography that "We lost 6–0. But everybody had a good time."[25]

Halas Has Some Bumps

By Saturday, December 2, 1922, plans were in place for the rematch scheduled for December 10: "Negotiations indicated that the Cardinals and Bears, not satisfied with a punishing game and two fights, which ended in victory for the Cardinals 6 to 0, Thanksgiving Day, will meet again on December 10 at the Cubs Park. Both Bears and Cardinals emerged from their fierce battle for the city championship undamaged, save in feelings. Driscoll has a split lip and Halas some bumps."[26]

On Sunday, December 3, the Bears (9–2) rebounded with a 22–0 win over the Toledo Maroons while the Cardinals (7–3) were upset 7–3 by the Dayton Triangles. Both squads still trailed the undefeated Canton Bulldogs (9–0–2) in the league title chase heading into the final week of the season. Just prior to the Bears-Cardinals clash, Halas received some disturbing news when it was learned that both he and Dutch Sternaman were being sued by former partner Bill Harley. The litigation was prompted by the Harley brothers seeking revenue from their perceived still-extant ownership agreement with the Bears as well as for the emotional duress inflicted upon Chic Harley during the 1921 campaign. Media coverage included reports of specific acts of manipulation by Bears managers: "William Harley, former business manager of the Staley football team, has brought an action in the Superior Court in behalf of himself and his brother [Chic] to recover one-half of the receipts of the present Bears season…. Harley alleges that the name of the team was changed; that he was never consulted upon any matter of management, and was gradually eased out of the club, which has this year been a tremendous money maker…. The Harley brothers, in a hearing in equity, seek to force a full accounting of the Bears' season and the allotment of their share of the proceeds as partners."[27]

Bill Harley also indicated that the emotional difficulties suffered recently by his brother, Chic, who was now receiving medical attention in a sanitarium, were the result of ill treatment by the Bears' owners in 1921. Even Chris O'Brien was mentioned in the discussion, as reported by the *"Rock Island Argus"*: Harley gives dates and instances in which Halas and Sternaman slowly brought about his ousting and asserts that in a final move Halas and Sternaman succeeded in getting Chris O'Brien of the Cardinals to sign their application for a transfer. This was necessary in order to permit them to take over the club and get rid of Harley, it appears, and in exchange for this favor they promised to play the Cardinals on Thanksgiving Day. This was the game played on Thanksgiving after O'Brien had used every possible means to keep Halas and Sternaman from getting out of their agreement."[28]

While this case would work its way through the courts for two more years, it was eventually dismissed, as mentioned in the previous chapter. However, with the newly filed lawsuit fresh in everyone's mind, the Cardinals and the Bears would meet for one final time in 1922 on December 10 at Cubs Park. Unfortunately, the management of the Chicago Cubs was forced to close the facility early in December due to needed excavation work on the field prior to the hard freeze of winter. The rematch would naturally be moved back to Comiskey…

Once again, it was a tight affair with the Cardinals shutting down the visitors 9–0 before another strong crowd of 12,000. In a bit of irony, Paddy Driscoll, the man whom Halas wanted so desperately on his team that he offered him an ownership deal, kicked all three field goals for the winners. "Paddy was very much in evidence, making a field goal in each of the first three quarters."[29]

With the victory, the Cardinals captured both wins against their rivals in 1922, taming the ambitions of the Bears, who were seeking to snare a second straight crown. On that same day, Canton disposed of Toledo 18–0 to finish undefeated for the year with a 10–0–2 mark. The Bears settled into second place (9–3) while the Cardinals eased into third with an 8–3 record. More important, the two victories over the Bears by O'Brien's crew enabled the Cardinals to clearly capture the mythical "city championship." In a sense, justice was served for O'Brien after the unsuccessful raid by Halas on the kingpin of the Cards' roster, Paddy Driscoll. But now, could O'Brien take that next step and grab an NFL title? To do so, he would need to retain the services of the inimitable Driscoll and avoid the financial woes that were threatening many of the members of the National Football League.

Nine

The Grange Effect

"Today brings a new era to professional football."
—*Chicago Tribune*, November 25, 1925

In the fall of 1923, a virtually unknown halfback by the name of Harold Grange showed up for varsity football practice at the University of Illinois. Nicknamed "Red" due to his colorful locks of hair as a child, Grange was a former high school track champion and a dominating rusher at Wheaton High School west of Chicago. He was impressive during his tenure with the Illini freshmen team in 1922, and then broke out quickly in his first varsity game in 1923. In the opener against Nebraska, the elusive Grange was unstoppable in leading Illinois to a solid 24–7 victory over the visitors. "It was Grange's superb open field running and clean handling of the ball that enabled him to make three touchdowns," reported Walter Eckersall of the *Chicago Tribune*.[1] Grange was on the road to stardom with that opening performance, which would eventually see him named to three straight All-American teams from 1923 to 1925. Illinois would finish the 1923 season undefeated with an 8–0 record, and with a valid claim to the national championship. The future seemed limitless for both Grange and the University of Illinois!

By the time he was a senior in 1925, Grange was perhaps the best-known athlete in the country, rubbing virtual shoulders with baseball's Babe Ruth and boxer Jack Dempsey. He was also the most highly sought pro football prospect in the land and when he signed a groundbreaking contract with the Chicago Bears, he was about to change the landscape of pro football forever. With Grange in the mix, attendance at Bears games exploded and pro football, the ugly stepchild of the sports world, was suddenly front-page news. While there have been many books on the life and career of Red Grange, the most comprehensive is author Chris Willis's effort, *Red Grange: The Life and Legacy of the NFL's First Superstar*. Willis explained why the addition of Grange was such a boost for the still-struggling National Football League:

> The signing of Red Grange in 1925 was important to the NFL for a few reasons. One, Grange was the best player in college football at that time, maybe the best ever, as college football was more popular than professional football. Most All-Americans bypassed playing pro football because of its reputation, so Grange deciding to play in the NFL gave the sport a shot in the arm. Second, Grange's signing with the Chicago Bears gave the NFL much-needed exposure. In an era where the public got their news through newspapers, radio, and newsreels, Grange

playing in the NFL made front-page headlines, broadcasted on radio and highlights shown in movie theaters. This mass-media exposure had never been seen for professional football or the NFL, so that's why his signing is very important in NFL history.[2]

Yet, the signing of Grange was not greeted with open arms and unbridled enthusiasm by all. With the NFL still grappling with seeds of discontent among college coaches, the signing of Grange provoked the opening of some wounds between the college and professional football interests. Grange joined the Bears immediately after his final collegiate game, which seemed like a stinging slap in the face to college coaches who had been assured previously by the NFL that the pros would not touch any player while he was still in college. Obviously, the recruitment of Grange was done before he graduated but *after* his football eligibility was concluded at the University of Illinois. It was a fine line that Chicago Bears owner George Halas had crossed with his interpretation that the addition of Grange was both legal and logical. The collegiate world disagreed and the NFL was now forced into a defensive mode to justify this decision. Ultimately, it would be another uphill battle for the professional interests.

If We Must Fight, We Will Fight

Back in 1921, the league had decreed that the employment of college players by its member clubs was prohibited. It was hoped that this would help silence the critics of the professional game. Even the *Staley Fellowship Journal* weighed in on this decision at the time: "While pro football will in all probability never be given much welcome by the college and university heads they will certainly appreciate the attitude of the pro leaders on this subject which in the past has been a source of much worry to them."[3]

And then, the newly minted Green Bay Packers went out and hired some college players and were promptly booted out of the league…

In 1922, the NFL attempted once more to underline its aversion to employing college players when the league president, Joe Carr, issued a statement intended to clearly delineate the NFL's position on "raiding" college athletes: "We are ready to enter an agreement with school authorities to stop any professional practices of college athletes until they have completed their studies. We would agree to bar a college star from playing with a team in our association until he had secured the release of his coach, if school officials would agree."[4]

Carr also refused to budge under the increasing consensus of the collegiate coaches that perhaps it would be best for all concerned if the pro game simply disappeared, saying: "We want to get along happily with the colleges, and we will go out of our way to do just this, but the colleges and their organizations do not need to think we are going to lay down and quit because they don't like us. We are in business to stay. Our game is clean and our principles are clean and above board. If we must fight, we will fight and we will fight hard."[5]

Any cooperative effort between the pros and the academic representatives was not in the imminent future. Instead, each circled the other warily, with the wildly embraced college game continuing to grow in popularity year after year while nearly all of the professional outlets continued to struggle financially. It was an interesting concept, since only professional football was targeted for revulsion as a reprehensible business while the matter of collegiate *baseball* players jumping to the major leagues after graduation was not questioned. Eventually, the legendary football coach Amos Alonzo Stagg from the University of Chicago steered his ship around and fired a blistering broadside at the professional game that rippled across the entire country. Stagg's emotional message hit the front pages in early November 1923 and left no doubt regarding his utter dislike for the professional game. His lengthy statement was addressed "to all friends of college football," and was picked up by dozens of newspapers around the country. In particular, two sentences summarized the ire of Coach Stagg:

> To patronize Sunday professional football games is to cooperate with forces which are destructive of the finest elements of interscholastic and intercollegiate football and to add to the heavy burden of the schools and colleges in preserving it in its ennobling worth.
>
> If you believe in preserving inter scholastic and intercollegiate football for the upbuilding of the present and future generations of clean, healthy, right minded and patriotic citizens, you will not lend your assistance to any of the forces which are helping to destroy it.[6]

On the other side of the verbal battle, Joe Carr was unperturbed and not reluctant to once again present his side of the discussion. Carefully addressing the key points in Stagg's diatribe, Carr confidently stated: "It is hardly fair to cast suspicion on the many creditable men who are leading teams as well as the attempt to discredit the many former college stars of the gridiron, as the pick and flower of the players of the last few years are to be found in the lineups of the various teams now playing post-graduate football. It is gratifying to know that the view [Stagg's] is not shared by all college men for there are many who feel that the postgraduate or professional game when properly conducted is an asset rather than a menace to the college branch of the sport."[7]

While there would be no quick solution to the "professional" situation in football, the *Green Bay Press-Gazette* proved to be an unabashed supporter of Carr. The newspaper first published an editorial from the *Ohio State Journal* that plainly stated: "The popularity of college football does not seem to be endangered by professional football (there appears to be lively demand for both)," then followed with its own opinion: "Coach Stagg sure kicked over a hornet's nest when he launched his attack on pro football. One thing has led to another and the sport world is sizzling with charges and counter charges. Personalities have cropped out rather lively in the argument and the end is not yet in sight. President Carr came back at Stagg point blank. His defense of pro football was superb. The league president bowled over Stagg's arguments one after another…. He has guided the sport successfully out of the infant period and we don't think that anything Stagg says will undermine the firm foundation."[8]

Not Knowingly Permit Any College Student to Play

While the NFL prepared for its 1923 season in late September, Chris O'Brien and George Halas were engaged in a sports battle of a different sort in Chicago:

baseball. During the summer "off-season" from football in 1923, O'Brien returned to the diamond with the Normals, no longer playing but managing the club. Halas was the starting right fielder for the Logan Squares from the North Side. In addition, Paddy Driscoll held down second base for the Pyotts, another of the exceptional semipro teams in the city. It was during this time that the lawsuit between the Harley brothers and Halas was still active in the court system. Yet Halas played for the Logan Squares, the previous affiliation for Bill Harley, while Harley performed as the center fielder for the Normals.[9] Based on game box scores from the time, the football representatives in question continued their baseball season right up until the start of the 1923 NFL grid campaign on September 30.

On the South Side prior to the beginning of the 1923 schedule, Chris O'Brien was negotiating with the Chicago White Sox to use Comiskey Park as the team's home field, while Halas was in the second year of a three-year agreement to utilize Cubs Park on the North Side. The agreement, reached by the Bears with William Veeck of the Chicago Cubs, allowed the team to use the facility from October 1922 through January 1, 1925. In an interesting sidelight, the contract included the following verbiage intended to help negate the use of college players in any game staged at Cubs Park: "Second party [the Bears] agrees that such games will be played by professional football players and that it will not knowingly permit any person who is a student at any college and who represents or has represented such a college upon its football team, to appear in any football game or games in which it may conduct at said Park during the periods covered by this agreement."[10]

While the contract is confusing in its language, since it also seems to prohibit any *former* college player, it does establish some parameters regarding player eligibility that the league would certainly endorse. Getting to the meat of the contract, the Bears could use the field for both practice and games during the last quarter of each year, as long as the Cubs baseball team was not involved in postseason activity. Overall, the price for the use of Cubs Park was favorable to Halas: "20% of the gross sum received for admission fees ... however, that if such gross receipts amount to less than Ten Thousand Dollars ($10,000) for any particular game, then the said first party [Cubs] shall be paid for such game only Fifteen per cent (15%) of the gross sum."[11] Not a bad deal for Halas. In case of awful weather, or simply poor attendance, he was protected from financial disaster since he would pay only a portion of the gate, not a fixed figure of $5,000 per game, for example. However, without solid attendance, achieving a profit would be difficult for any pro football team. Aside from the field rental, Halas still needed to meet other obligations, such as for salaries and equipment. One of the largest accounts on the expenditure side was the compensation for both Halas and Sternaman. According to documents found in the Sternaman collection, Halas and Sternaman each received $1,300 in salary for playing in 1922. In addition, both earned $2,000 apiece as officers of the corporation in 1922 and again in 1923. On September 17, 1923, Sternaman outlined the game salaries for Bears players in 1923. At the top of the list was George Trafton at $90 per game, followed by such key individuals as Hugh Blacklock ($85), Ed Healey ($75), Hunk Anderson ($75), and Ralph Scott ($85). At the bottom end was rookie Gus Fetz, earning $50 per contest.[12]

In 1924, Dutch Sternaman created another handwritten report on September 12, which indicated that players such as Scott ($85), Healey ($75), and Anderson ($75) did not receive a raise from the previous season and may even have earned a bit less. Sternaman left a small note attached to his report, simply stating "First game free."[13] Whether this meant that the players provided their services at no charge, or indicated something completely different, such was the mysterious accounting system of the 1924 Chicago Bears! Well before the age of computers and software, Dutch kept the books for the Bears by hand.

Mouthful of Mud

On the South Side, Paddy Driscoll stepped aside as the coach of the Chicago Cardinals in favor of Arnie Horween. Oddly enough, the game programs for the Cardinals in 1923 included photos of both Arnie and his brother Ralph, still under their pseudonym of McMahon. Team manager Chris O'Brien was excited about the Cards' prospects as he added several quality players to supplement a talented group of veterans led by Driscoll, the Horween brothers, big tackle Fred Gillies, end Eddie Anderson, and scrappy guard Clyde Zoia. A graduate of Notre Dame, where he played under legendary coaches Jesse Harper and Knute Rockne, Zoia was the antithesis of the giant linemen so common in 21st-century NFL ranks.

Zoia's prominence on the gridiron might be considered incredible compared with today's standards. Listed at just 5'7" tall and weighing a mere 175 pounds, Zoia was not a fleet-footed halfback, but rather a solid lineman for the Cardinals from 1920 through 1923. Zoia was a mainstay at either guard or center, cleverly and discreetly pushing around opponents weighing 50 to 100 pounds more. Even more telling about Zoia's devotion to the team was the fact that he did not live in the same South Side neighborhood around Normal Park as did most of Chris O'Brien's players. Rather, he commuted approximately 70 miles one way for practices twice each week from Woodstock, Illinois, and then returned to join the Cardinals wherever the Sunday game would be held. In addition, he worked as many as six days a week at his job in Woodstock (eventually joining the police force) while rarely, if ever, missing any of his football commitments. He was, by far, the smallest member of the Chicago Cardinals line during that time. His daughter, Mary Zoia Zentner, recalled her father and his reaction when people discovered he was a former NFL player, despite his stature: "He was a humble man. When he was recognized as being a former football player, he would often be asked, 'Were you big enough to survive in the trenches?' And he would say, 'Well, I guess so … here I am!'"

Since the NFL was still in its infancy in the early 1920s, in later life, Zoia was more often remembered for his career at the University of Notre Dame rather than for his time served with the Cardinals, according to Mary Zoia Zentner: "He rarely mentioned playing for the Cardinals, but he was an ardent follower of Notre Dame football because of his time playing under coach Knute Rockne. He was recognized mostly for his Notre Dame career both in his hometown of Woodstock, Illinois, and when he was part of a Notre Dame traveling alumni group as they attended road games throughout the country. On the train, it was a common time to visit with fans of Notre Dame, but also many recognized the fact that he played with the Cardinals in the early 1920s."[14]

Backing up Clyde Zoia in 1923 were newcomers in the backfield Johnny Mohardt and Roger Kiley from Notre Dame, former Englewood prep star Art Folz, and Illinois fullback Jack Crangle. The 1923 game programs sold by the Cardinals leaned heavily on the team's overall experience: "As you will note, these same men played an important part in the Cardinals double win over the Chicago Bears in 1922."[15]

In 1923, the Cardinals enjoyed a tremendous start by winning their first five games, including a 60-0 romp over the Rochester Jeffersons on October 7. The offensive total for the Cardinals would stand as the highest in team history until a 63-35 rout of the New York Giants in 1948. Rochester was managed by Leo Lyons, an unsung hero of the early NFL. Lyons maintained journals and his comments are quite insightful. John Steffenhagen, his great-grandson, has retained the journals and shared information specific to the 1923 game with the Chicago Cardinals. Lyons wrote that the playing field at Normal Park was a "field half grass and dirt. Looked like a sandlot." Regarding the 60–0 loss to the Cardinals, Lyons noted: "Couldn't stop Driscoll. Outplayed badly." Finally, Lyons described a disturbance that temporarily halted the game: "Driscoll [was] knocked out of bounds into crowd. Think he killed a fan; fence did not fare well! The umpire's white shirt was red with blood from fan. I think someone fired a gun at one of the houses overlooking the field—play stopped!"[16]

Driscoll was on a personal roll. Aside from the 27 points he compiled in the Rochester game, the clever halfback and kicker tallied all of his team's points in wins over Buffalo (3–0), Akron (19–0), Minneapolis (9–0), and Dayton (13–3). Now 5–0, the Cardinals entertained the equally undefeated Canton Bulldogs on November 4, 1923, to determine the frontrunner in the bloated 20-team NFL. It was a contest that had been eagerly awaited for some time: "Unless some of the weaker teams begin reconstructing soon, the race in the Professional Football League promises to become a lopsided affair. Canton [5–0], the Chicago Cardinals [5–0] and Duluth [4–0] continue to show the class of the organization. Canton, last year's champion, and the Cardinals are playing the most consistent football. Unless there is an upset in form, these two teams promise to fight it for the championship."[17]

By now, the Cardinals were playing their home games at Comiskey Park, and a nice audience of 6,000 showed up for the battle of the unbeatens. Driscoll continued his scoring dominance for the Cardinals when he was successful on a 47-yard dropkick field goal in the opening period. That was the only score of the game for the hosts as Canton pushed across the winning touchdown in the final stanza to capture a 7–3 victory and remain in first place in the league.

On the North Side, only 1,000 fans braved the rain to watch the Bears (3–2) bully the winless (0–5) Oorang Indians 26–0. The visitors, from tiny LaRue, Ohio, played all of their games on the road. Composed primarily of Native Americans, the team was the brainchild of Walter Lingo and served to help market Lingo's dog kennels in LaRue. The team was led by Jim Thorpe, whose presence provided George Halas with one of the greatest moments of his own playing career, as reported in the *Chicago Tribune*:

The big thriller of the game was provided by George Halas, the Bears' right end. In the second period, the Indians by means of some forward passing, had the ball on the home team's one-yard line. Long Time Sleeping, the redskin center, then dozed off and made a bad pass. Halas tore in, scooped up the loose pigskin on the three-yard line, and raced down the field all the way to the Oorangs' goal. Thorpe was on Halas' heels all the way, but the ex-Illini kept just out of the one-time Carlisle star's reach. Finally, Thorpe, realizing his speed isn't what it used to be, made a dive for the moving target, but his dive got him nothing more than a mouthful of mud, and Halas went merrily, but by this time wearily, on his way over the goal line.[18]

The big 98-yard fumble return by Halas established an NFL record that stood until Oakland's Jack Tatum returned a botched fumble 104 yards for a score in 1972. Now with a 4–2 record, the Bears won three more times in November to move into the battle with the Cardinals on Thanksgiving Day, November 29, on a five-game winning streak that improved the team's mark to 7–2. After the hot start to the season, the Cardinals limped into the Bears contest with the same 7–2 ledger after being upset by the Racine (Wisconsin) Legion 10–4 a week earlier. Without the injured Paddy Driscoll, the Cards knocked off Hammond 6–0 and then, with Driscoll returning, shut out Duluth 10–0. Since Canton had yet to be defeated, the two Chicago teams would be fighting for second-place honors in the championship race. While neither club was pleased with the option of praying for Canton to lose some games (the Bulldogs never did), at the very least the somewhat glittering city championship was still up for grabs. The Cardinals had won the previous two meetings and looked to maintain that advantage. In addition, the persistent efforts by both organizations in begging the local media for coverage seemed to have worked as several Chicago newspapers filed daily updates leading up to the contest: "The south siders expect a stormy session with the lads from the north side, but, despite the crippled condition of the Cardinals, they are banking on another victory. Since the two elevens have been in action, they have played five times, the Cardinals scoring three victories and the north siders one, while another battle terminated in a tie."[19]

In a bit of trivia, the two teams were in the midst of an unusual scoring pattern in their games. Beginning with the second game played in 1920, in each game played between the two through the final match in 1929, covering 17 games, one of the two teams would always fail to score! Such was the case in 1923, when the Bears squeezed out a 3–0 win behind Dutch Sternaman's 30-yard field goal in the first quarter.

In various game reports, the crowd was announced as somewhere between 12,000 and 14,000, making it the best-attended pro game in Chicago up to that point. Attendance figures were always murky in the early years of the league, but the availability of the Sternaman collection has now added a more definitive, and accurate, depth to the study of that activity. In a letter from M. Donahue, assistant secretary of the Chicago Cubs to the Bears, the total attendance for the game was listed as 13,172. Of that number, 3,802 were box seats, 7,271 were general admission tickets, and 1,965 fans were in the bleachers. Finally, 134 children were counted in the number, with total gate receipts of $20,602.[20]

With the victory over the Cardinals, the Bears claimed the city championship in a game that was bereft of fistfights, gouging, kicking, or other common practices seen in previous battles between the two teams. In fact, the *Decatur Herald* accused the adversaries of participating in a "hard fought, but cleanly played battle."[21] Quite unusual for the Bears and the Cardinals! Joey Sternaman, brother of Dutch, was back with the Bears for this game after Halas purchased his contract from Duluth. After being one of the instigators in the all-out brawl between the two teams in 1922, Joey Sternaman would soon grab a piece of the ownership of the Bears and almost as quickly desert the team in 1926 for what he envisioned would be much greener financial pastures.

Following the close loss to the Bears, the Cardinals dropped the Oorang Indians 22–19 and then surprisingly fell to the Milwaukee Badgers 14–12 to finish 8–4, good for only sixth place in the NFL. Paddy Driscoll missed both of the last two contests with an illness. Milwaukee also caught the Bears off guard, tying the Halas men 0–0, before Chicago rolled over Rock Island 29–7 in the final game of the season. Undefeated Canton (11–0–1) successfully defended its crown in 1923, edging out the Bears (9–2–1).

Something That Had Not Been Seen in Football Before

In Champaign, Illinois, the blossoming career of Red Grange was taking hold in 1923 for the University of Illinois, resulting in a wave of national acclaim: "Speaking of much-talked of footballers, Grange of Illinois, gets the chocolate coated pigskin. The pride of Urbana is being featured by every pigskin writer in the country. His remarkable performances on the chalk-marked field ... despite the fact that he is only a sophomore, we think he is headed for an All-American post."[22]

For the season, Grange scampered for 723 yards in just seven games and added 12 touchdowns for the consensus national champion (8–0) Illini. But the best was yet to come for the All-American.

On October 18, 1924, the legend of Red Grange became surreal. In a game against Michigan that also marked the opening of the new Memorial Stadium at Illinois, Grange went nuts! Scoring four times in the opening quarter alone, Grange pushed Illinois past the Wolverines 39–14 in a stunning performance:

> Grange had torn Michigan to pieces before the game had gone more than fifteen seconds because he received the first kickoff and from his own five-yard line ran and dodged and tore his way 95 yards for a touchdown. Right then and there, Michigan knew it was up against something it hadn't seen in football before. Three more times in that first period Grange got loose for long runs for touchdowns. His second one came after about five minutes of play and was 67 yards in length. The joyful Illini rooters were hardly through cheering that thrilling play before the red-headed Wheaton lad got loose again for another 56 yards in length, and before the quarter was ended, he took the ball on the Michigan 44-yard line and dashed through the whole team for a fourth touchdown.[23]

It didn't hurt Grange's reputation that a record crowd of over 67,000 was in attendance or that WGN Radio in Chicago broadcast the game to a national audience. With the four quick scores, Grange led Illinois to a 27–0 first-quarter advantage, which was shocking to both friend and foe alike. After all, Michigan arrived with a 20-game unbeaten streak (since 1921) and a stout defense that had allowed just three touchdowns in the last two years. Grange obliterated all of that in just 12 minutes of play. He would go on to add one more rushing touchdown from 11 yards out and then tossed a 20-yard passing score in the easy Illinois win. If any football follower in the country did not know of Grange before the Michigan explosion, they would now. "He stamped himself as one of the greatest football stars of all time, east or west."[24]

Grange became the subject of countless interviews and speculation about himself as both a football player and a human being. Readers would learn what classes he took in school, what he did in the off-season (hauling ice locally as the "Wheaton Ice Man"), and about his devotion to his family and his privacy. A nationally syndicated feature article by Margaret Dale appeared in mid–November 1924 around the country and provided an unusual insight into the home life of the Grange family in Wheaton, Illinois, including his widowed father, Lyle, who brought up Red and his brother, Garland. Focusing on Red's humility, Lyle told Margaret Dale, and the world, what it was like living with a superstar: "Lyle Grange likes nothing more than to talk about his boy. As the father of the big football hero of the age dusted off a chair for the writer, he pointed with pride to the four walls of the little bachelor living room. Clippings from dozens of newspapers and cuts of the college right halfback in action did service where wall paper had once done its duty. 'I pasted the clippings there,' said Mr. Grange. 'My son, Harold, that is 'Red' wouldn't have done it. He's too modest. He doesn't like all this adulation anyway.... But I like them where they are. They're finer than paintings to me.'"[25]

One effect of Grange's big day against Michigan was that it pushed the preview article on the first Bears-Cardinals game of the 1924 season to the back pages of the sports section, but it also prompted a spark of interest in the football-focused mind of George Halas. In November 1924, Halas decided to journey back to his alma mater for a personal look at Grange. He wrote in his autobiography: "One Saturday in November of 1924 [friend] Ralph Brizzolara and I decided to drive down to the University of Illinois to see Red run.... It is strange that I don't remember the game. Perhaps I was living in my own dreams. I assume Illinois won. We had seen the 'Galloping Ghost' in the flesh. As an owner, manager, coach and player, I was determined to have Red on the Bears. But how? For a year, I pondered. I wrote Grange a couple of letters, but received no reply. I spoke to him on the phone to no avail."[26]

The wait for Grange would continue. Grange would still need to complete two years of college football and then graduate from Illinois before the professional interests could sign him to a contract for the 1926 season. That is, if he was ready to play professional football. Halas added: "The pressures on Red were terrible. He did not know what to do. His father said he hoped Red would do something other than professional football. Fielding Yost said the same thing but [writer] Westbrook Pegler advised: 'Grange may bring a butcher shop many books of clippings but after he has exhibited them all, the butcher will say, 'The chops are still 68 cents.'"[27]

We Had Two Paydays Per Season

In comparison with the huge crowds attending college games, the professional contests were still struggling for recognition in 1924. Since the Bears and Cardinals seemed to attract better-than-average attendees to their contest, it was a wise move to schedule a pair of encounters in 1924 between the two rivals. Like the Bears and other NFL teams, the Cardinals were not awash in cash. Left-handed quarterback Art Folz played just one season as a freshman at the University of Chicago before enjoying a three-year career with the Cardinals from 1923 to 1925. Later in life, he recalled that the players received two checks per season based upon their per-game rate: "What I most remember is that we usually had two pay days a season. The first one was after the first game against the Bears, the next one after the rematch. But Chris O'Brien always came up with the checks. My first one was for $50, but later I made $75 [per game]. Par for an All-American lineman in my years with the Cards was $125."[28]

The statement by Folz certainly made sense, since the games with the Bears always attracted the most attendees each season. As an example, the Cardinals hosted the Green Bay Packers on October 5, 1924, before only 2,800 fans. For the first outing of the 1924 season between the Bears and the Cardinals on October 19, the Cardinals (3–0) were perched in first place while the Bears were enduring some early season struggles with a record of 0–1–2. Still, the gate at Cubs Park welcomed 20,000 attendees, the biggest crowd of the season to see the professionals in action. This battle took place a day after the incredible performance by Red Grange against Michigan, but in comparison, the pro game was lacking in the offensive firepower of Grange and his cohorts. The contest was billed as a battle of kickers by the local press: "In former years field goals have decided most of the games between these hot rivals. Paddy Driscoll is looked upon as the best drop kicker in the country. The Bears have two accurate goal kickers in Dutch Sternaman and his brother, Joe. Dutch specializes at place kicks and Joe at drop kicks."[29]

As predicted, the contest did come down to a war between dropkickers. Joey Sternaman connected from the 7- and the 18-, while Driscoll missed from the 25- and the 40-yard lines as the Bears escaped with a 6–0 victory. Once again, as had become customary, there was a shutout involved. This trend continued on Thanksgiving Day (November 27, 1924) when the crosstown competition was renewed at Comiskey Park. With the two clubs now meeting for the fifth season, each had grabbed three victories while one clash ended in a draw. Chris O'Brien scheduled a late-morning kickoff for a special reason: "The kickoff is listed for 11 o'clock, giving the fans plenty of time to get home and consume the turkey. There is much rivalry not only between the teams, but between the rooters of the north and south sides in this game."[30]

Entering the game, the Bears had rebounded to stand with a 4–1–4 record while the slumping Cardinals now sat on a 5–3–1 mark. Tie games still did not count in the official standings, which allowed the Bears to keep pace with the Cleveland Bulldogs (6–1–1) and the Frankford Yellow Jackets (9–2–1) as of November 23, 1924. A win over the Cardinals was critical for the Bears if Halas still hoped to stake a claim for the NFL title. Cleveland ended its season on Thanksgiving by clobbering Milwaukee 53–10 to finish 7–1–1, including an early season 16–14 win over the Bears.

That same day, the Bears (5–1–4) rolled over the Cardinals 21–0 to claim the city championship once again. In an unusual sidebar, the *Decatur Daily Review* claimed that Bears punter Frank Hanny enjoyed the finest day a punter ever experienced in the NFL: "It is doubtful if rooters had ever seen a 100-yard and a 92-yard punt on the same day, such as Hanny served to them. The roll after the ball struck the turf was included in each case."[31] While Hanny's name does not appear in the NFL record books for these voluminous kicks, even with the revised calculations used today to establish punting yardage, Mr. Hanny experienced a very successful afternoon! Three days later on November 30, Halas wrapped up his season (or so it appeared) by stopping the Milwaukee Badgers 31–14. Only about 1,000 fans attended the game, but one of those hardy individuals braving the cold weather was none other than Red Grange of Illinois. Grange had just completed his junior year at Illinois by being named an All-American for the second straight year while leading his club to a 6–1–1 record. Grange rushed for 743 yards and also passed for another 433 yards in just six games. It would not be his last visit to Cubs Park.

The victory over Milwaukee allowed the Bears to focus on still possibly grabbing the league title. However, at the league meeting in Chicago the previous August, the NFL released a fairly stable schedule and also voted to conclude the season on November 30, 1924. There had been league-ending deadlines in the past that had been largely ignored, especially in 1921 when the Chicago Bears managed to squeeze in some extra games to pull even with Buffalo. In 1921, the league allowed the late victories by the Bears and then voted the team as the league champion. If the 1924 season truly ended on November 30, Cleveland (7–1–1) would be safely in first place ahead of the Bears (6–1–4) and Frankford (11–2–1). In a script that looked oddly familiar to 1921, the Bears continued playing into December, beginning with hosting Cleveland on December 7. Apparently, the Bulldogs assumed that this postseason collaboration was an exhibition game, while the Bears stressed that it was a battle for the NFL title (as did most newspapers around the country) and won a convincing 23–0 decision over Cleveland. For some reason, Halas then contracted for a back-breaking double-header, playing at Frankford in the Philadelphia area on December 13 (a 13–10 win) and then returning back to Chicago the next day to host Rock Island (a surprising 7–6 defeat).

With the season finally over, it was now left up to the league owners and management to wade through the various claims for the title among Cleveland, Frankford, and the Bears. In the end, Joe Carr strictly enforced the previously established deadline date of November 30, 1924, and ruled that any games played after that date would not be considered in the final NFL standings. Carr stated: "The pennant of the National Football League is awarded to Cleveland on the basis of games played before and concluding November 30, and that post-season games wherein agreements are made between teams to play for a championship are positively forbidden and to insure conformity to this resolution the season is extended to December 20 for the season of 1925."[32]

Carr had now firmly taken control of the NFL and demonstrated that he was not reluctant to enforce the rules. The league itself was still battling to attract fans, but it was more stable financially, and recognition by national media was slowly emerging. College football was continuing to thrill its patrons as exemplified by the raw enthusiasm for Grange and the mammoth crowds appearing on a weekly basis. Joe Carr was fine-tuning his NFL vehicle by increasing rosters, personally assigning game officials, compiling a schedule *before* the season, and implementing a final date on the schedule after which any arranged games simply would not be considered in the standings. His dream of establishing two conferences within the league and then having the winners meet in the postseason for the overall championship was still elusive, but on the drawing board.

The Sternaman documents revealed some interesting facts about the 1924 season, including an accurate financial accounting of Chicago Bears games. For example, when the Bears hosted the Columbus Tigers on November 9, 1924 (a 12–6 win), a formal contract offered Columbus two options for receiving payment as the visiting team. The agreement, signed September 27, 1924, guaranteed the Tigers a flat fee of $1,200 plus $100 for hotel and travel expenses. Or, perhaps feeling confident, Columbus could accept 40 percent of "the entire gross receipts after 15 percent thereof has been deducted for park rental, not including war tax, to be paid at the conclusion of the game." In this case, Columbus opted to accept the 40 percent risk. For this game, it paid off well for the visitors as Sternaman documented gate receipts of $8,419.40 based on 6,203 attendees. The rental fee (15 percent) off the top to the Cubs was $1,262.91. The Tigers then left with 40 percent of the remainder ($7,156.49), which turned out to be $2,862.60, or more than double the flat guarantee/expense rate originally suggested in the contract.[33] With the larger crowds supporting the Bears, it was an easy decision for visiting teams to accept the risk of the 40 percent fee, especially in the warmer months earlier in the season. For the final NFL game of the season against Milwaukee, barely 1,000 braved inclement weather and showed up for the contest. In this case, probably both teams suffered a financial setback but such were the risks of professional football in 1924.

Although the Cardinals had faded down the stretch to finish 5–4–1 in 1924, the team was drawing fair crowds to Comiskey Park. Chris O'Brien's club would remain competitive as long as the gifted Paddy Driscoll remained in the lineup. Chris, with help from his brother Pat, continued to manage the Cardinals as well as operate small businesses in the area, including O'Brien & O'Brien: Men's Furnishings and Sporting Goods located a bit east of Normal Park at 5152 South Halsted. Aside from gate receipts, early NFL teams relied on additional income from advertising placed in their game programs. This was one of the important allowances that George Halas retained in his original negotiations to use Cubs Park. The Cardinals did likewise and the surviving programs contain intriguing information about the teams. In the Cardinals program, advertisements bragged that NFL teams visiting Chicago to play the Cardinals stayed at the now long-gone Pershing Hotel at 64th and Cottage Grove, where one could find "Quality accommodations at notably reasonable rates. One person $2.50 to $5 a day." Printing needs for the team were handled by the Bentley, Murray & Company, managed by Joseph E. Bidwill, a family name soon to become synonymous with the Cardinals for decades.[34]

O'Brien Bids on Four Horsemen of Notre Dame

While Joe Carr and the NFL brass defined a firm date (December 20) to conclude the upcoming 1925 season, that seemingly minor decision would somehow backfire and prompt a controversy in professional football that still lingers today. During the off-season, Chris O'Brien and George Halas were busy with both football and other related activities. In 1925, a "draft" of promising players was still over a decade away, but the Bears and the Cardinals were anxious to fine-tune their rosters and add recent qualified college graduates. O'Brien was perhaps the most ambitious, publicly positioning the Cardinals to add the famous "Four Horsemen" of Notre Dame. These four backfield mates (Quarterback Harry Stuhldreher, halfback Jim Crowley, halfback Don Miller, and fullback Elmer Layden) led Notre Dame to the 1924 national championship with an undefeated (10–0) record. During their three seasons together, Notre Dame lost only two games. Along with Red Grange, they were the most widely acclaimed collegiate players during the 1924 season. While Halas continued to monitor Grange from afar, since Red still had one more season of eligibility remaining, O'Brien was quick to initiate the recruitment process for the four Notre Dame grads, but he wasn't alone in that effort: "From the gossip heard in the league meeting, every club in the league has put in a bid for the 'Four Horsemen' of Notre Dame. Rumor has it that Chris O'Brien of the Chicago Cardinals made a proposal just about tossing in his Normal Park if the Notre Dame stars would don Cardinals uniforms. But it is said O'Brien returned empty handed."[35]

With O'Brien spending part of his winter in early 1925 wooing the Notre Dame stars, he was also preparing for another stint as manager of the Normals baseball club in Chicago. Meanwhile, Halas returned to one of his first loves, basketball, and signed on with the Chicago Bruins, a newly organized squad that he also managed. Once again, Halas was in the forefront in pushing for more national recognition of the sport, much like he had experienced recently with the founding of the American Professional Football Association: "Some of the strongest eastern teams in the pro fold will tackle the Bruins at the Armory this winter. Manager George Halas is now corresponding with the famous Holly Majors of New York City."[36] In an effort to bolster his roster, Halas added his Bears teammates George Trafton and Laurie Walquist, along with Paddy Driscoll, to the Bruins squad. Halas then scheduled pro clubs from around the Midwest as well as from New York, Washington, D.C., and other locations to fill out the Bruins' schedule. In an action that nearly mirrored the founding of the original National Football League, Halas was a proponent of a new professional basketball circuit. Called the American Basketball League, the new organization was born on April 25, 1925, and perhaps not ironically, Joe Carr was hired to serve as its president.[37] Halas maintained his interest in the Chicago Bruins until 1933, eventually leasing the mammoth Chicago Stadium briefly for the team's home games. The team succumbed that same year. Halas later explained: "Hope led me into taking the team into the vast Chicago Stadium, giving up half of the gate as rental. It was a sporting success but a financial disaster."[38]

The American Basketball League temporarily disbanded in November 1931 for two seasons before reorganizing and returning in 1933, but without the Bruins. Halas shares very little about his pro basketball endeavors in his autobiography, noting mistakenly that he was involved with the Bruins for only three years. The responsibility of running two separate pro franchises certainly must have been difficult for him. It appears that the suffocating presence of the Great Depression in the early 1930s finally forced him to relinquish his basketball interests and focus primarily on football.

Once the 1925 basketball season concluded, Halas jumped right into the local baseball campaign with the Logan Squares, teaming with his friend/foe Bill Harley. But football was what Halas was all about in the fall of 1925 as he prepared the Bears for a tough season while also working quietly in the background to secure the services of Red Grange. The NFL welcomed four new teams to the league by adding representatives from New York; Detroit; Pottsville, Pennsylvania; and Providence, Rhode Island. The reincarnated Canton Bulldogs also reappeared after sitting out the 1924 campaign. President Joe Carr predicted that the league would enjoy a successful year, particularly with the strong teams expected in the Chicago area: "The Chicago Bears should be as strong as ever while Chris O'Brien aims to place a much better Chicago Cardinal team on the new field. [Ambrose] McGurk, the Milwaukee manager, is building his club anew. He has sold many of his stars but has a bunch of promising youngsters lined up."[39]

The soon-to-be controversial 1925 season would conclude with an enormous impact on each of these clubs.

Coaching Was More Casual Then

Although Chris O'Brien was unsuccessful in recruiting the Four Horsemen, he bolstered his line with Harvard grad Buck Evans and Purdue's Ralph Claypool. These moves represented an effort to plug a very big hole left by the loss of giant guard Garland "Gob" Buckeye. Generously listed as a 238-pound lineman (but thought to be around 260), Buckeye had just completed a successful season as a pitcher for the Cleveland Indians. Buckeye finished with a 13–8 record on the mound in 1925 and decided that the rigors of playing two professional sports were too challenging. In failing to return to the Cardinals after three seasons, Buckeye said: "I have won more games than I have lost and I do not imagine the management would want me to play football. So, I shall go back to my old job in the Illinois Trust company and keep in shape by playing handball a few times a week."[40] As usual, Paddy Driscoll was back to steer the Cardinals offense and was still considered one of the best backs in the business. Taking over the coaching duties from Arnold Horween in 1925 was former Cardinal and Notre Dame star Norman Barry. In another example of how different pro football was nearly 100 years ago, Barry was also the head coach at nearby De LaSalle High School in Chicago. How could one man handle the coaching of two teams, albeit at different levels, at the same time? Years later, Barry provided the answer: "It wasn't actually as difficult as it sounds. The Cardinals practiced only two or three times a week and I had able help from Dr. Eddie Anderson running practices, and Fred Gillies, who coached the line. I could spend part of my day at De LaSalle and then take care of the Cardinals duties. Coaching was more casual then."[41]

Driscoll's 50-yard return after intercepting a pass led the Cardinals to their first score in the season-opening 14–6 exhibition win over Harvey, Illinois, on September 20, 1925. In Rock Island that same day, the Bears were surprised when they were handcuffed in a scoreless draw against the Independents. A missed Joey Sternaman field goal as time expired kept the Bears from claiming an opening-day victory. In fact, the Bears struggled a bit in the early part of the season, managing just a 2–2–1 record before the first meeting of the year with the Cardinals on October 25. On the other side of town, the Cardinals were cruising with a 3–1 league mark prior to the Bears encounter with only a 10–6 upset loss to Hammond in the opening NFL game marring the club's record. Driscoll was superb as always, pacing the Cards on both sides of the ball and even kicking a league-record four field goals in a 19–9 win over the Columbus Tigers.

Bears Went Back to Their Side of the River

It turns out that the Bears had "eyes" on the Hammond game as Dutch Sternaman continued his practice of scouting future opponents while also hiring the same external resource to chart the offense of each Bears game when possible. For both responsibilities, Sternaman usually used the services of auto mechanic Monroe Hamilton of Oak Park, Illinois. Whether he charted or scouted, Hamilton would almost immediately provide Sternaman with a fairly detailed, handwritten report on the game he just witnessed for the lofty sum of $3 per game. In a letter to Sternaman in 1924, Hamilton outlined the agreement: "I am enclosing the charts of today's game. I presume that the rate will be the same as last year, $3.00 and 2 passes. As it will be difficult to see you between games will you mail the passes to me? I am enclosing an envelope stamped and addressed."[42]

Hamilton's scouting report on the Cardinals-Hammond game on September 27, 1925, revealed the Cards' basic offensive alignment (looking similar to a T-formation) while noting that the "Cardinals huddle, walk into line, start calling signals and pass [the] ball while calling—usually on fourth number." In another set, Hamilton points out that an unbalanced line "was used extensively with either Paddy or [Red] Dunn doing all passing and end runs." He carefully documented various plays run by the Cardinals and observed some that simply did not work. Eventually, he summarized the day by concluding: "The Cardinals out-played Hammond but Hammond got all the breaks."[43] Indeed, the 10–6 defeat was possible only when Driscoll muffed a punt on his own 15-yard line and the visitors took it in for the only touchdown of the game.

Following the 0–0 tie with Rock Island to open the season and a 14–10 loss to Green Bay on September 27, the Bears (0–1–1) hoped to even their ledger in Detroit on October 4, 1925. Although the contest concluded with still another scoreless deadlock, Dutch Sternaman's carefully crafted financial report revealed some interesting specifics regarding pro football travel during that era. For example, the Bears brought 16 players along for the excursion and each received a total of $3 for meals during the trip. Dutch also itemized individual expenses for the train tickets to Detroit and then for taxis to Navin Field (later Briggs Stadium). Hotel rooms were not part of the equation, since the Bears secured sleeping berths for the traveling party, which left the Dearborn station in Chicago on Saturday, October 3, at 11:25 p.m. The team then returned to Chicago immediately after the game. Still, direct expenses for the rail travel were $417.36, with some players being reimbursed later for travel to other locations. The Bears owners elected to secure a guarantee of $2,500 for the game, including $200 in cash, rather than the standard 40 percent of gross receipts (after a $1,000 park rental fee). With the cash portion of the guarantee, Halas paid the players their per diem of $3 each as well as the cab fares in Detroit and Chicago. Due to heavy rain before and during the game, only 3,372 attended, for a total monetary gate of $4,281.58, leaving the Bears without a victory, but with a much larger share of the ticket sales than the host club.[44]

A week later (October 11), the Bears entertained Hammond in another contest that demonstrated some of the frustrations in terms of managing early pro football teams. The Bears were already blocked from using their home field of Cubs Park since the Chicago Cubs and the Chicago White Sox were competing in their postseason intracity series. Then, the original opponent scheduled by the Bears for this date, the Racine Legion, suspended its franchise in 1925 and the Bears scurried to locate an opponent, as well as a field, for October 11. Sternaman mentioned in his game notes that he "tried to stage this game at Grant Park Stadium [now Soldier Field]. As this was impossible on Wednesday [October 7] decided to play in DePaul Field."[45] On that same day, an agreement was reached to play the Hammond Professionals. While Hammond did not offer much resistance in a 28–7 Bears victory, the smallish stadium resulted in an ugly gate, with just 1,897 in attendance worth $2,788.50. The visitors claimed a 45 percent guarantee ($795.30 after park rental and game expenses), leaving the Bears with a woeful balance of $972.03, likely not enough to meet the club's payroll for the day.[46]

As the Bears were dismantling Hammond, Sternaman's favorite auto mechanic, Monroe Hamilton, was scouting the Cardinals game with the Columbus Tigers at Normal Park. "The Cards got a touchdown on a recovered fumble. Otherwise the teams were fairly well matched," reported Hamilton. "Their formation was same as last week and no new plays came into play."[47] Paddy Driscoll dominated the game by succeeding on four field goals, all by dropkicks, including one from 50 yards as the Cardinals eased past Columbus 19–9. With both teams grabbing wins the week before, the Bears (2–1–2) and the Cardinals (3–1) were set for their first encounter of the season on October 25, 1925, at Comiskey Park. Since Akron and Detroit were sporting undefeated (3–0–1) records and with ties still not counting in the standings, both Chicago clubs were anxious for a win to remain in the title hunt.

On game day, quarterback Red Dunn paced the Cardinals to a 9–0 win over the Bears in sloppy conditions. Dunn completed 7 of 13 passes for 147 yards and then intercepted two fourth-quarter tosses to secure the big victory. The *Chicago Tribune* reported: "The Bears went back to their own side of the river with an empty sack in one paw and a lesson in football in the other."[48] The *Evening Post* complimented the adversaries by stating: "Despite the rivalry between the two elevens, the game was cleanly fought and well handled by the officials."[49] Although no official financial records for the game could be located, it was reported in the media that about 13,000 attended the contest. Dutch Sternaman did leave behind an undated piece of scrap paper in his collection that indicated that the Bears took five taxis from the North Side for the trip to Comiskey Park that day and the round-trip total fare was $24.10 for all five vehicles!

I Haven't Made Any Plans to Play Professional Football

On the college front, the name of Red Grange continued to splash across the front pages of newspapers around the country. While Illinois was suffering through a tough year after losing most of its linemen due to graduation the previous year, Grange was still a superb back and quite the target for opposing defenses. After starting out with a 1–3 record, the Illini won their final four games to conclude the great career of Grange with a 5–3 mark. However, throughout the season, there were rumors floating about the country that college football's finest halfback would soon be turning professional. Grange appeared to be impervious to the "pro" chatter and deftly sidestepped any inference that he would soon fall victim to the lure of professional football riches. On September 30, 1925, he denied any association with the NFL, but provided some intriguing hints about his possible future in an interview with the Associated Press:

> I haven't made any plans whatever to play professional football. I haven't signed a contract nor have I made a verbal commitment to play, and right now I really don't know whether or not I would accept an offer to play for money. I will admit I have been approached by one man in Chicago. He talked to me about two minutes on the subject of playing professional football. I didn't say anything about it other than to say I didn't know yet what I would do. He didn't make any offer to me. I am not opposed to college men playing professional football after they have finished their college career on the gridiron…. But I wouldn't say I would not play professional football. I guess it all depends on how much money I might be offered.[50]

It was around this same time that Grange claimed to have first met his controversial personal manager, Charles C. Pyle, who owned a couple of movie theaters in Champaign, Illinois. In his autobiography (originally published in 1953), Grange wrote:

> The story behind my turning professional and my association with Charlie Pyle, who was responsible for the whole thing, begins the second week of my senior year [1925] at Illinois…. I went to the Virginia [Theater] again. As I entered the theater I was greeted in the theater by Mr. Pyle and invited up to his office. I had heard his name mentioned many times before, but never met him. After exchanging a few pleasantries, he got around to the real reason for his wanting to see me. "How would you like to make one hundred thousand dollars, or maybe even a million?" Pyle asked. I was momentarily stunned. Regaining my composure, I quickly answered in the affirmative.[51]

That meeting apparently set in motion a grand scheme by Pyle to market both the man and the reputation of Red Grange. Pyle's plan for Grange's lucrative future spread well beyond the football field. He envisioned a profitable partnership with Grange that would also include motion picture stardom, advertising opportunities, and personal appearances. The most famous person in the football world resided minutes from Pyle in Champaign and the two were about to embark on both a prestigious and lucrative partnership unlike any the sporting world had ever witnessed.

In reality, Pyle was developing an intriguing business management team to position Grange to secure and profit from numerous marketing opportunities that would elevate the football superstar even further above the mainstream sporting world. And—most of the heavy lifting already had been completed well before

Grange's senior year at Illinois. In his landmark book *Red Grange: The Life and Legacy of the NFL's First Superstar*, author Chris Willis indicated that Pyle and Grange likely were discussing future projects as early as 1924 and that Grange signed his first management contract on March 27, 1925, well before his senior season at Illinois.[52] Willis also pointed out that Pyle was not the only "manager" of Grange. Willis stated that two others would participate in the management of Red Grange and that this was done long before Pyle and Grange entered into contract discussions with professional football interests, who would turn out to be the Chicago Bears: "Red Grange actually did sign with C.C. Pyle (and Byron Moore and Marion Coolley) with a three-year contract on March 27, 1925. Grange's contract with Pyle, Moore, and Coolley called for him to get 50 percent of the earnings for all football games, endorsements, movie appearances, and other royalties. Pyle would get 25 percent and Moore-Coolley would get 12 and a half percent each."[53]

Moore was also a theater owner while Coolley (nicknamed Doc) was a friend of Grange's at Illinois, albeit a few years older. In a sense, this was a personal services contract since Pyle and his partners were careful to not link themselves specifically with professional football while Grange still retained his collegiate eligibility. But that did not stop Pyle from quietly initiating contact with his preferred personal target for the professional football services of Red Grange: the Chicago Bears. According to Willis, Pyle sent Dutch Sternaman a letter on August 9, 1925, requesting a meeting to discuss "a tour that I am interested in arranging for Red Grange this winter as soon as his season with Illinois is over."[54]

In his book, George Halas states that Grange first met Pyle in early November 1925, and that Pyle then contacted the Bears to discuss contract possibilities. Halas claimed that he, Pyle, and Sternaman then met secretly (on November 11, 1925) to avoid being seen publicly and risking possible accusations of professional improprieties while Grange was still representing the University of Illinois. After what Halas described as an all-night meeting that extended into the next afternoon, Pyle and the Bears finally reached agreement on a contract for Grange's services that would cover the last two games on the Bears' NFL schedule as well as two proposed postseason tours. "We would split the earnings fifty-fifty," said Halas, "I would provide the Bears and pay tour costs. Pyle would provide Red. Red would provide the crowds. It was a fair arrangement. We put it in writing. The last clause stated if any of us were asked about a contact we would declare none existed. The date was November 10, 1925."[55] The key portion of the agreement was that it was without the signature of Red Grange so as to not misstep over the fine line of the NFL's professional eligibility interpretations. At this point, Grange was the subject of two contracts: one with his management team, and one between Pyle and the Bears.

With the Illinois season scheduled to conclude on November 21, 1925, at Ohio State, the Halas version does not leave much time to finalize contracts among the various parties now involved in the proposed pro football career of Red Grange. It was a difficult time for Grange, with persistent whispers of his turning pro while he still attempted to maintain some semblance of college life. This, of course, was difficult, and became even more so when Grange appeared on the cover of *Time* magazine in October. If the country did not know of Grange previously, it would now. One Chicago newspaper described the reticent lifestyle of Grange due to his overwhelming popularity: "Football season is worse than Lent as far as he is concerned. It cuts him off from everything. Last year he attended the Orpheum [theater] after one of the conference games. He was recognized and the crowd wouldn't subside until he stood up and bowed. He's never attended a vaudeville show or movie during football season since."[56]

During November 1925, the University of Illinois would complete its season by winning its last three games to finish 5–3 overall. Grange would play his last home games against in-state foe University of Chicago on November 7 and tiny Wabash College on November 14. Playing before a huge crowd of 68,864 in Champaign against Chicago, Grange was unable to get untracked during wet, cold conditions. Although he was limited to negative yardage on 17 carries, Grange and his teammates prevailed over the visitors 13–6. There was such enthusiasm for the contest that 25 special trains filled with an estimated 18,000 football fans made the trip from Chicago to Champaign.[57] The following week, which was the final home game for Grange, the famous halfback made only a token appearance and wasn't needed to carry the ball in an easy 21–0 win over outclassed Wabash.

As Grange and Illinois approached the last game of the year at Ohio State on November 21, rumors and speculation increased regarding the future plans of Grange. During the week before the game, Grange was grilled by reporters, as well as his own coach, Robert Zuppke, in an effort to determine if he was not only intending to play pro football but also if he had already signed a contract. If he had done so, Grange would have forfeited his remaining college eligibility. Prior to his final game, Grange flatly stated: "As I said before, my actions after I am through here at the university are accountable to no one. I have done nothing to hurt my standing and I do not intend to do anything. I have not signed a contract and I have not received a penny for the use of my name."[58]

Two days before the Ohio State game, reporter Warren Brown of the *Chicago Herald and Examiner* claimed that he witnessed Pyle and Grange in a private conference in a Champaign hotel and then accurately predicted that not only was Pyle serving as Grange's manager but that Grange would also turn pro after the Ohio State game. In addition, Brown wrote: "The Chicago Bears, some say, have his word, if not his signature, that he will grace their backfield before the end of the current pro grid season. Mr. Pyle denies all this."[59]

Grange then went out and helped Illinois defeat Ohio State 14–9 before over 85,000 fans in one of his finest outings of the season: "Grange's last game was one in which he was content to allow his mates a share of the glory. During the entire game he gained 235 yards by every avenue of advance. He carried the ball 21 times from scrimmage for 113 yards. Nine times he threw successfully for a gain of 42 yards and once he ran 40 yards down the misty field after intercepting an Ohio pass."[60]

Following the game, Grange announced that he would be playing professional football, although original speculation centered on Grange forming his own touring team. When Grange embarked on a train ride for Chicago following the Ohio State game, news slowly leaked that he would soon be wearing the uniform of the Chicago Bears. The *Chicago American* tracked down Chicago Cardinals manager Chris O'Brien for his opinion on the Grange situation: "Chris denied any knowledge of the affair and said all he knows is that he [Grange] has signed to play for the Bears and hopes the North Side team gets the services of the great Grange. 'With Driscoll and my team going great, we will show that the Cards can beat the Bears with the "Great Red" in the lineup. I am just as anxious as you are for some official announcement of Grange's pro situation.'"61

The Crowd Stood Up and Roared a Deafening Tribute

All of the gossip landed with a thud on Sunday, November 22, when Grange sat on the Bears' bench during a 21–0 win over the Green Bay Packers. He was officially in the fold, contracts had been finalized with the Bears, and his recognized manager, C.C. Pyle, continued to line up potential opponents for the planned postseason tour. Grange would make his NFL debut against the Cardinals on Thanksgiving Day (November 26) at Cubs Park. Immediately, the city of Chicago was up for grabs in its excitement over the presence of Grange. Although fewer than 7,000 were in attendance for the Bears' 21–0 win over the Packers, Grange received an unusual standing ovation from the crowd early in the day: "'Red,' accompanied by his manager, Charley Pyle, sat on the Bears' bench. When the famous sorrel top, clad in a sumptuous raccoon coat, poked his head up from the dugout and took his seat, the crowd stood up and roared a deafening tribute, and it required immediate action on the part of the police to keep the fans from mobbing their idol."62

Tickets for the Thanksgiving Day battle went on sale Monday, November 23, and quickly sold out, leaving thousands without the means to witness the first appearance of Grange in the NFL. Unfortunately, this resulted in some unruly behavior from disappointed Chicagoans who were anxious to observe Grange play in person: "Fifteen policemen, battling against one of the longest—if not strongest—lines seen in conference circles this year, responded to a riot call yesterday to quell thousands of persons who fought to obtain tickets to see Harold 'Red' Grange in his first appearance as a professional football player."63

Local newspapers, with wild headlines such as "All Chicago Grange Mad," predicted that as many as 200,000 people were seeking tickets for the inaugural Grange professional appearance.64 Sternaman and Halas hoped to squeeze in about 35,000, including standing room, into cozy Cubs Park. Notes found in the Sternaman collection indicate that Sternaman was fidgeting with financial numbers as early as November 9, 1925. In these early estimates, Dutch was hoping for a gate windfall of $40,000 based on attracting 30,000 at an average admittance fee of $1.33. After park rental fees and other expenses, Sternaman planned to distribute $9,000 each to the Bears and the Cardinals, while Grange/Pyle would receive $5,600. Dutch also worked out a scenario with only 16,000 fans in attendance, but these tabulations were worked on well before the Grange contract was announced. Another example of the behind-the-scenes arrangements occurred on November 12, 1925, when Dutch authored a handwritten "addendum" to the original game contract that stated, "The Cardinals and Bears are to receive the first $14,000 net after deduction of war tax and park rental is made. Then Harold Grange is to receive 35% of the net balance. The 65% left is to be divided equally between the Cardinals and Bears. The Bears

Nine. The Grange Effect 133

Red Grange (sitting) was welcomed to the Chicago Bears in 1925 by team player/owner Dutch Sternaman (center) and quarterback Joey Sternaman. The arrival of Red Grange brought new life into the NFL and attracted the largest crowds to date to witness pro football games (courtesy Pro Football Hall of Fame, Dutch Sternaman Collection).

and Cardinals will stand expenses such as band, tickets, officials, park payroll, etc., equally."[65]

While both sides were anticipating a large crowd for the game, there was no precedent for an NFL contest in Chicago to reach those staggering attendance expectations. While huge crowds of over 50,000 were commonplace for college games, the pros were still struggling. The aforementioned Packers game drew just 6,800 while the Hammond encounter just a month earlier attracted fewer than 2,000. In a game at Detroit on October 4, only 3,300 witnessed the Bears in action. Would the emergence of Red Grange change that familiar pattern? Fortunately, the presence of the Cardinals as the opposition added both recognition and a bit of local glamour to the upcoming clash. The Cards were enjoying a successful season with a solid 8–1 mark prior to the Bears Thanksgiving engagement, with real hopes of capturing Chris O'Brien's first NFL title. The Cards rested atop the league standings with that 8–1 record, just a notch ahead of Detroit (7–1–2), Pottsville (7–2), and the Bears (6–2–2). While the national press waited impatiently for the debut of Grange, local media observers reminded their readers that the game would also be for the "city" title: "Next in importance to the fact that Red will play in the combat is that the Bears and the Cardinals will be playing their second game of the season for the city title, the south siders winning the first encounter 9–0. The Bears were caught off their guard that day and never threatened the Cards' goal line, but since that time it has been a different story, with the north siders showing vast improvement in every game while their rivals from the other side of town have maintained their fast pace which has carried them to the top of the national pro league heap, with the Bears close on their heels."[66]

Pro Football, That Wicked Pastime

While the acquisition of Grange by the Bears was huge news in Chicago, it was proving to be equally beneficial to the NFL. For the first time, the professional game was receiving positive publicity and interest across the country. Fans were literally fighting for tickets, and as word began spreading of a possible Grange tour, interest in pro football was increasing dramatically: "Pro football, that wicked pastime that has been mauled and kicked all over the country, has your upstanding, reforming citizen converted. And the promoters are chuckling. You may pan Grange and say that he is nothing more than a kid who doesn't know his own mind. Probably not. But the fact remains that the Middle West has gone Grange mad."[67]

On Thanksgiving Day, November 26, Red Grange emerged from the Cubs Park dugout for his first professional game with the Chicago Bears. In the mere five days since his last collegiate game representing the University of Illinois, Grange had seen his universe turned upside down. The rumors, the emotions, and the endless speculation were now swept aside and Grange could concentrate on what he did best: play football. All eyes would be on him. Outside the congested Cubs Park, ticket searching and scalping were widespread before the gates opened at 9:00 a.m. for the 11:00 a.m. kickoff. Over 300 police and 100 private security personnel were stationed both in and outside the park. Up above in the upper deck, radio stations WGN and KYX prepared for "the first time a professional football game will be radiocast by two Chicago stations."[68]

On the field, Paddy Driscoll's opening kickoff sailed into the end zone for a touchback. Grange scampered six yards off right tackle on the first play from scrimmage to the delight of the capacity crowd. After the game, Grange stated: "Of course I felt a bit strange in there during the first quarter, but soon shook off that nervousness and was just as much at home as if I were playing with my old mates at Illinois." The game itself was both exciting and dreadfully boring! For those who anticipated the brilliant flashes of Grange breaking away for an evasive run, they were disappointed. But for fans who enjoyed a tough, clean defensive battle, they were more than rewarded. Grange added: "It was the hardest, toughest game in which I have played in my career. At the start I didn't have any false hopes about staging long runs, because I knew that the Cardinals were powerful on defense."[69]

Overall, Grange picked up just 30 rushing yards on 14 carries and returned three punts for 75 yards. He also tossed six passes, but all fell incomplete. The Bears gained just two first downs and the Cardinals only one so it was only fitting that the game ended in a scoreless tie. Part of the reason for that was the expert punting of Paddy Driscoll, who punted 17 times that day. Unfortunately for Grange,

Paddy aimed 14 of those boots away from Red, or out of bounds, denying Grange the opportunity to consistently demonstrate his exquisite return abilities. It also earned Paddy a chorus of incessant "boos" throughout the afternoon since he clearly was avoiding kicking directly to Grange to prohibit any type of significant return. Surprisingly, the local media defended Driscoll's strategy: "Driscoll's repeated refusal to risk punting to the Phantom Flier [Grange] unquestionably saved his team from defeat. Three times during the contest, when it was absolutely unavoidable, Paddy kicked to Grange. Three times he saw 'Red' run wild through his entire team for brilliant and spectacular runs of 25 yards each.... Paddy deliberately refused to punt to Grange and was booed throughout the game by that football-mad mob that came to see 'Red' run. He stuck to his guns, however."[70]

George Halas later recounted the game's most prominent story: "Red didn't do much on Thanksgiving Day. Paddy Driscoll kept punting the ball away from him. The game was scoreless. At the end, people booed. When Paddy came home, he told Mary, his wife, 'Isn't it terrible the way people booed Red?' Mary said, 'Paddy, they were not booing Red. They were booing you for not giving Red a chance.'"[71]

Despite the rather dreary nature of the 0–0 deadlock in the game, everyone seemed to go home happy. One of the most pleased was William Veeck, president of the Chicago Cubs, who embraced a nice "rental" payday during the usual off-season for Cubs Park. Veeck was most enthusiastic about pro football, with or without the presence of Red Grange, and predicted a bright future for the sport: "Grange, of course, is unusual, in the way that he hit the public between the eyes. He has temporarily, at least, brought professional football into the 35,000 [attendance] class, but to my mind, he will neither make nor break professional football. The game, as a game, is too well established for one individual to alter its course for long."[72]

With the scoreless tie with the Bears, the Cardinals (8–1–1) maintained their slim lead in the NFL standings over Pottsville (8–2), Detroit (7–2–2), and the Bears (6–2–3). Both Pottsville and the Detroit Panthers also played a game on Thanksgiving with Pottsville emerging with a 31–0 win over Green Bay and the Panthers losing to Rock Island 6–3. Just three days after the scoreless draw with the Bears, the Cardinals hosted Rock Island with high hopes for the remainder of the season. The *Chicago Tribune* reported: "The Cards are in first place in the pro league now and a victory [over Rock Island] will clear the way to full claim to the title. The pro league schedule ends December 20."[73]

Almost immediately, the Bears' plans for an extensive gridiron tour with Grange at the helm were appearing in the press across the nation. Daily reports in the newspapers reported about upcoming Bears games in Detroit, New York, Washington, D.C., and other locations. Halas and Pyle were clearly focused on extending the popularity and the gate attraction of Grange. Meanwhile, Chris O'Brien and the Cardinals were dead set on securing the NFL title and then perhaps scheduling a return match with Grange and the Bears, but this time at Comiskey Park.

And then the fun began!

Ten

The NFL's First Scandal

"In any case, the pro game hasn't helped itself."
—*Collyer's Eye*, December 12, 1925

As the young defendants were marched to the front of the room, now hot, humid and overcrowded with too many bodies, to face their accusers, they could not help but hear the derision—and the passion—in the voices of the angry mob of self-righteous advocates.

There were just four of them … frightened and afraid, standing together against a dreary wall with shoulders hunched forward and heads facing down.

Alone.

It had come down to this, a one-sided fracas where good vs. evil stood steps apart and eyed each other warily. Yet in this case, identifying and separating good from evil (or vice versa) was both challenging and impossible. Mostly impossible.

It had already been determined that a "crime" had been committed. In a sense, the trial had already been completed in newspapers around the country, but not always with the same judicial decision. This hearing was merely a formality to ensure that justice was indeed served and that the perpetrators be punished fully for the serious transgressions that had been committed.

In the end, the proud, passionate protectors of the city of Chicago snuffed out and prevented any hint of a defense, and bullied the four defendants (all Chicago high school students) into accepting the most severe punishment allowed.

The four boys shuffled off after the verdict was announced, and could only silently accept the punishment that was intended to not only match the crime, but also establish an example for any others who might dare to duplicate that despicable activity both now and forever.

And so the book was quickly closed on this chapter that threatened the sanctity of the Board of Control. The four boys, it was hoped, would accept their punishment and move on to more fruitful life experiences; they would learn their lesson and never again commit such a heinous infraction.

Their crime?

They played in a football game…

It was just another episode in the wacky, confusing, and groundbreaking 1925 NFL season: four high school kids somehow landing a spot in an actual professional football game. How could this happen? Why was this allowed? And did this occurrence somehow connect with the appearance of Red Grange in the pro ranks?

Following the Thanksgiving Day clash between the Bears and the Cardinals, all sorts of possibilities emerged in the world of pro football. The Cardinals still maintained a secure lead in the league standings, while the Bears and their beguiling new partner, Charles C. Pyle, blasted ahead with plans to take the national football audience by force in what was otherwise known as a barnstorming tour.

The first Grange game in the NFL left little doubt that pro football could finally become a profitable venture. Both the Bears and the Cardinals enjoyed a much stronger financial return than was customary. The Sternaman collection in the Professional Football Hall of Fame revealed an "official" paid attendance of 31,180, resulting in a gate of $54,766.75. In addition, there were an unknown number of "passes" provided by the Bears, along with probable gate crashers. As such, the likely total attendance for the game was probably closer to 35,000—believed to be the biggest turnout to date for a pro football game. Chris O'Brien of the Cardinals wisely selected a favorable guarantee of $14,000 (actually $14,634.77), although part of that sum ($6,451.50) was exercised in the value of tickets provided to O'Brien for the game. This left O'Brien's final share of the proceeds at $8,183.27.

According to the Sternaman records, after taxes, park rental, team guarantees, and other expenses, Pyle and Grange walked away with 35 percent ($9,007.43) of the net figure ($25,735.51), a tidy sum but less than the predicted numbers that surfaced before the game in the media.[1] It was time for all parties to readjust their thinking and move forward with the cash cow, otherwise known as Red Grange, as the Bears began preparing for an East Coast "tour." Grange manager Pyle was seeking a much bigger piece of the football pie.

But first, previously scheduled games would need to be completed. On Sunday, November 29, the Cardinals defeated Rock Island 7–0 to improve the team's record to 9–1–1 and remain in first place. Pottsville rolled over the Frankford Yellow Jackets 49–0 to reach 9–2 on the season, while the Bears (7–2–3) edged Columbus 14–13. The Detroit Panthers (7–2–2) were also in the mix. If the Cardinals had decided to end their season on December 1, the 1925 NFL title would have been theirs. With just that lone defeat, no one else would have been able to capture the crown. Yet for some reason, Chris O'Brien contacted the managers of the Pottsville team on Monday, November 30, challenging the Maroons to a game in Chicago and framing the encounter as being for the NFL championship. Initially, the Pottsville newspapers thought the contest would be held later in December, but the date and the ground rules were established quickly and Pottsville grabbed the train to Chicago for the battle on Sunday, December 6, as noted by the local media in Pennsylvania: "The management of the Pottsville Maroons today definitely accepted the challenge issued last Monday [November 30] by the Chicago Cardinals to Pottsville to play for the national professional football championship. The Maroons were scheduled to play in Atlantic City next Sunday, but today were released from that engagement by [Atlantic City] Mayor Bader so that they could journey to Chicago to play the Cardinals."[2]

This confrontation had all of the makings of an NFL title game, without the benefit of it actually being a title game! However, both teams proclaimed it to be a battle for the NFL crown and newspapers in each location took up that cause as well, even with the league schedule not concluding until December 20. The *Chicago Tribune* stated:

> The National Professional Football League championship hangs in the balance today [December 6] when the Chicago Cardinals and Pottsville, Pa. elevens clash on the gridiron at Comiskey Park. The game was scheduled by Manager O'Brien of the Cardinals as a post-season contest to decide the championship, as the Cards and Pottsville elevens both have closed their regular league season. As the schedules worked out the Cardinals could claim the title without meeting Pottsville, but Manager O'Brien wanted his team to meet the eastern champs with the view of settling definitely the title claims of the rivals.[3]

For O'Brien, it was a move that he would soon regret. A fired-up Pottsville team smoked the Cardinals 21–7, moved into first place in the league standings, and boldly claimed the NFL title. Of course, since there was no such thing as a championship game in the NFL at the time, both teams would need to patiently await the final decision regarding the champion at the NFL's next league meeting in February. Based on the confusing experiences from the end of the 1924 season, critics were quick to question the "championship" status of games such as the Cardinals-Pottsville battle, although the suggested reasoning for such scheduling was easier to understand:

> The signing of Red Grange and other well-known gridiron players of this season is the impetus that is postponing the end of the professional season. The "pros" expect to cash in on the tail-end of the interest that has been aroused in the sport this year.... Because of the mix-up that ensued last year when the Chicago Bears and Cleveland played after the regular season, no post-series championship games are likely, unless there is a tie. Cleveland finished the regular season last year the winner, but after playing a game with the Bears and losing the latter claimed the title. The contest was advertised as a championship affair and the resulting dispute left a sour taste with many of the game's supporters.[4]

What a Tour!

While the Cardinals were preparing for Pottsville, the Chicago Bears embarked on the busiest week of football competition in history. Following the 14–13 victory over the visiting Columbus Tigers on November 29 with 24,285 in attendance, the Bears quickly embarked on their much-anticipated "Grange tour." Grange finally broke loose for some broken-field yardage against Columbus, picking up 78 yards on the ground, catching a couple of long passes, and returning one of the punts for 30 yards. Unlike Akron's brief postseason tour of the West Coast following the 1920 season, the Bears' odyssey in 1925 was much more rigorous. Between December 2 and December 13, Grange and the Bears would face eight opponents and attract the biggest crowd to ever see a professional football contest. Counting his last collegiate game with Illinois on Saturday, November 21, and his first two games with the Bears in Chicago on November 26 and November 29, Red Grange was expected to participate in 11 football games in just over three weeks. The physical demands on Grange and his teammates were brutal, but Halas did not incur any opposition in convincing the Bears' players to join the nonstop gridiron extravaganza: "I had no difficulty getting all sixteen players to agree to the tour. What a tour! There never has been one to match it. There probably never will."[5] While the tour was lucrative, the challenge of playing eight football games in such a short time span (and traveling almost daily) was difficult, if not questionable. The nonstop battering on every play, the crushing falls to the frozen turf, and the lack of recovery time for a player's body would all contribute to a challenging two weeks for the Bears players involved.

For Grange, who was the target each game of a fresh team of opponents eager to prove their worth against the newest American hero, the challenges of the tour were daunting. As the main object of attention on the field, Grange would endure massive blind-side hits and traumatic tackles on an almost daily basis. Eight games in 11 days in any sport would be questionable, but adding in the physical aspects of a sport such as football, the demands of the game became dangerous. Critical thinking regarding the health and durability of the athletes during the tour was obviously lacking in the planning of these contests. Red Grange and the Chicago Bears would soon discover that the scheduling of that many events during such a brief time frame was not only questionable but foolhardy. Pyle, of course, was not on the field, nor was he always on-site. But whenever there was a dollar to unearth, his presence was guaranteed.

Prior to the start of the tour, Pyle and the Bears worked out a new agreement to ensure that Grange and Pyle would be happy with their financial rewards from this football expedition. Pyle continued to actively market the personal services of Grange, madly targeting potential advertising and motion picture opportunities for his client. All of Pyle's efforts were about to pay off handsomely, both on and off the football field. However, it was the content of the new contract that virtually ensured riches for Grange but left the Bears organization basically as an employee of Pyle for the length of the tour. With Pyle serving as the "first party" and the Chicago Bears listed as the "second party," the contract stated:

> The party of the first part will produce Harold E. "Red" Grange … ready, able and willing to play in a football contest … and agrees that said Grange will participate in said game for a period of not less than twenty five (25) minutes, barring, however, accident, injury or other contingency beyond his control. Grange will be in the starting line-up.
>
> The second party agrees that it will furnish its entire present squad of football players known as the "Chicago Bears," fully uniformed, ready, able and willing to play … on which "Chicago Bears" team the said Grange will play…. The said second party will pay all the expenses of transportation, hotel bills, meals and other incidental and necessary expenses of its team and the said Grange…. Party of the first part agrees to pay to the party of the second part for the faithful performance of the agreements herein contained a sum of money equal to twenty five (25) percent of the balance of the total receipts of the sale of tickets for said game, after first deducting war tax and fifteen (15) percent for Park rent.[6]

In essence, Halas and Sternaman would absorb all team-related expenses for the tour, including the salaries of the 16 players, and in return, would receive 25 percent of the receipts after basic expenses had been withdrawn. A similar contract was created for each of the scheduled tour games, clearly indicating Pyle's vision of revenue sharing, although the precise division of receipts did seem to differ per location for some reason. It wasn't a great deal for Halas, but it did offer the Bears the opportunity to retain the connection to Grange, as well as enjoy a few games in the national spotlight. Thanks to the emergence of Red Grange, the NFL was finally receiving more than token interest around the country and Halas was pleased to be part of it all. Instead of wrapping up the 1925 season quietly in Chicago before a few thousand fans, Halas and Sternaman tagged along on Grange's coattails in a well-publicized tour that ultimately would pay off handsomely.

The grand tour was audacious, both in its scope and its expectations. Games were rapidly scheduled in St. Louis (December 2), Philadelphia (December 5), New York (December 6), Washington, D.C. (December 8), Boston (December 9), Pittsburgh (December 10), Detroit (December 12), and concluding with a home game in Chicago against the New York Giants on December 13. The Bears finished with a 4–4 mark overall on the tour, with three games included against nonleague clubs. Each day seemed to unveil a new challenge for the Bears and Grange, most obviously in the pronounced wearing down of the prized halfback. Again, not much thought was given to the overwhelming physical pressures placed on both Grange and the Bears players and slowly but surely, the ramifications of the nonstop games became apparent. Grange would later comment: "After the season we barnstormed playing eight games in 11 days. Before it was over, we were so near exhaustion that the players would match coins to see who would start the game. The losers had to start!"[7]

They Just Clobbered Him!

Bears quarterback Joey Sternaman was impressed with the composure of Grange, who endured screaming hits and aggressive defensive assaults on an almost daily basis during the tour:

> Well, when he came with the Bears, I was the play-caller, and I said to him, "Are you interested in doing well for yourself, or are you interested in winning ball games?" After all, he's been used to an offense down at Illinois that was built solely on opening a hole for him.... Well, Red was honestly interested in winning games and, as I found out, he was one of the finest team players around. So, what I did a lot after Red came with us was use him as a decoy. I'd fake handing the ball off to him and they would swarm after Red; why they'd just clobber him.... Red took a real beating, especially that first year, but he never complained, just played his best.[8]

By the time the Bears arrived in Boston on Wednesday, December 9, the constant battering on Grange was beginning to show. The team had knocked off a motley crew called the Washington All-Stars 19–0 on December 8 in the nation's capital, and Grange had looked less than extraordinary. Columnist Westbrook Pegler of the *Chicago Tribune* calmly observed: "Probably the wear and tear of his sudden and intensive professional career and the strain of trying to be a superman all the time have worn down Red's energy. This was his third game since last Saturday [December 5], and, furthermore, in each game there have been certain members of the opposition who felt sure that the great Grange would bust, if they threw him down hard enough, and were willing to use a lot of energy trying."[9]

Sadly, things became even worse for Grange in that Boston game against the Providence Steamroller. Although the Bears dropped a 9–6 decision, the real pain was endured by Grange, who, for the first time, was roundly booed by the crowd. He later stated:

> Arriving in Boston on Wednesday morning, December 9th, the Bears were in a pitiful condition, with many of us bandaged from head to foot. I was in particularly bad shape. I had hurt my arm in New York and it was still badly swollen.... Under such conditions it was to be expected the Bears would not fare well and the best I could do was eighteen yards on five tries. I was booed for the first time in my football career in the Boston game. It made me aware of something I had never thought of before—that the public's attitude toward a professional football player is quite different from the manner in which they view a college gridder. A pro must deliver, or else.[10]

Off the field, however, Grange's mood was brightened when his manager, C.C. Pyle, apparently finalized a movie deal for Grange that was publicized as paying the football hero a flat guarantee of $300,000 (with a check that was photographed and published widely) for the first film scheduled as part of an announced long-term contract. In his autobiography, Grange scoffed at the amount of the huge movie contract: "Unfortunately, the whole thing was just another one of Pyle's wild publicity stunts. In reality, the check was a phony. We received only a few thousand dollars for signing the contract and the promise of about $5,000 a week while making a picture."[11]

In addition, while in New York for the December 6 game, Pyle also engineered a series of endorsement commitments as outlined by the Associated Press: "Grange and Pyle were besieged at their hotel by agents of business firms seeking Red's endorsement of articles ranging from dolls to sweaters. Pyle said that $12,000 was received for endorsing a sweater, $10,000 for the use of Grange's name in manufacturing a football doll, $5,000 for a shoe and $2,500 for a cap. Although Grange himself never has smoked, he received $1,000 for the use of his name in connection with a tobacco advertisement."[12]

The financial windfall, with still more endorsements to come, was both impressive and unprecedented for a pro football collaboration. During the tour, while the crowds were basically inconsistent, the stop in New York on December 6 made everything worthwhile. An estimated 70,000 fans showed up at the Polo Grounds to watch the Bears smother the Giants 19–7. It was the biggest attendance to ever witness a pro football game and the crowd was thrilled as Grange intercepted a pass and returned it 30 yards for a touchdown. Unfortunately for Grange, the on-field pummeling continued as described by one New York newspaper: "The huge crowd at the Polo Grounds was out of sympathy with the exceedingly rough treatment the Giants accorded Red Grange on several occasions. Several times the fans joined in booing and hissing seemingly unnecessarily harsh play, such as twisting Red over backward and piling on him some seconds after the ball was out of play. One instance of slugging, after a tackle, was more obvious to those in the stands, but went unpenalized."[13]

Not all of the games were blockbusters in terms of attendance. For example, on December 10, 1925, the Bears played in Pittsburgh against the Pittsburgh All-Stars and suffered a lackluster 24–0 defeat. A crowd estimated at just 4,498 was on hand and Sternaman's careful records revealed a gate of only $9,384.85 after taxes. Pyle then received $6,256.57 of that amount, retaining $3,910.36 for himself and Grange, and remitting $2,346.21 to the Bears.[14]

C.C. Pyle Wrecked the Bears

Eventually, the injuries suffered by Grange proved to be so debilitating that he missed some games at the end of the tour. Throughout the series of games, Sternaman retained notes identifying significant events during these dates:

- Red hurt bad in Pittsburgh game, Thursday, December 10;
- Red did not play in Detroit Saturday, December 12;
- Red did not play in New York at Chicago Sunday, December 13;
- Why did we play December 12 and 13 games? Because they are members of league;
- Cost us [money] December 12 and 13 [with] Red not playing.[15]

As the team finally stumbled home in time for the final contest with the Giants (a 9–0 defeat) on Sunday, December 13, local writer Harry Neily described the arrival of the players at Cubs Park: "When the Bruins returned home from their hasty trip to the effete East they were as flat as the proverbial pancake. Ailing athletes limped into Cubs Park, dragging one foot after the other. There scarcely was a whole person in the party and the results were apparent on the field of play. The zip and the snap were gone."[16]

While the trip was financially rewarding, especially for Pyle and Grange, the media was not kind in the assessment of the packed schedule. Harry Neily added: "You can't conduct football like … a baseball outfit. The work is not the same, nor are the results. A baseball team can play a schedule of 154 games and with reasonable luck not crack under the well-known strain. The Bears have proved conclusively the uselessness of trying to make the Autumnal pastime a hippodrome. It can't be done. C.C. Pyle beyond doubt is making Red Grange rich but he wrecked the Bears."[17]

While the aches and pains from the tour eventually healed, fond memories remained for the players and coaches who endured this remarkable football carnival. Perhaps the most enjoyable tale was one that Halas enjoyed sharing throughout the years. During the tour's stop in Washington, D.C., both Grange and Halas were invited to the White house for a brief meeting with President Calvin Coolidge. As Halas wrote years later: "Senator [William] McKinley of Illinois sent his limousine to take Red and me to the White House to meet President Coolidge. The senator introduced us, 'Mr. President, this is George Halas and Red Grange of the Chicago Bears.' President Coolidge replied, 'How are you, young gentlemen. I have always admired animal acts.'"[18]

Pro Game Has Stepped Ahead with the Strides of a Goliath

President Coolidge may have been one of the few people in America by that time to be unaware of the true identities of Red Grange and the Chicago Bears. That brief interlude at the White House certainly demonstrated that recognition of pro football in the United States was still not a given. Things were now moving fast, perhaps too fast, for the NFL, which found itself squarely on the front pages after being relegated to anonymity during its first few years of existence. While one could scan the numerous available daily newspapers (morning, afternoon, and evening versions in some cases) for news on the Grange tour, others might notice an upcoming battle between the Pottsville Maroons and the 1924 Notre Dame All-Stars. It was a unique concept, taking one of the top professional clubs of the year and pitting that team against the undefeated collegiate national champions from the previous (1924) season. Would the world soon discover which version of the game was superior, the pro or the college version? Or would it be unfair to expect a disbanded college team to suddenly regroup a year later and become competitive in an actual game? The public relations possibilities were also significant, especially if the vaunted "Four Horsemen" from that 1924 Notre Dame team could reunite in a successful effort to conquer the professional league contenders.

Since their graduation from Notre Dame earlier in 1925, the members of the Four Horsemen quartet had initially sidestepped pro-football-playing opportunities and all had entered the college coaching ranks. Jim Crowley was at Georgia, Don Miller at Georgia Tech, Elmer Layden at Columbia, and Harry Stuhldreher at Villanova. As the college football season concluded late in 1925, Crowley, a native of Green Bay, decided to dip his toes in the professional ranks and signed with the Packers. Miller and Stuhldreher then joined the Hartford Blues, a semipro team in Connecticut. In their first game together, the pair of former Irish standouts paced the Blues to a 28–7 win over the All-New Britain squad on November 29, 1925. "The wonderful, broken field running of Miller was the feature of the game while Stuhldreher's uncanny forward passing were the telling strokes in the great victory."[19] Around this same time, it was announced that the defending national champion Notre Dame squad from 1924 would reunite with all of the Four Horsemen and challenge the current Pottsville Maroons club in what the *Philadelphia Inquirer* termed a "Bitter Battle Between Systems":

> Things that happen when Greek meets Greek smack of pacificism when one championship football machine collides head on with another. If you don't know just what we mean, be among those present at Shibe Park on the afternoon of Saturday, December 12, when the boss college team of 1924 mixes with the outstanding professional eleven of 1925.
> The pro game has stepped ahead with the strides of a Goliath. But never before has an all-conquering college team stepped onto professional ranks as a unit to play together as they did when they wore the colors of their alma mater.[20]

But first, Pottsville needed to complete its NFL commitment to play the Chicago Cardinals in Chicago on Sunday, December 6, in what the two teams erroneously termed a "championship" duel. The Cardinals, as noted previously, dropped that contest 21–7 while advertisements in the Philadelphia newspapers began to promote the upcoming December 12 battle between the Maroons and Notre Dame. Even on the long train ride home, H.C. Hoffman, assistant editor of the *Pottsville Evening Republican*, filed a dispatch and shared the excitement surrounding the upcoming contest: "Wearing gracefully but proudly their honors of champion football club of the world, the Pottsville Maroons reached Pittsburgh this morning, rather battered, but anxious for the fray Saturday with the famous Notre Dame club of 1924 at Philadelphia."[21]

Will You Play Us in Cubs Park?

Meanwhile, in Chicago, Cardinals manager Chris O'Brien was working behind the scenes to arrange a rematch with the Bears while also looking to schedule more games in an effort to bypass Pottsville in the league standings before the final league date of December 20. The Maroons were also hoping to add a date with Red Grange and the Chicago Bears before the end of the season. The *Chicago Evening American* reported on the possibility of conflicting dates: "Chris O'Brien is still dickering for a game with the Chicago Bears on December 20 at the Sox Park. The Cards now hold one win with a tie showing for the other games with the Bears. On top of this comes a report from the East that the Bears and Pottsville likely will play a game here [Chicago] on the same date."[22]

On Wednesday, December 9, 1925, O'Brien received a telegram from Dutch Sternaman and George Halas, who were in Pittsburgh where the Bears were continuing their East Coast tour. The telegram was brief and to the point regarding an invitation for the Cardinals to play the Bears for a third time that season. After the wonderful financial response from the previous game between the rivals, it would appear to be another windfall for both clubs:

> TO: Chris O'Brien
> Have opportunity to play Pottsville at Cubs Park December twenty. On what basis will you play us in Cubs Park on that date? Wire Hotel Schenley Pittsburgh tonight.
> Halas & Sternaman

O'Brien responded back to Halas on Thursday, December 10, with his plans, including an alternate proposal regarding the site of the game:

> TO: George Halas
> Am playing Milwaukee Thursday, Hammond Saturday. If we win both games will lead league race. Would toss coin to settle place to play. Terms would be three way split of net. Saw Pyle today, told him same. He was in favor of Sox Park.
> Chris O'Brien[23]

An agreement was quickly hammered out by O'Brien and the Bears for the teams to meet on December 20, leaving Pottsville out of the running for a game with Red Grange to finish off the season. As O'Brien's telegram indicated, he was also in the process of scheduling two more home games: one with the Milwaukee Badgers on December 10 and then a second contest against Hammond on Saturday, December 12. After the loss to Pottsville (10–2) the previous Sunday, the Cardinals (9–2–1) were just one-half game behind the front-running Maroons in the NFL standings. It seemed logical that both teams might wish to schedule additional games since the league season clearly would not be concluded until December 20, two weeks after the earlier tilt between the Cardinals and Pottsville had mistakenly been touted as the league "championship" game. In the eyes of Joe Carr and the NFL administration, the Cardinals-Pottsville clash was viewed as nothing more than a regular season game, albeit one with great importance in the title chase.

They Can Fire Us Out of the League If They Wish

The Cardinals easily vanquished both outclassed Milwaukee (58–0) and Hammond (13–0) to move ahead of Pottsville with an 11–2–1 record. Pottsville (10–2) was clearly focused on its imminent showdown with the "Four Horsemen" on Saturday, December 12, in Philadelphia to be followed by a league meeting with Providence on December 13 the next day. Meanwhile, there was some discouraging news from the NFL office that would cloud the playing of that widely anticipated game against the Notre Dame players. The idea for the contest originated in late November with Philadelphia promoter Frank Schumann. Not knowing that Red Grange was already locked in with the Chicago Bears, Schumann had hoped to lure Grange to his city for a game on December 5, according to the *Philadelphia Inquirer*: "The terms which Schumann offered Grange were $25,000 for his appearance here, and a suitable sum for the team that would accompany him to this city. It was Schumann's intention to bring some pro eleven like Pottsville to Shibe Park as opponents for Grange's troops."[24]

Schumann's hopes for coaxing Grange to Philadelphia were dashed when Grange signed with the Bears and Halas elected to meet the local NFL team, the Frankford Yellowjackets, on that December 5 day in Philadelphia as part of the Bears' tour. This decision did not hinder the efforts of Schumann, who then set his sights on another potentially lucrative gridiron attraction: the popular Four Horsemen, late of Notre Dame. Schumann dreamed of a huge gate if he could succeed in convincing the individual members of the former Notre Dame backfield to reunite for a special "one-time" appearance.

> Schumann sought Harry Stuhldreher, Elmer Layden, Jim Crowley and Don Miller and asked them to form a team among their colleagues of last season at South Bend and make their first appearance in this city intact. The Four Horsemen agreed, and then came the matter of obtaining an opponent. The Frankford Yellowjackets were tied with their Grange function. Schumann had signed a contract with the Four Horsemen, which naturally had to be fulfilled, so it was up to him to obtain some other team. He took a trip to Pottsville and laid the matter before Doc [John G.] Striegel who handles the Maroons' business affairs.[25]

Striegel and the Maroons—as well as the entire city of Pottsville—embraced the idea and plans moved ahead for the meeting on December 12 in Philadelphia. Ads were placed in local publications, special trains from Pottsville were arranged, and various newspapers provided news, updates, and gossip to eager readers excited to learn more about the upcoming pro vs. college clash. But all of this quickly became a potential problem. The game was scheduled to be staged at Shibe Park in Philadelphia, which was within the league "territory" of the Frankford Yellowjackets, and Frankford officials immediately expressed their concerns to the NFL office. The rapid result was that Pottsville was warned by the league office in Columbus, Ohio, to drop its plans to play the Four Horsemen or risk having its franchise suspended by the NFL. Doc Striegel, owner of the Maroons, claimed that he had personally contacted the league office to ensure that there was no difficulty in scheduling the game in Philadelphia. In the absence of President Joe Carr (due to illness), Striegel discussed the situation by phone with an individual named Jerry Corcoran, who

Striegel apparently thought was the league secretary. Corcoran was actually the manager of the Columbus Tigers and was likely helping out in the NFL league office during Carr's illness and fielded the call for the current league secretary, Carl Storck:

> According to Dr. Striegel the secretary [Corcoran] gave official sanction to the game and so Striegel signed the contract which bound the Maroons to the contest at Shibe Park.... Then came a snag. According to Striegel, Frankford suddenly found itself desirous of playing a game with the champions [Pottsville].... The doctor related to those who carried the message that he was bound by a contract with Schumann that he could not break. Then the territorial clause of the agreement was cited. Striegel admitted the justice of the territorial restrictions, but asserted that he had received the verbal sanction of the secretary.[26]

When notified of the league's decision that threatened both the Four Horsemen game and the Pottsville franchise, Dr. Striegel was both bewildered and upset. He once again phoned the league office and spoke to the same "secretary," as reported on Wednesday, December 9, by the *Philadelphia Inquirer*:

> Immediately that official, so Dr. Striegel says, suffered from lack of memory, and was as unable to recall his previous testimony as a prize witness in a bootlegging continuance. "He wound up by asking if I had any written permission," said the indignant doctor after the costly chatter over the patented wires of Ma Bell. "He knew dashed well that I didn't have, because he didn't give me any. I'm going to play this game anyway, permission or no permission," vehemently announced the Pottsville magnate. "The secretary said it was all right," he continued, "and I signed this contract in good faith. I'm going through with it, and they can fire us out of the league if they wish."[27]

Corcoran, of course, had no authority to approve any action on behalf of the league, but canceling the game at this point would not be a fiscally pragmatic decision for Striegel. Still, he had a choice: cancel the game or risk having his team booted out of the NFL. He chose the latter, and was applauded by the Pottsville media, especially since he stood up and refused to bend to the territorial demands of the rival Frankford Yellowjackets: "Regardless of any rumors to the contrary, the Pottsville Maroons will play the Notre Dame team on Saturday afternoon in Philadelphia. It appears that the only reason for the Frankford management objecting so strenuously is that the jealousy exists since the Maroons took the scalp of the yellow clad team and then went out to Chicago, where they won the national title.[28]

To complicate things further, Frankford was scheduled to play the Cleveland Indians at Frankford Stadium, also on December 12, meaning that Philadelphia fans, already confused by the "territorial" distractions, would be forced to choose between two competing NFL games in basically the same city on the same day. Another annoyed party was the University of Notre Dame, which released a statement disavowing any connection to the Pottsville-Four Horsemen spectacle, and clearly intimating that the Notre Dame name should not be used under any circumstances: "The scheduled appearance of the 'Four Horsemen' against the Pottsville Maroons ... is an independent enterprise and should not be interpreted as having any association whatever with the University of Notre Dame. Any reference to or use of the name of the University in connection with this game is unwarranted and unauthorized."[29]

So on Saturday, December 12, 1925, the dueling pro enterprises finished their respective games with Frankford losing to Cleveland 3–0 in front of 7,000 and Pottsville outlasting the Four Horsemen 9–7. With three minutes left in the contest, Pottsville's Charlie Berry booted a 30-yard field goal to pull out the 9–7 victory for the Maroons before a crowd of about 8,000, far from the Grange-like attendance numbers expected by both sides.

In response to Pottsville's refusal to adhere to his directives, Joe Carr's retribution was swift and decisive: Pottsville would forfeit its franchise and was no longer a member of the National Football League. In addition, Carr forced the cancellation of a game set for Sunday, December 13, between Pottsville and Providence, stating in a telegram to the latter club: "If Steamrollers play Pottsville Sunday, the club will be placed on the outlaw list and franchise forfeited. Manager Striegel has violated territorial rights of Yellowjackets by scheduling game in Philadelphia…. I warned Pottsville that the club would be put on the outlaw list and players declared free agents if game is played there, Striegel has defied the league."[30]

In a matter of hours, Pottsville won the battle against the Four Horsemen but lost the war with the NFL. To make matters worse, Doc Striegel soon discovered that the primary reason for playing the game in Philadelphia, a coveted large check from the promoter, bounced…

Football Public Anxious to See the Cards and Bears

By the time the Pottsville game was completed on Saturday, December 12, the Cardinals (11-2-1) were wrapping up their 13-0 conquest of Hammond and therefore nudging past Pottsville (10-2) for first place in the NFL with eight days remaining in the season. Since the Maroons had swept past the Cardinals on December 6 and claimed the league title, nine NFL teams had continued playing games deep into December. With another game set with the Bears on December 20, Chris O'Brien was intent on doing all he could to detour Pottsville's title hopes. Winning the NFL championship, along with securing another lucrative date with Grange and the Bears, was the best of both worlds for O'Brien. Now, with the Maroons apparently kicked out of the circuit, the Cardinals could rest and wait for the next edition of the competition with the Bears, while backing safely into the winner's circle with nary a worry. "The football public appears anxious to see the Cards and Bears in another contest before the season in Chicago closes," stated the *Chicago American*.[31] However, even with the challenges brought on by the early arrival of Grange, followed closely by the Pottsville eviction, league President Joe Carr was about to be blindsided by the biggest black eye experienced yet by the still-groping National Football League—and it landed squarely on the South Side of Chicago.

Most Uncalled for Occurrence Imaginable

Along with his anxious ambition to quickly schedule two games in an effort to bypass Pottsville in the standings, Chris O'Brien received some criticism from media both in Chicago and around the league. Even though most of the league members were still planning December games, O'Brien was targeted because his intent of securing the championship seemed a bit more selfish than simply playing for the money! Both the Milwaukee (December 10) and Hammond (December 12) dates were plotted rapidly after the loss to Pottsville on December 6. Milwaukee was rumored to have already disbanded its team (owned by former Cardinals player Ambrose McGurk). In fact, the Badgers (0–5) had played their last game on November 22, when the club was routed by Rock Island 40–7. On the other hand, Hammond (1–4) had last been on the field on November 1 but counted an earlier 10–6 win over the Cardinals as the team's only success of the season. Neither was expected to provide much opposition to the Cardinals and it showed in the pair of shutout wins by the Cards over that three-day period.

But any dreams of glory and fat paychecks for O'Brien exploded on Monday, December 14, when local newspapers broke the story that the Milwaukee Badgers had used four Chicago high school players in their December 10 game with the Cardinals. What? How could this happen? Why did this happen? It was bad enough that the professionals enticed Red Grange to leave school before his collegiate graduation, but what evil entity would willingly allow mere teenagers to participate? Mr. E.C. Delaporte, the director of athletics for the Chicago Public School System, told the *Chicago Daily Journal* that he would personally investigate rumors that several high school players were added to Milwaukee's roster for its game with the Cardinals on December 10. The *Daily Journal* stated: "If the report proves true the players will automatically be disqualified from further competition. Delaporte is of the opinion the story will prove unfounded, but the rumor has been so persistent that he instituted the investigation."[32]

Delaporte's investigation moved swiftly, and within 24 hours he had discovered the culprits as well as wrestled "confessions" from the teenage offenders. He then promised that he would not conclude his investigation until he could identify the representatives from the professional football interests who brazenly allowed this athletic travesty to occur. The story quickly became front-page news around the country with salacious details seeping out on a daily basis. According to the *Chicago Daily News*, the Badgers arrived in Chicago for the game without enough players, forcing the team to engage in a hurried search for additional players:

> The [Milwaukee] lineup was obtained in a pickup campaign that gathered in former high school players and college stars who were willing to compete for some small monetary award…. The four men that competed in the uniform of the Milwaukee Badgers were W. Thompson, all-city center selection; J.E. Snyder, halfback; Jack Daniels, halfback; and Charlie Richardson, quarterback selection for all-city honors by many of the experts. They entered the contest using the names of the Milwaukee players. Daniels, Richardson, and Snyder worked in the backfield as "Mooney, Blood and Mason," respectively, regular players in the Cream City outfit.[33]

All four of the players mentioned in the above article attended Englewood High School on the South Side of Chicago, and all were gifted athletes now facing permanent disqualification for both high school and college sports. Under questioning by Delaporte, the four admitted their role in the game, including showing up with dirt-covered faces to avoid identification. However, they insisted that they received no money for participating in the game and thought they were only playing in a practice session.

As Delaporte dug deeper, all fingers began to point to Cardinals quarterback Art Folz as the individual who recruited the players for Milwaukee once it became apparent that the visitors would not be able to field a complete eleven for the contest. With the potential loss of future eligibility facing each of the Englewood players, their parents began to share their side of the controversy. Roy Snyder, father of James Snyder, explained the process by which his son and his teammates became involved with the professionals:

> My son was visited by Art Folz, who used to be a star football player at Englewood High School. He represented that the Cardinal football team needed practice and wished to have that kind of a session behind closed gates. He assured my son that his amateur standing would be involved in no way. Consequently, he consented to play along with young Daniels, Thompson and Richardson. My son is less than 17 years old. After all the so-called scandal I asked the boy why he played. "Why," he replied, "Folz asked me to and, dad, I thought I'd learn something about football from practicing with the older men. It was only a practice game and nothing ever was said about money."[34]

If one was to have attended the Cardinals game with Milwaukee on December 10, it would certainly be noticeable that there was no admission fee, no advertising, and very few in attendance. Chris O'Brien was intent on quickly pulling in a couple of more opponents in order to ease past Pottsville in the standings. The four Englewood players maintained that they were misled or "framed" into thinking they were merely participating in a practice session. Delaporte would not consider that excuse and shared his unfiltered opinion with local newspapers regarding not only the Englewood students, but also pro football as a whole: "While there probably is an element of 'frameup' in the affair, I doubt whether any of the boys were so stupid as not to realize what they were doing. They saw a chance for a little easy money, tried to put something over, got caught, and must now pay the penalty. There is little wonder why we are so bitter against the professional game. This was the most uncalled for occurrence imaginable and it has absolutely wrecked the athletic careers of four promising boys. I can't express my contempt for such a trick as this pro team has been guilty of."[35]

Naturally, the professional game was raked over the coals, with Englewood High School Athletic Director Roy Quant offering his troubled view on the situation: "The game was the sort of thing that tends to be detrimental to professional football. The Cards booked it solely for the purpose of winning and boosting their average in order to have a claim to a return game with the Bears. This return game is wanted as Red Grange's presence in the Bears lineup makes a good gate certain."[36]

Once the four players admitted that they participated in the professional game, Delaporte immediately declared them ineligible for further high school competition. This decision was based solely on an existing rule that forbade amateurs from competing in the same competition with a professional. William Thompson and Charles Richardson were seniors and had just completed their final season for the Englewood football squad, while James Snyder was a junior and Jack Daniels just a sophomore. It was reported that Richardson would be heading to Ohio State to continue his career, and that Illinois was already eyeing Snyder to eventually join its football squad. Thompson and Daniels both hoped to play at the next level as well. Delaporte, however, intended to adhere strictly to the rules in this unusual case: "I understand these boys expected to attend college and this may bar them from partaking in athletics. There was nothing for us to do but declare them professionals and make them ineligible. Their only chance for reinstatement would be by the board of control. If that body would be convinced that the boys were blameless, it might reinstate them."[37]

While readers and media feasted on this gridiron scandal, none of the boys involved was heard from until halfback James Snyder was interviewed by the *Chicago Daily Journal* in its December 16 edition. Snyder told reporter Rocky Wolfe:

> They simply took advantage of us. Artie Folz came to me Tuesday at school and asked me if I wanted to practice against the Cardinals. I understand he asked the other three fellows the same thing. At no time was I under the impression we were to engage in a professional game. No mention was made that I was to be paid for playing or I most certainly would have refused. When we were taken to the Sox Park, I thought nothing of it, for I know that is where the Cardinals play. Folz took us up to Chris O'Brien and said "Here are the boys." Then we were given uniforms and sent out on the field. There were some people there to watch, but we were informed that no admission was being charged and it never struck me there was the slightest harm in playing under such conditions.[38]

If Snyder's testimony is accurate, and there is no reason to believe otherwise, then two significant items were revealed. The first is that Folz was recruiting players two days before the game in question. This would indicate that all parties involved would have clearly understood that Milwaukee would not be able to bring a full team of accomplished professional players to Chicago for the game on Thursday, December 10. Secondly, Snyder indicated that the Englewood players were introduced to Chris O'Brien before the game began. He almost certainly knew that they were not members of the Milwaukee team, but did he know that they were high school players, which would dramatically change this story?

Nobody Is More Sorry Over This Affair

On December 17, O'Brien's version of the escapade was shared by the *Chicago Evening American*, in which O'Brien acknowledged that he met the boys before the game:

> Nobody is more sorry over this affair than I am. While I was introduced to the four Englewood boys, their names meant nothing to me and I didn't realize the seriousness of the matter until it was too late. I didn't think it out carefully or it would never have happened. I was selfish in wanting the game so we could play the Bears again and in the hurry the boys were drawn in. I did not know it until late in the game. I should have stopped it right there, but I didn't. I am willing to take my share of the blame and to do everything in my power to square these kids who I realize are absolutely blameless.[39]

In the same article, Art Folz explained his role in the burgeoning situation and accepted all blame for what was turning into a fiasco for both the Cardinals and the National Football League. Following closely after the acclaimed debut of Red Grange and the nearly instant acceptance of pro football in this country, the Englewood scandal was earning national headlines and there was nowhere to hide from it. As such, Folz was both contrite and apologetic:

> It was my fault that this mix-up occurred and I don't want the Englewood boys or Mr. O'Brien to suffer the consequences. The thing came about in this way: Mr. O'Brien told me that we were to play the Milwaukee Badgers, but expressed fear that they might not be able to assemble a whole team on such short notice. I told him I knew several semipro players who would be willing to fill in. However, I was unable to find them. When the Milwaukee men came to town they were shorthanded, as we had expected. I was wondering where I could dig up a couple of men when I thought of Englewood. Because it had been announced that the game would be behind closed gates and without spectators, I never thought it would jeopardize the standing of the preps. I want to take all the blame and do anything in my power to have the boys restored to their amateur standings. It was not their fault.[40]

Although few, if any, looked upon the professionals with sympathy, there was a huge outpouring of concern for the Englewood players. The loss of their amateur eligibility, both in high school and college, seemed much too severe. If the boys did not receive money for their participation and did not realize that they were actually playing in an NFL game, the punishment did not fit the so-called crime. Meanwhile, local editorials sensed an imminent miscarriage of justice and publicly pleaded for the quick exoneration of the Englewood players. A typical message was published by the *Chicago Daily Journal*, which suggested: "Something is wrong here. The punishment does not fit. The right thing, the big thing is to exonerate them."[41]

All that the players could hope for at this point would be a careful review and understanding of the entire mess in a hearing before the Chicago Public Schools Board of Control on December 23. And, once the high school assessment was complete, NFL President Joe Carr was prepared to issue his own brand of justice to the Badgers, the Cardinals, and anyone else who may have touched this debacle. After the huge strides initiated by the NFL in 1925, any directives issued by Carr were expected to be tough and meaningful. The recent trend toward positive public acceptance of the pro ranks was in danger of slipping back into negative territory. The staunch opinion of reader Frank Boyd, published in the *Chicago Evening American*, was typical of the public's ire: "The efforts of the Cardinals and the Bears and Pottsville and New York and others to annex a claim to the championship this season were not only laughable but positively harmful. How much confidence can a fan have in a league where games are scheduled on the spur of the moment—where 'scrub' teams are formed overnight to furnish opposition and where a dozen other [such] things are practiced?"[42]

Treated to the Razzberry of Cross-Examination

The meeting of the Chicago Public Schools Board of Control was scheduled to begin at 2:00 p.m. on Wednesday, December 23. Most in the city hoped for an early Christmas present in the form of forgiveness, and understanding, that would find its way to the four Englewood boys. Folz, O'Brien, and others were present to provide explanations that were intended to be beneficial to the players. Any decision, either for or against the players, made at the meeting would have a wide-ranging national impact as well since the separation between amateurs and professionals was clearly defined at the time. The Board of Control would be expected to determine simply if the boys were professionals or amateurs.

But the session dissolved into much more than that, resembling a trial more than a hearing. A total of 24 preening, pompous bureaucrats representing the athletic interests of the Chicago public high schools battled for the spotlight in the tiny, humid, and suffocating meeting room. This assembly of academic prosecutors was not interested in embracing any words shared in defense of the boys. Rather, the preconceived intent that the meeting was held solely to protect lofty amateur ideals by "convicting" a group of teenagers was quickly evident. One speaker after another took the stage to present prepared statements that bordered on egocentric opinions instead of equitable discussions:

> The open meeting was frequently out of order when several members of the board and others tried to get the floor at the same time. Several rather unfair questions were put to the boys and at one time the Loeb and Leopold case [1924 murder trial in Chicago] was dragged in as an example of precedent to follow on this matter. It was the general opinion the boys were tricked into the game, and while the "buck" changed hands frequently in the meeting, the majority were in sympathy with the players, but under the conditions there was nothing else to do but to stick to the amateur rule. A few favored leniency but were quieted by the argument of setting a bad precedent.[43]

Charles Richardson was an All-City quarterback at Englewood High School in 1925 as well as a collegiate baseball prospect as a catcher. However, he became a part of pro football history when he played one game for the Milwaukee Badgers while still in high school. Richardson is shown catching for Englewood during the 1924 baseball season (SDN-064842, *Chicago Daily News* collection, Chicago History Museum).

Comparing the playing of a football game with a hideous murder trial was insidious and regrettable, but the Board of Control, representing all 24 Chicago public high schools, was adamant in its search for the truth. Going strictly by the book, the board needed to agree that the Englewood boys broke the most prominent aspect of the amateur rule: that an amateur player not participate on a team that includes paid players. Following the general discussion, the board members adjourned to a private session for over an hour to deliberate the fate of the Englewood football players. In the end, the vote was 23–0 to "convict," with Englewood High

School abstaining from the judicial melee. All four (Thompson, Richardson, Snyder, and Daniels) were deemed to be professionals and would be barred forever from playing high school or college sports (since colleges observed the same rules regarding professionalism).

According to newspaper reports, "witnesses" such as Chris O'Brien and Art Folz were treated rudely:

> Chris O'Brien, proprietor of the Cardinals arose thereupon and began to give his version. He was quite candid.... That was about as far as he got for various members of the board all started to examine him at the same time, and in the resulting confusion, Mr. O'Brien slumped into a chair and was silent. Art Folz, the recruiting agent of O'Brien, was next. He said that he told the boys they would not jeopardize their standing, and that the affair was to be merely a scrimmage behind closed gates. In very affable fashion, Mr. Folz declared that it was all his fault. He was then treated to the razzberry of cross-examination by the assembled members who severely demanded to know if he didn't know that he was doing wrong. And when the members got arguing among themselves again, he popped into a seat.[44]

With their athletic fates determined, the four Englewood students appeared stunned and without hope. Their mood was captured perfectly by reporter Guy High of the *Chicago Evening American*: "They realized that it was a life sentence and that the colleges would carry on from where the high schools left off. They said nothing, but stood staring at the floor with their hands in their pockets. They had played with professionals. Then they put on their coats and went downstairs to wait for their coach. Perhaps they thought of their dreams of being Granges, Hestons or Thorpes in future days. As they stood in the lobby, a street corner Santa Claus passed the door with his chimney box on his shoulder. He paused, looked in, and then went on."[45]

While the local media universally panned the decision to ban the boys from future athletic endeavors as being too harsh, bordering on the absurd, Chris O'Brien waited for the other shoe to drop with the expected punishment from Joe Carr and the National Football League. The highly anticipated game with the Bears on December 20 was canceled due to an arm injury to Red Grange and the possibility of severe weather. More likely, since the proverbial heat was really on pro football in Chicago, Halas and O'Brien may have decided that the adverse publicity was simply not worth it. The *Chicago Daily Journal* suggested that another influential source may have been behind the nixing of the contest: "It was reported here that President Carr frowned on the proposed December 20 game between the Bears and the Cardinals and that for that reason it was canceled. The Cardinals, it was said, had this very game in mind with its big gate because of Grange when they booked the 'Milwaukee' team."[46]

I Think Joe Carr Is Bluffing

Then on December 29, Carr slammed down the hammer and cleaned up the debris from the December mischief in the NFL. The results were not unexpected in Chicago as Chris O'Brien was fined $1,000 and placed on league probation for one year for his part in the placement of high school players on the Milwaukee roster.

Carr had decided that O'Brien did not realize the identities of the high school players before the start of the Milwaukee game; otherwise he faced much more severe punishment, including the loss of the Cardinals franchise. Art Folz fared much worse when he learned that he was being held responsible for the entire Englewood disaster and was now prohibited from ever playing in the NFL again. Next, Carr took aim at Ambrose McGurk and the Milwaukee franchise by fining McGurk $500 for adding the Englewood athletes to his roster. Carr ordered McGurk to dispose of his team and all of its assets within 90 days. Finally, Carr addressed the Pottsville situation and fined the Maroons $500 for violating the territorial rights of Frankford while also suspending Pottsville's membership in the league, effectively dropping the Maroons from the league. Carr was adamant in his attempts to preserve the integrity of his league, and his comments after the rulings clearly indicated that, if possible, he would have imposed even more severe punishments upon the offenders: "We are trying to build up the National Professional Football League by trying to merit confidence of the public and press through observance of all rules, especially that pertaining to the use of players who still are eligible for college competition. My only regret is that in this instance league rules do not permit more drastic fines, and I propose to ask that stringent regulations and much heavier fines be placed in the league rules when the league convenes in its annual meeting."[47]

Carr made it clear that no appeals would be allowed regarding his decisions. Any further league activity and discussions, including the determination of the 1925 champion, would be considered at the next league meeting in February 1926. But, after Carr's ruling, Pottsville was no longer in the NFL and the Cardinals, although with the questionable two additional wins, finished with the best record in the league. Following Carr's announcements, Chris O'Brien and Ambrose McGurk were silent, but Doc Striegel of the Pottsville Maroons remained confident in his own assessment of the situation as he told the *Pottsville Evening Republican*: "The matter is not over yet. I am not at all worried. I think Joe Carr is bluffing, and when the annual meeting is held next month [February, 1926], I will be on hand with plenty of evidence to demand a hearing and have our case passed upon by all the other managers. I am not worried about the outcome and tell our fans not to worry either."[48]

As the calendar year of 1925 finally stumbled to an ignominious close, NFL President Joe Carr welcomed what would prove to be a very brief respite from the internal squabbles that had threatened to strangle the very life out of the league. Yet even with the splurge of problems that erupted near the end of the year, Carr would face an even larger challenge in just over a month, when the league's biggest asset would likewise become its biggest problem.

Eleven

Betrayals and Empty Bank Accounts!

"If Driscoll should jump to the Grange league, his name would be blacklisted."—Chicago Tribune, September 9, 1926

On the same day (December 23, 1925) that the four Englewood players learned of their athletic fate, the Chicago Bears arrived in Miami, Florida, to begin a second football tour with the famous Red Grange. Lessons had been learned from the first tour, as the initial plan for six games on what was called the "Southern and Western Trip" included rest and travel periods between the contests. In addition, more players were added to the Bears' roster to ensure that there were adequate substitutes not only for the games but also in case of injuries. Grange pronounced himself fit to play after recovering from the numerous ailments he endured amid the rigors of the initial East Coast tour. This, of course, was excellent news for both the Bears and the individual promoters in each city who were confident that the appearance of Grange would result in substantial financial windfalls.

Eventually, the tour would extend through nine games, with the Bears succeeding in eight of those contests. Grange's manager, C.C. Pyle, arranged for most of the stops on the excursion and was by now savvy enough to demand flat guarantees from the local promoter for some of the games. Some, sadly, agreed to this one-sided proposition and gladly placed the full buying cost down before the game started. Such was the case on the tour's first stop in Coral Gables, Florida, where the local organizers forked over $25,000 to Pyle prior to the December 25 contest. What was even more surprising was that the game was even played, as Red Grange recalled: "Pyle, Halas, and Sternaman were unhappy upon discovering that the site of our initial gridiron venture in the southland was just a big, open sand field. Their concern soon changed to absolute amazement when an army of carpenters, working twenty-four hours around the clock, erected a 25,000-seat stadium in time for the contest."[1]

The fat advance/guarantee ensured a nice profit for Pyle and Grange but was a pronounced disaster for the organizers, as only an estimated 5,000 showed up for the battle between the Bears and "Tim Callahan's Coral Gables Collegians." While Grange scored the only touchdown in the 7–0 Bears victory, the promoters (and Pyle) frightened away many potential customers by establishing ticket prices well above the norm as observed by a local reporter: "Red did just about everything which was expected of him yesterday except run back a kick for a touchdown. But he couldn't drag the fans into that vast wooden arena at the current price of $13 and $11. And if Grange couldn't pack them in at those prices, who could?"[2]

The contract for the game had been finalized on November 12, 1925, between Pyle and the Coral Gables Recreational Department, represented by Director Henry Dutton. This was another example of the numerous efforts initiated by Pyle to capitalize on the name of Red Grange, even before his collegiate playing career was completed. No mention of the Chicago Bears was included in the agreement, but the pregame guarantee of $25,000 was stipulated as was the extravagant ticket pricing: "Both parties agree that the average price of a seat for this game shall be not less than $8.00 nor more than $10.00, unless a change be agreed upon by both parties."[3] Apparently, by the time the game was played, the "parties" had quietly bumped up the price of tickets even further.

The next stop on the tour would be in Tampa, Florida, on January 1, 1926. A slightly different contract was arranged between Pyle and J. Burris Mitchel of Tampa that would guarantee the Pyle-Grange partnership $15,000. Once again, the agreement was completed much earlier, on November 17, 1925, just before Grange turned professional. However, as the deadline for providing the guarantee to Pyle passed, Mitchel experienced some difficulty in making the guarantee and was ousted from the agreement and replaced by Dr. H.E. Opre of Tampa just two days before the game. A quick contract was drawn up the night before the contest that dropped Pyle's guarantee down to $13,000, with $3,000 of that number designated for the opposing Tampa Cardinals.[4] Many players on the opposing Tampa roster were actually members of the NFL's Rock Island Independents and featured the aging, but still well-known, Jim Thorpe. In a sense, Dr. Opre was the ideal choice to fill in as the local promoter. Ticket sales for the Bears game were sluggish, but Dr. Opre agreed to take on the unattractive contract as part of his personal effort to increase the visibility of the Tampa area. Earlier in the year, Opre purchased the struggling local minor league baseball team in Tampa along with a mountain of debt. At the time, Opre revealed a bit about his personal strategy: "I didn't take over the Tampa franchise for personal gain. I did it to give Tampa baseball. This city should have baseball every summer and it is my intention to see that she gets it."[5] And then on the first day of 1926, Opre bestowed the gift of pro football on his beloved hometown.

It might not have been an artistic success, and it certainly was not a financial one, but Opre watched as the Bears dismantled the Tampa Cardinals 17–3 in front of an estimated crowd pegged at just 7,000. While Thorpe was ineffective, Grange thrilled the fans with a spectacular 70-yard run that was glorified forever by the local press:

> When Red had finished a 70-yard run at Plant Field yesterday afternoon, he left in his wake a veritable furrow of fallen bodies. They had all dived at the fleeting form, and they had all missed. It was Kipling who told the world that when you have had your fun you must eventually pay for it. There is nobody to guarantee that when you have paid for your fun you will surely enjoy it. But Tampans were not disappointed yesterday. Some 7,000 of them paid good prices to see Red Grange run, and they saw him, at least those who were able to keep up with the flying form of the former Illinois star saw him.[6]

As for the generous Dr. Opre, he was optimistic and pleasantly at ease while witnessing the exploits of Grange in the half-empty stadium: "Even Dr. H.E. Opre, who assumed charge of the game only two days ago, in the face of certain losses, not once cast estimating glances at the crowd. He was asked whether he thought the 'gate' would cover expenses, and responded: 'That doesn't matter. We are seeing a good football game, and a good team trying to wallop a better one. There is enough good land in Florida to make up whatever I lose on today's game.'"[7]

Land! Plenty of land! And Dr. Opre was right in the middle of a wildly successful tenure as the owner of Finch Brothers, a real estate company in Tampa. Dr. Opre was snapping up, and reselling, large parcels of land in Florida. In particular, he was fond of Sanibel Island, and enjoyed the fruits of his speculation. If he could attract more possible buyers to Florida through his affiliation with sporting events, a few dollars lost on one Chicago Bears game would be insignificant. After the New Year's Day game, Dr. Opre moved on to new real estate ventures, while the Bears moved on to Jacksonville.

America's Greatest Line Smasher

The third game of the tour landed in Jacksonville, Florida, just a day later on January 2, 1926. Whereas Grange had faced the legend of Jim Thorpe the previous afternoon, his newest challenge would be in the form of Ernie Nevers, the Stanford star, who like Grange was intent on profiting from the pro game before his collegiate class graduated. Nevers was a first-team All-American (as was Grange) and was lured from the Stanford basketball court in mid–December by a very generous offer to play several games in Florida, in an article first reported by the *San Francisco Examiner*: "Ernie Nevers, Stanford grid captain and famed All-American fullback, has joined the ranks of the football professionals! Through a contract consummated with a group of Florida capitalists by telegraph last night, America's greatest line smasher agreed to do battle against the Chicago Bears and the sensational Red Grange in a series of games in Florida and California for a consideration in excess of $50,000."[8]

As more details emerged, it was learned that Nevers would play a total of five games in Florida with a hastily created team called the Jacksonville All-Stars. He received $25,000 up front and then was expected to benefit from 5 percent of the gate receipts at each game. If additional games were scheduled, Nevers would earn $5,000 per game and 10 percent of the gate.[9] Unlike Grange, Nevers did not have an agent/manager and his decision to turn professional seemed to be based solely on the opportunity to assist his parents. Nevers remarked: "I was sent to the university to prepare for life. This offer will help me to the same end. It will enable me to repay my parents immediately for the sacrifices they have made in sending me through school and college."[10]

Apparently, Nevers failed to share his good fortune with his parents. His mother was unaware of his decision when contacted by a newspaper: "Until 'The Examiner's' correspondent had telephoned the home of Mr. and Mrs. George E. Nevers this morning, they had not heard of the lad's big stride. 'I had heard nothing about it.

Ernie's at Stanford. Ernie will make good; we know that,' was what his mother had to say."[11]

Once the guaranteed funding of $25,000 was safely in the bank, Nevers embarked on the long cross-country train ride from California to Florida, arriving on December 26. This left less than a week for the Jacksonville All-Stars and Nevers to become acclimated and prepare for the seasoned Chicago Bears. Unfortunately, in what should have been a blockbuster at the gate for the battle between the two heralded superstars in Grange and Nevers, the game dissolved into a dismal financial failure as only 6,500 were in attendance. C.C. Pyle, however, had wrangled a $20,000 guarantee from the local organizers to ensure that all was not lost for him personally. The Bears easily won 19–6 and the *Chicago Tribune* noted the disparity on the field: "The Bears were a smooth working football machine while the All-Stars were a collection of stars imperfectly welded into a team by insufficient practice."[12] Grange played about one-half of the game and gained 29 yards in five carries while Nevers played every minute and delighted the crowd with his passing, rushing and especially his punting, averaging 54 yards on six kicks. Clearly, Nevers was the highlight of the game and the Bears remained true to their plan of not overextending Grange as had been the case on the first tour. Nevers picked up 46 yards on six carries and completed 8 of 16 passes, including one for a 40-yard gain. Defensively, "Nevers stopped the Bear plays right and left, ending up by intercepting a long pass," which led to Nevers scoring the only touchdown for the losers.[13]

Following the game, the Bears headed west for their next game in New Orleans on January 10 while the Jacksonville All-Stars dropped a 7–0 decision to the New York Giants on January 9. That would prove to be the final game for the All-Stars, as Nevers was injured in the game against the Giants and another poor gate prompted the team to disband on January 12. Nevers would, however, play Major League Baseball with the St. Louis Browns in 1926 and later join the NFL's Duluth Eskimos that fall.

Harold "Red" Grange (right) and his father, Lyle, await the departure of Red's train from Chicago in 1926. Lyle Grange was a huge influence in Red's life but was initially unsure if pro football was the best choice for Red to pursue after his collegiate playing days were over. Grange not only played football with the Chicago Bears but also became a regular in Hollywood (SDN-066116, *Chicago Sun-Times/Chicago Daily News* collection, Chicago History Museum).

We Were Pretty Hot Stuff

Red Grange and the Chicago Bears would enjoy the continuation of a very comfortable nine-game tour, both on and off the field. After the three wins in Florida, the Bears stopped in New Orleans (January 10), Los Angeles (January 16), San Diego (January 17), San Francisco (January 24), Portland (January 30), and Seattle (January 31). While not all games were successful financially, two (Los Angeles and San Francisco) were monetary bonanzas, and the team would suffer just one lone defeat to finish with an 8–1 mark. Quarterback Joey Sternaman later recalled the ambience of the tour and the adventures he and his fellow players experienced: "For that second tour, we were pretty hot stuff. C.C. Pyle, Grange's manager and the guy who put it all together, got us our own Pullman car and personal porter for the whole tour. Very fancy. This second tour lasted five weeks, a lot easier than that first one of two weeks. I think through it all I got $200 a game. It was quite something and we all enjoyed it, the second tour, that is. We saw all the nightlife in New Orleans and a lot of the stars in Hollywood and there was always something going on. Pyle saw to that. I had my first airplane ride while I was on it. That was really something."[14]

Easily the high point of the second tour was the stop in Los Angeles to face the Los Angeles Tigers on January 16. The Tigers would be paced by All-American halfback George "Wildcat" Wilson from the University of Washington and a selected crew from California colleges, prompting keen interest from football fans in the area: "All seats to the Los Angeles Coliseum had been sold this morning. This means that a record throng of at least 75,000 persons are paying to see Grange and Wilson do their stuff."[15] With the huge crowd in place and with a big smile on the face of C.C. Pyle, the Bears players noticed an aberration: they had not been paid recently and refused to take the field until payment was in hand. George Halas recalled the situation:

> The boys had been shopping. They bought belted camel-hair coats and snap brim hats. They became a classy lot. Not surprisingly, they felt a need for money. They looked out at the huge crowd and decided the time had come to collect a half game's pay I had owed from the start of the tour. They said they wouldn't go until they got the money. Pyle had not given me the Bears' share of receipts for the past two games. I went to the box office, confronted Pyle and told him that the Bears wouldn't play unless he gave me the overdue money, right now. He did so, I went back to the dressing room and told the boys to play.[16]

Although Grange was surpassed by Wilson in total-yardage performance for the day, Grange scored twice as the Bears survived a late surge by the Tigers to win 17–7. The *Los Angeles Times* observed: "Grange made both of the touchdowns, and, while he uncorked none of the long runs for which he was famous during the late college season, the red-head carried the ball often enough and brilliantly enough to pacify most of the midwinter customers. The crowd was the biggest ever assembled in the Coliseum for a football game ... it was good football all the way and everybody went home satisfied."[17]

Pyle and the Bears had signed a new agreement on December 16, 1925, just prior to the second tour, which ensured that the Pyle/Grange tandem would be well compensated for their efforts. Essentially, the Bears organization was along for the ride with the team receiving just 10 percent of the receipts, although Pyle agreed to also pay the salaries and expenses of the players (except for Halas and Sternaman) on the second tour.[18] In addition, Pyle prepared a contract with each venue on the tour, delineating the division of the game revenue and expenses. The local sponsor was responsible for the stadium rental, the opposing team's wages, advertising, tickets, officials, etc. The contract listed specific ticket prices, which near the end of the tour were much lower than earlier ticket costs. Pyle was the sole representative of the second party noted in the contract and his share of the receipts would be 65 percent after taxes were paid.[19] So, in this confusing realm of contracts, Pyle would receive his 65 percent share and then pay both the Bears and Grange (and the other Grange partners) from this amount. For the well-attended Los Angeles game, Pyle secured $47,711.84 from which the Bears and Grange would be paid, despite 20 percent of the overall gate ($144,556.66) going to charity off the top, along with taxes.[20]

Propinquity Lends Enchantment into Anybody's Life

The Bears suffered their only defeat on the tour in San Francisco on January 24, dropping a 14–9 decision to the San Francisco Tigers. Grange carried the ball just seven times, prompting some dismay from a nice crowd of 23,278. And rumors began to surface of some underlying unhappiness among the Bears players. A pair of San Francisco newspapers published separate "insider" articles on January 26 purporting to share locker room dissatisfaction with the whole Grange extravaganza: "Outside of Grange all of the players are on regular salary and to quote one of them, 'They are tired of seeing Pyle and Grange gathering in the big money.' Grange and Pyle are reported to have made about $75,000 out of the games in Los Angeles and San Francisco. The other Bear boys are said to be getting around $500 per month."[21]

A similar article in the *San Francisco Call and Post* was even more blunt:

> Little financial difficulties that crop up in all business affairs were threatening the fame of Harold "Red" Grange in his professional career, it was learned from reliable sources. The Chicago Bears, it seems, do not warm up to the idea of playing second ukulele, and a dispute is said to have arisen between its chiefs and "Cash and Carry" Pyle, manager of Grange…. A clearing up of the situation may come when the Bears and Grange part company for the season. It is possible that C.C. Pyle may seek a team of his own with which to travel next season if the fame of Grange is not already destroyed before that time.[22]

Even Halas recalled some disenchantment among the troops in the Bears locker room before the San Francisco game: "Tempers were rising. In the dressing room before the game, an old feud broke out between George Trafton and Dutch Sternaman. Dutch knocked George through the door into the runway filled with people. As Ed Healey said, 'It was a tiring season, long and arduous and rugged on manhood. There were a lot of things to laugh at. Propinquity lends enchantment into anybody's life, you might say.'"[23]

In the final two games of the elongated season, the Bears romped over the Portland All-Stars 60–3 on January 30 and the Northwest All-Stars 34–0 on January 31 in Seattle. The most astounding tour in the history of football was now complete. Grange could look forward to a three-week vacation at his home in Wheaton,

Illinois, before beginning his film career. Or could he? The next major change in his life was just days away…

Can't Sleep in Pullman Cars

In retrospect, the nine-game "Western" tour was certainly a financial success. The Sternaman collection revealed that the Pyle/Grange portion of the receipts was $146,556.69, ranging from a low return in Portland ($3,770.70) to a high in Los Angeles ($47,711.84).[24] An undated letter in the Sternaman collection indicated that both Halas and Sternaman benefited from the two tours as well. In addition to their annual salaries of $10,000 each in 1925, the Chicago Bears corporation awarded them both a bonus of $23,000 in December 1925.[25]

Grange remained a celebrity and, in an interview on the train trip back to Chicago, shared his yearning for some rest: "The gridiron hero is going to try to get some sleep in Wheaton these next few weeks, he says. 'I feel fine, but I can't sleep in Pullman cars or in hotels. But I'll bet I get less rest in Wheaton than I did away from home.'"[26]

That period of rest would need to wait, however, as Grange and Pyle jumped back on the train almost immediately to head for Detroit to attend the winter NFL league meeting beginning on February 6, 1926. This would be an important meeting for President Joe Carr since not only would the winner of the muddled 1925 championship be determined, but the league would need to respond strongly to the perception of the negativity of professionalism football. This was brought on by the early signing of Grange (before his college graduation) and the use of the four high school boys by the Milwaukee Badgers in the team's December 10 game against the Chicago Cardinals. In addition, the futures of both the Pottsville Maroons and the Chicago Cardinals franchises were at stake. Would Joe Carr revoke the franchises of both organizations for the embarrassing events that took place in December?

One of the biggest stories emanating from the meeting was the rumor that Red Grange was interested in purchasing the Chicago Cardinals from Chris O'Brien. In light of the recent league ruling against the Cardinals (and the accompanying fine of $1,000), the suggestion did make some sense, as reported in the *Green Bay Press-Gazette*: "It is believed that there is some truth to the Grange rumor although Chris O'Brien, manager of the Cards, was sitting mum. He refused to say a word but one of his associates hinted that Grange had been talking things over with O'Brien. The Cards got a black eye last fall in their 'hurry up' game with the so-called Milwaukee Badgers and O'Brien has not recovered from the shock yet. President Carr slapped a fine of $1,000 on O'Brien for his part in the affair and it is quite possible that O'Brien will get out from under if the Grange offer is big enough."[27]

Whatever the circumstances, O'Brien decided not to sell the Cardinals to Grange, which left the league with another dilemma: what to do with Grange and Pyle? Earlier, the relationship between Pyle and the Bears crumbled when Pyle suggested that Grange could continue his career with the Bears, but at a specific price. George Halas was quick to turn down the less-than-modest offer: "The Bears' contract with Mr. Pyle for Red's services ended with the Seattle game. I had hoped, and perhaps even somewhat expected, that Mr. Pyle would continue the very profitable cooperation with the Bears. He said yes, he would continue to provide the services of Mr. Grange to the Bears in return for one-third ownership of the Bears. One-third ownership? An equal partner with Dutch and me? No, no, no! In no way. No, first, last and always! A percentage of earnings, yes, that was negotiable, but a share of ownership, no!"[28]

At the league meeting, Pyle and Grange then petitioned for a franchise in New York, which, of course, was already in the realm of the New York Giants. Brimming with confidence, Pyle prematurely leased Yankee Stadium for five years to serve as the home base for his proposed team. Therefore, it must have been quite a shock for Pyle when the league representatives denied his franchise request. The reason was simple: the Giants were already positioned in New York. Pyle then determined that Grange would play in Yankee Stadium in 1926, whether his team was a member of the NFL or not. A new league would be established by Pyle in direct competition to the National Football League, with Grange leading the New York representative. New York Giants owner Tim Mara accepted the challenge and vowed that any rivalry between the two teams would be risky: "If Grange carries out his threat to promote a team in New York and conflicts with our Sunday dates, neither one of us will make a nickel. But we are in a better position to survive as we are in an organized league and any other team that invades our territory without a franchise will have to play as outlaws."[29]

In another nod to Grange, the league representatives also unanimously implemented a rule that would forbid member organizations from utilizing the services of any collegiate player before his class graduated. Ironically, George Halas, who initiated the overall eligibility disturbance with his signing of Grange immediately after the latter's final college football game, was appointed to help resolve this issue with the colleges: "There was a strong sentiment expressed against any act on the part of the league to injure either the colleges or the college players by professionalizing the stars. In furtherance of this sentiment a committee of which George Halas, manager of the Chicago Bears, as chairman, was named to confer with representatives of the National Collegiate Athletic Association in an effort to draw up a set for regulation for the protection of college players."[30]

Chris O'Brien Refused the Throne

During his "President's Report," Joe Carr acknowledged the progress made by the league members, but upheld the previous sanctions against the Milwaukee Badgers, the Chicago Cardinals, and the Pottsville Maroons. He clearly listed the actions in question and distinctly outlined his reasons for maintaining the previously assigned punishments, beginning with the Badgers and Cardinals:

> Milwaukee and the Chicago Cardinals engaged in a game of football at Chicago, in which four high school boys were permitted to play with the Milwaukee club.... I made a very thoro investigation and at its conclusion I fined the Milwaukee club the sum of $500.00 and gave the management ninety days in which to dispose of its assets at Milwaukee.... The Cardinal management was fined the sum of $1,000.00 and placed on probation for one year. I could not

find where the management of the Cardinal team had guilty knowledge of the status of the boys who played until after the game had been played.³¹

The plight of the Pottsville Maroons was also verified by Carr, who carefully explained his reasoning:

> In the case of Pottsville, I had been appraised through reports from league members and the press that the Pottsville team intended to play a game at Philadelphia on December 12. I immediately notified the management of the Pottsville club that the game should not be played under all penalties that the League could inflict. The Pottsville management wired me that they had signed a contract and that they desired the League to insure them against a damage suit. I advised that the League would give them every protection possible and again forbade them to play in the protected territory of another club, and with a team which was not a member of our organization. Three different notices forbidding the Pottsville club to play were given and the management elected to play regardless. Hence I fined the club the sum of $500.00 and suspended them from all rights and privileges, and declared their franchise forfeited in the league.³²

Cardinals quarterback Art Folz was swept along in the debris of penalties and chastisements when his lifetime banishment from the NFL was upheld. Folz had been identified previously as being the key contact in luring the Englewood High School boys to play for Milwaukee in that ill-fated game against the Cardinals. Finally, the league representatives awarded the 1925 championship to the Chicago Cardinals, based on compiling the best record for the season. However, O'Brien turned down the title, apparently in deference to the controversial way the schedule concluded: "Like Caesar, Chris O'Brien, owner of the Chicago Cardinals, refused the throne and as a result the league will play through 1926 without a champion. O'Brien stated that owing to the conditions under which his team had tied Pottsville and later was declared champion, he didn't feel that the honors had been earned."³³

With Pottsville no longer in the National Football League for ignoring league rules, and with

Art Folz was a strong-armed southpaw quarterback for the Chicago Cardinals before his career ended in conjunction with the 1925 scandal when Folz recruited four high school players to join the Milwaukee Badgers for one game. This photograph is from when Folz was a student at Englewood High School in 1921. Folz was banned for life by the NFL for his actions, but that decision was later rescinded. Folz, however, elected to "retire" from football and was a pioneer in promoting auto racing in the Chicago area (SDN-063018, *Chicago Daily News* collection, Chicago History Museum).

the Cardinals achieving the best record in the league, no matter how disputed, the decision to award the 1925 championship to the Cardinals was the correct one to be made by the NFL, even if Chris O'Brien respectfully declined the honor.

Both Want Their Pound of Flesh

Pottsville suffered another significant setback when a hearing began in Philadelphia on January 16, 1926, to sort through the claims relating to the "bounced" check received by the Pottsville management following the now infamous game with the former Notre Dame "Four Horsemen" on December 12. Harry Stuhldreher, one of the Four Horsemen, brought litigation against promoter Frank Schumann after Stuhldreher received only $8,000 of the expected $25,000 amount promised the ex–Notre Dame players. John "Doc" Streigel, manager of the Pottsville club, was also seeking $4,900, or the amount of the bad check that Schumann had given Streigel for his team's participation, as described by the local press: "Schumann had more vision than he had cash ... and there was something wrong with the promoter who figured two outside [of Philadelphia] teams could draw it. But anyway, Stuhldreher got all the money in sight, $8,000. Pottsville got a check for $4,900 and got kicked out of the National League, while Schumann went south. Stuhldreher and Streigel both want their pound of flesh, however, and have instituted suit against Schumann."[34]

Then, on March 25, 1926, it was reported that Schumann was acquitted on the charge that he issued a bad check to the Maroons. Apparently, his litany of excuses, including blaming Streigel for his problems, swayed the jury and the charges pertaining to issuing a bad check were dropped.[35] Neither Streigel nor Stuhldreher received a penny more from Schumann for their participation in the heralded December 12 battle. It was another blow for Streigel, whose marginal hope of acquiring the 1925 championship was snuffed out at the recent NFL meeting in Detroit. Now, the game that caused him to lose his NFL franchise ended up being a complete financial loss.

He Showed a Wealth of Football Brains

As the years, and the decades, have passed, the tumultuous events of the final month of the 1925 NFL season have been resurrected on occasion for renewed debate, but rarely are the four Englewood High School players and Art Folz ever mentioned. Their lives and individual stories after the scandal are both interesting and unique, with one player even reaching superstardom in another sport. Englewood High School (called the Purple) had been a powerhouse among Chicago high schools since the 1890s. Heading into the 1925 season under Coach Chuck Palmer, a former three-sport Northwestern standout, Englewood was expecting another strong campaign. Senior center Bill "Hoppy" Thompson was elected captain of the squad and he and versatile senior quarterback Charles Richardson were already stars. They were joined in the starting lineup by James Snyder, a junior right halfback, and sophomore fullback John "Jack" Daniels.

As the season progressed, all four were in the starting lineup and shared the spotlight. In a 27–0 drubbing of Tilden Tech, Snyder scored two touchdowns, while in a tight 15–0 escape over feisty Marshall, "Hoppy Thompson at center was the only Purple lineman who showed up well," lamented the *Southtown Economist*.[36] Englewood was so well respected on the football field that the team was invited to play two games out of state, a bit unusual at the time. On its way to an overall 6-2-2 record in 1925, Englewood traveled to Muskegon, Michigan, for a 6–6 tie, and then journeyed to Lock Haven, Pennsylvania, for a 3–0 loss on December 5, 1925, in the final game. Following the season-ending defeat at Lock Haven, winning coach Sol Wolf praised the effort to the visitors from Chicago: "Englewood showed the best fundamentally coached and smartest team which we have met in the past two years. The Englewood players proved themselves splendid sportsmen both throughout and after the game. It was a pleasure to play them."[37]

After the battle in Lock Haven, the Englewood team enjoyed a visit to Niagara Falls, New York, and then returned to Chicago on Monday, December 7, 1925. By that time, the players could read all about some of the honors that were pouring in following their successful season. Thompson and Richardson had both been named to the first team of the "All-Section" honor squad by the *Southtown Economist*, which praised the abilities of quarterback Richardson: "Richardson is unequalled as an open field runner. His change of pace and sidestepping have brought him many long runs. He is a brilliant passer, and as quarterback of the Purple eleven he showed a wealth of football brains. Because he is so adept at dodging, he averaged more yardage on the return of punts than any other player in the section. On defense he is a deadly tackle."[38]

Both were also named to the Chicago "All City" team by the *Chicago Tribune*, which was especially impressed by the interior line work of Thompson: "Thompson, Englewood's aggressive center, is placed in the pivot position. He was one of the best passers [centers] of the season. Offensively he opened large holes and defensively he was a veritable stone wall."[39]

While Richardson and Thompson were scheduled to graduate, Snyder and Daniels would return to anchor the 1926 Englewood High School football team. But then, of course, came the visit from Art Folz, the ill-fated recruitment of the players for the Milwaukee Badgers game, and the lifetime banishment for all four individuals who simply thought they were playing in a practice game. It was a horrible punishment for the kids and one that was loudly criticized throughout the country by various media members, such as by Don Maxwell, the sports editor of the *Chicago Tribune*:

> When the boys complete high school they may enter college. But they never can play on college teams. The board might have suspended the boys for six months or a year. It didn't do either. It showed no leniency whatever. The board was as drastic in its ruling as it might have been had the boys been paid to play and had they played with their eyes open to the consequences. Blacklisted in every college in the country, these four Englewood boys may lose their desire for a college degree. This may be bad logic but it's good dope. In conclusion, we beg to suggest to the athletic board that leniency is sometimes a virtue. High school boys have committed graver sins than playing for nothing in what they believed was a practice game.[40]

Richardson and Thompson graduated from Englewood earlier in 1926, but by the time the fall football season came around, Snyder and Daniels were surprisingly back out on the field. In a confusing reversal, E.C. Delaporte, the secretary for the Chicago Public Schools Board of Control, discussed the Englewood situation with the *Southtown Economist*: "As explained by Mr. Delaporte, the two boys [Snyder and Daniels] were never declared ineligible or disqualified by the league officials. The only thing barring them from competition again this year is the decision of [Englewood] Principal David M. Davidson in the matter."[41]

Huh? Under these circumstances, Snyder and Daniels were delighted to rejoin the team and promptly led Englewood to a spotless 3–0 record after a 13–9 win over host Pine Bluff, Arkansas, with Snyder scoring the winning touchdown. But then, probably because of a protest from an unnerved opponent, the careers of both Snyder and Daniels were derailed—again. Englewood Principal Davidson elected to flash his bureaucratic credentials and decided that both players were finished on the athletic field. Line coach Roy Quant explained the odd decision: "Mr. Davidson has decided to follow the suggestion of the Chicago principals' club that the boys be kept out of competition rather than risk difficulties within the league if they were allowed to play."[42] Englewood proceeded to drop its remaining five games and managed to score just one touchdown without Snyder and Daniels. If there is anything worse for an athlete than being prohibited from competing, it might be feeling the elation of being allowed back in the arena, then kicked out a second time. Such was the sad case of Snyder and Daniels. The Chicago public school principals did indeed show no mercy.

Once a Star at Englewood

So, whatever happened to the "Englewood Four" and their ambushed athletic careers? After playing in one NFL game against the Chicago Cardinals in 1925, all four are listed in the respected *Total Football II*, the hefty encyclopedia of the National Football League, as being members of the Milwaukee Badgers for that single game. After that lone appearance, the four would never again play together for Englewood High School in any sport, but three of them did manage to unite once more on the local semipro circuit in 1928, which will be discussed shortly.

William "Hoppy" Thompson graduated from Englewood High School in February 1926. Born August 12, 1905, Thompson lived at 325 West 59th Place while in high school and eventually became a Chicago policeman. His father, also named William, was a United States marshal "who escorted Al Capone to prison."[43] Tragically, the younger Thompson died on February 15, 1937, of pneumonia at the age of 31, but his obituary noted that he was "a football star at Englewood High School in 1925."[44] Thompson left behind a wife and two young children. Catherine Markee Smith, the granddaughter of William Thompson, was vaguely familiar with but not totally aware of her grandfather's "one-game professional and high school football career. Although I do like the truth vs. urban legends, the computer is teaching us that once again people are not good at transferring information over the years accurately. This was fascinating learning this information!"[45]

Charles A. Richardson, born September 12, 1906, in Fulton, Kentucky, was an exceptional athlete at Englewood, participating in football, basketball, and baseball, according to the 1926 *Purple and White* school yearbook. His father was a railroad worker and the family moved to St. Louis from Kentucky and eventually settled in Chicago at 5632 South Calumet Avenue. Like his teammate Thompson, Richardson graduated in February 1926. Before the so-called scandal, he hoped to attend Ohio State University. Richardson found employment in the baking industry, becoming a salesman for the Continental Baking Company in Chicago. He served in the U.S. Navy during World War II and eventually moved to California, where he was involved in a variety of service-related occupations before passing away on January 12, 2000.

John DeFrance "Jack" Daniels was given a middle name that was the same as his mother's maiden name. Born on December 24, 1906, in Kalamazoo, Michigan, Daniels, who resided at 224 West 60th Place, experienced a very unusual academic career at Englewood. He entered as a freshman in February 1920 but did not graduate until February 1928! According to school records, Daniels dropped out several times for work-related reasons before finally completing his academic work eight years after beginning. In the 1928 Englewood High School yearbook, Daniels indicated that his secret ambition was "to become a famous football coach, and he hoped to attend the University of Southern California."[46] Also known as "Pug," Daniels did return to play for Englewood in 1927 and boxed for a brief time. After finally graduating from Englewood, he initially found work as a teacher and then as a book manufacturer in Chicago before working for the Golden Nugget casino complex in Las Vegas in the 1950s. Daniels died in Evergreen Park, Illinois, on January 10, 1977.

In 1928, Richardson, Thompson, and Daniels were on the field together again as members of the semipro Amos Athletic Association team in Chicago. The club included former players from Notre Dame, Michigan, Indiana, Purdue, and other well-known universities. Yet the leader was quarterback Richardson. In a close 7–0 loss to the Hammond Boosters on December 2, 1928, his sterling effort was recognized by the *Hammond Times*: "Richardson, once a star at Englewood High, directed the Amos play from the quarterback post and was responsible for many gains."[47] But where was the missing member of the celebrated "Englewood Four?"

Former Chicago Milk Wagon Driver Broke All Records

As far as James Snyder was concerned, he did not wish to end his high school athletic career watching from the sidelines. After being limited to just three games during his senior football season (1926), Snyder grabbed a starting spot on the school's basketball team and led Englewood to the city championship in early 1927. Snyder, who lived at 342 West 61st Place, enjoyed a varied high school experience by also participating on the track squad, the ice-skating club, the rifle team, the drama club, and the Lettermen's Club.[48] After graduating from Englewood in 1927, he took his talents down to the University of Illinois, where he majored in physical education and was a member of the football team in 1928, playing exclusively on the varsity reserve team. His grades were average. He excelled in a basketball class but struggled with sessions in English history and modern industry.[49]

Following the first semester of the 1928–1929 academic year, sophomore Snyder departed Illinois and enrolled at Oglethorpe University in Georgia. However, Snyder left school and moved back to Chicago during the year and found work as a milk wagon driver, according to the 1930 U.S. census.[50] Perhaps he found the lethargic speed of the milk wagon disenchanting since by 1932, Snyder (now going by the name of Jimmy) was beginning to appear at local auto race tracks in the Chicago area. He enjoyed asking questions, probing drivers for information, and looking for any opportunity to slide behind the wheel of a race car. Arch Ward, sports editor of the *Chicago Tribune*, later described Snyder's entry into auto racing: "Jimmy Snyder, former Chicago milkman, got his start as a driver when he bought a helmet and a pair of goggles in 1932."[51]

Initially, Snyder drove "midget" race cars and became a consistent winner in both indoor and outdoor competitions. On October 8, 1933, Snyder won a 100-mile race at the long-gone Roby Speedway in Hammond, Indiana, and the following week captured shorter-length races at the Evanston (Illinois) Motor Speedway, prompting the *Chicago Tribune* to describe him as "a new star in automobile racing."[52] Snyder's star continued to ascend over the next few years. He dominated the popular indoor midget races at the 124th Field Artillery Armory in Chicago: "Jimmy Snyder, south side driver, took top honors in the second series of indoor auto races at the 124th Field Artillery Armory. [Chicago] Mayor Edward J. Kelly fired the starting gun. Snyder won four events and a match race."[53]

In 1935 Snyder graduated to the big time when he qualified for the prestigious Indianapolis 500, the first of five consecutive appearances in the brickyard for Snyder. The *Chicago Tribune* noted his Chicago ties: "Among the qualifiers today was Jimmy Snyder of Chicago, former Englewood High School athlete, who raced all winter in midget races in Chicago indoor arenas. Snyder qualified with an average of 112.249 miles an hour."[54]

Snyder, nicknamed "The Flying Milk Man," established a new track record at Indianapolis in 1937 and then repeated that feat in 1939 while grabbing the vaunted pole position as the fastest car in the field: "Jimmy Snyder, the former Chicago milk wagon driver, broke all qualifying records as well as the one-lap mark, in winning the No. 1 berth in the front row for the 500-mile race to be held May 30 at the famous brick and asphalt oval yesterday afternoon. He averaged 130.138 miles an hour for his

Jimmy Snyder was the 1939 pole sitter for the Indianapolis 500 race and one of the most famous race car drivers in the country. But before that, he was a hard-driving fullback for Englewood High School in Chicago. His prep sports career was derailed after he unknowingly played in one NFL game in 1925 as a member of the Milwaukee Badgers while still in high school (courtesy IMS Photo Archive).

10-mile sprint and showed 130.757 m.p.h. on his second turn of the two-and-one-half mile course."[55]

Snyder went on to finish second in the race behind Wilbur Shaw, and further fortified his reputation as one of the leading race car drivers in the world. Joe Skibinski, archivist and staff photographer at the Indianapolis Motor Speedway (IMS), provided the following comment from the IMS:

> Many racing historians consider Jimmy Snyder to have been one of the greatest drivers ever in Indianapolis 500-Mile Race history who never was able to win. The first driver ever to turn an official qualifying lap in excess of 130 mph (1937), Snyder led 24 of the 27 laps he completed before a transmission failed in 1937; 92 of the 150 laps he completed before a supercharger malfunctioned in 1938; and 65 of the full 200 on his way to finishing second in 1939. His total of 181 laps led during those three years remain to this day as the third-highest number ever by a driver who never was able to win.[56]

Sadly, just one month later on June 29, 1939, Jimmy Snyder lost his life in a midget car race in Cahokia, Illinois, at the age of 30. The startling news stunned the racing world:

> When the final checkered flag fell for smiling Jimmy Snyder, Chicago's premier racing car driver, last night at an obscure little midget track in Cahokia, Illinois, after he won years of spectacular speedway competition, it took one of the most popular and appealing figures in big time automobile racing. In 1932 he drove his first racing car on the historic Crown Point, Indiana, course. Since that time, he has blazed to the top of the American and international speed world, driving the dirt tracks, the Indianapolis 500-mile classics and the midget courses with a brilliance and fearlessness that has endeared him to thousands of race followers.[57]

Jimmy Snyder and his Englewood teammates all rose above the cruel hand that was dealt to them after the 1925 "scandal." If anything good resulted from the infamous game between the Milwaukee Badgers and the Chicago Cardinals on December 10, 1925, it was not the blemish that robbed the four Englewood boys from pursuing their collegiate dreams. However, there is an interesting sidebar from that ill-fated contest. When Jimmy Snyder joined the Badgers against the Cardinals on December 10, 1925, he was just 16 years old (born March 10, 1909) and it appears that he was, and remains, the youngest person ever to play in an NFL game!

We Intend to Protect Our Investment

With the NFL refusing to honor the request of C.C. Pyle and Red Grange to operate their own franchise in New York for the 1926 season, it forced Pyle to pursue an alternative arrangement intended to showcase the talents of Grange. Through a series of rapid contacts, introductions, and negotiations, Pyle was able to create the new American Football League (AFL) that would provide the existing NFL with its first real threat from a competitive professional outlet. Pyle inserted Red Grange as the star attraction of the AFL and rightly so. Pyle realized the drawing power of Grange and hoped to hammer the NFL into submission through dominant attendance figures and increased public support. Nine teams quickly joined the circuit, including the New York Yankees headed by Red Grange. The NFL became somewhat concerned when the Rock Island Independents deserted the older league and jumped to Pyle's waiting arms. In Chicago, both the Bears and the Cardinals would have their immediate futures impacted during the early jousting among the two leagues. Pyle and Grange strongly pursued Chris O'Brien to join the AFL, but O'Brien refused to budge from the older league. In fact, O'Brien quickly became a staunch defender of the NFL despite the recent "punishment" he had received as part of the fragile ending to the 1925 season. O'Brien grimly envisioned a bidding war for players between the two leagues, which did not portend a happy ending for the new AFL, as he told the Associated Press: "We have our own playing fields and most of the high-class stars under binding contracts and a war chest on which to draw—and we certainly intend to protect our investment to the best of our financial ability."[58]

Pyle then planted an AFL team in O'Brien's own backyard when the Chicago Bulls were created and Pyle wisely secured a lease for Comiskey Park, forcing O'Brien and the Cardinals back to Normal Park with its smaller seating capacity. Or did they? O'Brien had apparently already alerted the Comiskey Park managers that he would relinquish his lease in 1926 in favor of retaining his old home base of Normal Park: "O'Brien had previously given up the White Sox park and had announced that his team would play its home games at Normal Park. The Cardinals will play out of town games this season for the first time in three years."[59] Part of the reasoning behind this was that O'Brien planned to do something unusual with his scheduling during the upcoming season by taking the Cardinals on the road for at least one half of its schedule. Previously, the Cards rarely played an away game outside Chicago. His thinking was sound. Instead of renting a huge stadium and then remitting a guaranteed fee to the visiting team (with no assurance that he would be left with any margin, considering Chicago weather issues that could affect attendance), O'Brien would instead travel to several games, be reimbursed for much of his team's travel, and also pocket a reliable guarantee.

The emergence of the AFL also caused friction on the Chicago Bears when quarterback Joey Sternaman departed to become a player/coach/owner of the Chicago Bulls. Said Sternaman: "I started up a team in Chicago. Well, I owned the Bulls, coached them, and played quarterback. It was a big gamble, and I got talked into making it. It seemed like a real good thing at the time."[60]

Joey Sternaman's departure created some tension on the Bears side since Joey's brother Dutch was still the co-owner of the team. In fact, so was Joey! Following the failed attempt in 1922 to lure Paddy Driscoll to the Bears with promises of an equal ownership commitment, some of that stock designated for Driscoll was shared with Joey Sternaman and Frank Halas, brother of George Halas. At a special meeting of the organization's Board of Directors on May 14, 1926, Joey Sternaman resigned from his board seat. His handwritten letter was brief and succinct:

> To: Chicago Bears Football Club, Inc.
> Kindly take notice that I am this day tendering my resignation as Director of Chicago Bears Football Club, Incorporated, to take effect immediately. Dated this 14th day of May, A.D. 1926.
> Signed: Joseph T. Sternaman

The resignation was unanimously accepted and the board immediately elected Chester Sternaman, an older brother of Dutch, as its fourth member, joining Dutch along with George and Frank Halas.[61] More important, in a situation that was shaping up as a battle for survival, the Bears were now facing stiff competition from one of their own in the same city. Would Dutch Sternaman be able to navigate the breach in loyalty between his brother Joey and his partner George Halas? Early signs indicated this might not be possible. The partnership between Dutch Sternman and George Halas began to fray at the next NFL meeting, held in July 1926 in Philadelphia. One of the primary reasons for this meeting was to develop the 1926 league schedule as well as address the growing competitive presence of the American Football League. The polarization between Halas and Sternaman apparently was obvious to all at the league meeting: "First news of divergence in the views of Sternaman and Halas came when the franchise holders in the National League held their annual meeting in Philadelphia. Joe Carr, president of the league, is said to have been bewildered at the efforts of both owners to schedule games. He asked who had the authority to make the schedules. Each claimed that right. The league was then put to a vote of the other club owners and Halas was victorious."[62]

Evidently, the critical date in question was October 17, 1926. Halas wanted to schedule the Cardinals on that day, while Sternman insisted that the Bears and the Cardinals meet instead on Thanksgiving Day. George Halas later explained the reasoning behind both preferences:

> On my schedule, I had penciled in for that day [October 17] a game with our old rivals, the Cardinals, a match that usually produced the biggest gate of the season. Dutch wanted to play the Cardinals on the traditional date, Thanksgiving Day. When other league members learned that October 17 was the day Joey Sternaman had scheduled a game in Chicago between his new club and Mr. Pyle's New York Yankees starring the great Red Grange, the reason for differences between Dutch and me became obvious. A double bill in Chicago on the day I proposed would hurt the Bulls; keeping the Cardinals game on Thanksgiving Day would help them. The situation caused me heartache. Dutch, Joey and I had gone through hard times together. Now, when prosperity was here, we were divided. I was finding adversity more pleasant than prosperity.[63]

I Could Never Let the Bears Be Second Best in Chicago

While the Halas/Sternaman partnership was beginning to disintegrate, another Chicago football duo quietly separated. Chris O'Brien brought Paddy Driscoll to the Cardinals in 1920, and despite nearly rabid efforts by George Halas to procure the services of Driscoll over the years, he remained with O'Brien. Driscoll had been the anchor of the early years of the NFL, providing skill, leadership, and, most important, drawing power as the league struggled for recognition. Now, after six seasons on the South Side, Driscoll was the object of a bidding war between O'Brien and the new AFL. Pyle intended to place Driscoll in the backfield of the Chicago Bulls along with Joey Sternaman, while Chris O'Brien valiantly attempted to equal any offers to Driscoll, although his resources at the time were limited. As the involved teams waited, Driscoll evaluated his options, and the NFL mentors feared that the loss of another star player to the AFL would be devastating.

Not surprisingly, George Halas entered the bidding war when O'Brien reluctantly traded the rights to Driscoll to the Bears. This transaction would have been unfathomable a couple of years earlier, but O'Brien's fragile financial assets might have prevented the NFL from retaining the services of Driscoll. Understanding the situation and still wanting to add Driscoll to his roster, Halas was prepared to do all he could to keep Driscoll in the NFL: "His [O'Brien's] financial outlook was dismal. He had to cut expenses. The most expensive player was Paddy Driscoll, and common sense told Chris that Paddy deserved a raise, not a cut. Joey Sternaman offered Paddy a raise, and a big one, to join the Bulls. Alarms rang in my head. If they got Paddy, the Bulls might be a better club than the Bears. I could never let the Bears be second best in Chicago. I offered Chris O'Brien $3,500 if he would sell Paddy's contract to me. He accepted. Paddy wavered.... In the end, he decided to play for the Bears [in 1926] for $10,000."[64]

By signing with the Bears instead of the Bulls, Driscoll avoided being branded an "outlaw" by the NFL as the league dug in its heels for the upcoming battle with the AFL. The Chicago Bulls Inc. organization was incorporated on June 12, 1926. The three named stakeholders were all residents of Chicago: attorney Wadsworth Watts, real estate broker Charles Grauer, and structural engineer Norman Brunkow.[65] As noted previously, Joey Sternaman claimed to be the owner of the Bulls, even if his name was not on the original incorporation documents. Later, both Joey Sternaman and his twin brother, Paul, were listed as the officers of the now-defunct organization. Attorney Steve Thomas explained the possibility of how Sternaman could have assumed that role:

> Watts, Grauer, and Brunkow (the incorporators) are represented as having subscribed ($10,000) and paid in ($5,000) as an investment in the stock of the corporation. As original investors they could have retained or sold or transferred all or part of their original investment at any point in time without need for any public record of the transaction(s). They are also shown as the initial three-person board of directors.
>
> By the time an annual report is filed in 1928, the two Sternamans [Joey and Paul] are listed as the sole officers and directors, and the three original incorporators, subscribers, and directors are no longer listed. An annual report must disclose the names and addresses of officers and directors, but investors are not required to be identified, although it is not uncommon for directors or officers also to be investors. By 1928 the issued stock had increased from $5,000 to $10,000, according to the annual report. But the report itself tells nothing about the ownership of these shares.[66]

As the 1926 season unfolded, the threat of the AFL's presence may have persuaded NFL President Joe Carr to reevaluate some prior decisions. Instead of allowing the exiled Pottsville Maroons to be coaxed into the new league, Carr welcomed the scorned Maroons back into the NFL. Carr then refunded the $1,000 fine to Chris O'Brien originally levied due to the 1925 shenanigans and also lifted the lifetime ban from Art Folz on September 7, 1926, perhaps fearing that Folz would likely cross over the pro football border and sign with an AFL club. However, Folz elected to never play in the National Football League again. Instead, Folz, like Jimmy Snyder, became involved in auto racing. But unlike Snyder, Folz was not a driver, but an organizer: "Mr. Folz, who played with the Cardinals in the early 1920s ... is Chicago's leading entrepreneur of automobile racing, not only the stocks but the stripped-down hot rods, and the midgets. Soldier Field, where Art operates, as president of the Chicago Racing Association, is the largest stock car track in the country in attendance and purses paid."[67]

Folz was the founder and served as a president of the National Midget Automobile Racing circuit. In 1950, he was selected as the local "Promoter of the Year" by Chicago media.[68] During his racing tenure, Folz became a partner in the ownership of the *San Fernando Sun* newspaper and moved to California in 1953. Later he added ownership responsibilities for the *Antelope Valley Press*. Folz passed away on August 18, 1965, in Los Angeles at the age of 62.

Pyle Will Put Easter Bunnies Under Contract

With all of the parties from the 1925 Milwaukee Badgers catastrophe forgiven (except owner Ambrose McGurk of the Badgers and the least guilty party—the Englewood Four), the 1926 NFL season began with both the Bears and the Cardinals moving quickly out of the gate. And yet, all eyes were on the new competition in the form of the American Football League. As the latest brainchild of C.C. Pyle, the new organization promised stiff, if not consequential, competition where none was needed. The NFL was emerging from the most publicized season in its brief existence, from the glow of thousands turning out to watch Red Grange play, to the black eye of the Milwaukee Badgers scandal. Still Major League Baseball, as well as collegiate football, held a significant lead over pro football in terms of audience participation and fiscal success. Pyle was confident, if not arrogant, by this time and certainly believed in both his product and his own creative marketing skills. When the NFL repulsed his request for a New York franchise earlier in the year, he instinctively moved forward with his next plan, assured in his own mind that the Grange hysteria would easily carry over into 1926. Then he could prove the naysayers wrong and maneuver the NFL into whatever corner would be most financially beneficial to himself. But could the professional grid infighting possibly kill the sport as well?

Of course, the most accurate measuring stick to gauge the success of the new league would be a win not on the field but rather in attendance. On the opening week of the season, September 19, two games were scheduled in the Chicago area. The New York Yankees of the AFL, led by Red Grange, defeated the local Illinois All-Stars in the Chicago suburb of Aurora, where the Yankees held their preseason training camp. The game attracted "a crowd of 18,000, the greatest throng that ever witnessed a gridiron contest in the community." One of the dangers of leasing a Major League Baseball park for football was that no home games could be scheduled until the baseball club vacated the premises for the season. This was not an issue for the Chicago Cardinals in 1926 since the team was now relegated to hosting teams at cozy Normal Park. In the opening game on September 19, the Cards blanked the Columbus Tigers 14–0 but only 2,500 were in the crowd.[69]

The two Chicago teams that were based in baseball stadiums, the Bears and the Bulls, scurried out of town to open their respective seasons. The Chicago Bears needed some effort in edging the revitalized Badgers in Milwaukee 10–7 on September 19, while the Bulls and Joey Sternaman waited a week for their opener in Newark,

New Jersey, on September 26, tying the home club 7–7. Unfortunately, just 3,000 showed up.[70] While Grange and Joey Sternaman performed well on the field, overall attendance at AFL games was inconsistent. While the Yankees attracted 22,000 in Cleveland, the Bulls and Independents game in Rock Island was seen by a paltry 1,700. The big date on the calendar in Chicago would be October 17 when the undefeated Cardinals (4–0) and the Bears (3–0–1) would meet to determine first-place honors for the early season. At the same time, the Chicago Bulls would be hosting Red Grange and the New York Yankees, with both games being held in Chicago. Over 12,000 were in the crowd at Cubs Park as the Bears scorched the Cardinals 16–0 with their newly acquired superstar doing all of the scoring damage: "For six years one Paddy Driscoll, wearer of moleskins, sported the colors of Chris O'Brien's Cardinals, but when the Chicago Bears showed him the color of $10,000, Paddy and Chris became total strangers. Sunday, at Cubs Park, Chris must have felt some misgivings as he sat on the sidelines and watched this same Paddy Driscoll, whose home telephone number he once carried in his note book, ran rings around his old team mates. Paddy accounted for all of the Bears' 16 points."[71]

Down on the South Side at Comiskey Park, the Bulls surprised Red Grange and the Yankees in front of 17,000 fans, an observation that did not go unnoticed in the press: "Is Grange a drawing card? Well, if the figures given out on the attendance of the two pro games in Chicago are correct the Red Head is all of that. The Chicago Bears team was playing the Chicago Cardinals Sunday. It was two city teams clashing and 12,000 fans turned out. The Chicago Bulls, a team that hadn't set the world on fire to date and a new one in Chicago met Red Grange's New York Yankees and 17,000 came out. Draw your own conclusions."[72]

Was this a sign that the National Football League was in serious trouble? Had the clever C.C. Pyle pulled off another improbable financial success and outwitted his adversaries in the older circuit? For that one, brief shining moment in October 1926 he did ... and then the promising American Football League began to disintegrate. Pyle biographer Jim Reisler wrote: "Halfway through its inaugural season, Pyle's new league was having a full-fledged financial crisis.... Pyle engineered a quick fix, and just like that, dropped most of the league's teams. By early November, the American Football League had become a four-team league comprised of the Yankees, Philadelphia, Los Angeles, and Chicago."[73] Although Pyle presented an optimistic front, he realized that his pet project was not only in danger but was also draining him of his precious financial assets since he was the key investor in the organization. By the end of the season, it was clear that the AFL was doomed, but Pyle was already in the midst of a grandiose pro tennis tour and was looking to capitalize on other promising sporting ventures. However, Pyle was also feeling pressure to pay his bills and was becoming an easy target for satirists anxious to shrewdly skewer his ambitious efforts: "This will probably be the last year that Santa Claus will be an amateur. C.C. Pyle has talked him into turning professional. Mr. Pyle wants ten percent of everything Kris Kringle gives away. C.C. Pyle is a smart man and it's rumored that his next business deal will be to put the Easter bunnies under contract."[74]

By the time the 1927 NFL campaign began, the American Football League had disappeared.

15,000 Fans Chilled by Icy Gusts

After the Cardinals lost the showdown of unbeaten NFL teams to the Bears on October 17 to fall to 4–1 on the season, the team stumbled mightily down the stretch to finish 5–6–1. The only two success stories during that precarious fall from the top of the leader board were an unusual 3–2 win over Milwaukee on October 24 and a 0–0 tie with the Bears on November 25. Beginning with that first Bears game (of three that season), the Cardinals compiled a 1–6–1 mark to conclude the campaign and scored just one touchdown during that span. The lone victory over Milwaukee was an odd one and was enabled by the quick thinking of lineman Jerry Lunz, who recovered a blocked Cardinals punt in his own end zone for a safety, rather than affording the Badgers a touchdown. Earlier, the reliable Red Dunn booted a field goal in the opening period for the only other score of the game. It was only the second, and last, time in NFL history that a game has ended with a 3–2 final result.

While the 1926 Cardinals were slipping badly, the Chicago Bears were rampaging through the league, winning six straight games before meeting the Cardinals again on November 11. By that time, the Bears (10–0–1) were leading the NFL while the Cards had slumped to 5–4. The battle on November 11 was not only huge in terms of the Bears-Cardinals rivalry, but also in NFL history since it was the first professional game staged in the new Soldier Field in Chicago. The spacious lakefront stadium would later become the home for both the Cardinals (1959) and the Bears (from 1971 to the present). Back on November 11, 1926, the two teams managed to maintain their unusual string of one team not scoring as the Bears eased past their South Side adversaries 10–0 in miserable weather described by the *Chicago Tribune*: "Fifteen thousand fans shivered in the huge stone stands and were chilled by icy gusts across the soggy ground."[75] As with the previous collision between the two rivals, Paddy Driscoll was responsible for all of the Bears' points by tossing a 40-yard scoring pass, adding the extra point, and also kicking a field goal. The game also marked another "first" in Chicago pro football history. Not only was it the first professional one played at Soldier Field, but it was also played for the benefit of the nearby Rosary College (now part of Dominican University) building fund.

Less than a week later, on November 15, Chris O'Brien quickly signed a key player from the failing Rock Island Independents of the American Football league: Duke Slater. An All-American at the University of Iowa, Slater rarely left his tackle position and was a fixture on early NFL All-Pro teams during his career from 1922 to 1931. He played one more game for Rock Island in 1926 before joining the Cards on Thanksgiving Day for a third battle with the Bears, this one ending in a scoreless deadlock. For the year, the Cardinals slumped to 5–6–1, the first time the South Siders finished below the .500 mark while the Bears completed the campaign with a 12–1–3 finish. Normally, that superior record would have warranted another NFL title for the Bears, but a 7–6 loss to the Frankford Yellow Jackets of Philadelphia on December 4 was not only the sole loss of the season but it also allowed Frankford to sneak ahead of the Bears in the final standings with a 14–1–2 mark.

The last gasp of the American Football League occurred on December 12, 1926, when Red Grange and the New York Yankees edged the Chicago Bulls 7–3 at Comiskey Park. Almost immediately, speculation began regarding the future of not only the AFL but also pro football in general, including a dire accounting of the just-completed season from a financial perspective: "Only four clubs in the National league made any money the past year—the worst in the history of the game for two reasons: bad weather and the fight between the two rival organizations. Frankford, Chicago Bears, Providence and Green Bay of the National League alone made money.... Pyle's organization had a number of stellar gate attractions that would strengthen the other league. It is estimated he and his backers dropped $200,000 or more on the season and it is believed that if an equitable working agreement could be reached the rivals would be glad to join hands the coming year."[76]

Chris O'Brien Never Thoroughly Appreciated

For the time being, it appeared that the NFL had survived the onslaught of the AFL. The league was staggered but survived. Much of the credit for this welcome triumph was the staunch loyalty of Chris O'Brien to the league and the enthusiastic rejection by George Halas of Pyle's brazen ownership bid of the Bears. In particular, Dr. Harry March, once president of the New York Giants, wrote about the strength of O'Brien in rebuffing the advances of the new AFL: "President Carr, who can only represent the will of the club owners, was firm and tactful after war was declared and Chris O'Brien, of the Chicago Cardinals, stuck to the old league when every possible financial inducement was made to have him desert to the new outlaws. His loyalty and stability under the stress, in my opinion, have never been thoroughly appreciated by the team owners or by the public."[77]

With the AFL in shambles, O'Brien was approached with a different type of football proposal. As reported in some media outlets, the Chicago Bulls ownership, represented by Joey Sternaman, suggested that the Bulls and the Chicago Cardinals might merge prior to the 1927 season. That possibility was set aside when the parties apparently could not reach an amicable decision: "The deal whereby Sternaman sought to combine the Bulls with the Cards fell through when Sternaman and Chris O'Brien, owner of the Cards, could not agree on the terms of the merger."[78] So Sternaman returned to the Bears, hopefully placating the ill feelings between George Halas and Dutch Sternaman that erupted when Joey Sternaman fled the Chicago Bears the year before for what he presumed would be greener pastures. Speaking of the American Football League in retrospect, Joey Sternaman admitted: "It went under at the end of the year. I came out broke after it, it was a bum gamble."[79] The lone surviving team from the AFL would be the New York Yankees. After months of wrangling, the NFL allowed the Yankees to become the 12th member of the slimmed-down circuit. The Yankees would remain in New York for the 1927 campaign, but with tight restrictions on scheduling home games so as not to compete directly with the New York Giants. And, perhaps most important, Red Grange would be back in the National Football League.

Cardinals Pushed the Chicago Bears Out of the Spotlight

A key word was added to descriptions of Chris O'Brien in the off-season—*owner*. Although he obviously managed and operated the Chicago Cardinals for many years, O'Brien did not officially become an owner until April 25, 1927, when the "Chicago Cardinals Football Club" was incorporated in the state of Illinois. O'Brien listed his home address at 5712 South Racine Avenue in Chicago as the headquarters location of the corporation. Four directors were identified in addition to O'Brien: his wife, Frieda O'Brien; bookkeeper Thomas Burian; paper manufacturer John E. Taylor; and James P. Taylor. Basically, the corporation issued 3,004 shares of capital stock and Chris O'Brien owned 3,000 of those shares.[80] Still, even with a minimal piece of the ownership pie, Frieda O'Brien might still be considered the first female "owner" of an NFL team!

One of O'Brien's initial management decisions was to hire the respected Guy Chamberlin as player/coach of the Cardinals. Chamberlin was the hottest coach in the first decade of the NFL, winning four titles with three different teams, including Frankford in 1926. In fact, the Professional Football Hall of Fame credits Chamberlin with being one of the winningest NFL coaches of all time in terms of winning percentage: "Guy Chamberlin played and coached in the earliest days of the National Football League when the only meaningful statistic kept was the team's won-lost record. Winning was a category in which Chamberlin excelled. Of those coaches with 50 or more victories, Guy's 58-16-7 record and .759 winning percentage ranks among the best."[81]

Actually, that winning percentage (.759) is the most successful of any head coach of all time in the NFL.[82] Unfortunately, Chamberlin's brief time as coach of the Cardinals in 1927 was nothing short of a disaster. The Cards struggled out of the gate, going a mere 2-6-1, before Chris O'Brien surprisingly fired the most successful coach in NFL history after just nine games. In fact, since Chamberlin did not last the season, his overall coaching record should be changed to 57-15-7 since he did not coach the final two games of the 1927 schedule for the Cardinals (3-7-1). Most resources failed to note Chamberlin's early departure in 1927, when he was replaced by Ben Jones, and the two games coached by Jones (1-1) were erroneously credited to Chamberlin.[83]

As the Cardinals fluttered downward in the 1927 standings, the Chicago Bears posted a strong 9-3-2 mark. After defeating the Cardinals 9-0 in the season opener at Normal Park and running up a 7-1-1 record, the Bears were surprised 3-0 by the Cards (2-6-1) in the first game after the departure of Chamberlin on November 24, 1927: "The Chicago Cardinals, who have been defeated by nearly all the pro football teams between Lake Michigan and the Atlantic seaboard, flared back yesterday morning at Wrigley Field and pushed the Chicago Bears out of the spotlight now centering on the National league title. The Cards won 3 to 0, a place kick by [Evar] Swanson, Cardinal end, in the first three minutes of the game being the winning margin."[84]

Fastest Man in Baseball History!

In a bit of irony, it was the only field goal of Swanson's career, but it was successful in nudging the Bears out of championship contention! While the field goal may have been the highlight of Swanson's NFL career, which concluded after the 1927 season, he was just two years away from establishing one of the oldest records in professional sports. Swanson also played baseball and finally reached the major leagues in 1929 with the Cincinnati Reds. Between games of a doubleheader with the Boston Braves on September 15, 1929, Swanson participated in a contest to determine which player could round the bases the quickest. The *Cincinnati Enquirer* provided the results: "Evar Swanson, fleet left fielder of the Reds, showed his heels to all opposition and established a new mark for the journey around the paths when he was timed in 13.3 seconds for the trip of 120 yards, with a sharp turn at each of the three bases. Swanson clipped a full second off the ancient record of Honus Lobert, made here in a baseball field day about 20 years ago."[85]

A year later, Swanson lowered his mark to 13.2 seconds and since that time, no major leaguer has been able to equal his record, including attempts by speedsters Mickey Rivers and Ricky Henderson. As such a Chicago Cardinals football player remains the fastest man in baseball history![86]

With a final 9–3–2 record in 1927, the Bears finished in third place behind the surprising New York Giants (11–1–1) and the Green Bay Packers (7–2–1). Far down the list in ninth place sat the Chicago Cardinals with a troubling 3–7–1 mark. Chris O'Brien's noble experiment with the heretofore successful coach Guy Chamberlin had exploded prematurely. O'Brien's finances continued to be worrisome, but the clever promoter wasn't ready to surrender just yet. There were games to be played, victories to be captured, and loyal fans to attract. He just needed to discover a way to achieve all three in 1928.

Twelve

Programs and Sir Duke

"The giant Slater leaned to the left and the entire Bears' wall crumbled."
—*Chicago Daily Journal*, September 21, 1928

Jim Thorpe, Red Grange, Ernie Nevers, Paddy Driscoll…

As the so-called "Roaring Twenties" eased to a close, rosters in the National Football League were brimming with the illustrious names of future inductees in the still-distant Pro Football Hall of Fame, with many bringing their talents to the Chicago area with the Bears and Cardinals.

Duke Slater, George Halas, Ed Healey, George Trafton…

The NFL was maturing, with the competing American Football League a thing of the past and the rift between professional and collegiate football interests diminishing somewhat. With just 10 teams in the league in 1928, the NFL was ready for its stars to take a bigger stage on the American sports landscape. Under the leadership of President Joe Carr, the NFL had brushed past both internal and external squabbles to finally position itself as a growing influence on the sporting scene. Carr had trimmed down the number of league members from a bloated 22 in 1926 to emerge with a tight group from mostly larger cities that would hopefully survive likely financial challenges in the upcoming season.

Life was still not luxurious for NFL owners and players. Salaries were low, with typical wages of around $100 per game, and players and coaches needed to find off-season (and often in-season) work in order to survive. The owners usually did not have deep pockets to sustain severe losses at the gate, especially in the case of inclement weather. With no domed stadiums or warm-weather team venues at the time, it took a very hardy fan to show up for an outdoor NFL game in the northern part of the country in early December. With the majority of team income coming from ticket sales, NFL owners cringed when temperatures dipped or heavy rains were predicted. Owners simply did what they could to survive. Later in life, the great Red Grange acknowledged the significant contributions to the early pro game of both George Halas and Chris O'Brien: "It was a great honor to play for Halas. George has to be the No. 1 man in professional football. He held on to the Bears' franchise when many people, including myself, thought he was nuts—losing $25,000 to $30,000 a year. People would say, 'That dumb Halas; why does he keep going?' And I didn't think pro football had a bright future. Men like Halas and Chris O'Brien set the stage for the game's greatness."[1]

As mentioned earlier, the careful financial records maintained by Dutch Sternaman provide us with previously unknown details concerning the often-difficult fiscal world of an early NFL team owner. Most important, they demonstrate just how very close the Chicago Bears came to folding, and where would the NFL be today without the ever-present influence of George Halas?

In 1928, both Halas and Sternaman were still coaching and managing the Bears, as well as playing for the team on the field. Although the Bears, and to a lesser extent the Cardinals, enjoyed a brief respite from financial worries after the arrival of Red Grange in 1925, the never-ending slog to make ends meet continued throughout the end of the decade. Halas always figured that he should continue playing, since it saved at least one player's salary when he was on the field!

But by 1928, his shaky partnership with Dutch Sternaman continued to deteriorate, Halas admitted:

> My biggest problem was personal. My relationship with Dutch Sternaman was worsening. Mutual trust had almost vanished. The split hurt the team. The consequence was that I would tell the team to do this and Sternaman would tell them to do that. The results soon began to show. In the 1927 season, we won only nine and placed third; in 1928, we won seven and in 1929 only four. Receipts, too, were off. We lost $3,486.35 in 1927, $563.71 in 1928, and $1,082.92 in 1929. We couldn't pay our guarantee to the visitors from Frankford. The Bears were kept solvent thanks to program sales. These little sheets steadily earned about $2,000 a year.[2]

Program sales? It did make sense that the little booklets sold at each home game that included rosters, league gossip, and local advertising would be a suitable, if limited, revenue opportunity for each club. Aside from ticket sales, the possibility of program advertising and individual copy sales would be about the only other way for a team to attract revenue in the days before television rights, marketing partnerships, apparel sales, etc. For the Bears, Dutch Sternaman supervised the production of the game programs and the commercial advertising. It was a time-consuming process and Dutch maintained handwritten ledgers to help identify sales volume, delinquent advertisers, and other issues. For example, Sternaman once received a letter from a Mr. D.H. Howard of the Commonwealth Edison Company of Chicago complaining (albeit nicely) about a miscommunication regarding advertising in the Bears game program:

> Dear Mr. Sternaman:
> We are in receipt of yours of the 10th with enclosure of statement for $40.00 covering 1930 advertising and regret, as explained to Mr. Halas, that no order was ever issued for this advertising. I am always for you, but our Advertising Committee many times disagrees with me, especially when it comes to program advertising. If there is anything I can do, even at this late date, you may be assured that I will gladly do it, although no Purchase Order was ever issued nor contract signed.[3]

Generally, Sternaman retained a detailed, comprehensive record of all program advertising, including delinquent accounts. The inadvertent errors, such as the one dealing with Commonwealth Edison noted above, were also adjusted by Sternaman. The collection of delinquent accounts was always difficult, but Dutch kept the laggards on the books for two years and rarely wrote them off completely.

Program sales were included in contracts signed by the Bears and William

Veeck for the rental of Wrigley Field in 1927 and repeated in 1930. These three-year contracts offered the Bears the use of "said Wrigley Field, including the field, grandstands, box office and dressing rooms on each Sunday and holiday during said periods, from on and about October 15 to December 31."[4] Even nine years after the original agreement was signed between the two organizations, the Bears still enjoyed a very attractive deal. The contract stipulated that the Bears would remit 20 percent of the gross amount of ticket revenue to Wrigley Field after each game EXCEPT if such gross revenue dipped below $10,000 in total. In that case, only 15 percent rental payment would be required. Finally, the agreement allowed the Bears to sell programs under the following circumstances: Each program would be sold for 10 cents by the Wrigley Field staff. At the end of the day, the Bears would return 25 percent of the program sales to the landlord for that service! Of course, this arrangement was for program sales only. The Bears retained all advertising revenue.[5] However, still another separate contract between the Bears and salesman William C. Hauk signed in 1927 paid Hauk a hefty commission of 33⅓ percent for his role in selling advertising and preparing the program for printing.[6]

So, what did all of these contracts, percentages, and commissions really do for the Chicago Bears? According to Sternaman's year-end financial report in 1929, the program project did quite well. Advertising revenue for the season was $3,288 and sales of the programs over eight games was $2,731.39, or $6,019.39 in total income. The aforementioned Mr. Hauk earned $1,150 in commissions, which rolled up to a 35 percent cut of the sales. Total expenses, including printing and the agreed-upon 25 percent portion of sales to Wrigley Field, equaled $3,339.88, leaving a tidy profit of $2,679.51 for the year—verifying the number indicated in the Halas autobiography.[7]

On the South Side, the Cardinals usually produced a 16-page program that was updated for each home game held at either Normal Park or Comiskey Park. While financial information has not survived regarding the preparation of the Cardinals' programs, a few print copies are still in existence. With advertising consisting entirely of local businesses, the program included marketing overtures from a variety of establishments. These included the owner's O'Brien & O'Brien Men's Furnishing located at 5112 South Halsted ("8 Bowling Alleys and 10 Billiard Tables"); Normal Park Inn across from the Normal Park Field at 6101 South Racine ("See Us Before and After the Game"); The Hotel Halwood ("Home of the Cardinals") at 62nd Place and Halsted; and Miller's Place, found at 6136 South Racine, also across from the team's home field ("Before and After Games").[8]

Entire Bears Wall Crumbled

In 1928, the Bears and the Cardinals met on the opening day of the NFL season for the first time. Since Comiskey Park was in use by the Chicago White Sox, the game was moved to Normal Park. Familiar players such as Paddy Driscoll, George Trafton, Link Lyman, and Dutch Sternaman still guided the Bears, who looked for some redemption in the initial game on the schedule: "The Bears who last year fought splendidly to annex the league flag which finally was won by the New York Giants, will seek vengeance for the injury suffered last Thanksgiving when the south side's underdogs took a 3–0 contest at Wrigley Field. All calendars for these two professional elevens date [point] for that game."[9]

The Cardinals were now coached by longtime tackle Fred Gillies, who lined up on the left side opposite from the fearsome Duke Slater at right tackle for the hosts. Optimism reigned supreme for both clubs, but especially on the South Side: "Gillies, who is coaching the Cardinals this year, has one of the best aggregations working in harmony that ever donned one of Chris O'Brien's uniforms."[10] Back in 1928, there was no such thing as the Professional Football Hall of Fame, but in that battle between the Chicago rivals to kick off the season, an amazing five players on the field would eventually find their way into the Hall of Fame: Slater, Lyman, Trafton, Driscoll, and George Halas.

Slater was certainly a groundbreaker in the National Football League when he became the first African American lineman to play in the circuit. As an All-American coming out of the University of Iowa (with an aversion to playing with a helmet!), Slater was a dominant force in the NFL from the moment he stepped onto the field with the Rock Island Independents in 1922.

In a game against the Bears that season, the blocking strength of Slater was noted on the offensive front line: "The giant [Slater] leaned to the left and the entire Bears' wall crumbled, Gavin rushing by the line for the necessary fourteen yards over the goal."[11] As noted, when the Independents folded after the 1926 campaign, Chris O'Brien quickly signed Slater and he remained with the Cardinals through the 1931 season, racking up seven "All Pro" honors during his career. Slater also proved to be one of the most resilient players in the league, playing both offense and defense and rarely taking a breather during a game. In his excellent biography of Duke Slater, author Neal Rozendaal explained: "Slater had astonishing durability. He was famous for playing complete games, going wire to wire in nearly every contest. Duke often discussed how substitutes were much rarer when he played. 'You were expected to play the whole game unless you got hurt,' he pointed out. He also never missed a game due to injury in his long career, despite being a frequent target as one of the few Black players and occasionally the only Black player in the NFL."[12]

Slater was such an enormous force in the early days of the NFL that it was an utter calamity that he was not inducted into the Professional Football Hall of Fame until 2021.

But in 1928, Slater was expected to help propel the Cardinals back into title contention following a two-year absence after the trade of Paddy Driscoll to the Bears before the 1926 season. After an opening 12–0 exhibition win over the less-than-formidable Hammond Boosters, the Cardinals would slam into a series of increasingly frustrating outings against NFL opponents. In fact, the 1928 Cardinals were so incompetent that the team failed to score an offensive touchdown the remainder of the year in league action. Perhaps the most ignominious performance of the season took place on September 30, 1928, when the Cardinals filled an open date by bowing 7–6 to the semipro Chicago Mills club. End Swede Erickson grabbed a touchdown toss from Mickey MacDonnell for the club's only score of the game, but a missed extra point proved to be the difference in the final outcome. The following week, the Cards captured their only NFL win of the season when Swede Erickson intercepted a pass and ran it back 30 yards for the score in a 7–0 decision over the Dayton Triangles. Sadly, the Cardinals would not win another game, nor score a point, the rest of the campaign.

Yet part of that problem was that O'Brien's team virtually disappeared after a 20–0 loss to the Green Bay Packers on October 14 and did not play another game for six weeks. It was one of the strangest vanishing acts in the history of the game and there is little evidence pertaining to the reason. Even more baffling was the fact that when the team did return to action on November 24, the Cardinals played three games in five days, including back-to-back road outings against the Frankford Yellow Jackets and the New York Yankees.

Much of the bizarre scheduling circumstances during the Cardinals 1928 season might be linked to the precarious financial situation of owner Chris O'Brien. As an owner of a few small businesses in the Englewood neighborhood, O'Brien did not rely on a plush financial cushion to absorb the expenses of his football team. O'Brien was with the original Morgan Athletic Association in 1899 that eventually morphed into the Chicago Cardinals, but his role had been primarily as the manager of the team as it evolved into its various forms throughout the years. Now, in 1928, it appeared that his fiscal capabilities were nearing the end of the line in terms of the Cardinals football organization. The loss of Paddy Driscoll in 1926, followed by the in-town rivalry with the neighboring Chicago Bulls that same year, had unveiled some leaks in O'Brien's gridiron life raft. As he clung for the survival of his franchise in 1928, O'Brien settled for three road games to complete the schedule rather than host any opponents (along with the required guarantee) during the middle six weeks of the season. If there was a sliver of hope for O'Brien, it would be the season finale on Thanksgiving Day with the Chicago Bears. Although just 5,000 showed up for the season opener between the two rivals at Normal Park, the *Daily Journal* generously predicted that there were "hopes for a crowd of 50,000 people" for the rematch.[13] The Cardinals' share of that massive gate would certainly help the club through the winter—but look again…

In a gesture that was both benevolent and painful, the Bears and the Cardinals agreed to surrender their shares of the receipts from the Thanksgiving Day game to a local charity: "The feud started in 1920, and in all seasons except 1921 and 1923, two games have been played each year, with the Bears holding the edge in victories, seven to five, with three scoreless ties on the record, too. Chris O'Brien, boss of the Cards, and Dutch Sternaman and George Halas, mentors of the Bears, agreed to donate the proceeds, which will run into a tidy sum, to Chris Paschen's annual Christmas fund for the poor."[14]

Toughest, Meanest, Most Ornery Critter Alive

For the Cardinals (1–4), the contest at Wrigley Field would mercifully bring to an end an unsuccessful, and unusual, season. On the other side of the scrimmage line, the Bears (5–3–1) were enduring what would become the least impressive campaign in the team's history with an unanticipated rough landing waiting in the remaining three games following the affair with the Cardinals. Although any meeting between the two clubs attracted interest, two off-the-field moves right before the game raised a few eyebrows. Each team shared a surprise announcement, although the one offered by George Halas would appear to be more detrimental to the Bears when the following personnel movement was hidden in the pregame coverage: "The Bears announced the suspension of center George Trafton for the balance of the season for breaking training rules. He also was fined $200."[15] No other explanation was offered.

Trafton, as mentioned previously on these pages, was a no-nonsense lineman who was considered one of the roughest players in pro football. Columnist Jim Bell once wrote: "A center, Trafton was Dick Butkus' predecessor. One of his teammates once described him as 'the toughest, meanest, most ornery critter alive.' Extreme violence was his forte. He was hated in every city he ever played in, particularly Rock Island and Green Bay."[16]

As tough as he was on the field, Trafton was also never reluctant to engage all comers in any "after hours" skirmishes. The reason for Trafton's suspension was the result of a Trafton altercation in the wee hours of the morning on Sunday, November 25. When Trafton left a local Chicago watering hole, he discovered a young man sitting on Trafton's car with no intention of vacating that position. In addition to ignoring Trafton's polite request to move away from the car, the fender offender, 21-year-old Daniel Delagio, unwisely challenged Trafton then and there to a duel of fists. Trafton, later a heavyweight boxer, was ever so happy to participate and quickly decked his opponent, who politely slid away from the car in a dream-like state. As far as Trafton was concerned, the matter was closed until someone notified the local police: "George was caught by authorities trying to push a young man down through the concrete sidewalk of a West Side street in the small hours of the morning. George explained that the man had been sitting on the running board of his automobile and had refused to get off. Also, that several friends of this man, who gave his name as Daniel Delagio, were in all probability trying to help themselves to the battery of his car. Trafton and Delagio were hauled down to the Maxwell Street station and locked up in cells."[17]

Trafton was released from police custody around 4:00 a.m. and played the entire game later that same day in a 14–7 loss to the Detroit Wolverines. However, when the predawn exploits of Trafton were shared by wire services around the country, Halas really had no choice but to suspend his gifted center, especially since the transgression occurred hours before a game. It would not be Trafton's last excursion with his fists...

Thorpe Played a Few Minutes for the Cardinals

With the big Thanksgiving Day with the Bears quickly approaching, Cardinals owner Chris O'Brien looked for some edge that might provide his team with the spark to upset the North Siders. While the opportunity to contend for the NFL title was long gone, O'Brien could still save face by knocking off the Bears to claim the city championship. As was common in the 1920s, O'Brien grabbed the phone and began to solicit talented players to join the Cardinals in the team's final outing of the year against the Bears. On the eve of the game, there were persistent rumors that O'Brien was prepared to sign former University of Minnesota fullback Herb Joesting for the clash: "Joesting will be long remembered for his performance against the Bears early this Fall while playing with the Minneapolis Marines. The Bears won 12–6, but the former Minnesota star was a threat throughout the game. Although there may seem to be quite a difference in the two teams this year, the addition of Joesting should make the contest more even."[18]

For whatever reason, the recruitment of Joesting failed, but the inventive O'Brien called in an even bigger name to assist with the team's efforts against the Bears: Jim Thorpe. Although now over 40 years old and well past his prime, Thorpe was still ready to play a few minutes for a team in need (and a paycheck). He was in the general neighborhood as well after playing with the Hammond Semco team in a 7–6 loss to the Hammond Boosters earlier in the month.[19] Virtually at the last minute, O'Brien reached agreement with Thorpe to play against the Bears on November 28, 1928. The *Chicago Tribune* shared the reasoning behind the decision of the Cardinals' owner: "Despite the handicap of age, O'Brien thinks Thorpe will be of value in stopping the Bears end runs. Thorpe still possesses the phenomenal kicking ability that was his a decade ago."[20] Unfortunately, neither the absent Trafton nor the arrival of Thorpe could help the Cardinals as the Bears romped to an easy 34–0 victory. Thorpe was on the field for just a short time, replacing Ed Allen at left end and then heading back to the bench when Don Yeisley replaced Thorpe. His brief appearance would prove to be his last in an NFL game and the Associated Press was quick to write Thorpe's football obituary: "Jim Thorpe, former Indian star, played a few minutes for the Cardinals but was unable to get anywhere. Forty-four years old and muscle bound, Thrope was a mere shadow of his former self."[21]

In Jim Thorpe's home state of Oklahoma, the Oklahoma Sports Hall of Fame in Oklahoma City also houses the Jim Thorpe Museum. Museum Curator Justin Lenhart provided some additional insight into that final game of the great Jim Thorpe's professional football career: "By the fall of 1928, Jim was growing financially desperate. He had solicited several baseball and football teams for work but most viewed him as beyond his prime. With no job prospects and a growing family to support, Jim agreed to play one last football game. The Chicago Cardinals were at the end of their third losing season and needed to inject some enthusiasm in their fanbase. So, they hired Jim, who was still very popular, to play in one game, the charity benefit Thanksgiving game against the Chicago Bears."[22]

With the overwhelming defeat, the Cardinals completed the season with an underwhelming 1–5 record, and being outscored 107–7. In Chicago, the local press was no longer tiptoeing around the obvious noncompetitive nature of the club, even more glaring in that final Bears game: "About the only excuse for thankfulness the Cardinals could muster after the debacle was that the score was only 34–0. Watching the Bears score four times in the second period, the hapless Cards doubtless were surprised that the defeat was by no greater margin. The defeat, however, could not have been more convincing."[23]

With the loss, the Cardinals groveled near the bottom of the final league standings, just ahead of the winless Dayton Triangles (0–7). The 1928 Cardinals were disappointing to management, fans, and even the usually supportive local press: "Two of the teams proved only schedule fillers, Dayton and the Chicago Cardinals. Dayton had a colorful squad with a lot of individual ability, but, as a team, it was just 11 fellows dressed in uniforms. The Cardinals never were anything else."[24]

After the Cardinals game, the aging Bears dropped Frankford 28–6, before losing games against Green Bay (6–0) and Frankford (19–0) to finish the season with a 7–5–1 mark, easily the worst in team history.

For some of the players on both teams, the off-season could not come soon enough, although a few found time to participate in one last game. On December 2, two teams in western Illinois battled to a scoreless tie in an encounter that was intended to determine the championship of the Illinois Valley. The host LaSalle Pony Express recruited heavily and lured Duke Slater and Swede Erickson of the Cardinals to play in the game against the Spring Valley Wildcats along with the still-suspended George Trafton and Laurie Walquist of the Bears. With all of this professional talent, LaSalle was still unable to generate any type of offense in the surprising deadlock, which was tainted by an unfortunate episode of racial taunting from members of the crowd numbering about 6,000, which forced Slater out of the game for his own safety.[25]

It Broke His Heart to Sell the Cardinals

Everything changes. Or so it seemed in the world of professional football in Chicago in 1929. The Cardinals and the Bears both experienced significant adjustments intended to improve both the stability and the on-field performances of each organization. For the Bears, an ugly 1929 campaign prompted a change of head coaches, while the respected Chris O'Brien was finally convinced to sell his beloved Cardinals. And, to ensure that things continued to be interesting in the Windy City, Red Grange wandered back to the Chicago Bears after a dreadful knee injury sidetracked his career.

For O'Brien, the signs of a precarious financial position with the Cardinals were everywhere, from the "selling" of Paddy Driscoll in 1926, to the wacky six-game schedule in 1928 with a noncompetitive team. O'Brien had been a founding father of the team back in 1899 and then was the primary influence behind the scenes as the club had moved through its various iterations over the past 30 years. Without a bundle of cash at his disposal, and little incoming revenue aside from gate receipts, O'Brien needed to make a very painful decision in the summer of 1929. "Owning the Cardinals meant everything to Chris and it dominated his life for many years," said O'Brien's granddaughter Carol Judge. "My dad [Edward O'Brien] would tell us that he was much loved by the neighborhood and all his football friends, but he was taken advantage of money-wise and that's how he lost the Cardinals."[26]

Not surprisingly, George Halas was involved with the sale of the Cardinals, looking no further than his partner with the Chicago Bruins basketball team: "It [Cardinals team] was losing money and Chris O'Brien could not subsidize it. I was concerned the buyer might be undesirable. I induced a great Bear fan, Dr. David J. Jones, to buy the club. He had served as city physician [of Chicago] under four mayors. I promised him that if the losses continued, I would absorb 40 percent; if there was a profit, I would take none of it. That was some partnership! Heads you win; tails I lose."[27]

A handwritten contract discovered in the archives of the Professional Football Hall of Fame and dated June 14, 1929, outlined the terms of the agreement: "I, Chris O'Brien, as owner of the Chicago Cardinals Football Club, agree to sell the said club, and corporation and players and all stock and assets of club to Dr. David Jones for the sum of twelve thousand five hundred dollars. The corporation is to be turned over to Dr. David Jones by Chris O'Brien free of all bills, liens and liabilities. Any debts that Chris O'Brien cannot settle at this time it is agreed to put money in escrow with satisfactory party to cover these amounts until settled. It is understood that Dr. David Jones is to signify his intention in regard to this contract within ten days."[28]

An addendum to the letter of agreement, dated June 26, 1929, acknowledged that O'Brien received a deposit of $500 with the "balance of money to be turned over to Geo. S. Halas as Escrow Officer within ten days."[29] Newspapers speculated that the actual cost of the sale was significantly more than $12,500, with the Associated Press indicating that the selling price was actually $25,000.[30] But the loyal, dedicated reign of the personable Chris O'Brien was over as owner of the Cardinals. His late granddaughter Carol Needham said: "He sold the team so that he could pay his players. It broke his heart to sell the Cardinals."[31]

Mr. Pyle Did Not See Fit to Attend This Meeting

The announcement of the transaction was shared with the media on July 18, 1929, with the NFL approving the sale at the league meeting in Atlantic City on July 27. During that meeting, O'Brien was not the only familiar face missing. C.C. Pyle, who had burst onto the football landscape with his management of Red Grange beginning in 1925, failed to attend the meeting on behalf of his beleaguered New York Yankees franchise. NFL President Joe Carr and the other team representatives apparently were not pleased with Pyle's absence, as they quickly dropped the Yankees from league membership: "The franchise of the New York Yankees," Joseph A. Carr, president of the league, said, "has been forfeited. Mr. Pyle did not see fit to attend this meeting. Therefore, there was nothing left for officials of the league to do but to declare the franchise forfeited."[32]

The departure of Pyle did not appear to sadden any league members, many of whom were not fond of his stubbornness and egocentric personality: "It is understood that the league had been looking for an excuse to oust Cash-and-Carry [Pyle], who came in when the American and National Leagues were consolidated, and his recent financial reverses gave them the opportunity."[33]

In 1925, Pyle had emerged from out of nowhere and produced both massive crowds and attractive gates for the NFL, but after a series of monetary setbacks (including the Yankees), Pyle had lost his bargaining advantage and simply appeared satisfied to abandon the franchise. His partnership with his biggest asset had dissipated as well, according to Red Grange. The sterling halfback with the evasive moves on the field injured his knee in a game against the Bears in October 1927. After sitting out the 1928 season to rest his knee, the football future of Grange was in doubt. In May of that year, Grange decided to conclude the business relationship with Pyle: "Since my football future was in doubt, due to my injured knee, I decided it unwise to continue our pact. I also elected to withdraw my interest in the New York Yankees football team. The Yankees had been losing heavily and I could no longer afford to continue pouring money into the property. I thus ended a memorable three-year association with perhaps the greatest sports impresario [Pyle] the world has ever known."[34]

Despite the injury, and his own wariness, Grange was eagerly pursued by George Halas in hopes of coaxing Grange out of his mini-retirement. Robbed of his ability to initiate sharp cuts while running, Grange nonetheless evolved into a valuable defender with the Bears, making several All-Pro teams from 1930 to 1932 as the team returned to NFL prominence.

Overall, the 1929 season was not kind to either the Bears or the Cardinals, but it did produce a phenomenal individual performance that has been unmatched to this day. Immediately after the league meeting concluded in Atlantic City on July 28, owner Dr. David Jones of the Cardinals announced the surprise signing of rugged fullback Ernie Nevers, most recently with the Duluth Eskimos during the 1927 season. Nevers had "retired" from football in 1928 in order to return to Stanford to help coach the football team. With Nevers in the fold, Jones exuberantly predicted good times ahead for the downtrodden Cardinals: "I believe the South Side will support winning football and I'm going to give 'em that or bust. And I believe the North Side fans will come to see our games when they see what we have."[35] If anyone could help the Cardinals achieve those goals, it would be the multitalented Ernie Nevers, whose greatest professional triumph was only weeks away.

In addition, Jones was in the forefront of a determined effort among owners to not only increase the visibility of the league, but to also attract better coaches, in this case, prime collegiate leaders: "Several owners believe this will give the sport more of a college aspect. Dr. David Jones, who purchased the Cardinals from Chris O'Brien, is a leader of this movement. 'It may be a year, but some day we will convince college instructors [coaches] there is no difference between professional football and other sports. In baseball, various players assist in coaching colleges, and I can see no wrong for grid mentors to uplift professional football.' Dr. Jones is ready to pay a leading coach $25,000 to lead his Cardinals."[36]

For his first coaching hire, Jones avoided the temptation (and the cost) of recruiting a major college name and brought in Dewey Scanlon, who last coached the Duluth Eskimos in 1926, and Ole Haugsrud, also from Duluth, as team manager. More important, Scanlon was the coach of Nevers when the latter began his NFL career with Duluth that season. Dr. Jones was brimming with ideas, innovations, and ambition. He quickly secured Comiskey Park as the team's home field and announced that the Cardinals would hold their preseason training camp in Coldwater, Michigan—believed to be the first time that an NFL club moved out of state for its preseason endeavors. Haugsrud gathered the troops in a form letter sent out to all players prior to the start of training camp: "Please be advised that the Chicago

Cardinals football team will meet at the Planters Hotel Chicago, Illinois, at nine AM Chicago Daylight Savings time on Sunday, September 15, 1929. Let's all try and be as prompt as possible as we expect to leave in a bus for a nearby summer resort shortly after our meeting time. Wish to say that we would appreciate it very much if you have all your baggage with you and a complete football outfit as our uniforms will not be available until the first game."[37]

As Haugsrud's letter indicated, the pro players were expected to provide their own practice pads and gear during training camp in Coldwater. Meanwhile the *Coldwater Daily Reporter* was ecstatic about having the Cardinals in town, even forgetting that their previous season had been nothing short of a debacle: "One of the greatest collections of football material ever to invade Coldwater arrived here Sunday to remain ten days during which time they will practice twice daily at Waterworks Park. The men compose none other than the nationally famous Chicago Cardinals whose gridiron accomplishments have startled the lovers of sport for several seasons."[38]

In reality, Scanlon and Haugsrud rebuilt the 1929 version of the Cardinals with only three players returning from the unsuccessful (1–5) 1928 outfit. However, one of that trio was the immovable Duke Slater at tackle on both sides of the line. Slater would remain a menacing presence on the offensive side and a reliable lead blocker for the hard-driving Nevers. Together, they would help the Cardinals rebound with a 6–6–1 record in 1929, including two grueling battles with the Bears, and a contest with historical ramifications for the National Football League. But first, a much bigger influence would soon have an enormous impact on both the NFL and the country as a whole.

Everybody Was Expecting to Get Rich

In the fall of 1929, when squads were just beginning to unveil their rosters for the season, an economic development shook the world and threatened to undermine every aspect of American life. George Halas distinctly remembered this crisis: "Wall Street collapsed. I had bought stocks on margin with my Grange earnings. Everybody was doing that, expecting to get rich. Stock values fell so fast that J.J. O'Brien of Paine, Webber and Co. sold me out. He didn't even ask. Of course, it was their privilege. My partner, Dutch, had played safe, buying an apartment house and a super gas station. Life does have its ups and downs and a man must accept them and try to make the best of it all…. Misery extended to the football field."[39]

As Halas watched his savings evaporate, so did the Bears' impressive annual winning record. In 1929, the club slipped to 4–9–2, including a woeful 0–8–1 mark during the final nine games. It was the first losing season for the Bears since the NFL began and would prompt Halas to implement some difficult decisions in an effort to right the ship: "As the 1929 season deteriorated … loss after loss drove home two lessons. First, the time had come for me to stop playing. I was thirty-four. I no longer had speed. Dutch had ceased playing regularly. Secondly, the time had come for Dutch and me to stop coaching, or more accurately, miscoaching. We had to put coaching under one mind."[40]

After three seasons of unspectacular football, the Cardinals in 1929 were much more competitive. This led to a pair of interesting matches with the Bears where, in the first encounter, the behavior of the North Siders so infuriated Ernie Nevers that it pushed him to extraordinary heights in the second contest. On October 20, 1929, the two Chicago clubs met for the first time that season as the Bears (3–1) hosted the Cardinals (1–2) in a battle that quickly became quite contentious. Although the game ended in a 0–0 tie, there were some in the Cardinals contingent who thought that perhaps the Bears were a bit overaggressive on the defensive side in this roughhouse meeting as aptly reported by the *Chicago Tribune*: "But what might have been doesn't tell the story of the battle. It was hard fought, broken only by breathing spaces in which the perspiring players called for the water buckets and the sopping sponges. Some unidentified Bear lineman pushed Nevers' nose a trifle with his open hand to draw first blood early in the game. Jake Williams, a soft spoken but exceedingly earnest southerner, kept up a drawling conversation through a split lip. And Capt. Don Murry of the Bears had first aid for a gash in his eyebrow received in a bit of hardy scrimmage. So much for the earnestness of the play."[41]

Shaking off the surprising deadlock with the Cardinals, George Halas and the Chicago Bears easily swept past the Minneapolis Red Jackets 27–0 the following week as Red Grange continued on his personal comeback trail with an impressive effort: "The noted red head threw his hips through the opposition, tossed passes, leaped into the air to snag 'em, squirmed and romped all over the field."[42] Now 4–1–1, the immediate future looked extremely bright for the Bears, especially with the rejuvenated Red Grange partnered with the still-speedy Paddy Driscoll in the backfield. Unfortunately, the team would fail to notch another victory in 1929, managing just a single tie in the final nine games.

Panicky Feeling That Player Would Be Splattered with Egg Yolk

On the South Side, the Cardinals quickly dropped two more contests, falling to 1–4–1 before experiencing a rebirth of sorts in a game of historical importance against the Providence (Rhode Island) Steam Roller. In a rare Wednesday tilt (which was originally scheduled for Sunday, November 3, but postponed due to inclement weather), the Cardinals participated in the NFL's first night game on November 6, 1929. The home field of the Steam Roller was usually a bicycle racing facility called the Cyclodrome, but due to the field condition, the game was moved to Kinsley Park Stadium, where ample floodlights were available to accommodate a nocturnal NFL game. The Pro Football Hall of Fame provided a glimpse into the proceedings of that historic night, including the use of a white football to increase its visibility: "Although the Steam Roller lost 16–0, the game was declared a success because 6,000 fans attended. The local newspaper reported that the ball, which had been painted white for the night game, 'had the appearance of a large egg,' and whenever either team passed, 'there was a panicky feeling that the player who made the catch would be splattered with egg yolk.' The floodlights, the newspaper concluded, were 'just as good as daylight for the players.'"[43]

Ernie Nevers accounted for all of the Cardinals' points during the victory with a 50-yard touchdown toss, a rushing score, a field goal, and an extra point. Then, on November 24, Nevers tallied all of the points in the Cards' 19–0 romp over the Dayton Triangles, setting up the important Thanksgiving Day match with the Bears between two teams on opposite trajectories: "Rivalry as keen as any existing between big college elevens features the hookup of the two local clubs who played a 0–0 tie early in the season. For the first time in many seasons the Cards are leading the Bears in the league standings, and the south siders are given the edge over their long-time rivals."[44]

Although the Cardinals (4–5–1) were slightly ahead of the Bears (4–6–1) in the NFL standings, the impending duel between Ernie Nevers and the revitalized Red Grange was both heavily debated and greatly anticipated: "The Nevers-Grange duel will be the one that will attract attention, for the great fullback [Nevers] has been rated as one of the finest all-around football players who ever booted a ball. Red Grange has been accorded a great reception this season in the pro game and has performed well."[45]

While both teams were clearly out of the running for the NFL title, the bragging rights for the city of Chicago were still a valuable commodity. Nevers also seemed to still be somewhat indignant over the scoreless result from the first meeting, a game in which he was continually pounded upon by the Bears' defense. Nevers was quoted as saying: "I told my players, the next time we meet the Bears, we'll beat the hell out of 'em. I knew we could. I just knew it!"[46] Nevers may have also been inspired by a questionable wire service article that appeared in newspapers around the country on the morning (November 28, 1929) of the Bears game. For some reason, reporter Davis S. Walsh unleashed unwarranted vitriol on Nevers and other NFL stars, claiming that their individual performances in the pro wars were inferior to their collegiate accomplishments: "I mean that the riot of the campus, the lad who sets the world agog with his deeds for the dear old school, generally turns out to be just another football player once he finds himself in the unromantic atmosphere of the professional game. There are few exceptions to this rule."

Walsh lambasted players such as Red Grange, Jim Thorpe, and Wildcat Wilson, but was even more focused in his assessment of Nevers: "Ernie Nevers afforded an even more poignant example of post-college retrogression. In fact, I doubt whether he even stood out too boldly as the individual star of his team."[47]

Let Nevers Take It

If Nevers entered the game in frustration, he left it in triumph by scoring all of the Cardinals' points in a 40–6 destruction of the Bears. Nevers scored six rushing touchdowns and booted four extra points in the impressive win, establishing NFL records for most points scored by an individual in one game, as well as for most touchdowns in a single outing. The scoring total has never been surpassed in over 90 years, while only three players since that time have equaled the record six touchdowns established by the Cards' fullback. Dub Jones of the Cleveland Browns was the first to do so in 1951 on four rushes and two pass receptions. Then, in 1965, Gale Sayers of the Bears blitzed San Francisco with four tallies on the ground, one pass reception, and one on an 85-yard punt return. The rushing record of six in one game was finally matched by running back Alvin Kamara of New Orleans in 2020.

Following the lead blocking of indomitable tackle Duke Slater, Nevers evaded the Bears' defense throughout the afternoon on his way to the record 40 points: "Before this coast terror [Nevers] was through galloping about the snow-blanketed field, the 7,000 holiday spectators saw the formidable Bears of other years almost on the verge of complete demoralization. Six touchdowns, the result of slashes ranging from one yard to ten, were registered by Nevers with such grace that the crowd took up the chant of 'Let Nevers take it' before the game was very old. As testimony to his prowess is the fact that he tallied four of those half dozen markers standing up."[48]

For the record, Nevers scored twice in the first quarter on runs of one and three yards. His onslaught continued in the second period when Nevers eased in from one yard out, boosting the lead to 20–0 with Nevers adding a pair of extra points. He completed his scoring barrage with runs of one, three, and 10 yards in the second half, along with two more extra points. After the game, Nevers shared the limelight with his offensive line, especially Duke Slater, Herb Blumer, and Walt Kiesling. The overpowering work of the front wall was praised by the media as well: "The Cardinal line was the foundation on which these ball carriers built their successes. There was no question of its superiority. And it played no favorites."[49]

Slater, as usual, was an immovable force at tackle on both sides of the ball and initiated the huge gaps for Nevers to follow: "Duke Slater, the veteran tackle, seemed the dominant figure in that forward wall which had the Bear front wobbly. It was Slater who opened the holes for Nevers when a touchdown was in the making."[50]

It was interesting that the only Bears score resulted from a long pass reception by Garland Grange, brother of the illustrious Red Grange. With the Garland Grange touchdown, it marked the first time since 1920 that both of the Chicago teams scored in the same game when meeting each other. As for Red Grange, the anticipated offensive fireworks expected between himself and Nevers failed to materialize: "Harold 'Red' Grange didn't get anywhere yesterday which probably isn't surprising. The Cardinals had the ball about three-fourths of the time and it was Nevers who was the unstoppable instead of the former Galloping Ghost of the Illini."[51]

With the offensive carnage concluded and the victory safely tucked away, Nevers finally left the Comiskey Park field late in the game to a rousing chorus of happy yells and applause from the home crowd: "Then Ernie left the game and how those south siders cheered! And well they might. Forty points plus nineteen points against Dayton last Sunday gave him fifty-nine in a row which is some kind of record, but the south side didn't care. For the Cardinals had defeated the Bears!"[52]

The Team Had Lost Its Morale

Following the big win over the Bears, the Cards stumbled at New York 24–21 but rebounded with a season-ending 26–0 romp over the Orange (New Jersey) Tornadoes that was highlighted by a 40-yard interception return for a touchdown by Duke Slater. The victory over Orange evened the Cardinals' slate at 6–6–1 for the 1929 campaign, a nice conclusion after the disastrous 1928 season. Meanwhile, the

Bears managed just a tie in their final three outings to finish 4–9–2, the worst season under the coaching tenure of George Halas and Dutch Sternaman.

Rumors had surfaced during the season regarding conflicting, and confusing, coaching messages shared with the team by Halas and Sternaman. In an interview prior to the 1930 season, Halas explained the woes of the dismal 1929 campaign and the hopes for the immediate future: "We believe our hope for the development of a winning team would be increased if we could turn the squad over to a professional coach. Neither Ed nor I had time to coach the Bears. Last season, the worst since we entered professional football with the old Staleys, the coaching responsibility was divided between us. As a result, our offense was ragged and by midseason the team had lost its morale."[53]

Halas wasted little time in hiring Ralph Jones, a high school football coach at nearby Lake Forest (Illinois) Academy, to lead the Bears in 1930. But there was more to the story than Jones merely being a prep coach suddenly hoisted up the ladder to mentor a leading professional eleven. Jones was previously the freshman football coach at the University of Illinois while both Halas and Sternaman were at the school. He served as the Illini's head basketball coach as well as at Butler and Purdue, where he was also a football assistant. During his 10 years at Lake Forest Academy, Jones compiled an 82–8 record on the gridiron and was widely respected for his innovations on the field. Although his time with the Bears would be limited to three years by the impact of the Great Depression, Jones remains the team's winningest coach (percentage-wise) in its long history with a .706 mark.

Trafton Can Take a Punch

But back to the conclusion of the 1929 season, which ended with a thud for Halas on December 15 with a 14–9 loss to the New York Giants. For most of the players, the season was over, but for one Chicago Bear, a new endeavor was just beginning. Center George Trafton, a rugged individual both on and off the field, was compelled to accept a sizable check to appear in a charity boxing match with Chicago White Sox baseball player Art Shires on December 16, 1929, just a day after the conclusion of the Bears' season. Years after the event, Red Grange shared his thoughts in an interview on the battle that was once termed the "Fight of the Century," but later simply appended to the "Battle of Clowns":

> I actually helped promote it. On this night we were helping Trafton celebrate his birthday. He had never lost a fight in a night club. After midnight, someone brought in a copy of the *Chicago Tribune*. Its big sports story announced that Art Shires, then trying to make some extra bucks in the ring to carry him through the winter, had signed to fight some chump. "I can beat him with one hand," Trafton snorted. Why not, we thought.
>
> My brother Garland was in the party and he was a neighbor of Jim Mullen, who was promoting the Shires' bouts. So, along about 2 am he called up Mullen. "Great," Mullen said, "we'll sign the contracts tomorrow." Next day, we'd forgotten all about it, but not Mullen. And Trafton suddenly remembered when he was offered a $1,000 guarantee for three rounds. A few days later, when Trafton was going through the motions of training, a couple of harsh looking characters walked into the gym. "Who's going to win?" one of them asked. "Trafton," one of our group replied. "He'd better not," one of them growled.

A day or two later, a slick young fellow walked in and asked the same question. My brother replied: "Up until yesterday, we thought Trafton was" and then told him about the visitors the day before. "Forget 'em," the guy told us. "They'll never bother you again. I'll take care of them. All I want to know is the fight on the up and up. If it is, I'll bet on Trafton." We learned later who the young man was: it was Machine Gun Jack McGurn [one of Al Capone's leading henchmen].[54]

When the day of the fight arrived, Trafton pounded Shires, the confident first baseman of the White Sox, and easily won the five-round match before 5,000 spectators. Neither "fighter" appeared to be in the best of pugilistic shape: "From the first bell there was good reason to suspect that neither would go the full five. Shires, obviously hoping for a quick knockout, came out like a bear but walked into the real Bear's long left. He went down, but bounced back without a count. Trafton dropped him twice more before the bell. Trafton's endurance was little better. Yells of 'hit him!' came from the Bear cheering section, but all Trafton could give was an ex post facto reply that 'I couldn't get my hands up. They weighed 100 pounds apiece!'"[55]

As for Shires, he vowed to return to the ring quickly (which he did) but without giving away over a 30-pound weight advantage to his opponent as he did with Trafton. "I want to give Trafton the credit due him for the fight he put up. He can take a punch and I am here to testify that he can sock," said Shires.[56] But what about Jack McGurn? Was it possible that the suave gangster was really in conversations with Red Grange? McGurn had been a prime suspect in the horrible St. Valentine's Day massacre in Chicago earlier in 1929 that left seven dead. However, charges against McGurn in conjunction with that unfortunate event were dropped on December 2, 1929. Still, the Capone group began to distance itself from McGurn in the aftermath of the Valentine's Day investigation. Richard J. Shmelter, the author of *Chicago Assassin*, which chronicled the life of McGurn, indicated that it was indeed possible for McGurn to be involved in local Chicago boxing matches: "I truly believe that anything was possible to make money, and fixing boxing matches has been commonplace probably since the sport began. As to McGurn's involvement in fixing fights, I personally think he could have, seeing that he was deeply involved in the lucrative gambling business for the Capone organization. However, I do not know of any concrete evidence to back up McGurn fixing fights."[57]

In addition, Shmelter noted that the actions of McGurn in reassuring Red Grange and the other Bears that there would be no interference with the Trafton fight would have been consistent with McGurn's personality:

McGurn was just cleared of involvement in the massacre two weeks prior to the Trafton-Shires fight. For this reason, it seemed to me that he would not have looked to draw more attention to himself over a boxing match at that time. Strictly in my own opinion, with his star starting to dim within the Capone organization, McGurn might have spouted off about not allowing anyone to "fix" the fight just to make himself still feel relevant. After all, being on top of his business for a few years, with Capone admiring him for his athletic prowess and ability to protect him, that type of power would have been extremely hard to see fading away. Once again, that is only my observation. I do believe that McGurn might have visited the training camp, and even watched the fight. For he was a huge sports fan, as well as an incredible athlete himself.[58]

Money Was Short Everywhere

As the 1929 season closed, the early impact of the Great Depression was beginning to take its toll on all aspects of American life. Jobs were lost, investments disappeared, banks closed, and the overall economy staggered. Professional football was not unscathed as well since attendance dropped, advertisers eased away, and budgets were stretched. Even George Halas admitted that funds were very scarce and that he was not above "borrowing" from his children's savings accounts: "Money was short everywhere, including the Halas household, [We] had given the children money every Christmas and birthday. Almost all had gone into savings. I raided their accounts. I fell behind with the apartment rent."[59]

The year-end financial statement of the Chicago Bears reflected some of that instability. The organization was battered financially by less income as well as not being successful in receiving funds owed to the team. That, of course, led to an inability to remit payment for bills in a timely manner. As of December 31, 1929, the Bears counted just $1,876.40 available in cash at the Sheridan Trust and Savings Bank. Total cash receipts for the season were $138,638.90 against expenses of $139,721.92. However, the additional income from program sales, although minimal, allowed the club to demonstrate a surplus of $2,101.18 for the year. Home games with the Giants ($30,338.50) and the Cardinals ($23,834) provided the biggest financial boost on the schedule. On the expense side, the Bears paid out $43,929.16 in player salaries plus a separate salary of $3,337.75 to Red Grange. In terms of individual player salaries, Walter Holmer was the highest paid at $5,200 while Paddy Driscoll and Joey Sternaman each earned $3,944.33. Reliable center George Trafton was farther down the list at $2,595.82 for his efforts. Travel expenses were nicely documented as well with the trips ranging in cost from $15 for bus transportation to the Chicago Cardinals game to $1,157.28 for train fare and meals to Minneapolis. Hotel costs were small since the team slept on the train, both coming and going to a destination. Finally, Halas and Sternaman each received $3,000 for the season and Harry Hazelwood, the "club house boy," earned a robust $5 in 1929![60] Noticeably absent in 1929, however, were the large bonuses that Halas and Sternaman usually enjoyed after a successful financial season.

Nagurski Was Most Bruising Fullback

By the time the 1930 season rolled around, Halas, Dutch Sternaman, and Paddy Driscoll had all hung up their cleats and retired from the playing field. With Ralph Jones now in charge on the gridiron, and Halas and Sternaman focused on the business of running an NFL club, the Bears rebounded with a 9–4–1 NFL record. The Cardinals also initiated a coaching change with superb fullback Ernie Nevers assuming the coaching reins while continuing to toil in the backfield. Nevers celebrated the birth of the new year by heading back to his hometown of Santa Rosa, California, to play for the local Bonecrushers grid team. Nevers scored a pair of touchdowns to pace the Bonecrushers to a 25–6 win over Antioch for the California American Legion state title on January 5, 1930.[61] The appearance of Nevers with the local club might be compared to having Michael Jordan, in his heyday, show up to play some hoops with the local park district team!

Once again, the Cardinals established their preseason training camp in Michigan, this time in Sturgis. A new arrival for the 1930 season was undersized (5'11", 190 pounds) guard Phil Handler from Texas Christian University. He would go on to play seven seasons for the Cardinals, making an All-Pro team during four of those campaigns; but in 1930, Handler was just another rookie hoping to continue his playing career as a member of the Chicago Cardinals. In his later years, Handler shared that first training camp experience with Coach Ernie Nevers as told to *Chicago Tribune* columnist David Condon:

> When the Cardinals went to Sturgis, Handler was with them and he recently recounted the jaunt in 1930. Today the pro teams are housed in air-conditioned quarters and have central dining areas with he-man food available. In 1930, Handler recalled: "At Sturgis, we lived in rooming houses all over town. Meals were in the back room of a downtown restaurant." Handler remembered the restaurant's specialty was gravy. Today pro football practice sessions are as organized as were the plans for D-Day. But in 1930, Handler recalled, "The Cardinals practice was sort of hit or miss. Ernie Nevers was our coach, and we practiced as he felt like it. He felt like scrimmaging the first year we were there. I'll say this for Ernie, tho. He went out there and scrimmaged with us."[62]

On the North Side of Chicago, Coach Ralph Jones and the Bears greeted a rookie whose name would become one of the most revered in team history: Bronislau "Bronko" Nagurski, an All-American tackle and fullback from the University of Minnesota. During training camp at Mills Stadium in the city, Jones initially penciled in Nagurski as a tackle, where he performed on defense in college. But Nagurski became quickly invaluable on the offensive side at fullback due to his potent blocking and his ramming, battering, rushing style. His teammate Red Grange once said: "Running into him was like getting an electric shock. If you tried to tackle him anywhere above the ankles, you were liable to get killed."[63] At 6'2" tall and weighing around 230 pounds, Nagurski was uncommonly large for a running back in 1930 and was never one to shy away from initiating contact. Former Green Bay Packer Clark Hinkle once said of Nagurski: "My greatest thrill in football was the day Bronko Nagurski announced his retirement. There's no question he was the most bruising fullback football has ever seen. I know because I've still got the bruises!"[64]

George Halas quickly signed Nagurski to a hefty $5,000 contract in March 1930 after the player entertained offers from several other NFL clubs. His rookie salary dwarfed those of future Hall of Famers Link Lyman ($2,300) and George Trafton ($2,345.68) on the Bears' 1930 roster. To accommodate the higher salaries of individuals like Nagurski and Coach Ralph Jones ($7,500), the Bears implemented a system of promissory notes to spread the payments out over several months.[65] But Nagurski was worth it, proving to be a scourge to opponents on either side of the line and helping the resurgence of the Bears in the early 1930s.

Both the Bears and the Cardinals played their early season games away since both used Major League Baseball stadiums, keeping the gridders locked out until the baseball season concluded. The Cardinals' schedule in 1930 was quite unusual, with the team playing seven games during the month of October, including a four-game

East Coast swing in only 11 days that resulted in just one win and a tie. Star fullback Ernie Nevers saw limited action on the trip due to an injury but was expected back three days later on October 19 when the Cardinals (1–3–2 overall) opened their home season at Comiskey Park by hosting the Bears (1–2–1). As usual, the bluster of the local media predicted a magnanimous battle, ripe with exciting offensive talent and outstanding defenders: "Stonewall defenses, always the rule in pro football, will be more in evidence than usual in the city championship clash at Sox Park Sunday…. Experts who saw Bronko Nagurski as defensive fullback against the New York Giants branded his exhibition as one of the greatest ever recorded. Halas and Sternaman offer him as their answer to the problem of how to stop Ernie Nevers, who walked through the Bears last Thanksgiving for forty points unaided."[66]

Although this would be the fifth game for the Cardinals in two weeks, the hosts were expected to prevail with a healthy Nevers back in the lineup. Instead, a still-limited Nevers played little in the freezing environment of early fall and the vengeful Bears rolled over their rivals 32–6. While Nevers managed one touchdown, Red Grange scored twice and Walt Holmer added three more for the victors. The excellent performance by Grange provoked memories of his halcyon collegiate days: "It was very reminiscent of certain old plays made for Illinois back in 1924 and 1925, and brought tears to the eyes of the customers. Or maybe it was the cold that brought tears to the eyes!"[67]

Lambeau Was Furious

Just a week later, the Cardinals bounced back with a pair of victories enabled by another wild scheduling maneuver. On Saturday, October 25, Ernie Nevers scored twice to lead the Cardinals over Frankford 34–7 in Philadelphia. The team then grabbed a long train ride back to Chicago and hosted the Portsmouth (Ohio) Spartans the next day. Once again, Nevers crossed the goal line twice and the Cardinals slipped past the visitors 23–13. By the time the Bears and the Cardinals met for the second time, on Thanksgiving Day (November 27), both were nonfactors in the league standings with the Bears checking in with a 6–4–1 mark and the Cardinals at 5–5–2. And then, as was quite common in this rivalry, something new and different popped up right before the game.

In this case Halas surprised the football world by signing controversial Notre Dame fullback Joe Savoldi on November 22. Savoldi was caught up in an unusual scandal that would be commonplace today. While a student at Notre Dame, Savoldi was married but kept the marriage secret and claimed that he not only did not live with his wife but had not seen her since the ceremony in April 1929. When the cover-up was made public, Savoldi became the subject of a national controversy: should he be allowed to not only play football at Notre Dame, but also remain a student? Apparently, married students at Notre Dame were forbidden at the time. After days of conjecture, Savoldi dropped out of school on November 17, although it was assumed that he had been expelled. Savoldi renounced the marriage immediately, but later admitted: "I had expected it [the discovery of his marriage] to come any time, but I was praying ardently that it might be delayed at least until my college football career was ended. I remember I was standing on the sidelines when a newspaper reporter walked over to me and handed me a slip of paper. I looked at it a minute and then felt shaky around the knees. Naturally, I was so surprised that all I could say was I did not know anything about it."[68]

Coincidentally, Curly Lambeau of the Green Bay Packers visited the Notre Dame campus right around the time that Savoldi surrendered his eligibility and rumors swirled that Savoldi would sign with the Packers. Lambeau rejected that possibility by noting NFL teams were not allowed to contract with a player until that athlete's class graduated. And that's when the surprise from Halas and company arrived. It was announced on November 22 that Savoldi would be joining the Bears in time to face the Cardinals. A furious Lambeau told the press: "President Joe Carr of the National League notified me to lay-off Savoldi until his class graduated next June. I have followed his instructions completely. I can't see how the Bears can use Savoldi. It would be in direct violation of the National Football League regulations which provide that no player can be signed or used by a National League club until his class graduated."[69]

Once again, as had been the case in 1925 with Red Grange, George Halas interpreted the collegiate eligibility as not being in effect if the player dropped out of school. And for Cardinals fans, the result was immediate. In the Bears' 6–0 victory over the Cards on Thanksgiving Day, Savoldi scored the only touchdown of the game. In the true tradition of the Bears/Cardinals battles, Savoldi was also quickly involved in some nonfootball skirmishes on the field:

> In the fourth period George Kenneally, Cardinal end, apparently decided that Savoldi had dumped [tackled] him with too much vigor. Kenneally sought out Savoldi on the next play and belted him in the mouth. This procedure failed to intimidate "Jumping Joe" however, and the next play he sought out Mr. Kenneally. The Cardinal end anticipated the attack and succeeded in tying up the infuriated Italian in a cinch. Meanwhile "Bullet" Baker of the Cardinals, rushed up and let loose with a right-hand uppercut. Fortunately, he missed the punch. Savoldi was ready to battle the whole Cardinal team single-handed but his teammates dragged him away from the battle zone.[70]

Two days later, President Carr fined the Bears $1,000 for violating the league rules against utilizing a player before his college class graduated, a rule that had been instituted after the uproar caused by Halas for signing Red Grange in 1925 under similar circumstances. "The hiring of Savoldi was in direct violation of the league's rules," explained President Carr. "The Bears officials knew the rule and the fine was necessary."[71] As for Savoldi, he played just two more games for the Bears before leaving football behind for a long wrestling career that lasted until 1950. And, because of his ability to speak several languages, he served in a valuable espionage role during World War II for the United States military. For his three games in the NFL back in 1930, the Bears paid Savoldi a cool $4,000, according to the Sternaman financial records.[72]

I Even Had to Buy a Ticket for My Wife!

When the door finally slammed shut on the 1930 NFL season, Cardinals owner Dr. David Jones conceived a rather innovative idea that likely changed the way we watch football today. In the midst of the Great Depression, Jones contacted Halas and Sternaman and challenged the Bears to one more game—an exhibition that would be played for charity. The idea was a sound one, but became even more attractive when Jones, because of nasty weather conditions, suggested that the game be conducted indoors, specifically at the massive Chicago Stadium. The Bears accepted the challenge and the media jumped all over the concept of playing a football game inside during the winter. In fact, it would be the first time that two NFL clubs would play under a roof, an odd concept that is now quite common.

However, there were myriad challenges facing the organizers of this event. The stadium was also used as the home base for the Chicago Blackhawks hockey club. Monday, December 15, was selected as the date of the game so that the football contest would not conflict with any regularly scheduled hockey games. Inside the Chicago Stadium, the area designated for the football game was literally covered by a hockey rink. In addition, the length of a full-sized football field could not be accommodated indoors. And, would the ceiling be high enough to allow punting, passing, and extra points? Careful, advanced planning for staging such an extravaganza was not possible, but by working with the stadium crew and hashing out pragmatic possibilities, the Bears and the Cardinals settled upon some workable solutions. The biggest obstacle was the ice itself, especially since the Blackhawks hosted the Montreal Maroons in a match the day before (December 14), leaving plenty of frozen stuff and nothing resembling a football field! The *Chicago Evening Post* described the breakneck process that would be needed to convert the ice rink into a football field in such a short period of time: "Next Sunday night, the Black Hawks and the Montreal Maroons meet in a hockey game. Immediately after this game and when the enclosure is cleared, steam will be run through the refrigeration pipes to melt the ice. When the arena is drained then trucks will haul earth to cover approximately 47,500 square feet of surface about six inches in depth, which will be rolled to make the football playing surface. All of this must be done in about eighteen hours."[73]

The next challenge would be less of a physical demand, but still critical in order to ensure the game's success. As hard as the organizers tried, there was no way a regulation 100-yard field could be dropped into Chicago Stadium. Instead, the teams agreed upon some rules that would facilitate playing the game on an 80-yard surface:

- With an 80-yard field, it was determined that kickoffs would be initiated from the goal line.
- Since the field was shorter than usual, any offensive drive would have 20 yards subtracted before crossing midfield.
- In order to increase visibility for both players and fans, a white football would be used during the game.
- Because of ceiling height concerns, dropkicks and placekicks for field goals would not be allowed.
- Surprisingly, there would not be any limitations on punting. Stadium officials indicated that there would be about 94 feet of open space above the field.[74]

Newspapers and fans viewed this game in 1930 as quite the novelty at the time, but the anticipation of watching stars such as Grange, Nevers, and Savoldi up close and personal attracted a crowd estimated at 12,500. The charitable aspect of it was also well-timed, promising a substantial contribution to the state's unemployment commission, as emphasized by Halas: "Every cent above operating costs will go to the unemployment fund. I even had to buy a ticket for my wife. No free tickets will be issued except to writers and photographers who have been assigned to the game."[75]

The large crowd enjoyed the activity as both Nagurski and Nevers scored touchdowns for their teams in a tight 9–7 Bears win. The difference in the outcome resulted when Nevers was caught in his own end zone for a safety. Adding to the "giving" nature of the evening, the teams auctioned off a football at halftime that was autographed by both Grange and Nevers. It may have been one of the earliest examples of an NFL memorabilia sale with the lively bidding resulting in another $180 for the unemployment fund in addition to the estimated $15,000 from the game itself. While the footing may have been slippery at times for the players, the indoor experiment failed to disappoint those in attendance. About the only occasion where the building itself impaired a play occurred when Nevers unleashed an impressive extra point attempt, according to the *Chicago Tribune*: "Nevers then kicked directly at the world's greatest pipe organ, the bull's eye for the seventh point, and it was good, although deflected by Ralph Waldo Emmerson, the organist."[76]

After this very first "inside" game featuring NFL teams, absolutely no one could have foreseen the boom in building indoor football stadiums in the future. Ironically, the Cardinals now have one of the more prominent edifices in pro football. Situated outside Phoenix, Arizona, the Cardinals' home field even has a movable roof designed to protect the participants from inclement weather. But unlike the cold and snow that threatened Chicago in December 1930, the Cardinals' stadium roof today can be adjusted to block out the searing heat of the Arizona desert.

With the success of the first experience of playing pro football inside, George Halas was not averse to following that possibility again in the future. The Bears would play indoors once more in 1932 in a contest that would significantly alter the direction of the National Football League and enable the Bears to reclaim the professional title. But would Halas be able to survive a brutal financial onslaught in the coming months that might wrestle away his control of the Chicago Bears?

Thirteen

Bidwill Saves the Bears!

"Professional football is motion without emotion."
—Robert Zuppke, Coach, University of Illinois

Bounced checks, overdrafts, and IOUs.

The financial future of the Chicago Bears in 1931 was both precarious and disheartening. Under new coach Ralph Jones in 1930, the Bears had returned to prominence, but now Coach Jones was somewhat unhappy. Not totally angry but concerned. In late 1931, Jones had still not been paid completely for his efforts during the 1931 season.

Being the reasonable sort, Jones composed a polite letter on December 17, 1931, to the warring faction known as George Halas and Dutch Sternaman, and asked nicely for any compensation due from his employers:

> Dear Dutch:
> I spoke to George Halas about getting the balance and interest on the note. He said to write you giving the amount and that you would take care of it. There is a balance of $200.00 and as I figure it the interest amounts to $44.50. Will appreciate it if you will take care of this at once. You paid $200.00 June 18th, $200.00 August 12th, $200.00 August 31st, and $200.00 October 15th. I expected to see you around football this fall. We certainly had the worst season of injuries I ever saw. Knees and shoulders, and they were the bad ones.[1]

Jones had been coaxed into taking the Bears job a year before with just one condition, according to George Halas. "I'll take the job," Jones stipulated, "if you two stay put in the front office. I want to be boss on the field. Let me do things my way and I'll win the championship in three years."[2] Jones had signed his new annual contract with the Bears on March 20, 1931, which allowed him complete authority on the field: "He is to be in absolute charge and control of the discipline, conditioning, practice, conduct and play of the members of the football squad and the formations and plays used by said football team."[3] Coach Jones was to be paid $7,500 for the season, due in its entirety by December 15, 1931. Somehow, either before or during the season, the salary schedule turned into a promissory note with the Bears churning out smaller bits of compensation for an unspecified amount of time. Apparently, the Bears fell behind quickly in this process, as indicated by a letter to Jones dated June 19, 1931:

> Dear Ralph:
> Enclosed find our check No. 1153 for $200.00 to apply to our note due June 1, 1931. Philadelphia has not paid us as yet although we expect to have it settled before the league meeting is called, which is July 11th and 12th here in Chicago.[4]

In truth, the Bears, along with all of the teams in the National Football League, were feeling the squeeze of the Depression throughout 1931. Earlier in the year, the Bears organization sent out letters to its players (this one going to Bronko Nagurski) warning of the bleak financial picture surrounding the league:

> Dear Bronko:
> We are adopting a new policy this year, in that we expect to mail contracts for the 1931 season within the next ten days.... Last season was mighty bad financially, and due to the depression, all over the country, next season does not look very rosy from a financial standpoint. In studying the auditor's report we find that we have a salary list that is prohibitive. Most of the clubs lost money last year and unless general business conditions improve greatly, it looks like the league is in for a bad season this fall.[5]

The letter encouraged each player to return his signed contract quickly, and for those who might not accept the terms, the team would attempt to trade them to a more accommodating organization. Nagurski, who became a member of the first class of the Pro Football Hall of Fame in 1963 along with Red Grange and Halas, years later looked back fondly at the career of his former boss, saying of Halas: "A wonderful guy to play for but tough to deal with. I never had to worry about being overpaid!"[6]

While the overall ledger for the 1930 season showed the Bears with a slight profit of $1,695.93, cash flow was tight and notes were extended into 1931 to cover the salaries of Jones, Nagurski, Dan McMullen, Walt Holmer, and even Joe Savoldi, who exited after those three games in 1930.[7] Indeed, by the end of 1930, the bank account of the Chicago Bears was nearly dry with just $1,323.48 remaining in the Sheridan Trust & Savings Bank as of December 10, 1930.[8] The Chicago Bears, it seems, were precariously close to careening over into insolvency prior to the 1931 campaign, with mounting debts still needing to be addressed. The letter above dated December 17, 1931, from Ralph Jones was written to Dutch Sternaman and lingered over the question of the whereabouts of Sternaman during the season. Apparently, the backroom negotiations were protected from outside eyes, but paperwork found in the Sternaman collection indicates that Halas and his partner began the long process of ending their relationship early in 1931. Halas recalled: "We had a drawerful of bills and we were overdrawn at the bank by $1,147.44. Altogether the Bears owed $11,791.88, and no change was in sight. The depression was deadly for many league teams. In the summer of 1931, my partner, Dutch Sternaman, couldn't meet mortgage payments on his apartment house and his super gas station. His only other asset was his partnership in the Bears. He asked if I would buy him out for $38,000, enough to meet his financial needs. I did want control of the Bears. My faith in the Bears was boundless. I scurried around to find the money."[9]

On April 22, 1931, Edward C. "Dutch" Sternaman resigned from his position as president of the Chicago Bears, as well as from his seat on the Board of Directors. The announcement of the sale did not appear in the newspapers until September 15, 1931, when the reorganization of the Chicago Bears corporation was disclosed.

By this time, Dutch's brother Joey Sternaman had also resigned from the Board of Directors, generating the following corporate realignment:

> Ed "Dutch" Sternaman, who was associated with George Halas in the management of the Chicago Bears football club since its origins, has sold his interest in the North Side organization. The retirement of Sternaman necessitated a new formation in the management of the club. George Halas is president, treasurer, and also on the board of directors; James McMillen, a star with the Bears and now a prominent wrestling star, is vice president; Charles Bidwill, secretary of the Illinois Turf Association, is secretary of the club. The other director is Ralph Brizzolara, chief engineer of the American Steel Foundries.[10]

The Worst Was Worse Than Any Worst I Could Conceive

Oddly enough, there was still more going on behind the scenes, according to the Sternaman collection. An unexecuted document, dated May 21, 1931, was prepared that would allow Dr. David Jones, owner of the Chicago Cardinals, to purchase stock owned by Joey and Chester Sternaman (brothers of Dutch Sternaman) in the Chicago Bears corporation. The price would not be cheap. The tentative agreement delineated the details of the proposed transaction: "In the event said option is exercised, the party of the second part [Dr. Jones] is to pay for said stock forty thousand dollars ($40,000.00) in cash and, in addition, ten thousand dollars ($10,000.00) which is to be represented by a judgement note executed by the party of the second part [Dr. Jones] and payable on or before ten (10) months after the date of this agreement and bearing interest at five per cent (5%) per annum. It is further expressly agreed, by and between the parties hereto, that the stock hereinabove described, represents one-half (½) interest in said corporation."[11]

This would have been a highly suspect and potentially controversial transaction. The surviving documents from the Sternaman collection do not reveal if George Halas was aware that Dr. Jones might become the owner of both the Chicago Cardinals and an equal owner of the Chicago Bears. The deal with Dr. Jones did not materialize and eventually Joey Sternaman sold his stock in the Bears to Dutch Sternaman, as recorded in the minutes from a special stockholders' meeting on July 3, 1931. With this sale, Dutch Sternaman now owned a controlling share in the corporation with six shares. George Halas possessed five shares and Frank Halas one. A second meeting of the Board of Directors followed immediately on July 3, 1931, at 3:00 p.m. During this session, the resignation of Dutch Sternaman as a director was accepted. The organization now included just two directors: Frank Halas and George Halas.[12]

The complicated negotiations between Halas and Edward "Dutch" Sternaman for the sale of the Sternaman stock were addressed next. Halas explained his unique method for raising the funds necessary to procure the shares (priced at $38,000) owned by Dutch Sternaman:

> On July 3, 1931, I did buy out Dutch. I paid him $25,000 in cash and promised to pay $6,000 on January 25, 1932, and the final $7,000 on July 31, 1932. I placed my Bears' stock in the bank as collateral. I paid off pressing bills and had $6,000 left for the January payment. I always went to the bank to borrow money for the new season and I assumed that if worse came to worst, I could borrow the final $7,000. The fine print said if I failed to make the payment the

stock would go to Sternaman. I considered the clause merely legal hocus-pocus, something I was soon to learn a person must never do.[13]

The recollection of Halas regarding the collateral statement above is accurate. In an undated letter to the Cicero State Bank, Halas provides the following guidance:

> You are holding as collateral to my loan of $5,700.00 certain certificates for six shares of common stock of Chicago Bears Football Club, Inc. You are instructed to hold the same even after payment of loan to you, as escrow agent, to be delivered to the undersigned upon the joint order of Edward G. Sternaman and the undersigned or upon exhibiting to you notes numbered one and two, made by the undersigned, payable to the order of bearer, for $6,000.00 and $7,000.00 respectively due January 25, 1932 and July 31, 1932.
>
> In event said Edward G. Sternaman shall after either of the maturity dates above mentioned, exhibit said notes and show to your satisfaction that the same have not been paid, then you are authorized to deliver said certificates of stock to said Edward G. Sternaman provided the said $5,700.00 has been paid in full to Cicero State Bank.[14]

Indeed, the date of July 3, 1931, was a busy one for the directors of the Chicago Bears. In addition to the two meetings held to discuss stock transactions and ownership responsibilities, the contract between Halas and Sternaman was also finalized. The selling price of the six units of stock from Sternaman to Halas was $38,000, with $25,000 due up front and the remainder of the agreement due on January 25, 1932 ($6,000), and July 31, 1932 ($7,000), as mentioned by Halas.[15] But Halas found it difficult to raise the funds necessary for the final payment due on July 31, 1932. Halas claimed that he possessed only $2,000 of the needed $7,000 to complete the sale by the deadline and hoped to secure the remainder through a bank loan. If not, his ownership of the Bears was certainly in danger of disappearing: "By the next July, the worst was worse than any worst I could conceive. Many banks were closed and those open would make no loan. I was $5,000.00 short and, as the fine print stated, the stock passed into the control of Sternaman. On August 3, his lawyer wrote a letter informing me that the stock would be put up for public auction in his office at 12 o'clock sharp on August 9. I tried everywhere to raise the $5,000. I called everyone I knew. No one could help me. August 9 came. I was desperate. At noon I would lose my Bears. Years of effort would be negated."[16]

Although some of the interpretations have differed over the years, Halas did offer this explanation to the *Chicago Tribune* in 1967 on how he managed to secure the remaining amount of cash needed to retain his ownership of the Bears: "From this desperate situation, I was rescued by the joint efforts of my mother and my good friend Charley Bidwill. Mother [of Halas] bought $5,000 worth of stock from her savings, Bidwill purchased $5,000 in stock and also arranged a bank loan for the remaining $5,000 needed to pay off Sternaman. But it was a mighty close call. As I remember, I finally got all the money together at 11:10 am on the day the final note came due. Forfeit time was 12 o'clock noon."[17]

Charles Bidwill had indeed saved the day for George Halas. Bidwill, a local Chicago lawyer, successful businessman, and sports enthusiast, would shortly become an even bigger player in the NFL landscape as the future owner of the Cardinals. His son, the late William V. Bidwill, stated: "Halas and my father were very good friends. And he did help Halas and the Bears. The financial numbers would seem insignificant in today's economy, but they were big back then."[18] But for now, Halas was the primary owner of the Chicago Bears and ready to address the usual problems of a pro football team as well as the unusual problems facing a business during the Great Depression.

Pro Football Is the McHooey

As for the Cardinals, the team would be in the headlines even before the 1931 season started. Three significant events attributed to the organization emerged before a down was played in 1931. On August 26, Dr. David Jones, the owner of the Cardinals, announced that Leroy Andrew, the successful coach of the New York Giants, had been hired to the same position with the Cards. Andrew had compiled an impressive 24–5–1 record with the Giants over the previous two seasons and moved to Chicago with seven years of head coaching experience in the NFL. Jones was elated with the addition of Andrew: "Dr. David Jones, in securing the services of the successful pro mentor, voiced the belief that Andrew would boom the south side eleven into a formidable contender."[19] Ernie Nevers, who served the team as player, captain, and coach in 1930, would relinquish his coaching duties in 1931 but continue in his on-field roles. This was the second big announcement from Dr. Jones that week. On August 20, he dropped the surprising decision that the Cardinals would move their home games to Wrigley Field on the North Side. This would mean that the Cardinals would share Wrigley Field with both the Chicago Cubs baseball team and the Chicago Bears. As such, with most prime dates already gobbled up, the Cards did not entertain a league opponent at "home" until November 15.

Apparently, Dr. Jones was of the opinion that by moving his team into the lair of the Chicago Bears, he would be able to duplicate the recent strong attendance experienced by the North Side club. But from a marketing viewpoint, the move was certainly questionable. Bears fans were unlikely to support the Cardinals while South Side fans were equally unlikely to follow their team north. In a sense, the Cardinals nation felt abandoned. One anguished supporter fired off a scorching letter to the *Chicago Tribune* expressing his frustration with the decision: "I read with surprise that this coming season all home games of the Chicago Cardinals will be played at Wrigley Field, which leaves the south side out in the cold as far as professional football is concerned. The writer and four of his friends saw every home game of the Cardinals on the south side last season, but for reasons peculiar to true south siders we have made up our minds that if the Cardinals' games must be played on the north side, they will have to rely on the north side for trade. I wonder how many other fans feel the same way about the snubbing."[20]

Jones countered by publicly stating that the Cardinals had been informed the previous April by Charles Comiskey that Comiskey Park would not be available for football games in 1931, necessitating the move to Wrigley Field.[21] As difficult as it was for South Side followers to comprehend, the Cardinals would remain entrenched in Wrigley Field for the remainder of the decade. But Dr. Jones was not finished with his preseason headline-grabbing maneuvers. Jones reacted with anger and disdain when, for some reason, University of Illinois football coach Robert Zuppke decided to bash the burgeoning world of pro football with a less-than-praiseworthy evaluation. In comments published in the *Chicago Tribune*, Zuppke flatly stated: "My Illinois football team of last year [which was by no means his best] could play the Bears, the Cardinals, or any other pro club to a standstill. A team like the 1930 Notre Dame eleven would score four touchdowns on the best pro eleven before the latter knew what was going on." In a final verbal assault, columnist Arch Ward added: "Whatever their opinions about the formidability of the other's team, Zuppke and [Northwestern coach Dick] Hanley were one in their appraisal of professional football. They agree it is the McHooey."[22]

In one of those rare examples of Chicago gridiron unity, both Dr. Jones and George Halas responded quickly to Zuppke's surprise broadside. "George Halas, former intercollegiate and pro star, now manager of the Bears, thinks Mr. Zuppke is 'talking through his hat.'"[23] Dr. Jones was even more emphatic. He suggested that the University of Illinois play the Chicago Cardinals in a charity event to prove the superiority of one level of football over the other. Seizing on the Zuppke comment that Illinois "could play the Bears, the Cardinals, or any other pro club to a standstill," Jones issued a prompt challenge to his collegiate brethren: "Now if Mr. Zuppke is of the opinion that his team this fall can do the same, I will gladly post $10,000, the amount to be donated to charity if his team, or any other college football team designated by Mr. Zuppke will play and beat the Cardinals. I know Mr. Zuppke will hide behind the cloak of the rules of the Big Ten conference and say 'We are not allowed to play.'"[24]

Of course, such a game would never be considered and the sniping between Zuppke and his professional rivals continued for a few weeks before largely disappearing. Zuppke's persistence in addressing a seemingly innocuous issue continued in September 1931, when he stated: "Professional football is motion without emotion. That's why I believe it never can excel the college game and why I object to any statements that the pro teams are better than the colleges."[25] Perhaps the final word should be left with the elusive C.C. Pyle, the erstwhile former manager of Red Grange. Now six years after his wild athletic excursion with Grange, Pyle confidently stated: "In my opinion any national professional league team can beat any college eleven by four touchdowns. I would love to see a game between Illinois or Northwestern and one of the Chicago professional teams ... the college coaches would be wiser after the game."[26]

Old Red Just Would Not Be Stopped

As the NFL season commenced on September 23, 1931, new Cardinals coach Andrew was very pleased with his prospects. The Cards had knocked off a pair of local teams in preseason activity and traveled to Portsmouth, Ohio, to take on the Spartans for the team's league opener. "I have so many great players I don't know where to put them," said Andrew.[27] Unfortunately, the vastly improved Spartans stunned the talented Cardinals 13–3, with an Ernie Nevers field goal accounting for the only points for the losers. With over two weeks off until the next game against the Green Bay Packers on October 11, it was assumed that Coach Andrew would use the time to revitalize his squad. Instead, on October 5, Andrew (sometimes called *Andrews* in the media) suddenly resigned as head coach of the Cardinals after just one NFL contest. The *Chicago Daily News* attributed the abrupt transition to reasons that were simply "business and financial."[28] There was speculation that Andrew was the victim of a player "revolt" specifically connected to his choice of offense. When he arrived in Chicago, Andrew implemented a single-wing offense whereas Ernie Nevers favored a double wing the year before. Andrew responded to inquiries about this possibility by stating: "There probably was some dissatisfaction with the single wing back I installed. I don't believe though, that Nevers started the trouble. I have regarded him as one of my best friends."[29] Nevers was then appointed as the Cardinals head coach for the remainder of the season as the team finished 5–4 in the league and 14–4–1 overall, including a six-game tour to conclude the season. The Cardinals dropped both games to the Bears in 1931 and were mired in a 13-game winless streak against their North Side rivals that would not be broken until the 1936 season.

A couple of the more intriguing aspects of the season were the final matchups between Ernie Nevers and Red Grange. Nevers would retire from his playing career at the conclusion of the 1931 campaign while Grange seemed to be enjoying a renaissance of his offensive skills, scoring three touchdowns in the Bears' 26–13 win over the Cardinals on October 18. The presence of the durable and sturdy Bronko Nagurski in the same backfield helped Grange tremendously: "Old Red just would not be stopped and with assistance of the big Nagurski, who bowled over the opposition as interference, the redhead at the end of the sixty minutes had crossed the Cardinal goal line three times. Nagurski added the fourth marker with a brilliant 62-yard run from scrimmage."[30]

Nagurski's presence in the Bears backfield was appreciated by Halas, who acknowledged the fullback's toughness and ferocity throughout his career. Halas enjoyed sharing a recollection about Nagurski from a game at Wrigley Field that exemplified the durability of Bronko:

> Because it was designed as a baseball stadium, at one end of the field, the outfield wall was not very far from the end line. The Bears were on about the two-yard line. Nagurski got the handoff. With head down and legs churning, he plunged into the line. Nagurski blasted through two would-be tacklers as though they were a pair of old saloon doors, and kept on going right through the end zone. His head still down, Nagurski ran full speed into the brick outfield wall. He went down, then got up and trotted off the field. As he approached me on the sideline, he shook his head and said, "That last guy really gave me a good lick, coach."[31]

In the return match, set for Thanksgiving Day, November 26, 1931, Nevers was optimistic about his team's chances against the Bears (6–3). The Cardinals (4–3) were enjoying a four-game winning streak, including a 21–13 upset over the undefeated, and defending champion, Green Bay Packers, and Nevers shared his assured viewpoint: "I think we can beat them. In the first game [26–13 loss], we had so many injured players that we couldn't feed reserves into the game. We're all o.k. now, and they'll know they've had a football game, anyway."[32]

The Chicago newspapers treated each clash between the Bears and the Cardinals as something very special. Even if one team or the other was well out of contention in the NFL standings, the battles between the two clubs would always be for the "city" championship. Typical of this enchantment, even in 1931 after the rivalry was reaching maturity, was the opening sequence of the game preview by the *Chicago Daily News*: "The oldest and most intense rivalry in professional football will fare again Thursday morning when the Bears and Cardinals clash at Wrigley Field in their twenty-third meeting. Interest in the game has skyrocketed following the great showing of the Cardinals in their last two games in which they defeated the Green Bay Packers and the Portsmouth Spartans, the two leading teams in the league. The Cards are confident of furnishing another upset, while the Bears are equally confident they can put an end to the winning streak of their rivals."[33]

Unknown at the time was the fact that both Nevers and sterling lineman Duke Slater of the Cardinals would be playing in their final game against the Bears. Both would one day be inducted into the Pro Football Hall of Fame, Nevers in 1963 and Slater in 2021. Slater had earned his law degree in 1928 and elected to pursue that path after an outstanding career in professional football where he earned All-Pro honors in seven of his 10 seasons. Prior to the Bears game, columnist Edward Geiger wrote: "Duke Slater … will be among those present. Nevers calls him the best lineman he ever saw and there are plenty of fans who will put their O.K. on that statement. Duke is a giant, with long arms and tremendous power. He has speed, knows how to take it easy when he's not in a play but he works like a Trojan when it is necessary. He, like Nevers, usually plays the full sixty minutes."[34]

Behind the rushing of Red Grange, the Bears swept to an easy 18–7 win over the Cardinals in front of 15,000 fans. The final league game of the Cardinals' season, and of Nevers's career, took place two days later, on Saturday, November 28. Nevers rushed for a pair of touchdowns, tossed a scoring pass for a third, and booted three extra points to account for all of the scoring in a decisive 21–0 victory over the Cleveland Indians at Wrigley Field. Sadly, just 1,500 spectators turned out to watch Nevers in his last NFL appearance. For the 1931 season, the Cardinals finished 5–4 in league play, which was good enough for a fourth-place finish in the NFL standings. The Packers captured their third straight NFL title with a 12–2 mark, while the Bears coasted into third with an 8–5 record.

World's Finest Fullback

The Cardinals then embarked on a six-game postseason tour, winning five of those (and tying one) to complete a fairly successful 14–4–1 ledger. On the first tour stop in Grand Rapids, Michigan, on December 5, 1931, the Cards were held to a 7–7 deadlock by the Grand Rapids Maroons. After the contest, Nevers provided a glimpse of his future plans: "Nevers says he is going to continue playing football until he is no longer able to run with a ball in his arm."[35] Yet a little over a month later, Ernie Nevers was finished with his playing career. In San Francisco on January 24, 1932, before 40,000 fans, Nevers endured a broken arm in a 26–14 decision over a group of all-stars headed by Frank Carideo of Notre Dame. In typical Nevers fashion, the big fullback was the whole offensive show for the Cardinals: "Nevers, who scored all four of the Cardinal touchdowns and converted two of them, suffered his injury on the last play of the game. Nevers said after the game that it was his last."³⁶ The *San Francisco Examiner* provided a fitting tribute to the outgoing local native: "A 60-minute boy he was in college, and a 60-minute boy he still is. He broke his arm, on the last play of the game, as hundreds of the crowd rushed to the field to mob him for autographs. He 'passed out' twice in the shower room from exhaustion due to hard play and the shock of a fractured radius bone. It will be at least a month before he can be active in any game again, but 40,000 will tell you that he never need touch another football to prove to their satisfaction who is the world's finest fullback."³⁷

As for the Bears' final 8–5 mark, the season did not result in any type of salvation from the mounting financial problems. There was precious little cash on hand. In fact, on December 29, 1931, the Bears received an overdraft notice from the Continental Illinois Bank and Trust Company in the amount of $124.53.³⁸

We Lost $18,000

In 1932, Halas maintained his majority ownership of the Bears once the Sternaman deal was completed. It was apparent that economic difficulties swept through the league that season and the Bears were not immune. "We lost $18,000, and I couldn't get a dime out of the bank," Halas complained.³⁹ But, the saving grace for Halas was the performance of the Bears on the field. Coach Jones returned the team to dominance and fulfilled his promise of bringing back a championship within three years of his hiring. Unfortunately for Jones, that title would also prove to be his occupational downfall despite his lofty success. It was indeed an unusual season, especially with the league's archaic rules still ignoring any value for tie games, which were especially prevalent in determining the 1932 NFL champion.

In a sense, the Cardinals played a key role in the postseason discussions when they played to a scoreless tie with the Bears on October 9, 1932. Including non-league games, the Cardinals jumped off to a 6–1–2 mark under new coach Jack Chevigny, a former player and assistant coach at Notre Dame. The Bears remained under the direction of Ralph Jones, "one of the leading coaches in the country ... and his work, which featured lateral plays and a back field man in motion...," but the Bears were having difficulty scoring.⁴⁰ After four NFL games, including a 0–0 deadlock with the Cardinals on October 9, the North Side representatives were just 0–1–3 and failed to cross the goal line in those four contests: zero points and zero wins! The Cardinals match was the third in that quartet of opening games for the Bears and the deadlock seemed to be consistent with two problems that the league would need to address: a plethora of tie games and a lack of scoring. In his book *Pioneer Coaches of the NFL*, author John Maxymuk noted: "In the decade of the 1920s, the average points-per-game ranged from a low of 7.6 in 1926, to a high of 10.4 in 1924. Fifty-seven NFL games in the 1920s ended in 0–0 ties. That's 7.2 percent of the decade's contests producing zero points ... the low scoring continued into the 1930s with the average points-per-game for pro teams running 10.6, 9.9, and 8.2, from 1930 to 1932 respectively."⁴¹

The league itself was running on fumes in 1932, with just eight teams in the race, tied for the lowest number in its history (during World War II, the NFL consisted of just eight members as well). With the Great Depression still raging, attracting attendees to games continued to be a challenge, especially with a rather conservative product on the field in terms of numerous ties and the dearth of scoring. The Chicago Cardinals attempted to enliven their offense when the team signed gifted running back Joe Lillard the week before the first Bears game on October 9. Lillard was a promising backfield star at the University of Oregon who lost his collegiate eligibility in 1931 under questionable circumstances. Lillard was apparently "convicted" for playing semipro baseball under an assumed name: "President W.B. Owens, of Stanford, president of the [Pacific Coast] conference, issued a formal statement announcing the faculty representatives' findings. His statement did not say in what sport Lillard 'had played under an assumed name,' but it has been known generally that Lillard played semi-professional baseball with the Gilkerson Colored Giants. He was employed as a driver for the team but on occasions he 'filled in' for players who were not in physical condition to play."[42]

Shortly thereafter, Lillard left Oregon and pursued an independent sports career, eventually bringing him to the Cardinals for an in-game tryout against Portsmouth on October 2, 1932. In the next game against the Bears, Lillard earned great reviews in the scoreless tie: "Joe Lillard stole the show when the Chicago Bears and Cardinals played to a scoreless tie Sunday. Lillard performed with the Cardinals and he made Grange and the other notables look feeble by comparison. Lillard passed, ran and kicked and outshone Nagurski, Joesting and the other stars."[43]

Lillard stayed with the team through the 1933 season but was an unfortunate victim of the NFL's shameful, albeit unwritten, ban on Black players that existed from 1934 through 1946. Ray Kemp of Pittsburgh and Lillard were the last two Black players in the league prior to the 1934 season. But for a brief time, Lillard was one of the brightest stars in the NFL, a dangerous triple threat, according to Kemp: "Joe could do it all—punt, pass and run. He did it all with great abandonment."[44]

A Very Swell Brand of Dirt

As the 1932 season progressed, three teams battled for the NFL title amid a flurry of tie games. After a solid start (2–1–2 in league competition), the Cardinals dropped their final five games to stumble out of championship contention, finishing with a disappointing 2–6–2 record and seventh place in the eight-team circuit. And that is why the tie game between the Bears and the Cardinals was so significant. The Bears completed their schedule with a puzzling 6–1–6 mark, in a virtual deadlock with Portsmouth (6–1–4) since tie games did not count in the standings and would not be considered as such until 1972. Also in the mix was Green Bay (10–3–1), the three-time defending NFL champion. Since the standings in 1932 did not consider tie games at all, the Bears and Portsmouth finished with identical winning percentages of .857. The Packers completed the schedule with a .769 mark, good only for third place despite having 10 wins. Ironically, tie games are now considered as one half of a win and one half of a loss, meaning that using the current interpretation, the Packers of 1932 would have ended with a winning percentage of .750, well ahead of Portsmouth (.727) and Chicago (.692). But since the old rules were still in place regarding tie games, it was decided by the NFL that the Bears and the Spartans would meet in a one-game playoff in Chicago to determine the league champion.

With the title tilt scheduled for Sunday, December 18, at Wrigley Field, the city of Chicago was locked in the midst of a nasty cold front. When temperatures dipped below zero degrees in the early morning hours of Thursday, December 15, a decision was made to move the game from Wrigley Field to Chicago Stadium. George Halas recalled the indoor playing conditions: "The Salvation Army had sponsored a circus there so the concrete floor had a thick covering of what the management described as a very swell brand of dirt. Permanent seats limited the length of the playing field to 80 yards and the width to 45. That required special rules. We put the posts on the goal line. To avoid solid-plank four-foot-high walls, we moved out-of-bounds balls inward 10 yards."[45]

Prior to the game, the local media debated whether or not the indoor setting might provide the Bears with a bit of an advantage, especially with strong-armed quarterback John "Bull" Doehring in the fold: "Bringing the title battle indoors not only is a break for the customers, but it will help the Bears' passing attack which centers around John Doehring."[46] Doehring was one of those unique characters who dotted the Bears' roster over the years. He never played in college, but Doehring caught the eye of George Halas during a tryout with the Bears in November 1932. Although listed as a halfback, he was not unlike other running backs during that time who also did a great deal of passing for their team. But Doehring possessed quite an unusual skill for the time: he could throw the ball almost 100 yards! And yet throwing a long forward pass with a watermelon-type football was not Doehring's only talent, as revealed by the *Los Angeles Times*, which said: "Halfback John Doehring, who never played college football, can throw the porker more than 100 yards and he is the only man in the world who can toss 'em from behind his back, his record for this being 60 yards by spiral!"[47] Author Richard Whittingham, in his book *What a Game They Played*, verified this unique skill set of Doehring as shared by Bears end Luke Johnsos:

> Bull took a lateral and started out towards the sidelines. He was supposed to throw a long pass to me, but he was in trouble, the defense was all over him. He didn't even have room to raise his arm. I looked away, figuring the play had failed. Then I happened to look up and there, coming straight into my hands, was the ball. I was so surprised I dropped it! As we were walking to the dressing room later, I asked him how he got rid of the ball. "Well, they were rushing me so I threw it behind my back." And that's what he had done, thrown the ball behind his back. Forty yards. Right into my hands.[48]

A nice crowd of over 11,000 attended the indoor contest, which was won by the Bears 9–0. The only touchdown of the game occurred in the fourth quarter when Red Grange snared a two-yard pass from Bronko Nagurski, not Bull Doehring! At the time, the league rules required that any pass be thrown from at least five yards beyond the line of scrimmage, and Portsmouth complained that Nagurski, after faking a run, had launched his toss from just a couple of yards behind the line. "The touchdown immediately was protested by Coach Potsy Clark of Portsmouth, who rushed to the field shouting that Nagurski was not five yards behind the line of scrimmage and that the forward pass was illegal. Referee Bobby Cahn of New York ruled that Bronko had complied with the rules."[49] After the protest was disallowed, the Bears added the extra point, and later a safety, to complete the 9–0 victory for the team's first championship in 11 years.

Although the victory in this unofficial "playoff" ensured that the Bears would wear the 1932 NFL crown, the decision still counted in the regular season standings, thus allowing the Packers to move into second place ahead of Portsmouth in the final league pecking order. More important, the indoor game itself, and its unusual ground rules, provided the league with the opportunity to contemplate significant changes in the professional game that would allow it to differentiate itself from the collegiate version. George Halas, who was quite influential in the changing of the rules, outlined the more prominent adjustments adopted in 1933: "At the league meeting two months later, we made three fundamental rules changes: 1. Passing was permitted anywhere behind the line. Potsy Clark's attitude was common. 'Nagurski will pass from anywhere so why not make it legal.' 2. An out-of-bounds ball was moved in 10 yards, eliminating the usual waste of a down to gain room to maneuver (this, of course, was the birth of hash marks). 3. The goal posts, which had been moved 10 yards behind the goal line three years earlier following the colleges, were restored to the goal line."[50]

The relaxation of the passing rules, the "closer" goalposts, and the placement of the hash marks on the interior of the field opened up the pro game a bit, resulting in more scoring and fewer tie games. A year later, the physical size of the football itself was reduced, thus making the actual passing procedure somewhat easier. In 1933, the NFL also decided that a year-end meeting of the top two teams might continue to be attractive (and eliminate any postseason "voting" to determine the champion). Two divisions were established, each including five teams. The Eastern Division consisted of the New York Giants, the Pittsburgh Pirates, the Philadelphia Eagles, the Brooklyn Dodgers, and the Boston Redskins. The Bears and the Cardinals were part of the Western Division, which also included the Green Bay Packers, the Cincinnati Reds, and the Portsmouth Spartans. At the conclusion of the 1933 season, the top team in each division would then play the other in the first "official" NFL playoff game. NFL President Joe Carr was confident that the changes would prove to be beneficial: "Professional football has progressed steadily. In a decade the helter skelter assortment of teams, several of which could not afford to play at home, has been reduced from 22 to an organization which has financial backing in all of its cities and which now will be big league from start to finish. Professional teams are well coached, practice daily, and offer superlative football at prices less than those charged for college games. These have been the factors in the growth of attendance. We confidently expect our greatest season this fall."[51]

A Football Field Is No Place for Saints!

Before the 1933 season started, both Chicago teams watched as their head coaches departed. Jack Chevigny of the Cardinals, who had finished 2–6–2 in the NFL (7–6–2 overall), decided that greener pastures smiled at tiny (500 students) St.

Edward's University in Austin, Texas. Chevigny, also an attorney, left the Cardinals in January 1933 to become the athletic director and head football coach at St. Edward's, and did so with the blessing of Cardinals owner Dr. David Jones. Upon learning that Chevigny had been offered $4,200 per annum for his expertise, Jones stated: "I am sorry to lose Chevigny, for I have the highest regard for his coaching ability. I understand that he has been offered a full-time position with a salary which the club cannot afford to meet in our three months' season. Chevigny has the best wishes of the Cardinals in his new position."[52]

One of his first acts as head coach at St. Edward's was to change the name of the team from "Saints" to "Tigers," or as Coach Chevigny explained: "A football field is no place for saints!"[53] After a single season at St. Edward's, Chevigny was named head coach at the University of Texas in 1934. By 1937, he was out of football and appointed deputy attorney general of Texas. When World War II broke out, Chevigny attempted to enlist but was turned down because of knee problems. Even so, in 1943, at the age of 36, Chevigny entered the service and eventually sought an assignment that was more than a public relations post. Instead of understandably helping his country in that manner, Chevigny pursued a slot in the dangerous Pacific arena. He was eventually part of the invasion of Iwo Jima, where on March 19, 1945, he lost his life on the first day of fighting. Chevigny was not expected to serve in the heavy action but did so anyway. Reporter Jim Costin remembered the bravery of Chevigny when learning of his passing: "The fierce competitive fires that always burned in Jack's breast wouldn't allow him to remain in camp. Even though he was 38 … he asked the marines to send him to where the fighting was going on. He met his death that day in the bloody fighting. He was a rough, tough, two-fisted competitor who was at his best when the chips were down."[54]

It took Dr. David Jones a few months to identify Chevigny's replacement as Cardinals coach, but he settled on the well-respected Paul Schissler on May 12, 1933. Schissler, who had resigned after nine years as the head coach at Oregon State over a financial dispute, accepted a three-year pact with the Cardinals. "I believe we have found a man with sufficient experience and background to give the Cardinals the necessary push toward at least a first division berth in the pro league. Schissler will be with us for three seasons and in that time, I am certain we will reach the top," proclaimed Jones.[55]

I Hate to Leave the Bears

As the Cardinals looked to Schissler to greatly improve their status in the NFL standings, the Bears moved on without Ralph Jones, the coach who led the team to the 1932 NFL title. As promised, Jones won a championship within three years, but apparently decided that he had seen enough IOUs from Halas during that time. So, on March 21, 1933, Jones surprised the pro football world by leaving the Bears for a position with Lake Forest (Illinois) College. Jones agreed to take on the responsibilities of athletic director, and to coach the football, basketball, and baseball teams at the school. "I hate to leave the Bears," said Jones. "The work at Lake Forest appeals to me."[56]

Immediate speculation on a successor for Jones centered on Red Grange who had flirted with talk of retirement after the 1932 season. According to one local newspaper, the hiring of Grange was a done deal just two days after the departure of Jones was announced: "From an authoritative source it was learned last night that the former Illinois star will be tendered the position by George Halas, owner of the Bears. Grange captained the Bears thru the past several seasons and has as much inside knowledge of the pro sport as any man in the game and has won the confidence of all the Bears players. His selection, no doubt, would be extremely popular with the fans and a wise move on the part of the Bears' management."[57]

Halas sifted through nearly 30 coaching resumes before finally deciding on the most ideal candidate to run the Chicago Bears: himself! Halas slid into the driver's seat, saved an "outside" coach's salary, and steered the Bears on a remarkable two-year run, adding another NFL championship in 1933 and securing the team's first undefeated regular season in 1934. Apparently, he enjoyed the job so much that he kept it for over two more decades, stepped aside in 1956 and 1957, and then jumped back in until his coaching retirement after the 1967 season. As for Red Grange, he played two more years with the Bears as the club finished 10–2–1 in 1933 and then waltzed through the 1934 schedule with a perfect 13–0 mark.

The Halas announcement regarding his return to coaching hit the streets on August 31, 1933. Just a week later, Halas finalized a deal that he hoped would strengthen pro football in Chicago when Charles Bidwill purchased the Chicago Cardinals from Dr. David Jones. One may question why Halas was involved with the sale of the Cardinals, but his explanation seemed reasonable:

> Dr. David Jones was losing interest in football. He saw a dark financial future for football and his Cardinals. Undesirable characters again sniffed about. I looked around for another owner. I favored my old friend Charlie Bidwill. One night Dr. Jones and I were guests aboard Charlie's boat. Bidwill said he heard Dr. Jones might be willing to sell the Cardinals. "If I get my price," Dr. Jones said. Bidwill asked the price. "Fifty thousand," Dr. Jones said. The doctor thought Bidwill was only making polite conversation but a couple of nights later Bidwill called Dr. Jones and told him he'd take the club for $50,000. I rejoiced. The Cardinals remained in good hands.[58]

In recent years, current Arizona Cardinals owner Michael Bidwill, grandson of Charles Bidwill, shared a different version of the transaction: "After a few drinks, the then owner of the Cardinals [Dr. Jones] was complaining about how much money he was losing. And my grandmother said, 'Well, sell it to Charley.' As I understand it, we purchased it for $5,000—$2,000 cash right there on the boat. My dad told me there was $45,000 of debt on the team at the time. It was recorded as a $50,000 sale."[59]

Either way, the control of the team quickly changed. Whether the selling price was $5,000 or $50,000, the Cardinals franchise is now worth $2.325 billion, according to *Forbes* magazine.[60] But, back in 1933, it was tough for Dr. Jones to give up his ownership of the Cardinals: "I regret to withdraw from the ranks of professional football owners. I believe it is the fastest developing sport in America. I can't do justice to two jobs and I feel at the moment that I am more valuable to the community as city physician than as a football leader."[61]

These Folks Love Their Athletic Idols

During his time with the team, the enthusiasm of Dr. Jones brought Ernie Nevers to Chicago, sent the Cards out of town for preseason training, and moved the team's home base to Wrigley Field. On the field, the Cardinals won just 18 league games in four years (18–22–5) but snared 36 victories (36–24–6) overall due to an expanded nonleague slate implemented by Dr. Jones that included the team's first trip to California in the postseason. However, the Cardinals were not even remotely close to contending for an NFL championship during his tenure. With Charles Bidwill, the club would benefit from some deeper pockets and from an owner already familiar with the business of pro football due to his connection to George Halas and the Bears. Of course, Bidwill was expected to separate himself from his responsibilities with the Bears, including his position as secretary of the North Side club. However, with Halas securing ownership of the Bears, and Bidwill acquiring the Cardinals, the two oldest teams in the National Football League established ownership families by 1933 that are still in place today.

In contrast to the grim departure of Dr. Jones, Charles Bidwill was absolutely delighted to become involved with the Cardinals and shared a promising message regarding the expectations for the team and its fans:

> We think the Cardinals will hold their own with the leading teams in the league this season. If we are proved wrong, we shall try to strengthen the club for 1934. Nothing less than a championship will be satisfactory. Our appeal will be particularly to the popular fan— the everyday gent with no collegiate affiliation. We hope to attract letter carriers, street car conductors, clerks, and above all, kids. In brief, the success of professional football depends in no small measure upon its ability to draw the workaday sports fan who either have been ignored by the colleges or who can't get away to Saturday games. These folks love their athletic idols and must have them. Professional football supplies that need.[62]

Bidwill's proficiency at identifying market segments for his new business had been cultivated from an enormous presence on the Chicago sports scene. At the time of his acquisition of the Cardinals, Bidwill was director of the Illinois Turf Association; secretary of the Chicago Business Men's Racing Association; president of the Chicago Stadium Operating Company; and the owner of Bentley, Murray and Company (which printed schedules, passes, stationery, etc., for the Bears). Bidwill, it appeared, was riding a golden financial stretch where his numerous investments and interests were all bringing ample revenue returns. The Cardinals did not join that group, suffering from casual attendance and the lost fan base by continuing to be based in Wrigley Field throughout the remainder of the 1930s. At one point, asked about the continuing losses from the Cardinals (rumored to be in excess of $500,000), Bidwill's response was curt and to the point: "What the hell. What good is that dough if you can't have fun with it?"[63]

And yet, Bidwill exhibited a keen promoter's sense of marketing and product exposure. In a lengthy interview with the *Chicago Daily News* on October 16, 1933, Bidwill spoke on a wide range of athletic topics but continued to veer back to his main objective: attracting the "average" fan to his events, especially during the Depression: "Here's the idea. Madison Square Garden and Chicago Stadium were built with everyone in mind but the little one-dollar fellow. The real money, good solid money that you could count before it came in, used to come from the $2 and $3 boys. There are no more of them. They are all $1 fellows now and we aren't doing anything for them. I think that all sports will be patronized more when normal times return, but right now it is up to us to get something that will interest the little one-buck fellow and let him in for a buck."[64]

Greatest Game of Football Ever Played

Bidwill would not be able to analyze his football market immediately, as the 1933 Cardinals (including exhibitions) opened up with seven straight road games (and 10 out of the first 11), interrupted only by a battle with the Bears at shared Wrigley Field on October 15. While the Cards romped over the Aurora Ideals (65–0) and the Freeport Lions (29–0), less success was found once the NFL season began. Coach Paul Schissler's first edition stumbled to a 1–9–1 league mark and easily captured last place in the new Western Division. The Chicago Bears swerved into another trajectory and finished at the top of the division with a 10–2–1 record under their "rookie" coach, George Halas. Under the new setup for the NFL, the Bears then qualified to meet the New York Giants (11–3), champions of the East Division, in the first "official" league title game.

The pregame buildup for the championship game on December 17, 1933, was remarkably strong, especially in New York and Chicago. Since the teams had split a pair of games during the regular season, the interest in the final game for all of the honors was significant. For the NFL to host teams from the two largest markets in both the league and the country for the inaugural title contest was in itself significant. NFL President Joe Carr took the opportunity of being in the limelight to hold a league meeting the day before the game in Chicago's Wrigley Field. In a widely circulated interview, Carr promised more football thrills for the fans in 1934 prompted by the success of the more open passing game in 1933: "It is the tendency in our league to open the game up. Football fans want to see that football; they want to see spectacular plays, kicks, and long runs for touchdowns. We are going to do our best to give 'em what they want."[65]

Because of the closeness of the previous games, in which the Bears won in Chicago 14–10 and the Giants prevailed in New York 3–0, the title tilt was expected to be tight, and the two adversaries did not disappoint. In a highly competitive battle that included six lead changes, the Bears managed to slip past the Giants 23–21 in what the *New York Daily News* described as "undoubtedly the greatest game of football ever played."[66]

In what was likely the largest crowd (21,000) to witness a pro football contest in Chicago since the debut of Red Grange eight years earlier, the Bears used a trick play in the waning minutes to sabotage any hopes for a New York victory. Bronko Nagurski, whose short jump pass to Red Grange defeated Portsmouth in the "unofficial" title game in Chicago Stadium the year before, rocked the Giants with both his running and passing. With the Bears trailing 21–16 and with under four minutes to play, Nagurski took advantage of the new rules that allowed passing anywhere behind the line, faked a plunge, and instead tossed a short pass to Bill Hewitt, as described by the *Chicago Tribune*: "Nagurski started as if to hit the line, stopped and leaped into the air. Then he threw to Bill Hewitt as he raced through the New York defense behind the center of the line. Two defenders rushed to tackle Hewitt, but he relayed the ball laterally to Bill Karr, who swept down the east side of the field, swerved to avoid the safety man as this last opponent went down under a perfect block, and then he continued to the goal for the winning points."[67]

Nagurski's heroics followed an equally improbable score by the Giants that provided the invaders with their final lead in the game. Earlier in the fourth quarter, halfback Ken Strong headed left on a sweep, only to encounter an avalanche of Bear defenders. Strong suddenly pulled up and tossed the ball back to quarterback Harry Newman in the center of the field, but still behind the line. As the defense swarmed toward Newman, Strong hesitated, then raced downfield, where Newman found him all alone in the end zone. "It was a play which had never before been attempted in football," raved the *Tribune* of the unusual lateral-forward pass, which was most uncommon for the day.[68] One of the heroes for the Bears was sure-handed end Bill Karr, who scored twice for the winners, including one on a lateral for the deciding touchdown. Karr was a favorite of Halas, and the coach mentioned that when Karr reported for his first training camp, he was underweight and hungry. Gradually, Karr regained his strength and became an All-Pro for the Bears. George King, the grandson of Bill Karr, confirmed the "hunger" story: "The story I heard is in George Halas's book, about him showing up to try out for the Bears and after a few days, getting weak. It turns out he didn't have any money and hadn't eaten anything. So, they took him out for a steak dinner."[69] The investment paid off for Halas!

The nifty passing throughout the championship game convinced one profound critic of the professional game that perhaps the recent changes that separated the pro rules from the collegiate set might not be a bad idea. "I advocated this forward pass rule for the colleges last year," admitted Northwestern football coach Dick Hanley. "The Bears-Giants game is proof that it produces a more open contest with resulting thrills for the spectators. I wanted that rule adopted last year and I hope it is included in the college rules for next season."[70] Hanley, of course, teamed with Illinois mentor Robert Zuppke earlier in 1931 to question the quality and talent of the pros. The brief skirmish with former Cardinals owner Dr. David Jones did no lasting damage at the time, but the bold change in the professional passing rules quickly grabbed the attention of the collegiate bosses. Despite the lack of pep bands, co-ed cheerleaders, and loyal alumni, the professional game had suddenly become a bit more entertaining than the college version!

Following the championship game, George Halas wasted little time and quickly ushered the Bears onto a train for an extensive postseason tour. After tying the St. Louis Gunners 0–0 on Christmas Eve, the Bears ran off eight straight wins as the team cavorted through Louisiana, Texas, Arizona, and California for victories. The fresh brand of football was appealing to the media, who had never witnessed a professional exhibition with the relaxed passing rules: "Brother, those Chicago Bears really do things with a football and it's even money that they could run any of last year's college elevens right out of a stadium. They're big, fast, smart, and they put on a show. The fans got a real kick out of the contest, which provided more thrills than anything ever seen on a football field around here."[71]

In what was the longest season for the Bears up to that point, the team finished with an overall 21–2–2 record (including exhibitions). The city of Chicago was pleased with the success of its gridiron representatives and a formal welcome was planned on February 20, 1934, for the players and coaches: "The players will be given an official greeting today at the city hall by Mayor Kelly, and will be guests of George Halas, coach and owner of the team, tonight at Red Grange's "77" club on the north side."[72]

Big Kies Knows His Business

As the Bears said hello to the team's second straight championship, the Cardinals bid farewell to a pair of their most important linemen from the past few seasons. Both Walt Kiesling and Herb Blumer decided to conclude their playing careers with the Cardinals. Kiesling played for the Cards for five seasons (1929–1933) and simply moved across town to join the Bears as the starting left guard in 1934. At 6-3 and 260 pounds, Kiesling was one of the bigger players in the NFL at the time, and one of the most rugged. The All-Pro lineman played in the NFL from 1926 to 1938 and was once asked what finally convinced him to retire after so many successful seasons. Kiesling replied, "Each year, you get a little softer and the ground gets a little harder. It even feels frozen in the summer!"[73]

Kiesling then embarked on a long coaching career in the NFL, including a couple of stints as the head man for the Pittsburgh Steelers. Although his overall record (30–55–5) was not entirely successful, Kiesling was respected for both his passion and understanding of the game. Steelers owner Art Rooney once praised Kiesling by stating: "He's one of the smartest coaches in the business. Ask anybody. Ask the coaches. They'll all tell you the same thing—Big Kies knows his business. The coaches all respect him."[74] One regrettable decision that Kiesling took as a coach was releasing a young quarterback named Johnny Unitas! After being cast off by Pittsburgh, Unitas became a three-time NFL MVP for the Baltimore Colts and eventually was elected to the Pro Football Hall of Fame.

Herb Blumer, on the other hand, voiced little interest in an NFL career, but quietly became an MVP in a totally different world. While toiling in the trenches for the Cardinals from 1925 to 1930, and again in 1933, Blumer pursued his doctoral degree from the University of Chicago. After completing his degree program, Blumer remained on the faculty of Chicago until 1952 and served as the line coach on the school's football team under head coach Clark Shaughnessy.[75] After leaving the University of Chicago, he became the chairman of the sociology department at the University of California, Berkeley and was the president of the American Sociological Association. In his chosen field, the former lineman "was considered an expert in the fields of collective behavior, social movement, race relations, social problems and public opinion."[76] And so, the tough lineman from the University of Missouri who specialized in defending his quarterback moved successfully into his intellectual pursuit of sociology, in particular symbolic interactionism. Blumer was the first to use this term and is known as the founder of symbolic interactionism. He passed away on April 13, 1987, at the age of 87.

Most Unusual Football Game Ever

As the Chicago Bears recovered from their arduous postseason tour, the football world was pleasantly surprised and thrilled on July 6, 1934, with the announcement of an upcoming game based on an exciting concept that immediately intrigued all lovers of the gridiron. Arch Ward, the innovative sports editor of the *Chicago Tribune*, released details of a proposed football game to be held in Chicago pitting the best of the graduating college seniors from the previous season against the Chicago Bears, defending NFL champions. At last, the decades-long argument over whether the pros or the collegians were superior was likely to be answered. Ward, a marketing genius in the pre-internet days, had previously initiated the major league All-Star baseball game in 1933, but his proposal for what would become the Chicago Charities College All-Star Football Game was a mammoth undertaking. Ward set the date for the game on August 31, meaning that there would be less than two months to prepare for this extraordinary event and ensure that it came to life successfully.

He first worked behind the scenes with George Halas to determine if the Bears were willing to participate in this unknown and untested event. Next, Ward and Halas worked with other NFL clubs to make sure that collegiate players who had already signed with pro teams would be allowed to take part in the All-Star game. Ward also needed to secure a location for the game and decided upon Soldier Field, the huge landmark on the Chicago lakefront. But what about fans? Ward pulled out a key to unlock that market as well by putting together a network of over 30 newspapers across the country to help market the event. More important, the collegiate players would not be selected by coaches, but rather by fans through a nationwide voting process. Lists of possible college players were created, and write-in candidates were encouraged, with mail votes due back to the *Tribune* by July 25. Players would then be notified of their selection with plenty of time before the All-Star training camp set to open up at Northwestern University in nearby Evanston, Illinois, on August 15, 1934. Ward's announcement captured the essence of his concept as well as requested the immediate response by readers: "This is an announcement of the most unusual football game ever scheduled. It will bring together the Chicago Bears, champions of the National Professional league, and the strongest team of last year's college seniors that can be recruited…. It is up to you, the football fans of Chicago and America. Never before have you had a chance to pick the starting players for a college team. We hope you make the most of it."[77]

Using the scope and the power of the *Chicago Tribune* as a daily battering ram (other local newspapers in the city barely mentioned the game), Ward continued to push, promote, and beatify the upcoming All-Star game. His well-conceived network of affiliated papers helped with the push in an unprecedented promotion for the game. The results were simply astounding. By July 25, 1934, when the final consumer votes were collected, over 165,000 ballots (each including 11 choices for All-Star players) were returned, and Ward was overjoyed with the results: "America knows this morning who were the football heroes of 1933. Their names are not the opinion of a limited number of self-styled experts who annually attempt to name the country's leading players. They are the favorites of 165,000 fans who participated in the coast-to-coast poll conducted by the *Chicago Tribune* and 30 associated newspapers. And no part of the land was slighted in the nation-wide balloting. Returns rolled in from the Pacific coast, the south, the east and the middle west."[78]

At this point, Ward could handle the invitations to the All-Star players, and another poll would soon select the coach (over 617,000 total votes were cast with Purdue's Noble Kizer receiving 261,485 to top the list), leaving his primary concern to be the game itself.[79] Would the attraction of placing the leading collegians against the top professional club be enough to secure a worthy crowd? A year before, an exhibition between the Bears and the Notre Dame All-Stars fell far short of expectations, as only 8,800 attended to watch the pros prevail 14–0, also at cavernous, but nearly empty, Soldier Field. Still, Ward envisioned some promise for a football spectacle for the ages, especially if done right. Ward intended to promote the heck out of the game and position it as the "can't miss" event of the summer. With those daily articles full of glowing reports on the prowess of the players and coaches, Ward mixed in some old-fashioned, although subtle, trash talk. One of his first entries into that realm included the glib comments of the legendary Red Grange, who actually spoke from the heart when queried as to whether or not he was looking forward to the game against the collegians: "Play 'em? Bring 'em on. What a treat! All my life I have wanted to see the real All-American team in action, not one of those so-called All-Americans picked by Joe Bloke of the New York Crier or I.M. Expert of the Los Angeles Bugle. This team will be America's team, the people's choice, and there can be no question of the superiority of professional football after we whip them. All I can say is I hope the old bones stand up against these young punks!"[80]

The bravado of Grange would soon play out in front of a larger-than-expected crowd. Much larger, in fact! On August 31, an hour before game time, traffic was backed up solid for more than a mile in each direction (north and south) from Soldier Field, necessitating street closures and detours through nearby Grant Park in an effort to ease the congestion. In total, 79,432 showed up for the game, clogging streets, sidewalks, and parking lots. "Otto Jelinek, traffic engineer for the south park district, estimated that it was the largest gathering of automobiles in the history of Chicago sports," announced the *Chicago Tribune*.[81] With a huge crowd, national attention, and anxious rivals, Arch Ward succeeded in fulfilling his dream of staging a "dream" game that very few likely thought possible. Ward's summer classic would continue until 1976, when player contracts and the fear of injuries helped end the spectacle. Audiences were always strong and games featuring the Chicago Cardinals and the Chicago Bears against the collegians in the 1940s would attract over 100,000 attendees.

The combat on the field in 1934 was just as auspicious as the two teams battled to a scoreless tie that left both teams, and the huge audience, wishing for more. For Bears owner/coach George Halas, the tie likely hurt as much as a loss. The pros had failed to clearly dominate the college stars. Halas could merely shrug and remark:

"They had a great team and were in better physical shape than we were. The Bears have always been slow to develop in the early season."[82]

Bears quarterback Carl Brumbaugh admitted that the outcome was a bit unexpected: "Well, it was a surprise to me. They had a good ball club and I'll give them credit, but I know we would welcome another crack at them."[83] On the other side, tackle Ed "Moose" Krause of Notre Dame, who was the leading vote-getter among the college players with over 65,000 votes, felt that the All-Star team was the better football squad on the Soldier Field gridiron that night: "Our boys charged harder and straighter. They were easier than we expected. It was a clean game, but if anyone should have won it, we should, and we feel a little disappointed that we didn't. Just say that college football stands supreme."[84]

And so, the discussion continued…

Return of Chris O'Brien

Two days after the Bears battled to the scoreless deadlock with the collegians, the Cardinals opened up their preseason camp at Loyola Stadium in Chicago and welcomed seven members from the All-Star team to their roster. Coach Paul Schissler opted for a complete rebuild of the squad that finished in last place in 1933 and retained only six players from the previous year: Phil Handler, Dick Nesbitt, Howard Tipton, Frank McNally, Lou Gordon, and Milan Creighton. Both the Cardinals and the Bears were restricted from using Wrigley Field early in the year due to ongoing baseball commitments with the Chicago Cubs, so both teams elected to use familiar, old favorite Normal Park for early exhibition outings.

The opposition for both clubs on successive weekends at Normal Park would be the newly organized Chicago Tigers, a local club that nonetheless recruited athletes from places like Notre Dame, Washington State, Northwestern, and DePaul. However, the most intriguing part of the Tigers was the team's founder/organizer Chris O'Brien. After moving on from his ownership of the Cardinals in 1929, O'Brien eventually became involved with the Tigers as a means to temper his attraction to football! Before the Bears game, the *Chicago Daily News* reported: "Chris O'Brien, for many years identified with the promotion of professional athletics in Chicago, is making plans to return to football in the role of club owner. He is busy signing former college stars to play on a team to be known as the Chicago Tigers, with Normal Park as the home grounds. With the exception of games in September, however, the team will travel."[85]

O'Brien's welcome return was tarnished when the Bears spanked the Tigers 41–0 on September 9, 1934, followed by the Cardinals' easy 33–0 romp one week later. Although the Tigers played a few more games with teams such as the Indiana Harbor Gophers, the La Crosse Lagers, and the St. Louis Gunners, it appears that O'Brien's journey with his new team was short-lived as the Tigers disappeared from the sports pages by late October. Meanwhile, the Chicago Bears (13–0) enjoyed an extraordinary season, becoming the first NFL team to complete an unbeaten and untied schedule in league history, including a pair of wins over the rival Cardinals. While the Bears continued their recent dominance over the Cards in 1934 with a pair of victories, it was also becoming apparent that the latter's decision to share Wrigley Field with the Bears was no longer successful. When coupled with the enormous publicity provided courtesy of the Bears' appearance in the initial All-Star game, along with the Cardinals' questionable decision to desert the South Side, the gap in popularity between the two Chicago clubs became even more significant. This disparity continued throughout the time that the Cardinals remained in Chicago.

Although the Cardinals were fairly competitive (5–6) in 1934, fans were not tripping over themselves to gain entrance to Wrigley Field on home game days. In just three home games, including one with the Bears, the Cards attracted 28,500 attendees, although 17,500 showed up for the Bears game. Based on approximate attendance figures reported by Chicago newspapers, the Cardinals averaged only 9,500 fans for home games during that 1934 season, while the Bears averaged 19,882. If the "home" game against the Bears was dropped from the configuration, the average number of fans for the remaining two Cardinal contests in 1934 was a meager 5,500. By 1936, the Cardinals hosted five home games that attracted 31,639 fans for an average of 6,329. But if the attendance for the Bears game (13,704) was removed, the average for the other four football games was just 4,484.

During the 1936 season, the peril of sharing Wrigley Field with the Cubs and the Bears was evident as the opening home game for the Cardinals did not take place until November 8, 1936, when a lonely group of only 1,500 witnessed the Eagles game. The Chicago Bears, however, enjoyed a brisk turnstile in 1936 as 99,853 fans were in the stands for four home games—an average of 23,773.

The 1934 season truly demonstrated the disparity in the two Chicago teams. While the Bears strolled through their undefeated (13–0) campaign, led by the NFL's first 1,000-yard rusher, rookie Beattie Feathers, the Cardinals struggled to obtain either touchdowns or victories. The Cards tallied just 80 points that year and were shut out on four occasions. The ultimate measure of the athletic separation (or disrespect) occurred on Thanksgiving Day (November 29, 1934), when the starting time of the Cardinals home game against the Packers was pushed back. This was not because of travel delays or to accommodate late fan arrivals. Instead, the time change was implemented so that fans might be able to follow the earlier exploits of the Bears! "Today's game will start at 2 o'clock. The traditional Thanksgiving Day starting time at 11 o'clock has been foregone on this occasion to permit professional fans to hear radio reports of the Bears game in Detroit."[86]

Although the beleaguered Cardinals finished with a 5–6 record, two of those wins were against the winless, and hopeless, Cincinnati Reds (0–8). Yet due to a generous addition of nonleague games and a lengthy postseason tour, the Cardinals collected 11 more wins for an overall 16–6 finish.

Abe Ransacked the Manhattan Lockers

The 1934 Bears glided to the Western Division title despite tight wins to close out the regular season against the Giants (10–9), the Cardinals (17–14), and twice against the Detroit Lions (19–16 and 10–7). Under the still-new playoff format, this superb finish allowed the Bears to meet the Giants, champions of the Eastern

Division, for the NFL title on December 9, 1934. New York hosted the game at the old Polo Grounds, with the Giants still feeling the sting of the recent one-point loss to the Bears. New York coach Steve Owen was bothered by the late Bears rally on November 18 and blamed himself for the defeat: "It was my fault that the team lost. I know what licked us and when we meet the Bears again, the Giants will win."[87] The high-scoring Bears had also romped over the Giants 27–7 on November 4 in Chicago, so Owen was certainly seeking some answers in response to the Bears' recent dominance. And he did find such a resource in the title game from an unexpected ally by the name of Abe Cohen.

Cohen played a pivotal role in what became known as the "Sneakers Game," a phenomenal battle for the NFL crown that was unduly influenced by both foul weather and one team's choice of footwear on the slick, frozen field. The Bears charged to a quick 10–3 halftime advantage thanks to a Nagurski touchdown plunge and a field goal from Jack Manders that offset an earlier three-pointer by the Giants' Ken Strong. In the third quarter, Manders added a 23-yard field goal to boost the Bears' lead to 13–3 entering the final stanza. While the Bears appeared to be dominating the game despite the treacherous footing, something prompted the Giants to quickly reverse the fortunes of the game. End Ray Flaherty, captain of the Giants, was credited with inspiring the fourth-quarter turnaround. It was the shoes! The Giants wisely donned basketball shoes (aka "sneakers") on offense in the final quarter and literally swept the Bears off the frozen gridiron. In one of the most amazing and overpowering comebacks in NFL history, the Giants scored 27 unanswered points in the fourth quarter to stun the Bears 30–13. After the game, Flaherty, who would later be selected to the Pro Football Hall of Fame as one of the more successful coaches in the history of the NFL, modestly explained his game-changing suggestion: "We used to wear them [sneakers] out on the Coast when the fields were frozen. When Jack Mara [son of team owner Tim Mara] called me up this morning and told me that the field was frozen, I immediately thought of the rubber shoes. But as you know, you can't get a sporting goods store open on a Sunday and we didn't know what to do. Finally, Ken Strong thought of sending up to Manhattan [College] for the shoes of the basketball team and an auto was sent for them."[88]

And this is where the heretofore unknown Abe Cohen grabbed his little slice of NFL history. According to the *Brooklyn Times Union*, Cohen's instant reaction in addressing the shoe issue was at least partly responsible for the Giants' "giant" comeback win: "The unsung hero of the Giants-Bears game was Abe Cohen, Manhattan College property man. It was Abe who ransacked the Manhattan lockers and popped back with an armful of rubber-soled basketball shoes which the Giants donned to give them more secure footing on the frozen turf of the Polo Grounds. After cleaning out the Manhattan lockers, Abe continued to Ken Strong's sporting goods store and wiped-out Ken's supply, returning in time for the Giants to don their new footwear for the second half. It was the first time a team in rubber soled shoes ran roughshod over an opponent."[89]

On the field, Giants halfback Ken Strong was clearly the hero, scoring 17 of his team's points (14 in the fourth quarter) on two touchdowns, a field goal, and a pair of extra points. Strong's unerring performance on one of his scores attracted a rather picturesque description of his running ability from the *New York Daily News*: "Did you ever see a goldfish wiggle its way through a coral labyrinth and then scoot through the green plant into open water? Well, that was Strong sneaking through the Chicago backs. His rubber soles padded 41 thrilling yards and every step of the way a growing chant rose hoarsely until it reached a deafening din as he crossed the last chalk line."[90]

The slipping, sliding Bears were unable to keep pace with the more sure-footed Giants in the last quarter of the championship contest. Years later, a story of the shoe switch and the reaction of George Halas was circulated. Whether the following was totally accurate or not, it does seem to define the reaction of both sides to the "sneaker" issue: "In some versions of the game, they write that Walt Kiesling of the Bears saw the tennis shoes and nudged coach George Halas to 'look at the sneakers.' George is said to have sniffed a bit and said: 'Good, step on their toes!'"[91] Of course, there were some who scoffed at the idea that the unbeatable Bears could be blown out so decisively in just one quarter. There were reports of gamblers smiling after the game, which prompted immediate denials by both teams and the league itself. Halas adamantly declared: "We just got licked in the fourth quarter, that's all. It had to come sometime. We're sorry we are no longer champions, but remember, we beat the Giants twice this year."[92]

Rather than heading home for a much-deserved break from a season that began in early August prior to the All-Star game, the Bears simply kept playing, defeating the Eagles in an exhibition game 28–14 on December 15 and then toppling the Brooklyn Dodgers 20–6 on a baseball field in Knoxville, Tennessee, on December 22. The latter game was originally planned for the University of Tennessee's football stadium, but this request was refused because of the university's "opposition to professional football."[93] Despite the enormous success of the 1934 College All-Star Game, there clearly remained some pockets of opposition to the professional game, even when the exhibition was slated for the benefit of local charities. After the Bears steamrolled the Dodgers, Halas headed west with his club, joining the Cardinals, who were already in the middle of a seven-game tour that would culminate with a pitched battle against the Bears on January 13, 1935.

The crisp rivalry between the two warring clubs was about to become more caustic, even in a distant environment.

Fourteen

Bronko, Spies, and Foolish Magnates

> *"Two men in buildings opposite the park were relieved of field glasses and notebooks."—Chicago Tribune*, October 13, 1934

They looked like spies...

Two suspicious men lurked in the shadows of Wrigley Field while the Cardinals practiced on the afternoon of Friday, October 12, 1934. The intruders were discovered and quickly removed from the premises but their presence reinforced the sense of danger, real or imagined, that seemed to hide behind every corner when two competitive rivals shared the same facility in the National Football League. This situation was likely not a random occurrence since the Bears experienced a similar episode during their morning session on the same turf: "Both teams practiced at Wrigley Field yesterday. The Cardinals completed their drill in the afternoon after twice being interrupted to clear the field of suspected Bear spies. The Bears' drill in the morning was held up while two men in buildings opposite the park were relieved of field glasses and notebooks. These were said to have been Cardinal scouts, but the Cardinals denied they had scouts."[1]

While the possible flurry of "spies" did not affect the outcome of the game between the two Chicago teams the following Sunday (the Bears won easily 20–0), it did demonstrate the continuing distrust between the clubs. Since George Halas helped enable the purchase of the Cardinals organization by Charles Bidwill in 1933, there appeared to be no animosity among the ownership. However, the rivalry being waged on the gridiron continued unabated and in the next game between the two opponents on November 26, 1934, the game, once again, dissolved into an alley brawl as the Bears prevailed 17–6: "For a half it was a football battle, with the champions [Bears] holding a huge edge. From that point on, it was a real battle with no holds barred. Several times fists were flying and Mike Mikulak, big Cardinal fullback, finally brought a chorus of boos on his head by wrestling the ball from [Gene] Ronzani and kicking it into the stands in disgust. The Bears today showed visible effects of the bruising tussle, and Beattie Feathers and Joe Kopcha were in the hospital for x-ray examinations."[2]

As the Bears fell prey to the frozen elements in the now famous "Sneakers" game on December 9, the Cardinals embarked December 1 on a lengthy (seven games) postseason trip to the West Coast after the conclusion of their 1934 NFL schedule. The key game on the trip would be the final outing, a match with the hated Bears on January 13, 1935, in Los Angeles, California. "All our club needs is experience," said Coach Paul Schissler of the Cardinals, "and we hope to give the boys what amounts to a season's play together on this trip."[3] The Bears quickly followed the Cardinals westward but with a much different objective: a rematch with the now NFL champion Giants on January 27, also in Los Angeles. Actually, the Bears' revenge tour might have also included some plans for retaliation against the Cardinals. Due to injuries suffered in the last game against the Cardinals, both leading rusher Beattie Feathers and three-time All-Pro lineman Dr. Joe Kopcha sat out the title game with the Giants and were sorely missed. Kopcha completed medical school while playing pro football for eight years, and with his expertise off the field is credited with developing the premise for the shoulder pad that is still used today. As Dr. Kopcha later explained: "Shoulder pads in those days were nothing more than epaulets—like a hotel doorman wears. I resurrected a set to actually fit my shoulders and protect my collarbone and the acromio-clavicular joint. Shoulder joint injuries occurred from tackling. My concept of the shoulder pads generated from an injury to my left shoulder. As a result of the injury, I pinpointed where the fault was and covered my shoulders with an extra 'cup' of leather and felt, overlapping the shoulder joint."[4]

Boys Came Close to Settling Dispute Via Fisticuffs

Kopcha would miss the brief tour after accepting an intern position at a Detroit hospital, but Feathers would be back on the field for the three games scheduled in California. In the ever-changing discourse between the collegiate and professional football interests, a slight problem emerged prior to the Bears and Cardinals game. Vic Dana, commissioner of the Pacific Coast Conference, declared that any official who worked a professional game such as the Bears/Cardinals tilt would "lose their standing." Dana stated: "The men who handle varsity games are expected not to handle pro games." When asked about the reason for this mandate, Dana replied: "The reason was not given to me—that's the law as far as the conference is concerned. It was decided by the ten colleges of the conference. It is the same rule the Big Ten has had for several years, so there is nothing new about it."[5]

Four college officials crossed the line, however, and the game went on as scheduled in Los Angeles with a fair crowd of 18,000 interlaced with Hollywood types enjoying the physicality of the event. Surprisingly, the Cardinals dropped the Bears 13–9 thanks to an 80-yard touchdown run by Homer Griffith and a pair of dropkick field goals by Paul Pardonner. As usual with the two Chicago teams, it was a rough, physical battle. For the most part the players behaved themselves as West Coast fans appeared to be thoroughly entertained by the on-field antics of the warriors: "The tackling and blocking was absolutely brutal most of the time and it's a wonder how the participants stood up under the terrific battering they gave each other without being maimed. It was the most bitterly fought game seen in these parts for years and on several occasions the boys came close to settling the dispute via fisticuffs."[6]

Although the great Bronko Nagurski was not on-site for the game due to a wrestling commitment, the Cardinals' upset was well-deserved. The win helped the club to its seventh straight, and final, victory on the long postseason tour, allowing Coach Schissler to finish with a 16–6 mark for the elongated year. As the Cardinals departed for home, the Bears remained in California for the eagerly awaited rematch with the NFL champion New York Giants. The Bears still fretted about the anomaly of the championship game when the Giants smartly wore tennis shoes in the second half to roar from behind and capture the NFL crown 30–13 back on December 9, 1934. Coach Steve Owen of the Giants added to the competitive ill will between the clubs prior to the Los Angeles game when he stated: "Of course, we don't think the Bears are a bunch of daisies, but they will be up against a faster and smarter team."[7] Those were the only words the Bears needed to hear as they rolled over the Giants 21–0, scoring all of their points in the first half. Nagurski, back at his powerful fullback post, bulled through for a score from the one with just three minutes gone in the game, and the Bears never relented on both the offensive and defensive sides of the ball. Revenge was sweet, especially with the sting of the "Sneakers" game still fresh in the memories of the players. The play of the Bears was so decisive that one writer dared to question the previous game's result with the Giants: "The big mystery to 15,000 fans who saw yesterday's game is how the Giants ever beat the Bears at all."[8]

Enough Football to Last a Lifetime

In the glow of the huge victory over the Giants, albeit in an exhibition game, the Bears accepted the expected when both Red Grange and tackle Link Lyman retired from football. Grange would join the Bears as an assistant coach for the 1935 season, while Lyman would assume the same position at the University of Nebraska. William Roy "Link" Lyman, at 6'2" and 233 pounds, entered the professional ranks in 1922 with the Canton Bulldogs and later joined the Bears in time for the Red Grange tours following the 1925 season. He then remained with the Bears through the early 1935 slate of games in California, although Lyman did "retire" twice previously and missed the 1929 and 1932 NFL campaigns. Sportswriter Ed Prell once noted: "The best description of Link was that he was an enormous man who always was in the thick of things."[9] Lyman, who played both ways, often confused opposing offensive linemen by "shifting" while anticipating the snap. The gifted Nebraska native was inducted into the Pro Football Hall of Fame (established in 1963) in 1964 as part of just the second class of honorees.

The departure of Grange had been anticipated since before the "Sneakers" championship game against the Giants. Still, his retirement after the revenge game against those same Giants on January 27, 1935, brought a close to a very special era in professional football. The signing of Grange by the Bears in 1925, while the vaunted halfback was still in college, offended the collegiate ruling class but opened the doors wide for pro football in the country. The popularity, and affability, of Grange bought him a special place in the hearts of football fans, even if some questioned, or were jealous of, his instant marketability and cash-generating opportunities. Grange provided one last thrill for the populace when he broke off a 41-yard gain but was stopped short of the goal line in the closing moments of the Giants game, disappointing teammates who were hoping for the "Galloping Ghost" to go all the way in his final appearance. His long football career would need to end sometime, and Grange chose the 1934 season to be his last by stating on January 28, 1935: "And now I've played enough. I'm going to get out of the game before they kill me. It's the old legs. They can't take it anymore. I want to get out of the game before people start feeling sorry for me. I figure I've played 265 games—nine seasons of professional football and before that, 25 college games and forty high school games. That's enough football to last a lifetime."[10]

The accomplishments of Grange have lasted far longer than a lifetime. He was an All-American and an All-Pro, along with being a charter member of both the Pro Football Hall of Fame (1963) and the College Football Hall of Fame (1951). So great was his reputation and influence that noted writer Damon Runyon once said: "On the field, he is the equal of three football players and a horse."[11]

There Have Been No Profits

Shortly after the Cardinals returned to Chicago from the California trip in early 1935, Coach Schissler delivered a surprising message that once again revealed the precarious financial position of pro football organizations. Schissler abruptly resigned from his position as head coach of the Cardinals and in a media interview, he cited economic challenges as the primary reason behind his decision: "When I signed a contract with Dr. David Jones [previous Cardinals' owner] I was hired for a rather nominal salary. However, I was supposed to receive a percentage of the profits. This arrangement was satisfactory except that there have been no profits. I can't afford to continue coaching the Cardinals for the present salary."[12]

According to Arch Ward of the *Chicago Tribune*, Schissler was paid $3,500 per year and was to receive a favorable 25 percent of all profits, which did not materialize during the 1934 season.[13] No decision on replacing Schissler was rendered until August 10, when Cards owner Charles Bidwill promoted end Milan Creighton to serve as player/coach of the squad. Creighton joined the club in 1931 after a stellar career at the University of Arkansas. In his new role, Creighton resurrected the player/coach position that had largely disappeared after the first decade of the NFL. He also became the youngest coach in the circuit at the age of 27. Schissler, meanwhile, was hired as the head coach of the Brooklyn Dodgers of the NFL, where he would serve for two seasons.

By the time Creighton was hired by the Cardinals, the Bears were already knee-deep in practice for the second College All-Star Game. The premise of this honored exhibition contest, first staged in 1934, was to pit the defending professional champion against an all-star conglomerate of recently graduated collegiate players who were selected by the vote of football fans across the nation. In 1935, the voting totals exploded from the 165,000 that sent in ballots from the inaugural battle. For the 1935 game, the sponsoring *Chicago Tribune* tallied 737,918 voting selections for the all-star players and an astounding 7,317,821 ballots for the head coach candidates (won by Frank Thomas of Alabama).[14] In a decision that was never really explained, Arch Ward selected the Bears, rather than the defending NFL champion Giants, to meet the College All-Stars in 1935 stating: "This is an announcement of the most colorful football game of all time. It will bring together the College All-Americans of 1934, and the strongest team in the National Professional League, the Chicago Bears."[15]

In this battle, the Bears used a Jack Manders field goal, a safety, and the stop of a late All-Star offensive drive to secure a victory by the unusual score of 5–0. Another superlative crowd of 77,450 turned out at Soldier Field in Chicago as the Bears turned back a fired-up collegiate squad led by future Hall of Famer Don Hutson and future U.S. President Gerald Ford, a center from Michigan. The professionals prevailed on the field, achieving some notoriety as the first actual winner of an All-Star game after the initial scoreless tie in 1934.

With the Bears edging the All-Stars and with returning stars such as Bronko Nagurski and Beattie Feathers, the team was securely the favorite to nab another NFL title in 1935. However, in one of the more surprising aspects of that season, the Chicago Cardinals proved to be a contender under new player/coach Creighton. Even with a nearly complete turnover of the roster from 1934, Creighton maneuvered his young club into first place after twice defeating the Green Bay Packers early in the season. Heading into the final two weeks of the season, the Cardinals were in a first-place tie with the Detroit Lions. Due to a scheduling quirk with the Bears (an earlier game slated for October 6 was postponed when the Cubs were in the World Series and using Wrigley Field), the two Chicago teams were forced to face off twice in the last two scheduled games. On Sunday, December 1, 1935, the Cardinals (6–3–1) were tied with Detroit (6–3–2) at the top of the Western Division standings, while Green Bay (7–4) and the Bears (5–4–1) lurked closely behind.

With a crowd of 12,167 watching at Wrigley Field on December 1, the two rivals left the gridiron with a rugged 7–7 deadlock as Bronko Nagurski scored for the Bears and Al Nichelini did likewise for the Cards. At the same time, the Lions (now 7–3–2) cruised past Brooklyn 28–0 to move one-half game ahead of the Cardinals (6–3–2) in the standings. However, since the Detroit season was completed with the Brooklyn game, the Cardinals could still maneuver into a playoff with the Lions via a victory over the Bears in the game on December 8. It was a remarkable achievement for rookie coach Milan Creighton of the Cardinals, especially with so many new faces on his roster, earning the praise of writer George Strickler: "Starting out with a squad composed of two veterans, Lou Gordon, tackle, and Phil Handler, guard, 22 youngsters only one season removed from college campuses, and a coach who had no previous experience in handling football teams, the Cardinals fought their way free from four years of cellar occupancy into the thick of the championship race and stayed there."[16]

Just one win. Just one. That was the only objective for the Chicago Cardinals on December 8, 1935. With a win over the Bears the Cards would qualify for a playoff with Detroit to determine the Western Division crown and the right to meet the New York Giants for the NFL title. Instead, wiry Bears halfback Keith Molesworth broke through for a pair of touchdowns, pushing the Bears to a 13–0 advantage in the last game of the 1935 season for both teams. For the Cardinals, it was a devastating disappointment to an otherwise long and surprising season and squashed their title hopes. Both the Bears and Cardinals finished with 6–4–2 records in 1935 as Detroit clinched the division title with a 7–3–2 mark. A week later, the Lions would defeat the New York Giants 26–7 in the NFL championship game. While the Cardinals were pleased with the team's performance in 1935, George Halas expected more from his Bears: "We slipped in 1935, winning only half of our twelve games."[17]

Frenzied Quest for New Material

In early 1936, the NFL implemented one of its more sterling innovations: the "draft" of eligible collegiate players. Previously, the signing of players was a free-for-all. Pro teams could contact graduating seniors and entice them to join their club. Usually, these offers consisted of a predetermined game salary, as well as possible contacts for a job in the off-season. However, this system was certainly not equitable. Teams with stronger finances could reach out to college stars with potential and present a contract that was more financially inviting than could some of their struggling brethren. Most NFL teams were still not in a position to profit financially from games played each season so the jousting for key collegiate players was an inexact science. Recruitment and scouting of players was less formal, with some teams relying on local recommendations or magazine articles to inform them of possible roster candidates.

In Green Bay, Coach Curly Lambeau scouted postseason college games in his efforts to secure top-notch players. For example, in early 1935, Lambeau scored perhaps his greatest pre-draft signing when he convinced the great All-American receiver Don Hutson to join him in northern Wisconsin. The elated *Green Bay Press-Gazette* reported on February 22: "Coach Lambeau contacted Hutson while on the west coast and after corresponding with him he came to terms."[18] It sounds simple, but the signing of Hutson was far from it. In fact, the controversy surrounding the Hutson recruitment was a major factor in the creation of the first NFL draft a year later. Hutson allowed himself (and rightly so) to become the object of a bidding war between the Packers and the Brooklyn Dodgers. As noted, bidding on a specific player was commonplace, and a few clubs were part of the early Hutson recruiting process: "Several teams, including George Halas of the Bears (he dropped out at $75 a game) made offers."[19]

In the end, Hutson signed with the Packers. Or did he? He also signed with the Dodgers. Maybe? "Last night Shipwreck Kelly, of the Brooklyn Dodgers, announced that the All-American end [Hutson] of Alabama had signed a contract with his outfit. A few hours earlier, Coach Curly Lambeau of the Green Bay Packers had announced that Hutson had signed a contract to play with him next fall."[20] If the situation was already confusing, it became even more so when both teams continued to claim Hutson as their own, leaving the final decision up to NFL President Joe Carr. It was determined by Carr that Hutson, for some reason, had indeed inked contracts with both teams. In order to decipher the winner amid the confusion, Carr awarded the rights to Hutson to the Green Bay Packers based on the time stamp of the postmark for when the contracts were forwarded to the league office by both organizations. For now, the issue was settled, but Carr, and others around the NFL, were probably thinking that there must be a better way to handle the recruitment of graduating collegiate seniors.

The antics of the recruitment sideshow were exemplified even further in the pursuit of Minnesota fullback Stan Kostka, who was the beneficiary of an escalating bidding war between Brooklyn and Philadelphia, with Kostka in the middle turning the screws on the checkbooks of both bidders. Apparently, Brooklyn indicated that it would match any offer made to Kostka and the Eagles "offered a fabulous sum to the Gopher battering ram. Stan [Kostka] tried to hold Brooklyn to its promise and the furor over the case brought the foolishness of the magnates into the limelight."[21] The worst part of this entire scenario was that the competing clubs were driving up the salaries of players at a time when very few were showing a profit. As the league meeting approached in Pittsburgh on May 19, 1935, the irritating subject was certain to be finally addressed: "A frenzied quest for new material [players] which has shot prices for 1934 college stars sky high and created no end of bitter feelings among the magnates, seems certain to bring the question of salaries to the forefront … it is known that only three entries, Green Bay, New York Giants and Chicago Bears made money last season, with the rest of the owners going into the red for various sums."[22]

And then along came Bert Bell…

Bert Bell's Monument to Football

Bell was the founder and owner of the Philadelphia Eagles (and future commissioner of the NFL from 1946 to 1959). But in 1935, his team was struggling on the field and failing to achieve financial success. Bell was a pragmatic businessman and grasped the reality of a very dire outlook for the league if the teams continued to blast away at each other in their immodest pursuit of high-tier college athletes. Of course, there were no complaints from the players themselves, but the lawless and often pointless chase for top gridders by teams with deep pockets could eventually suffocate NFL clubs with a less-than-fruitful financial base. It had to stop somewhere, and Bell had a solution. He proposed a rather simple, but realistic, suggestion to his league cohorts: create a selection process of eligible college players beginning in inverse order with the last-place team choosing first. The player selected or "drafted" by an NFL organization would then be bound to that club, thus eliminating the wild bidding process that emerged in recent years. Upton Bell, the son of Bert Bell noted: "I'm convinced that if he didn't invent the draft in 1935, we would be talking about something else right now instead of the NFL. He told the owners that they could either hang separately or hang together."[23]

Upton Bell, himself a former general manager of the Boston (now New England) Patriots, and a team owner in the World Football League, recalled the persuasive nature of his father and his critical input into securing a draft for the NFL: "My father said, 'I'm one of those teams that can't win and if we can't find a way, we're going to sink.' He was saying that 'we're going under as a league unless you accept my proposal.' He convinced George Halas of the Bears and Tim Mara of the Giants to support his proposal."[24]

Ironically, Bert Bell was the owner of the reigning last-place team (Philadelphia) in 1936 when the first draft was held. According to the structure of the new selection process, the last-place team in the overall standings from the previous season would be "rewarded" with the first pick of the draft. This was probably not the scenario that Bell preferred for the Eagles, but the intent of the draft was to allow poorer-performing squads to have the first access to the rich collegiate talent pool and therefore have an opportunity to improve. But there were a few obstacles.

At the time, a career in pro football was still not a choice that many players would follow. Even if a player was selected, there was no guarantee that he would sign with the team that picked him in the draft. Also, with no formal scouting procedures in place, teams often worked primarily on intuition, recommendations, and a few magazine clippings to determine their choices. The first draft was finally held on February 8, 1936, in Philadelphia. A general pool of 90 players was compiled and the owners agreed on nine rounds for the initial effort. In the end, 81 players were selected by the nine NFL teams, but ultimately, only 24 prospects actually appeared in the National Football League.[25] But now, the draft was in place and today it stands as probably the second-biggest event on the NFL calendar behind the Super Bowl. It's a three-day television bonanza with significant fan interest and unbridled emotion among the gasps, groans, and cheers reacting to the numerous individual team selections. "I'll always look at him as a great visionary," said Upton Bell when discussing his father, Bert Bell. "He saw things in the future that could be beneficial to the league such as television, draft bonus choices, and 'sudden death' in tie games. Arthur Daley of the *New York Times* once said that the NFL draft was Bert Bell's 'monument and the key to the continuous success of the NFL.'"[26] Later, both the National Basketball Association and Major League Baseball instituted player drafts based on Bert Bell's model.

As the team leaders adjusted to this strange new concept of a "draft," there was little doubt as to who would become the first player selected. Jay Berwanger, a rousing, deceptive, All-American halfback from the University of Chicago, was the recent winner of what would become the very first Heisman Trophy following the 1935 season. With the first choice in the draft, the Philadelphia Eagles (and Bert Bell) did pick Jay Berwanger. Unfortunately, a great big ball of confusion accompanied that selection, which almost immediately threatened the fledgling draft. In what was intended to be an orderly and polite sharing of alternating draft choices, the Eagles suddenly faced a crisis in their pursuit of Berwanger: it seems that the highly respected Berwanger simply wanted too much money to play pro football. This forced the Eagles (and Bert Bell) to shy away from Berwanger and to trade his rights to the welcoming Chicago Bears. George Halas had admired the skill level of Berwanger and was confident that he would fit in nicely with the Bears' offensive plans. However, Halas failed to convince Berwanger to join his club and the first player ever drafted by the NFL never played a down in the league.

For years, there has been speculation that Berwanger simply wanted more compensation for his services than either the Eagles or the Bears were willing to offer, but Upton Bell and Berwanger himself have revealed differing scenarios. Upton Bell indicated that the question of salary was not the only reason Berwanger turned his back on pro football: "My father talked to Jay Berwanger, who told my father that he could make more money in business than he could playing pro football. Basically, he didn't want to play. Ironically, my father invented the draft, then got the first pick but was unable to sign Berwanger. His rights were then traded to Halas."[27]

Now with the rights to the talented local product cradled in his grasp, Halas actively pursued Berwanger before also failing to agree on financial terms. Or did he? Nearly 40 years later in 1974, Berwanger explained the situation: "At this time, the important thing was to have a job that could develop into a career. I felt if I were to play football for two-three years, I'd just have to start at the bottom when I quit."[28]

Berwanger also revealed that the rumored lengthy negotiations with Halas were somewhat overstated, as revealed in the *Chicago Tribune*: "And so he [Berwanger] faced another moment of truth when George Halas took him aside at a party. At a time when players still were in the $100-a-game range, Halas asked what it would take for him to play with the Bears. 'A two-year contract for $25,000,' Jay said, his blue eyes unblinking. 'Goodbye,' Halas said softly, and that was that. Jay insists he would not have changed the price in subsequent negotiation. 'And I have no regrets,' he said."[29]

And so, apparently after just one informal meeting, the Bears and Berwanger never spoke again and pro football's most prized prospect simply walked away. Berwanger did go on to become a very successful businessman in the Chicago area and returned to play football for one more game in 1937. On September 10, 1937, Berwanger was the starting halfback for the local Calumet Gunners-All Stars in an exhibition game against the Bears held in Hammond, Indiana. Despite Berwanger's presence, the All-Stars were limited to a net of 15 yards rushing and were hammered 34–0 by the Bears. "The illustrious Jay Berwanger, slated to engineer the ground and air attack, had to get his glory by brilliant punting," reported the *Hammond Times*.[30]

Although the Bears were unable to sign Berwanger, the team did score a winner in the first round of that draft. Picking sixth overall, Halas selected tackle Joe Stydahar from West Virginia, who is now a member of the Pro Football Hall of Fame. Then in the ninth and final round, the Bears chose another future Hall of Famer in Colgate guard Danny Fortman. Guard Eddie Michaels (Villanova) also enjoyed a nice career with four teams (just one with the Bears), but four other draft picks never played a minute in the NFL for Halas.

As for the Cardinals, the pickings were very slim. Six of the nine selections did not appear in an NFL game. Fourth-round pick Jeep Brett from Washington State lasted one game with the Cards before being moved to Pittsburgh, leaving first-rounder Jimmy Lawrence and eighth-round choice Ross Carter as the only two draftees who spent significant time with the Cardinals. Lawrence was a speedy back from Texas Christian who rushed for 357 yards on 130 attempts during his three years with the Cardinals (1936–1938) and a final year split between the Cardinals and Green Bay. Carter, a guard from Oregon, played in 42 games for the Cardinals from 1936 to 1939, making him the most prolific of the nine players pursued by the Cardinals in the first NFL draft.[31] Perhaps as an omen from the ugly draft results, the Chicago Cardinals entered a downhill spin, failing to achieve a winning season for a decade from 1936 to 1945. Under promising coach Milan Creighton, the Cardinals finished 3–8–1 in 1936, 5–5–1 in 1937, and 2–9 in Creighton's final season as coach in 1938.

Both Benched for Getting Frisky with Their Fists

After a disappointing record of 6–4–2 in 1935, the Bears rebounded with a 9–3 mark in 1936. Whereas the Bears had crushed the Cardinals' late title hopes in 1935, the South Siders returned the favor a year later. Behind the powerful rookie line duo of Stydahar and Fortmann, the Bears surged to a league-leading 9–1 record before a Thanksgiving Day date with the Detroit Lions on November 26. Although Detroit was 7–3 in the hotly contested NFL Western Division, the Lions managed to outlast the Bears 13–7, leaving the losers (9–2) slightly behind Green Bay (9–1) following the Turkey Day festivities. With a 12-game schedule in play back in 1936, the Bears needed just a victory over the last-place Cardinals in their final game to perhaps catch Green Bay, while hoping the Packers would stumble at least once in their last two contests.

In 1935, Doug Russell of the Cardinals led the NFL in rushing with 499 yards. Then, in 1938, he completed just one pass for the Cards, but it was for a 98-yard touchdown to Gaynell Tinsley. That long scoring toss is still tied for the longest in team history (author's collection).

But all of those hopes were dashed by the Cardinals, who were suddenly on a late-season hot streak. After dropping their first seven games of the campaign, the Cardinals finished up with three wins, a loss, and a tie in the final five contests, including a pleasing 14–7 win over the Bears on November 29, 1936. The Cardinals had not defeated their in-town rivals in NFL competition since 1929, when the great Ernie Nevers established his individual scoring record by notching all of the Cardinals' points in a 40–6 rout. Since that time (except in an exhibition match), the Bears had thoroughly dominated the series. The hero of the hour for the winners was George Grosvenor, a former bench warmer for the Bears until his services were purchased by the Cards earlier in the 1936 season. Not only would Grosvenor bury the Bears with his 66-yard winning touchdown in the victory, but he would become the fifth-leading rusher in the league in both 1936 and 1937. Then, in 1938, he abruptly retired from the NFL to accept a coaching and teaching position at a high school in Colorado.

The surprising Cardinals win at the end of the 1936 season wiped out the Bears' hopes of catching Green Bay and left the North Side contingent (9–3) out of the running behind the Packers (10–1–1) in the final standings. Just to prove that their win over the Bears was not a fluke, the upstart Cardinals then battled the champion Packers club to a 0–0 tie in the NFL season finale on December 6, 1936. A week later,

Green Bay knocked off the Boston Redskins 21–6 to capture the overall NFL title for 1936. Improvement, it seemed, was on its way for the Chicago Cardinals.

As an added incentive, along with a $4,000 check for the club's coffers, Charles Bidwill sent the Cardinals out west once again for one more postseason excursion. The opponent, and host, would be the Los Angeles Bulldogs, a solid club hoping to be considered for NFL membership that very weekend at the league meeting in New York. But the Bulldogs faced one significant obstacle in the form of physical "distance" from the other members of the circuit: "Representatives of the Los Angeles club were staging numerous lobby huddles with the post graduate loop executives. The far westerners are after a league franchise (informally they have been on probation this fall) but the cross-country jump does not look so good to some of the pro league veterans who know what it costs to move a team even from Chicago to New York."[32]

While the Bulldogs were ultimately unsuccessful in securing an NFL franchise, the team did succeed in knocking off the Cardinals 13–10 on December 13, 1936. It was a battle, literally, as penalties derived from the Cardinals' aggressive play helped the hosts to secure advantageous field position in the second half that led to the winning score in a pugilistic setting. The aftermath was described by a bemused *Los Angeles Daily News* reporter: "It was the fiercest melee of the year, and after the game the dressing rooms housed the worst bruised-up players you ever saw. The game turned into a free-for-all on several occasions, and [Hal] Wickersham, of the locals and Billy Wilson of the Cards, were both benched for getting frisky with their fists."[33]

The result was not that surprising since Los Angeles was a competitive team that had already defeated both Philadelphia and Pittsburgh in earlier games. However, on January 10, 1937, the NFL received some retribution when the Bears edged the Bulldogs 7–0 and then the Packers blasted Los Angeles 49–0 on January 17. Although the mighty Bulldogs were unable to secure membership in the league in 1936, it would be another decade before an NFL team established permanent residence in California when the Cleveland Rams migrated to Los Angeles in 1946.

Nothing Protecting His Noggin

During the same weekend of the Cardinals-Bulldogs game, the NFL honchos held their second draft of collegiate players on December 12, 1936. After a humdrum first effort earlier in 1936, the Cardinals fared a little better in the procedure intended to bolster rosters for the 1937 season. With 10 teams now in the league, the NFL extended the draft to 10 rounds, leaving exactly 100 players to be selected. Of the 10 draftees added to the Cardinals' list, only three would ever play for the South Side club. Yet in that sea of gridiron talent morass, the Cards uncovered one gem in the second round: receiver Gaynell "Gus" Tinsley from Louisiana State University. Tinsley would blossom into one of the elite ends in the NFL in a brief but remarkable career that will be discussed shortly.

On the North Side, just five of the 10 players drafted by the Bears played with the team, including Les McDonald (Nebraska end), Henry Hammond (Rhodes College end), Bill Conkright (Oklahoma center), and Del Bjork (Oregon tackle). The fifth survivor (third-round pick Dick Plasman) became a legend in the league and won titles with both the Bears and the Cardinals. Plasman was a big, rangy end from Vanderbilt (6'3", 218 pounds) with great hands and an aggressive temperament. But Plasman is best known as the last person NOT to wear a helmet in an NFL game! With time out for his service during World War II, Plasman still managed to play in the league from 1937 through 1947, and was twice named an All-Pro.

His insistence on not wearing a helmet came into question after an encounter with the Wrigley Field end zone wall while with the Bears in 1938. Syndicated columnist Ira Berkow recalled the episode: "Dick Plasman ... clumped into battle with nothing protecting his noggin but a thick shock of blondish hair. Skull untrussed and hands outstretched, Plasman ran into the end zone as he followed the flight of the ball. It was a certain touchdown. However, he never caught the ball as he ran into the end zone because he simultaneously ran into the wall. The outfield wall in Wrigley Field encroached two feet into the end zone in those days. Today, the field is situated totally in the field and there are mats up on the wall. Too late, though, for Plasman's pate."[34]

Although he was supposedly knocked out for two days after that collision, Plasman continued to distrust helmets because they tended to hinder his vision on the field. He also shunned hip pads during his playing days. As the years went by, Plasman continued to avoid the use of a helmet and every so often encountered an opponent who seemed intent on causing physical harm to the head of the helmet-less wonder. Plasman shared a particular experience with Ira Berkow regarding an opponent who wouldn't listen to the pleas of fairness expressed by Plasman: "He was a defensive tackle for the Washington Redskins. The guy kept bashing me with his elbows. I told him I was getting sick of it. He kept on. So one day he was on the ground and I stepped on a vulnerable part of him. He stopped after that. I mean, I was justified. I got tired of his antics after two years!"[35]

On the other side of town, the Cardinals' first pick of the 1937 draft was Marquette quarterback Ray Buivid. The All-American would go on to establish an NFL passing record later in the season by tossing five touchdown passes in one game. Unfortunately, it was *against* the Cardinals! This achievement was possible after the Cards traded the rights to Buivid to the Bears but he remained unsigned until after the College All-Star Game. George Halas was anxious to secure this talent, with one source stating, "George Halas, coach of the Bears, rates Ray Buivid of Marquette the best forward passer in football."[36] Then, surprisingly, Buivid agreed to join the rival (and very shaky financially) American Football League (AFL). It did not appear to be a wise move at the time, but Buivid was apparently swayed by the opportunity to become a player/coach. Some members of the media simply could not believe that one of the best passers in the country would risk everything with the financially challenged AFL: "The big laughing stock of all football is Ray Buivid, ex-All American from Marquette. Refusing a fine opportunity and exceptional salary to play with the Chicago Bears, Buivid jumped to the outlaw league. He is now barred by the National League."[37]

For whatever reason, Buivid jumped back to the Bears on October 11, 1937. He was neither barred nor ostracized. Rather, the NFL welcomed the young quarterback with the amazing passing skills. Seeing limited action as the understudy to veteran Bernie Masterson for most of the year, Buivid finally burst into the spotlight in the final game of the regular season against the Chicago Cardinals. The Bears had raced to an 8–1–1 mark and had clinched first place in the Western Division when the Windy City rivals clashed on December 5, 1937. The Cardinals were an improved 5–4–1 at this point and looked to secure a rare winning campaign with a win over the favored Bears. It was a cold, dark, gloomy day more fitting for the backdrop of a horror movie than a football game, but certainly a perfect setting for a Bears-Cardinals duel. After a long week of practice, the Cardinals appeared ready to spring the upset: "The Cards have been working hard, for they see a chance to salvage some solace from a disappointing season by whipping the Bears Sunday. It would not be overly surprising, either, if the Cards succeeded in their aims, for they always rise to unexpected heights against the Bears."[38]

Later, Cardinals coach Milan Creighton was pleased by the angry atmosphere during the team's lengthy practice sessions leading up to the game: "They scrimmaged until tempers were on edge and then I called them off. Now if they only take it out on the Bears…"[39]

Since the Bears were already safely positioned as the champs of the Western Division, Coach Halas made the decision to finally unleash the passing talents of Ray Buivid. Buivid had been chafing on the bench since his arrival in October. He was both anxious and confident for this opportunity to start against the Cardinals and demonstrate his solid passing skills. On the Cardinals' side, the tandem of quarterback Pat Coffee and receiver Gus Tinsley had already earned notice around the league. On the day before the Bears game, Tinsley was named as the left end on the All-Pro team selected by one publication. At the right end slot was Green Bay's Don Hutson, already a mythical figure on the gridiron. Yet, the rookie Tinsley earned even more plaudits than Hutson: "Gaynell Tinsley and Don Hutson stood out [at end]. The latter is best known for his ability as a pass receiver. He has an edge on Tinsley in this respect, but the Cardinals ace is a better all-around end."[40]

Not bad for a freshman receiver, but it was another rookie, the Bears quarterback Buivid, who stole the show in the final game of the 1937 regular season in what would become one of the more unique and entertaining contests in the league up to that time. Records fell, new marks were established, coaches chased each other around the field, and half-frozen, albeit playful, fans set fire to the bleachers. All in all, the game contained the typical ingredients of a Bears-Cardinals face-off!

Backs Went Skidding in Undignified Positions

The temperature at game time (2:00 p.m.) dipped to just 16 degrees, leaving the field frozen and nearly unplayable. Both teams wore tennis shoes in an effort to secure better footing. This led to some easy gains by both pass-happy quarterbacks when defenders were unable to turn quickly enough to adjust to the routes of the receivers. That helped the Cardinals to grab a 14–13 halftime lead behind Pat Coffee's scoring tosses to Doug Russell and Pete Tyler. Meanwhile, Buivid connected with end Les McDonald for touchdown passes of 16 and 42 yards to narrow the gap after the Cardinals had opened up a 14–0 advantage. The latter grab by McDonald was most impressive, as reported the *Chicago Daily News*: "Buivid pitched one which McDonald pulled in with an amazing one-handed knee-high catch and raced on to score again employing the baseball slide to cross the final line."[41]

The second half, however, was all about the Chicago Bears. Buivid took advantage of the inability of the Cardinals' pass defenders to react spontaneously and accurately picked apart the helpless secondary on an atrocious field of play that befuddled both defenses: "A solid coating of ice covered the end of the field extending from the 30-yard line on through the end zone. The frozen condition of the remainder of the playing surface made it impossible for linemen to get leverage or backs to drive, nullifying running plays. All of the touchdowns were made on the ice over the baseball infield, where defenders, once they started could not turn or stop. This heightened the hilarity as backs went skidding along in undignified positions and linemen, coming out of the huddle, often arrived at the line of scrimmage on their bloomers."[42]

Buivid conquered the elements that day in one of the most dominating offensive performances in NFL history. He threw for five touchdown passes, then an NFL record, and also caught a touchdown pass to account for all six of the Bears' touchdowns in what became a 42–28 rout. The North Siders actually rolled up 40 straight points to put the game out of reach at 40–14. A late Cardinals rally interrupted by a safety left the final tally at 42–28. Unofficial statistics revealed that the two teams combined for 658 yards in total offense, including 501 yards via the air. Yet the game featured a few other unusual activities as well. With a 2:00 p.m. starting time in December, daylight was fleeting and the game was ended about three minutes early when it became too dark for the contest to continue. However, it did help the Cardinals add one final memorable touchdown as Gus Tinsley scored on a 95-yard dash (later adjusted to 97 yards) that no one apparently witnessed, as reported by the *Chicago Tribune*: "Tinsley … whose 95-yard run was a comical, but fitting climax to a remarkable season. The field was enveloped in complete darkness and the Cardinals were back on their own five-yard line when he took a shovel pass from Coffee on an end around. He ran up the sidelines and was at midfield before the Bears realized anyone was loose. Even then they had their doubts for all that was visible of the runner in the darkness was a pair of silver pants. Some Bear hero, whose identity was hidden by night, then realized pants seldom go running around without a sponsor and gave futile chase."[43]

Due to the darkness, the Cardinals were automatically given the extra point and the game was called with 2:51 to play due to both the arrival of nightfall and the swarming of the field by legions of frozen fans from both teams: "The ludicrous battle wound up with the fans, who had lined the field for the last period, finally swarming on the gridiron in the dark as others less hardy huddled around bonfires in the stands."[44] And, that last statement was accurate. Fun-loving Chicago football fans decided that the best way to combat the miserable cold was to set fire to various sections of the Wrigley Field bleachers!

The crowd of 7,313 witnessed the highest-scoring game in league history to that date and marveled at the talent of Tinsley, who grabbed six passes for 155 yards, thus establishing a new NFL record with 693 receiving yards for the season. But there was more...

Cardinals coach Milan Creighton was apparently not in agreement with the officiating throughout the afternoon and late in the game was also seen attempting to physically confront George Halas: "With dusk coming at about four o'clock, it was very difficult to follow play in the final period and teams and officials had several arguments, including some fistic exchanges and one disagreement between coaches which resulted in Milan Creighton, Cardinals mentor, chasing George Halas, the Bear tutor across the gridiron and Halas winning the race."[45]

Years later, Creighton was credited with another lively exchange with referee Jim Durfee believed to have occurred in this game: "It was in Wrigley Field that Milan Creighton, coach of the Chicago Cardinals, raced down the sidelines all the way to the goal to protest the call by referee Jim Durfee. When Durfee stepped off another ten yards, Creighton demanded: 'What's that for?' 'For unsportsmanlike conduct,' Durfee explained. 'Why you stupid ass!' Creighton screamed. 'You never did know the rules. Unsportsmanlike conduct is 15 yards.' 'Not for you,' Durfee replied, 'You're only worth ten!'"[46]

A week later on December 12, 1937, the Bears (9–1–1) were upset 28–21 by Washington (8–3) in the NFL title game as Sammy Baugh of the Redskins ripped apart the Chicago defense with his impressive aerial display. In a league where the running game was beginning to lose its long-held dominance, Baugh shattered the defensive secondary by completing 17 of 34 passes for a whopping 352 yards. Baugh was so inspiring that the Associated Press released a nationwide story featuring some lofty opinions about the passer: "Earl (Dutch) Clark, Detroit Lion's brilliant playing coach and Ray Flaherty, Washington coach, agreed that Baugh's passing in Washington's 28–21 victory over the Chicago Bears for the championship 'was the greatest one-man show ever put on by professional football.'"[47]

Mixing Knuckles and Scrimmages

Once again, the Bears' season did not end with the defeat in the title game. It was a tour reminiscent of the one taken after the loss to the Giants in the "Sneakers" game of 1934 when the Bears then upended the New Yorkers a month later in California. This time around in early 1938, George Halas scheduled a five-game trip down south, including a pair of rematches with the champion Redskins and the dangerous Sammy Baugh. The Bears would win four of the five contests, losing only 13–0 to Washington once again on January 23, 1938, in Dallas, Texas. The team then traveled over to New Orleans on January 30 and easily eclipsed the Southern All-Stars 41–20, despite the presence of Don Hutson and Gus Tinsley in the lineup of the All-Stars. A highlight of the game was the performance of one of the Bears' quarterbacks: "John Doehring, sensational southpaw passer for the Bears, flipped one behind his back to Lester McDonald for twenty-five yards and the pro team's final touchdown as the Bears made a show of the game."[48]

One stop remained on the tour, this time in Miami, for yet another rematch with the Redskins on February 6, 1938. With Baugh limited by a leg injury, the Bears ousted Washington 16–10 in a battle that featured the expulsion of several players for fighting: "Chicago's bristling Bears whipped the champion Washington Redskins 16–10 between fist fights. A paid gathering of 7,774—a darned good crowd for a February football game—saw eight players, four from each side, benched for mixing knuckles and scrimmages. Six of 'em were set down in the fourth quarter and it looked for a moment as if the game would wind up in a free-for-all as the Chicago substitutes stormed on the field with fists flying."[49]

Now that it was over, the 1937–1938 season for the Chicago Bears was truly remarkable. In addition to the NFL slate (9-2-1) and the postseason tour (4-1), the Bears also completed an eight-game preseason schedule, finishing with seven wins and just one defeat. Taking all of these games into consideration, the club racked up 20 wins against just four losses and one tie for the astounding 25 games played. Before Coach Halas could rest, however, he needed to address one nagging issue: the future of Bronko Nagurski. The incomparable fullback, still just 29 years old, was adamantly seeking a pay raise while Halas was just as stubborn that such an increase was not possible. Already recognized as a world champion wrestler in his "side" job, Nagurski and Halas failed to negotiate a new agreement and the big fullback simply walked away from football. In 1989, an article in *Sports Illustrated* provided some insight into Nagurski's reasoning: "I played during the depression and my salary went down every year. I asked George Halas [in 1938] for something like a $700 raise and he turned me down, and I said fine. I wanted to go home anyway. I was tired of knocking myself out, going on the wrestling tour between games to make extra money. It took its toll."[50]

In another interview, Nagurski further explained the situation: "They upped my pay to $5,000 in 1937 when I talked about retiring and when I asked for $6,000 in 1938, they turned me down. I went home figuring they'd call me, but they never did—not until five years later."[51]

After much speculation, the news about Nagurski was announced in sports pages around the country on August 18, 1938: "Pro football fans are going to have to get along without old Bronko Nagurski this season. He's off on a world's tour to show the boys and girls the latest wrestling grips. Chicago's Bears won't seem the same without him."[52]

For others around the NFL, the departure of Nagurski would not be missed. "Steve Owen, coach of the New York Giants, calls Bronko Nagurski the only back he ever saw who runs his own interference!" claimed Arch Ward of the *Chicago Tribune*.[53] Famed Packers fullback Clark Hinkle once admitted: "He was the most bruising runner ever. The first time I tackled Nagurski, I had to have five stitches in my face. My biggest thrill in football was the day he announced his retirement!"[54]

Nagurski did return to the Bears for one more amazing season in 1943 when rosters were askew due to military service in World War II. Of course, Nagurski is remembered today as one of the very best players in the history of the National Football League and a charter member (1963) of the Pro Football Hall of Fame.

As the 1938 season rolled around, the Cardinals once again looked like homeless waifs. The team managed to schedule only two games as hosts (in late November) in the friendly confines of Wrigley Field and also elected to play other "home" games in Buffalo, New York, Charleston, West Virginia, and Erie, Pennsylvania. None of this wanderlust helped on the field as the Cards dropped with a thud to the bottom of the heap in the Western Division with a 2–9 record. The Bears fared little better, falling from an appearance in the NFL title game in 1937 to a disappointing 6–5 mark in 1938, good for just third place in the division. Instead of finishing the season as usual, the Bears and the Cardinals opened the 1938 schedule with an unusually early date (September 11, 1938) for a night game at Soldier Field in Chicago. In a contest staged in part for the benefit of the Denver Sanitarium, the Cardinals burst out to a 13–0 lead in the first half after tackle Tony Blazine chugged 14 yards into the end zone with a fumble recovery and Doug Russell scored on a one-yard plunge. The Bears retaliated when Bill Karr hauled in a nine-yard scoring toss from George Corbett to lower the deficit to 13–7 at the half. The Bears knotted the score in the third period when Ray Nolting scored from 15 yards out, leaving the game deadlocked until the fourth quarter, when reliable Jack Manders connected on a field goal from the 24-yard line with less than four minutes remaining for the final points in a 16–13 Bears win.

Before the teams met once again on October 16, Cards coach Milan Creighton

Bill Smith (#40) leads the way for Cardinal Jimmy Lawrence (#8) during an exhibition game with the Cincinnati Bengals in 1938. The two teams battled to a 14–14 deadlock, and as typical for those days, the game included a major brawl between the teams (author's collection).

grabbed the attention of the NFL world by dropping five veterans from the roster of the 1–4 club. Creighton was apparently not impressed with the early season effort provided by his team and was insistent in his effort to change the culture immediately by stating: "This is only the beginning. We are not running a rest haven for athletes. I have no quarrel with men who play to win, but lose. But I am convinced that we have a better football team than the standings indicate and the players will prove it Sunday starting with the Bears or they will be given a chance to do their loafing in some other line of endeavor."[55]

Cards Rushed Referee Tommy Hughitt

It didn't work. By this time, the Bears had become enormously dominant in the city series. The Cardinals captured just one win in 18 attempts from 1930 through 1938. Two games did end in ties, but there was no question that the Bears were the superior team in the 1930s and they fortified that position with a wild 34–28 victory over the Cardinals in the final meeting of the two teams in 1938. While the losses were mounting for Coach Creighton and the Cardinals during the dreary 1938 campaign, a flash of feistiness appeared a week later during a 7–0 loss to the Philadelphia Eagles in a game played during a driving rainstorm in Erie, Pennsylvania. Buoyed by the frustration of a sixth straight loss, tempers flared at the conclusion of the contest: "At the end of the game, a Chicago coach, halfback Doug Russell and other Cards rushed referee Tommy Hughitt to protest several of his decisions. It took a half dozen policemen to break up the fracas, but not until Hughitt had been slugged."[56]

As the Cardinals limped home to finish 2–9, more changes were imminent. A day after the season ended on November 29, both Head Coach Milan Creighton and assistant Phil Handler resigned their positions with the Cardinals. Creighton had been in charge for four seasons and compiled a 16–26–4 record. Owner Charles Bidwill needed just three days to find a replacement that he was certain would return the Cardinals to glory. On December 1, 1938, Bidwill announced the signing of Ernie Nevers as the new coach of the Chicago Cardinals: "I consider myself extremely fortunate to obtain Nevers. I pledge him the full cooperation of the Cardinal staff in the attempt to bring the team to the front in the National league, where it belongs. I haven't been any more pleased with a losing team than the fans. In fact, not as much. I pay the bills."[57]

On the North Side, George Halas eyed the 1939 NFL draft hoping to add enough talent to reverse the disappointing 6–5 1938 finish. Held on December 8, 1938, in New York, the bloated selection process stretched into 12 rounds but Halas landed two individuals who would quickly guide his team through perhaps the most magical era in Bears history. The Cardinals owned the very first pick of the draft and promptly grabbed Ki Aldrich, a center/linebacker from the undefeated Texas Christian eleven. Aldrich was a unanimous All-American choice and was named his club's most valuable player over lauded quarterback Davey O'Brien. Despite winning the Heisman Trophy as the nation's most outstanding football player in 1938, O'Brien agreed with the crowning of Aldrich as the team's MVP: "Ki Aldrich has always been our most valuable player. It was his fight and hustle that kept us going when it was tough."[58] Aldrich would spend only the first two years of his career with the Cardinals before being traded to Washington. New coach Ernie Nevers added another big name in the second round when he selected Pittsburgh All-American Marshall Goldberg with the 12th overall pick. The elusive halfback would enjoy a long career with the Cardinals, before eventually evolving into the NFL's first defensive specialist.

But it was the pair of rookie standouts who instantly pumped new life into the Bears. With the second choice of the draft, Halas chose quarterback/halfback Sid Luckman from Columbia, who was initially reluctant to play pro football but ended up shattering most of the Bears' passing records during his aerial reign of terror. Luckman still holds the team mark for most touchdowns in one game with seven and also continues to retain second place on the team's all-time passing yardage charts. It is now more than 70 years since he last put on a Bears uniform! With the sixth pick of the draft, Halas acquired fullback Bill Osmanski from Holy Cross. Osmanski made an immediate impact in the NFL in 1939 by topping the league in rushing and earning All-Pro honors. He was especially effective in the two games that season with the Cardinals, both won by the Bears by wide margins.

My Boys Aren't Overconfident

Coach Nevers could not have started the season with worse news than when five players (all backfield men) decided not to report to the Cards' training camp in Duluth, Minnesota. Meanwhile, star draftee Marshall Goldberg reported for camp with a cast on his foot that would be bothersome during the season. Finally, in a real stunner, two-time All-Pro selection Gus Tinsley decided to accept the football coaching job at Haynesville High School in Louisiana. This surprise departure occurred just a week after camp began. Tinsley still holds the Cardinals team record (since tied) for the longest touchdown reception with a 98-yarder in 1938. With four key players already sidelined by injuries, the outlook for the Cardinals looked bleak indeed. Things never did get better...

The Cardinals were a woeful 1–4 when they met the Bears (3–1) on October 15, 1939. At this early point in the season, the Bears' Osmanski was more of a threat for Halas than was Luckman, who was still learning the ropes of the NFL behind Bernie Masterson. In fact, Masterson was fourth in the NFL in total passing yards (458) after the first four games while Osmanski was second in rushing yards behind teammate Joe Maniaci. Although the Cardinals were wallowing at the bottom of the standings, George Halas insisted that he was fearful of the Cardinals under Coach Nevers: "That offense Ernie Nevers has worked up for the Cards is tricky. It has tremendous possibilities, and from what our scouts brought back from the Cards' game with Green Bay last week, it's going to realize those possibilities just in time to cause an unpleasant afternoon. Luckily, my boys aren't overconfident. They know they're in for a battle."[59]

Halas should not have worried about the outcome. Before a good crowd of nearly 30,000, the Bears routed their rivals 44–7 at Wrigley Field in the most lopsided win in the long series between the two clubs. The biggest concern for Halas, however, was the loss of footballs that were leaving Wrigley at an alarming rate. For the man who walked away from both Jay Berwanger and Bronko Nagurski because of financial concerns, the cost of the lost footballs was becoming frightening as the Bears jumped off to a 17–0 advantage in the first quarter: "Three new footballs were kicked out of the park, bringing the cost of the Bears' first 17 points to $2.35 per point. At the time, it seemed quite reasonable, but in view of later developments, the purchasing department was a little put out about the whole thing.... On orders from the purchasing department, the Bears didn't risk the loss of another ball thru strong-footed kicking for the [other] extra points."[60]

The highlight of the game for the Bears (aside from the dramatic cost savings from non-kicked footballs!) was a fourth-quarter touchdown by Osmanski. Behind the blocking of big Jack Torrance and Dick Brassi, Osmanski burst through a hole and scampered 86 yards for the final score of the game. To this day, no other member of the Chicago Bears has been able to equal the length of Osmanski's touchdown jaunt. The two teams met once again to close out the 1939 season on November 26 at Wrigley Field. The result was even more hideous for the Cardinals this time, as the Bears walloped the South Siders 48–7. With the victory, the Bears finished with an 8–3 mark, just a game behind the eventual NFL champion Green Bay Packers in the Western Division title chase. The Cardinals fell to 1–10 for the season with eight straight losses to conclude the schedule. It was the worst record in team history. Predictably, changes were forthcoming.

After weeks of rumors and gossip, it was reported on February 20, 1940, that Ernie Nevers had resigned as head coach of the Chicago Cardinals after just one season: "In resigning as coach of the Cardinals, Nevers gave up a position which paid him an estimated $8,000 per year. He quit, he said, because he wanted to make his home in California and also because he wanted to be free to negotiate 'several propositions now on the fire.'"[61]

As the decade concluded, the Cardinals had nowhere to go but up. The team was safely ensconced at the bottom of the standings, barely clinging to life as a football squad, and with no firm plan in sight for a revival. The Bears, meanwhile, were drafting well, playing well, and looking to recapture the recently elusive NFL title. Two teams. Two directions. Would they ever meet in the middle? Perhaps the best hope for the Cardinals would be if the two Chicago rivals merged forces. It almost happened...

Fifteen

Mergers, Titles, and Missing Halfbacks

"He called me on the phone and suggested that we merge with the Bears. I answered, kiddingly, that it would be a swell idea. Maybe he took me seriously."—Charles Bidwill, Owner, Chicago Cardinals, 1943

No coach. No home. No plan.

Charles Bidwill, the owner of the Chicago Cardinals, demonstrated consistent business success in his many ventures. With a keen sense for recognizing market shifts and customer bases, Bidwill entered the new decade of the 1940s with a renewed will to reverse the lagging fortunes of the Cardinals. In recent years, the innovative player draft initiated by Bert Bell had failed to benefit the Cardinals, as noted by Edward Cochrane of the *Chicago Herald-American* in late 1939: "Stars don't always report to professional teams. If they did Charley Bidwill would have had a championship contender instead of a bust this year. Eight of the best players in the land, drafted by the Cardinals last fall failed to sign contracts, leaving the Red Birds in about the same position physically as they were a year previous."[1]

Winning was elusive and attendance was in the dumpster with so few "home" games at Wrigley Field. The last two games of the 1938 season hosted by the Cardinals drew paltry crowds of 8,279 and 2,200, respectively. Thanks to the opponent being the Bears, the final contest in 1939 attracted 16,055, but the team largely survived on the guarantees received from being the NFL's most prominent "away" team. Two home games at Wrigley Field and one at Soldier Field were clearly not offering enough local visibility for the Cardinals.

Since its inception in 1899, the Cardinals team had been associated with the South Side of Chicago. That is, until the surprise move to Wrigley Field on the North Side in 1931, which gutted the loyal fan base following for the team. In addition, the departure of Coach Ernie Nevers and the tardiness in identifying his replacement had delayed any concrete plans for the 1940 season. Nevers was still around and in charge of the most recent draft selections, so the new coach would be forced to bundle those picks in an effort to somehow fit the pieces together for his football vision for the future. And why were players either quitting the team, or deciding not to join the club as draft picks?

Had the Cardinals lost touch with the reality of the NFL? Had the team curled up in comfort and accepted its recent role as a perennial also-ran in the professional ranks? Or, had the organization simply lost its identity?

In early 1940, Charles Bidwill decided to implement several significant changes to the organization with the firm goal of returning the Chicago Cardinals to relevance in the National Football League. His first and likely most important objective was to bring in a respected head coach—preferably one with knowledge, experience, and personality. The brief sojourn with Ernie Nevers as the head man did not succeed and Bidwill needed to mend some fences when he learned that there had been several scrapes between Nevers and his players. Most important, Nevers had actually released All-Pro Gus Tinsley after a disagreement during training camp the year before, forcing Tinsley to accept the high school coaching position previously mentioned. Nearly two months after the resignation of Nevers, Bidwill reeled in his preferred head coach, the ebullient Jimmy Conzelman.

Most Versatile Man in the Country

Conzelman was fresh off a successful season at Washington University in St. Louis, where he spent eight seasons, winning three conference titles, the most recent in 1939. However, Conzelman was not a newcomer to the NFL. He had been an outstanding player, coach, and owner in the league during its formative years and knew just about everyone connected with the NFL. Upon his hiring on April 10, 1940, Conzelman stated: "I'm looking forward to my return to the pro game and to renewing associations I formerly enjoyed before I entered the college sport."[2]

Conzelman was a member of the famed Great Lakes Naval Training Center football team with George Halas and Paddy Driscoll that captured the 1919 Rose Bowl. Later he played for the Decatur Staleys and then was a member of, and coached, the Rock Island Independents. He coached the Milwaukee Badgers and the Providence Steam Roller, winning the NFL title in 1928 with Providence. Conzelman was also the owner of the Detroit Panthers club in the mid–1920s. Yet football was only a small part of Conzelman's repertoire. He was a writer, composer, and a popular after-dinner speaker known for his dry wit and insightful sense of humor, motivating 1940 Pulitzer Prize winner Bart Howard of the *St. Louis Post-Dispatch* to write: "Has anyone since Leonardo DaVinci had as many talents in his portfolio as Conzelman?" Sportswriter B.A. Bridgewater of Tulsa, Oklahoma, added: "Football coach, magazine writer, raconteur, musician, ex-amateur boxing champion, radio star, actor, the most versatile man in the country: Jimmy Conzelman."[3]

With Conzelman now in the fold and quickly hitting the recruiting trail for prospects, Bidwill waited less than 10 days before making another difficult decision. The Cardinals, he determined, would no longer be homeless as he signed a lease moving the team back to Comiskey Park on the South Side of Chicago. For Cardinals fans, it seemed that the natural order of things was finally back in place. The Cardinals were home! The transition back to Comiskey Park reversed the bewildering decision by then-owner David Jones to transfer the club away from its traditional neighborhood fan base, as reported in the *Chicago Tribune*: "Signing of the lease yesterday successfully concluded a campaign waged by south side fans and business interests since Dr. David Jones sought to stimulate attendance by moving north, where Bears prosperity seemed to indicate professional football was more popular. Professional football was extremely popular on the north side, provided it was Bears football."[4]

Meanwhile, Conzelman hit the road, making personal visits to potential roster additions such as center Andy Chisick, a seventh-round draft pick from Villanova. Chisick was on the fence as to whether to play pro football or to pursue a coaching career. Conzelman flew into Philadelphia to extoll the benefits of the Cardinals' organization, hoping to convince Chisick by offering him the best of both worlds:

> Andy Chisick, Villanova College football center for three years, has signed a contract to play professional football with the Chicago Cardinals. Jimmy Conzelman, the Cardinals' new coach, signed Chisick yesterday on a flying visit to the Villanova campus. Chisick rejected two previous offers from Conzelman, but was unable to resist the opportunities held out to him when Jimmy made a personal visit. Andy preferred to give up the playing end and seek a coaching berth. In the event such a position should be offered before the football season opens, a clause in Andy's contract permits him to withdraw from the pro ranks.[5]

Conzelman's persuasive powers were essential if Bidwill's plan to rebuild the team was to be successful. But Bidwill proved to be just as mobile, reaching out to former star Gaynell Tinsley, who was ousted by Coach Ernie Nevers after Tinsley's 1938 All-Pro season. "Bidwill has agreed to pay Gay Tinsley, Louisiana State's All-American end, $1,000 more than he was getting as a coach in a Louisiana prep school last year, and the great end of the Bayou Tigers will be back in the pro ranks this fall."[6] Next, Conzelman vowed to use the services of running back Marshall Goldberg more extensively in 1940. Goldberg, a three-time All-American at Pittsburgh, ran the ball only 56 times in 1939 with Conzelman claiming that Goldberg would be more effective with a change to fullback or right halfback. Finally, Bidwill focused on reacquiring several players who slipped away from both the Cardinals and football in 1939. His efforts were certainly noticed: "Charles W. Bidwill, leading Chicago sports enthusiast, already is looking forward to the coming football season. Several star performers who refused to join the Cardinals last fall are expected to trek to camp when newly appointed Coach Jimmy Conzelman issues orders in August. This includes Gaynell Tinsley, greatest end in football, Bill Daddio, famed Pitt All-American, and Al Wolff, outstanding tackle at Santa Clara two years ago."[7]

The Bidwill/Conzelman partnership was returning enthusiasm to the fan base, and more important, a connection with the players. But would it translate to success on the field? Perhaps, but the foundation was prepared for an eventual return to NFL supremacy later in the decade. After spending the previous training camp in Duluth, Minnesota, Bidwill arranged for the team to sequester back on the South Side of Chicago for the 1940 preseason preparation. Returning to Morgan Park Military Academy, the players were housed in the non-air-conditioned dormitories used during the school year for the "boarding" students attending the school. Since the facilities were not needed during the summer months, the academy found the concept of hosting an NFL team for three weeks to be very advantageous. Each member of the Cardinals' party was charged a daily fee for lodging, meals, and the opportunity to access the practice fields (and the pristine Abell Field football stadium) available on campus: "It is further agreed that room and board for the players, numbering about fifty men, will be supplied by the Academy at the rate of $2.50 per day basis per man. It is further agreed to allow the party [Cardinals] to use Abell Athletic Field three times per week for scrimmage, it being understood by both parties that the field will not be in use more than one and a half hours at a time. The party agrees to reimburse [the Academy] … for any damages done to any property … by any one in connection with the Chicago Cardinals Football Club in any capacity."[8]

Bears Came Up with New Formations Football Never Saw

The Cardinals remained on the Morgan Park Military Academy campus from August 18 through September 11, 1940, when the squad headed east for opening games against the Pittsburgh Steelers and the Detroit Lions, the latter to take place in Buffalo, New York. For the Cardinals, the season outlook was promising, but unknown, while the Bears were expecting big things out of their improved roster, which now included talented rookies (and future Hall of Famers) Bulldog Turner at center and speedster George McAfee. Sid Luckman was back at the offensive helm to manage the intricate "T" formation. George Halas was one of the first in the league to tinker with the "T" formation as a method to increase the team's offense efficiency. While other teams continued to employ the aging single-wing offense, Halas contemplated ways to improve the potential of the "T" and worked closely with Clark Shaughnessy, the former head coach at the nearby University of Chicago, to tinker with the various options that the offense could provide. For that very reason, Halas felt a bit unprepared before the team's 1940 opener at Green Bay: "There is no denying that the Bears' offense is the most complicated and difficult system to master in football. Schooling the rookies in all the various formations has been a slow, tedious task and it has progressed so poorly that Halas and his assistants consider the men to have attained only 50 per cent of its efficiency."[9]

However, the bleak assessment provided by Halas before the Green Bay game was purely deceptive. The Bears pelted the Packers 41–10 behind a dazzling offense that left one reporter virtually awe-struck: "I saw the greatest pro football team that ever strode out onto a gridiron Sunday. It was the Chicago Bears. The Bears came up with some new formations that football never saw before, they were the cat's whiskers and how. They put on a shimmy stunt. Their heads and shoulders shook in perfect harmony and their feet and ball went the other way. All they need is an orchestra with that stuff. It's perfect."[10]

In reality, the "T" formation had been around for decades, but Halas and Shaughnessy managed to squeeze the most out of it, especially when the talent on the field matched the potential of the powerful offense. As the 1940 season progressed, Halas was elated with the product, especially with Sid Luckman assuming more of a major role. Longtime collegiate coach Jon Cooper has spent 45 years in the profession, including a decade as the head of the Benedictine College (Illinois) program. As a student of the game, and currently working as a scout for Ourlads NFL Scouting Service, Cooper provided some insight into the history of the "T" formation and why the Bears pursued this option:

With the elimination of the five-yard passing rule in the early 1930s, the "T" formation was revived. Clark Shaughnessy at the University of Chicago was an early proponent as well as a friend and consultant to George Halas. Halas liked the idea because the three backs could now be balanced and could attack quickly downhill. Misdirection was also possible along with power runs and halfback and fullback lead plays. The passing game could become more diverse with the quarterback throwing quick tosses with one- and three-step drops. The deep drop for longer routes took the place of the short punt formation snap of the single wing. With the easing of the passing rules, the quarterback could also roll out and attack the line of scrimmage and be able to run or pass before he got to the line. Splitting one end and motioning one of the halfbacks put two receivers wide on the snap. In 1939, Halas signed University of Chicago Quarterback Solly Sherman as a backup and tutor to fellow rookie Sid Luckman in the "T" formation. Bernie Masterson was the Bear quarterback who would be replaced by Luckman in 1940. In Luckman, Halas had the right athlete to run the T. The rest is history.[11]

The powerhouse put together by Halas was certainly no accident as by now, he was carefully plotting his draft selections and wheeling and dealing behind the scenes with fellow owners prior to the annual draft. Football author and historian Bob Carroll explained the superlative maneuvers orchestrated by Halas in 1940:

> The Bears' 1940 draft was one of the best any team ever had. They chose center Clyde "Bulldog" Turner, ends Ken Kavanaugh and Hamp Pool, tackles Ed Kolman and Lee Artoe, and running back Harry Clark. All of them would gain All-Pro recognition in their careers and Turner would wind up in the Hall of Fame. But the biggest blast of all came from one of those patented George Halas-Bert Bell deals. The Eagles tabbed breakaway wonder George McAfee out of Duke and immediately packed him off to the Bears for a couple of long-forgotten tackles. For the next two seasons, McAfee would be arguably the greatest runner the NFL had ever seen. They called him "One-Play" because that's all it took to get him from anywhere on the field into the end zone. Amazingly, Bell later explained, "We had [passing star] Davey O'Brien then and couldn't have used McAfee anyway." Like a skydiver couldn't use a parachute![12]

While the Bears handed the Packers their worst defeat in team history in the 1940 opener, the Cardinals were quietly putting together the beginnings of what the club thought might be an undefeated season. Surprisingly, the Cards tied both Pittsburgh and Detroit on successive weekends to set up an early season showdown with the unblemished Bears, although the Lions game may have been the ugliest in NFL annals. Played in Buffalo, New York, on September 15, 1940, when Comiskey Park was unavailable, the Cardinals and Detroit brought football down to one of its lowest points in the 0–0 tie. Usually, a scoreless result is caused by an absence of offense. Somehow, this contest was even more horrifying in that department. Playing in a driving rainstorm accompanied by high winds and limited visibility, neither team could generate any offense, and in the second half, neither appeared to have any desire to move the ball. In short, some may consider this "battle" as the worst game ever played in the NFL!

Besides the failure to score, the ugly stat line for the game revealed a total yardage accumulation of just 30 yards for both teams in total! That excruciating low figure remains an NFL record for fewest yards in a game over 80 years later. In addition, there were seven turnovers and a parade of punts that were both bewildering and boring. Neither team, it seems, was anxious to initiate an offense from deep in its own territory in very peculiar weather conditions: "A terrific thunderstorm burst on the stadium with the opening kickoff and the downpour continued throughout the game to drench some 18,000 fans and turn the gridiron into a virtual quagmire. By the third quarter, both teams were so water-logged the contest developed into a punting duel between Whizzer White and the Cardinals' Beryl Clark. The final period saw eight successive exchanges of punts between the two without a single intervening play."[13]

Fiery Little Band of Unknowns

It would be difficult to comprehend such an unusual contest today, especially in the wake of those eight straight punts that were delivered without the response of a single play from scrimmage! But the tie with the Lions did allow the Cardinals to remain both undefeated and winless for their first two outings. The Cards also enjoyed 10 days off between games before the showdown at Comiskey Park on Wednesday, September 25, with the Bears (1–0). There was little hope for a Cardinals victory, but fans from the South Side embraced the return of their team after a decade's absence: "It is a confident, fiery little band of unknowns who can play good football that Conzelman will introduce to the Cardinals' south side constituency in what amounts to a homecoming in several respects for the Cardinals. The Cardinals were a south side team ten years ago before taking up their residence in Wrigley Field with the mistaken idea that more people would come to their games because more people went to see the Bears there."[14]

In a completely unexpected result, the Cardinals proved to be inhospitable hosts, turning away the favored Bears 21–7 before a crowd of over 23,000. In the game program, the Cardinals featured a full-page illustration of Gaynell "Gus" Tinsley, revealing that Tinsley received the nickname of "Gus" due to his perpetual sad look.[15] Now back on the Cards' roster after a year coaching high school football, Tinsley was anything but sad as he snared a 10-yard scoring toss from Hugh McCullough in the second half to put the game away for the winners. Earlier, McCullough, who had just joined the Cards after being placed on waivers by Cleveland, opened the scoring by drilling a 36-yard touchdown pass to rookie John Hall. Marshall Goldberg, running with confidence under Coach Conzelman, also scored on a seven-yard burst around left end in the second quarter. All in all, it was a satisfying homecoming for Bidwill and Conzelman and their rebuilt roster: "Chicago's young Cardinals, 22 of them new to the team and 19 making their third starts as professionals, last night fought their way to what will survive the season as one of football's major surprises. With a starting lineup that included three rookies and seven veterans who have salvaged a deep affection for the game out of the reorganization of the coaching staff, the Cardinals set out with the opening kick-off to establish their superiority over the team that is being hailed as the finest aggregation in the history of the national league."[16]

Lost in the headlines proclaiming the stunning accomplishment of the Cardinals was the acknowledgment that the midweek victory was the first for the South Siders over the Bears since 1936, and just the second since 1929 in league play. Of course, since this was a standoff between the Bears and Cardinals, a few fistfights broke out, one of which led to the ejection of Bears tackle Joe Stydahar and Cards rookie end Billy Dewell.

So, after the first three weeks of the NFL season, the Cardinals stood atop the Western Division standings. Would Conzelman's charges be able to sustain this momentum? Were the highly lauded Bears finished? The answer to both questions would be a resounding "no" as the two Chicago clubs took wildly different paths for the rest of the 1940 season. The Cardinals, unfortunately, would savor just one more win that year while falling to a 2–7–2 record. On the other hand, the Bears reversed course quickly and rebounded to finish in first place in the Western Division with an 8–3 mark. One of those losses, however, occurred at the hands of Washington, leading to some confrontational words between the owners of the two organizations.

Ready to Tear the Referee Limb from Limb

On November 17, 1940, the Bears (6–2) traveled to Washington to take on the Redskins (7–1) in a battle of division leaders. Washington escaped with a 7–3 win in a defeat that didn't bother the Bears as much as the way the game ended. The Redskins clung to a slim 7–3 advantage with just 20 seconds remaining in the game. The Bears had one last chance to score from midfield. Arch Ward of the *Chicago Tribune* reported on the hectic last few seconds of the battle: "Bob Snyder faded deep, gave George McAfee plenty of room to get down the field and then threw a long pass directly into his arms. McAfee was brought down on the one-yard line where Coach George Halas stopped the clock by sending in a substitute. The Bears were penalized for excessive time outs. There was time for only one more play. Sid Luckman passed to [Bill] Osmanski in the end zone, but the former Holy Cross star couldn't lift his arms because of what appeared to be interference on the part of [Bob] Titchenal, Washington's center."[17]

Bill Osmanski was in disbelief at the "no call" and looked to the officials for justice, none of which was forthcoming and the Redskins celebrated their hard-earned victory as time ran out. He later recalled the circumstances in the waning seconds of the defeat: "There I was, hands out, just waiting for the ball. Sid Luckman's pass was perfect. Someone grabbed me from behind and pulled my arms tight against my sides. The ball hit my chest and flopped to the ground. The gun went off. I shouted a protest to the referee. Mr. Halas came running."[18]

Halas discussed his immediate reaction and the aftermath from his futile complaints in his autobiography: "I was furious! I was ready to tear the referee limb from limb. I probably used all the words I had learned on the Chicago streets and in ball parks and training camps and maybe even made up a few new ones. George Preston Marshall [owner of the Redskins] heard of my protests. 'The Bears are a bunch of crybabies,' he said. 'They can't take defeat. They are a first-half club. They are quitters. They are the world's greatest crybabies!'"[19]

Tough words and sometimes those words can take on a life of their own. Normally, postgame comments are quickly forgotten as the teams move on to their next opponent with a rematch unlikely for a few weeks or even until the next season. However, the Bears and the Redskins continued to march forward to the NFL championship game by both winning their divisions. Washington finished 9–2 to top the East while the Bears rebounded from the Redskins defeat to complete the 1940 campaign with an 8–3 ledger. With the title tilt scheduled for December 8, 1940, in Washington, D.C., the war of words (mostly from George Preston Marshall) continued unabated. He told reporters prior to the game: "The Bears are a great team. We'll kill 'em!"[20]

We Almost Broke Down the Door!

Halas was careful to direct his comments internally, but after the loss to the Redskins, he boldly stated: "We are not going to lose another game, and that includes the championship playoff, too."[21] Meanwhile, he quietly collected each and every negative comment tossed his way by the Redskins owner. Halas was a master motivator and shared the clippings with his players as the championship game drew closer. Were the Bears really crybabies? Did they quit after the first half? Halas was keen to turn the tough loss in Washington, and the ensuing negative outbursts from Marshall, into an advantage for his team: "His comments were reported coast to coast. The words burned into my mind. I did not let the players forget them. You can understand why the game for the championship took on special importance."[22]

Meanwhile, ticket sales were going through the roof, mostly through scalpers since all 36,000 seats for the game itself sold out in a matter of hours. The Associated Press sifted through the unusual circumstances for tickets to a pro football game being so difficult to acquire: "From the way things looked today it's going to be a lot harder to get into the Washington Redskins-Chicago Bears football game Sunday than it is to get into the White House. Tourists who want to see the Executive Mansion merely have to stand in line and try to keep from looking like suspicious characters when they reach the door. Senators and representatives—who usually can get into anything in the Capital—are frantically making calls trying to round up tickets."[23]

Everyone was anxious to see the game but most would need to take advantage of the first nationwide radio broadcast of an NFL championship game by the Mutual Broadcasting System. Mutual hooked up with approximately 125 local stations, including WGN in Chicago, to call the game from Griffith Stadium with advertising support from the Gillette Safety Razor company.[24]

By now, the offensive success of the "T formation" preferred by Halas and supplemented by Shaughnessy, who was now the coach at Stanford, was beginning to attract interest on a national level:

> You have heard how the secret of the Palo Alto [Stanford] success was the introduction of the Bears' T-formation offense. This is a fact, but Stanford hardly swiped the Chicago stuff, since it belonged to Clark Shaughnessy all the time. According to another version, Shaughnessy has been chairman of the Bears' board of strategy and chief mapper-out of their plays for several seasons. All he did was take it along to the west, leaving enough for the pros. What with one of Mr. Shaughnessy's eleven in the Rose Bowl and another in the national professional championship, the supply of touchdowns on hand must have been ample for all concerned.[25]

With all of the pregame excitement, the game itself quickly became anti-climactic. If there was any doubt about the ability of Halas to motivate a team, that was quickly dispersed when the Bears walked into the visiting team's locker room and discovered that the coach had used all of the negative clippings about his team as wallpaper, according to fullback Bill Osmanski: "When we came into the dressing room we saw that Mr. Halas had pinned the clippings to the wall. When we were ready to go out, he pointed to the clippings and said, 'That's what the people in Washington are saying about you gentlemen. I know you are the greatest football team ever. Now go out and show the world.' We almost broke down the door!"[26]

The Chicago Bears were ready and, seeking immediate retribution for the controversial loss to Washington earlier, jumped all over the Redskins; knocked quarterback Sammy Baugh out of the game temporarily; and pounced on an unbelievable nine turnovers, including eight interceptions. It took just three plays for the Bears to score as Osmanski swept around right end on a 68-yard scoring scamper. In quick order, Sid Luckman scored on a one-yard rush, and then Joe Maniaci rolled around end for a 42-yard tally—all in the first stanza. In the second quarter, Luckman connected with Ken Kavanaugh with a 30-yard touchdown reception, leaving the score a shocking 28–0 at the half. From there, things only became worse for Washington.

The Bears totally obliterated the Washington defense in the second half and walked away with a stunning 73–0 victory and the 1940 NFL championship. The dominance of the Bears was so stifling that Luckman was strapped to the bench in the final half, allowing Bernie Masterson, Sollie Sherman, and Bob Snyder to finish off the opposition at quarterback. The Washington defeat was both overwhelming and embarrassing: "Not since the British sacked this city more than a 100 years ago has Washington seen such a rout. The thousands of loyal Redskin rooters, who had come to boo the Bears, stayed to roar bravos in spontaneous tribute to the incredible Chicago eleven. And finally, in resentment at the pitiful collapse of the Redskins, those fans booed the men who had been their heroes."[27]

With the final 73–0 count, the Bears established a record (which still stands) for both the most points and the largest margin of victory in an NFL game. The usually vocal George Preston Marshall was distraught after the game and unusually quiet after his pregame predictions. All that could be coaxed out of him was a brazen comment on the efforts of his players: "My players must have had their fountain pens out, figuring the winners' shares," meaning they were more concerned with their share of the receipts rather than the task at hand.[28] Another good quote from the Washington side has survived over the years. Right after the first score by the Bears, Sammy Baugh led the Redskins downfield and hit open receiver Charley Malone with a pass in the end zone for what would have tied the game. But the ball was dropped and Washington never did dent the end zone that day. Later, when asked if Malone had caught that ball for a touchdown would it have made a difference in the game, Baugh simply responded, "Hell, yes, the score would've been 73–6."[29] Washington coach Ray Flaherty was also shocked by the outcome. When asked what happened, Flaherty could only say: "I'm not sure, but I do know that every time we got the ball the Bears scored."[30]

Bears' Most Successful Run in Team History

The NFL as a whole was becoming a more prominent fixture on the American sporting scene. The Bears' huge victory, coupled with Clark Shaughnessy and Stanford's win over Nebraska in the Rose Bowl, led to increased interest in the "T" formation. The league released its attendance figures later in December 1940. Over 1.3 million watched the regular season games (1,600,000 with exhibitions) and the championship contest, a 2.5 percent increase from the previous season. The New York Giants topped all teams in attendance for the year with 247,645 (seven home games), while the Bears were third with 143,471 (five home games) and the Cardinals last with 64,006 for four games.[31] Although the Cardinals were still struggling at the gate, the product on the field under Jimmy Conzelman was improving, despite the 2–7–2 record in 1940. Conzelman intended to maintain that upward curve of improvement in 1941. But after three years at the helm (1940–1942), Conzelman, like others before him, was unable to break through to NFL prominence (or even a winning season) and he retired from coaching following losing records in 1940 (2–7–2), 1941 (3–7–2), and 1942 (3–8).

Swinging over to the North Side of Chicago, the Bears were set to continue their positive run in what was the most successful era in team history. Following the rewarding destruction of the Redskins in 1940, the Bears moved on to capture NFL titles again in 1941, 1943, and 1946. That impressive stretch resulted in four titles in the decade. In a bit of an aberration, the 1942 team, which might have been the strongest of the Bears units during the 1940s, went through an undefeated season only to drop the championship game to the revenge-minded Redskins. During this same time frame (from 1943 to 1945), the Cardinals suffered through a succession of horrible seasons and managed to establish the NFL's longest losing streak along the way.

The Bears raged out of the box in 1941, running to a 6–1 record, including a 53–7 stomping of the Cardinals on October 12. The effort by the Cardinals mirrored the final score, as the Bears rolled up a league record of 613 total yards. Quarterbacks Sid Luckman and

Coach Jimmy Conzelman was hopeful his second-round draft choice in 1941, Paul Christman, would be able to assist the Cardinals that season. However, the All-American quarterback enlisted in the Naval Reserve and did not return to the Cardinals until 1945. He then helped the club grab the 1947 NFL championship as part of the "Dream Backfield" (author's collection).

Young Bussey each tossed a pair of touchdowns as the Bears jumped out to a 33–0 lead at the half and coasted to the easy victory in which a couple of other records were also established: "A perfect football day brought out 34,668 to Wrigley Field, the largest crowd which has watched these teams since they started playing each other in 1920. There was another record, too. Those 53 points were the most either team has amassed in the 42 times they have met."[32]

As the Bears continued to rampage through the schedule, Halas and his crew could not shake the pesky Green Bay Packers. The Bears opened the 1941 schedule with a 25–17 win over the Packers in Green Bay, the only blemish on the Packers' record. In the second meeting between the two clubs during the regular season, the Packers outlasted the Bears 16–14 to hand the Chicagoans their lone defeat of the season. Moving into the final game on December 7, 1941, the Bears (9–1) would need to claim a victory over the Cardinals (3–6–1) in order to forge a tie for the division title with the Packers (10–1). Green Bay had completed its regular season a week earlier with a 22–17 decision over Washington for the team's eighth straight win. The Cardinals, of course, had nothing to lose in their final game except the opportunity to eliminate the rival Bears from title contention.

Ejected from the Game for Slugging

With the memory of the not-too-distant 53–7 whipping from the Bears earlier in the year still fresh, the Cardinals astounded the attendees by jumping out to a 14–0 lead in the second quarter: "A crowd of 18,879 sat in amazement as an embattled bunch of Cardinals led by Marshall Goldberg and Ray Mallouf and featuring a hard-charging line, outplayed the Bears and threatened to knock the champions right out of the title picture. With less than 10 minutes remaining, the Cards were ahead 24–21 and the Bears were acting like a beaten team. But then luck turned their way and the Bears, like the [baseball] Yankees, will knock another team's brains out if given as much as one break."[33]

As usual, the two teams engaged in some extended personal battles, including one incident that benefited the Cardinals in the first half: "The south siders were aided, too, by the over exuberance of the Bears, especially Ray 'Muscles' Bray, who was ejected from the game for slugging. After this show of pugilism, the Bears were assessed two more penalties in a row for unnecessary roughness, this loss of yardage putting the Cards down close enough for Bill Daddio to kick a field goal just before the half ended to put the Cardinals ahead 17–14. It also earned for the champions a chorus of lusty boos as they went to their dressing room at intermission time."[34]

The Bears did bounce back to secure a 34–24 win over the Cardinals and tie the Packers atop the Western Division. In victory, the Bears shared their admiration for the plucky fight put up by the Cardinals. Bears line coach Luke Johnsos stated: "The Cardinals played the greatest game of any Cardinal team I ever saw. If we play like that next Sunday against Green Bay, we'll win."[35] George Halas pointed to Jimmy Conzelman of the Cardinals and praised: "There is the man who did the best coaching job in the National league this season."[36]

The Bears' victory over the Cardinals necessitated the first "playoff" game since the NFL separated into two divisions in 1933. A week later, the Bears hosted the Packers and walked away with a 33–14 win, qualifying to meet the New Yorks Giants for the 1941 NFL championship on December 21. The title game, also at Wrigley Field, was almost an afterthought for the Bears (11–1) after battling the Cardinals and Packers, while the Giants (8–3) rested with just one game since November 23. However, the Bears brushed aside any concerns and rumbled over the Giants for the 1941 crown with a surprisingly easy 37–9 trouncing. It was the second straight title for the Bears and completed a lengthy season in which the club won 18 of 19 games, including exhibitions. Once again, the star power of quarterback Sid Luckman led the way as his pinpoint passing kept the Giants off-balance all afternoon. This was noticed even by the local New York press: "Of all the Bears there is just one who stands above the others. It's the Brooklyn boy Luckman. While he's at the helm the team does move ahead, relentlessly."[37]

The entire NFL was now in awe of the Bears, including the league office, which was surprisingly generous when dishing out accolades about the team in a press release following the title game: "The story of professional football in 1941 was the story of the Chicago Bears, a fabulous aggregation of artists who swept through a divisional playoff and the championship contest to establish themselves as the greatest team ever assembled."[38]

About the only thing to infringe on the joy of winning a second straight title for the Bears was the disappointing cash shares, which were based on the attendance at the title battle. The smallest Wrigley Field crowd (13,341) of the year was on hand to view the NFL championship game, thus dramatically decreasing the anticipated player shares for the championship honors: "Each member of the Bears collected only $430.94, considerably under the $606.25 that players on the losing Washington club drew in the 1940 championship game. Each Giant earned $288.70."[39]

Yet wins, losses, and shares meant little amid the harsh realities with the outbreak of World War II hostilities. The mayhem and destruction experienced in other parts of the world came home with the attack on Pearl Harbor on December 7, 1941. The surprise raid on Pearl Harbor in Hawaii took place during the Bears-Cardinals game: "Wave after wave of Japanese planes streaked across Oahu Island in an attack which the army said started at 8:10 a.m. Honolulu time, and which ended at around 9:25, an hour and 15 minutes later (at 1:55 p.m. Chicago time)."[40]

Participating players did not recall any formal announcement of the attack being made during the game, although there were several requests made for any military personnel to report to their units. Marshall Goldberg of the Cardinals later stated: "We found out about it after the game. We never thought it would happen. We were stunned. We didn't know what to think."[41] It was much the same story in New York, where the Giants were playing football's Brooklyn Dodgers. Center Mel Hein of the Giants recalled: "We knew something was going on because every few minutes during the game the PA announcer would call for some military person to report to his post. Then after the game the word came that the Japanese had bombed Pearl Harbor."[42]

The response of NFL players, coaches, and administrators to the war effort was overwhelming. Players from every team quickly joined the military, creating an immediate manpower shortage on the rosters of most clubs. Sadly, the Pro Football Hall of Fame reported on the casualties endured by League members through the course of the war: "World War II claimed the lives of 21 NFL men—19 active or former players, an ex-head coach and a team executive."[43] The former coach who bravely lost his life was Jack Chevigny, who was the head coach of the Cardinals in 1932. He was killed in the initial assault at Iwo Jima in 1945. The Bears lost promising quarterback Young Bussey, also in 1945.

Perhaps the most notable member of the Bears to volunteer for the military was George Halas, who had lamented that during his service in World War I, he had not seen any "action" due to his athletic duties with Great Lakes. In his autobiography, he wrote that he intended to reverse that experience: "The Japanese attack brought to the fore a commitment I had made to myself at the end of World War I. I had gone into the navy as a volunteer and asked for sea duty but the navy had assigned me to the sports program at the Great Lakes Naval Training Station, playing on the base teams and helping to coach football. On discharge I pledged myself that if another war came, I would get myself where the action was. The time had come to make good that commitment."[44]

Halas was called into service in the middle of the 1942 season at the age of 47. His last game with the Bears before departing for his assignment at Norman, Oklahoma, was a 45–14 blasting of the Eagles on October 25, 1942. He was caught off guard at halftime with the presentation of a sword by Lt. Commander Carl Olson of the naval aviation selection board. In response, Halas said: "This indeed is a complete surprise and I do feel honored by this presentation and I wish to thank my friends. As you all know, it is difficult to leave the Bears at this time, but nevertheless, I am looking forward to my naval duties. I hope I will be a credit to naval aviation."[45]

Maybe We Could Find Some Cardinal Spies

After making the necessary arrangements to provide for his family, his team, and the NFL, Halas was reactivated on November 1, 1942, to serve as a lieutenant commander. In doing so, Halas was leaving perhaps the most powerful squad in the history of the Chicago Bears. The team rolled through the 11-game season undefeated while averaging over 34 points per game. Two of those victories came at the expense of the Cardinals. At this point in time, the two Chicago rivals were headed in distinct opposite orbits. The Cardinals started off with a surprising 3–2 record before dropping their final six contests. The first of those losses was at Cleveland when the Rams took advantage of Cards quarterback Bud Schwenk by intercepting four of his passes. With that defeat, the Cardinals initiated the longest losing streak in NFL history, a drought that would cover 29 games and not end until the 1945 season. Meanwhile, the Bears would finish the 1942 schedule undefeated (11–0) and with a 16-game winning skein, the second longest at the time. But it all came crashing down in the 1942 NFL championship game when the Redskins surprised the Bears 14–6 to derail the Bears' two-year run as the NFL championship team. Sid Luckman later lamented the shocking defeat and the missing influence from Halas:

"We were beginning to think of ourselves as unbeatable. Coach Halas would never have allowed that. He always told us we must go into every game prepared to meet a superior team. We did not work as before. The inevitable occurred. We ceased being the champions."[46]

As usual, the two battles between the Bears and the Cardinals in 1942 (both won by the Bears) provided some unusual circumstances. Even publications outside the Chicago area, such as the *Dixon* (Illinois) *Evening Telegraph*, were struck by the jousting between the two NFL clubs in Chicago: "For naked unabashed bitterness no game in the league season after season and regardless of the situation, surpasses the annual meetings of the Bears and the Cardinals. It is civic pride—the north vs. the south—and as usual they'll get just as personal as the law allows."[47]

The buildup to the October 11 matchup was especially intriguing. The rejuvenated Cardinals were a respectable 2–1 at the time while the Bears entered the contest with a 2–0 mark. So, for the first time in eons, a game between the Bears and the Cardinals had championship ramifications, even this early in the season. Any meeting between the two local rivalries inspired spirited reactions, real or imagined. But this time the first pitched verbal skirmishes took place a few days before the kickoff when the two coaches waged a wacky war of words.

Conzelman started things off with a riveting tale about two "mysterious" figures who tried unsuccessfully to enter the Cardinals' practice facility at 83rd and Yates on Chicago's South Side but were rebuffed by the locked gates. Instead, they observed the practice and began to scribble furiously in their notebooks, documenting the plans and strategies of the Cardinals, or so said Conzelman. The coach then claimed that he chased the intruders, described as "big, broad-shouldered fellows, wearing top coats," who then jumped into a green car and sped away. But there was more, as reported by Edward Prell in the *Chicago Tribune*: "Conzelman said one of the Cardinal players obtained the license number and that the name and address of the owner was traced. Furthermore, said Conzelman, the car's owner is a friend of at least two Chicago Bears."[48] As expected, Halas was not amused at the hint of impropriety on his part and responded accordingly: "Ridiculous stuff! I haven't the slightest idea where the Cardinals practice and care less. We're too busy getting ready for Sunday's game to pay any attention to that. I guess maybe we could find some Cardinal spies around us if we looked hard enough."[49]

Once the game began on October 11, 1942, the Bears quickly swept aside the visitors from the South Side and scored a 41–14 victory. After the mirth of the spy episode, Halas and Conzelman were probably enjoying a cold one after the game and agreeing that perhaps the whole "misunderstanding" was worth it now that 38,426 crammed into Wrigley Field to witness the latest renewal of the city feud. The two alleged spies were never caught, unlike the Bears, who committed a few misdemeanors on the field: "The Bears were ready for this game, too. They were so overzealous that an alert group of officials penalized them 12 times for a total of 150 yards, a league record."[50]

But, within a couple of weeks, Coach Halas was off to the military and the Cardinals made a minor player transaction that no one really noticed. As an example of the means by which teams attempted to circumvent the player shortage, the

Cardinals had signed 19-year-old Ross Nagel from Maplewood High School in Missouri. Nagel appeared in just one game for the Cards before his release on October 26, 1942. After his brief tenure in the NFL, he entered the military and then became an All-American for St. Louis University following his service in World War II. Nagel also earned a spot on the 1951 New York Yankees pro football roster, but his small niche in Cardinal history remains. Nagel was likely the youngest person ever to play for the Cardinals.

Nagel's daughter, Toni Nagel Mason, shared some memories from her father's football career:

> We knew our dad played pro football at an early age, but just did not comprehend what that meant until we were much older. My dad talked about being recruited right out of high school, and then was called off to WWII. When he came back, he went to St. Louis University and played for the Billikens on the GI Bill. He is listed amongst those who played, stayed out the longest, and then came back after eight years. He also mentioned that they made a football card of him when he played for the Chicago Cardinals, but I have never been able to find one. He played linebacker and tackle and was a great punter as well.[51]

Coach Conzelman summed up his roster woes following the season when he had been forced to use the services of youngsters like Nagel and other untried players: "We opened the season with high hopes and wound up with yard rationing. At the start we had eighteen bouncing boys. Most of them are still bouncing!"[52]

Cardinals and Bears Consolidate?

By the time the 1943 season rolled around, the manpower shortages in the NFL were even more evident. Teams were having difficulty filling roster spots due to military commitments and the league itself began to shrink. The depleted Cleveland Rams actually took the year off. The NFL would downsize to eight teams by the time the season started and would be missing one very recognizable coach. On June 3, 1943, Conzelman decided to leave football and accepted a position with the St. Louis Browns baseball team. He stated: "I have resigned as coach of the Chicago Cardinals football team to accept what I believe to be an excellent opportunity in a new field."[53]

Conzelman's departure in June arose at an unusual time, with the baseball season already in full swing and football festivities about to begin. Conzelman may have chosen this window to explore other opportunities because it was becoming clear that the NFL was staggering toward the 1943 starting line. No team appeared to be well positioned, either financially or in terms of a competent roster. Speculation was rampant that the NFL was shaky and no team was safe from possible suspension of its football activities: "Consensus is that if the league decides to operate it will likely have to do so as a five or six club circuit. Even such a solid organization as the Bears may not be fielded for 1943 and Jimmy Conzelman's move to the St. Louis Browns certainly indicated all wasn't well for the Chicago Cardinals."[54]

The next league meeting would begin on June 19, 1943, to address both scheduling and membership status. But a week before then, more specific "news" was being released by interested media outlets, adding to the bevy of rumors drifting in abundance regarding the 1943 season: "The Chicago Bears probably also will be ready to go, perhaps by consolidating with the Chicago Cardinals. Whatever develops in pro football next fall, it is a foregone conclusion that the league will bear only a slim resemblance to the pro league of pre-war days."[55]

Initially, Cardinals owner Charles Bidwill scoffed at the idea of a merger with his biggest rival, which was apparently the suggestion of Art Rooney, the owner of the Pittsburgh Steelers: "He [Rooney] called me on the phone a couple of days ago and during our conversation suggested that we merge with the Bears. I answered him back, kiddingly, that it would be a swell idea. Maybe he took me seriously. I don't know how we would go about combining with the Bears. Each of us has a ball park and there would be other complications. And, what would the league say about it?"[56]

The *Chicago Tribune* indicated that the Bears were indeed receptive to the idea of merging with the Cardinals: "Ralph Brizzolara, acting general manager of the Bears, said he would be willing to talk over the proposed merger with Bidwill. Brizzolara thought it might be a good idea."[57] Not surprisingly, by the time the NFL meetings opened up on June 19, 1943, in Chicago, the Bears and the Cardinals petitioned for permission to merge for the 1943 season. The proposal was met with resistance from Washington owner George Preston Marshall as the league honchos parried over possible mergers between the two Chicago teams as well as with Pittsburgh and Philadelphia. The Chicago request was later withdrawn in the midst of some unusual backroom maneuvering: "Apparently because of the power that would be concentrated should the Cardinals and Bears consolidate, the league cut off their attempt by passing a rule forbidding the merging of player talent. Later, however, this was relaxed, allowing the Steelers and Eagles to pool their players but at the same time retain only a single vote in league affairs. The merger will be effective only for the 1943 season."[58]

According to the minutes from the June 19, 1943, meeting, the Chicago proposal was withdrawn shortly after 5:00 p.m.: "Mr. Conzelman withdrew Bear merger request and stated Chicago Cardinals would operate."[59] This was the same Jimmy Conzelman who had resigned as the head coach of the Chicago Cardinals earlier in the month, but anything was possible in the NFL during the turbulent days of World War II. With the Bears and Cardinals continuing to operate as separate entities in 1943, the NFL membership included just eight teams, including the recently merged Philadelphia Eagles and Pittsburgh Steelers (known as the Steagles).

Bronk Is Full of Business

Charles Bidwill eventually appointed longtime assistant Phil Handler as the new head coach for the Cardinals. For Handler, the dream job he accepted in 1943 would turn out to be a nightmare. The Cardinals dropped all 10 of their games and were rarely competitive. On the other side of town, the Bears also struggled to build a complete roster, but surprised everyone by bringing back 35-year-old Bronko Nagurski to serve on the line. Nagurski had left football after Halas refused to meet his salary requests after the 1937 season. Nagurski had then continued his career as a pro wrestler but was susceptible to the pleas of the Bears to return for the 1943 season. Team secretary Frank Halas (brother of George) enticed Nagurski back to the fold by assuring him his playing time would be limited to the tackle position, and not his old fullback slot. It was a remarkable acquisition for the Bears, since this would fill one of the bigger holes on the roster: "Bronk is full of business and taking his football comeback in the vigorous manner of a young Fuller Brush salesman tackling his first customer. He figures he can help the Bears and partly adjust the only weak spot in the present cast—at tackle. Asked if he desired to try his hand at fullback, Bronk said: 'I doubt if my legs would permit it. I've been off too long to get back there and take that pounding. As a tackle I'll be aiming at the fullback. If I am the fullback these big tackles would be aiming at me.'"[60]

With Nagurski back, the Bears, now under coaches Heartley "Hunk" Anderson and Luke Johnsos, roared through their schedule to compile an 8–1–1 record. Nagurski maintained his role in the line successfully but, due to team injuries, was coaxed into the backfield against the Cardinals in the last regular season game of the year on November 28, 1943. The Cardinals were 0–9 at this point but still posed a threat to the Bears, who were already assured of a spot in the NFL title clash. The surprising Cardinals jumped out to a 24–14 lead before Nagurski scored from one yard out and then proceeded to baffle the opposing defense with his hard-driving running style: head down, feet churning, and no stopping until he was lassoed by a swarming group of tacklers. Nagurski finished with 15 carries for 84 yards in the 35–24 win, prompting the following accolade from the defense: "As for Nagurski ... even the Cardinals shook their heads at the mere mention of his name, as so many other battered rivals have. 'He isn't 35,' an innocent blurted out. 'That guy's lying. He hits as hard and he's just as tough as that Nagurski of ten years ago.'"[61]

As another sign of the difficult times, eight of the 11 Cardinals' starters were on the field for the entire game. With another Western Division title in hand, the Bears earned the right to meet Washington for the NFL championship. The Bears flattened the Redskins 41–21 in the title match to grab the team's third crown in four years. In his final game, Nagurski scored one more touchdown in the rout.

We Were Terrible!

However, the manpower issue remained a distinct problem in 1944 and it finally began to whittle down the Bears' roster enough that there was a danger that the team might need to fold for the 1944 season. Luke Johnsos, co-coach of the Bears, recalled how bad the personnel situation had become in 1944 for the defending champion Bears:

> We lost 19 of our 28 players to the armed forces. Bulldog Turner joined the Air Force. George McAfee went into the Navy. Dan Fortman joined the Navy. Sid Luckman joined the Merchant Marine in Washington. For a while Admiral Land let him come to Chicago on weekends to play but then he was assigned to a tanker carrying gasoline in Europe, a risky job. During the Normandy invasion, he was on a transport ferrying troops from Britain to France. We held tryouts at Cubs Park and signed up anybody who could run around the field twice. We had players forty years old, fifty years old. We had a very poor ball club.[62]

When the possible merger between the Bears and the Cardinals failed to materialize in 1943, there was no hope that the two struggling Chicago teams might combine in 1944. Instead, the NFL softly announced that the Cardinals and the Steelers would combine forces for the 1944 season. Under the less-than-imaginative name of the "Card-Pitts," the team was a preseason favorite to claim a division title, at least according to Turk Edwards, the line coach of the Washington Redskins: "The war has been a great equalizer among pro teams, and any two teams which merge, no matter what their standing the preceding year, have a tremendous advantage."[63] Somewhere, somehow, that advantage disappeared as the Card-Pitts managed to drop all 10 of their games in 1944. The Cardinals' losing streak had now reached a suffocating 26 straight games with no end in sight. Although the 1944 Card-Pitt combination was certainly an aberration, the squad provided some humor and may have qualified as the worst team in the history of the National Football League!

Aside from dropping all 10 games, the Card-Pitts were outscored 308–108 and, unfortunately, led the league in two areas: most points allowed and most turnovers (53). Chet Bulger, a holdover from the Cardinals, recalled those ugly days: "We were terrible. You'd get beat so bad, you'd cry!" Lineman Vince Banonis added: "That was true. We got massacred every week."[64] With the Cards' Phil Handler and Pittsburgh's Walt Kiesling sharing head coaching chores, the team stumbled through

Johnny Grigas (#66) was vying for the NFL rushing title in 1944 for the Card-Pitts when he failed to show up for the last game of the season. Grigas was working on his feet full-time in a military supply company while practicing and playing pro football. In the end, he admitted that he was emotionally not ready to play. His actions forced the league to examine the mental, as well as the physical, aspects of a player's health (author's collection).

its schedule hopefully, but haplessly. After an opening-day 30–28 loss to the Cleveland Rams, the new combo team was unable to lose a game by less than 14 points all season. Week after week, the squad was getting drubbed and after a 23–0 loss to the New York Giants on October 22, 1944, the *Chicago Tribune* provided an insulting but accurate description of the squad that has managed to supersede the Card-Pitts name: "The Card-Pitts played the role of a red plush rug this afternoon as the undefeated Giants paraded over and past them for a 23–0 triumph in their home debut before 40,734."[65] And just like that, the Card-Pitts name evolved into the "Carpets"—insinuating that every other team in the NFL walked all over them!

He Finally Gave Up

One of the stranger escapades for the year occurred just before the final game against the Bears. Halfback Johnny Grigas had performed admirably for the Card-Pitts all season and was battling for the NFL rushing title, after leading the Cards in rushing the year before. He was a workhorse for the team and did double duty on both sides of the ball, as was usual for the time. In other words, he was on the field for just about every minute of every game. His plucky rushing efforts behind a patched-together offensive line resulted in an excellent performance on November 12 against the Detroit Lions. Despite still another loss, Grigas picked up 123 yards on the ground and took over as the NFL's leading rusher.

But on December 3, 1944, Grigas, for some reason, failed to show up for the final game of the season against the Chicago Bears. After taking part in the team's final practice session the day before in Pittsburgh, Grigas returned to his hotel room and teammate Don Currivan found him asleep later that evening. However, when Currivan awoke the next morning, Grigas was nowhere to be found, but he did leave a brief note. In it, Grigas wrote:

> Dear Don:
> Did not want to wake you up. Funny thing: everything seems so mixed up. I'm going home now. Can't change my plans. Take care of my bags. Best of luck. Johnny.[66]

As might be expected, Grigas was the object of derision and ridicule after the game, which was won by the Bears (6–3–1) 49–7. He was labeled a quitter and a coward in some corners of the media world, but eventually his side of the story opened some eyes. In a letter to the Cardinals management, Grigas explained that his departure, while perhaps not done in an ideal manner, was prompted by a combination of both physical and emotional concerns:

> My action for what I just did, may not be the best in regard to good, ethical business. Think what you may of me, but I sincerely believe that in all justice it is for the best. I had that desire, but how long a person can have any desire depends upon the frame of mind under which he plays. The human mind is the faculty of the soul, which is influenced by the human body. When your mind is changed because of the physical beating, week in and week out, your soul isn't in the game. My mind has been influenced this past week and I tried to stick it out, but it has reached the stage where the mind is stronger than the will. In all justice to the management and myself, I am leaving because I couldn't play the whole game. I played every game from start to finish and never said a word because it was my job.... I tried to win

and work hard, but the workhorse, as I was termed by the newspapers, is almost ready for the stud farm. In closing all I can say is that I'm deeply sorry—but there are things which can't be fully explained.[67]

For one of the first times in NFL history, the emotional side of a player's health was being considered. Grigas was beaten down physically by being almost the sole offensive provider for the Card-Pitts, but the mental side of this experience was also affected. Sports Editor Havey J. Boyle of the *Pittsburgh Post-Gazette* was quick to recognize this challenge: "Outside observers will go a little slow in putting the backfield star [Grigas] in the grease as a result of his action for certainly the tone of his letter indicated that whatever his physical condition for the final contest, he was not geared psychologically to give out with his best ... it might be well for the bosses to study the background of the whole situation before treating Grigas' case as one that is set out clear—either all black or all white."[68]

As more information became available, it became clear that Grigas had more on his plate than just the demands of football. His coach, Phil Handler, provided some additional insight a few weeks after the incident: "He worked days in a steel mill at a job where he had to stand all the time. The team practiced at night and because of the shortage of backs, Grigas had to work out both on offense and defense. Then Sundays he played sixty-minute football. The strain was too great, and he finally gave up."[69]

It now all added up. Grigas worked full-time, practiced daily, and rarely stepped off the field on game days. He then arranged for special train transportation so that he could report on time for work Monday morning where the company provided supplies for the military. Instead of derision, Grigas began to receive some applause. He was traded by the Cardinals to the Boston Yanks prior to the 1945 season and played three more years in the NFL but never approached his 1944 accomplishments, when he was named All-Pro, finished second in the league in rushing, and was first in all-purpose yards.

Seemed Like Some Prehistoric Monster

While the Bears were dethroned as NFL champions in 1944, the return of veteran players following the conclusion of World War II provided new hope for the immediate future for both Chicago teams. With the Cards looking to finally snap that lengthy losing streak and the Bears hungry to return to championship form, the 1945 season was critical, both in Chicago and elsewhere. Most important, the NFL had survived during the war years. Team mergers, player shortages, and unanticipated roster losses to the military were finally in the past. Yet both the Bears and the Cardinals were looking at a difficult climb back to contention. The Cards, however, were seeking only improvement and not the giant step over the rest of the division: "The Cardinals have been the collective 'little fellow' of the NFL the past two seasons ... everybody has kicked them around, with no quarter asked or given. So, it is more than a little zeal that [Coach Phil] Handler and Boss Charley Bidwill are actually looking forward to a football campaign instead of wishing it was over."[70]

Three opening defeats suffered by the Cardinals in 1945 stretched the NFL's longest losing streak to 29 games when the South Side contingent (0–3) prepared to face

Fifteen. Mergers, Titles, and Missing Halfbacks 265

Charles Bidwill, owner of the Chicago Cardinals, was an avid supporter of women's sports. He was also the owner of the Chicago Bluebirds of the National Girls Softball league. In this photograph, he is discussing an upcoming 1945 game with catcher Betty Moczynski (left) and pitcher Agnes Schlueter (right) (author's collection).

the Bears (0–2) on October 14, 1945. Coach Phil Handler was giddy over the potential of new quarterback Paul Christman, while a vastly improved Chet Bulger anchored the Cards line. Bulger had terrorized the Detroit Lions in a 10–0 loss on September 23, which was especially impressive since he broke his back against that same team in 1942 and his football future was in doubt. But he was back with a vengeance in the tight game against Detroit:

> Bulger saved the day. He played 60 minutes ... he was in and out of the Detroit backfield all afternoon. With a steady rain streaking the mud all over him in the final period, he must have seemed like some prehistoric monster to the desperate Lions. Five times yesterday he shook would-be Detroit blockers off his massive shoulders ... and in those five smashes he smacked down would-be Lion passers or runners for a total of 42 loss yards. As the [unnamed] scout said on Bulger's fifth trip into the Detroit backfield: "If they scored this game on Bulger's 'offense,' the Cards would be leading the league."[71]

Bulger, Christman, and two new running backs (Frank Seno and Leo Cantor) provided the spark as the Cardinals ended their 29-game losing streak with a satisfying 16–7 win over the stunned Bears before 20,784 at Wrigley Field. Cantor scored twice and the defense kept dangerous Bears quarterback Sid Luckman in check as the Cards grabbed their first victory since 1942. It was a brief respite for the Cardinals, however, as Handler's squad dropped its final six games to conclude the 1945 campaign with a 1–9 mark. The Bears struggled as well, finishing 3-7 after winning their final two games, including a 28–20 conquest over the Cardinals in the season finale. Before that game, Bears co-coach Luke Johnsos commented on the anticipated rough battle expected from the Cardinals: "I've never seen a Cardinal game, especially in Comiskey Park, which wasn't a rough one. Those fellows seem to save up all their best punches for us."[72] Over 50 games (including exhibitions) had now been played in the Bears-Cardinals rivalry. While the names would constantly revolve, the intensity between the two Chicago teams never wavered.

It's Like a Dream—a Bad Dream

As players slowly returned home from military service in 1945 and rejoined their former teams, one individual quietly slipped back to Chicago after enduring a horrific wartime experience. Mario "Motts" Tonelli had volunteered for the service in 1941, forgoing that season with the Chicago Cardinals. In early 1942 he was captured by the Japanese on the Bataan Peninsula and survived the brutal Bataan Death March, an over 60-mile trek under a blazing sun with little food or water. Tonelli, a former 210-pound fullback from Notre Dame, spent the entire war in captivity. When his camp was liberated on August 27, 1945, he weighed barely 100 pounds. After 42 months of incarceration, Tonelli arrived back in Chicago for further hospitalization and was still attempting to absorb everything that he had experienced when interviewed in October 1945: "He is the first professional football star to return to the gridiron from a prisoner-of-war camp. It marked a saga of determination and courage which even Tonelli doesn't yet realize. 'You know,' he frowned, 'even now—just two months away—I still can't remember (or want to remember) everything that happened. It's like a dream ... a bad one.'"[73]

Mario "Motts" Tonelli survived the Bataan Death March and 42 months in Japanese captivity during World War II. When he returned home after the war in 1945, Cardinals owner Charles Bidwill insisted that Tonelli sign a new contract with the organization, and he did appear in one game that season (author's collection).

Tonelli received a very welcome visitor when Cards owner Charles Bidwill visited him in the hospital. Tonelli later related the reason for the visit: "When Mr. Bidwill visited me in the hospital after my return from the war, he did something for me for which I will always be grateful. When he renewed my contract after the war, he provided me with a wonderful opportunity. Back in those days, under the rules of the NFL, you had to play both before and after the war in order to get credit for your pension for the seasons you missed during the war. I will always be grateful to the Bidwills. I owe them a lot."[74]

When the Cardinals dropped a 33–14 decision at Green Bay on October 28, 1945, Tonelli did make a brief appearance on defense, thus completing his return to the NFL and securing his future pension benefits. It would be the last game he would play with the Cardinals, but for Tonelli, his resilience, bravery, and determination will always mark him as one of the greatest of all Cardinals players.

Although the Cardinals managed to snap their 29-game losing streak in 1945, the three-year record under Coach Phil Handler was just 1–29. Handler was plagued by lack of talent and the merger with Pittsburgh during his tenure as head coach. In late 1945, Charles Bidwill announced that Jimmy Conzelman would return to coach the Chicago Cardinals for the 1946 season, although the trusted Handler would be retained as an assistant. Conzelman's job would be to meld the current roster with the abundance of experienced talent returning from the military, along with the surplus of draft picks now eligible for the professional ranks. Conzelman met those expectations by turning in a 6–5 record in 1946, the Cardinals' first winning season since 1937, when they finished 6–5–1 under Milan Creighton. Players such as end Billy Dewell, halfback Elmer Angsman, center Bill Blackburn, end Mal Kutner, tackle Stan Mauldin, halfback Marshall Goldberg, fullback Pat Harder, and quarterback Paul Christman were all on the Cardinals' roster and ready to continue the resurrection of the team in 1947.

Then Our Defense Cracked

On the North Side of Chicago, George Halas returned after 39 months in the service to take over the Bears. His roster blossomed with familiar names such as record-setting quarterback Sid Luckman, center Bulldog Turner, halfback Hugh Gallarneau, end Ken Kavanaugh, back George McAfee, and linemen Ed Sprinkle and Joe Stydahar. As usual, the two Chicago clubs would meet twice during the 1946 season with the first contest set for Comiskey Park on October 6. Ironically, it would be the first meeting between the two squads with both Jimmy Conzelman and George Halas on the sidelines since October 11, 1942. The Cardinals (1–1) erupted for a 17–7 lead early in the third quarter when Christman nailed Dewell with an 84-yard scoring pass, delighting the home crowd of 39,263. Luckman then directed his team (1–0) to a 34–17 victory by rallying for 27 points in the last 20 minutes of the game, leaving the Bears with a tough, but welcome, 34–17 decision.

The rematch was slated for December 1, 1946, at Wrigley Field. By that time, the Cardinals had fallen to 5–5 while the Bears were 7–1–1 and on their way to the NFL title game after clinching the division crown a week before. This was due, in large part, by the Cardinals' upset of the second-place Green Bay Packers 24–6 on November 24. The Bears rematch was the final game of the campaign for the Cardinals, and Jimmy Conzelman was anxious to reverse the results from the previous encounter even if the game would have no bearing on the final standings: "Our offense has worked well all year. We were ahead of the Bears 17–7 the first time we played them—then our defense cracked."[75] On the other side of the field, George Halas was hoping to avert a letdown from his troops: "They're in shape. It's time to find out whether they have the championship stuff they'll need later on."[76]

Although the Bears were heavily favored, the Cardinals pushed across a last-minute score to sneak past the Bears 35–28 in one of the more heart-stopping battles between the two teams. A crowd of 47,511 was jammed into Wrigley Field for the intracity squabble. When Joe Osmanski of the Bears danced into the end zone with just 55 seconds left to tie the game at 28 apiece, it was expected that Halas would rely on his sturdy defense to fashion a draw in this meaningless game. But it was, after all, the Bears and the Cardinals, and Halas risked a loss for the thrill of victory. On the ensuing kickoff, the Bears attempted an onside kick that was attacked from all sides at the 50-yard line. It took the officials a few minutes to sort out the pile before awarding the ball to the Cardinals. The Bears disagreed a bit too strongly regarding this decision and were assessed a 15-yard penalty, bringing the ball down to the Bears' 35-yard line. From there, quarterback Paul Christman succeeded on a 30-yard pass to Mal Kutner and followed that with the winning five-yard toss to Kutner. It took Christman just 41 seconds to steal the victory for the Cardinals.

The Bears bounced back to defeat Detroit 45–24 the following week, and then knocked off the New York Giants in the championship, behind the talents of Sid Luckman, before 58,346. This was the biggest audience up to that point to witness an NFL playoff game. Luckman was a gifted passer but a reluctant runner. In fact, he had carried the ball intentionally only once all season, but with the score tied 14–14 early in the fourth quarter, Halas unleashed a trick play where Luckman faked a handoff to George McAfee to the left side. As the entire defense forgot about Luckman and converged on McAfee, the quarterback bootlegged quickly around the unguarded right side and waltzed 19 yards into the end zone. The Bears, and Halas, grabbed their fourth—and final—NFL championship of the 1940s. The Bears were reborn with the return of Halas and winning the seventh title in team history. But with the rapidly improving Cardinals, and the league itself, would the Bears be able to continue that success in 1947?

As with the Bears, the Cardinals under Jimmy Conzelman were enjoying a renaissance as well, moving from 1–9 in 1945 to a vastly improved 6–5 in 1946. The team possessed a solid line, a dangerous quarterback, and a fleet of capable running backs. However, there was just one piece missing that might propel the Cardinals into the upper echelons of the NFL, and owner Charles Bidwill was determined to secure it. The object of his gridiron affection was halfback Charley Trippi, perhaps the most prized athlete on the collegiate level in 1946. But Trippi was no bright-eyed youngster. He would turn 25 during the 1946 season. Although he was still in college, Trippi served in the military during World War II, and then returned to the University of Georgia upon his discharge. The Cardinals had drafted Trippi as a "future" selection in 1945 (the year he would have graduated from college), but the team was happy to wait patiently for his arrival ... if Bidwill could sign him.

Aside from his extraordinary football talent (Trippi was named as the Maxwell

Fifteen. Mergers, Titles, and Missing Halfbacks

In 1946, the National Football League was threatened by the presence of the new All-America Football Conference. Plotting strategy at the NFL meeting in January 1946 were (from left) Harry Thayer, business manager of the Philadelphia Eagles; Jimmy Conzelman of the Cardinals; and George Halas of the Bears. The two leagues soon tired of the expensive bidding wars for players and merged in 1949 (author's collection).

Award winner in 1946 for being the best overall player in the country), he was also a potential superstar in baseball. In addition, the new professional All-America Football Conference (AAFC) also made the signing of Trippi a priority. So Bidwill expected plenty of competition in his quest to land Trippi from both Major League Baseball and a competing pro football league. It would be a tough, grueling process, but Bidwill was about to demonstrate his crafty negotiating skills. His opposition from the AAFC would be the New York Yankees, who wisely teamed up with baseball's New York Yankees to offer Trippi the opportunity to stay in New York and play professionally for both clubs. Trippi was now in the enviable position of being the hottest recruit in the country with the option of choosing both his preferred team and his preferred sport. Aside from the baseball Yankees, the Boston Red Sox also began contacting Trippi.

The New York football-baseball partnership made the first move and invited Trippi to visit the city and tour the facilities. His time in town was carefully monitored by the media, and the *New York Daily News* optimistically published an article predicting that Trippi would sign with the New York teams: "The most wanted athlete of the hour, All-America Charley Trippi of Georgia, is expected to sign a lucrative Yankee football-baseball contract sometime this morning. Trippi said late last night, following a three-hour conference, that 'I don't think we will have much trouble reaching an agreement tomorrow. The Yankees definitely gave me the best offer I have received and I simply want to talk things over with Wally Butts [Georgia coach] and several other people before signing.'"[77]

One of those "other people" alluded to by Trippi was Bidwill, who had secretly traveled to New York with Trippi. In fact, Bidwill had been actively following Trippi in his pursuit to land the Georgia star and met with him following the conference with the Yankees. In the end, Trippi announced that he would sign with the Cardinals, thus rejecting a generous offer from New York. Later, it became known that Trippi had agreed to join the Cardinals even before his visit to New York. Ray Benningsen, Bidwill's chief assistant, said of the surprise Trippi signing: "Nobody in the Cardinals organization had any contacts with Trippi outside of Charlie. It was his greatest victory. Yet, I knew every move in advance. During the time when he was carrying on his cross-country dickering with Trippi, I'd hear from him five or six times a day. He'd call from New York, or Florida, or New Orleans."[78]

Jimmy Conzelman added: "Bidwill had already bagged Trippi while Dan Topping [the New York owner] was putting on his hunting jacket and practicing bird calls.[79] Even the opposition enjoyed the success of Bidwill. Curly Lambeau, coach of the Green Bay Packers, sent Bidwill a telegram on January 17, 1947, which simply stated: 'Congratulations on signing Trippi! Great victory for our league.'"[80] Trippi's contract was worth an estimated $100,000 over four years, an unheard of sum back in 1947, but it allowed Bidwill not only to repulse the efforts of the new league but also add another valuable piece to his talented roster. With Trippi on the squad, Bidwill envisioned the potential of his dangerous backfield, which became known as the "Dream Backfield." Each of the four starters—quarterback Paul Christman (Missouri), fullback Pat Harder (Wisconsin), and halfbacks Marshall Goldberg (Pittsburgh) and Trippi (Georgia)—had been an All-American in college. Later Goldberg would switch exclusively to defense while Elmer Angsman of Notre Dame filled in superbly at halfback. The stage was set; the pieces were in place. Charlie Bidwill was about to enjoy the rewards of his ambitious efforts to rebuild the Chicago Cardinals and place the team in a position to finally capture an NFL title.

Then sadly on April 19, 1947, the energetic Charles Bidwill passed away. Bidwill had been suffering from a cold for a few days, which developed into bronchial pneumonia before he fell into a coma. His death was unexpected, especially at the young age of 51. The loss of Charles Bidwill would alter the landscape of the National Football League, especially in Chicago, where the carefully cultivated spirit of cooperation between the teams of old friends Bidwill and Halas would soon disintegrate into a sea of acrimony.

Sixteen

Windy City Warriors

> "It was rather awkward to have the key man in our key play getting into condition by sleeping in a chair every night."
> —Jimmy Conzelman, Chicago Cardinals Coach, 1947

It was only a few months after the passing of Charles Bidwill that the Chicago Cardinals began preparing for the 1947 season. The team would be loaded, as would the Chicago Bears, and several other clubs in the National Football League. It had been over 20 years since the Cards had won their last NFL crown, but Bidwill clearly developed a roster that would be exceptionally dangerous in 1947. Veteran Chicago sportswriter Bill Gleason lauded the efforts of the late owner: "Bidwill got smart during the war. He started squirreling draft picks and made some good ones. He already had Marshall Goldberg as his showcase man in the backfield. Then he added [quarterback] Paul Christman from Missouri and [fullback] Pat Harder from Wisconsin."[1]

Of course, the signing of Charley Trippi earlier in the year added to a backfield brimming with talent, including local product Elmer Angsman. A graduate of Notre Dame and Mt. Carmel High School on Chicago's South Side, Angsman was a favorite of both the fans and the Cardinals' coaching staff. Coach Jimmy Conzelman appreciated the speed, and the toughness, of Angsman, especially after learning of an incident during a game at Notre Dame in 1945. Notre Dame coach Hugh Devore reported that Angsman lost 11 teeth that afternoon but was not slowed down by the inconvenience: "Angsman illustrates pretty well what I've been trying to tell you about this team. He had the stumps of those eleven teeth yanked Tuesday morning, and that afternoon he was out there practicing and tearing around like nothing had ever happened to him."[2]

Conzelman was impressed with his roster, but also cognizant that he was not shepherding a bunch of schoolkids. Many on the team were military veterans who were not bothered by the harshness of the sport they played. Chicago writer Bill Gleason recalled: "Conzelman was a very colorful human being. He used to play the piano during team meetings. And don't forget, this was a team made up of war veterans, so playing football for money was very much a go-to-hell sort of activity for them. I can remember seeing some of them in the locker room with scars from bullets still visible from the war."[3]

The Chicago Bears had high hopes as well for the 1947 campaign after winning the

NFL title in 1946. The team did stumble, however, in the 1947 College All-Star Game, when the Bears fell to the collegians 16–0 before a record crowd of 105,840. It was a bit of an embarrassment for the NFL since the league champions had begun to distance themselves a bit from the All-Stars in previous engagements. This was the second straight defeat inflicted on the NFL titlists. The misfortunes of the Bears continued into the regular season when the club dropped a 29–20 verdict to Green Bay in the opener. Meanwhile, the Cardinals began their schedule with an impressive 45–21 walloping of the Detroit Lions before the two Chicago

Prowling the sidelines for the Cardinals in 1947 were head coach Jimmy Conzelman (left) and his assistant, Phil Handler. The two led the Cardinals to the NFL title in 1947, and Handler was also an assistant for the Chicago Bears when that team secured the 1963 championship (author's collection).

teams met in the second week of the schedule on October 5, 1947. It was a special day for the Cardinals as reliable veteran Marshall Goldberg was honored for his lengthy service to the team. Goldberg was the recipient of a new car by the team's fans while his fellow Cardinals presented Goldberg with the latest in 1947 technology: motion picture equipment.

Game films for this encounter would reveal a definite changing of the guard in Chicago professional football ranks. In the battle of quarterbacks, Paul Christman surpassed Sid Luckman to lead the Cards to a convincing 31–7 landslide over the Bears. The North Siders had scored first to grab a quick 7–0 advantage, before the Cardinals derailed what many thought would be still another blowout by the Bears:

> A crowd of 51,123, largest to witness a National Football League game in Chicago, expected to see a repeat performance by the Bears of old after that first period touchdown. As the game wore on, the thousands who expected the champions to get up off the floor after that defeat by Green Bay last Sunday, looked on in amazement as the Cardinals calmly followed their plotted course to victory. Yesterday's game was the old story of age and experience against youth, ability, and competitive spirit as exemplified by the Cardinals. Famous Bear backfield performers were out there, but age apparently had caught up with them.[4]

Christman passed for two scores and ran for another as the Cardinals peeled off 31 straight points to snare the victory. Rookie punter Jeff Burkett averaged 50 yards for each of his booming punts to constantly keep the Bears deep in their own territory throughout the afternoon. And, since it was a Bears-Cardinals clash, at least one player was ejected for misconduct. In this case, it was Bears lineman Mike Jarmoluk, who was dismissed from duty for kicking Charley Trippi! Now 0–2, were the 1947 Bears finished? Far from it, as the team under Coach George Halas then piled up eight straight wins before dropping a tight 17–14 decision to the Los Angeles Rams on December 5. The Cardinals, meanwhile, started with a superior 7–1 mark before surprisingly losing away games at both Washington and New York to fall to 7–3. However, the club rebounded with a convincing 45–21 destruction of the Philadelphia Eagles on December 7, setting up the final game of the regular season on December 14 against the Bears. Both Chicago teams were sporting 8–3 records, and the battle would be staged at Wrigley Field for the Western Division title and the right to advance to the 1947 NFL championship game.

It would likely be the most important encounter between the two clubs in the history of the NFL's oldest rivalry. Short of playing for the NFL title itself, this game would be for division honors, with the winner expected to emerge as the favorite over the eventual Eastern champion. Naturally, the entire city of Chicago was abuzz with excitement over the impending brawl. Since the NFL split into divisions in 1933, the Cardinals had never qualified for a playoff appearance. Meanwhile, the Bears' vaunted history included seven NFL titles, with four in the 1940s alone. With the recent eight-game winning streak, the Bears had proved that the powerful squad was not shedding any of its luster. Indeed, the North Side franchise was carefully maneuvering for its second straight NFL title. Both clubs were evenly matched by the end of the 1947 campaign, with the Bears earning a slight nod as favorites, owing primarily to their role as host in this important match.

We Would Use This Play at The Start

Well before game day, Cards coach Jimmy Conzelman was brimming with ideas on how to take advantage of certain habits within the Bears' defense. Nothing major; just an opportunity here and there that could possibly succeed only once before the Bears would initiate a quick remedy to avoid further danger. Conzelman, the wily veteran of three decades in the NFL as both a player and coach, spotted something that, if attacked early, could knock the Bears off-balance and perhaps lead to a quick score. From there, Conzelman hoped, the strength of the Cardinals team should be enough to hold off whatever George Halas might throw at his squad.

Conzelman's plan involved attacking what he perceived as a "slow" spot in the Bears' defense by moving his quickest back into position against a defending linebacker:

> They were stronger than we were. So, we thought we'd have to score first to have a chance. We studied our scouting reports, and they showed that one of the Bears' linebackers was not as fast as the others. We decided to devise a play that would run our fastest halfback—Babe Dimancheff—at such an angle that this particular linebacker would have to cover him. So, we designed a pass play, taking into account the defense our scouts said the Bears would use deep in our territory. Now, ideally, we would use this play right at the start, and that meant we were hoping to win the toss and elect to receive.[5]

Everyone on the coaching staff was certain that this play would work successfully with the right amount of practice and preparation. By the Tuesday practice before the Sunday game, the responsibilities of each player were explained and outlined. Conzelman wanted to ensure that everything was in place well before kickoff. However, a slight problem ensued when the key actor in the plot, Babe Dimancheff, failed to appear for practice. It turned out that his wife was expecting and Dimancheff was with her in the hospital. Conzelman was not worried, figuring a delay of one day in the rehearsal of the play would not be harmful. But then Dimancheff was not present on Wednesday, or Thursday, or Friday. Conzelman began to worry and talked with Babe on the phone and learned that Dimancheff was sleeping in a chair in his wife's room: "I said 'Have you got a room out there at the hospital, Babe?' The Babe said, 'No, coach, I'm sleeping in a chair.' I said that this game Sunday was pretty important to all of us and although I understood his feelings perfectly it was rather awkward to have the key man in our key play getting into condition by sleeping in a chair every night. He agreed that it was a shame."[6]

Conzelman never did pressure Dimancheff to leave the side of his wife (who delivered a beautiful baby girl) but was concerned if his strategy would work after only reviewing the basic fundamentals with Dimancheff prior to the game. But luck would be there for the Cardinals as they won the toss, elected to receive, and began the first drive on their own 20 as quarterback Paul Christman called the initial play. The plan was for Cardinals right end Mal Kutner to lure the left defensive back to the middle of the field, leaving Dimancheff in a one-on-one situation with the linebacker the scouts had identified. Right on cue, Dimancheff blasted past the defender and Christman hit him with a pass at the 40-yard line and Dimancheff streaked down the field unmolested for the opening touchdown in the Cardinals' 30–21 win: "The Bears never completely recovered from the shock of Paul Christman's 80-yard touchdown pass to Babe Dimancheff on the first scrimmage. And when they did exhibit intermittent flashes of their famed power, they shackled those efforts by penalty and by errors of judgement and execution. It was a north side crowd and the Cards have been also-rans for 22 years, which goes back to Paddy Driscoll's last season with Chris O'Brien's team."[7]

The "surprise" play was even a surprise to the one player who would carry it out. Babe Dimancheff later recalled his role: "My wife was in the hospital with a baby due, and I was with her all week. I never knew about the play. I guess the coaches were afraid to tell me because I might get nervous. I usually ran from left halfback, and they called me out at right halfback. I knew the plays, but nobody had told me anything about it."[8]

With the win, the Cardinals qualified to face off with Philadelphia on December 28, 1947, at Comiskey Park for NFL honors. The Eagles and the Giants tied for the Eastern Division lead so a special playoff was held on December 21, with the Eagles prevailing 21–0. Despite defeating Philadelphia twice during the year, including in the preseason, Coach Conzelman was wary of the invaders: "[Coach] Greasy Neale has a fine team. It's a lot stronger than most folks around credit it with being. The Philadelphia line rates as one of the best in the league."[9]

Eagles Were Wearing Very Unusual Cleats

Conzelman was aware that the Eagles utilized an unusual eight-man front line on defense and was confident that the Cardinals' attack could expose that line, even though Philadelphia's defense allowed the fewest yards in the NFL in 1947. Offensively, the Eagles relied on the passing of quarterback Tommy Thompson (106–211, 1,680 yards) and the timely rushing of Steve Van Buren. Yet it was that solid front wall of Philadelphia that might make or break the game for the Eagles, predicted *Pittsburgh Press* writer Les Biederman: "The six to eight man line the Eagles use may run into trouble for the first time. If the Cards start throwing short passes and force the linebackers to deploy a few yards to the rear, the Eagles will find themselves contending with the hardest runners in the league."[10]

In the days leading up to the championship game, Philadelphia coach Greasy Neale was optimistic that his club could reverse the recent trend of losses to the Cardinals *if* the Eagles could stop two of the opposing offensive threats: "First, we have to stop those passes of Paul Christman to Mal Kutner and Billy Dewell, and second, we must halt the hard-running Pat Harder. If we do that, and I say this sincerely and not hopefully, the Eagles will be the NFL champions."[11] Jimmy Conzelman, on the other hand, was somewhat pessimistic about his club's chances based on the personalities of his players: "The boys are working good. They feel fine. But they're not grim enough. That's a little frightening to me. We felt fine before we played Washington and we lost, 45–21. We were happy as clams before the New York game and we tumbled, 35–31."[12]

With weather reports indicating that below-freezing temperatures were imminent before game time, the Comiskey Park field was covered with 18 tons of hay underneath a tarp. The goal was to keep the field itself from freezing should temperatures drop further, which would make life challenging for the gifted Cardinal running backs if the turf was frozen. But freeze it did, and Conzelman quickly made the decision that the Cardinals would wear gym shoes on the frozen Comiskey Park turf. Meanwhile, in the Philadelphia locker room before the game, a ball boy from the Cardinals noticed that the Eagles were busy sharpening their cleats, a forbidden act in the National Football League. Conzelman recalled the discussions that followed:

> One of our locker room boys came in and told me the Eagles were wearing very unusual cleats. They were very long and they were filing them, he said. One of our owners got all excited and wanted to go to the commissioner. I calmed him down and told the players what to do. Right after the kickoff one of our men grabbed an official and pointed to one of the Eagles. The official looked at the player's shoes and walked off a five-yard penalty. We did the same thing on the next play and the next. Well, pretty soon Greasy [Neale] called the players off the field and they changed the shoes right there.[13]

Sure, it was a bit of gamesmanship by Conzelman, but the early penalties appeared to disrupt the Eagles' offense. Meanwhile, the Cardinals attacked the eight-man defense quickly and effectively as Charley Trippi broke through and scored on a 44-yard run in the first quarter. Then in the second period, Elmer Angsman zipped through an opening and added a 70-yard touchdown run to provide the hosts with a 14–0 advantage. While the Eagles whittled that down to 14–7 at the half, thanks to a long touchdown pass by Philadelphia quarterback Tommy Thompson to Pat McHugh, the Cardinals were back at it in the third stanza. Charley Trippi fielded a punt at his own 25 and raced through the defense to push the lead to 21–7 with his 75-yard return. Steve Van Buren scored on a one-yard plunge later in the period before Angsman broke away on his second 70-yard scoring jaunt of the day to extend the lead to 28–14. Philadelphia scored one more time in the final period to close the gap to 28–21 but could get no closer. Finally, after 22 years, the Chicago Cardinals reigned as the undisputed NFL champions!

In the locker room, assistant coach Phil Handler, who had guided the team through the ugly Card-Pitts experience, was ecstatic: "How did you like what we did to that line? We put in special blocking last week. Just wanted to show those guys we could run through their eight-man line."[14] Years later, Angsman described the situation on the field: "Half the time, we had the linebackers going one way when we were carrying the ball the other way. We ran a lot of misdirection and trap plays. We two-timed Eagle nose tackle Bucko Kilroy, trapped the tackle, and I gave a little stutter step and ran smack up the middle."[15]

Happiness was found all over the South Side of Chicago, which wildly embraced

Three stars for the Chicago Cardinals during the championship season of 1947 were (from left) Elmer Angsman, Billy Dewell, and Marshall Goldberg. Dewell topped the NFL in touchdown passes (seven) and average receiving yards (23.8) in 1946 (author's collection).

the new champions. Perhaps the most lasting, and exuberant, comment regarding the win was from Cardinals President Ray Benningsen: 'Ray Benningsen, Cardinals' president, sat on one of the uniform trunks and glowed like a sunrise. 'How did it feel, Ray?' a reporter asked, and Benningsen said: 'I can tell you in two words: Wonderful!'"[16]

The satisfying victory helped offset two tragedies suffered by the Cardinals during 1947. Of course, the passing of owner Charles Bidwill was a devastating loss that was recognized throughout the country: "For 15 long, disappointing years, the late Charles Bidwill threw all of his financial resources into the business of developing a team capable of giving the Chicago Bears real competition, but he died before realizing his hope."[17] With the big win over the Eagles, the dreams, work, and dedication of Charles Bidwill were finally realized. Even in victory, however, the thoughts of the tight-knit group of Cardinals were never far from the family of Jeff Burkett. The rookie punter actually led the NFL in that category after the first three games (all Cardinals victories) with a 47.4 average. The following week (October 19), the team took the long train ride to Los Angeles, primarily because Coach Conzelman was not fond of flying cross-country.

During the train ride, Burkett began to feel some stomach discomfort that was diagnosed as appendicitis. When the club arrived in Los Angeles, Burkett underwent an appendectomy on Saturday, October 18, and thus missed the game with the Rams, which the Cardinals dropped 27–7 to snap the early season undefeated streak at three. When the Cards departed town on Monday, October 20, Burkett requested permission to join his teammates for the ride back to Chicago. His doctors denied the request and Burkett reluctantly agreed to remain in Los Angeles for a few more days of recuperation before taking a flight back to Chicago. On Friday, October 24, Burkett boarded a United Airlines DC-6 for the nonstop trip to Chicago. Sadly, the plane never made it, crashing into Bryce Canyon (Utah), and all 52 on board were lost. Burkett's ability and personality would be missed by the Cardinals, both on and off the field. Harry Sheer of the *Chicago Daily News* wrote: "Burkett was not only the most promising rookie in the Cardinal entourage, with the possible exception of Charley Trippi, he

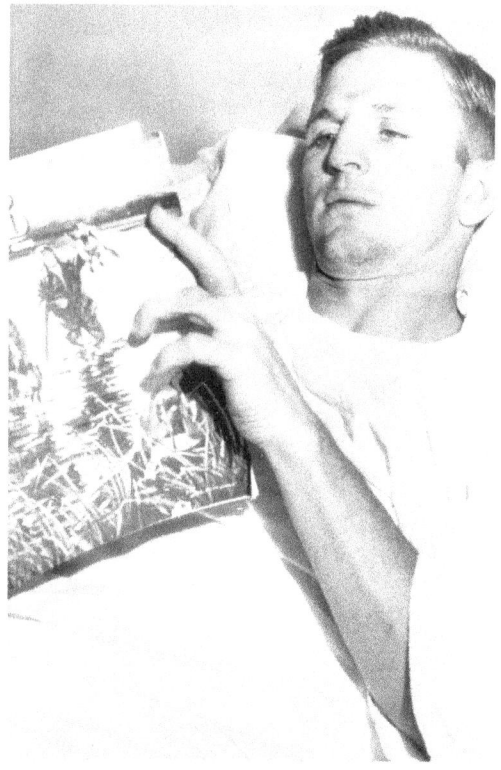

Jeff Burkett was the leading punter in the National Football League early in the 1947 season. Sadly, Burkett passed away in a plane crash in Bryce Canyon, Utah, after missing the Cardinals' team train from Los Angeles due to an appendicitis attack. This is the last known photograph of Burkett (author's collection).

was a pepper pot, a fiery competitor, a typical 1947 Cardinals. There hadn't been a punter in recent National Football League history like Burkett.... He was averaging 47.4 yards in the top football circuit in the world, He was developing into a dangerous end, a hard-playing, deadeye defensive halfback ... obviously into future stardom."[18]

After the championship win over the Eagles, the Cardinals divided the winner's share of the proceeds, with each team member, including the widow of Jeff Burkett, receiving $1,132.47. But the Cardinals were not done yet. As the prize for capturing the 1947 NFL title, the Cardinals would now represent the league in the next annual preseason battle with the College All-Stars. Since the NFL champs had dropped the previous two contests, there was some pressure on both Conzelman and the Cardinals to not only win the All-Star game but to win it convincingly in order to uphold the honor, and superiority, of the professional clan. The 1948 game would bring together two of the most gifted coaches in the business: Jimmy Conzelman of the Cardinals and Frank Leahy of Notre Dame. Early on, Leahy paid his respects to the defending NFL champs and their capable backfield: "I read recently that the Cardinals last fall literally burned up the grass at Comiskey Park by the roots with their great speed and I surely hope Jimmy Conzelman will slow them down a bit on August 20."[19]

Mother Had a Dream

Even though the All-Star game was technically a preseason affair, the publicity and nationwide interest in the contest might be compared to today's Super Bowl.

During the summer of 1997, the Chicago Cardinals reunited to celebrate the 50th anniversary of the team winning the 1947 NFL title. Each player was presented with a championship ring in honor of their accomplishment. From left: center Bill Blackburn, halfback Elmer Angsman, and former team owner Stormy Bidwill (author's collection).

In a twist of irony, a rivalry had been born between players who had never seen each other before and teams that tended to change each year. Still, the continual argument over whether the pros or the collegians were superior still existed. With the NFL taking a bath from the college upstarts in 1946 and 1947, the reputation of the professionals was beginning to quiver.

Interest in the game was so strong for the game on August 20, 1948, that all seats were sold a month before and 101,220 were in attendance, the biggest crowd to ever watch the Cardinals in the United States. In addition, the contest attracted one of the biggest television audiences to date: an estimated 500,000 viewers: "Television's largest Midwest audience saw WGN-TV's broadcast of the All-Star football game. It was a smash hit. An estimated half a million persons saw the game. All over the city and suburbs, radio, appliance, and furniture stores put sets in the windows. And the crowds that gathered on the sidewalks forced passing pedestrians to detour to the streets. Many set owners reported that at a tense moment, telefans forgot it was a picture and began to yell just as they would at the game."[20]

The Cardinals made quick work of the All-Stars as Elmer Angsman scored from two yards out in the first quarter and Vic Schwall added a 14-yard touchdown in the second period for a 14–0 halftime advantage. Before the game, Schwall predicted a victory for the Cardinals based on a reliable source: "We haven't a thing to worry about. Mother had a dream about our winning the game. Her dreams never miss."[21] Lineman Vince Banonis and Charley Trippi added the Cards' two final scores in the fourth quarter. Banonis returned an interception 31 yards and Trippi was on the receiving end of a Ray Mallouf pass to complete the decisive 28–0 win.

In 1948, the Cards were simply the best edition in the history of the franchise, conquering nearly all comers with an 11–1 record and capturing another Western Division title. Beginning with that impressive win over the College All-Stars on August 20, the Cardinals were almost unstoppable.

A 28–17 loss to the Bears in the second game of the season was the only blemish on the Cards' record during the regular season in 1948. It was a rare Monday night game at Comiskey Park when the two heavyweights squared off in still another robust battle. But the hearts of the Cardinals family members were heavy since it was the first game since tackle Stan Mauldin passed away in the Comiskey Park locker room after a season-opening 21–14 win over the Eagles. Mauldin complained of being dizzy after taking a shower and collapsed. Medics worked for two hours to revive Mauldin but he was dead at age 27. Clubhouse attendant Jim Muting was in the locker room when an apparent heart attack took Mauldin: "It was a shocking thing to see. They didn't let us get too close, but he was dead when he hit the floor."[22] Fullback Pat Harder, the NFL's Most Valuable Player in 1948, simply said, "He was the best tackle in the National League."[23]

In the Bears game, the Cardinals fell behind 14–0 before rallying to grab a 17–14 lead. Frank Minini then returned a Cardinals kickoff 95 yards to put the Bears ahead for good as they snared a 38–17 victory in front of another record crowd of 52,765. The Cardinals then reeled off 10 straight wins to finish 11–1, still the best record in team annals. During a midseason four-game offensive extravaganza, the Cards put away the New York Giants 63–35, the Boston Yankees 49–27, the Los Angeles Rams 27–22, and the Detroit Lions 56–20 in one of the foremost offensive explosions in team history, netting nearly 50 points per game during that stretch. Yet the Bears were no slouch, either, losing only a mid–October game to the Eagles 12–7 to keep pace with the Cardinals all season. When the two rivals met in the final regular season game at Wrigley Field on December 12, 1948, both clubs entered with 10–1 records and the winner would advance to the NFL title game. With two such exemplary representatives, Chicago was truly the centerpiece of pro football in 1948. As it was in 1947, the final game between the two gridiron beasts attracted substantial interest around the country. In Wisconsin, columnist Henry McCormick attempted to explain to his readers why fans in Chicago would sit in frigid temperatures to watch this particular game: "The game is a complete sellout and has been for some time, and any persons who wish to dispose of their tickets can do so at a fancy price in spite of the fact that the weather promises to be of the kind that would endanger the health of a bronze statue. The Bears-Cardinals thing is something different. This is one of the red-hot, spine-tingling rivalries of professional football."[24]

With everything at stake, the Bears quickly moved ahead 14–3 at the half in a duel that pitted the NFL's best offense (Cardinals) against the league's top defense (Bears). But in this game, those strengths seemed to evaporate as the Bears rambled for 240 yards in the first half while limiting the Cardinals to a paltry 64 yards of total offense. After the game, Coach Conzelman admitted that his players needed just a touch of guidance after the discouraging first half when the Cards trailed by 11: "I had to get the boys unwound. An odd situation, I must admit. But in that first half they were too steamed up. I told 'em to relax and if they settled down in the second half the Bears might make some mistakes. That's what happened."[25]

The first error occurred when the Bears failed on an onside kick to open the second half, allowing the Cardinals to score in just three plays, culminating in Pat Harders's three-yard touchdown. Behind sensational rookie quarterback Johnny Lujack (15–24, 237 yards passing), the Bears came right back and scored early in the fourth period to extend the lead to 21–10. With 51,283 watching, the Cardinals then mounted an incredible comeback with reserve quarterback Ray Mallouf at the helm. Starter Paul Christman had suffered an injury earlier in the game, thus yielding to Mallouf, who patiently led the Cardinals to two scores in the fourth quarter to secure a 24–21 lead. Then, in a bit of a surprise, the hot-handed Lujack was replaced at quarterback for the Bears by the dangerous, but aging, Sid Luckman. Luckman proceeded to march the Bears downfield for a chance at victory but threw an interception to defensive back Johnny "Red" Cochran to extinguish any hope for the Bears. Cochran's theft secured the Cardinals' 24–21 win and the 1948 Western Division title. Later, Cochran, who enjoyed a long coaching career in the NFL, remained in awe of Conzelman and his subtle ploys to inspire his team, such as the request to "relax" at halftime of the Bears game: "Playing for Jim was a lark. Whenever I speak to young coaches at clinics, I tell them about Conzelman because I consider him a master psychologist who could get the most out of a player without having to drive it out of him."[26] The 1948 Western Division title game proved to be an exciting and memorable affair for both the fans and the media: "The game was as near perfection as possible in football: vicious line play, crisp blocking, and heady signal calling. It was so close that the huge audience seldom was off its feet."27

In the 1948 finale, the Bears and the Cardinals had delivered another solid effort, but unfortunately, it would be the last game between the two that would be played with playoff consequences while both teams remained in Chicago. But in December 1948, the Bears packed their bags for the off-season while the Cardinals prepared for a rematch of the 1947 championship battle with the Eagles, only this time it would be played in Philadelphia.

Wound Up with My Face Buried in Snow

The 1948 title game turned out to be one that was never forgotten by anyone who was there, especially the players. It turned out to be more than a football game, although certainly some form of football was on display that day. Still, when one mentions the 1948 NFL title tilt on December 19, 1948, a follower of the Cardinals might wince. Just a little. The Cards were deemed as the favorites by most observers, based primarily on the team's victorious effort over the Bears the week before. And, once again, they had defeated the Eagles handily in the opening game of the season. But ever the pessimist, Coach Jimmy Conzelman would only admit: "We are a little tired from the Bears game last Sunday. I really fear the worst."28 On the other side, Philadelphia coach Greasy Neale was careful not to provide any bulletin board material when he was asked about his opponents: "Those Cardinals are a fine team," was all he said.29

Coach Jimmy Conzelman of the Cardinals reacts in excitement as the Cardinals grab a 24–21 win over the Bears on December 12, 1948. The victory gave the Cards the Western Division championship. Assistant coach Buddy Parker is on the left. The battle at Wrigley Field in Chicago was attended by 51,283 (author's collection).

The Eagles (9–2–1) were loaded on offense again with Tommy Thompson reigning as one of the top signal callers in the league and halfback Steve Van Buren returning as the NFL's leading rusher. The Cardinals (11–1) had knocked off the Eagles five straight times, but the final bout of the 1948 season was expected to be close. Although the weather in Philadelphia was unseasonably warm just prior to the game, both coaches were keeping an eye on the forecast, particularly the threat of a graupel, which was explained by Wilfrid Smith of the *Chicago Tribune*: "Wednesday [December 15] Philadelphia had its deluge of graupel—the weather bureau's technical name for a combination of rain, hail, and snow. The storm disrupted traffic, grounded planes and delayed trains, and sent the football players indoors."[30]

Indeed, the weather did play a key role in the outcome of the 1948 championship game—a huge role. Snow began falling during the night before the game and did not ease up, draping the city of Philadelphia, and Shibe Field, with several inches of the white stuff. Neither team was certain that the game would be played, or even if it should have been played. But one of the more splendid sights, and one that will never be duplicated, was that both teams helped clear the field of snow before the NFL title game: "In an afternoon of amazing happenings, the players joined a ground crew of 50 to help slide the protective tarpaulin from the turf. They tugged at the heavy canvas while the fans chanted a methodical 'heave-ho.'"[31]

With the heavy accumulation of several inches continuing in an unrelenting fashion, both teams agreed to specific ground rules for the game. Since yardage markers, and the field itself, were covered by snow, the clubs agreed to trust the judgment of the referee on ball placement and first downs. Extra officials were corralled to stand on the sidelines and in the end zone to serve as an indication of the field of play. Once the game began, it was clear that the ensuing battle would be a comedy of errors with slippery footing, impossible passing conditions, and limited visibility. It would likely come down to a lucky break to determine the winner, and that's exactly what happened. An errant fumble by the Cardinals on their own 17 early in the fourth period led to the only score of the game, a five-yard rumble by Steve Van Buren, as Philadelphia claimed its first NFL title by the score of 7–0. Afterward Van Buren described the conditions of the game: "Cold! I'll never get warm again. And it seems that every time they tackled me, I wound up with my face buried in the snow."[32] Ever gracious in defeat, Jimmy Conzelman stated: "We knew a break would win the game. The Eagles got it and capitalized. They outplayed us and the better team on the field won."[33]

Sadly, the game now known as the "Snow Bowl" would turn out to be the last game ever coached by Jimmy Conzelman. The 1948 season was a long, arduous journey for Conzelman. It began with the early start to training camp in preparation for the College All-Star Game and through the tightness of the Western Division race with the Bears, and then still another team tragedy suffered by the Cardinals with the death of Stan Mauldin. Since Conzelman first joined the team in 1940 after the Cards won just a single game in 1939, he brought the Cardinals into the NFL spotlight with back-to-back title game appearances during his second stint (1946–1948) with the club. Not surprisingly, he was selected for induction into the Pro Football Hall of Fame in 1964.

His resignation on January 7, 1949, came as a surprise to the Cardinals organization, since the team was expected to remain a contender for the NFL title in 1949 under Conzelman. There was still a year left on his contract at an impressive $25,000 per year. Team owner Violet Bidwill said: "I am sorry to see Jim go. When he left Chicago at the end of the season he did not indicate that he would not return. His resignation has come so suddenly that naturally we have no idea who will succeed him."[34] But Conzelman apparently had enough, explaining in his resignation letter that family was foremost in his future: "It has become increasingly difficult the last few years to take my family back and forth between St. Louis and Chicago. The situation has not been helped by having a school age son as part of that twice-a-year change. Because I think that it is about time that I take root in one locality, I have decided to tender my resignation as coach of the Chicago Cardinals. I have decided to tender my resignation effective January 12, 1949, and to take a job with the D'Arcy Advertising Company."[35]

Among others shaking their heads in disbelief that Conzelman would retreat from football was Cardinals President Ray Benningsen, who wondered: "Will he be happy out of football?"[36] Conzelman never would return to the NFL, perhaps answering the innocent query of Benningsen. Whether Conzelman was completely happy or not would be difficult to determine, although he continued to be in demand as a prized after-dinner speaker. But would the Cardinals, in turn, be "happy" or even competitive without their old coach? Following the bright lights of the Conzelman era, the Cardinals experienced a decade of disdain, confusion, and losing as the fearsome championship roster quickly disappeared. About the only thing that went well for the Cards in the post–Conzelman years was the persistent ability to defeat the Bears! The rivalry between the Bears and the Cardinals continued into the 1950s, but under totally different circumstances.

Seventeen

The Last Hurrah

"The Cardinal game has always been a nightmare for us, and I guess it always will be."—George Halas, November 26, 1959

Maybe it was a right jab? Or perhaps a right cross?

Whatever it was, it quickly ended one of the more storied of the many on-field brawls that marked the long, intense rivalry between the Cardinals and the Bears. On December 16, 1951, Hall of Famer Charley Trippi of the Cardinals decked Bears Hall of Famer Ed Sprinkle, known at the time as the "meanest man in football." Sprinkle had been in Trippi's face the entire afternoon and Trippi finally called a halt to the proceedings. "Trippi knocked out the Bears' Ed Sprinkle with a terrific swipe late in the game," reported Edward Prell of the *Chicago Tribune*. "He was tossed out for this act, but what he had done to the Bears was beyond repair."[1]

Following the death of Charles Bidwill in 1947, the rivalry between the two Chicago clubs accelerated immensely as the players clashed on the field while the owners did likewise off the turf. Neither team generated enough firepower to claim an NFL championship during the 1950s, but both embraced the opportunity to beat the heck out of each other during the decade. Surprisingly, even in a downward spiral for most of the 1950s, the Cardinals were usually competitive in their outings with the Bears, often getting the best of the match, much to the chagrin of the Bears organization.

Then, with the departure of coach Jimmy Conzelman following the 1948 season, the confusion in the Cardinals' front office was apparent as two coaches were hired in 1949 to maintain the recent glory of the team. The double coach pairing didn't work for the winless Card-Pitts in 1944, and it didn't work for the Cards in 1949 as the team slid to 6–5–1 under head coaches Buddy Parker and Phil Handler. While this uneasy experiment failed, the Cards took another step backward in 1950 by naming estranged Packers founder and longtime coach Curly Lambeau to lead the team. Lambeau's reign on the South Side lasted less than two seasons as the team continued to slide further back in the standings, finishing 5–7 in 1950 and 3–9 in 1951. Lambeau was long gone by the time the Bears and the Cardinals squared off in the final game of the 1951 season. For some strange reason, the Cards were ensconced in a brief period of domination over the Bears, and the 24–14 spanking of the Bears to conclude the 1951 schedule would be the third of four straight victories for the Cardinals over the North Siders in an unseemly change of direction for the competing clubs.

Seventeen. The Last Hurrah

Before he knocked out Sprinkle, Trippi was the dominant force for the Cardinals (2–9) in that upset over the Bears (7–4) in December 1951: "That old Eskimo from Georgia and Pennsylvania, Charles Louis Trippi, was the hottest person, man, woman, or child, in Wrigley Field, a refrigerator registering one below zero. In his greatest pro afternoon, he ran 13 times for 145 yards, scored two touchdowns, and passed for the other one in completing nine of 20 pitches for 106 yards in a 24–14 triumph."[2]

Despite his heroics lugging the ball, all anyone wanted to discuss after the game was Trippi's quick KO of Sprinkle, and his teammates were prepared to assist Trippi with any fiscal punishment that might be imminent for his fistic activity: "A movement was started by the Cardinals for a 'Five Dollar Club.' The dues, of course, would be turned over to Trippi to pay the $50 fine, automatic for an athlete who strikes an opposing player and is thrown out of the game."[3]

For Trippi, there was no regret for his action: "It was worth it," he said.[4]

As the Cardinals finished 3–9 in 1951, it was a steep drop from the 11–1 record as recently as 1948. The resignation of Coach Conzelman after the 1948 season was impactful, as was the retirement of All-Pro Marshall Goldberg following the 1948 campaign. Quarterback Ray Mallouf, who expertly handled the offense when Paul Christman was injured, was traded to New York in 1949, while Christman himself was traded to the Packers in 1950. Star end Billy Dewell retired after the 1949 season and invaluable tackle Chet Bulger, a member of three All-Pro teams, signed with

Quarterback Jim Hardy hands off to halfback Elmer Angsman during a 1951 Cardinals practice at Stagg Field in Chicago. Other Cardinals in the backfield (from left) are fullback Pat Harder and halfback Charley Trippi. Hardy took over as the team's quarterback after new coach Curly Lambeau traded Paul Christman to the Green Bay Packers (author's collection).

Detroit for the 1950 season before retiring. Dewell caught 177 passes for the Cardinals during his career and led the NFL in receiving touchdowns (7) and yards per reception (23.8) in 1946. Center Vince Banonis, a three-time All-Pro with the Cards, was also traded to Detroit in 1950 and won two more NFL titles while with the Lions. Another acquisition by Detroit in 1951 was fullback Pat Harder, the 1948 league MVP, who topped the NFL in scoring for three years (1947–1949) while also being named to six All-Pro teams. All in all, the glory years of the Chicago Cardinals in 1947 and 1948 vanished quickly amid player departures and coaching changes. The decade of the 1950s was not kind to the Chicago Cardinals. The team would spin through five different head coaches who combined for a meager 33–84–3 record from 1950 through 1959. In six of those seasons, the Cards would win three games or less. Things were so tough that only the 1956 team (7–5) would escape the season with a winning record. For the decade, the Cards managed a winning percentage of just .288, likely the lowest of all time (for a decade) in NFL history and solely occupied (or tied) for last place in the division seven times…

I Prayed and Then Called George Halas

The status change of the Chicago Bears was less discernable as the team finished with 9–3 records in both 1949 and 1950, both good for second place in the Western Division. It was also time to say goodbye to the amazing Sid Luckman, who retired following the 1950 season after revolutionizing the passing game in the NFL. Luckman was an All-Pro five times and led his team to four NFL titles, all while taking time out to serve in World War II. Joining Luckman in retirement in 1952 (and also inducted into the Pro Football Hall of Fame) was longtime center and linebacker Clyde Douglas "Bulldog" Turner. Turner joined the Bears as a rookie in 1940 and quickly became the starting center. One of his biggest thrills was intercepting a pass and returning it for a touchdown in the 73–0 rout of Washington in the 1940 championship game. Like Luckman, Turner was a part of four NFL titles with the Bears and was named to All-Pro teams in eight seasons. Turner retired in 1952 but was always the subject of countless stories regarding his escapades during his NFL career. Although the two often clashed over contract details, there was a mutual admiration between Bulldog Turner and George Halas. Turner once commented on his relationship with his coach: "Oh, I've heard all the stories. I guess old George must have been a little bit of a Jekyll and Hyde. He was always great to me. I used to tell people that when I got in trouble, I prayed to the Lord and then called George Halas. Halas usually answered first!"[5]

Probably the biggest change in the league, and one that certainly affected the Bears-Cardinals rivalry, was the "merger" in late 1949 of the NFL with the competing All-America Football Conference. The latter league, founded by Arch Ward of the *Chicago Tribune* (the impetus behind the Major League All-Star Game and football's College All-Star Game), began play in 1946. By the end of the decade, the battle over players and the resulting salary concerns forced the NFL to grudgingly recognize its counterpart. In his autobiography, George Halas offered a different viewpoint: "By 1949 everyone was hurting from the bitter competition. Raiding was cutting into team morale. A team could carve the heart out of a player in the rival league by offering him a lot of money even though it had no intention of hiring him. In 1950, the American Football Conference folded. We took in Paul Brown's Cleveland Browns, the San Francisco '49ers and Baltimore. Again, we were a united league, with thirteen teams, coast to coast."[6]

League bosses toyed around with names for the new endeavor, like the National American Football League and the North American Football League, before retreating to the more familiar National Football League in early 1950. There was a significant change in the alignment of the new circuit's 13 teams that affected the rivalry of the Chicago teams. Instead of the previous Eastern and Western Divisions, the two sections would be known (albeit temporarily) as the National and the American Conferences. With the new setup, the Cardinals would be sent to the American Conference while the Bears were placed in the National Conference, an eye-opener that was addressed by the *Green Bay Press-Gazette*: "It can be noticed that the rivalries of the two big towns—New York and Chicago—are in separate divisions. This idea seems to have been patterned after baseball—the Chicago White Sox and Cubs—to create separate interest and thus form a natural 'world series' atmosphere. Bears coach George Halas is understood to be disinterested in such a setup since he would like to continue the two-game series with the Cardinals. Card Prexy Ray Benningsen agrees with Halas."[7]

In 1949, the two encounters between the Chicago teams attracted crowds of 52,867 and 50,101, wonderful numbers for a cash-challenged league. The separation of the two due to the new conferences meant that after the 1952 season, following three decades of playing at least twice per year against each other, the Bears and the Cardinals would enjoy just a single meeting every year. The attendance numbers for Bears-Cardinals battles would remain strong during the remainder of the 1950s, but a bit of the luster on the rivalry was lost because of the move to one lone game each season. Yet that seemed to make this single match each year even more intense.

Lambeau Will Do a Grand Job with the Cardinals

During the extensive league merger discussions in early 1950, the Cardinals were still without a head coach until a decision was announced on February 1, 1950: Curly Lambeau would be the man. The arrival of Lambeau in Chicago was somewhat of a surprise since it came less than a day after Lambeau resigned from his position as head coach and general manager of the Green Bay Packers, where he was employed for 31 years. While citing a difference in opinion within the Green Bay organization in his letter of resignation to the Packers, Lambeau was welcomed to Chicago at a press conference at the Blackstone Hotel. "Lambeau is a great coach and he'll do a grand job with the Cardinals," said George Halas.[8] But not all were enamored with the long-term prospects for the Lambeau/Cardinals partnership, according to Associated Press columnist Hugh Fullerton Jr.: "Another source says Green Bay grid fans are predicting that Curly Lambeau won't last more than one season as Chicago Cardinals coach. Reasoning is that after 31 years as the boss, Curly won't find it easy to take orders."[9]

Although Lambeau departed late in the 1951 season with two games remaining, it was not only his record (7–15) that likely influenced his decision, but also several skirmishes with the front office. This time, in his letter of resignation to the Cardinals, Lambeau noted: "No man can do a satisfactory job if he constantly is harassed by front office second guessing."[10] It was the second major resignation within the Cardinals family in 1951. Longtime Charles Bidwill ally Ray Benningsen also decided to vacate the premises in July 1951. Benningsen had assumed most of Bidwill's managerial responsibilities after the passing of the latter in 1947, including running the Cardinals, the Bentley-Murray Printing Company, Hawthorne Race Track, and others. Violet Bidwill, the widow of Charles Bidwill, had recently married Walter Wolfner and indicated that there were no differences of opinion between her and Benningsen. She told the *Chicago Tribune*: "Ray was just overworked and tired. He has wanted to resign for some time. There was absolutely no dissension."[11] However, in the same article, the *Tribune* alluded not only to problems experienced by Benningsen, but also by former coach Jimmy Conzelman: "It has been no secret, for some time that all was not harmonious between Benningsen and Bidwill's widow and her business advisor Walter Wolfner.... Benningsen is the second major official to leave the Cardinals since Bidwill's death. Head coach Jimmy Conzelman resigned after the 1948 season and it was reported at the time he quit because of differences with Wolfner."[12]

With Curly Lambeau resigning later in 1951, three key team managers had voluntarily fled the Cardinals' premises in recent years. Speculation might suggest that the only common thread between those departures might be Walter Wolfner, who was now seemingly running the Cardinals organization as managing director following his marriage to Violet Bidwill. Wolfner brought absolutely no football experience to the club, yet he quickly maneuvered into a position of authority within the organization, bringing with him the ability to aggravate personnel both within and outside the Cardinals organization. Or, as one unnamed former player told *Sports Illustrated*: "Making him [Wolfner] managing director of the team just because he married the owner is like you should send me to manage the New York Philharmonic."[13]

And his dislike for George Halas was poorly hidden. Although the two clubs worked together for the good of the NFL, the potshots from the owners and the on-field antics by the players betrayed any softened public perception that Wolfner and Halas might be good buddies. Halas and Charles Bidwill had been friends, very good friends, and so the rivalry between the Bears and the Cardinals never sank to unsavory depths. Once Bidwill was not around, the temperature rose, the gloves came off, and the battle for Chicago football supremacy ignited very quickly.

Never Have the Bears and Cardinals Had So Few Victories

While the owners were battling, some very good football players were on display in Chicago during the 1950s. For the Cardinals, Trippi, Harder, and Angsman were still around, but the team later added Hall of Famers Ollie Matson and Dick "Night Train" Lane. The Bears enjoyed the last years of the careers of Bulldog Turner and George McAfee, and introduced some excellent talent in Doug Atkins, George Connor, Rick Casares, Willie Galimore, and Bill George. No matter who the players were on each sideline, the desire to not only win, but to dominate, was evident when the Bears and the Cardinals met during those final years together in the Windy City.

Matson was an immediate success on the South Side when he arrived in 1952 after claiming a pair of medals at the 1952 Helsinki Olympics. The speedster thrilled crowds with his fabulous kick returns, his agility with the ball, and his insightful defense. Matson's first taste of the rivalry took place on October 5, 1952, under new Cardinals coach Joe Kuharich. Although the Bears were 13-point favorites, Matson teamed with Charley Trippi to scorch the Comiskey Park invaders 21–10. It was the fourth straight victory in the series for the Cardinals and Matson promised to be an exciting part of future battles when he scored on a 100-yard kick return and then on a 34-yard scoring jaunt with an errant fumble. Trippi added a 59-yarder for the final touchdown of the day for the winners. It was one of the better scoring displays of the year for the Cardinals as they finished 4–8 during Kuharich's only season but averaged only 14.3 points per game. The Bears did manage to finally snap their four-game skid against the Cardinals on December 14, 1952. Quarterback George Blanda accounted for all of the points for the winners by tossing a seven-yard touchdown pass to Chuck Hunsinger and also adding a field goal in the 10–7 win. Bruce Morrison of the *Chicago Sun-Times* wrote: "It was not a brilliant victory. But it put an end to Cardinal domination that had stretched over four games."[14]

Ollie Matson would spend the 1953 season in the military, where he was named as the most valuable player among all U.S. Army football participants. His presence was sorely missed by the Cardinals as the team had only a tie to show for its first 11 games in 1953 (0–10–1). The Bears (3–7–1) were suffering from rare back-to-back losing campaigns after finishing 5–7 in 1952. When the teams met on December 13, 1953, there was nothing on the line except good old pride. Both teams were well out of the limelight enjoyed by the conference contenders, which was noticed quickly by the beat writers covering the teams: "Never since their first meeting in 1920 have the Bears and the Cardinals come down to their traditional final with so few victories between them—exactly three in 22 National League starts!"[15]

As if on cue, the Cardinals saved their best for last by taking advantage of several turnovers to shock the Bears 24–17 and avoid a much-feared winless season. The many "gifts" provided by the Bears fit right in with the Christmas season, prompting George Halas to quip: "As long as I had to play Santa Claus, I'm glad that [Cardinals coach] Joe Stydahar was the recipient. He's a nice guy and after all, he is a former Bears [player]."[16] Stydahar was a decorated player for the Bears, earning All-Pro honors five times and being elected to the Pro Football Hall of Fame in 1967. After winning the NFL championship as head coach of the Los Angeles Rams in 1951, Stydahar was a welcome addition as coach of the forlorn Cardinals in 1953. However, in his two seasons as the head man for the Cards from 1953 to 1954, he suffered through two ugly seasons and an overall 3–20–1 record.

One of Stydahar's final games was against the Bears on December 5, 1954. With Ollie Matson back from the military, the Cardinals (2–8) hoped that the late-season invasion by the Bears (6–4) would provide some bliss in what had been a very

The Cardinals dropped a 28–6 decision to the New York Giants on November 2, 1952, before a sparse crowd at Comiskey Park in Chicago. Don Paul (#22) of the Cardinals moves in to stop fullback Ed Price (#31) of the Giants. The Cardinals would finish 4–8 that season under new coach Joe Kuharich (author's collection).

unhappy year. Instead, a barrage of pass interceptions scuttled the Cardinals' hopes early as the Bears breezed to an easy 29–7 win. For the Bears, Bones Weatherly, Stan Wallace, and Bill George each picked off two passes while McNeil Moore added another, giving the winners a total of seven takeaways. Quarterback Lamar McHan was victimized on six of those thefts, while George Blanda of the Bears kicked three field goals.

Cardinals Will Share Profits with Players

As the schedule wound down, Walter Wolfner announced an incentive plan for the Cardinals that was embraced enthusiastically by his team. Wolfner shared plans to distribute profits to Cardinals players and coaches in 1955: "The Cardinals will set aside 50 percent of net profits from all football operations, including receipts from radio and television, which will be distributed as follows: 33 percent to the players and 17 percent to the coaching staff."[17]

Reaction to Wolfner's bold statement was mixed among players and NFL management. Team co-captain Leo Sanford was enthusiastic in his response: "This is further proof of something we players already knew. Mr. and Mrs. Walter Wolfner are interested in bringing a championship team to Chicago and are sparing no expense to do just that. If the players need any incentive next year, this should be it."[18] George Halas, however, was not quite as receptive to Wolfner's scheme: "If Mr. Wolfner included his race track profits in the deal, I think he would have something tangible to offer. If more money is the answer to better player performance, I think he should double every player's salary immediately."[19] NFL Commissioner Bert Bell did not find anything wrong with Wolfner's plan, declaring it similar to other teams that offered bonuses for individual performances during the season. Such rewards were legal, as long as they were awarded for the entire schedule and not on a game-by-game basis. The only trouble with Wolfner's vision was not a simple one: the Cardinals would need to make money in 1955 in order to finance a profit-sharing program.

One other item surfaced in late 1954 that has been gradually lost in time. A new Chicago police station opened on the land formerly occupied by Normal Park, the home field at 61st and Racine for the Chicago Cardinals for many of the early years. Local newspapers fondly remembered the history of that forgotten piece of real estate: "The old field, called Normal Park, was the site on which the Chicago Cardinals began their existence. In the early days, the south side pro football club was known as the Racine Cardinals and was owned by Chris O'Brien, who usually had more rough and tough neighborhood boys on the roster than he did college graduates."[20]

Halas Is Becoming a Mean Old Man

In 1955, both Chicago teams rebounded slightly in terms of wins and losses. The Bears improved to 8–4 and finished just one-half game behind the Los Angeles Rams (8–3–1). It should have, could have, or would have been another conference title for the Chicago Bears, except for one unexpected occurrence: another unsightly loss to the Cardinals. The 1955 version of the rivalry was one of the most entertaining episodes in the series. It started innocently enough when four days before the game (scheduled for November 27, 1955), George Halas publicly lambasted the Cardinals for what Halas determined was a deteriorating field at Comiskey Park. Slamming his fist down while addressing 400 attendees at the Chicago Bears Alumni Fan Club, Halas spared nothing in exercising his wrath: "We sent a scout out there [Comiskey Park] this morning. He reported back that the condition of the field was disgraceful. We do not know whether it was covered Tuesday night during the rain or not. Chicago fans are deserving of a better break!"[21]

Cardinals publicity man Eddie McGuire caustically responded: "What is he beefing about? We are more anxious about a dry field than he is. We got more speed than he has and it is to our advantage to have fast going. Halas is just becoming a mean old man!"[22]

Above all, Halas was genuinely concerned the Cardinals (3–5–1) might derail the Bears' (6–3) title hopes with a big upset: "In my 36 years of football, I have never encountered a team in better position for staging an upset than the Cardinals."[23] Unfortunately for the Bears, the personal prophesy of Halas eerily came true. The underdog Cardinals, under new coach Ray Richards, attacked early and often, grabbing a 21–0 lead after one quarter and romping to a surprisingly easy 53–14 win: "Before an ulstered and unbelieving throng of 47,314, the largest in recent seasons in Comiskey Park, the Cardinals swept up and down the snow-blown field scoring almost at will to stop the Bears' six game winning streak and knock them out of first place in the Western Division. It was the largest score ever run up on the Bears. At the end they [Cardinals] climaxed the one-sided, but bitter contest by challenging the entire Bears squad in an altercation that threatened for a moment to become a free-for-all, then carried their coach, Ray Richards, off the field."[24]

After the game, Halas was asked about the condition of the field that he so ardently complained about earlier: "It was in pretty good shape. Four or five days of good weather fixed it up. And the snow didn't bother us. We should be able to play in snow."[25] Of course, Walter Wolfner could not resist tweaking his rival: "I'd like to nominate George Halas as coach of the year. He really brought the Cardinals 'up' for this one."[26] The win enabled the Cardinals to close out the 1955 campaign with an improved 4-7-1 record despite losing four out of their final five ball games. During that 1955 contest, several fistfights broke out and a couple of players were ejected—typical for a Bears-Cardinals game. But what happened the next season in 1956 took the on-field altercations to a whole new level and one not seen since the near riot between the two teams in 1922. But first, George Halas was about to make a significant decision that was surprising to both players and fans alike.

Old-Timers Were Scratching Their Heads

It was time, Halas decided. The NFL championships were stuck in the rearview mirror, but Halas desperately wanted to bring the Bears back into that enchanted circle of winners. Perhaps some new blood could do the trick? Maybe a younger man? And so it was that on February 2, 1956, that Halas announced that he was stepping down as the head coach of the Bears. Speculation for his replacement centered on younger, and very successful, college coaches such as Frank Leahy (formerly of Notre Dame) and Bud Wilkinson of Oklahoma. Even the name of Terry Brennan, the youthful coach of Mt. Carmel High School in Chicago, was mentioned. Sid Luckman, now an assistant for the Bears, was also a possibility. In the end, Halas turned over the keys to longtime friend and assistant coach Paddy Driscoll. It was a logical selection considering Driscoll's lengthy history with the Bears, but some questioned the age factor of the new leader: "Football's old-timers were scratching their heads today trying to remember when a man as old as Paddy Driscoll, who is 60, ever achieved appointment as head coach of a major gridiron power. Many think it is unprecedented. George Halas, on his 61st birthday, named Driscoll his successor as head coach of the Chicago Bears."[27]

Halas made no apologies for his decision and was lavish in praising his old friend: "I have great confidence in Driscoll's ability to keep the Bears in the title running. I know of no one who has made a greater contribution to football."[28] True to form, Driscoll directed the Bears to a sparkling 7-2-1 record before the annual Cardinals game on December 9, 1956, and into the thick of a battle for the Western

Conference title with the Detroit Lions (8–2). Under Coach Ray Richards, the Cardinals enjoyed a resurgence with a 6–4 mark and were hoping to catch the New York Giants at the top of the Eastern Conference. In an intriguing sidebar, Rick Casares of the Bears and Ollie Matson of the Cardinals were engaged in a neck-to-neck race for the NFL rushing honors. Casares held a slim lead of just one yard over Matson entering the game and the crowd of 48,606 at Wrigley Field anticipated more fireworks between the two relentless runners, especially with both clubs still in their respective title chases.

The scoreboard would ultimately reflect a 10–3 victory for the Bears, but this singular contest may have been the working model for the long, bitter rivalry between the two franchises. Writer George Strickler of the *Chicago Tribune* summed up the activity precisely:

> Play was as even as it was bruising and vicious. Feelings ran high and tempers were short almost from the opening kickoff. Officials striving mightily to keep matters on a legitimate basis, broke up a dozen incipient brawls before both teams and several hundred spectators clashed in a free for all in the last minute of play. Bill George of the Bears and Carl Brettschneider of the Cardinals were ejected for the flareup, but not before George had landed the best punch since [boxer] Floyd Patterson upset Archie Moore, and Harlon Hill, the Bears' quiet, personable pass catching star, had given end Pat Summerall of the Cardinals a thorough going over with professional rights and lefts.[29]

In between the numerous fistfights and general animosity, the game was scoreless until midway through the second quarter when George Blanda of the Bears nailed a 36-yard field goal, his only successful kick in four tries throughout the day. Later in that period, Pat Summerall of the Cardinals knotted things up at the half with his 42-yard three-pointer. But the real hero of the day was rookie J.C. Caroline of the Bears:

> J.C. Caroline, a football refugee from the Canadian league and the University of Illinois, led the Chicago Bears back into the championship spotlight in the most bitterly fought contest of the National League this season. Starring on offense as well as defense, he scored the third period touchdown that gave the Bears a 10–3 triumph over the Chicago Cardinals. Then on the last play of the day, he raced back to make the game-saving tackle on one of the Cardinals' speediest ball carriers [Dick "Night Train" Lane], halting a 75-yard pass play that brought this 67th Donnybrook between embattled cross-town rivals to a dramatic close.[30]

Caroline's timely, late-game tackle was surprising in that he trailed, and then nailed, one of the fastest men in the NFL in future Hall of Famer "Night Train" Lane. Years later, Driscoll's reaction to Caroline's heroics was recalled: "Driscoll slapped Caroline on the back afterwards in the locker room and asked, 'How fast ARE you, anyway, J.C.? That Lane is a 9.8 man [for 100-yard dash], isn't he?' Caroline's answer was concise and truthful: 'I don't know how fast I am, but I catch those 9.8 men!'"[31]

It was a disheartening finish for the Cardinals, since it appeared that no one would catch Lane on his 75-yard sprint after catching a tight pass in the secondary from quarterback Lamar McHan. But Caroline sprinted out of nowhere to stop Lane, thus preserving the close win as well as the Bears' title aspirations. As the final seconds ticked away, hundreds of fans joined the players from both teams in an old-fashioned slugfest. Perhaps the maelstrom of anger was touched off by Cardinals fans stunned by the last-minute heroics of J.C. Caroline (who was chased off the field by a bereaved spectator), or maybe some of the followers of the Bears were simply in a celebratory mood. Whatever the case, it was the most hostile ending for an event in the rivalry's recent years: "The teams left the field apparently without animosity, but at the end of the day the Cardinals had reason to curse the penalties that were more potent, perhaps, than the Bears' defense and the Bears had reason to feel lucky. It was the kind of game best described by a gray-haired old Bear in the upper deck who said: 'Just a good old-fashioned Bear-Cardinal fight. It's been going on for 36 years!'"[32]

But there was more. In the battle for NFL rushing honors, Casares widened the gap by picking up 117 yards in 25 carries while the speedy Matson gained only 26 yards in his nine attempts. Casares thus expanded his margin to 92 yards over Matson with just one game remaining on the schedule. Casares would go on to grab the rushing title for 1956 with 1,126 yards while Matson would finish a distant second with 924 yards. Yet there were two disputed penalties during the game on December 9, 1956. In that contest, on two occasions, Matson broke free on scoring runs of 65 yards in the first quarter and 83 yards in the third period only to have both scoring runs called back by penalties. Assistant Bears Coach Sid Luckman was impressed, but relieved, after witnessing the extraordinary speed of Ollie Matson during the game: "Sid Luckman, a hero in the Cardinals-Bears games of not long ago, was thinking of the two nullified touchdown runs by Ollie Matson, the Cardinals speedster, and he said: 'That Matson needs only one shot. He dances and wiggles and doesn't give you a chance at him, and then he sees an opening and he's away. Matson worries you, but look—we won.'"[33]

The 65-yard scamper was victimized by a "backfield in motion" call while the 83-yard run was canceled by a holding call on the Cardinals and an offside penalty on the Bears. With those two scores, the Cardinals might have won the game and increased the team's playoff hopes. In addition, Matson may have eventually captured the league rushing title with the lost yardage. A week later, Matson would also lose a 68-yard touchdown run due to an offside penalty when the Cardinals defeated the Cleveland Browns 24–7, completing their best record (7–5) since 1948 and only winning campaign of the 1950s.

However, the two lost touchdowns in the Bears game still rankle longtime Cardinals fans over 60 years later. Current scout, and former college coach, Jon Cooper grew up as a fan of the Cardinals. Using modern technology and the availability of old game film, Cooper questioned the "motion" call: "I went and froze the two runs. For example, in the game article and the signal I saw on film, the penalty was backfield in motion. This was wrong because it was on Ollie Matson who started early laterally, which is acceptable since one back could go in motion as long is it wasn't forward. Clearly Matson started early but it was perfectly legal. The call was incorrectly called 'backfield in motion' on Matson where the play can continue. I won't get into the specifics but in any interpretation of the rule, what Matson did was perfectly legal."[34]

The reason for examining this film so many years later was to determine if evidence remains of any obvious officiating errors from the game in question.

According to Cooper, the penalty calls on the Cardinals that nullified both of the Matson touchdown runs might be questionable. At the time, the Cardinals felt that there were problems with the officiating and the team lodged an official protest with Commissioner Bert Bell on December 13, claiming that there were 23 "infractions" from the Bears game that were misplayed by the officials. Paddy Driscoll, head coach of the Bears, also provided his opinion on the game film: "We studied movies of the game, too. And we certainly didn't see any flagrant violations committed by the Bears. On Ollie Matson's two runs, the films clearly show a holding infraction by the Cards on one of them and a man pulling out of the line too quickly on the other."[35] This left the final rebuttal to Walter Wolfner, who stated: "We have made a general protest on the conduct of the game. The films show out and out violations which were not called. A little boy could see them. The officials cannot say they didn't see them because they are in the pictures and the violations happened right in front of them."[36]

Two days later, Commissioner Bell dismissed the protest, thus ending still another controversy in the great Bears-Cardinals rivalry. Bell announced, "These are judgement decisions and there are 50 to 60 judgement plays a game. It wouldn't

Paddy Driscoll (far right) was the successful coach of the Chicago Bears in 1956 and led the team to the NFL championship game against the New York Giants, which the Bears dropped 47–7. In keeping with the holiday spirit of the time, this photograph from December 21, 1956, shows these angelic Bears (complete with halos) before the big game. From left: Ed Meadows, Harlon Hill, Bill McColl, Joe Fortunato, and Bill George (author's collection).

make any difference if there were a formal protest or not."[37] Another chapter with the Cardinals was closed, but the win allowed the Bears (8–2–1) to entertain the first-place Detroit Lions (9–2) on December 16, 1956, for the right to participate in the NFL championship game. The Bears secured the Western Conference title by defeating Detroit 38–21 and then moved on to the championship game on December 30 at Yankee Stadium in New York to face the Giants.

Although favored by three points in the battle, the Bears were shocked and bewildered by the Giants as the New Yorkers easily jumped out to a 34–7 halftime lead. Gene Ward of the *New York Daily* news wrote: "The Bears didn't know what hit 'em, and that was their state of mind throughout the afternoon."[38] By the end of the day, the Giants had overwhelmed the Bears 47–7 and secured their first NFL crown in 18 years. Although not pleased with the outcome, Coach Driscoll had brought the Bears back among the NFL elite, and the Cardinals under Ray Richards appeared to be just a step behind.

But the 1957 season did not serve either team well. Instead of vying for first place, both clubs struggled to stay out of the cellar. The Cardinals dipped to 3–9, while the Bears dropped sharply after the 1956 conference championship by finishing 5–7. When the Cardinals started slowly (2–3), Walter Wolfner unabashedly took the opportunity to vilify his club (and coaches) in the *Chicago Sun-Times*: "There's

Members of the 1920 Staley team are shown during a reunion in 1956 arranged by Bears team owner George Halas. In front are Ross Petty, left, and Jack Mintun. Second row, from left: George Halas, George Trafton, Jimmy Conzelman, Lennie High, Roy Adkins, Andy Feichtinger, and Walter Pearce. Back row, from left: Randolph Young, Leo Johnson, Kyle MacWherter, Jake Lanum, Walter Veech, and Charles Dressen (courtesy *Decatur [IL] Herald & Review*).

no leadership on the field, either from the coaches or the players. I've been very disappointed at the Cardinals' showing. With the personnel we have we should be doing a lot better. I think we've got the best personnel in the league. But I don't think the personnel is being used right. I don't feel we're getting the full potential out of our ball club."[39]

Besides alienating his organization, Wolfner was also sidestepping around rumors that the Cardinals might soon be leaving Chicago. This was nothing new since the Cardinals had experimented with playing "home" games away from Chicago for many years. And, previous rumors purported that the club was leaving for Buffalo, Houston, Atlanta, or myriad other locations. In his autobiography, George Halas even mentioned that he was personally against the NFL expanding to the West Coast in the early 1940s for a specific reason: "I had promised Charlie Bidwill I would back him when Los Angeles opened."[40] However, the rumors this time did not seem to diminish, despite the wave of denials from Wolfner. Yet by late 1957, Wolfner was already plotting a move, although not one out of the greater Chicago area.

I'd Be a Terrific Witness!

George Halas, thought to be retired from coaching, appeared regularly on the Bears' sideline during the 1957 season, offering encouragement, advice, as well as coaching! During the annual meeting between the two Chicago squads on December 8, 1957 (won by the Bears 14–6), Halas was spotted cavorting near the Bears' bench: "Owner George Halas of the Bears, although officially retired from coaching, was bustling on the sidelines with his staff headed by Paddy Driscoll."[41]

Halas was ready to respond when queried about his obvious appearances on the Bears' bench:

> "I made up my mind when I quit coaching that I'd always be on the sidelines in Comiskey Park and in Detroit—where both benches are on the same side of the field—just so I'd be there in case trouble started."
> "What good would you do?" a jesting bystander asked.
> "I," said George with great dignity, "will be a terrific witness!"[42]

Despite the lack of championship hopes in Chicago during the 1957 season, the showdown between the Bears and Cardinals still managed to attract a nice crowd of 43,735 to Comiskey Park on December 8, 1957. Rookie Willie Galimore of the Bears broke free for a 67-yard scoring run in the first quarter and later quarterback Ed Brown tossed a four-yard touchdown pass to Jim Dooley to increase the lead to 14–0 at the half. The Cardinals rallied with a short touchdown pass from Lamar McHan to sure-handed Gern Nagler but the Cards never could solve the Bears' defense as they fell 14–6: "Until the Cardinals' successful drive, which survived on a 43-yard pass from McHan to Ollie Matson, the Bears defense provided the outstanding highlight of the 68th game in professional football's oldest rivalry. Bears defenders operated as if they were as well versed in the Cardinals attack as the Cardinals themselves."[43] Coach Paddy Driscoll of the Bears was both pleased, and relieved, with the victory: "I'm very happy to win. The Cardinals are always dangerous. It looked as if we had it in the bag until they completed that long pass to Ollie Matson. Then we were in trouble again, but our defense played well."[44] Matson, in another rough game with the Bears, left without a touchdown but did depart with a couple of stitches over his left eye.

With the team's dip to 5–7 in 1957, Halas decided to make his presence on the field more permanent and replaced Paddy Driscoll with himself as head coach of the Chicago Bears. The Cardinals, as expected, moved on from the competitive Ray Richards (14–21–1) after three seasons and brought in former player Frank "Pop" Ivy, to coach the team. Richards had clashed with Walter Wolfner during his three-year tenure with the Cardinals, primarily regarding an issue where Wolfner dipped into Richards's jurisdiction and insisted on fining a player for what he perceived as a lack of effort. Ivy, on the other hand, was an end for the Cardinals in the 1940s and was a member of the 1947 championship squad before moving into coaching. When Wolfner reached out to Ivy and offered him the head coaching job, Ivy had just completed a phenomenal four-year run guiding the Edmonton Eskimos in the Canadian league. He compiled a 50–14 record and snared three Grey Cup championships (equivalent to the NFL title). Ivy was well respected for his innovations in Edmonton and the local press was sad to see him depart: "Frank 'Pop' Ivy, regarded as the greatest American coach to enter the Canadian game to date, was lost to the Edmonton Eskimos. He signed to coach the Chicago Cardinals, the team with which he played for seven years. Frank usually was a year ahead of his coaching colleagues in Canada. He perfected the double halfback system to become the first American coach to take full advantage of the 12th man, or extra backfielder, in Canadian football. He exploited the backfield motion, allowed in Canada, to a great degree."[45]

Those coaching moves by each Chicago team would play out merely as a sidebar to an unprecedented battle between Halas and Wolfner off the field as 1958 dissolved into 1959. During the 1950s, the Cardinals were losing money on an annual basis and there was no Band-Aid big enough to treat that problem. From 1952 through 1956, the organization suffered an overall deficit of $799,000.[46] Although persistently denying that the Cardinals were looking to leave the city, Wolfner and his wife, Violet Bidwill, devised a plan to move the club's home games to what might be considered a more attractive part of the Chicago area. The change in scenery would also eliminate the scheduling challenges encountered when the Chicago White Sox were still active during the baseball season at Comiskey Park.

Specifically, the Wolfners were intrigued by the possibility of hosting NFL contests at Dyche Stadium on the campus of Northwestern University in nearby Evanston, Illinois. Northwestern seemed interested in preliminary discussions as well until George Halas voiced his objections and the Cardinals threatened litigation. Halas cited an ancient agreement between the two teams as his reason for not allowing the Cardinals to move to the northern suburb of Evanston. Basically, the original 1931 agreement (signed by Dr. David Jones and reaffirmed in 1937 and 1939 by Charles Bidwill) determined that Madison Street in Chicago would be the dividing line for games hosted by each team. In other words, the Cardinals would be required to play all of their games south of Madison Street, while the Bears were restricted to playing their home schedule north of Madison Street. Soldier Field would be available to both teams, however.

Ray Geraci, the former public relations director for the Cardinals, recalled that representatives from the Cardinals initially were quietly doing some research in Evanston, both with Northwestern and then with some local residents to determine if there was any opposition to holding the Cardinals' home games in Dyche Stadium: "Basically, it was favorable. The move was just about set to go. Halas got wind of it. He literally blew his stack because he knew that if [the Cardinals] went into Evanston, we'd have a better stadium and would probably become dominant in the market. So, lo and behold, he pulls out a document that he had signed with Charley Bidwill ... no one in the Cardinal organization knew existed. Mrs. Bidwill didn't know. Wolfner didn't know. Not even old Arch Wolf, who was there during Charley Bidwill's era, knew about it."[47]

When Halas blocked the way, the Cardinals, in turn, filed a lawsuit on September 26, 1958, to nullify the 1931 "Madison Street Agreement" in order to allow their move to Northwestern: "The Chicago Cardinals filed suit in Superior Court to break a 1931 agreement with the Chicago Bears which has stymied an attempt by the Cardinals to move from Comiskey Park to Dyche Stadium in Evanston, Illinois. The agreement, signed by George S. Halas, president of the Bears, and David T. Jones, former owner of the Cardinals, specified that the Cardinals would play their games south of Madison Street, the city's north-south dividing line."[48]

Without abandoning the lawsuit, the Wolfners also petitioned NFL Commissioner Bert Bell to rule on the dispute. Basically, Bell was asked to determine if the "Madison Street Agreement" was legal, since it was signed by previous owners of the Chicago Cardinals. In what Bell called the "toughest decision I have ever had to make," Bell ruled that the contract was still valid, and that it was an agreement between NFL member teams, not only individual owners.[49] Before announcing his decision at the league meeting on January 22, 1959, Bell explained the process utilized to reach his conclusion: "I am going to make a report here as far as the league is concerned, and I am going to make a decision. I have to make a decision and I am making it as honestly and justly as I can. I was advised in this decision; I spent long hours discussing the case with my brother [John C. Bell] who is a Pennsylvania Supreme Court Justice."[50]

Today, Upton Bell, the son of Bert Bell, acknowledges that it was an extremely tough deliberation for his father. Upton Bell, who was once an NFL general manager, stated: "He knew he had to do something about the Chicago issue. The whole thing was decided by his brother since it was a legal matter. Probably what exacerbated the situation was that the Cardinals were not that far away from when they were winners in the league. There was a need to understand the egos on both sides. Was it the right decision for the Cardinals in 1959? It probably was the right thing for the Cardinals."[51]

Players Like Ollie Come Along Once in Years

Back to the 1958 season... Behind rookies like Bobby Joe Conrad, John David Crow, King Hill, and M.C. Reynolds, the Cardinals under Pop Ivy started strongly at 2–2 before spiraling down the stretch with just a single tie to show for the final eight contests. One of those losses occurred on December 7, 1958, to the Bears on a frigid afternoon at Wrigley Field. The Bears (8–4 for the season) piled up a 30–0 halftime lead thanks to a suffocating defense that allowed just one first down and 19 total yards during the first two periods. The Cardinals picked up the slack in the second half by scoring twice to narrow the final margin to 30–14. As usual, circumstances on the field often became belligerent: "But the one-sidedness, like the stiff west wind that wafted a fine sifting of snow into the arena, had little effect on the torrid tempo of the engagement. Rookies Erich Barnes of the Bears and Ken Gray of the Cardinals were ejected for exchanging punches, and trainers were kept busy administering to combatants who fell victims to the treacherous footing and the fierce play."[52]

After the game, Pop Ivy admired the overall effort of the Bears in throttling his young team so decisively: "We were simply overpowered. We couldn't get a passing play off. We couldn't pass. But our fellows never quit, and I'm happy about that. They could have given up in the second half, but instead they came back stronger."[53]

Before the improving Cardinals (2–9–1) in 1958 could seek to return the favor against the Bears in 1959, massive changes were about to engulf the pro football scene in Chicago, including an enormous trade of a superstar and a move to a new home field. After receiving Bert Bell's verdict in January 1958 regarding the proposed departure from Comiskey Park, Walter Wolfner was momentarily silent.

Cardinals assistant coach Chuck Drulis (left) reviews the defensive game plan with his team prior to a game with the Los Angeles Rams on November 30, 1958. The Rams captured a 20–14 win in what would be the final game ever for the Cardinals at Comiskey Park in Chicago. The next season, the club would call Soldier Field home (author's collection).

Seventeen. The Last Hurrah

With the option to play in Evanston eliminated, Wolfner looked for another venue to house the Cardinals. His search was brief but not surprising: the Cardinals would play the 1959 season in Chicago's cavernous Soldier Field. With a few improvements, such as moving the field more toward the south end of the stadium and then building bleachers on the north end to allow the field to be encircled (rather than open at the north end), the Cardinals found the location satisfactory.

The team then sent another wave through the NFL world when it was announced on February 28, 1959, that superstar Ollie Matson had been traded to the Los Angeles Rams. Not only was Matson traded, but he was exchanged for nine players in one of the league's largest transactions. Wolfner explained the huge deal: "Our entire coaching staff feels that these additional top-flight players will, without a doubt, make the Cardinals a strong contender this year. Although we gave up, in my book, the greatest back that ever played in the National Football League."[54]

Pete Rozelle, the business/general manager for the Rams (and future NFL commissioner), engineered the swap with Wolfner and was delighted with the outcome: "I was hoping there would be some way to get Matson to Los Angeles ever since I became business manager. Football players like Ollie come along once in years and years."[55] Although initially surprised by the prospect of the trade, Ollie Matson was humbled by the immensity of the deal: "I just hope I prove worthy of the men they're giving up. I'll say this. I'm looking forward with enthusiasm to at least three more good years of pro ball. I played hard for Chicago, too, and have always tried to do my best wherever I've been."[56] Matson was sorely missed in Chicago, but he did go on to play until 1966 with the Rams, the Lions, and the Eagles before being inducted into the Pro Football Hall of Fame in 1972.

Now, as the 1959 season approached, although it was unknown at the time, the Bears and Cardinals would skirmish just one more time while both teams were in Chicago. While the rivalry has diminished in recent years since the Cardinals are now in Arizona while the Bears remained in Chicago, the annual battles that began in 1920 finally drew to a close on November 29, 1959. The Bears (5–4) were in the middle of a seven-game winning streak that would allow the team to close the season with an 8–4 record. Meanwhile, the Chicago Cardinals (2–7) had swerved into the opposite direction that would see them drop their final six contests to finish the 1959 campaign with

Hall of Fame running back Ollie Matson signed his sixth contract with the Cardinals in June 1958. In 1959, Managing Director Walter Wolfner (left) traded Matson to the Los Angeles Rams for nine players (author's collection).

a lackluster 2–10 mark. It would be the 70th NFL clash between the two clubs since that 1920 debut in Normal Park. As part of his usual, and effective, motivational techniques, Halas reminded his charges of a recent game with the Cardinals where the Bears came in a bit overconfident: "In 1955, we were heavy favorites to beat the Cards. We went into Comiskey Park sublimely confident. It snowed on us heavily, but apparently, it didn't snow on the Cardinals. They won 53–14. We all still carry the stigma of that embarrassment. I hope you remember that Sunday."[57]

For the Cardinals, this would be the fourth, and final, home game in 1959 held at Soldier Field. The Cards elected to sacrifice two more "home" games, transferring them to Metropolitan Stadium in Minneapolis, Minnesota, perhaps in an effort to test the waters for a possible move to the Twin Cities. However, word leaked out that the Cardinals would actually "profit" by staging the games in Minnesota where the organization would receive a nice guarantee of $240,000 for the two battles. This brought a smile to Walter Wolfner's face: "The guarantee, plus television revenue, will give us one of our most profitable seasons in years."[58]

Just prior to the game on November 29, Pop Ivy expressed confidence in his troops, despite their lackluster record: "We're such an unpredictable team we're liable to do anything. The fellows have appeared to be intense and serious in practice this week. Naturally, I'm not going to predict a Cardinal victory, but I've never gone into a game expecting to be beaten."[59] George Halas was equally cautious when addressing his players: "I hope that by now all of us are aware of the importance of beating the Cards Sunday. The Cardinal game has always been a nightmare for us, and I guess it always will be."[60] Halas did not need to worry this time. Helped by six fumbles by the Cardinals, the Bears waltzed to a 31–7 victory over the Cardinals before 48,687 at Soldier Field. Quarterback Ed Brown tossed two scoring passes to Willard Dewveall. The last touchdown scored by the Cardinals while the team was based in Chicago was a 25-yard pass play from King Hill to Perry Richards. The extra point was booted by Bobby Joe Conrad.

And so it ended. The superlative neighborhood rivalry that began in the looming darkness of Normal Park in 1920 concluded in frigid Soldier Field in 1959. In total, 70 NFL games had been played between the two clubs, with the Bears winning 45 and the Cardinals securing 19 victories. Six games ended in ties. For the first time since 1960, the Bears and the Cardinals would not meet on the football field in 1920. The reason? The Chicago Cardinals left town…

Still the Chicago Cardinals

After a long and winding series of denials from Walter Wolfner, the Cardinals accepted a generous offer to move the franchise to St. Louis in March 1960. The announcement came as part of the NFL winter meetings in Los Angeles on March 13, 1960, and left thousands of Chicago Cardinals fans shocked, speechless, disbelieving, and crushed. Part of this reaction was due to Wolfner's continuous disavowal of any story that might pop up mentioning a move. For example, on March 10, 1960, Wolfner denied the latest rumor that the club was moving, this time to St. Louis. Wolfner asserted: "Someone is always trying to move us some place. Some time ago we were approached by a St. Louis group. We talked but nothing came of it. We've been approached by many people but we're still the Chicago Cardinals."[61] Then on March 12, 1960, a story broke that a minority share in the ownership of the Cardinals was procured by Joseph Griesedieck, president of the Falstaff Brewing Company. With the arrival of Griesedieck into the Cardinals' management profile, it seemed a sure indication that the team would be uprooted to a new home in St. Louis. But once again, Wolfner was quick with a denial: "This has nothing whatsoever to do with any contemplated move we might make. It would cost the Cardinals too much money to move and I don't think it is necessary."[62] Wolfner also added that the Cardinals would play all of their home games again in 1960 at Soldier Field in Chicago.

On March 13, 1960, the morning edition of the *Chicago Sun-Times* reported that Wolfner was pleased with the addition of Griesedieck but that any thoughts of moving to St. Louis to accommodate the wishes of Griesedieck were not planned. He also disparaged any thought that George Halas had suggested in any way that the Bears would compensate the Cards if the South Side club would leave the Windy City. "Any stories to that effect are untrue," claimed Wolfner.[63]

But, on March 13, 1960, the dam holding back the truth about the Cardinals crumbled when the departure of the team to St. Louis became known. With all things considered, the announcement came as no surprise to those closest to the hub of activity in the National Football League. One reason was that with two professional clubs being in Chicago, a "blackout" rule was in effect. Basically, if one Chicago team was playing at home, the other club was prohibited from televising its road games back to its Chicago fans. Chicago was the only NFL hub with two teams at the time and the "blackout" rule resulted in a loss of revenue from television rights as well as became a hindrance to increasing fan support. Visiting teams to Comiskey Park or Soldier Field were also weary of meager guarantees when traveling to engage the Cardinals: "Eastern division owners in the National league, faced with expanding expenses, had sought for several years to have the

Following the 1959 season, Managing Director Walter Wolfner (right) was instrumental in moving the Cardinals to St. Louis. Seated with Wolfner is coach Frank Ivy. The Cardinals had been in Chicago since the team's inception in 1899 (author's collection).

Cardinals move out from under the shadow of the prosperous and successful Chicago Bears to some location where it would be possible for visiting clubs to come nearer to breaking even than on Chicago visits. The Cardinals seldom were able to pay teams visiting Chicago more than the $20,000 guarantee. Some clubs lost that much when they went calling in the Loop. When the league raised the guarantee to $30,000 in January, the problem was intensified.[64]

As part of the decision to encourage the Cardinals to fly to St. Louis, the team was provided with $500,000 to assist with moving expenses as well as to pay off certain debts to the Chicago Park District for renovations done to Soldier Field prior to the 1959 season. Of course, one of those most pleased with the move was none other than George Halas. And it was Halas who was pleased to help in preparing the large monetary send-off package for the Cardinals, as noted in the *Chicago Daily News*: "The Cardinals are moving to St. Louis and George Halas is paying their way. That about sums up the pro football story in Chicago. Halas, owner of the Bears, has been trying to get rid of the Cards for some time now and he finally made it with the help of the other National Football League owners. Halas was happy to put up a major share of $500,000 that the NFL will present to the Cards so they can make the move this season. The Bears can now televise road games into Chicago."[65]

After the dust settled, there was still speculation as to why the Cardinals really departed, even though there was a litany of good reasons for such a move. Legendary Chicago sportswriter Bill Gleason stated: "The league wanted the Cardinals out, plus the fact that Wolfner wanted the team in St. Louis. That was how it worked out."[66] Bill Bidwill, the late owner of the Cardinals, explained the primary motive for the move: "Basically, it was because of television. It wasn't necessarily a move to anywhere, but a move out of Chicago because of the television problems."[67]

The Cardinals were gone. The rivalry was over. But the memories would remain, as the media remembered the "fun" times of the more recent past: "In recent years, the Cardinals, no matter how they fared during the season, took special delight in attempting to halt the Bears on the gridiron. The feud even carried into the front office with Halas and Wolfner embroiled in verbal charges and counter-charges."[68]

Charles "Stormy" Bidwill Jr., the son of Charles Bidwill, enjoyed an up-front view of the rivalry as a young man: "Those were the games that everyone in Chicago, North Side or South Side, wanted to see. There was an intense rivalry, but more of a fan's rivalry than the players. There were always fights in the stands. The players would get hot-headed and fight, too, but I remember after one of the games that we won I ended up at a place where some of the Bear players and some of the Cardinal players had gone. They were laughing and joking and kidding around with each other."[69]

While there was a healthy respect between the opposing players, most realized that each time they played, it would be the game of the year in Chicago! Bears Hall of Famer Ed Sprinkle remembered some of his favorite encounters with the Cardinals: "I never had any particular dislike for the Cardinals, but I had some pretty good run-ins with their players. Charley Trippi and I had quite a thing going. We went back and forth with each other all of the time."[70]

And so it goes. The weeks pass, the months pass, the years pass. The stories disappear. Memories. That is all that remains of the Bears-Cardinals rivalry. Forty years of frozen fields, head-banging, and slugfests. They were the ones wearing floppy leather helmets and little padding. They spit out teeth, fought each other, fought in wars, and lived through the Depression. The muffled sounds of Halas, O'Brien, Luckman, and Matson have slipped away. But we know they are there, the names reminding us of the giants who served as the foundation of the sport today and the inspiration for generations to follow. They were heroes, they were men, they were us … the fiercest and oldest rivals and, without fail, they always will be…

Chapter Notes

Chapter One

1. www.barrypopik.com. Theodore Roosevelt quotation may be found at "Roosevelt to Try Again if Defeated," *New York Times*, April 9, 1912, 2. Accessed November 18, 2019.
2. https://www.profootballhof.com/teams/arizona-cardinals/team-history/. Accessed July 14, 2018.
3. https://www.azcardinals.com/news/2019-arizona-cardinals-media-guide, 246. Accessed January 8, 2020.
4. https://en.wikipedia.org/wiki/History_of_the_Chicago_Cardinals. Accessed July 15, 2019.
5. *Official Guide of the National Football League*. New York: American Sports Publishing Company, 1935, 33.
6. McGuire, Eddie. *Chicago Cardinals 1947 Press and Radio Guide*. Chicago: Bentley, Murray & Company, 1947, 6.
7. "Hold Funeral Services for Seys Today," *Chicago Tribune*, January 26, 1938, 19.
8. Condon, David. "Eddie McGuire Is Dead at 69," *Chicago Tribune*, October 30, 1971, 71.
9. Rollow, Cooper. "Leo Sugar Sweetens Eagle Training Camp with Crushing Play," *Chicago Tribune*, July 22, 1961, 42.
10. *Spalding's Official Football Guide*. New York: American Sports Publishing Company, 1899, 173.
11. *Spalding's Official Football Guide*. 200.
12. Hopper, James. "We Really Played Football in the Gay Nineties," *Saturday Evening Post*, November 1945, 43.
13. McKinley, Michael. "The Greatest Football Game I Ever Saw," *Chicago Herald-Examiner*, October 14, 1932.
14. Home addresses for various individuals listed throughout this book were located through specific United States Census searches on Ancestry.com.
15. "They Claim the Game," *South Side Daily Sun*, November 13, 1899.
16. Author interview with Dr. Dominic Pacyga on July 17, 2020.
17. "Stock-Yards Stench Again," *Chicago Daily News*, November 10, 1899.
18. "Victory for the Morgans," *Chicago South Side Daily Sun*, October 16, 1899. For a complete listing of Cardinals games and scores from any season in Chicago, please refer to my previous book on the topic: Ziemba, Joe, *When Football Was Football: The Chicago Cardinals and the Birth of the NFL*. Chicago: Triumph Books, 1999.
19. "Was a Tie Game," *Chicago South Side Daily Sun*, December 6, 1899.
20. "A New Athletic Club," *Chicago South Side Daily Sun*, August 27, 1900, and "New Athletic Club," *Chicago South Side Daily Sun*, September 13, 1900.
21. Pearson, Ray. "General Sporting News and Comment," *Chicago Tribune*, June 15, 1907, 7.
22. Author interview with Dr. Dominic Pacyga on July 17, 2020.
23. Morgan Athletic Club. *State of Illinois, Secretary of State, Articles of Incorporation*. Springfield, IL, 1901.
24. "Morgan Athletic Club's First Ladies' Night Proves a Success," *Chicago South Side Daily Sun*, September 15, 1900.
25. "Baseball," *Chicago South Side Daily Sun*, September 10, 1900.
26. "Football," *Chicago South Side Daily Sun*, October 8, 1900.
27. Sullivan, Floyd, editor. *Old Comiskey Park* (Jefferson, NC: McFarland, 2014), 134.
28. "Thomas Clancy, Central Police Sergeant, Dies," *Chicago Tribune*, December 29, 1936, 19.
29. "Nicholas Bruck Killed as Auto Strikes Truck," *Chicago Tribune*, January 10, 1934, 20.
30. "Sees No Rival of Bezdek," *Chicago South Side Daily Sun*, December 3, 1905.
31. "Career of Hugo Bezdek Reads Like a Romance; Always Star Athlete," *La Crosse Tribune*, June 30, 1918, 14.
32. "The Gangster and the Politician." https://homicide.northwestern.edu/docs. Accessed December 16, 2019.

Chapter Two

1. "Social and Athletic Club in Good Shape," *Chicago South Side Daily Sun*, September 27, 1901, 1.
2. "Will Play the Kicking Game," *Chicago Tribune*, September 28, 1901, 6, and "Associated

Football Clubs," *Chicago Tribune*, October 12, 1901, 6.

3. *Chicago South Side Daily Sun*, November 21, 1901.

4. "Stagg Turns Guns on Pro Grid Games," *Chicago Herald-Examiner*, November 2, 1923.

5. "Giants Are Beaten," *Michigan City Evening News*, November 17, 1902.

6. *Chicago South Side Daily Sun*, November 21, 1903.

7. *Chicago South Side Daily Sun*, October 19, 1903.

8. Normal Athletic Association. *State of Illinois, Department of State, Articles of Incorporation*. Springfield, IL, 1903.

9. Fisher, Henry G., Editor. *The Chicago Amateur Base Ball Annual and Inter-City Base Ball Association Year Book*. Chicago: A.G. Spalding & Brothers, 1905, 21.

10. "Circuses Played at 69th and Halsted Streets in the Old Days," *Southtown Economist*, November 10, 1940, 12.

11. "Normal Athletics Win," *The Inter Ocean*, November 21, 1904, 4.

12. "Sound Knell of Brutal Football," *Chicago Tribune*, November 27, 1905.

13. "Roosevelt's Football Reform Platform," *Los Angeles Express*, December 4, 1905, 6.

14. Roosevelt, Theodore. "What We Can Expect of the American Boy," *St. Nicholas Magazine*, May, 1900, 571–574.

15. "How They Felt in Chicago and Ann Arbor," *The Decatur Herald*, December 2, 1905, 5.

16. *Chicago South Side Daily Sun*, December 2, 1905.

17. "Weight to Rule Game," *Chicago Tribune*, December 15, 1905, 5.

18. *Chicago Englewood Times*, October 9, 1908, 1.

19. "Ansons and Normals Again," *Chicago Tribune*, December 20, 1908, 15.

20. "O'Brien Veteran of Twenty-One Football Years," *Chicago Herald and Examiner*, December 15, 1918.

Chapter Three

1. Halas, George S., with Gwen Morgan and Arthur Veysey. *Halas: An Autobiography* (Chicago: Bonus Books, 1986), 15–16.

2. American Sports Publishing Company, *Official Indoor Base Ball Guide Containing the Constitution*. American Sports Publishing Company, New York, 1911.

3. Interview with Robert Pruter, July 14, 2020.

4. "Crane Looms Up as Pennant Contender," *Herald-Examiner*, February 16, 1910, 11.

5. "Seward Park, 1; Pilsens, 0," *Inter Ocean*, March 7, 1910, 8.

6. "Pitcher Halas Fails to Secure His Reinstatement," *Chicago Tribune*, March 23, 1910, 14.

7. "Crane Retains Baseball Title," *Chicago Tribune*, April 7, 1911, 24.

8. "Lane Takes Indoor Honors," *Chicago Tribune*, April 7, 1912, 31.

9. "Crane's Indoor Nine Wins Sectional Title," *Herald-Examiner*, March 13, 1913, 10. "Crane Tech Nine Gets into Final," *Herald-Examiner*, March 19, 1913, 14. "Crane Tech Beats Lane in Battle for Indoor Title," *Herald-Examiner*, April 6, 1913, 30.

10. "Hyde Park Wins First of Prep Elimination Meets," *Herald-Examiner*, March 12, 1912, 21.

11. "Crane Seeks Double Honors in Gridiron," *Herald-Examiner*, September 20, 1912, 7.

12. "Football," *Science and Craft*, October, 1912, 22.

13. Halas, with Morgan and Veysey. *Halas: An Autobiography*, 28.

14. "Barry Nine Takes K.C. Title; Swamp Columbus Team, 10–2," *Chicago Tribune*, March 23, 1914, 11. "Sigmas Beat Crescents, 8–3, In Indoor Title Contest," *Chicago Tribune*, March 30, 1914, 14.

15. Halas, with Morgan and Veysey. *Halas: An Autobiography*, 30.

16. http://www.eastlanddisaster.org/history/what-happened. Accessed March 14, 2020.

17. "Western Electric Employees Missing and Possibly Dead," *Chicago Tribune*, July 27, 1915, 4.

18. "Illinois is Easy Victor Over Indians," *Champaign Daily Gazette*, October 4, 1915, 2 and "Steam Rollered," *Champaign Daily Gazette*, October 11, 1915, 8.

19. "Footballers Form New Society, 'The Order of the Broken Jaw,'" *Fairmont West Virginian*, November 8, 1915, 9.

20. "Macomber is Captain of '16 Team," *Champaign Daily Gazette*, November 30, 1915, 1.

21. "Illinois Winner of First Game," *Daily Review*, April 12, 1916, 5.

22. "Illini Team Holds Initial Scrimmage," *Rock Island Argus*, September 22, 1916, 18.

23. "Zuppke Reticent on Team Makeup," *Champaign Daily News*, September 23, 1916, 2.

24. "How Yale and Army Bowed to Colgate," *Urbana Daily Courier*, October 9, 1916, 6.

25. "East and West Clash Today," *Daily Illini*, October 14, 1916, 1. "Injured Leg Stops Halas," *Chicago Tribune*, October 13, 1916, 10.

26. "Buckeyes Beat Illinois, 7 To 6, In Fast Finish," *Chicago Tribune*, October 22, 1916, 21.

27. "Weakened Team Battles Purdue," *Daily Illini*, October 28, 1916, 1.

28. Halas, with Morgan and Veysey, *Halas: An Autobiography*, 34.

29. Halas, with Morgan and Veysey, *Halas: An Autobiography*, 35.

30. http://www.fightingillini.com/sports/m-baskbl/records/year-1916.html. Accessed January 16, 2020.

31. "Halas Becomes New Captain as Wood Trio Takes Leave," *Daily Illini*, March 22, 1917, 1.

32. "Reserve Lists for Three Eye League Are Out," *Daily Times*, September 19, 1916, 10.

33. "Hitting the Maroons," *La Crosse Tribune*, May 14, 1917, 8.

34. "Zuppke Returns to Coach Illinois Eleven," *Herald-Examiner*, September 17, 1917, 19.

35. "Zup Smiles as Halas Appears," *Daily Illini*, September 25, 1917, 1.
36. "Zup at Work on Illini Weak Spots," *Daily Illini*, October 23, 1917, 1.
37. "Zuppke's Toilers Use Maroon Plays," *Quad-City Times*, October 31, 1917, 7.
38. "Illinois Interest Has Turned to Basketball," *Grand Forks Herald*, December 12, 1917, 8.

Chapter Four

1. Halas, George S., with Gwen Morgan and Arthur Veysey. *Halas: An Autobiography* (Chicago: Bonus Books, 1986), 37–38.
2. "Halas Goes Into Navy After Game Tomorrow," *Daily Illini*, January 13, 1918, 1.
3. Gonzalez, Therese. *Great Lakes Naval Training Station* (Charleston: Arcadia Publishing, 2008), 21.
4. "Jackies State They Have All-Star Team," *Rock Island Argus*, January 18, 1918, 14.
5. "Basketball Game Tonight Expected to Be City's Best Yet," *Sheboygan Press*, March 8, 1918, 3.
6. "Garden City Drops Rip Roaring Tussle to Jackie Nine, 8–6," *Chicago Tribune*, June 9, 1918, 19.
7. "Great Lakes Team Wins Ball Game," *Daily Review*, July 26, 1918, 5.
8. "World's Biggest Jackie School at Great Lakes," *Chicago Tribune*, May 29, 1917, 7.
9. "Navy Wants Players," *Collyer's Eye*, August 3, 1918, 2.
10. Author interview with Chris Serb on September 19, 2020.
11. "Blacklock to Be on Jackie Eleven," *Lansing State Journal*, August 13, 1918, 10.
12. Author interview with Chris Serb on September 19, 2020.
13. Prell, Edward. "The Story of the Big, Bad Bears," *Chicago Tribune*, October 21, 1941, 21.
14. Eckersall, Walter. "Bluejackets and Iowa Varsity Usher In Football Season," *Chicago Tribune*, September 28, 1918, 11.
15. "Jackies Defeat Illinois 7–0," *Champaign Daily News*, October 13, 1918, 7.
16. "Notre Dame Holds Boys of Navy to 7–7 Tie," *South Bend Tribune*, November 11, 1918, 10.
17. Taylor, Charles A. "Western Boys Spring Surprise of Season," *New York Tribune*, November 17, 1918, 21.
18. "Navy Nearly Equals Georgia Tech's Record," *Baltimore Sun*, November 17, 1918, 28.
19. "Great Lakes Team May Come to the Coast for Game," *Los Angeles Record*, November 23, 1918, 8.
20. "Great Lakes Gobs Defeat Annapolis Midshipmen In Bitterly-Fought Contest," *Democrat and Chronicle*, November 24, 1918, 39.
21. Brand, Harry R. "Mather Field Eleven One of Best on Pacific Coast," *Evening Express*, December 1, 1918, 8.
22. Lark, E. Thomas. "Strong Station Eleven Blanks Seventh Regiment Team 26–0," *Great Lakes Bulletin*, December 11, 1918, 8.

23. "American League Jots," *Evening News*, December 16, 1918, 11.
24. "Great Lakes Team at Highest Power for Pasadena Game," *Chicago Tribune*, December 22, 1918, 21.
25. Henry, William M. "Mighty Tars Crush the Marines," *Los Angeles Times*, January 2, 1919, 11.
26. *Ibid.*, 17.
27. *Ibid.*, 17.
28. Eckersall, Walter. "Attacks in Air Reduce Marines of Mare Island," *Chicago Tribune*, January 2, 1919, 9.
29. "Bachman, Driscoll and Halas Play One Final Game," *Des Moines Tribune*, December 31, 1918, 9.
30. Halas, with Morgan and Veysey. *Halas: An Autobiography*, 42.
31. "Paddy Driscoll to Report to the Cubs," *San Francisco Examiner*, March 12, 1919, 11.
32. "Huggins Says He Will Not Trade Leonard, Anyway," *Boston Globe*, April 4, 1919, 8.
33. https://www.baseball-almanac.com/boxscores/boxscore.php.
34. "Diamond Dust, *Courier Journal*, July 18, 1919, 8.
35. Halas, with Morgan and Veysey. *Halas: An Autobiography*, 43.
36. "Batting Records," *Cincinnati Enquirer*, September 14, 1919, 23.
37. Halas, with Morgan and Veysey. *Halas: An Autobiography*, 50.
38. Chayken, Irving. "Hammond Team Going After National Professional Championship," *Hammond Times*, September 19, 1919, 11.
39. Wallace, Bruce. "Hammond Football Team Signed to Meet Rock Island Here on October 12; Many Stars on List," *Daily Times*, October 7, 1919, 14.
40. "Detroit, Hammond Game Off," *Hammond Times*, October 8, 1919, 7.
41. "Large Crowd of Rooters Will Also Make the Jaunt Here in Two Special Cars with Squad," *Rock Island Argus*, October 9, 1919, 18.
42. "Parduhn in Trouble," *Indianapolis News*, December 16, 1919, 26.
43. *Evansville Press*, December 17, 1919, 6.
44. Fitz Gerald, J.V. "The Round-Up," *Washington Post*, February 25, 1920, 10.

Chapter Five

1. Halas, George S., with Gwen Morgan and Arthur Veysey. *Halas: An Autobiography* (Chicago: Bonus Books, 1986), 53.
2. Halas, with Morgan and Veysey. *Halas: An Autobiography*, 54.
3. "Star Players Try Out for Staley Quintet," *Decatur Herald*, November 19, 1919, 4, and "Woodworth Wins Net Tournament," *Decatur Herald*, September 3, 1920, 4.
4. Author interview with Jon Kendle, December 8, 2020.
5. Sternaman, Edward. "Dutch's Own Story

of the Arcola Game Significance," Unpublished. Transcribed by Peg Holmes, May 12, 2002 based on recording made February 9, 1972. Dutch Sternaman Collection, Professional Football Hall of Fame. Box 8, folder 8.
6. Author interview with Mark Sorensen, July 13, 2020.
7. "Dutch Sternaman Is Signed by Staleys," *Dispatch*, June 14, 1920, 14.
8. "Staleys Win State Football," *Staley Fellowship Journal*, December, 1919, 14.
9. Halas, with Morgan and Veysey, *Halas: An Autobiography*, 58–59.
10. "Staleys Sign Paddie Driscoll for Eleven," *Decatur Daily Review*, July 26, 1920, 9.
11. "Driscoll Signs with Racine Team," *Decatur Herald*, September 11, 1920, 4.
12. Racine Cardinal Pleasure Club. *State of Illinois, Department of State, Articles of Incorporation*. Springfield, IL, 1917.
13. *Sanborn Fire Insurance Map from Chicago, Cook County, Illinois*. Sanborn Map Company, Vol. 15, 1926.
14. Engel, Otto A. "South Side Preps to Combine Games," *Chicago Tribune*, October 18, 1916, 18.
15. Author interview with Patrick Glynn, September 7, 2020.
16. "Racine Cardinals to Hold First Dance Tonight," *Day Book*, February 2, 1917, 12.
17. "The Sports Spyglass," *Hammond Times*, November 23, 1917, 11.
18. "Two Ties in Indoor Grid Games," *Hammond Times*, December 24, 1917, 3.
19. Pasley, Fred. "Our Town," *Chicago Tribune*, November 25, 1928, 13.
20. Walker, Johnny. "Cardinals May Spring Upset in M.F.A. Game," *Dispatch*, October 18, 1919, 16.
21. Walker, Johnny. "Giant Guard Is Out of Sunday Game for M.F.A.," *Dispatch*, October 18, 1919, 14.
22. "Moline Team in Hair Raising Finish, Ties Racine, 7–7," *Quad City Times*, October 20, 1919, 7.
23. "Hammond Books Cub Park for Season," *Daily Times*, October 18, 1919, 17.
24. "Racine Cardinal Secretary Dead," *Hammond Times*, December 23, 1919, 13.
25. Author interview with Patrick Glynn, November 20, 2020.
26. "Lakota Cardinals Lose 32–17 Game," *Capital Times*, January 2, 1920, 3, and "Beloit Fairies Stop Whiting's Victories, 27–18," *Chicago Tribune*, January 3, 1920, 10.
27. "Paddy Driscoll in Indoor Grid Contest Today," *Chicago Tribune*, January 4, 1920, 18.
28. Condon, David. "In the Wake of the News," *Chicago Tribune*, December 8, 1956, 34.
29. "To Have Great Football Eleven This Fall," *Staley Fellowship Journal*, October, 1920, 10.
30. "Staley Eleven to Start Work on Next Monday," *Decatur Herald*, September 12, 1920, 8.
31. "Driscoll Joins Team," *South Bend Tribune*, September 9, 1920, 12.
32. Halas, with Morgan and Veysey. *Halas: An Autobiography*, 59–60.
33. "Independents Are Given Great Send-Off," *Rock Island Argus*, September 14, 1920, 15.
34. "Football Managers Make Plans," *Akron Beacon Journal*, August 21, 1920, 10.
35. "Grid Plans of Staleys Seek Title," *Rock Island Argus*, September 16, 1920, 11.
36. "Strong Grid League Plan, *Decatur Herald*, September 17, 1920, 4.
37. Halas, with Morgan and Veysey. *Halas: An Autobiography*, 60.
38. "Staleys Enter Grid League," *Decatur Herald*, September 19, 1920, 4.

Chapter Six

1. "Chicago Tigers Engage Cub Lot for Grid Games," *Rock Island Argus*, September 22, 1920, 14.
2. "All-American Man Plays at Fullback on Hammond Team," *Dispatch*, October 6, 1920, 18.
3. "Join Strong Football League for 1920 Play," *Staley Fellowship Journal*, October, 1920, 10.
4. Copeland, Bruce. "Independents Denied Clash on Home Grid," *Rock Island Argus Leader*, September 21, 1920, 11.
5. Author interview with Mark Sorensen, July 13, 2020.
6. Roeser, Thomas F. *Father Mac: The Life and Times of Ignatius D. McDermott, Co-Founder of Chicago's Famed Haymarket Center* (Chicago: McDermott Foundation, 2002), 17.
7. Gleason, William F. *The Liquid Cross of Skid Row* (Milwaukee: The Bruce Publishing Company, 1966), 167.
8. "Profesh Gridders to Play," *Chicago Daily News*, October 6, 1920.
9. "Grid Pros Open Season Today at Home of Cubs," *Chicago Tribune*, October 10, 1920, 20.
10. "Staleys Win from Kewanee Walworths," *Decatur Herald*, October 11, 1920, 4.
11. "Hammond Pros Snowed Under Pile," *Hammond Times*, October 18, 1920, 7.
12. Copeland, Bruce. "Racine Cards Next Foes at Douglas Park," *Rock Island Argus*, October 19, 1920, 20.
13. "Tiger-Staley Game to Be Held at Cub Park Next Sunday," *Dispatch*, October 19, 1920, 18.
14. Barron, Lee. "Independent Players Fight for Grid Lives; Defeat Will Mean Blue Slip Distribution," *Daily Times*, October 23, 1920, 13.
15. "Six New Stars in Rock Island Lineup Sunday," *Quad-City Times*, October 21, 1920, 7.
16. "Crippled Rock Island Eleven Meets Hard Foe," *Quad-City Times*, October 24, 1920, 22.
17. Copeland, Bruce. "Paddy Driscoll's Vaunted Men Yield to Spectacular Flashes of Smart, Out-Rushing Tactics," *Rock Island Argus*, October 25, 1920, 14.
18. Author interview with Mark Sorensen, July 13, 2020.
19. "Staleys Leave for Chicago," *Dispatch*,

October 23, 1920, 16; "Bethany Grid Squad Getting into Condition," *Pittsburgh Daily Post*, September 16, 1923, 30.

20. "Heralds Beaten by Large Score," *Detroit Free Press*, November 1, 1920, 15.

21. McGuire, Eddie. *Chicago Cardinals 1955 Press, Radio and Television Guide*. Chicago: Bentley, Murray & Company, 1955, 6.

22. Copeland, Bruce. "Starch Moguls Yield to Plea of Flanigan for Return Game Sunday on Douglas Park Grid," *Rock Island Argus*, November 2, 1920, 11.

23. Halas, George S., with Gwen Morgan and Arthur Veysey. *Halas: An Autobiography* (Chicago: Bonus Books, 1986), 64.

24. "Sidelights of Staley-Islander Game," *Quad-City Times*, November 8, 1920, 7.

25. "Held to Tie Score," *Staley Fellowship Journal*, December, 1920, 8.

26. Halas. *Halas*, 64.

27. "Held to Tie Score," *Staley Fellowship Journal*, December, 1920, 8.

28. Copeland, Bruce. "Staleys Win World's Dirt Title," *Rock Island Argus*, November 8, 1920, 12.

29. Halas. *Halas*, 64.

30. "Driscoll's Father Dies; Cards Game Called Off," *Chicago Tribune*, November 25, 1920, 29.

31. Smith, Red. "Papa Bear Still a Wonder," *Courier Journal*, December 24, 1979, 8.

32. "Staleys Bow to Cardinals," *Chicago Herald and Examiner*, November 29, 1920.

33. "Cards Met Staleys Again," *Chicago Daily News*, November 30, 1920.

34. "Staleys Schedule Return Game with Chicago Cardinals," *Decatur Herald*, November 30, 1920, 4.

35. "Staleys Turn on Cards, 10–0," *Chicago Herald and Examiner*, December 6, 1920.

36. "Offers for Pros Halts Trip West," *Akron Beacon Journal*, December 7, 1920, 19.

37. "Staleys to Play Akron for Title," *Chicago Herald and Examiner*, December 8, 1920.

38. "Great Elevens Struggle for Grid Honors of Country," *Decatur Herald*, December 8, 1920, 4.

39. "Staleys in 0–0 Tie with Akron," *Chicago Herald and Examiner*, December 13, 1920.

40. Prell, Edward. "Fans Awaken to Birth of Pro Football, *Chicago Tribune*, October 27, 1948.

41. Gibbons, Jack. "Akron Pros Arrange to Leave Thursday on Trip to California," *Akron Beacon Journal*, December 21, 1920, 23.

42. "Akron Professional Grid Team Works Out for Big Pasadena Game Saturday," *Los Angeles Record*, January 10, 1921, 10.

43. "Stayms to Have Many Grid Stars in Lineup," *Chicago Herald and Examiner*, December 18, 1920.

44. Rollow, Cooper. "Staleys, Shades of Early Bears, To Meet," *Chicago Tribune*, October 17, 1956, 68.

45. "Some Facts, Thoughts, Records on the A.E. Staley Manufacturing Company and Football 1919–1922 Era," Unpublished, August 1, 1956. Professional Football Hall of Fame Archives.

Chapter Seven

1. "Driscoll Ready for Outdoor Grid Game," *The Courier*, January 8, 1921, 14.

2. "Islander Team Outplays Fast Chicago Eleven," *Quad-City Times*, January 10, 1921, 7.

3. Copeland, Bruce. "Starchmakers Reject Terms of Islanders," *Rock Island Argus*, January 20, 1921, 13.

4. *Ibid*.

5. Copeland, Bruce. "Proposed Grid League Likely to be Adopted," *Rock Island Argus*, January 28, 1921, 22.

6. "Pro Football Notes," *Chicago Tribune*, September 25, 1921, 22.

7. "Parking Space for Autos at Cardinal-Hammond Game," *Chicago Tribune*, November 4, 1921, 17.

8. "George Halas Named New Athletic Head," *Staley Fellowship Journal*, March, 1921, 12.

9. Author interview with Chris Willis, January 29, 2021.

10. "Diploma Says Walt Is Boss of R.I. Eleven," *Rock Island Argus*, June 22, 1921, 14.

11. "Staleys Lease Cubs' Park for Next Football Season," *Chicago Tribune*, June 29, 1921, 18.

12. "Staley Plant Is Closed to Await Orders," *Decatur Herald*, June 8, 1921, 3.

13. "Times Are Good Because They Force Us to Think Says Ford," *Decatur Herald*, June 26, 1921, 3.

14. "Will Break No Records This Month," *Decatur Herald*, October 9, 1921, 18.

15. "Staley Man Named Officer of Pro Grid Association," *Staley Fellowship Journal*, June, 1921, 9.

16. Phillips, Larry. "Chic Harley Helped Put Ohio State on the Map," *News-Journal*, October 5, 2003, 27.

17. *Ibid*., 31.

18. Halas, George S., with Gwen Morgan and Arthur Veysey. *Halas: An Autobiography* (Chicago: Bonus Books, 1986), 68.

19. "Stinchcomb and Harley to Play with Staleys Eleven," *Chicago Tribune*, August 16, 1921, 13.

20. Horrigan, Joe. "*NFL Century: The One-Hundred-Year Rise of America's Greatest Sports League*," (New York: Crown, 2019), 25.

21. "Cardinals to Open Season Tomorrow," *Chicago Daily News*, September 24, 1921.

22. "Three Scouts Try to Get Hold of Baumann," *Journal Times*, September 26, 1921, 11.

23. "Harley Stars as Staleys Open Big," *Wisconsin State Journal*, October 3, 1921, 6.

24. Halas, George. "The Inside Story of Pro Football by Papa Bear," *Chicago Tribune*, January 24, 1967, 41.

25. Halas, George. "The $71.63 Lost in Debut Season, Halas Didn't Return to Railroad," *Chicago Tribune*, January 25, 1967, 49.

26. Author interview with Mark Sorensen, January 27, 2021.

27. Copy of A.E. Staley letter to the Staley Football Team, dated October 6, 1921, provided by Mark Sorensen.

28. Author interview with Mark Sorensen, July 13, 2020.
29. Whittingham, Richard. *What a Game They Played: An Inside Look at the Golden Era of Pro Football* (Lincoln: University of Nebraska Press, 2001), 6.
30. "Staley Forced to Turn Down German Order," *Decatur Herald*, October 27, 1921, 3.
31. "Staley Finds New Yorkers Are Hopeful," *Decatur Herald*, December 11, 1921, 27.
32. Halas, with Morgan and Veysey. *Halas: An Autobiography*, 74.
33. Hughes, J.L. "Driscoll is Outwitted by J. Conzelman," *Rock Island Argus*, October 17, 1921, 10.
34. "Rock Island Eleven Beats Cardinals, 14–7," *Chicago Tribune*, October 17, 1921, 18.
35. Goldstein, Richard. "Ralph Horween, 100, the Oldest Ex-NFL Player," *New York Times*, May 29, 1997, 19.
36. Curran, Bob. *Pro Football's Rag Days* (New York: Bonanza Books, 1969), 49.
37. "Coughlin Is Released by Independents," *Daily Times*, October 19, 1921, 13.
38. Hughes, J.L. "Driscoll is Outwitted by J. Conzelman," *Rock Island Argus*, October 17, 1921, 10.
39. Halas, George. "The $71.63 Lost in Debut Season, Halas Didn't Return to Railroad," *Chicago Tribune*, January 25, 1967, 53.
40. "Lose Money at Canton; Local Card Is Dropped," *Evening Review*, November 10, 1921, 10.
41. "Packer-Cardinal Game, Play by Play, Over Wire," *Green Bay Press-Gazette*, November 18, 1921, 13.
42. "Sports News and Views," *Post-Crescent*, November 18, 1921, 18.
43. "Watching the Parade," *Green Bay Press-Gazette*, November 21, 1921, 13.
44. "Cardinals Book Gary Elks for Game Tomorrow," *Chicago Tribune*, November 26, 1921, 11.
45. Author interview with Jeff Miller, February 21, 2021.
46. "Buffalo-Staleys Again," *Buffalo Morning Express*, December 2, 1921, 16.
47. Author interview with Jeff Miller, February 21, 2021.
48. Wolf, Jason. "Was Buffalo Robbed of the First Two NFL Championships?" *Buffalo News*, January 31, 2020.
49. Author interview with Jeff Miller, February 21, 2021
50. "Buffalo Disputes Staleys' Claim of Professional Football Title," *Buffalo Times*, December 5, 1921, 10.
51. "Staleys Battle Cardinals for Pro Grid Title," *Chicago Tribune*, December 18, 1921, 3.
52. Halas, with Morgan and Veysey. *Halas: An Autobiography*, 75–76.
53. Millard, Howard. "Fans Need Not Worry About 1922 Baseball," *Decatur Daily Review*, January 8, 1922, 8.
54. "Staley Company Drops Professional Sport," *Decatur Daily Review*, February 1, 1922, 13.
55. "Passing of Professionalism," *Decatur Herald*, February 2, 1922, 6.
56. Author interview with Jeff Miller, February 21, 2021
57. Halas, with Morgan and Veysey. *Halas: An Autobiography*, 76.
58. "Birth and Rebirth," *Coffin Corner*, Volume 7, 1985, 1.
59. "In the World of Sport," *Muncie Evening Press*, January 30, 1922, 5.
60. "O'Brien Urges That Pros Bar College Player," *Rock Island Argus*, February 15, 1922, 12.
61. "Copy of Statement of Incorporation," Sternaman Collection, Professional Football Hall of Fame, Box 7A, Folder 8.
62. Author interview with Steve Thomas, March 29, 2021.
63. APFA Meeting Minutes, June 24–25, 1922, Professional Football Hall of Fame.
64. Hughes, James. "The Sport-O-Graph," *Rock Island Argus*, September 7, 1922, 12.

Chapter Eight

1. Koenig, Wally. "Independents Will Play Bears with Their Usual Lineup of College Aces," *Daily Times*, November 18, 1922, 17.
2. "Team Which Put Dayton to Rout Will Be Used Against Halas' Outfit," *Rock Island Argus*, November 17, 1922, 26.
3. "Rock Island Independents Tackle Bears at Cub Park," *Chicago Tribune*, November 19, 1922, 25.
4. "Big Game on Argus Grid Board at 2:15," *Rock Island Argus*, November 18, 1922, 1.
5. Koenig, Wally. "Place-Kick by Sternaman Results in 3–0 Trimming for Rock Island Machine," *Daily Times*, November 20, 1922, 10.
6. Hughes, James. "The Sport-O-Graph," *Rock Island Argus*, October 30, 1922. 10.
7. Koenig, Wally. "Members of Independent Eleven Desire Release; Claim Can't Collect Pay," *Daily Times*, November 22, 1922, 15.
8. Koenig, Wally. "Independent Stars Preparing to Sign with Other Squads," *Daily Times*, November 23, 1922, 26.
9. "Racine Gets Pair of Flanigan Aces," *Daily Times*, November 25, 1922, 16.
10. Cope, Myron. *The Game That Was*. Cleveland: The World Publishing Company, 1970, 25–26.
11. Halas, George, with Gwen Morgan and Arthur Veysey. *Halas: An Autobiography; The Autobiography of George Halas*. New York: McGraw-Hill, 1979, 83.
12. "Bears Buy Healey; Thought First Sale of Gridiron Player," *Rock Island Argus*, November 27, 1922, 12.
13. "Sale of Gridiron Player Is Latest," *Tennessean*, November 28, 1922, 10.
14. "Bears Pay Sum for Ed Healey," *Rock Island*

Argus, December 2, 1922, 12. Author Myron Cope notes that there were indications that Buffalo may have purchased the services of Akron's Bob Nash in 1921, but most researchers, including this author, feel that Healey was indeed the NFL's first free agent signing. In fact, Art Ranney, owner of the Akron Pros, stated on September 10, 1921, that he had not been able to reach an agreement to trade Bob Nash to Buffalo. Ironically, the day before (September 9), Buffalo announced that Nash would be playing for the All-Americans in 1921, apparently because of his interest to play for an eastern team, not because of a trade or purchase transaction. See "All-Americans to Be Stronger, Says F. M'Neil," *Buffalo Times*, September 9, 1921, 20, and "Pro Football Players Here," *Akron Beacon Journal*, September 10, 1921, 7.

15. "Bear, Cardinal Elevens in Clash Tomorrow," *Chicago Tribune*, November 29, 1922, 15.

16. "Cards and Bears in Wrangle Over Turkey Day Tilt," *Chicago Tribune*, November 23, 1922, 17.

17. "October Gets All Triangle Games at Home," *Dayton Daily News*, August 21, 1922, 8; "Complete Pro Football Schedule Drawn Up," *Green Bay Gazette*, September 1, 1922, 13; "How Schedules Compare," *Rock Island Argus*, September 30, 1922, 24.

18. "Bears and Cards Clash at Sox Park," *Chicago Herald and Examiner*, November 30, 1922.

19. Johnson, Harold. "Cards Defeat Bears 6–0; Play Again on Dec. 10," *Chicago Evening American*, December 1, 1922.

20. "Cardinals in 6 to 0 Win Over Bears," *Chicago Herald and Examiner*, December 1, 1922.

21. Halas, with Morgan and Veysey. *Halas: An Autobiography*, 84.

22. Cope, *The Game That Was*, 26–27.

23. Halas, with Morgan and Veysey, *Halas: An Autobiography*, 84.

24. "Rowdyism Mars Pro Game," *Chicago Daily News*, December 1, 1922.

25. Halas, with Morgan and Veysey. *Halas: An Autobiography*, 85.

26. "Cardinals and Bears to Meet Again on December 10, *Chicago Tribune*, December 2, 1922.

27. "Mental Collapse of Harley Is Charged to Gridiron Plot, and Owners of the Bears Are Sued," *Rock Island Argus*, December 5, 1922, 14.

28. Ibid.

29. "Driscoll Boots Three Field Goals to Win Championship for Cardinals Sunday, 9 to 0," *La Crosse Tribune*, December 11, 1922, 7.

Chapter Nine

1. Eckersall, Walter. "Grange is Illinois 'Punch' That Fells Nebraska, 24 to 7," *Chicago Tribune*, October 7, 1923, 21.

2. Author interview with Chris Willis, January 29, 2021.

3. "Staley Man Named Officer of Pro Grid Association," *Staley Fellowship Journal*, June, 1921, 9.

4. "Would Co-Operate to Put an End to All Professionalism," *Modesto Evening News*, February 1, 1922, 1.

5. "In the World of Sport," *Muncie Evening Press*, January 30, 1922, 5.

6. "Stagg, Maroon Coach, Condemns 'Pro' Football," *Chicago Tribune*, November 2, 1923, 28.

7. "Carr Says Pro Football No Menace to Colleges," *Green Bay Press-Gazette*, November 6, 1923, 13.

8. "Amateur and Professional," *Green Bay Press-Gazette*, November 6, 1923, 13; "Cal's Comments," *Green Bay Press-Gazette*, November 7, 1923, 16.

9. "Normals Twice Lose in Week-End Games," *Englewood Economist*, September 12, 1923, 4.

10. "Memorandum of Agreement Between Chicago National League Ball Club and Chicago Bears Football Club," Sternaman Collection, Professional Football Hall of Fame. June, 1922.

11. Ibid.

12. "1923 Player Contracts," Sternaman Collection, Professional Football Hall of Fame.

13. "1924 Player Contracts," Sternaman Collection, Professional Football Hall of Fame.

14. Author interview with Mary Zoia Zentner, March 20, 2021.

15. *Chicago Cardinals Football Club Official Scorebook and Program*, November 4, 1923.

16. Author interview with John Steffenhagen on June 11, 2021.

17. Brands, E.G. "Lop-Sided Race in National Pro Football League Looms," *Collyer's Eye*, October 20, 1923, 8.

18. Vaughan, Irving. "Bears Rout Thorpe's Oorang Indians, 26–0," *Chicago Tribune*, November 5, 1923, 28.

19. "Cardinals Train Hard for Game with the Bears," *Chicago Daily News*, November 27, 1923.

20. M. Donahue Letter to Chicago Bears Football Club, November 8, 1925. Sternaman Collection, Professional Football Hall of Fame.

21. "Chicago Bears Blank Cards," *Decatur Herald*, November 30, 1923, 15.

22. "Illinois and Michigan May Go Through Big Ten Season Without Any Grid Upsets," *Green Bay Post-Gazette*, November 6, 1923, 13.

23. Crusinberry, James. "Grange Thrills Huge Crowd by Racing to 5 Touchdowns," *Chicago Tribune*, October 19, 1924, 25.

24. Ibid., 26.

25. Dale, Margaret. "Dad, a Six-Footer, Wrestled with Boy," *Springfield News-Leader*, November 23, 1924, 7.

26. Halas, George S., with Gwen Morgan and Arthur Veysey. *Halas: An Autobiography* (Chicago: Bonus Books, 1986), 102.

27. Halas, with Morgan and Veysey. *Halas: An Autobiography*, 103.

28. Ward, Arch. "In the Wake of the News," *Chicago Tribune*, June 30, 1952, 49.

29. "Kicks Likely to Decide Victor in Card-Bear Tilt," *Chicago Tribune*, October 19, 1924.

30. "Bears Clash with Cards for City Pro Title," *Chicago Tribune*, November 27, 1924, 37.
31. "Chicago Bears Trim Cardinals," *Decatur Daily Review*, November 28, 1924, 20.
32. "Cleveland Bulldogs Awarded Pro Football Title," *Green Bay-Gazette*, January 26, 1925, 13.
33. "Columbus Tigers Game Contract," September 27, 1924. Sternaman Collection, Professional Football Hall of Fame. Box 9B, Folder 77.
34. *Chicago Cardinals Football Club Official Score Book and Program*, November 16, 1924.
35. "Cleveland and Philadelphia May Be Seen Here This Fall in Games Against Packers," *Green Bay-Gazette*, January 27, 1925, 12.
36. "Chicago Bruins to Meet Columbus Five Thursday," *Capital Times*, January 17, 1925, 13.
37. "Form a League of Basketball," *Star Press*, April 26, 1925, 11.
38. Halas, with Morgan and Veysey. *Halas: An Autobiography*, 130.
39. "Pro League Season Opens Sunday; Two Games Scheduled," *Green Bay Press-Gazette*, September 17, 1925, 16.
40. "Buckeye, Giant Pitcher, Spurns Place on Grid," *Tampa Bay Times*, September 28, 1925, 9.
41. Condon, David. "Judge Could Sum Up Bear-Card History, *Chicago Tribune*, December 6, 1975, 3.
42. Monroe Hamilton Letter to Dutch Sternaman, October 12, 1924. Sternaman Collection, Professional Football Hall of Fame. Box NA.
43. "Cardinals vs. Hammond," September 27, 1925. Sternaman Collection, Professional Football Hall of Fame. Box 9A, Folder 5.
44. "Detroit, October 24, 1925." Sternaman Collection, Professional Football Hall of Fame. Box 9B, Folder 23.
45. "Chicago Bears vs. Hammond," October 11, 1925. Sternaman Collection, Professional Football Hall of Fame. Box NA.
46. Ibid.
47. "Cardinals vs. Columbus," October 11, 1925. Sternaman Collection, Professional Football Hall of Fame. Box 9A, Folder 5.
48. Vaughan, Irving. "Dunn's Passes Give Cardinals Win Over Bears," *Chicago Tribune*, October 26, 1925, 23.
49. McBroom, Robert. "Cards Beat Bears with No Trouble," *Chicago Evening Post*, October 26, 1925.
50. "Grange Passes Up Pro-Grid Inducement," *Chicago Herald and Examiner*, October 1, 1925.
51. Grange, Harold, as told to Ira Morton. *The Red Grange Story: An Autobiography* (Urbana: University of Illinois Press, 1953), 91.
52. Willis, Chris. *Red Grange: The Life and Legacy of the NFL's First Superstar* (Lanham: Rowman & Littlefield, 2019), 93.
53. Author interview with Chris Willis, January 29, 2021.
54. Willis, Chris. *Red Grange*, 139.
55. Halas, with Morgan and Veysey. *Halas: An Autobiography*, 105–106.
56. Walker, Betty. "'Red' Terror on Gridiron: Harold Modest Senior," *Chicago Herald and Examiner*, November 7, 1925.
57. "Twenty-Five Trains Carry Maroon Rooters to Game," *Chicago Tribune*, November 9, 1925, 30.
58. "Grange and Britton Deny Signing as Pros," *Chicago Herald and Examiner*, November 18, 1925.
59. "Fall Dates of Grid Star Up to Pyle," *Chicago Herald and Examiner*, November 19, 1925.
60. Powers, Francis. "Red Grange Sparkles in Last Appearance on College Gridiron," *Dayton Daily News*, November 22, 1925, 49.
61. "Grange Comes to Bears; To Play Here Thursday," *Chicago Evening American*, November 21, 1925.
62. MacNamara, Harry. "Crowd Roars Noisy Tribute to Sorrel Top," *Chicago Herald and Examiner*, November 23, 1925.
63. "Riot for Grange Game," *Chicago Herald and Examiner*, November 24, 1925.
64. Corcoran, Jimmy. "200,000 Fans Would See 'Red' in Action," *Chicago Evening American*, November 24, 1925.
65. "Dutch Sternaman Original Letter to Chicago Cardinals," November 12, 1925. Sternaman Collection, Professional Football Hall of Fame. Box 9B, Folder 24.
66. McBroom, Robert. "Can Great Red Head Run Wild Against the Cards As He Did for the Illini?" *Chicago Evening Post*, November 24, 1925.
67. Corcoran, Jimmy. "200,000 Fans Would See 'Red' in Action," *Chicago Evening American*, November 24, 1925.
68. "Will Put Grange's Exploits on 'Air,'" *Daily Review*, November 25, 1925, 1.
69. Grange, Harold as told to Harold Johnson. "Red Finds Pro Game Fast," *Chicago Evening American*, November 27, 1925.
70. MacNamara, Harry. "Pro Debut Ends in Scoreless Tie," *Chicago Herald and Examiner*, November 27, 1925.
71. Halas, with Morgan and Veysey. *Halas: An Autobiography*, 108.
72. "Pro Game Here to Stay—Veeck," *Chicago Herald and Examiner*, November 28, 1925.
73. "Cards VS. Islanders," *Chicago Tribune*, November 29, 1925, 33.

Chapter Ten

1. "Chicago Cardinals at Cubs Park," November 26, 1925. Sternaman Collection, Professional Football Hall of Fame. Box 9A, Folder 5.
2. "Pottsville Accepts Chicago's Challenge," *Morning Call*, December 3, 1925, 24.
3. "Cardinals Play Pottsville for Pro Title Today," *Chicago Tribune*, December 6, 1925, 32.
4. Field, F.B. "Barn-Storming Junkets for Pro Football," *Collyer's Eye*, November 28, 1925, 3.
5. Halas, George S., with Gwen Morgan and Arthur Veysey. *Halas: An Autobiography* (Chicago: Bonus Books, 1986), 108.
6. "Donnelly Stars," November 25, 1925.

Sternaman Collection, Professional Football Hall of Fame. Box 9B, Folder 33.

7. Prell, Edward. "Grange Recalls Glory Days," *Chicago Tribune*, December 14, 1968, 45.

8. Whittingham, Richard. *What a Game They Played: An Inside Look at the Golden Era of Pro Football* (Lincoln: University of Nebraska Press, 2001), 9.

9. Pegler, Westbrook. "Washington's Powerful Pros Maul Grange," *Chicago Tribune*, December 9, 1925, 29.

10. Grange, Harold as told to Ira Morton. *The Red Grange Story: An Autobiography* (Urbana: University of Illinois Press, 1993), 103–104.

11. Grange, Harold as told to Ira Morton. *The Red Grange Story: An Autobiography*, 102.

12. "Football Star Gets a Flat Guarantee," *Chicago Daily News*, December 7, 1925.

13. "N.Y. Giants Used No Gloves in Handling Grange," *Daily News*, December 7, 1925, 92.

14. "SETTLEMENT: Chicago Bears vs. Boston" (includes Pittsburgh game report), November 26, 1925, Sternaman Collection, Professional Football Hall of Fame.

15. Untitled document, February 15, 1928, Sternaman Collection, Professional Football Hall of Fame. Box 9A, Folder 8. Prepared in conjunction with a lawsuit filed by Cleveland representatives regarding a Chicago Bears game canceled in that city on December 19, 1925, due to injuries suffered by Red Grange previously.

16. Neily, Harry. "Can't Play Daily Football; Bears Prove This," *Chicago Evening American*, December 15, 1925.

17. *Ibid.*

18. Halas, with Morgan and Veysey. *Halas: An Autobiography*, 109.

19. "Hartford Wallops New Britain, 28–7; Two Horsemen Star," *Meriden Record*, November 30, 1925, 12.

20. Lewis, Perry. "Notre Dame of 1924 Opposes Pro Forces," *Philadelphia Inquirer*, December 1, 1925, 21.

21. Hoffman, H. C. "Proud and Happy Maroons Enroute Home," *Pottsville Evening Republican*, December 7, 1925, 1.

22. "Cardinals Play Milwaukee Tomorrow," *Chicago Evening American*, December 9, 1925.

23. Original telegrams dated December 9, 1925, and December 10, 1925. Sternaman Collection, Professional Football Hall of Fame. Box 9B, Folder 24.

24. Mackay, Gordon. "Red Grange Will Play at Shibe Park on December 5," *Philadelphia Inquirer*, November 23, 1925, 12.

25. Mackay, Gordon. "Pottsville Defies League to Play Here," *Philadelphia Inquirer*, December 9, 1925, 26.

26. "Maroons Going Through with Game at Shibe Park in Spite of Officials," *Daily News*, December 9, 1925, 6.

27. Mackay, Gordon. "Pottsville Defies League to Play Here," *Philadelphia Inquirer*, December 9, 1925, 26.

28. "Maroons Will Not Cancel Game with Notre Dame," *Evening Herald*, December 10, 1925, 7.

29. "Are Perturbed Now," *Philadelphia Inquirer*, December 11, 1925, 26.

30. "Striegel Denies the Maroons Are Outlawed," *Mount Carmel Item*, December 14, 1925, 5.

31. "Red May Play Cards Here Dec. 20," *Chicago American*, December 12, 1925.

32. "Probe Story Preps Played on Card Team," *Chicago Daily Journal*, December 14, 1925.

33. "Englewood Players Confess," *Chicago Daily News*, December 15, 1925.

34. Neily, Harry. "Claim Boys Victims of Folz," *Chicago Evening American*, December 16, 1925.

35. *Ibid.*

36. "Englewood Boys Play with Pros," *Southtown Economist*, December 16, 1925, 1.

37. Crusinberry, James. "Preps Confess Pro Grid Charge," *Chicago Tribune*, December 16, 1925.

38. Wolfe, Rocky. "Snyder Says Folz Sought Him for Game," *Chicago Daily Journal*, December 16, 1925.

39. High, Guy. "Folz Exonerates Englewood Grid Stars," *Chicago Evening American*, December 17, 1925.

40. *Ibid.*

41. "A Plea for Four Boys," *Chicago Daily Journal*, December 17, 1925.

42. "Sidelines," *Chicago Evening American*, December 17, 1925.

43. Wolfe, Rocky. "Pro Charge Upheld for Four Preps," *Chicago Daily Journal*, December 24, 1925.

44. Morgenstern, W.V. "Englewood Boys Barred for All Time," *Chicago Herald and Examiner*, December 24, 1925.

45. High, Guy. "4 Englewood Gridders Get Gate," *Chicago Evening American*, December 24, 1925.

46. "Alarmed Over Anti-Feeling in Prep Case," *Chicago Daily Journal*, December 29, 1925.

47. "Drastic Action Is Taken Against Professional Clubs by Football League Head," *Cincinnati Enquirer*, December 30, 1925, 11.

48. "Carr Fines and Fires the Maroons, But His Authority is Questioned by Striegel," *Pottsville Evening Republican*, December 30, 1925, 7.

Chapter Eleven

1. Grange, Harold as told to Ira Morton. *The Red Grange Story: An Autobiography* (Urbana: University of Illinois Press, 1993), 109.

2. Richman, Alan. "5,000 Fans See Just What Pro Football Is All About," *Miami Tribune*, December 26, 1925, 13.

3. "Coral Gables Golf and Country Club Contract," November 12, 1925, Sternaman Collection, Professional Football Hall of Fame. Box 9A, Folder 20.

4. "Tampa Agreement," December 31, 1925, Sternaman Collection, Professional Football Hall of Fame. Box 9B, Folder 32.

5. "Dr. H.E. Opre Acquires Ownership of

Tampa Baseball Club," *Tampa Times*, May 14, 1925, 6.

6. McCarthy, Marvin. "Grange Comes Through with Touchdown," *Tampa Tribune*, January 2, 1926, 8.

7. Ibid.

8. Leiser, William. "Nevers Turns Pro; Gets $50,000 Contract," *San Francisco Examiner*, December 12, 1925, 1.

9. "Guarantee to Nevers Will Be Posted Soon," *Tampa Tribune*, December 15, 1925, 9.

10. "Nevers Signs to Play Against Red Grange in Florida," *Miami Herald*, December 15, 1925, 13.

11. "Santa Rosa Has One Topic of Conversation—Ernest Nevers," *San Francisco Examiner*, December 13, 1925, 115.

12. "Nevers Stops Red, But Bears Win, 19–6," *Chicago Tribune*, January 3, 1926, 27.

13. Ibid.

14. Whittingham, Richard. "*What a Game They Played*," (Lincoln: University of Nebraska Press, 2001), 10–11.

15. "Grange-Wilson Tilt Attracts 75,000 Crowd," *Santa Ana Register*, January 16, 1926, 17.

16. Halas, George S., with Gwen Morgan and Arthur Veysey. *Halas: An Autobiography* (Chicago: Bonus Books, 1986), 113.

17. Lowry, Paul. "Tigers Beaten in Great Game," *Los Angeles Times*, January 17, 1926, 21.

18. "Charles C. Pyle and Chicago Bears Football Club Agreement," December 16, 1925, Sternaman Collection, Professional Football Hall of Fame. Box 9B, Folder 44.

19. "Portland Baseball Club, Inc. Agreement," January 29, 1926, Sternaman Collection, Professional Football Hall of Fame. Box 9B, Folder 35.

20. Willis, Chris. *Red Grange: The Life and Legacy of the NFL's First Superstar* (Lanham: Rowman & Littlefield, 2019), 201.

21. "The Second Guess," *San Francisco Examiner*, January 26, 1926, 27.

22. Frayne, Pat. "Money Row Is Seen in Flops," *San Francisco Call and Post*, January 26, 1926, 1.

23. Halas, with Morgan and Veysey. *Halas: An Autobiography*, 115.

24. "Southern and Western Trip Settlement," December 21, 1925 to February 4, 1926, Sternaman Collection, Professional Football Hall of Fame.

25. Undated letter to E.C. Sternaman and G.S. Halas. Memoranda on Salaries Paid to Officers 1922–1925. Sternaman Collection, Professional Football Hall of Fame.

26. Armstrong, Gail. "Red Grange to Wed—But Not Before June of 1931," *Minneapolis Star*, February 4, 1926, 1.

27. "Pro Footballers Open Their Meet in Detroit Today," *Green Bay Press-Gazette*, February 6, 1926, 16.

28. Halas, with Morgan and Veysey. *Halas: An Autobiography*, 121.

29. Farrell, Henry. "Giants Eleven's Official Says Invasion of Grange Would Hurt Grid Game Here," *Brooklyn Citizen*, February 9, 1926, 8.

30. "Will Not Take College Men in Pro League," *Quad-City Times*, February 7, 1926, 53.

31. "President's Report," NFL Meeting Minutes, February 6–7, 1926.

32. Ibid.

33. "Pro Grid Title Goes a Begging," *The Tennessean*, February 15, 1926, 9.

34. "Horsemen and Maroons Walk," *Mount Carmel Item*, January 28, 1926, 5.

35. "Acquitted on Charge of Giving Bogus Check," *Evening Herald*, March 26, 1926, 4.

36. "Purple Scores in All Periods; Tilden Humbled," *Southtown Economist*, October 14, 1925; "Purple Downs Marshall by Score of 15–0," *Southtown Economist*, October 21, 1925.

37. "Wolf's Warriors Down Englewood of Chicago, 13–0," *Lock Haven Express*, December 7, 1925, 1.

38. Gibbons, Thomas. "Two Players from Lindbloom, Three from Englewood Placed on Section 2 All-Star Team," *Southtown Economist*, December 1, 1925, 11.

39. Martin, Howard. "Lindbloom Rates 4 Players on All-Star Team, *Chicago Tribune*, December 8, 1925, 29.

40. Maxwell, Don. "Views and News of Sports," *Chicago Tribune*, December 24, 1925, 15.

41. "Sportorials," *Southtown Economist*, September 15, 1926.

42. "Purple and Eagles Clash in Feature," *Southtown Economist*, October 13, 1926.

43. "William G. Thompson," *Rockford Morning Star*, May 2, 1947, 4.

44. "Burial Today for Policeman William G. Thompson, Jr.," *Chicago Tribune*, February 18, 1937, 22.

45. Author interview with Catherine Markee Smith, June 20, 2021.

46. Chicago Public Schools Student Records Services, Englewood High School, Jack Daniels; "Four-Year, February," *Purple and White Yearbook*, 1928, 20.

47. "Boosters Beat Amos A.A. 'Andy' Stars," *Hammond Times*, December 3, 1928, 14.

48. *Purple and White Yearbook*, 1927, 77.

49. "Snyder, James Leroy: 1927–1928 Transcripts," University of Illinois at Urbana-Champaign.

50. Year: *1930*; Census Place: *Chicago, Cook, Illinois*; Page: 8A; Enumeration District: 0648; FHL microfilm: 2340178.

51. Ward, Arch. "In the Wake of the News," *Chicago Tribune*, May 27, 1939, 17.

52. "Snyder Drives in Races Today at Evanston," *Chicago Tribune*, October 15, 1933, 31.

53. "Snyder Sweeps Auto Card; Wins Four Races," *Chicago Daily News*, November 30, 1934.

54. "Complete Auto Race Field; 33 to Start," *Chicago Tribune*, May 29, 1935, 21.

55. Patton, W. Blaine. "Snyder Wins No. 1 Post at 130.138," *Indianapolis Star*, May 21, 1939, 1.

56. Author interview with Joe Skibinski, June 29, 2021.

57. Jenkins, John. "Auto Racing World Mourns

Snyder, Killed in Midget Crash," *Chicago Daily News*, June 30, 1939.

58. "Salary War is Threat in Pro Grid Conflict," *Rock Island Argus*, February 10, 1926, 20.

59. "Joe Sternaman Gets Franchise in Red's League," *Chicago Tribune*, July 17, 1926, 13.

60. Whittingham, Richard. *What a Game They Played: An Inside Look at the Golden Era of Pro Football*. University of Nebraska Press, 2001. 11.

61. Joseph T. Sternaman Letter to Chicago Bears Football Club; Minutes: Special Meeting of the Board of Directors, May 14, 1926. Sternaman Collection, Professional Football Hall of Fame. Box 12A, Folder 2.

62. "Owners of Bears Pro Grid Team Disagree, Report," *Chicago Tribune*, July 20, 1926, 17.

63. Halas, with Morgan and Veysey. *Halas: An Autobiography*, 122.

64. *Ibid.*, 124.

65. Chicago Bulls, Inc. *State of Illinois, Department of State, Articles of Incorporation*. Springfield, IL, 1926.

66. Author Interview with Steve Thomas April 23, 2021.

67. Ward, Arch. "In the Wake of the News," *Chicago Tribune*, June 30, 1952, 49.

68. "Death Takes Arthur Folz," *Van Nuys News and Valley Green Sheet*, August 20, 1965, 8.

69. "18,000 Fans See Grange's Yanks Win 20–0 Game," *Chicago Tribune*, September 20, 1926, 21. "Cards Upset Columbus Pro Eleven in 1926 Debut, 14–0," *Chicago Tribune*, September 20, 1926, 21.

70. "Milwaukee Badgers Drop 10–7 Contest to Chicago Bears," *Green Bay Press-Gazette*, September 20, 1926, 14. "Chicago, Newark Play to 7–7 Tie," *Daily News*, September 27, 1926, 30.

71. "Driscoll Too Much for Old Team Mates as He Runs Amuck," *Southtown Economist*, October 20, 1926, 11.

72. Millard, H.V. "Bait for Bugs," *Decatur Daily Review*, October 18, 1926, 4.

73. Reisler, Jim. *Cash and Carry: The Spectacular Rise and Fall of C.C. Pyle, America's First Sport Agent* (Jefferson, NC: McFarland, 2009), 99.

74. Medbury, John. "Famous Riders," *El Paso Herald*, December 24, 1926, 8.

75. "Dunn Hurt as Bears Batter Cards, 10–0," *Chicago Tribune*, November 12, 1926, 23.

76. Brands, E.G. "Decide Fate of Professional Grid Game at Meet Next Month," *Collyer's Eye*, December 25, 1926, 8.

77. March, Dr. Harry. *Pro Football: Its Ups and Downs*. J.B. Lyon Company, 1934. 121.

78. "Cards, Bears Are Ready for Pro Grid Tilt," *Chicago Tribune*, September 24, 1927, 23.

79. Whittingham, Richard. *What a Game They Played: An Inside Look At the Golden Era of Pro Football*. 11.

80. Chicago Cardinals Football Club (1927). *State of Illinois, Department of State, Articles of Incorporation*. Springfield, IL.

81. https://www.profootballhof.com/players/guy-chamberlin/.

82. https://www.pro-football-reference.com/coaches/ChamGu0.htm.

83. *Ibid.*

84. Smith, Wilfrid. "Cards Defeat Bears, 3 to 0, On Swanson's Kick," *Chicago Tribune*, November 25, 1927.

85. Ryder, Jack. "Our Boys Find Cellar Champs Easy Mark," *Cincinnati Enquirer*, September 16, 1929.

86. Doxsie, Don. "Fastest Man in Baseball History," *Quad-City Times*, August 21, 2001, 45.

Chapter Twelve

1. Prell, Edward. "Grange Recalls Glory Years," *Chicago Tribune*, December 14, 1968, 45.

2. Halas, George S., with Gwen Morgan and Arthur Veysey. *Halas: An Autobiography* (Chicago: Bonus Books, 1986), 132.

3. Original Letter from D.H. Howard to Edward Sternaman, October 12, 1931, Sternaman Collection, Professional Football Hall of Fame.

4. "Memorandum of Agreement" between Chicago National League Ball Club and Chicago Bears Football Club, Inc., April 1, 1930, Sternaman Collection, Professional Football Hall of Fame. Box 7A, Folder 1.

5. *Ibid.*

6. "Memorandum of Agreement" between William C. Hauk and Chicago Bears Football Club, November 4, 1927. Sternaman Collection, Professional Football Hall of Fame. Box 7A, Folder 1.

7. "Chicago Bears Football Club, Inc. Balance Sheet, December 31, 1929." Sternaman Collection, Professional Football Hall of Fame.

8. "Official Program," Chicago Cardinals Football Club, September 23, 1928.

9. "Bears, Cards to Renew Feud on Pro Grid Today," *Chicago Tribune*, September 23, 1928, 32.

10. "Cards Out to Stop Senn of Bears Sunday," *Chicago Daily Journal*, September 21, 1928.

11. Anderson, Curley. "Superiority of Bear Backfield Tips Islanders," *Dispatch*, October 9, 1922, 11.

12. Rozendaal, Neal. *Duke Slater: Pioneering Black NFL Player and Judge* (Jefferson, NC: McFarland, 2012), 187.

13. "50,000 May See Bears and Cards in Charity Tilt," *Chicago Daily Journal*, November 16, 1928.

14. "Bear-Card Tilt Thursday; Proceeds to Xmas Fund," *Chicago Evening Post*, November 27, 1928.

15. "Pro Elevens Clash Early for Charity," *Chicago Daily Journal*, November 28, 1928.

16. Bell, Jim. "A Butkus of Yesterday," *Alton Evening Telegraph*, September 24, 1971, 17.

17. "Trafton, Bears' Center Arrested in Street Fight," *Chicago Tribune*, November 26, 1928, 27.

18. "Cardinals May Have Joesting for Bear Game," *Chicago Herald and Examiner*, November 28, 1928.

19. "Indian Jim Thorpe, World's Greatest Athlete, Joins Semco Gridders," *Hammond Times*, November 1, 1928, 17.

20. "Bears, Cardinals Settle City Title Dispute Today," *Chicago Tribune*, November 29, 1928.
21. "Jim Thorpe Plays; Proves a Shadow of Former Self," *Spokane Chronicle*, November 29, 1928, 20.
22. Author interview with Justin Lenhart, June 9, 2021.
23. Smith, Wilfrid. "Bears Romp Over Cards; Win, 34 to 0," *Chicago Tribune*, November 30, 1928.
24. Craven, Archie. "Pro Football Drops Curtain," *Collyer's Eye*, December 22, 1928, 3.
25. "Duke Slater, Former Iowa Negro Star, Is Booed Out of Game," *Gazette*, December 3, 1928, 8.
26. Author interview with Carol Judge, April 10, 2021.
27. Halas, with Morgan and Veysey. *Halas: An Autobiography*, 135.
28. Untitled letter of agreement between Chris O'Brien and Dr. David Jones, June 14, 1929. Professional Football Hall of Fame.
29. *Ibid*.
30. "Chicago Cardinals Are Sold by Chris O'Brien," *Dispatch*, July 19, 1929, 28.
31. Author interview with Carol Needham, 1998.
32. "Pyle and N.Y. Yanks Lose Pro Grid Franchise," *Chicago Tribune*, July 28, 1929, 28.
33. "3 New Members Come In; Pyle Frozen Out," *Collyer's Eye*, August 3, 1929, 12.
34. Grange, Harold as told to Ira Morton. *The Red Grange Story: An Autobiography* (Urbana: University of Illinois Press, 1993), 142.
35. Geiger, Edward. "Sports," *Chicago Evening American*, September 13, 1929.
36. Korch, Frank. "League Magnates Plan Uplift of Pro Football," *Collyer's Eye*, August 10, 1929, 12.
37. Ole Haugsrud letter reprinted with permission of Michael Moran, son of Cardinals player Hap Moran.
38. "Football Stars to Train Here," *Coldwater Daily Reporter*," September 16, 1929.
39. Halas, with Morgan and Veysey. *Halas: An Autobiography*, 134.
40. *Ibid*. 136.
41. Smith, Wilfrid. "Driscoll's Toe Fails; Cards Tie Bears, 0–0," *Chicago Tribune*, October 21, 1929, 21.
42. "Bears Trounce Minneapolis; Grange in Form," *Chicago Tribune*, October 28, 1929, 25.
43. "NFL's First Night Game," https://www.profootballhof.com/news/nfl-s-first-night-game/. Accessed February 15, 2021.
44. "Grange, Nevers Ready to Mix on Gridiron," *Chicago Herald and Examiner*, November 27, 1929.
45. "Pros Battle Tomorrow," *Chicago American*, November 17, 1929.
46. "Nevers," undated clipping found in archives of Pro Football Hall of Fame.
47. Walsh, Davis. "Friedman Only Grid Star to Shine as Pro," *Tampa Times*, November 28, 1929, 6.
48. Munzel, Edgar. "Famous Coast Star Plunges and Kicks All 40 Points," *Chicago Herald and Examiner*, November 30, 1929.
49. Smith, Wilfrid. "Ernie Nevers Whole Show as Cards Win, 40–6," *Chicago Tribune*, November 29, 1929.
50. "Cards Swamp Bears, 40–6," *Chicago American*, November 29, 1929.
51. Munzel, Edgar. "Famous Coast Star Plunges and Kicks All 40 Points," *Chicago Herald and Examiner*, November 30, 1929.
52. Smith, Wilfrid. "Ernie Nevers Whole Show as Cards Win, 40–6," *Chicago Tribune*, November 29, 1929.
53. "Bears and Their New Coach Get 1st Test Sunday," *Chicago Tribune*, September 18, 1930, 17.
54. Prell, Edward. "Grange Recalls Glory Years," *Chicago Tribune*, December 14, 1968, 45.
55. Murphy, Raymond. "'29 Battle of Clowns Proved Shires a 21 Second Fighter," *Chicago Tribune*, December 16, 1951, 67.
56. MacNamara, Harry. "Quit Ring? I've Only Begun to Fight—Shires," *Chicago Herald and Examiner*, December 18, 1929.
57. Author interview with Richard Shmelter, June 12, 2021.
58. *Ibid*.
59. Halas, with Morgan and Veysey. *Halas: An Autobiography*, 146.
60. "Chicago Bears Football Club, Inc. Balance Sheet, December 31, 1929." Sternaman Collection, Professional Football Hall of Fame.
61. "Santa Rosans Win Legion Grid Flag," *Oakland Tribune*, January 6, 1930, 16.
62. Condon, David. "In the Wake of the News," *Chicago Tribune*, December 12, 1968, 89.
63. Wicker, Brian. "A Football Legend," *Star Tribune*, October 24, 1999, 46.
64. Reinmuth, Gary. "Bear Great Nagurski Dies at 81," *Chicago Tribune*, January 9, 1990, 37.
65. "Chicago Bears Football Club, Inc. Salaries of Players, Season of 1930." Sternaman Collection, Professional Football Hall of Fame.
66. "Big Lines to Meet in Pro Game," *Chicago Evening Post*, October 17, 1930.
67. Rudy, William. "Grange Gallops Again and Bears Bump Cardinals," *Chicago Evening Post*, October 20, 1930.
68. Corken, Maurice. "Joe Savoldi Talks About Notre Dame and Other Things During Visit Here," *Rock Island Argus*, December 18, 1930, 18.
69. "Bears Sign Savoldi; Claim He is Eligible to Play this Season," *Green Bay Press-Gazette*, November 24, 1930, 14.
70. MacNamara, Harry. "Bears Defeat Cards, 6–0; Savoldi Scores," *Chicago Herald and Examiner*, November 28, 1930.
71. "Bears Fined $1,000 for Using Savoldi," *Chicago Tribune*, November 30, 1930.
72. "Chicago Bears Football Club, Inc. Salaries of Players, Season of 1930." Sternaman Collection, Professional Football Hall of Fame.
73. "Rules for Indoor Tilt Decided On," *Chicago Evening Post*, December 12, 1930.

74. "Bears and Cards Adopt Rules for Indoor Grid Play," *Chicago Tribune*, December 14, 1930, 3.
75. Ward, Arch. "Charity Gets $20,000 if Pro Game Fills Stadium Tonight," *Chicago Tribune*, December 15, 1930, 31.
76. Smith, Wilfrid. "Safety Brings Victory Over Cardinal Team," *Chicago Tribune*, December 16, 1930, 25.

Chapter Thirteen

1. Letter from Ralph Jones to Dutch Sternaman. December 17, 1931. Sternaman Collection, Professional Football Hall of Fame. Box 12A, Folder 19.
2. Halas, George. "New Coach, Fresh Idea Bring Bears Title," *Chicago Tribune*, January 29, 1967, 70.
3. "Contract Between Ralph R. Jones and the Chicago Bears Football Club, Inc.," March 20, 1931. Sternaman Collection, Professional Football Hall of Fame. Box 12A, Folder 19.
4. Letter from Chicago Bears Football Club to Ralph Jones, June 19, 1931. Sternaman Collection, Professional Football Hall of Fame. Box 12A, Folder 19.
5. Letter from Chicago Bears Football Club to Bronko Nagurski, undated. Sternaman Collection, Professional Football Hall of Fame. Box 7A, Folder 6.
6. "Grange, Nagurski Endorse Series," *Chicago Tribune*, January 21, 1967, 45.
7. "Chicago Bears Football Club, Inc. Balance Sheet, December 31, 1930." Sternaman Collection, Professional Football Hall of Fame. Box 12A, Folder 19.
8. "Chicago Bears Football Club Program Account," December 10, 1930. Sternaman Collection, Professional Football Hall of Fame.
9. Halas, George S., with Gwen Morgan and Arthur Veysey. *Halas: An Autobiography* (Chicago: Bonus Books, 1986), 147.
10. "Ed Sternaman Leaves Bears," *Chicago Evening American*, September 15, 1931.
11. "Agreement," May 21, 1931. Sternaman Collection, Professional Football Hall of Fame.
12. "Special Meeting of Stockholders" and "Special Meeting of Directors," both held July 3, 1931. Sternaman Collection, Professional Football Hall of Fame. Box 7A, Folder 1.
13. Halas, with Morgan and Veysey. *Halas: An Autobiography*, 148.
14. Letter from George Halas to Cicero State Bank, undated. Sternaman Collection, Professional Football Hall of Fame.
15. Agreement Between Edward C. Sternaman and George S. Halas, July 3, 1931. Sternaman Collection, Professional Football Hall of Fame.
16. Halas, with Morgan and Veysey. *Halas: An Autobiography*, 148.
17. Halas, George. "Halas Once 50 Minutes from Losing Bears," *Chicago Tribune*, January 30, 1967, 45.
18. Ziemba, Joe. *When Football Was Football: The Chicago Cardinals and the Birth of the NFL* (Chicago: Triumph Books, 1999), 176.
19. "Andrews Is New Card Mentor," *Chicago Evening American*, August 27, 1931.
20. Ward, Arch. "Talking It Over," *Chicago Tribune*, September 4, 1931, 27.
21. Ward, Arch. "Talking It Over," *Chicago Tribune*, September 15, 1931, 17.
22. Ward, Arch. "Talking It Over," *Chicago Tribune*, August 17, 1931, 23.
23. "Did You Know That," *Scranton Republican*, August 27, 1931, 17.
24. Ward, Arch. "Talking It Over," *Chicago Tribune*, August 20, 1931, 23.
25. Zuppke, Bob. "Zuppke Staunch Supporter of College Football Game," *Dispatch*, September 15, 1931, 16.
26. Ward, Arch. "Talking It Over," *Chicago Tribune*, August 28, 1931, 23.
27. Ward, Arch. "Talking It Over," *Chicago Tribune*, September 18, 1931, 29.
28. "Andrew Resigns as Coach of Cardinals Pro Football Team," *Chicago Daily News*, October 5, 1931.
29. "Andrew Resigns as Card Coach; Reasons Differ," *Chicago Tribune*, October 6, 1931, 25.
30. "Grange Leads Bears to Easy Triumph Over Cards, 26 to 13," *Chicago Herald and Examiner*, October 19, 1931.
31. Whittingham, Richard. *The Bears: A 75-Year Celebration* (Dallas: Taylor Publishing, 1994), 159.
32. "Bears, Cards Ready for Turkey Day Tilt," *Chicago Evening American*, November 24, 1931.
33. "Old Pro Rivals, Bears, Cards, to Meet Thursday," *Chicago Daily News*, November 24, 1931.
34. Geiger, Edward J. "That Annual Grid Classic—Bears vs. Cards—Tomorrow," *Chicago Evening American*, November 25, 1931.
35. Martin, Heinie. "Sport Chatter," *Grand Rapids Herald*, December 6, 1931.
36. "Nevers Retires from Pro Grid; Breaks Wrist and Wins Bay Game," *Sacramento Bee*, January 25, 1932, 17.
37. Leiser, William. "Blond Giant Alone Masses 140 Yards on Line Plunges," *San Francisco Examiner*, January 25, 1932, 17.
38. "Continental Illinois Bank and Trust Company Notice," December 29, 1931. Sternaman Collection, Professional Football Hall of Fame. Box 12B, Folder 47.
39. Davis, Jeff. *Papa Bear: The Life and Legacy of George Halas* (New York: McGraw Hill, 2005), 106.
40. Smith, Wilfrid, "Bears Rise to Pro Heights with Signing of Nagurski," *Chicago Tribune*, December 7, 1934, 33.
41. Maxymuk, John. *Pioneer Coaches of the NFL: Shaping the Game in the Days of Leather Helmets and 60-Minute Men* (Lanham: Rowman & Littlefield, 2019), xxii.
42. "Joe Lillard is Held Ineligible in Coast Ruling," *Eugene Guard*, October 16, 1931, 1.
43. Casserly, Hank, "Hank Says," *Capital Times*, October 11, 1932, 11.

44. Buehner, Kristin. "He Did It All," *Globe-Gazette*, February 24, 2002, 1.
45. Halas, with Morgan and Veysey. *Halas: An Autobiography*, 168.
46. "Bears, Spartans Find Stadium Perfect As Grid," *Chicago Tribune*, December 17, 1932, 21.
47. "Bears Boast 6 Daddies," *Los Angeles Daily News*, January 8, 1937, 19.
48. Whittingham, Richard. *What a Game They Played: An Inside Look at the Golden Era of Pro Football* (Lincoln: University of Nebraska Press, 2001), 152.
49. Smith, Wilfrid. "Bears Win 9-0; Pro Football Champions," *Chicago Tribune*, December 19, 1932, 19.
50. Halas, with Morgan and Veysey. *Halas: An Autobiography*, 170.
51. Smith, Wilfrid. "National Pro Grid League Admits 3 Clubs," *Chicago Tribune*, July 9, 1933, 21.
52. "Chevigny Signs as St. Edward's Football Coach," *Chicago Tribune*, January 19, 1933, 25.
53. Hart, Weldon. "Jack Chevigny, Ex-UT Coach, Killed on Iwo," *Austin American*, March 24, 1945, 1.
54. Banks-Hernandez, Nancy. "An All-American Hero Remembered," *Hammond Times*, February 19, 1995, 84.
55. "Schissler to Coach Cardinals for Three Years," *Chicago Tribune*, May 12, 1933, 21.
56. "Ralph Jones Takes Position as Athletic Director at Lake Forest," *Pantagraph*, March 22, 1933, 8.
57. "Resignation of Jones Gives Red Big Opportunity," *Waukegan News-Sun*, March 23, 1933, 7.
58. Halas, with Morgan and Veysey. *Halas: An Autobiography*, 150.
59. Fearnow, Dawson. "Cardinals Sin: The Shady Roots of the NFL's Oldest Team," *Phoenix Magazine*, September 17, 2020.
60. https://www.forbes.com/teams/arizona-cardinals/?sh=5300b3303d28. Accessed March 9, 2021.
61. Ward, Arch. "Sport Leader Takes Control from Dr. Jones," *Chicago Tribune*, September 6, 1933, 23.
62. "Chi-Cardinals Football Team Sold by Jones," *Green Bay Press-Gazette*, September 6, 1933, 9.
63. Kogan, Rick. "Thoroughbreds," *Chicago Tribune*, April 29, 1993, 71.
64. Farrell, Henry. "Bidwill Has Eyes on Dollar Guys," *Chicago Daily News*, October 16, 1933.
65. "Pro Grid League Plans Wide Open Game Next Year," *New York Daily News*, December 15, 1933, 535.
66. "Bears Rally to Defeat Giants for Title, 23-21," *New York Daily News*, December 18, 1933, 214.
67. Smith, Wilfrid. "Bears Whip Giants, 23-21; World Champions," *Chicago Tribune*, December 18, 1933, 23.
68. *Ibid.* 25.
69. Author interview with George King, July 31, 2021.
70. "Hanley Hails Pro Forward Passing Rule," *Chicago Tribune*, December 18, 1933, 25.
71. Ray, Bob. "Pro Elevens Give 20,000 Fans Thrill," *Los Angeles Times*, January 15, 1934, 9.
72. "Mayor Kelly to Greet Chicago Bears Today," *Decatur Herald*, February 20, 1934, 4.
73. Drum, Bob. "Holiday Bowls Filled with Southeastern Conference Cheer," *Pittsburgh Press*, December 14, 1962, 39.
74. Bradis, Joe. "Pittsburgh Steeler Confidence Rests with Walt Kiesling," *Jackson Sun*, October 19, 1954, 10.
75. "Maroon Luck Is All Bad; Meet Ohio State Next," *Chicago Tribune*, October 26, 1937, 19.
76. "Herbert Blumer," *San Francisco Examiner*, April 15, 1987, 19.
77. Ward, Arch. "College Football Stars to Battle Bears," *Chicago Tribune*, July 6, 1934, 23.
78. Ward, Arch. "165,000 Pick College Team to Face Bears," *Chicago Tribune*, July 27, 1934, 23.
79. "617,000 Fans Elect Kizer All-Star Coach," *Chicago Tribune*, August 13, 1934, 21.
80. Ward, Arch. "Grange Eager for Test with College Stars," *Chicago Tribune*, July 7, 1934, 15.
81. Foust, Hal. "Huge Concourse of Cars Chokes Paths to Game," *Chicago Tribune*, September 1, 1934, 19.
82. Roberts, Howard. "Stars Shine in 0-0 Battle with Bears," *Chicago Daily News*, September 1, 1934.
83. Vaughan, Irving. "Bears Offer No Alibis, But Wish Another Chance," *Chicago Tribune*, September 1, 1934, 19.
84. Shaffer, George. "College Boys Jubilant Over Playing Pros to Standstill," *Chicago Tribune*, September 1, 1934, 19.
85. "O'Brien Starts Pro Eleven to be Known as Chicago Tigers," *Chicago Daily News*, August 25, 1934.
86. Strickler, George. "Green Bay Game Ends Cardinal Season Today," *Chicago Tribune*, November 29, 1934, 47.
87. Niss, Lou. "Change in Tactics Brings Giants Professional Football Crown," *Brooklyn Times Union*, December 10, 1934, 13.
88. Reil, Frank. "Jasper's Shoes Help Football Giants to Pro Gridiron Title," *Brooklyn Daily Eagle*, December 10, 1934, 11.
89. "Strong! Huh, the Real Hero of the Game Was Abe Cohen," *Brooklyn Times Union*, December 10, 1934, 13.
90. Powers, Jimmy. "Canvas Sneakers Won," *New York Daily News*, December 10, 1934, 46.
91. Carmichael, John. "Football Kept Owen from Growing Old," *Daily Oklahoman*, May 20, 1964, 43.
92. "Deny Report of Gambling Coup in Title Game," *Chicago Tribune*, December 10, 1934, 25.
93. "Bears Conquer Dodgers, 20-6, in Knoxville Game," *Chicago Tribune*, December 23, 1934, 15.

Chapter Fourteen

1. Strickler, George. "Cardinals Plan Surprise Attack for Bear Game," *Chicago Tribune*, October 13, 1934, 23.
2. Roberts, Howard. "Bears Need One Victory to Win Division Title," *Chicago Daily News*, November 26, 1934.
3. "Cards Start on Pro Football Trip to Coast," *Chicago Daily News*, November 30, 1934.
4. Braunwart, Bob, and Carroll, Bob. "Dr. Joe: A Guard's Guard," *Coffin Corner*, Vol. 2, No. 5, 1980, 1.
5. "No Coast Conference Official Can Work Pro Grid Games," *Sacramento Bee*, January 15, 1935, 15.
6. Bastajian. "Cardinals Beat Bears, 13–9, In Vicious Pro Grid Battle," *Illustrated Daily News*, January 14, 1935, 9.
7. Shaffer, George. "Can Bears Get Even? Take on Giants Today," *Chicago Tribune*, January 27, 1935, 23.
8. Dyer, Braven. "Bears Get Revenge, Beat Giants, 21–0," *Los Angeles Times*, January 28, 1935, 9.
9. Larkin, Will. "#31 Link Lyman," *Chicago Tribune*, August 6, 2019, 8.
10. "Grange Says He's Through," *Decatur Daily Review*, January 29, 1935, 25.
11. Reinmuth, Gary. "Red Grange: Greatness and Humility," *Chicago Tribune*, January 29, 1991, 32.
12. "Paul Schissler Resigns Job as Cardinal Coach," *Chicago Tribune*, February 8, 1935, 27.
13. Ward, Arch. "Talking It Over," *Chicago Tribune*, February 12, 1935, 19.
14. Ward, Arch. "Four Coaches Accept Positions on All-Star Staff," *Chicago Tribune*, August 8, 1935, 17.
15. Ward, Arch. "Bears Play College All-Stars Aug. 29," *Chicago Tribune*, July 2, 1935, 21.
16. Strickler, George. "Cards Battle Bears Today; Seek Title Tie," *Chicago Tribune*, December 8, 1935, 33.
17. Halas, George S., with Gwen Morgan and Arthur Veysey. *Halas: An Autobiography* (Chicago: Bonus Books, 1986), 183.
18. "Green Bay Packers Secure Don Hutson," *Green Bay Press-Gazette*, February 22, 1935, 13.
19. Zimmerman, David. *Curly Lambeau: The Man Behind the Mystique* (Hales Corners: Eagle Books, 2003), 112.
20. "Don Hutson Claimed by Two Professional Leaguers," *Nashville Banner*, February 23, 1935, 10.
21. Sell, Jack. "Salary Fuss Comes to Head at Grid Meet," *Pittsburgh Post-Gazette*, May 18, 1935, 15.
22. *Ibid.*
23. Author interview with Upton Bell, August 3, 2021.
24. *Ibid.*
25. https://operations.nfl.com/journey-to-the-nfl/the-nfl-draft/the-history-of-the-draft/. Accessed July 27, 2021.
26. Author interview with Upton Bell, August 3, 2021.
27. *Ibid.*
28. Husar, John. "Jay Berwanger Made Success of Life," *Chicago Tribune*, October 24, 1974, 75.
29. *Ibid.*
30. Kott, Doc. "Three Grid Charity Tilts Mean $25,000 to Hospital," *Hammond Times*, September 12, 1937, 37.
31. Carroll, Bob, with Michael Gersham, David Neft, John Thorn. *Total Football II: The Official Encyclopedia of the National Football League* (New York: Harper Collins Publishers, 1999). Player statistics and draft status included were listed in various sections of this publication.
32. "Annual Draft Meet Starts," *Green Bay Press-Gazette*, December 12, 1936, 13.
33. Macker, Gordon. "Bulldogs Upset Cardinals, 13–10," *Los Angeles Daily News*, December 14, 1936, 19.
34. Berkow, Ira. "Last of the Bareheaded Boys," *Times-Tribune*, November 10, 1974, 51.
35. *Ibid.*
36. Ward, Arch. "Talking It Over," *Chicago Tribune*, February 13, 1937, 19.
37. "New Grid Loop Tottering?" *Collyer's Eye and the Baseball World*, October 9, 1937, 3.
38. Roberts, Howard. "Bears Resume Practice After Two-Day Rest," *Chicago Daily News*, December 1, 1937, 27.
39. Roberts, Howard. "Civil Warfare on Pro Gridiron Closes Season," *Chicago Daily News*, December 4, 1937, 21.
40. Korch, Frank. "Five Chicago Bears, Two Green Bay Packers on All-Pro Grid Team," *Collyer's Eye and the Baseball World*, December 4, 1937, 2.
41. Roberts, Howard. "Bears Get Hot on Icy Field; Cards Get Burnt," *Chicago Daily News*, December 6, 1937, 17.
42. Strickler, George. "Bears Roll Up 42–28 Victory Over Cardinals," *Chicago Tribune*, December 6, 1937, 21.
43. *Ibid.*
44. Roberts, Howard. "Bears Get Hot on Icy Field; Cards Get Burnt," *Chicago Daily News*, December 6, 1937, 17.
45. McConnell, Mickey. "Sideline Slander," *Kearney Daily Hub*, December 7, 1937, 6.
46. Strickler, George. "Grange, Bronko Now Only Memories," *Chicago Tribune*, September 19, 1971, 166.
47. "Baugh Hero of Victory by Redskins," *Daily Mail*, December 13, 1937, 9.
48. "Chicago Bears Thump Dixie Rivals, 41–20," *Los Angeles Times*, January 31, 1938, 27.
49. Clay, Everett. "Chicago Bears Trip Washington Redskins," *Miami Herald*, February 7, 1938, 9.
50. Zimmerman, Paul. "The Bronk and the Gazelle," *Sports Illustrated*, September 11, 1989.
51. Bierig, Joel. "The Bronk," *Minneapolis Star*, March 1, 1982, 25.
52. Brietz, Eddie. "Bronko Nagurski Quits Chicago Bears," *Chattanooga News*, August 18, 1938, 7.

53. Ward, Arch, "In the Wake of the News," *Chicago Tribune*, August 16, 1938, 15.
54. Oates, Bob, "The Best Bear of All," *Journal Herald*, May 7, 1984, 9.
55. Strickler, George, "Five Fired in Shakeup of Cardinals Eleven," *Chicago Tribune*, October 12, 1938, 27.
56. "Philadelphia Eagles Defeat Chicago Cardinals at Erie, PA, 7 to 0," *Philadelphia Inquirer*, October 27, 1938, 23.
57. Strickler, George. "Nevers Returns to Pro Ranks as Coach of the Cards," *Chicago Tribune*, December 2, 1938, 27.
58. "Ex-TCU Star Ki Aldrich Dead at 66," *Fort Worth Star Telegram*," March 13, 1983, 52.
59. Roberts, Howard. "Bears Wary of Trick Offense in Card Tilt," *Chicago Daily News*, October 13, 1939.
60. Strickler, George. "Bears Rout Cardinals, 44–7, Before 29,592," *Chicago Tribune*, October 16, 1939, 19.
61. Sullivan, Prescott. "Nevers Quits Chicago Pro Post," *San Francisco Examiner*, February 20, 1940, 22.

Chapter Fifteen

1. Cochrane, Edward. "Sports," *Chicago Herald-American*, December 8, 1939.
2. "Conzelman to Coach Chicago Cardinals," *Belvidere Daily Republican*, April 11, 1940, 6.
3. "What Others Think of Jimmy Conzelman, Star Here Tonight," *Mount Carmel Item*, December 11, 1941, 10.
4. Strickler, George. "Cardinal Pro Team Moves to Comiskey Park," *Chicago Tribune*, April 21, 1940, 39.
5. "Villanova's Chisick Signs with Chicago Cardinals," *Philadelphia Inquirer*, April 26, 1940, 31.
6. "Young's Yarns," *Pantagraph*, May 8, 1940, 14.
7. Field, F.B. "Pro Grid Cards See Hope for a Comeback," *Collyer's Eye and The Baseball World*," June 22, 1940, 2.
8. Ziemba, Joe. *Cadets, Cannons and Legends: The Football History of Morgan Park Military Academy* (Columbus: Gatekeeper Press, 2018), 270.
9. Strickler, George. "Tricky Offense Causes Problem in Bears' Camp," *Chicago Tribune*, September 20, 1940, 31.
10. "Chicago Bears Greatest Pro Team, Van Every Green Bay's Best Pickup," *Minneapolis Star*, September 23, 1940, 18.
11. Author interview with Jon Cooper, August 21, 2021.
12. Carroll, Bob. "When Halas Cornered the Draft," *Coffin Corner*, Volume 18, Number 5, 1996, 1.
13. "Storm Drenches Crowd of 18,000," *Democrat and Chronicle*, September 16, 1940, 19.
14. Strickler, George. "30,000 to See Cards Play Bears in Sox Park Tonight," *Chicago Tribune*, September 25, 1940, 25.
15. "Bears vs Cards," *Official Cardinal Football Magazine*, September 25, 1940.
16. Strickler, George, "Cardinals Score 21 to 7 Upset Over Bears," *Chicago Tribune*, September 20, 1940, 21.
17. Ward, Arch. "Chicago Pass Goes to 1 Yard Line At Finish," *Chicago Tribune*, November 18, 1940, 21.
18. Halas, George S., with Gwen Morgan and Arthur Veysey. *Halas: An Autobiography* (Chicago: Bonus Books, 1986), 187.
19. Ibid. 188.
20. Lardner, John. "Alumni of Redskin Tech Boast; But It Looks Tough," *Argus-Leader*, December 3, 1940, 10.
21. "Chicago Bears Through Losing," *Minneapolis Star*, November 20, 1940, 13.
22. Halas, with Morgan and Veysey. *Halas: An Autobiography*, 188.
23. "Pro Tilt Harder to Crash Than White House," *New York Daily News*, December 7, 1940, 168.
24. "WGN, Mutual to Broadcast Bear, Redskin Battle," *Chicago Tribune*, December 4, 1940, 38.
25. Smith, Chester L. "Sutherland Rates Bears Best He Has Seen," *Pittsburgh Press*, December 5, 1940, 27.
26. Halas, with Morgan and Veysey. *Halas: An Autobiography*, 190.
27. Smith, Wilfrid. "Sid Luckman's Generalship Key to Victory," *Chicago Tribune*, December 9, 1940, 21.
28. "Redskins Roasted by Fans, Wits of Press Box," *New York Daily News*, December 9, 1940, 56.
29. Whittingham, Richard. *What a Game They Played: An Inside Look at the Golden Era of Pro Football* (Lincoln: University of Nebraska Press, 2001), 177.
30. Smith, Chester L. "The Village Smithy," *Pittsburgh Press*, October 22, 1954, 41.
31. "Records Tumble as Pro Football Draws 1,600,000," *Chicago Tribune*, December 24, 1940, 14.
32. Prell, Edward. "34,668 Watch Bears Rout Cardinals 53–7," *Chicago Tribune*, October 13, 1941, 23.
33. Roberts, Howard. "Bears to Battle Packers in Title Playoff," *Chicago Daily News*, December 8, 1941.
34. "Cardinals Are Heroes Despite Their Defeat," *Chicago Tribune*, December 8, 1941, 28.
35. Prell, Edward. "Bears Whip Cards, 34–24; Playoff Sunday," *Chicago Tribune*, December 8, 1941, 27.
36. "Big Bad Bears of Old Come Out of Hibernation for Night," *Chicago Tribune*, December 8, 1941, 28.
37. Trost, Ralph. "All on Those Bears!" *Brooklyn Daily Eagle*, December 22, 1941, 15.
38. "Sports," National Football League Release, December, 1941. Professional Football Hall of Fame.
39. "Snyder's 3 Field Goals Lead Bears to Victory in Title Game," *St. Louis Post-Dispatch*, December 22, 1941, 12.

40. "U.S. and Japs at War," *Chicago Tribune*, December 8, 1941, 1.
41. Ziemba, Joe. *When Football Was Football: The Chicago Cardinals and the Birth of the NFL* (Chicago: Triumph Books, 1999), 235.
42. Barnhart, Tony. "The '40s: NFL Goes to War," *Coffin Corner*, Vol. 9, No. 8, 1987.
43. https://www.profootballhof.com/footballs-wartime-heroes/. Accessed October 17, 2020.
44. Halas, with Morgan and Veysey. *Halas: An Autobiography*, 203.
45. "Halas Receives Sword at Last Game as Big Bear," *Chicago Tribune*, October 26, 1942, 23.
46. Halas, with Morgan and Veysey. *Halas: An Autobiography*, 204.
47. "Bears Open with Cards On Oct. 11," *Dixon Evening Telegraph*, September 1, 1942, 9.
48. Prell, Edward. "Cards, Bears Feud Flares for 44th Game," *Chicago Tribune*, October 8, 1942, 29.
49. *Ibid.*
50. Prell, Edward. "Bears Rout Cardinals, 41–14," *Chicago Tribune*, October 12, 1942, 23.
51. Author interview with Toni Nagel Mason, August 26, 2021.
52. "Sports," National Football League Release, December 5, 1942. Professional Football Hall of Fame.
53. "Conzelman Quits Football Post for Job with Browns," *Rock Island Argus*, June 3, 1943, 2.
54. Millard, Howard V. "Bait for Bugs," *Decatur Daily Review*, June 13, 1943, 13.
55. Gunderman, Ken. "The Sports Parade," *Escanaba Daily*, June 10, 1943, 11.
56. Prell, Edward. "Cardinal and Bear Merger Rooney's Idea," *Chicago Tribune*, June 9, 1943, 25.
57. *Ibid.*
58. "National Football League Will Start 1943 Season With Eight Contestants," *Hartford Courant*, June 20, 1943, 43.
59. "Meeting Minutes," National Football League Meeting, June 19, 1943, 3. Professional Football Hall of Fame.
60. Enright, James. "Cards Vacate Camp, Bears Move In," *Chicago Herald-American*, September 18, 1943.
61. Sheer, Harry. "Bronko Writes New Chapter in His Grid Career," *Chicago Daily News*, November 29, 1943, 19.
62. Halas, with Morgan and Veysey. *Halas: An Autobiography*, 214.
63. "Cards-Steelers Will Capture Western Title, Edwards Says," *Green Bay Press-Gazette*, July 27, 1944, 17.
64. Walker, Ben. "Car-Pitts Merger Made for Memories, Not Wins," *Rutland Daily Herald*, January 27, 2009, 15.
65. "40,734 Watch Giants Rout Card-Pitt, 23–0," *Chicago Tribune*, October 23, 1944, 23.
66. Birks, Tom. "Grigas' Letter Explains Quitting Club," *Pittsburgh Sun-Telegraph*, December 4, 1944, 15.
67. *Ibid.*
68. Boyle, Havey J. "The Departure of Grigas," *Pittsburgh Post-Gazette*, December 5, 1944, 14.
69. "What Happened to Johnny Grigas?" *Detroit Free Press*, January 7, 1945, 11.
70. Sheer, Harry. "Wee Collins Puts Hope in 'Little' Grid Cards," *Chicago Daily News*, September 21, 1945, 25.
71. Sheer, Harry. "Bulger Shines as Lions Beat Cards," *Chicago Daily News*, September 24, 1945.
72. Prell, Edward. "Speak of Card-Bear Series and You Talk of Driscoll," *Chicago Tribune*, November 29, 1945, 28.
73. Sheer, Harry. "Tonelli, P.O.W. to C.H. (Cover Hutson)," *Chicago Daily News*, October 24, 1945, 33.
74. Ziemba. *When Football Was Football: The Chicago Cardinals and the Birth of the NFL*, 269.
75. Fay, William. "Cards Whet Their Appetites for Turkeys and Bears, Too," *Chicago Tribune*, November 29, 1946, 35.
76. Fay, William. "Cards, Bears to Wind Up Chicago Schedule Today," *Chicago Tribune*, December 1, 1946.
77. McCulley, Jim. "Trippi, Yanks Near Agreement," *New York Daily News*, January 16, 1947, 360.
78. Ziemba, *When Football Was Football: The Chicago Cardinals and the Birth of the NFL*, 311.
79. "Charley Trippi," undated document. Professional Football Hall of Fame.
80. Original copy of telegram in Chicago Cardinals Records (Chicago History Museum). Accession Number: M1962.0329.

Chapter Sixteen

1. O'Donnell, Jim. "One Ace Among Bidwill's Cards," *Southtown Star*, January 25, 2009, 30.
2. Ward, Gene. "Army 20-Pt. Pick to Rip ND for 2d Year in Row," *New York Daily News*, November 10, 1945, 58.
3. O'Donnell, Jim. "One Ace Among Bidwill's Cards," *Southtown Star*, January 25, 2009, 30.
4. Warren, Harry. "Cards Win, 31–7; Bears Fade in 2d Half," *Chicago Tribune*, October 6, 1947, 31.
5. Curran, Bob. *Pro Football's Rag Days* (New York: Bonanza Books, 1969) 56.
6. *Ibid.*, 56.
7. Smith, Wilfrid. "Opportunity Knocks and Cards Reply," *Chicago Tribune*, December 15, 1947, 63.
8. Pierson, Don. "When the Cardinals Flew High," *Chicago Tribune*, August 15, 1997, 62.
9. Effrat, Louis. "Cards Prepare for Aerial Battle With Eagles in Chicago Tomorrow," *New York Times*, December 27, 1947.
10. Biederman, Les. "Eagle Backfield to Battle Cardinal Line for Title," *Pittsburgh Press*, December 28, 1947, 19.
11. "Coach Neale Tells of Eagles' Success," *Harrisburg Telegraph*, December 23, 1947, 17.
12. "Cards-Eagles Battle for NFL Championship," *The Mercury*, December 27, 1947, 9.
13. Curran. *Pro Football's Rag Days,* 57.
14. Cromie, Robert. "Cards, All Aces on Field,

Howl Like the Deuce," *Chicago Tribune*, December 29, 1947, 25.

15. Kearns, Patrick. "'47 Cards Relive the 'Dream' Team," *Chicago Tribune*, December 28, 1987, 34.

16. Cromie, Robert. "Cards, All Aces on Field, Howl Like the Deuce," *Chicago Tribune*, December 29, 1947, 26.

17. Birks, Tom. "Cards Choice Over Eagles in Pro Football Playoff," *Pittsburgh Sun-Telegraph*, December 28, 1947, 24.

18. Sheer, Harry. "Burkett Death 3d in Cardinal Family," *Chicago Daily News*, October 25, 1947.

19. Ward, Arch. "Cardinals Foes in Soldier Field," *Chicago Tribune*, May 9, 1948, 67.

20. "Half Million See All-Stars on Television," *Chicago Tribune*, August 22, 1948, 61.

21. Warren, Harry. "Cards' Spirit Won Game, Says Charley Trippi," *Chicago Tribune*, August 22, 1948, 59.

22. Cronin, Tim. "The Glory Days—From the Inside," *Southtown Economist*. Undated.

23. Hanson, Ed. "Looking 'Em Over," *Daily Tribune*, September 27, 1948, 5.

24. McCormick, Henry. "Playing the Game," *Wisconsin State Journal*, December 12, 1948, 33.

25. "Conzelman Cools Off Team At Half; Cards Go On to Beat Bears, 24–21," *Dispatch*, December 13, 1948, 14.

26. Broeg, Bob. "Big Red's Red Cochran Couldn't Shake Football," *St. Louis Post-Dispatch*, August 6, 1968, 24.

27. Chamberlain, Charles. "Cards Rally in 4th Quarter to Defeat Bears, 24–21," *Decatur Herald*, December 13, 1948, 8.

28. "Cards, Browns Favored in Pro Playoffs Today," *New York Daily News*, December 19, 1948, 292.

29. Welsh, Charles. "Neale Knocks Again on Door for Grid Title," *Cumberland Sunday Times*, December 19, 1948, 37.

30. Smith, Wilfrid. "Bad Weather Hits Eagles' Title Drills," *Chicago Tribune*, December 18, 1948, 17.

31. "Eagles Show Cards Tricks," *Daily Chronicle*, December 20, 1948, 10.

32. Fraley, Oscar. "Eagles Want No More, Thanks," *Quad-City Times*, December 20, 1948, 18.

33. "Browns and Eagles Take Pro Crowns," *Decatur Daily Review*, December 20, 1948, 10.

34. Prell, Edward. "Conzelman Quits as Cardinals' Coach," *Chicago Tribune*, January 6, 1949, 17.

35. Ibid., 17.

36. "Jimmy Conzelman Quits as Coach of Grid Cards for Ad Firm Job Here," *St. Louis Post-Dispatch*, January 8, 1949, 6.

Chapter Seventeen

1. Prell, Edward. "Cards, Trippi Stop Bears, 24–14," *Chicago Tribune*, December 17, 1951, 57.

2. Ibid.

3. Warren, Harry. "Triple Dream Comes True for Cardinal Aids," *Chicago Tribune*, December 17, 1951, 61.

4. Frisk, Bob. "Bears vs. Cardinals ... Classic Collisions," *Daily Herald*, November 5, 1976, 23.

5. "The Dry Days of Bulldog Turner," *Gatesville Messenger and Star-Forum*, January 24, 1985, 7.

6. Halas, George S., with Gwen Morgan and Arthur Veysey. *Halas: An Autobiography* (Chicago: Bonus Books, 1986), 237.

7. Daley, Art. "New Pro Grid League to Be Set Thursday," *Green Bay Press-Gazette*, January 18, 1950, 17.

8. Daley, Art. "Packers Start Hunt for New Coach-First Time in 31 Years," *Green Bay Press-Gazette*, February 2, 1950, 21.

9. Fullerton, Hugh Jr. "Fans Give Lambeau One Season in 'Chi,'" *Green Bay Press-Gazette*, March 1, 1950, 50.

10. "Curly Lambeau Quits as Coach of Pro Cardinals," *Daily Register*, December 8, 1951, 5.

11. "Benningsen Breaks with Bidwills Over Policies," *Chicago Tribune*, July 13, 1951, 45.

12. Ibid.

13. Olsen, Jack. "The Unhappiest Millionaire," *Sports Illustrated*, April 4, 1950.

14. Morrison, Bruce. "Bears Nip Cards, 10–7," *Chicago Sun-Times*, December 15, 1952.

15. Strickler, George. "Bears, Cards to Bury 1953 Hopes Today," *Chicago Tribune*, December 13, 1953, 61.

16. Warren, Harry. "Santa Claus Halas Brings Glee to Cards," *Chicago Tribune*, December 14, 1953, 70.

17. "Grid Cardinal Players Due Profit Slice," *Miami Herald*, December 8, 1954, 49.

18. Warren, Harry. "Cards Plan to Share Profit with Players," *Chicago Tribune*, December 8, 1954, 55.

19. "Owners Point Out Hitches in Profit Sharing," *Chicago Tribune*, December 8, 1954, 3.

20. "New Police Station Recalls Sport Scenes of Past," *Southtown Economist*, September 8, 1954, 57.

21. Strickler, George. "Halas Blasts Site of Bear, Card Battle," *Chicago Tribune*, November 24, 1955, 101.

22. Ibid.

23. "Halas Charges Cards Neglect 'Sloppy' Gridiron," *Des Moines Register*, November 24, 1955, 24.

24. Strickler, George. "Cards Upset Bears in Snowstorm, 53–14," *Chicago Tribune*, November 28, 1955, 1.

25. Cromie, Robert. "Their Good Game, Our Bad One-Halas," *Chicago Tribune*, November 28, 1955, 69.

26. Ibid., 70.

27. "Driscoll's Age Big Puzzle to Fans of Bears," *Decatur Daily Review*, February 3, 1956, 11.

28. Smith, Wilfrid. "Driscoll Bears' New Head Coach," *Chicago Tribune*, February 3, 1956, 43.

29. Strickler, George. "Bears Beat Cards, 10–3; Players in Fight," *Chicago Tribune*, December 10, 1956, 77.

30. Ibid.

31. Rollow, Cooper. "Paddy Builds Suspense in Card, Bear Thrill Series," *Chicago Tribune*, December 5, 1958, 49.

32. Strickler, George. "Bears Beat Cards, 10–3; Players in Fight," *Chicago Tribune*, December 10, 1956, 80.

33. Condon, David. "In the Wake of the News," *Chicago Tribune*, December 10, 1956, 77.

34. Author interview with Jon Cooper, August 27, 2021.

35. Strickler, George. "Cardinals Protest Defeat by Bears," *Chicago Tribune*, December 14, 1956, 59.

36. *Ibid.*, 61.

37. "Bell Throws Out Protest by Cardinals," *Chicago Tribune*, December 15, 1956, 29.

38. Ward, Gene. "56,836 See Giants Rip Bears, 47–7," *New York Daily News*, December 31, 1956, 56.

39. Agrella, Joe. "Cardinals' Wolfner: No Leadership," *Chicago Sun-Times*, November 1, 1957.

40. Halas, with Morgan and Veysey. *Halas: An Autobiography*, 205.

41. Liska, Jerry. "Bears Triumph Over Cardinals," *Pantagraph*, December 9, 1957, 16.

42. "Bears' Owner Explains Value Along Sideline," *Chicago Tribune*, December 9, 1957, 79.

43. Strickler, George. "43,735 See Bears Beat Cards, 14–6," *Chicago Tribune*, December 9, 1957, 79.

44. Cromie, Robert. "Gift of Ball Eases Pain for Casares," *Chicago Tribune*, December 9, 1957, 82.

45. Pawson, Hal. "Coach Pop Ivy Ends Successful Eskimo Reign," *Edmonton Journal*, January 10, 1958, 12.

46. Surdam, David George. *Run to Glory and Profits: The Economic Rise of the NFL During the 1950s* (Lincoln: University of Nebraska Press, 2013), 307.

47. Sullivan, Floyd, editor. *Old Comiskey Park* (Jefferson, NC: McFarland, 2014), 165.

48. "Cards File Suit to Break Bears Pact," *Oakland Tribune*, September 27, 1958, 15.

49. "NFL Meeting Minutes," January 21–23, 1959, Professional Football Hall of Fame.

50. *Ibid.*

51. Author interview with Upton Bell, November 7, 2020.

52. Strickler, George, "Bears Beat Cardinals in Snow, 30–14," *Chicago Tribune*, December 8, 1958, 63.

53. Rollow, Cooper. "He Came From El Paso for a Prize in the Show," *Chicago Tribune*, December 8, 1958, 66.

54. "Rams Swap 9 for Ollie," *San Francisco Examiner*, March 1, 1959, 47.

55. Brachman, Bob. "Ollie Tells How Deal Began," *San Francisco Examiner*, March 1, 1959, 52.

56. *Ibid.*

57. Rollow, Cooper. "Halas U. Gets Lessons from Papa Bear; Across Town—Cards Told of 'Cute' Foes," *Chicago Tribune*, November 26, 1959.

58. "49ers Picked Over Bears; Cards 'Test' Minneapolis," *Chicago Tribune*, October 25, 1959, 48.

59. Rollow, Cooper. "Ivy Gives Cards 'Good' Chance," *Chicago Tribune*, November 28, 1959, 33.

60. Rollow, Cooper. "Cards Loom as Key Game: Halas," *Chicago Tribune*, November 27, 1959, 57.

61. "Owner Denies Grid Card Shift," *Pittsburgh Press*, March 10, 1960, 37.

62. "Chicago Grid Cards Have No Plans to Move to St. Louis," *St. Joseph News-Press/Gazette*, March 13, 1960, 38.

63. "St. Louis Interests Purchase 10 Per Cent of Football Cards," *Chicago Sun-Times*, March 13, 1960.

64. "St. Louisan Buys 10% of Chicago Cards," *Chicago Tribune*, March 13, 1960, 1.

65. "Here's Why Cards Left," *Chicago Daily News*, March 14, 1960.

66. Davis, Jeff. *Papa Bear: The Life and Legacy of George Halas* (New York: McGraw Hill, 2005), 343.

67. Ziemba, Joe, *When Football Was Football: The Chicago Cardinals and the Birth of the NFL* (Chicago: Triumph Books, 1999), 387.

68. "Football Cards Made Home Here Since '99," *Chicago Sun-Times*, March 17, 1960.

69. Sullivan, Floyd, editor, *Old Comiskey Park* (Jefferson, NC: McFarland, 2014), 158.

70. Whittingham, Richard. *What Bears They Were: Chicago Bears Greats Talk About Their Teams, Their Coaches, and the Time of Their Lives* (Chicago: Triumph Books, 1991), 222.

Bibliography

Books

Carroll, Bob, Michael Gersham, David Neft, and John Thorn. *Total Football II: The Official Encyclopedia of the National Football League*. New York: HarperCollins, 1999.

Curran, Bob. *Pro Football's Rag Days*. New York: Bonanza Books, 1969.

Davis, Jeff. *Papa Bear: The Life and Legacy of George Halas*. New York: McGraw-Hill, 2005.

Englewood High School. *Purple and White, 1926, 1927, 1928*. Harold E. Washington Library, Chicago.

Fisher, Henry G., editor. *The Chicago Amateur Base Ball Annual and Inter-City Base Ball Association Year Book*. Chicago: A.G. Spalding & Brothers, 1905.

Gonzalez, Therese. *Great Lakes Naval Training Station*. Charleston, SC: Arcadia, 2008.

Grange, Harold, as told to Ira Morton. *The Red Grange Story: An Autobiography*. Urbana: University of Illinois Press, 1993.

Halas, George S., with Gwen Morgan and Arthur Veysey. *Halas: An Autobiography*. Chicago: Bonus Books, 1986.

Horrigan, Joe. *NFL Century: The One-Hundred-Year Rise of America's Greatest Sports League*. New York: Crown, 2019.

March, Dr. Harry. *Pro Football: Its Ups and Downs*. Albany: J.B. Lyon Company, 1934.

Maxymuk, John. *Pioneer Coaches of the NFL: Shaping the Game in the Days of Leather Helmets and 60-Minute Men*. Lanham, MD: Rowman & Littlefield, 2019.

Official Guide of the National Football League. New York: American Sports Publishing Company, 1935.

Official Indoor Base Ball Guide Containing the Constitution. New York: American Sports Publishing Company, 1911.

Pacyga, Dr. Dominic. *Slaughterhouse: Chicago's Union Stock Yard and the World It Made*. Chicago: University of Chicago Press, 2015.

Pruter, Robert. *The Rise of American High School Sports and the Search for Control*. Syracuse: Syracuse University Press, 2013.

Reisler, Jim. *Cash and Carry: The Spectacular Rise and Fall of C.C. Pyle, America's First Sport Agent*. Jefferson, NC: McFarland, 2009.

Roeser, Thomas F. *Father Mac: The Life and Times of Ignatius D. McDermott, Co-Founder of Chicago's Famed Haymarket Center*. Chicago: McDermott Foundation, 2002.

Rozendaal, Neal. *Duke Slater: Pioneering Black NFL Player and Judge*. Jefferson, NC: McFarland, 2012.

Sanborn Fire Insurance Map from Chicago, Cook County, Illinois. Sanborn Map Company, Vol. 15, 1926.

Science and Craft. Chicago: Richard T. Crane Technical High School, 1916.

Serb, Chris. *War Football: World War I and the Birth of the NFL*. Lanham, MD: Rowman and Littlefield, 2019.

Shmelter, Richard J. *Chicago Assassin: The Life and Legend of "Machine Gun" Jack McGurn and the Chicago Beer Wars of the Roaring Twenties*. Nashville: Cumberland House, 2008.

Spalding's Official Football Guide. New York: American Sports Publishing Company, 1899.

Sullivan, Floyd, editor. *Old Comiskey Park*. Jefferson, NC: McFarland, 2014.

Surdam, David George. *Run to Glory and Profits: The Economic Rise of the NFL During the 1950s*. Lincoln: University of Nebraska Press, 2013.

Whittingham, Richard. *The Bears: A 75-Year Celebration*. Dallas: Taylor, 1994.

Whittingham, Richard. *What a Game They Played: An Inside Look at the Golden Era of Pro Football*. Lincoln: University of Nebraska Press, 2001.

Whittingham, Richard. *What Bears They Were: Chicago Bears Greats Talk About Their Teams, Their Coaches, and the Time of Their Lives*. Chicago: Triumph Books, 1991.

Willis, Chris. *Joe Carr: The Man Who Built the National Football League*. Lanham, MD: Rowman and Littlefield, 2010.

Willis, Chris. *Red Grange: The Life and Legacy of the NFL's First Superstar*. Lanham, MD: Rowman and Littlefield, 2019.

Ziemba, Joe. *Cadets, Cannons and Legends: The Football History of Morgan Park Military Academy*. Columbus: Gatekeeper Press, 2018.

Ziemba, Joe. *When Football Was Football: The*

Chicago Cardinals and the Birth of the NFL. Chicago: Triumph Books, 1999.

Zimmerman, David. *Curly Lambeau: The Man Behind the Mystique.* Hales Corners, WI: Eagle Books, 2003.

Periodicals

"Birth and Rebirth," *Coffin Corner,* Volume 7, 1985, 1.

Chicago Cardinals Football Club Official Program, September 23, 1928.

Chicago Cardinals Football Club Official Scorebook and Program, November 4, 1923.

"Dr. Joe: A Guard's Guard," Coffin Corner, Volume 2, No. 5, 1980, 1.

Fearnow, Dawson. "Cardinals Sin: The Shady Roots of the NFL's Oldest Team," *Phoenix Magazine,* September 17, 2020.

"Football," Science and Craft, October, 1912, 22.

Hopper, James. "We Really Played Football in the Gay Nineties," Saturday Evening Post, November 1945, 43.

Olsen, Jack. "The Unhappiest Millionaire," *Sports Illustrated,* April 4, 1960.

Roosevelt, Theodore. "What We Can Expect of the American Boy," *St. Nicholas Magazine,* May 1900, 571–574.

"Staleys Win State Football," Staley Fellowship Journal, December, 1919, 14.

Zimmerman, Paul. "The Bronk and the Gazelle," Sports Illustrated, September 11, 1989.

Websites

Ancestry.com. *1930 United States Federal Census* [database on-line]. Provo, UT, USA: Ancestry.com Operations Inc, 2002.

en.wikipedia.org/wiki/History of the Chicago Cardinals

homicide.northwestern.edu/docs

operations.nfl.com/journey-to-the-nfl/the-nfl-draft/the-history-of-the-draft/

www.azcardinals.com/news/2019-arizona-cardinals-media-guide

www.barrypopik.com

www.baseball-almanac.com/box-scores/boxscore.php?boxid=191905140DET

www.eastlanddisaster.org/history/what-happened

www.fightingillini.com/sports/m-baskbl/records/year-1916.html

www.forbes.com/teams/arizona-cardinals/?sh=5300b3303d28

www.pro-football-reference.com/coaches/Cham Gu0.htm

www.profootballhof.com/news/nfl-s-first-night-game/

www.profootballhof.com/players/guy-chamberlin/

www.profootballhof.com/teams/arizona-cardinals/team-history/

Newspapers

Akron (Ohio) Beacon Journal
Alton (Illinois) Evening Telegraph
Anderson (Kentucky) News
Argus-Leader (South Dakota)
Austin (Texas) American
Baltimore (Maryland) Sun
Belvidere (Illinois) Daily Republican
Boston (Massachusetts) Globe
Brooklyn (New York) Daily Eagle
Brooklyn (New York) Times Union
Buffalo (New York) Morning Express
Buffalo (New York) News
Buffalo (New York) Times
Capital (Wisconsin) Times
Champaign (Illinois) Daily Gazette
Champaign (Illinois) Daily News
Chattanooga (Tennessee) News
Chicago (Illinois) Daily Journal
Chicago (Illinois) Daily News
Chicago (Illinois) Englewood Times
Chicago (Illinois) Evening American
Chicago (Illinois) Herald and Examiner
Chicago (Illinois) South Side Daily Sun
Chicago (Illinois) Sun-Times
Chicago (Illinois) Tribune
Cincinnati (Ohio) Enquirer
Coldwater (Michigan) Daily Reporter
Collyer's Eye (Illinois)
Courier (Iowa)
Courier (Kentucky) Journal
Cumberland (Maryland) Sunday Times
Daily Chronicle (Illinois)
Daily Herald (Illinois)
Daily Illini (Illinois)
Daily Mail (Maryland)
Daily News (California)
Daily News (New York)
Daily News (Pennsylvania)
Daily Oklahoman (Oklahoma)
Daily Register (Illinois)
Daily Times (Iowa)
Day Book (Illinois)
Dayton (Ohio) Daily News
Decatur (Illinois) Daily Review
Decatur (Illinois) Herald
Democrat and Chronicle (New York)
Des Moines (Iowa) Register
Des Moines (Iowa) Tribune
Detroit (Michigan) Free Press
Dispatch (Illinois)
Edmonton (Canada) Journal
El Paso (Illinois) Herald
Englewood (Illinois) Economist
Escanaba (Michigan) Daily
Eugene (Oregon) Guard
Evansville (Indiana) Press
Evening (California) Express
Evening (Ohio) Review
Evening (Pennsylvania) Herald
Evening (Pennsylvania) News
Fairmont (West Virginia) West Virginian
Fort Worth (Texas) Star Telegram

Gatesville (Texas) Messenger and Star-Forum
Gazette (Iowa)
Globe-Gazette (Iowa)
Grand Forks (North Dakota) Herald
Grand Rapids (Michigan) Herald
Great Lakes (Illinois) Bulletin
Green Bay (Wisconsin) Gazette
Hammond (Indiana) Times
Harrisburg (Pennsylvania) Telegraph
Hartford (Connecticut) Courant
Hastings (Michigan) Banner
Illustrated (California) Daily News
Indianapolis (Indiana) News
Indianapolis (Indiana) Star
Inter Ocean (Illinois)
Jackson (Tennessee) Sun
Journal Herald (Ohio)
Journal Times (Wisconsin)
Kearney (Nebraska) Daily Hub
La Crosse (Wisconsin) Tribune
Lansing (Michigan) State Journal
Lock Haven (Pennsylvania) Express
Los Angeles (California) Express
Los Angeles (California) Record
Los Angeles (California) Times
Mansfield (Ohio) News Journal
Mercury (Pennsylvania)
Meriden (Connecticut) Record
Miami (Florida) Herald
Michigan City (Indiana) Evening News
Minneapolis (Minnesota) Star
Modesto (California) Evening News
Morning (Pennsylvania) Call
Mount Carmel (Pennsylvania) Item
Muncie (Indiana) Evening Press
Muskegon (Michigan) Chronicle
Nashville (Tennessee) Banner

New York (New York) Times
New York (New York) Tribune
Oakland (California) Tribune
Pantagraph (Illinois)
Philadelphia (Pennsylvania) Inquirer
Pittsburgh (Pennsylvania) Daily Post
Pittsburgh (Pennsylvania) Post-Gazette
Pittsburgh (Pennsylvania) Press
Pittsburgh (Pennsylvania) Sun-Telegraph
Post-Crescent (Wisconsin)
Pottsville (Pennsylvania) Evening Republican
Quad-City (Iowa) Times
Rock Island (Illinois) Argus
Rockford (Illinois) Morning Star
Rutland (Vermont) Daily Herald
Sacramento (California) Bee
St. Joseph (Missouri) News-Press/Gazette
St. Louis (Missouri) Post-Dispatch
San Francisco (California) Call and Post
San Francisco (California) Examiner
Santa Ana (California) Register
Scranton (Pennsylvania) Republican
Sheboygan (Wisconsin) Press
South Bend (Indiana) Tribune
Southtown (Illinois) Economist
Southtown (Illinois) Star
Spokane (Washington) Chronicle
Springfield (Missouri) News-Leader
Tampa (Florida) Times
Tampa (Florida) Tribune
Tampa Bay (Florida) Times
Tennessean (Tennessee)
Times-Tribune (Pennsylvania)
Van Nuys (California) News and Valley Green Sheet
Washington (D.C.) Post
Waukegan (Illinois) News-Sun
Wisconsin State Journal

Index

Adkins, Roy 296
Akron Pros 6, 64–66, 78, 80–82, 97–98
Aldrich, Ki 242–243
All-America Football Conference (1946) 269, 286
All-Star Football Game; *see also* Chicago Charities College All-Star Football Game
American Basketball League (1925) 125
American Basketball League (1961) 11
American Football League (1926) 169–170, 172–174, 176,
American Football League (1937) 236
American Professional Football Association 9, 59, 66, 70–71, 81, 125
American Sociological Association 218
Amos Athletic Association 167
Anderson, Dr. Eddie 117, 126
Anderson, Heartley "Hunk" 45, 116, 261
Anderson, Lefty 41
Andrew, Leroy 205–207
Angsman, Elmer 267, 270–271, 275–276, 279, 288
Artoe, Lee 249
Atkins, Doug 289
Aurora Ideals 216

Bachman, Charley 44, 63
Baker, Roy "Bullet" 198
Banonis, Vince 262, 279, 286
Barnes, Erich 300
Barry, Norman 89, 95, 126
Baugh, Sammy 239, 253,
Bell, Bert 231–232, 245, 249, 291, 295, 299–300
Bell, John C. 299
Bell, Upton 231–232, 299
Benecke, Frieda; *see also* O'Brien, Frieda
Benningsen, Ray 270, 277, 288

Bentley-Murray Printing Company 288
Berkow, Ira 236
Berry, Charlie 147
Berwanger, Jay 232–233, 244
Bezdek, Hugo 19, 20, 23, 26
Bidwill, Charles 11, 204, 214–215, 225, 228, 235, 242, 245–247, 260, 265, 266–268, 270–271, 277, 284, 288, 298–299, 304
Bidwill, Charles "Stormy," Jr. 278, 304
Bidwill, Joseph 124
Bidwill, Michael 214
Bidwill, Violet 282, 287–288, 299
Bidwill, William 204, 304
Biederman, Les 275
Bjork, Del 236
Blackburn, Bill 267, 278
Blacklock, Hugh 43, 50, 56, 68, 78, 82, 84, 116
Blackout Rule (television) 303
Blanda, George 289–290, 293
Blazine, Tony 241
Blumer, Herb 192, 218,
Boston Redskins 212, 235
Boyd, Frank 151
Boyle, Havey J. 264
Brassi, Dick 244
Bray, Ray "Muscles" 255
Brennan, Terry 292
Brett, Jeep 233
Brettschneider, Carl 293
Bridgewater, B.A. 246
Brizzolara, Ralph 121, 203, 260
Brooklyn Dodgers (baseball team) 42
Brooklyn Dodgers (football team) 212, 224, 228, 230–231, 256
Brown, Ed 297, 302
Brown, Paul 287
Brown, Warren 131
Bruck, Nick 19
Brumbaugh, Carl 221
Brunkow, Norman 172
Buckeye, Garland "Gob" 126

Buffalo All-Americans 6, 66
Buivid, Ray 236–237
Bulger, Chet 262, 265, 285
Burian, Thomas 177
Burkett, Jeff 272, 277–278
Bussey, Young 255, 257
Butkus, Dick 184
Butts, Wally 269

Cahn, Bobby 212
Callahan, Tim 155
Calumet Gunners-All-Stars 233
Canton Bulldogs 6, 51, 64–65, 66, 68–69, 71, 95, 98, 111–112, 118, 120, 126
Cantor, Leo 265
Capone, Al 110, 166, 194
Card-Pitts 262–264, 276, 284
Cardinals Social and Athletic Club 22–24, 57
Carideo, Frank 208
Carlson, C.H. 24
Caroline, J.C. 293–294
Carr, Joseph 82, 86–87, 101, 108, 114–115, 124–126, 145–147, 151, 153–154, 161–163, 171–172, 179, 187, 198, 212, 216, 230
Carroll, Bob 249
Carter, Ross 233
Casares, Rick 289, 293–294
Casey, John 17
Chamberlain, George 53, 56, 64, 89
Chamberlin, Guy 56, 177, 178
Chevigny, Jack 209, 212–213, 257
Chicago Bears 1–4, 7, 9, 11, 55, 76, 79, 90, 96, 99, 101–114, 116–128, 130–135, 137–142, 144–145, 147, 149–150, 153, 155, 156–162, 170–186, 188–244, 248–268, 271–274, 280–281, 283–304
Chicago Black Hawks 199
Chicago Bruins 125, 186
Chicago Bulls (football team) 170–173, 176, 183

331

Index

Chicago Business Men's Racing Association 215
Chicago Cardinals 1–4, 7, 10–12, 56, 73–75, 77–82, 85–86, 88–90, 93–96, 98, 101–103, 107–112, 117–122, 124–128, 131–135, 137–138, 143–145, 147–151, 153–154, 161–164, 169–179, 181–192, 195–200, 203, 205–210, 212–216, 218, 221–222, 224–251, 254–262, 264–268, 270–304
Chicago Charities College All-Star Football Game 219, 224, 228–229, 236, 272, 278–279, 282, 286
Chicago Cubs 7, 11, 42, 48–49, 58, 61, 63, 83, 87, 90–92, 99, 112, 116, 119, 128, 135, 205, 221
Chicago Football League 24, 26–27, 57, 59–60, 63
Chicago Majors 11
Chicago Mills 182
Chicago Public Schools, Board of Control 151, 152
Chicago Stadium 125, 199, 211, 215–216
Chicago Staleys 98–100
Chicago Tigers (1920) 6, 66, 68–76
Chicago Tigers (1934) 221
Chicago White Sox 7, 18, 25, 41, 70, 116, 128, 170, 181, 193–194, 287, 298
Chisick, Andy 247
Christman, Paul 254, 265, 267–268, 270–272, 274, 280, 285
Cicero State Bank 204
Cincinnati Bengals 241
Cincinnati Reds (baseball team) 178
Cincinnati Reds (football team) 212, 222
Clancy, Tom 14, 16–18, 22
Clark, Beryl 250
Clark, Earl "Dutch" 239
Clark, Harry 249
Clark, Potsy 35, 39, 211
Claypool, Ralph 112
Clemons, Vern 41
Cleveland Bulldogs 6, 122
Cleveland Indians (baseball) 126
Cleveland Indians (football) 66, 95, 146, 208
Clover Athletic Club 25, 59
Cochran, Johnny "Red" 280
Cochrane, Edward 245
Coffee, Pat 237–238
Cohen, Abe 223
Columbus Panhandles 6, 66
Columbus Tigers 124, 127–128, 138, 146, 173
Comiskey, Charles 18, 205

Commonwealth Edison Company 180
Condon, David 11, 196
Conkright, Bill 236
Connor, George 289
Conrad, Bobby Joe 299, 302
Continental Illinois Bank 209
Conzelman, James "Jimmy" 1, 246–247, 250–251, 254–255, 258–260, 267–275, 278, 280–285, 288, 296
Coolidge, Pres. Calvin 142
Cooley, Marion "Doc" 130
Cooper, Jon 248, 294–295
Copeland, Bruce 76–77, 85
Corbett, George 241
Corcoran, Frank 17
Corcoran, Jerry 145–146
Costin, Jim 213
Coughlin, Frank 93–95
Coyne, William 24
Crane Technical High School 29–33, 36
Crangle, Jack 118
Creighton, Milan 221, 228, 233–234, 237, 239, 241–242, 267
Creighton University 1
Croutch, B. 32
Crow, John David 299
Crowley, Jim 125, 143, 145
Currivan, Don 263

Daddio, Bill 247, 255
Dale, Margaret 121
Daley, Arthur 232
Dana, Vic 226
Daniels, Jack 148–149, 152, 164–167
D'Arcy Advertising Company 283
Davidson, David 166
Dayton Triangles 6, 64–66, 97, 105, 111, 183, 185, 191
Decatur Staleys 2, 6, 9, 54–56, 63, 69–70, 72, 76, 78–79, 84, 91, 96, 100, 103
DeGroot, Edward 27
Delagio, Daniel 184
Delaporte, E.C. 148–150, 166
De LaSalle High School 89, 126
Des Jardiens, Shorty 50, 52, 68
Detroit Heralds 6, 50–51, 66, 75
Detroit Lions 1, 35, 222, 229, 234, 248, 263, 265, 272, 280, 293, 296
Detroit Panthers 135, 137, 246
Detroit Wolverines 184
Devlin, Mark 61
Devore, Hugh 271
Dewell, Billy 251, 267, 275–276, 285

Dewveall, Willard 302
Dexter Park Pavilion 59, 63, 84–85
Dimancheff, Boris "Babe" 273–274
Doehring, John "Bull" 211, 239
Donahue, M. 119
Dooley, Jim 297
Dressen, Charles "Chuck" 56, 296
Driscoll, John "Paddy" 41–51, 56–57, 59–60, 63–64, 68, 71, 75, 78–82, 84, 87, 89–90, 93, 96, 101–103, 108–112, 116–120, 122, 124–128, 132, 134–135, 155, 170–172, 174–175, 179, 181–183, 186, 190, 195, 246, 174, 292–293, 296–297
Drulis, Chuck 300
Duluth Eskimos 118–120, 158, 188
Dunn, Joseph "Red" 127–128, 175
Durfee, Jim 239

Eastland, S.S. 34, 35
Eckersall, Walter 44–45, 47–48, 50, 81, 113
Edwards, Turk 262
Eileson, Harry 46
Emmerson, Ralph Waldo 200
Englewood, IL (neighborhood) 13, 15, 58, 183
Englewood High School 93, 118, 148–154, 163–169, 173
Erickson, Swede 182, 186
Evans, Buck 126
Evansville Crimson Giants 87

Faber, Red 41
Fall, Eddie 41
Feathers, Beattie 222, 225–226, 229
Feichtinger, Andy 296
Fetz, Gus 116
Fisk, S.J. 24
Fitz Gerald, J.V. 52
Flaherty, Ray 223, 239, 253
Flanigan, Walter 66, 69, 73, 87, 105, 106–107
Florence, Paul 59
Folz, Art 118, 122, 149–151, 153–154, 163, 164, 172–173
Forbes Magazine 214
Ford, Pres. Gerald 229
Fortman, Danny 233–234, 261
Fortunato, Joe 295
Four Horsemen 124–126, 143, 145–147, 164
Frankford Yellow Jackets 122, 137, 175, 183
Freeport Lions 216
Fullerton, Hugh, Jr. 287

Index

Galimore, Willie 289, 297
Gallarneau, Hugh 267
Geiger, Edward 208
George, Bill 289–290, 293, 295
Geraci, Ray 299
Ghee, Milt 50, 68
Gillies, Fred 63, 117, 126, 182
Gipp, George 45, 62, 90
Gleason, Bill 271, 304
Glynn, John "Jack" 58, 60–63
Glynn, Patrick 58, 63
Glynn, Sister Helen 58
Goldberg, Marshall 243, 247, 250, 256, 267, 270–272, 276, 285
Gordon, Lou 221, 229
Grange, Garland 192–193
Grange, Harold "Red" 2, 7, 26, 54, 113–114, 120–123, 125, 129–135, 137–143, 145, 147, 149–150, 153, 155–162, 169, 173–174, 176, 179, 187–188, 190–200, 202, 206–208, 214, 216, 220, 227–228
Grange, Lyle 121, 158
Grauer, Charles 172
Gray, Ken 300
Great Lakes Naval Training Station 40–50, 56, 60, 78, 246, 257
Green, Kirk 16–18
Green Bay Packers 4, 95–96, 101, 114, 122, 132, 178, 183, 198, 206–208, 212, 229–230, 244, 255, 267, 270, 287
Griesedieck, Joseph 303
Griffith, Homer 226
Grigas, Johnny 262–264
Grosvenor, George 234

Halas, Barbara 29
Halas, Frank 29, 31, 34, 170–171, 203, 260
Halas, Frank J., Sr. 29, 33
Halas, George 1, 2, 4, 5, 11, 29–45, 47–50, 52–55, 56–57, 60, 63–69, 71–72, 74, 77–103, 106–112, 114–116, 119, 121, 123–126, 130, 132, 135, 138–140, 142, 144, 153, 155, 159–162, 170–172, 176, 179–184, 186, 188–189, 193, 195–204, 206, 207, 209, 211–214, 220, 224–225, 230–233, 236–237, 239–240, 242–243, 246, 248–249, 251–253, 255, 257–258, 260, 267–269, 284, 286–289, 291–292, 296–299, 302–305
Halas, Walter 29–35
Hall, John 250
Halstrom, Bernie 84
Hamilton, Monroe 127–128
Hamilton Athletic Club 24
Hammond, Henry 235

Hammond Bobcats/All-Stars 50–52, 56, 59–63, 68, 71, 119, 127–128, 133, 144–145, 147–148
Hammond Boosters 167, 182, 185
Hammond Pros 6, 66
Hammond Semco 185
Handler, Phil 196, 221, 229, 242, 260, 262, 264–267, 272, 276, 284
Hanley, Dick 206, 217
Hanny, Frank 122–123
Harder, Pat 270–271, 275, 279, 285–286, 288
Hardy, Jim 285
Harley, Bill 100–101, 111–112, 116, 126
Harley, Chic 37, 39, 88–90, 100, 111
Harper, Jesse 117
Haugsrud, Ole 188–189
Hauk, William 181
Hawthorne Race Track 288
Hay, Ralph 65–66, 81–82, 95
Hayes, Dave 94
Hazelwood, Harry 195
Healey, Ed 94, 104–107, 109–110, 116–117, 160, 179
Hegewisch 1
Hein, Mel 256
Hesseltine, William B. 9
Hewitt, Bill 217
High, Guy 153
High, Lennie 296
Hill, Harlon 293, 295
Hill, King 299, 302
Hinkle, Clark 196, 240
Hoffman, H.C. 143
Holmer, Walter 195, 197, 202
Holmes, Margaret 54
Hopper, James 14
Horrigan, Joe 54, 89
Horween, Arnie 94, 117, 126
Horween, Ralph 94, 111, 117
Howard, Bart 246
Howard, D.H. 180
Huggins, Miller 40, 49, 52
Hughitt, Tommy 97, 242
Hunsinger, Chuck 289
Hutson, Don 229–230, 237, 239

Illinois All-Stars 173
Illinois Turf Association 203, 215
Indiana Harbor Gophers 221
Indianapolis Motor Speedway 169
International Amphitheater 59, 84
Ivy, Frank "Pop" 298–300, 302–303

Jacksonville All-Stars 157–158
Jarmoluk, Mike 273

Jelinek, Otto 220
Jim Thorpe Museum 185
Joesting, Herb 185, 210
Johnson, Bill 41
Johnson, Jerry 106
Johnson, Leo 296
Johnsos, Luke 211, 255, 261, 266
Jones, Ben 177
Jones, Dr. David 11, 186–187, 198–199, 203, 214–215, 228, 246, 298
Jones, Jerry 50
Jones, Johnny 47
Jones, Ralph 37, 39, 193, 195–196, 201, 209, 213–214
Judge, Carol 185

Kamara, Alvin 192
Kane, E.J. 24
Karr, Bill 217, 241
Kavanaugh, Ken 249, 253, 267
Kelly, John "Shipwreck" 230
Kelly, Mayor Edward 11
Kemp, Ray 210
Kendle, Jon 54
Kenneally, George 198
Kensington Tigers 16, 18
Kewanee Walworths 71
Kiesling, Walt 192, 218, 224, 262
Kiley, Roger 118
Kilroy, Francis "Bucko" 276
King, Dick 50
King, George 217
Kizer, Noble 220
Koehler, Bob 78–79
Kolman, Ed 248
Kopcha, Joe 225–226
Kostka, Stan 231
Krause, Edward "Moose" 221
Kuharich, Joe 289–290
Kutner, Mal 267–268, 274–275

La Crosse Lagers 221
Lake Forest Academy 193
Lake Forest College 213
Lambeau, Curly 45, 95, 101, 197–198, 230, 270, 284–285, 287–288
Landis, Keneshaw M. 11
Lane, Dick "Night Train" 288, 293
Lane Tech High School 32–33, 81
Lanum, Jake 296
Lauer, Dutch 106
Lawrence, Jimmy 233, 241
Lawrence College 96
Layden, Elmer 125, 143, 145
Leahy, Frank 278, 292
Lenhart, Justin 185
Leonard, Dutch 41
Leonard, Joe 41–42
Lillard, Joe 210

Lingo, Walter 118
Loeb and Leopold 152
Logan Square Athletic Club (Logan Squares) 78, 85, 116, 126
Long Time Sleeping 119
Los Angeles Bulldogs 235
Louisville Brecks 87
Louisville Colonels 49
Luckman, Sid 243, 248–249, 251, 253–254, 256–257, 261, 265, 267–268, 272, 280, 286, 292, 294, 305
Lujack, Johnny 280
Lunz, Jerry 175
Lyman, Link 181–182, 196, 227
Lyons, Leo 118

MacConnell, Mickey 182
MacWherter, Kyle 296
Madison Street Agreement 298–299
Maher, Donald 58
Majors, Holly 125
Mallouf, Ray 255, 279–280, 285
Malone, Charley 253
Malone, Grover 94
Manders, Jack 223, 229, 241
Maniaci, Joe 243, 253
Mara, Jack 223
Mara, Tim 162, 223, 231
March, Dr. Harry 176
Marquardt, Rube 90
Marshall, George Preston 251–253, 260
Mason, Toni Nagel 259
Massillon Tigers 6, 64, 66
Masterson, Bernie 243, 249, 253
Matson, Ollie 288–289, 293–295, 297, 301, 305
Mauldin, Stan 267, 279, 282
Maxwell, Don 165
Maxwell Award 268
Maxymuk, John 209
McAfee, George 248–249, 251, 261, 267–268, 289
McArthy, John 58
McColl, Bill 295
McCormick, Henry 280
McCullough, Hugh 250
McDermott, Monsignor Ignatius 70
McDonald, Les 235, 238–239
McGinnity, "Iron Joe" 53
McGreavy, Lt. C.J. 44
McGuire, Eddie 11–12, 23, 75, 291
McGurk, Ambrose 61, 126, 148, 154, 173
McGurn, "Machine Gun" Jack 194
McHan, Lamar 290, 293, 297
McHugh, Pat 276
McKinley, Judge Michael 14

McKinley, Sen. William 142
McMillen, James 203
McMullen, Dan 202
McNally, Frank 221
McNeil, Frank 97,
Meadows, Ed 295
Michaels, Eddie 233
Mikulak, Mike 225
Miller, Don 125, 143, 145
Miller, Jeff 97–98, 100
Mills Stadium 101, 196
Milwaukee Badgers 105–106, 120, 123–124, 126, 144–145, 148–151, 153–154, 161–163, 165–166, 168–169, 173, 175, 246
Minneapolis Marines 90, 106, 185
Minneapolis Red Jackets 190
Mintun, Jack 296
Mitchel, J. Burris 156
Moczynski, Betty 265
Moffet, Captain William 42
Mohardt, John 118
Moline Athletic Club 70–71
Montreal Maroons 199
Moore, Archie 293
Moore, Byron 130
Moore, McNeil 290
Morgan Athletic Association 2, 5, 12–16, 183
Morgan Athletic Club 9, 10, 17–20, 22, 24–27
Morgan Park Military Academy 247–248
Morrison, Bruce 289
Mt. Carmel High School 1, 271, 292
Mullen, Jim 193
Muncie Flyers 66, 70
Murphy, Cornelius 17
Murry, Don 190
Muting, Jim 279

Nagel, Ross 259
Nagler, Gern 297
Nagurski, Bronislau "Bronko" 195–197, 200, 202, 207, 210–212, 216–217, 223, 225–227, 229, 240, 244, 260–261
National American Football League 287
National Midget Automobile Racing 173
Neale, Alred Earle "Greasy" 274–275, 281
Needham, Carol 187
Neily, Harry 142
Nesbitt, Dick 221
Nevers, Ernie 157–158, 179, 188–192, 195, 197, 199–200, 205–208, 215, 242–247
Nevers, Mrs. George 157
New Mexico State University 1

New York Giants (baseball team) 56–57, 59
New York Giants (football team) 118, 140, 158, 162, 176, 178, 181, 193, 197, 205, 212, 216, 227, 229–231, 240, 254, 263, 268, 279, 293, 296
New York Yankees (baseball team) 29, 40, 48–49, 269
New York Yankees (football team) 169, 171, 173–174, 176, 183, 187–188, 259, 269
Newman, Harry 217
Nichelini, Al 229
Nied, Frank 66, 80, 82
Nolting, Ray 241
Normal Athletic Association 24
Normal Park 57–58, 68–69, 71, 74, 78–79, 84, 86, 90, 93, 95, 108, 117–118, 124–125, 128, 170, 173, 177, 181, 183, 221, 291, 302
Normals 10, 24–25, 27, 57, 116, 125
North American Football League 287
Notre Dame All-Stars (1925) 143
Notre Dame All-Stars (1933) 220

O'Brien, Chris 4–5, 10–12, 14, 16–19, 20–21, 23–28, 57–64, 66, 68, 70–71, 73, 75, 78–79, 81, 82, 84–86, 89, 93, 95–96, 101–103, 107–108, 112, 115–118, 122, 124–126, 131, 135, 137–138, 144, 147–151, 153–154, 161–164, 170–172, 174–179, 181–188, 221, 305
O'Brien, Davey 242, 249
O'Brien, Edward 27, 186
O'Brien, Frieda 25, 27, 177
O'Brien, Morgan 65, 86
O'Brien, Pat 12, 14, 16–17, 19, 22–23, 25–27
O'Connor, Red 59
Oklahoma Sports Hall of Fame 185
Olcott, Herman 41, 43–44
Olson, Lt. Commander Carl 257
Oorang Indians 118–120
Opre, Dr. H.E. 156–157
Orange Tornadoes 192
O'Shea, Maurice 23
Osmanski, Bill 243–244, 251, 253
Osmanski, Joe 268
Owen, Steve 223, 227, 240
Owens, W.B. 210

Pacyga, Dr. Dominic 15, 17
Palmer, Chuck 164

Index

Pardonner, Paul 226
Parduhn, Paul 50–52, 60–61
Parker, Raymond "Buddy" 281, 284
Paschen, Chris 183
Patterson, Floyd 293
Paul, Don 290
Pearce, Walter "Pard" 74, 296
Pearl Harbor 256
Pegler, Westbrook 121, 140
Petty, Ross 296
Pfeffer, Jeff 42
Philadelphia Eagles 12, 212, 222, 224, 231–232, 242, 249, 257, 260, 273–277, 279–282, 301
Pittsburgh Pirates (baseball team) 20
Pittsburgh Pirates (football team) 212
Planters Hotel 106, 189
Plasman, Dick 235
Pollard, Fritz 81
Pool, Hamp 249
Portsmouth Spartans 197, 206, 208, 210–212, 216
Pottsville Maroons 126, 133, 135, 137–138, 143–148, 151, 154, 161–164, 172
Prell, Edward 44, 81, 227, 258, 284
Prendergast, Joe 85
Price, Ed 290
Providence Steamroller 126, 140, 145, 147, 176, 190, 246
Pruter, Robert 30–31
Pullman Thorns 60, 84
Pyle, Charles C. 129–130, 135, 137, 139, 141–142, 144, 155–156, 158–162, 169–171, 173–174, 176
Pyotts 56, 63, 90, 116

Quant, Roy 149, 166

Racine Cardinal Pleasure Club 5, 57
Racine Cardinals 5, 11, 27, 57–63, 66, 68–72, 77, 79, 291
Racine (WI) Cardinals 6
Racine Horlicks 90, 106
Racine Legion 128
Ragen, Frank 19, 20, 24
Ragen, James 26
Ragen Athletic and Benevolent Association 20
Ragen's Colts 19–20, 110
Ranney, Art 66–67, 82
Reeves, Andrew 48
Reichle, Richard 48
Reins, O.H. 24
Reisler, Jim 174
Reker, George 17
Reynolds, M.C. 299
Richards, Perry 302

Richards, Ray 292–293, 296, 298
Richardson, Charles 148–149, 151–152, 164–167
Rochester Jeffersons 6, 66, 92, 94, 118
Rock Island Independents 6, 64, 66, 69, 73, 76–77, 84–85, 87, 93, 94, 104–105, 106–107, 126, 156, 170, 174–175, 182, 246
Rockne, Knute 45, 117
Ronzani, Gene 225
Rooney, Art 218, 260
Roosevelt, Pres. Theodore 9, 25–26
Rose Bowl 20, 44, 46, 49–50, 60, 246, 252, 254
Rozelle, Pete 301
Rozendaal, Neal 182
Runkel, Gil 44
Russell, Doug 234, 237, 241–242

Sachs, Len 75, 78–79
St. Benedict's College 1
St. Edward's University 213
St. Louis Browns 41, 158, 259
St. Louis Gunners 217, 221
St. Rita High School 71
Sanford, Leo 290
Savoldi, Joe 197–199
Sayers, Gale 191
Scanlon, Dewey 188–189
Schissler, Paul 213, 216, 221, 226–228
Schumann, Fred 145–146, 164
Schwall, Vic 279
Schwenk, Bud 257
Scott, Ralph 56, 116
Seno, Frank 265
Serb, Chris 42, 44
Seys, John 11
Shaughnessy, Clark 218, 248–249, 252, 254
Shaw, Wilbur 169
Sheer, Harry 277
Sheridan Trust and Savings Bank 195, 202
Sherman, Sollie 253
Shermans 16
Shires, Art 193–194
Schlueter, Agnes 265
Shmelter, Richard 194
Shoemake, Hub 74, 82
Skibinski, Joe 169
Slater, Frederick "Duke" 45, 104, 175, 179, 182, 186, 189, 192, 208
Smith, Bill 241
Smith, Catherine Markee 166
Smith, Marston 59–60
Smith, Red 78
Smith, Wilfrid 282
Snyder, Bob 251, 253

Snyder, James "Jimmy" 148–150, 152, 164–169, 172
Snyder, Roy 149
Sorensen, Mark 55, 70, 74, 92
South Park Commission 26
Spitzel, Herman 47
Sports Illustrated 240, 288
Spring Valley Wildcats 186
Sprinkle, Ed 267, 284–285, 304
Stagg, Amos Alonzo 19–20, 23, 26, 115
Staley, A.E. 5, 53–56, 65, 69, 72, 83–84, 88–92, 99, 100
Staley Fellowship Journal 56, 64, 69, 77, 86, 88, 99
Stayms Football Team 82, 84
Steagles 260
Steffenhagen, John 118
Sternaman, Chester 171
Sternaman, Edward "Dutch" 2, 36, 54–55, 71, 79, 81, 84, 89–90, 92–93, 96, 100–102, 105–109, 111–112, 116–117, 119, 122, 124, 127–128, 130, 132–133, 137, 139–142, 144, 155, 160–161, 171, 176, 180–181, 183, 193, 195, 197–199, 201–204, 209
Sternaman, Joey 92, 109–110, 120, 122, 126, 133, 140, 159, 170–173, 176, 195, 203
Sternaman, Paul 172
Stinchcomb, Pete 88–89
Storck, Carl 108, 146
Stow, Ralph 94
Strickler, George 229, 293
Striegel, John "Doc" 145–147, 154, 164
Strong, Ken 217, 223,
Stuhldreher, Harry 143, 145, 164
Stydahar, Joe 125, 234, 251, 267, 289
Sugar, Leo 12
Sullivan, Floyd 18
Summerall, Pat 293
Swanson, Evar 177–178
Symbolic Interactionism 218–219

T-Formation 127, 248–249, 252
Tampa Cardinals 156
Tatum, Jack 119
Taylor, Charles 45
Taylor, James 177
Taylor, John E. 177
Taylor, John "Tarzan" 88–89
Taylorville 56
Thayer, Harry 269
Thomas, Frank 228
Thomas, Steve 102, 172
Thompson, Tommy 275–276, 281
Thompson, William 148–150, 152, 164–167

Index

Thompson, William, Sr. 166
Thorn-Staleys 84
Thorpe, Jim 51, 64–66, 68–69, 71, 80, 82, 85, 87, 95, 118–119, 153, 156–157, 171, 184–185, 191
Tinsley, Gaynell "Gus" 234–235, 237–239, 243, 246–247, 250
Tipton, Howard 221
Titchenal, Bob 251
Tonelli, Mario "Motts" 266–267
Topping, Dan 270
Torrance, Jack 244
Trafton, George 68, 72, 76–78, 84, 116, 125, 160, 179, 181–182, 184–186, 193–194, 196, 296
Trippi, Charley 268–271, 273, 275–277, 279, 285, 288–289, 304
Troller, Honora 58
Turner, Clyde "Bulldog" 248–249, 261, 267, 286, 288
Tyler, Pete 237

Unitas, Johnny 218
University of Chicago 6, 10, 17, 19–20, 23, 25–26, 35, 38, 41, 50, 60, 74, 115, 122, 131, 218, 232, 248–249
University of Notre Dame 1, 45, 50, 56, 61–63, 89, 93, 117–118, 124–126, 143–146, 164, 167, 197–198, 206, 208–209, 220–221, 266, 271, 278, 292
University of Oregon 20

Van Buren, Steve 275–276, 281–282
Veech, Walter 296
Veeck, William, Sr. 91–92, 99, 116, 135, 181
Voss, Tillie 106

Wallace, Stan 290
Walquist, Laurie 125, 186
Walsh, Davis 191
Ward, Arch 168, 206, 219–220, 228, 240, 251, 286
Ward, Gene 296
Ward, Willie 16
Warner, P. 24
Washington All-Stars 140
Washington Redskins 236, 239–240, 243, 251–253, 255–256, 260–261, 273, 275, 286
Washington Senators 87
Watts, Wadsworth 172
Weatherly, Gerald "Bones" 290
Western Electric Company 34, 36

Western Professional Football Association 85, 87
WGN 120, 134, 252, 279
Whalen, Bill 59, 61
White, Byron "Whizzer" 250
Whittingham, Richard 211
Wichita State University 1
Wickersham, Hal 235
Wilce, John 43
Wilkinson, Bud 292
Williams, Jake 190
Willis, Chris 87, 113, 130
Wilson, Billy 235
Wilson, George "Wildcat" 191
Wolf, Arch 299
Wolf, Sol 165
Wolfe, Rocky 150
Wolff, Al 247
Wolfner, Walter 288, 290–292, 295–303
Woodworth, Buster 53
Wrigley, William, Jr. 11, 91, 99

Yost, Fielding 121
Young, Doc 72
Young, Randolph 296

Zentner, Mary Zoia 117
Zoia, Clyde 117–118
Zuppke, Robert 35–38, 43, 131, 201, 205–206, 217

www.ingramcontent.com/pod-product-compliance
Lightning Source LLC
Chambersburg PA
CBHW060335010526
44117CB00017B/2837